A-Z MIDD

G000298959

Key to Map Pages	2
Map Pages	4-1
Postcode Map	170-1

REFERENCE

Motorway	A1(M)
A Road	A19
B Road	B1365
Dual Carriageway	
One-way Street Traffic flow on A Roads is also indicated by a heavy line on the driver's left.	
Road Under Construction Opening dates are correct at time of publication.	
Proposed Road	
Restricted Access	
Pedestrianized Road	
Track & Footpath	
Residential Walkway	
Railway	Level Crossing, Station, Tunnel
Built-up Area	STONE ST.
Local Authority Boundary	
National Park Boundary	
Posttown Boundary	
Postcode Boundary (within Posttown)	
Map Continuation	18

Airport	
Car Park (selected)	P
Church or Chapel	†
Cycleway (selected)	
Fire Station	■
Hospital	H
Information Centre	i
National Grid Reference	$^{4}45$
Police Station	▲
Post Office	★
Safety Camera with Speed Limit Fixed Cameras and long term road works cameras. Symbols do not indicate camera direction.	30
Toilet without facilities for the Disabled with facilities for the Disabled	
Viewpoint	
Educational Establishment	
Hospital or Healthcare Building	
Industrial Building	
Leisure or Recreational Facility	
Place of Interest	
Public Building	
Shopping Centre or Market	
Other Selected Buildings	

SCALE

0 — ¼ — ½ Mile

0 — 250 — 500 — 750 Metres — 1 Kilometre

1:15,840 4 inches (10.16 cm) to 1 mile 6.31 cm to 1km

EDITION 8 2015

Every possible care has been taken to ensure that, to the best of our knowledge, the information contained in this atlas is accurate at the date of publication. However, we cannot warrant that our work is entirely error free and whilst we would be grateful to learn of any inaccuracies, we do not accept responsibility for loss or damage resulting from reliance on information contained within this publication.

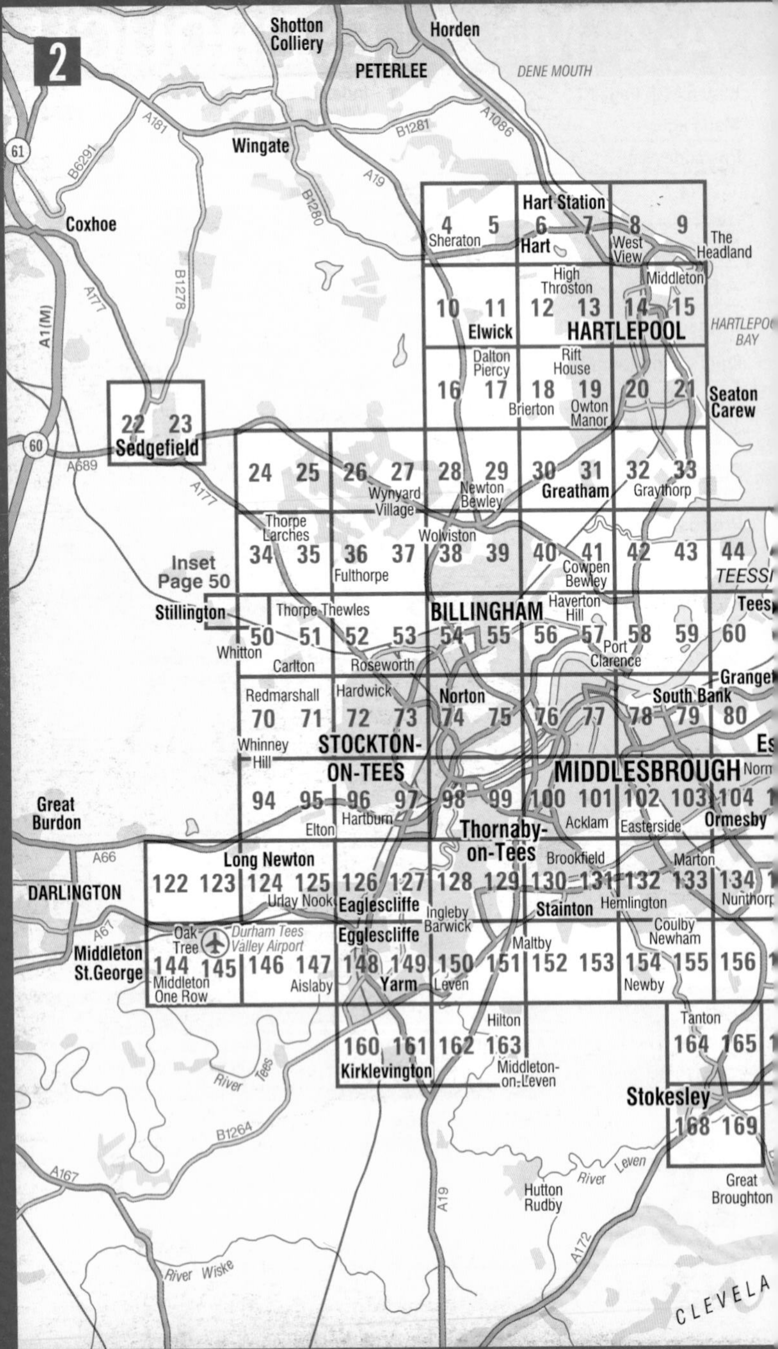
2
Shotton Colliery
Horden
PETERLEE
DENE MOUTH
Wingate
Coxhoe
A181
B1281
A1086
B6291
A19
B1280
B1278
A177
A1(M)
61
60
A689
Hart Station
Hart
Sheraton
West View
The Headland
Middleton
High Throston
Elwick
HARTLEPOOL
HARTLEPOOL BAY
Dalton Piercy
Rift House
Brierton
Owton Manor
Seaton Carew
Sedgefield
Wynyard Village
Newton Bewley
Greatham
Graythorp
Thorpe Larches
Wolviston
Fulthorpe
Cowpen Bewley
TEESSIDE
Inset Page 50
Stillington
Thorpe Thewles
BILLINGHAM
Haverton Hill
Whitton
Carlton
Roseworth
Port Clarence
Redmarshall
Hardwick
Norton
South Bank
Grangetown
Whinney Hill
STOCKTON-ON-TEES
MIDDLESBROUGH
Great Burdon
Elton
Hartburn
Thornaby-on-Tees
Acklam
Easterside
Ormesby
A66
Long Newton
Brookfield
Marton
DARLINGTON
Urlay Nook
Eaglescliffe
Ingleby Barwick
Stainton
Hemlington
Nunthorpe
A67
Oak Tree
Durham Tees Valley Airport
Egglescliffe
Maltby
Coulby Newham
Middleton St.George
Middleton One Row
Aislaby
Yarm
Leven
Newby
Hilton
Tanton
Kirklevington
Middleton-on-Leven
Stokesley
River Tees
B1264
A167
River Leven
Hutton Rudby
Great Broughton
A19
A172
River Wiske
CLEVELA
4 5 6 7 8 9
10 11 12 13 14 15
16 17 18 19 20 21
22 23
24 25 26 27 28 29 30 31 32 33
34 35 36 37 38 39 40 41 42 43 44
50 51 52 53 54 55 56 57 58 59 60
70 71 72 73 74 75 76 77 78 79 80
94 95 96 97 98 99 100 101 102 103 104
122 123 124 125 126 127 128 129 130 131 132 133 134
144 145 146 147 148 149 150 151 152 153 154 155 156
160 161 162 163 164 165
168 169

KEY TO MAP PAGES

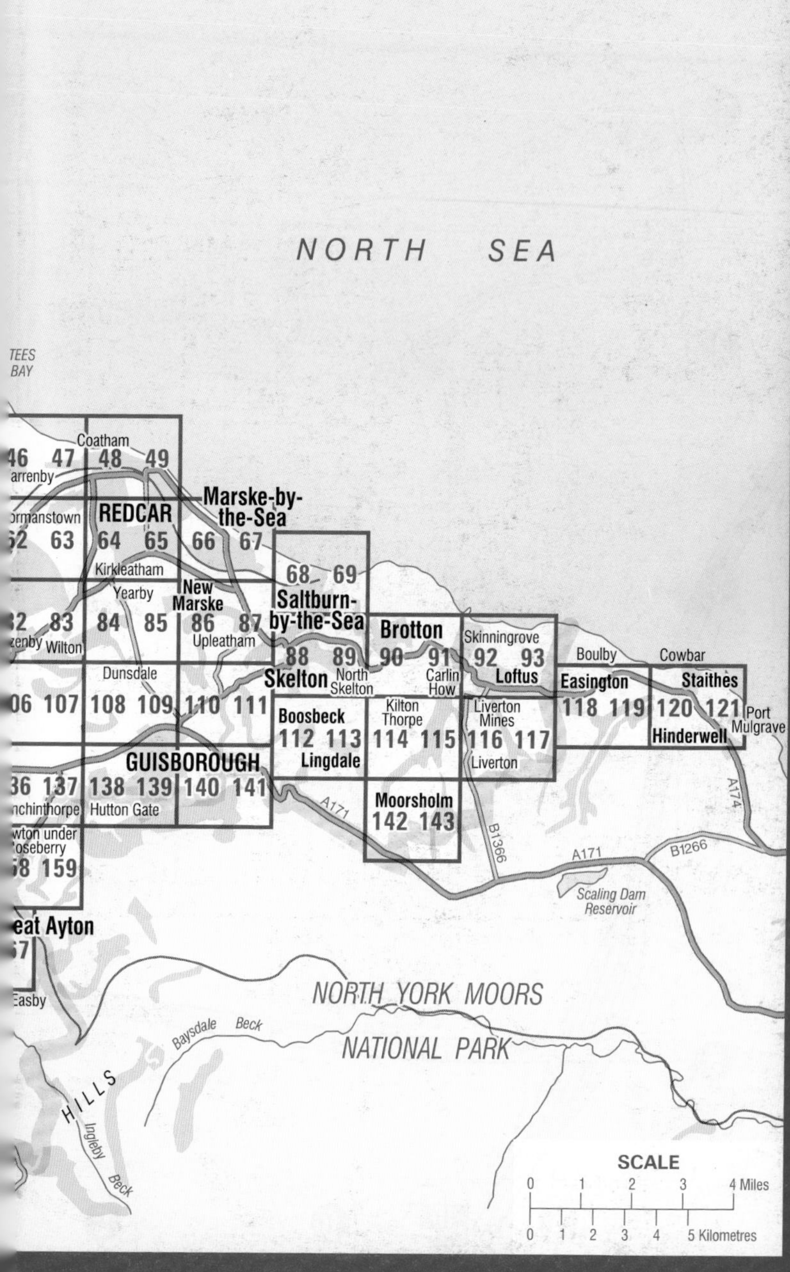

4
Hulam
44
A
B
C
4 45
Nesbitt Hall
Porrit's Close Plantation
Porrit's Close Hill
BELLOWS BURN LANE
1
36
Sheraton Hill
Hartlepool
TS27
2
SHERATON BANK
A19
3
White House
The Green
Burn
Ford
Sheraton Farm
Bellows
5 35
Sheraton Hall Estate
Sheraton House
Sheraton
Sewage Works
Sheraton Hall Farm
Hallgarth House
4
HARTLEPOOL
DURHAM
Fox Hill
Hart Moor Farm
BUTT
The Bungalow
East Grange Farm
5
B1280
A179
Whelly Hill
Whangdonhill Plantation
Whelly Hill Farm
34
Whangdon Hill
Whangdon Belt
Whangdo
44
A
10
B
C
4 45

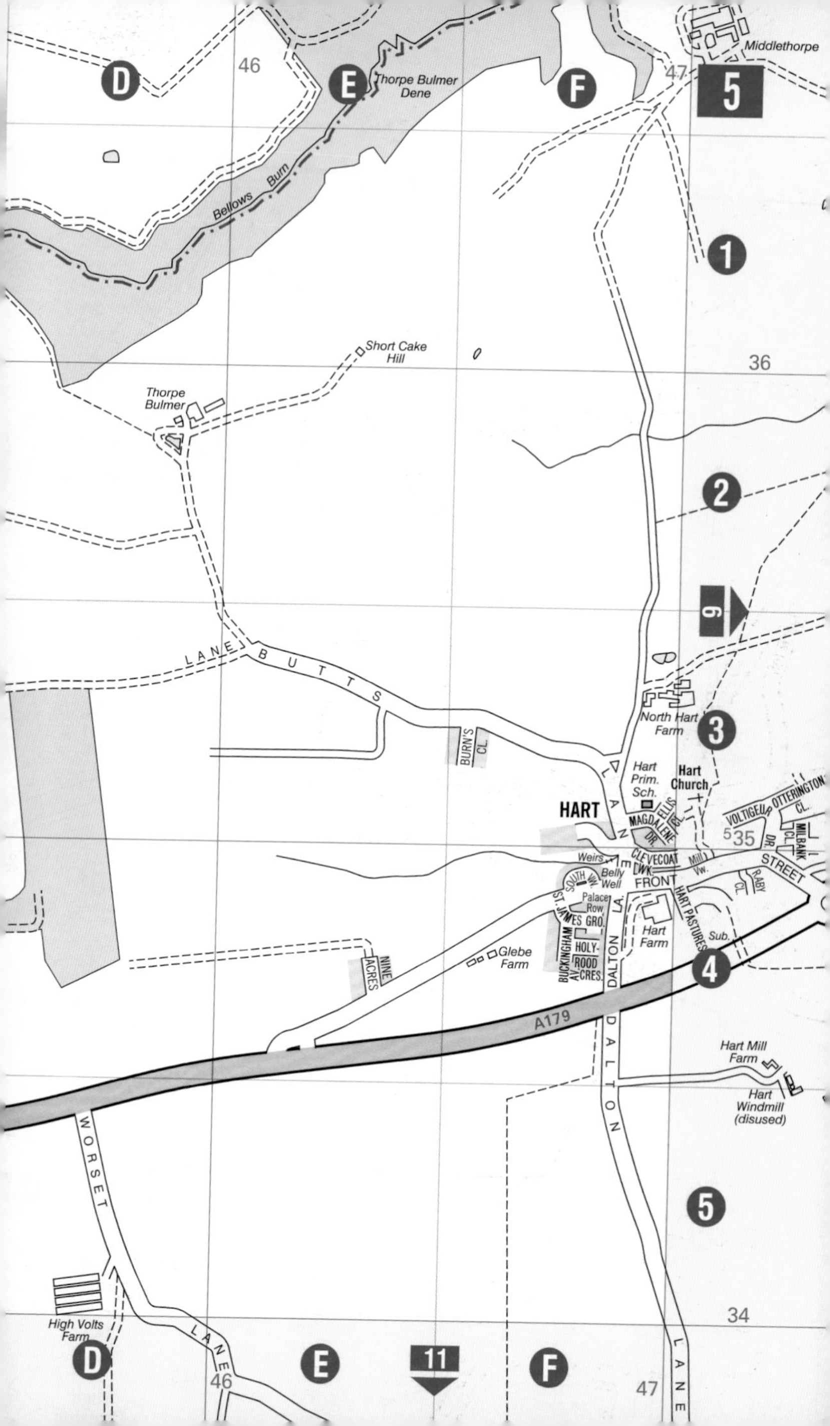
Middlethorpe
5
46
47
D
E
F
Thorpe Bulmer Dene
Bellows Burn
1
36
Short Cake Hill
Thorpe Bulmer
2
9
LANE
BUTTS
BURN'S CL.
North Hart Farm
3
Hart Prim. Sch.
Hart Church
HART
ELLIS CL.
MAGDALENE DR.
VOLTIGEUR
OTTERINGTON CL.
MILBANK CL.
35
DR.
STREET
CLEVECOAT WK.
Mill Vw.
Weirs
Belly Well
SOUTH VW.
FRONT
RABY CL.
Palace Row
ST. JAMES GRO.
HART PASTURES
BUCKINGHAM AV.
HOLY-ROOD CRES.
DALTON LA.
Hart Farm
Sub.
Glebe Farm
NINE ACRES
4
A179
DALTON
Hart Mill Farm
Hart Windmill (disused)
WORSET
5
34
High Volts Farm
LANE
11
LANE

6
Middlethorpe
North Pasture Farm
A
B
C
47
48
COAST ROAD
A1086
Crimdon House Farm
DURHAM
HARTLEPOOL
1
2
3
4
5
36
35
34
Seaview Park Homes
HARTVILLE ROAD
OCEAN
VERNER RD.
VERNER CL.
REDWOOD CL.
SILVERWOOD GRO.
LANE
FARM
NELSON
Ash Vale Holiday Park
Nelson Farm
Nelson Lodge
APPLEWOOD
JAYWOOD CL.
RAVENWOOD CL.
ALDERWOOD CL.
BLACKWOOD CL.
COPWOOD CL.
AMBERWOOD CL.
WOODSTOCK WAY
MIDDLEWOOD CL.
LINDRICK DR.
MUIRFIELD
Pannell Pl.
ASHWOOD
PINEWOOD CL.
WESTWOOD
THORNBURY CL.
CARNOUSTIE GRO.
TURNBERRY GRO.
TS27
OAKWOOD CL.
TEMPLETON CL.
TAVISTOCK
TOTNES CL.
TORCROSS CL.
TALLAND CL.
Clavering
TREMAINE CL.
TEIGNMOUTH CL.
TINTAGEL CL.
WEST VIEW ROAD
Hart Prim. Sch.
Hart Church
North Hart Farm
OTTERINGTON CL.
VOLTIGEUR DR.
MILBANK CL.
MAGDALENE DR.
ELLIS GR.
HART
CLEVECOAT WLK.
Mill Vw.
FRONT STREET
RABY CL.
Weirs
Belly Well
SOUTH VW.
Palace Row
ST. JAMES GRO.
BUCKINGHAM AV.
HOLYROOD CRES.
HART PASTURES
Hart Farm
Sub.
A179
DALTON LA.
THE FENS
HART LANE
Keeper's Cottage
Hartlepool
Strawberry Apartments
Hart Mill Farm
Hart Windmill (disused)
Hart Quarry
Hart Reservoir Cottage
Bishop Cuthbert
NIGHTINGALE CL.
Craggy Bank
HIGH THROSTON GOLF COURSE
Club House
12
High Throston
DALTON
LA

NORTH SEA
NORTH SANDS
HARTLEPOOL GOLF COURSE
Hart Station
Club House
TS24
HART WARREN
HARTLEPOOL GOLF COURSE
Barnard Grove Primary School
RAVENSWORTH CRES.
BARNARD GRO.
Bowes Green
BOURNEMOUTH DR.
SANDBANKS DRIVE
STUDLAND
SWANAGE GRO.
LULWORTH GRO.
WEYMOUTH DRIVE
PORTLAND GRO.
PARKSTONE GRO.
DORCHESTER DR.
SNOWDON GRO.
HYDMAN GRO.
SPEEDING DR.
SRIDLINGTON WAY
HOWDEN
LAZENBY
PORRETT CL.
HUTONE PL.
HOOD CL.
GOLDSMITH AV.
PERT RD.
ROAD RD.
WHITROUT
DOWSON
Playing Field
MILLER GRO.
GIBSON
MILLER CRES.
Merriman Green
FULTHORPE AV.
BUTTWICK
NICHOLSON WY.
MARSHALL CL.
GREYFRIARS
BARNES CT.
JOYCE RD.
DOBSON PL.
TEMPEST
WILLINGTON DR.
Brancepath Wk.
ROGERI PL.
NESBYT RD.
St. John Vianney RC Prim. Sch.
St. Hild's C of E Sch.
DICKENS
BRUNTOFT AV.
LAMBERD RD.
GILBERTI PL.
Playing Fields
MEADOWS
WHIN
GRAFTON
ST. ANDREWS GRO.
SANDWICH
Dollsworth
Belfast Gro.
Sunningdale
Spearman Wk.
CLAVERING
BAMBURGH CT.
LINDISFARNE CL.
CASTLE
HOWARD CL.
KNARESBOROUGH CL.
PARRISH CT.
BROUGH
Baker Cl.
Leighton Ter.
A1086
A179
HART ROAD
WEST VIEW ROAD
A1049
New Cemetery
West View
Mayfield Park (Hartlepool RUFC)
JOHN HOWE GDS.
ANNANDALE
CLIFFORD CL.
DAVISON
SKELTON
BRADSHAW CT.
EMERSON CT.
MIERS
ELLETT CT.
CRES.
CARRICK
BRUCE ST.
BRUCE CRESCENT
Comm. Cen.
Boagey Wk.
AVENUE
WINTERBOTTOM
SHARP CRES
GARSIDE
Brus Chr.
WINGFIELD
ATKINSON CT.
West View Prim. Sch.
DRIVE
SKERNE RD.
JONES
JOWITT
HARSNET PL.
HASTINGS PL.
HORLYE PL.
RUNCIMAN
POUNDRIT PL.
BULMR PL.
WARREN
LIGHTFOOT
CRESCENT
UNIVERSITY HOSPITAL OF HARTLEPOOL
HOLDFORTH
Hospice
WELLS
SURGY LA.
RAWLINS CT.
ROUTLGE CT.
RSN CT.
OAKESWAY BUS. PK.
THAMES
THOMPSON GRO.
HOWBECK
Holdforth Ct.
WARREN CL.
Kensington Court
KIRKSTONE GRO.
Army Res. Cen.
EASINGTON ROAD
JESMOND GARDENS
PINE GROVE
IVY GROVE
CRICKETHOLLOW
LIME CRESCENT
BERRY
BUCKLE
HAZEL GRO.
Hawthorn Wk.
WILLOW GRO.
Willow Walk
Cherry Wk.
Jesmond
Birch Walk
RABY ROAD
Factory
ROSEBUD CL.
SILVERBIRCH
ROAD
POPPY CL.
TULIP CL.
THISTLE CL.
Willow Flats
WATERCRESS CL.
CORNFLOWER
PRIMROSE RD.
EVERGREEN CL.
BLUEBELL
HONEYSUCKLE
WATERLILY CT.
MEADOWSWEET RD.
LIME
BROOK
VIOLA CL.
SNOWDROP ROAD
EYEBRIGHT CL.
DEWBERRY CL.
MERLIN WAY
DAISY CL.
BUTTERCUP CL.
SPEEDWELL
ORCHID ROAD
GOOSEBERRY CL.
ROSEBAY CL.
COLTSFOOT CL.
CRANESBILL AV.
JASMINE CL.
GARDENS
CELANDINE
RING STONES
DEAN
FALL
MEADOWS WK.
Wethers Nook
Parsley Nook
Rosemary Nook
Hart Reservoirs Nature Reserve
LARKSPUR
FOXGLOVE CL.
OSPREY WAY
CROCUS
TS26
Hartfields Manor
Play-ground
Throston Park
Throston Grange
SHER
CLOSE
GREENSHANK CL.
REDSHANK CL.
GOSHAWK
OUZEL CL.
MERGANSER
HAZELHEN
GOLDCREST CL.
GUILLEMOT
KITTIWAKE CL.
MOORHEN
LAPWING
HARRIER
BUNTING
DUNLIN R.
GREENFINCH CL.
LINNET RD.
CHAFFINCH CL.
SKYLARK CL.
FIELDFARE
REDSTART
STONECHAT CL.
WHINCHAT CL.
THROSTON CL.
GRANGE LANE
Supermarket
PEMBROKE GR.
MONMOUTH GRO.
CARDIGAN GRO.
Chepstow Walk
Gower Walk
WILTSHIRE WY.
ANGLESEY
MONTGOMERY
GLAMORGAN
THROSTON
Harlech
Conway Walk
Flint Walk
Springwell Flats
Plymouth Wk.
Throston Prim. Sch.
Tredegar
Springwell
Pavilion
Grayfields
Pavs.
HEATHER GRO.
49
450
36
535
34

8
13

450
A
B
51
C
1
NORTH
36
HARTLEPOOL GOLF COURSE
2
7
Outfall
Outfall
Pier
3
BRUNTOFT AV.
GILBERT PL.
WEST VIEW A1049 RD.
WEST VIEW ROAD
WEST VIEW
North
Sands
WEST VIEW RD.
Old Cemetery
OLD CEMETERY
SKELTON
ANNANDALE
DAVISON
EMERSON CT.
MIERS AVENUE
BRUCE CRESCENT
BRUCE ST.
Comm. Cen.
WINGFIELD CL.
ATKINSON CT.
SEDGEWICK CL.
WALLER CT.
LIDDELL CT.
Tennis Cts.
Playground
Sports Grd.
Boagey Wk.
PURVES PL.
GARSIDE DR.
ARKLEY CRES.
CARRICK ST.
WINTERBOTTOM CRES.
SHARP CRES.
New Friarage (Rugby Football Grd.)
4
West View Prim. Sch.
Play. Fld.
RUNCIMAN RD.
SKERNE ROAD
Warehouse
Hartlepool
TS24
Works
Factories
OAKESWAY INDUSTRIAL ESTATE
Factory
WARREN
WELLS
WINTERBOTTOM AV.
SKERNE RD.
THAMES AV.
THAMES AV.
OAKESWAY BUS. PK.
OAKESWAY
Club
GRITTEN SQ.
HEORTNESSE RD.
ROMAINE PK.
BRIDGEPOOL CL.
ROCKPOOL CL.
MANSEPOOL CL.
SOMERSBY CL.
UNION RD.
SHIELDS TER.
VINCENT ST.
ROKEBY ST.
HUTTON ST.
BRUNEL CL.
TELFORD CL.
A1049
Comms Cen.
Abdiel Ct.
Haxby Wk.
FIRBY CL.
HERONSPOOL CL.
MOUNTBATTEN CL.
UNIVERSITY HOSPITAL OF HARTLEPOOL
Hospice
HOLDFORTH RD.
HOLDFORTH CL.
5
HOWBECK LANE
THOMPSON GRO.
Army Res. Cen.
KIRKSTONE GRO.
KIRKSTONE CT.
HARTLEPOOL INDUSTRIAL ESTATE
Factory
Ten. Ct.
Bowl. Grn.
Factory
GATESGARTH CL.
WASDALE CL.
ROSTHWAITE CL.
STONETHWAITE CL.
VISCOUNT CL.
LANCASTER RD. NTH.
CLEVELAND ROAD
A1048
GREENLAND RD.
The
EASINGTON A179 ROAD
POWLETT ROAD
Bakers Ct.
Works
JESMOND
34
CRICKETHOLLOW
BERRY
BUCKLEY
CRESCENT
Hawthorn Wk.
Cherry Wk.
Jesmond
Birch Walk
HAZEL GRO.
RABY ROAD
Dyke House
14
Playing Field
MILBANK
APPLEBY GRO.
AMBERTON ROAD
MARINA WY.
51
Works
Dyke Ho. S. & T.
Grayfields

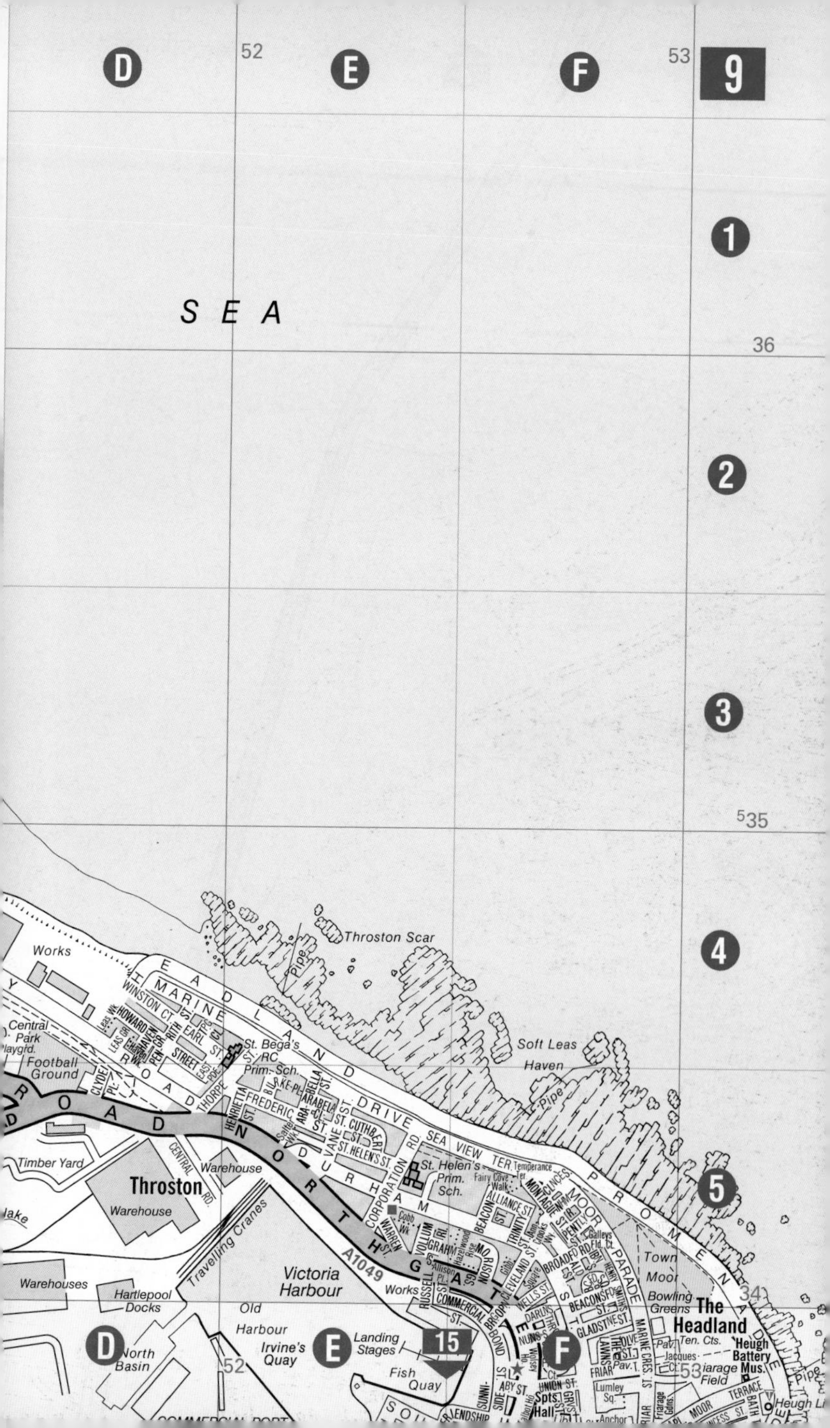
D
E
F
52
53
1
2
3
4
5
36
35
34
SEA
Throston Scar
Soft Leas
Haven
Pipe
Works
HEADLAND
MARINE DRIVE
WINSTON CT.
HOWARD ST.
EARL ST.
STREET
PEN-GRITH
HAVEN
Leas Wk.
Central Park Playgrd.
Football Ground
CLYDE PL.
ROAD
THORPE
St. Bega's RC Prim. Sch.
HENRIETTA ST.
FREDERIC ST.
ARABELLA ST.
VANE ST.
ST. CUTHBERT ST.
ST. HELEN'S ST.
DURHAM ST.
NORTHGATE
A1049
CORPORATION RD.
SEA VIEW TER.
Temperance Ter.
St. Helen's Prim. Sch.
Fairy Cove Walk
ALLIANCE ST.
BEACON ST.
TRINITY
MONTAGUE ST.
PRINCES ST.
MOOR PARADE
PROMENADE
Town Moor
Bowling Greens
The Headland
Ten. Cts.
Heugh Battery Mus.
Jacques Ct.
Friarage Field
Heugh Lt.
TERRACE
BATH
MOOR
Lumley Sq.
Anchor
MARINE CRES.
FRIAR
GLADSTONE ST.
BEACON ST.
BROADFIELD ST.
PENTLY ST.
Galleys Fld. Ct.
HENRY SMITHS
WELLS ST.
CLEVELAND ST.
MORISON
Hazelwood Rise
GRAHAM
VOLLUM
WARREN ST.
Cobb Wk.
Allison Pl.
RUSSELL ST.
COMMERCIAL ST.
BOND
NUNS
UNION ST.
Spts. Hall
SUNNISIDE
FRIENDSHIP
Timber Yard
Throston
Warehouse
CENTRAL RD.
Warehouses
Hartlepool Docks
Travelling Cranes
Victoria Harbour
Works
Old Harbour
Irvine's Quay
Landing Stages
Fish Quay
North Basin
COMMERCIAL PORT

15

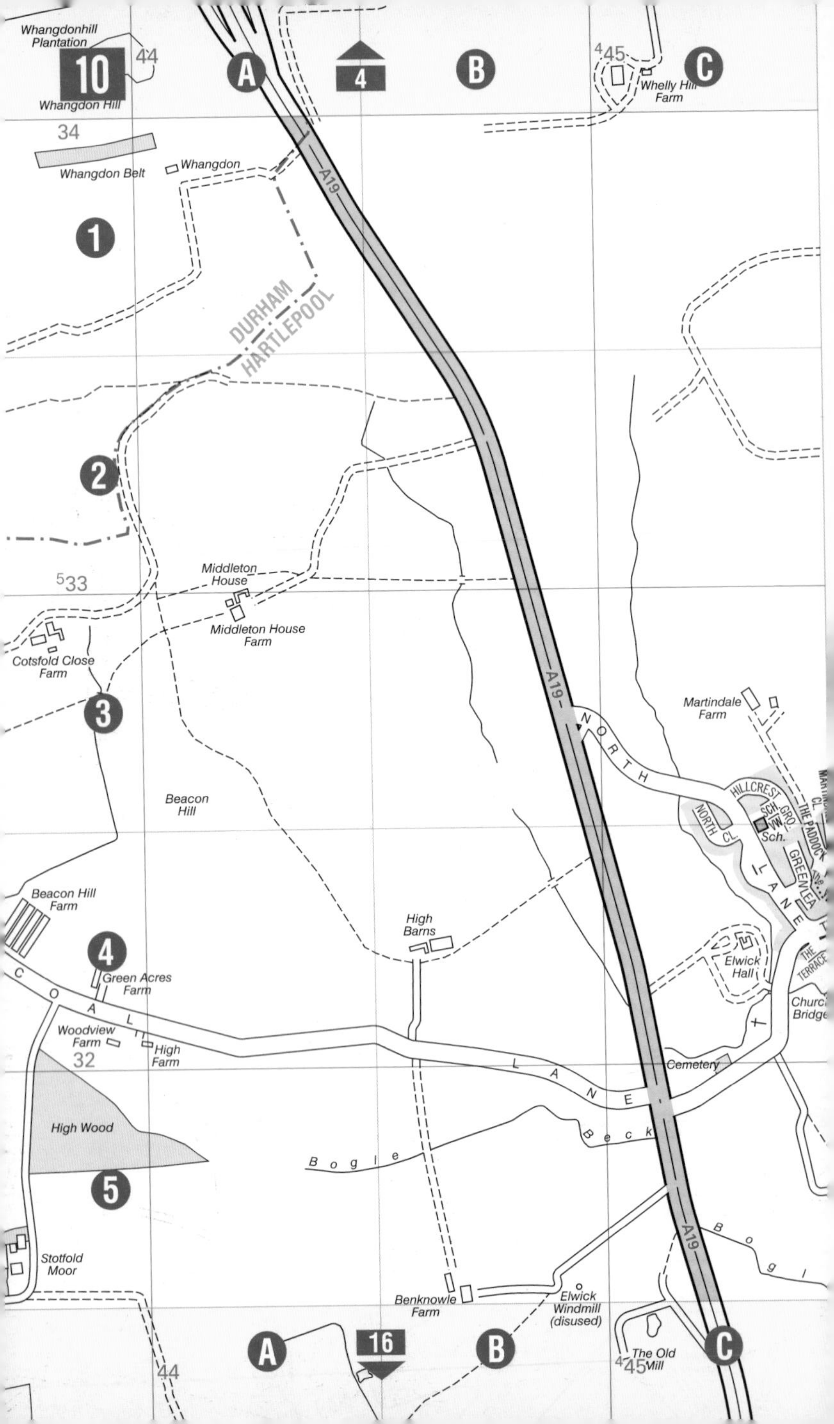
Whangdonhill Plantation
Whangdon Hill
A
4
B
C
Whelly Hill Farm
Whangdon Belt
Whangdon
A19
DURHAM
HARTLEPOOL
Middleton House
Middleton House Farm
Cotsfold Close Farm
Beacon Hill
Martindale Farm
NORTH LANE
HILLCREST
NORTH CL.
SCH. VW.
GRO.
Sch.
THE PADDOCK
GREENLEA
LANE
Beacon Hill Farm
High Barns
Elwick Hall
THE TERRACE
Green Acres Farm
COAL LANE
Woodview Farm
High Farm
Cemetery
High Wood
Bogle Beck
Stotfold Moor
Benknowle Farm
Elwick Windmill (disused)
16
The Old Mill
1
2
3
4
5
44
34
445
533
32

11
D
E
5
F
46
47
34
33
32
WORSET
High Volts Farm
Tilery Farm
Claypit Farm
Reservoirs (covered)
LANE
Naisberry
1
2
3
4
5
Hartlepool
TS27
North Urn Farm
North Urn Cottage
ELWICK LANE
ROAD
Lambs House Farm
Weir
Dalton Beck
ELWICK
North Farm
MANOR CL.
NORTH GREEN
Home Farm
The Ghyll
12
Sewage Works
Char Beck
Mayfield House
Abbey Hill Cotts.
Abbey Hill Farm
Hart on the Hill
DALTON LANE
Dove Cote
The Howls
Beck
Reservoir (covered)
Dalton Piercy
17
The Grove
Dalton Piercy

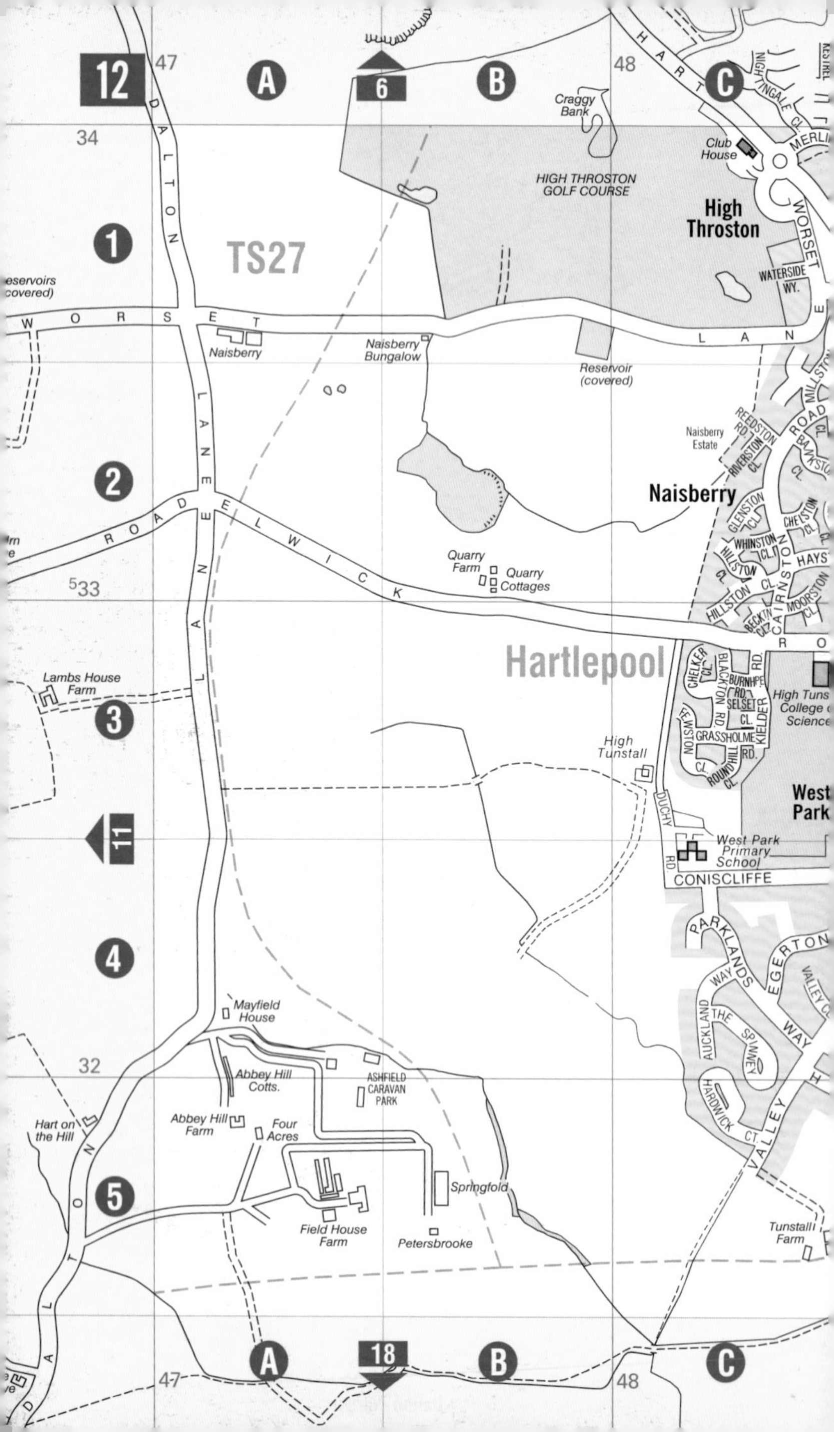
12
47
48
A
B
C
6
18
11
34
33
32
1
2
3
4
5
TS27
Hartlepool
High Throston
Naisberry
DALTON LANE
WORSET LANE
ELWICK ROAD
HART
Craggy Bank
Club House
HIGH THROSTON GOLF COURSE
Reservoirs (covered)
Reservoir (covered)
Naisberry
Naisberry Bungalow
Naisberry Estate
Quarry Farm
Quarry Cottages
Lambs House Farm
High Tunstall
West Park Primary School
High Tunstall College of Science
West Park
Mayfield House
Abbey Hill Cotts.
Abbey Hill Farm
Four Acres
ASHFIELD CARAVAN PARK
Springfold
Field House Farm
Petersbrooke
Hart on the Hill
Tunstall Farm
NIGHTINGALE CL.
MERLIN
WORSET
WATERSIDE WY.
REEDSTON RD.
RIVERSTON CL.
MILLSTON
ROAD
GLENSTON CL.
WHINSTON CL.
HILLSTON CL.
CHEISTON CL.
HAYSTON
CAIRNSTON
MOORSTON CL.
BECKTN CL.
CHELKER CL.
BLACKTON RD.
BURNHPE RD.
SELSET CL.
KIELDER RD.
FEWSTON CL.
GRASSHOLME
ROUNDHILL CL.
DUCHY RD.
CONISCLIFFE
PARKLANDS WAY
EGERTON
VALLEY
AUCKLAND WAY
THE SPINNEY
HARDWICK CT.
VALLEY DRIVE

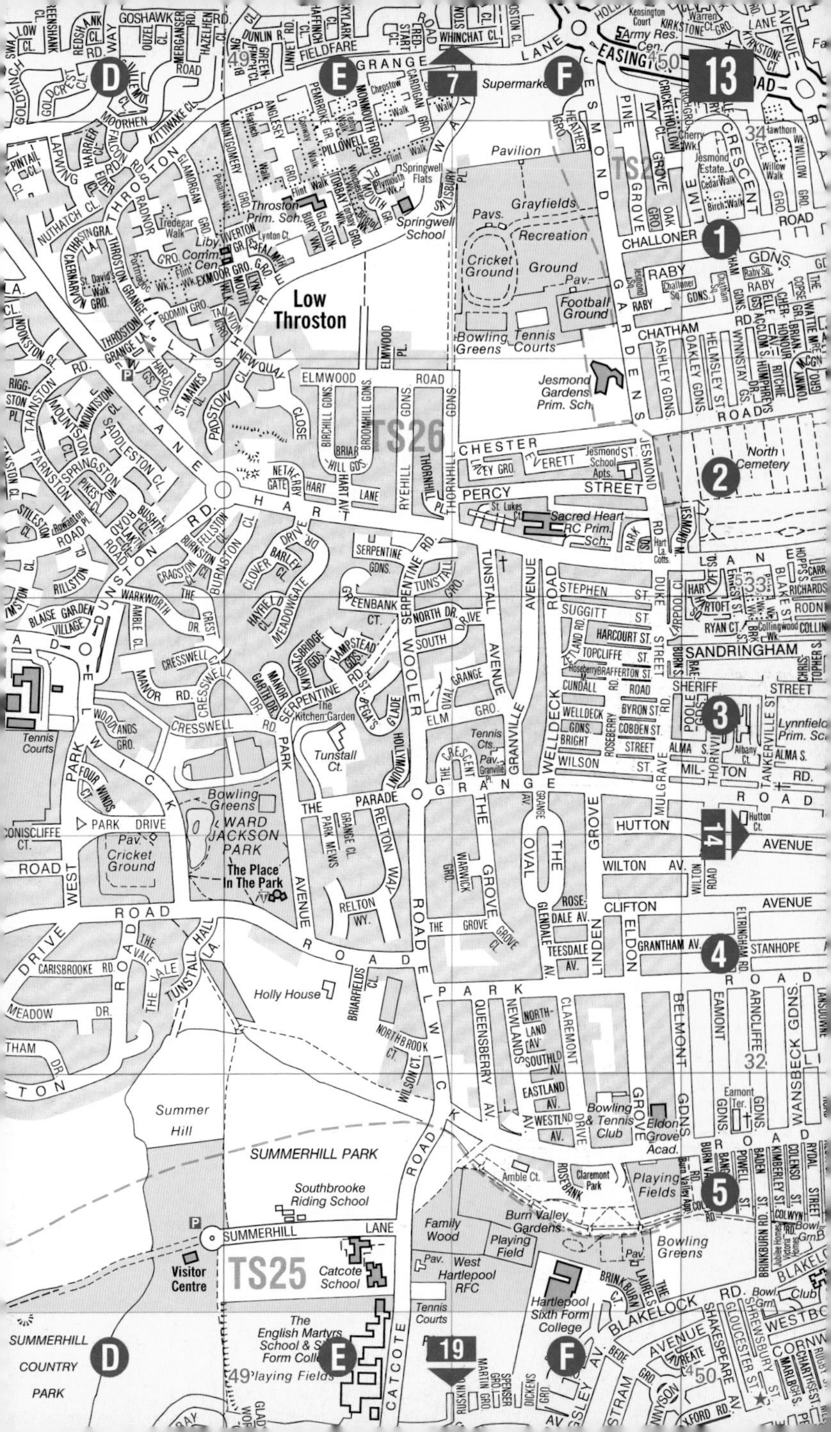

13
D
E
F
1
2
3
4
5
7
14
19
49
450
TS26
TS25
Low Throston
GRANGE ROAD
WHINCHAT CL.
FIELDFARE
Supermarket
EASINGTON ROAD
Army Res. Cen.
Kensington Court
KIRKSTONE
Pavilion
Grayfields
Pavs.
Recreation Ground
Cricket Ground
Football Ground
Bowling Greens
Tennis Courts
Jesmond Gardens Prim. Sch.
JESMOND GARDENS
CHALLONER ROAD
RABY GDNS.
CHATHAM ROAD
North Cemetery
CHESTER ROAD
PERCY STREET
Sacred Heart RC Prim. Sch.
Jesmond School Apts.
HART LANE
THROSTON GRANGE LA.
Throston Prim. Sch.
Springwell School
Springwell Flats
Liby. Comm. Cen.
ELMWOOD ROAD
SERPENTINE RD.
TUNSTALL AVENUE
GRANVILLE AVENUE
WELLDECK ROAD
STEPHEN ST.
SUGGITT ST.
HARCOURT ST.
SANDRINGHAM RD.
SHERIFF STREET
Lynnfield Prim. Sch.
MILTON RD.
HUTTON AVENUE
WILTON AV.
CLIFTON AVENUE
GRANTHAM AV.
STANHOPE AV.
PARK ROAD
WOOLER ROAD
ELWICK ROAD
DUNSTON RD.
WARKWORTH DR.
CRESSWELL RD.
MANOR RD.
The Kitchen Garden
Tunstall Ct.
THE PARADE
GRANGE ROAD
WARD JACKSON PARK
Bowling Greens
The Place In The Park
Pav. Cricket Ground
PARK DRIVE
WEST PARK
Tennis Courts
Holly House
Summer Hill
SUMMERHILL PARK
Southbrooke Riding School
SUMMERHILL LANE
Visitor Centre
Catcote School
SUMMERHILL COUNTRY PARK
The English Martyrs School & Sixth Form College
Playing Fields
CATCOTE ROAD
Family Wood
West Hartlepool RFC
Tennis Courts
Burn Valley Gardens
Playing Field
Claremont Park
Amble Ct.
Playing Fields
Bowling & Tennis Club
Eldon Grove Acad.
BURN VALLEY ROAD
Bowling Greens
Hartlepool Sixth Form College
BLAKELOCK RD.
SHAKESPEARE AV.
Eamont Ter.
WANSBECK GDNS.

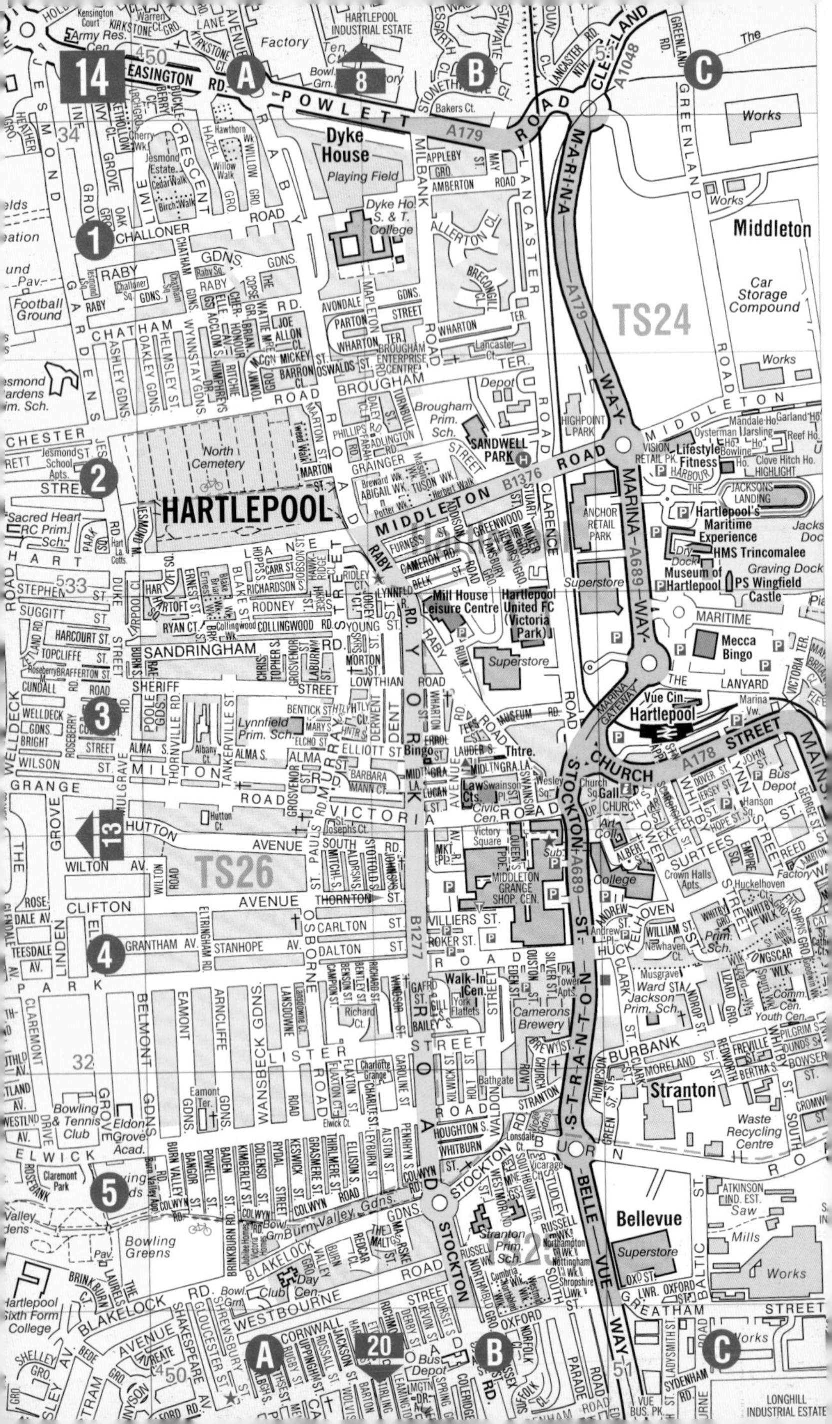

14
8
13
20
A
B
C
1
2
3
4
5
HARTLEPOOL
Dyke House
Playing Field
Dyke Ho. S. & T. College
Middleton
Car Storage Compound
TS24
TS26
North Cemetery
HARTLEPOOL INDUSTRIAL ESTATE
Factory
Works
POWLETT ROAD
A179
CLEVELAND ROAD
A1048
EASINGTON RD.
MARINA WAY
A689
MIDDLETON ROAD
B1376
CHURCH STREET
A178
STOCKTON ROAD
STOCKTON ST.
STRANTON
BELLE VUE WAY
YORK ROAD
B1127
RABY ROAD
VICTORIA ROAD
HUTTON AVENUE
PARK ROAD
ELWICK RD.
GRANGE ROAD
MILTON ROAD
BROUGHAM ROAD
CHALLONER ROAD
JESMOND GARDENS
JESMOND GROVE
HART LANE
CHESTER RD.
CLARENCE ROAD
LANCASTER ROAD
GREENLAND ROAD
MILBANK ROAD
MAPLETON ROAD
MURRAY STREET
LISTER STREET
OSBORNE ROAD
BLAKELOCK ROAD
WESTBOURNE ROAD
OXFORD ROAD
GREATHAM STREET
BURBANK ST.
Sandwell Park
Brougham Prim. Sch.
Lynnfield Prim. Sch.
Sacred Heart RC Prim. Sch.
Jesmond Gardens Prim. Sch.
Football Ground
Mill House Leisure Centre
Hartlepool United FC (Victoria Park)
Superstore
Anchor Retail Park
Highpoint Park
Vision Retail Pk.
Lifestyle Fitness
Jacksons Landing
Hartlepool's Maritime Experience
HMS Trincomalee
Museum of Hartlepool
PS Wingfield Castle
Graving Dock
Mecca Bingo
Vue Cin.
Hartlepool
Marina Gateway
The Lanyard
Maritime Avenue
Bus Depot
Art Gall.
Art Coll.
College
Church Sq.
Victory Square
Middleton Grange Shop. Cen.
Civic Cen.
Law Cts.
Thtre.
Bingo
Walk-In Cen.
Camerons Brewery
Jackson Prim. Sch.
Stranton
Waste Recycling Centre
Bellevue
Atkinson Ind. Est.
Mills
Stranton Prim. Sch.
Bowling & Tennis Club
Eldon Grove Acad.
Bowling Greens
Burn Valley Gdns.
Hartlepool Sixth Form College
Day Cen.
Bus Depot
Longhill Industrial Estate
Vue Bus. Pk.
Crown Halls Apts.
Huckelhoven Ct.
Comm. Cen.
Youth Cen.
Depot
Lancaster Ct.
Brougham Enterprise Centre
Army Res. Cen.
Kensington Court
Jesmond Estate
Claremont Park
Valley Gdns.

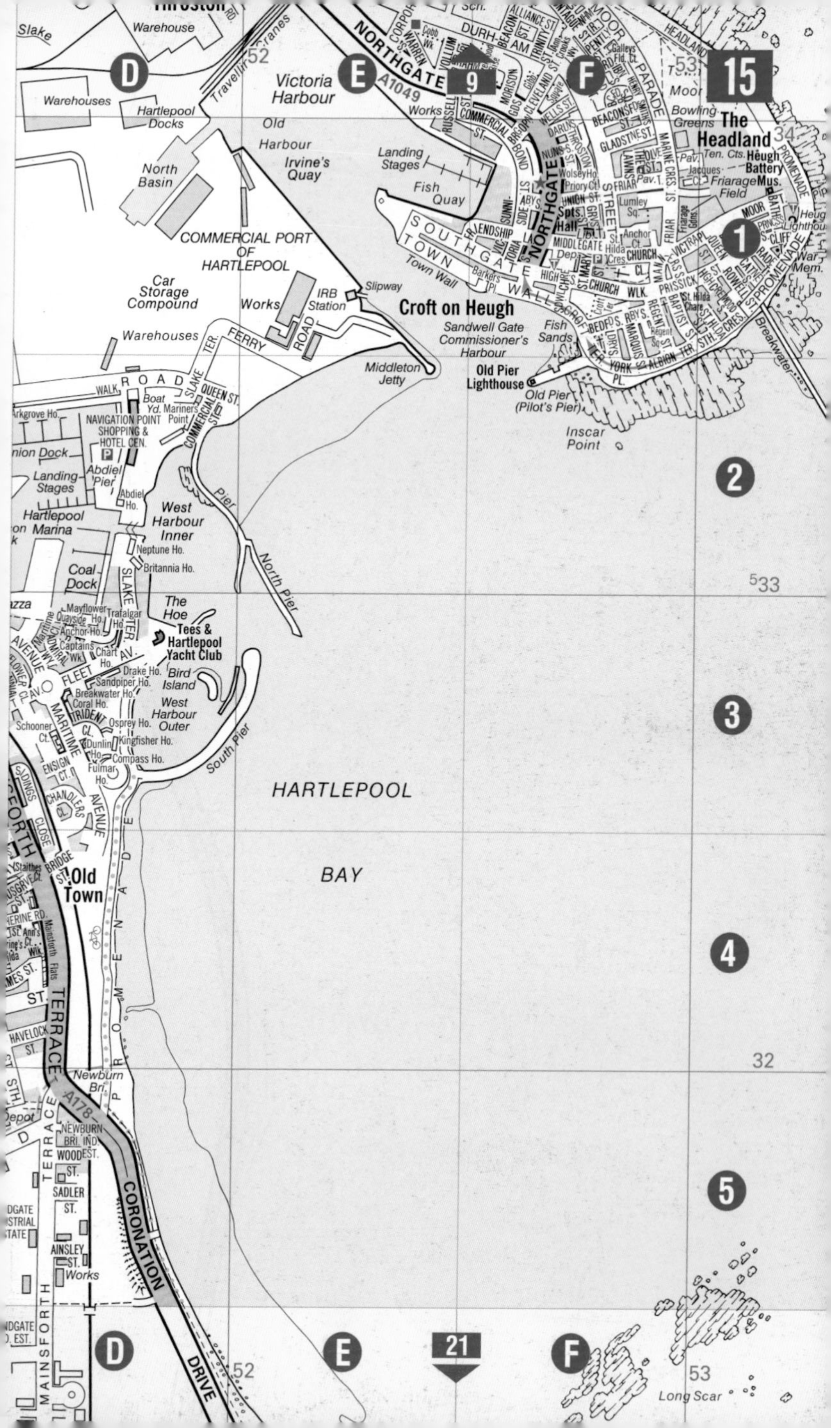
Warehouse
Slake
D
E
F
Victoria Harbour
NORTHGATE
A1049
9
Warehouses
Hartlepool Docks
Travelling Cranes
52
53
Old Harbour
Irvine's Quay
Landing Stages
Fish Quay
North Basin
Works
COMMERCIAL
RUSSELL ST.
DURHAM ST.
BEACON ST.
TRINITY ST.
ALLIANCE ST.
MORISON GDS.
CLEVELAND ST.
WELLS ST.
HEADLAND
PARADE
Moor
Bowling Greens
The Headland
34
Ten. Cts.
Pav.
Jacques Ct.
Friarage Field
Heugh Battery Mus.
PROMENADE
Heugh Lighthouse
War Mem.
MOOR
BATHS
PRINCES
CLIFF
BEACONSFIELD ST.
GLADSTONE ST.
LAWNS
OLIVE ST.
MARINE CRES.
FRIAR ST.
Lumley Sq.
Anchor Ct.
CHURCH CL.
VICTORIA PL.
QUEEN ST.
THROSTON ST.
NUNS ST.
NORTHGATE
Wolsey Ho.
Priory Ct.
UNION ST.
Spts. Hall
MIDDLEGATE
ST. MARY
Hilda Cres.
CHURCH
HIGH ST.
FRIENDSHIP
SUNNISIDE
VICTORIA
SOUTHGATE
TOWN WALL
Town Wall
Barkers Pl.
CHURCH WALK
PRISSICK
HIGH CROFT
ROWELL ST.
ST. HILDA CRES.
St. Hilda Chare
BAPTIST ST.
REGENT ST.
MARQUIS ST.
BEDFORD ST.
YORK PL.
ALBION TER.
Regent Sq.
Croft on Heugh
Sandwell Gate
Commissioner's Harbour
Fish Sands
Breakwater
Old Pier Lighthouse
Old Pier (Pilot's Pier)
Inscar Point
COMMERCIAL PORT OF HARTLEPOOL
Car Storage Compound
Works
IRB Station
Slipway
Warehouses
FERRY ROAD
SLAKE TER.
QUEEN ST.
COMMERCIAL ST.
ROAD
WALK
Middleton Jetty
Boat Yd.
Mariners Point
NAVIGATION POINT SHOPPING & HOTEL CEN.
Union Dock
Landing Stages
Abdiel Pier
Abdiel Ho.
Hartlepool Marina
West Harbour Inner
Pier
North Pier
Neptune Ho.
Britannia Ho.
Coal Dock
SLAKE TER.
The Hoe
Tees & Hartlepool Yacht Club
Mayflower Ho.
Trafalgar Ho.
Quayside
Anchor Ho.
Captains Wk.
Chart Ho.
FLEET AV.
Drake Ho.
Sandpiper Ho.
Breakwater Ho.
Coral Ho.
TRIDENT CL.
Osprey Ho.
Kingfisher Ho.
Dunlin Ho.
Compass Ho.
Fulmar Ho.
Bird Island
West Harbour Outer
South Pier
Schooner Ct.
ENSIGN CT.
MARITIME AVENUE
CHANDLERS CL.
AVENUE
HARTLEPOOL
BAY
PROMENADE
Old Town
Staithes Ct.
BRIDGE ST.
TERRACE
HAVELOCK ST.
Newburn Bri.
A178
NEWBURN BRI. IND. EST.
WOOD ST.
SADLER ST.
AINSLEY ST.
Works
CORONATION DRIVE
MAINSFORTH TERRACE
Depot
1
2
3
4
5
533
32
21
Long Scar

Stotfold Moor
44
A
10
B
4 45
C
Bogl
Benknowle Farm
Elwick Windmill (disused)
The Old Mill
A19
1
Cow Pasture Wood
Wyncroft
31
Winterly Hill Plantation
2
DAL
Red Lion Farm
Teesview
A19
TS27
3
High Stotfold
5 30
Black Wood
4
Middle Stotfold
RED GAP MOOR
5
A19
Gunnersvale Farm
Stotfold Crest Stables
29
A
28
B
C
44
4 45

Dove Cote
46
The Howls
Reservoir (covered)
11
LANE
47
17
D
E
F
Beck
Dalton Piercy Crag
TS25
The Grove
DALTON
Dalton Piercy
DALTON HEIGHTS
Dene Gth.
GREEN
NORTH VW.
THE TER.
COLLEGE CL.
THE
ABBOTS LEA
MANOR FIELDS
Hall
1
LANE
Dalton
31
Three Gates Farm
2
ON
Hartlepool
DALTON
18
Three Gates
Woodside
Poultry Houses
Brierton Heights Farm
Beck
3
Brierton Rush
530
BACK
4
Cheviot Hill
Crow's Meadow Farm
5
LANE
Billingham TS22
Weir
Low Stotfold
29
29
46
47
D
E
F

18
47
A
12
B
48
C
Field House Farm
Petersbrooke
Tunstall Farm
1
Dalton Nook Plantation
Hartlepool
Horse Clos
Plantation
31
2
TS27
17
Four Ace
Meadow Bungalow
Marite
Tees View
BRIERTO
Dalton
3
Cherry Tree Cottage
Brierton
Brierton North Farm
Brierton Farm
530
Brierton Farm
Quads 4 All
Leahills View
Beck
4
DALTON
LANARK RD.
Lennox
Milne Walk
MILNE WK.
ROAD
MACRA
MONKTON
Owton Grange
Billingham
BACK
Crow's Meadow Farm
5
TS22
Blue House
LANE
Greatham
29
West Pasture
A
30
B
C
47
48

Riding School
SUMMERHILL LANE
Visitor Centre
Family Wood
Burn Valley Gardens
Playing Field
Bowling Green
13
Tennis Courts
Playing Fields
Hartlepool Sixth Form College
The English Martyrs School & Sixth Form College
Playing Fields
SUMMERHILL COUNTRY PARK
BLAKELOCK RD.
SHAKESPEARE AV.
GLOUCESTER ST.
SHREWSBURY ST.
BRINKBURN RD.
OXFORD RD.
THACKERAY ROAD
POPE GRO.
GLADYS WORTHY CL.
KIPLING AV.
BURNS GRO.
CAXTON GRO.
BROWNING AV.
CHAUCER AV.
OXFORD ROAD
KINGSLEY AV.
TRISTRAM AVENUE
TENNYSON AV.
SHELLEY GRO.
WORDSWORTH AV.
SHERIDAN GRO.
WAVERLEY TERRACE
HEATHFIELD
FERNWOOD
KYLE AV.
Prim. Sch.
FERNVILLE CL.
CHESTERTON RD.
WALPOLE RD.
HUXLEY WLK.
SWALEBROOKE AV.
TAYBROOKE AV.
Kingsley Prim. Sch.
Rift House Recreation Ground
Pav.
MARLOWE ROAD
DRYDEN ROAD
SWINBURNE
Laurel Gds.
Rift House
TRENTBROOKE AV.
KINGSLEY AVENUE
OAKLAND
GRETA
THE MEADOW
GULLIVER WALK
LEWIS GRO.
MASEFIELD
MACAULAY ROAD
WESTBROOKE AVENUE
TYNEBROOKE AV.
TEESBROOKE AV.
SOUTHBROOKE AVENUE
War Memorial
SINCLAIR
Sitwell Walk
Hartlepool PRU
CATCOTE ROAD
TS25
20
Stranton
Hartlepool Crematorium
Cemetery
WESTFIELDS
Gardner House
Esha Ness
Brierton Shops
Brierton Sports Centre
BRIERTON LANE
EARLSFERRY
EAGLESFIELD
ERSKINE RD.
ENDRICK
DUNCAN RD.
DURNESS GRO.
CLOSE
ELMFIELD GDS.
WHITWORTH GDS.
PICKTREE GDS.
CLARKSON CT.
ARBROATH
ARGYLL
AIRDRIE
ARMADALE
ABERDEEN RD.
ARDROSSAN
DALKEITH ROAD
DUNBAR RD.
FULBECK RD.
DUNDEE
DUMFRIES RD.
Owton Manor Primary Sch.
ESKDALE
FORFAR ROAD
FIFE GRO.
FORDYCE
FALKIRK
DUNOON
GREENOCK
Com. Cen. Lib.
Youth Cen.
ROSSMERE WAY
Swim. Pool
Rossmere
Recreation Ground
Ten. Cts.
ROSSMERE PARK
BRAEMAR
St. Teresa's RC Prim. Sch.
Rossmere Prim. Sch.
WYNYARD ROAD
LAIRD
LOCH GRO.
LEVEN GRO.
KEBOCK WALK
KELSO WALK
HAMILTON RD.
HIGHLAND RD.
Heriot Grange
CALLANDER ROAD
BENMORE ROAD
BALMORAL
CAMPBELL RD.
OWTON MANOR LANE
KINTRA RD.
KINBRACE
KILMARNOCK
JAMESON
HOLYROOD
HARRIS GRO.
HIBERNIAN GRO.
IBROX GRO.
MANOR ROAD
OWTON ROAD
CAITHNESS ROAD
COMRIE RD.
CLAYMORE RD.
MARDALE AV.
BERKELEY AV.
AVENUE
STOCKTON ROAD
MAXWELL ROAD
Grange Prim. Sch.
Manor College of Technology
Owton Manor
Playing Fields
INVERNESS
IVANHOE CRES.
IRVINE RD.
INNES RD.
TORQUAY
WAY
FENS CRES.
TRURO DRIVE
BOSTON CL.
HONITON DRIVE
SALCOMBE DR.
PAIGNTON DR.
DAWLISH DR.
40
A689
KESTEVEN ROAD
LINCOLN
CRANWELL ROAD
MOWBRAY RD.
INGHAM GRO.
FENTON
SPALDING
WINTHORPE GRO.
THURSBY
WELLAND RD.
HOLLAND
UPTON WLK.
BURWELL WLK.
THETFORD ROAD
31
CROXTON AV.
CHICHESTER CLOSE
CAISTOR
FAREHAM
Milestone Garden Nurseries
Nursery
D
E
F
1
2
3
4
5
49
50

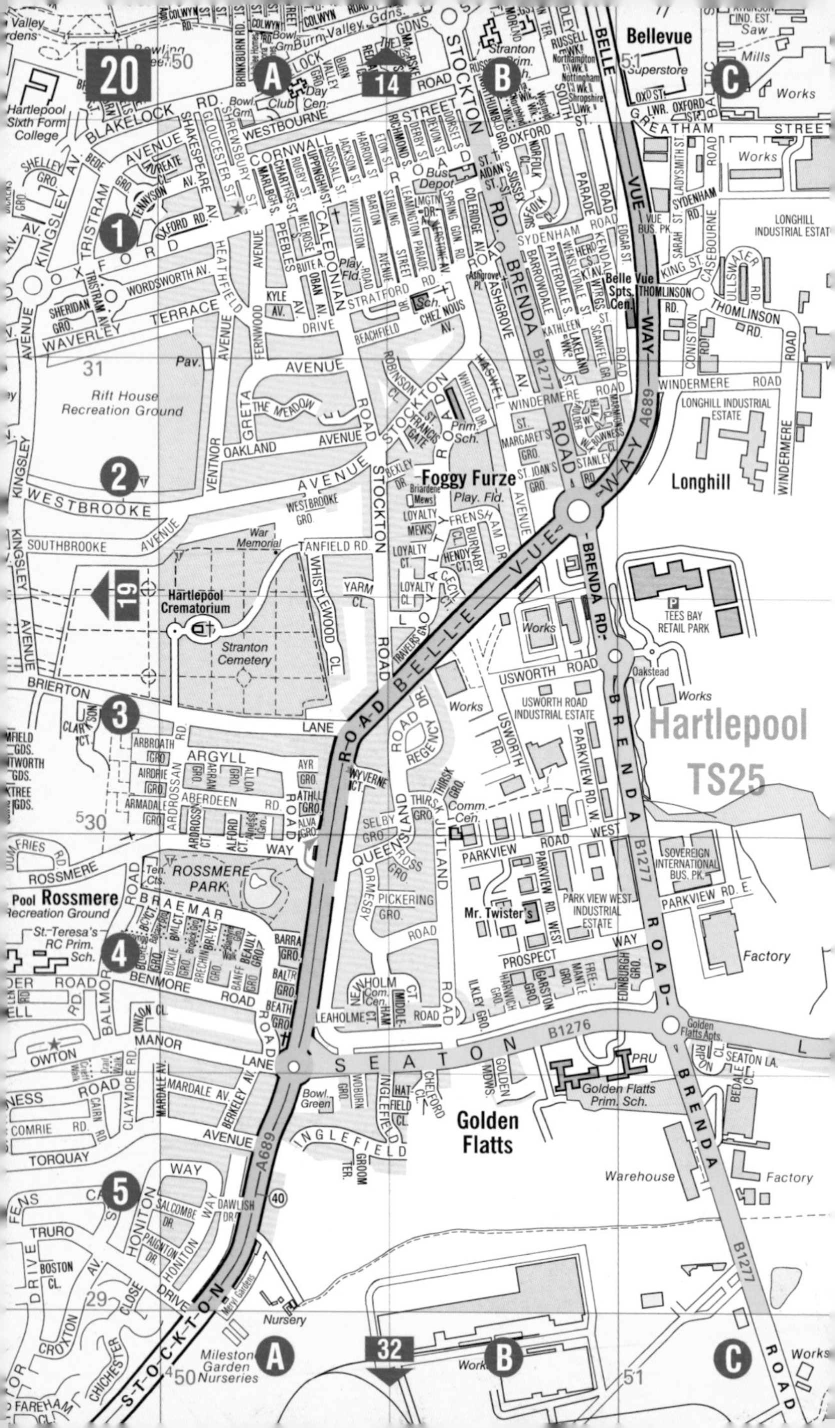

20
14
19
32
A
B
C
1
2
3
4
5
Bellevue
Superstore
Works
Mills
Saw
Hartlepool Sixth Form College
Stranton Prim. Sch.
Day Cen.
Club
Bowl. Grn.
Burn Valley Gdns.
BLAKELOCK RD.
WESTBOURNE
CORNWALL
STREET
OXFORD
OXFORD RD.
TRISTRAM AV.
KINGSLEY AV.
WORDSWORTH AV.
WAVERLEY TERRACE
HEATHFIELD
FERNWOOD
CALEDONIAN
STRATFORD RD.
BEACHFIELD
CHEZ NOUS AV.
DRIVE
Bus Depot
ST. AIDAN'S ST.
STOCKTON ROAD
BRENDA RD.
B1277
SYDENHAM
GREATHAM STREET
LWR. OXFORD ST.
VUE BUS. PK.
LONGHILL INDUSTRIAL ESTATE
KING ST.
THOMLINSON RD.
Belle Vue Spts. Cen.
WINDERMERE ROAD
Longhill
BELLE VUE WAY
A689
31
Rift House Recreation Ground
Pav.
THE MEADOW
GRETA AVENUE
OAKLAND AVENUE
WESTBROOKE AVENUE
SOUTHBROOKE AVENUE
Foggy Furze
Play. Fld.
Prim. Sch.
LOYALTY MEWS
LOYALTY CT.
LOYALTY CL.
YARM CL.
WHISTLEWOOD CL.
TANFIELD RD.
War Memorial
Hartlepool Crematorium
Stranton Cemetery
BRIERTON LANE
TEES BAY RETAIL PARK
Works
USWORTH ROAD
USWORTH ROAD INDUSTRIAL ESTATE
Hartlepool
TS25
ARGYLL
ABERDEEN RD.
REGENCY DR.
Comm. Cen.
PARKVIEW ROAD WEST
SOVEREIGN INTERNATIONAL BUS. PK.
PARKVIEW RD. E.
PARK VIEW WEST INDUSTRIAL ESTATE
Mr. Twister's
Factory
PROSPECT WAY
ROSSMERE WAY
ROSSMERE PARK
Rossmere
Recreation Ground
St. Teresa's RC Prim. Sch.
BRAEMAR
BENMORE ROAD
MANOR LANE
OWTON
PICKERING GRO.
SEATON
B1276
SEATON LA.
Golden Flatts Apts.
PRU
Golden Flatts Prim. Sch.
Golden Flatts
INGLEFIELD
Bowl. Green
Warehouse
Factory
TORQUAY AVENUE
WAY
DAWLISH DR.
HONITON
TRURO
BOSTON CL.
CROXTON
CHICHESTER CLOSE
29
STOCKTON
Nursery
Milestone Garden Nurseries
Works
ROAD
450
51
530

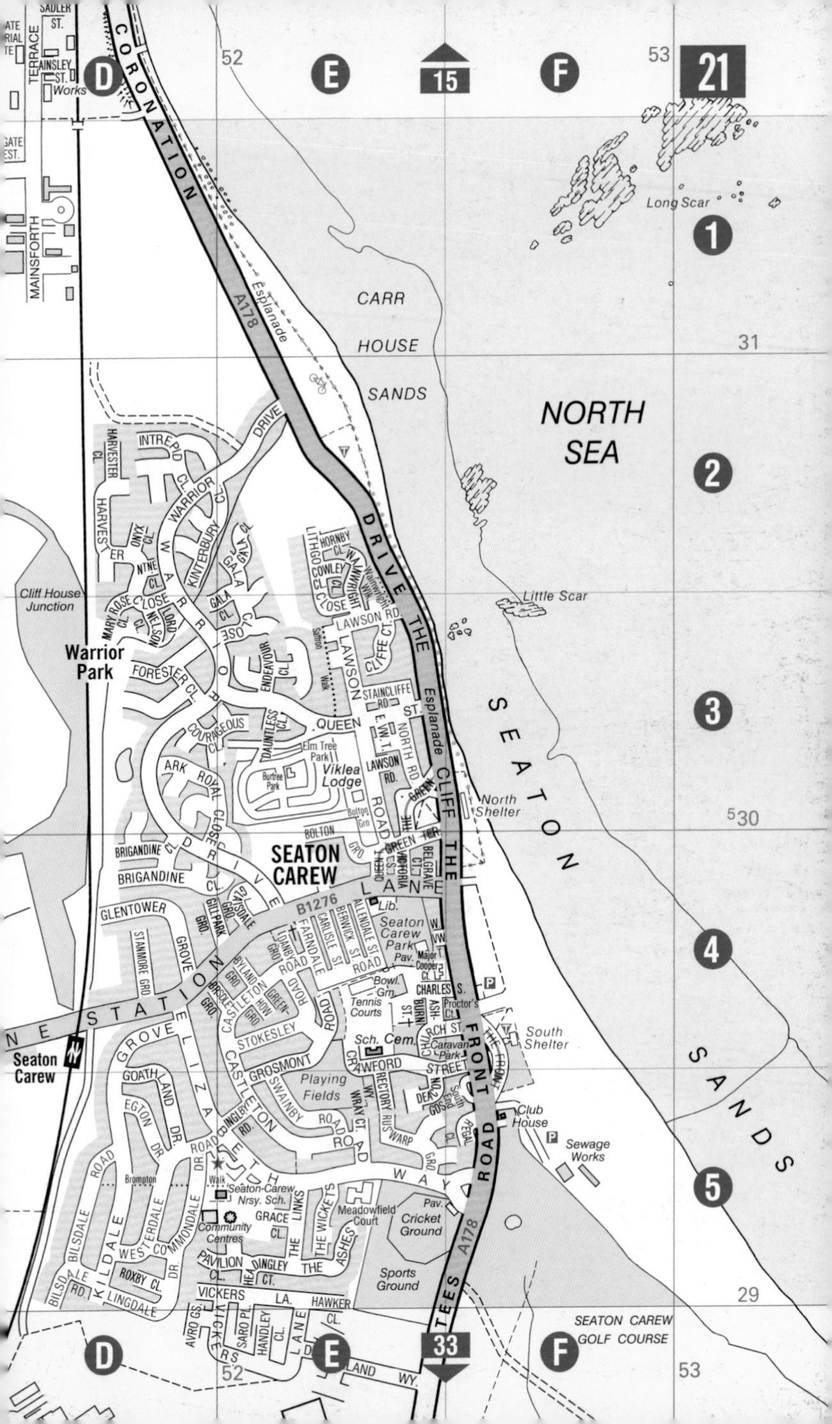
15
D
E
F
52
53
1
2
3
4
5
31
30
29
NORTH SEA
Long Scar
Little Scar
CARR HOUSE SANDS
SEATON SANDS
CORONATION DRIVE
THE CLIFF
THE FRONT
TEES ROAD
A178
B1276
Esplanade
SADLER ST.
TERRACE
AINSLEY ST.
Works
MAINSFORTH
Cliff House Junction
Warrior Park
HARVESTER CL.
HARVESTER
INTREPID CL.
WARRIOR DRIVE
WARRIOR CL.
KINTERBURY CL.
ONYX CL.
GALA CL.
GALA CLOSE
ROSE CLOSE
MARY ROSE CL.
NELSON CL.
LORD
FORESTER CL.
ENDEAVOUR CL.
DAUNTLESS CL.
COURAGEOUS CL.
ARK ROYAL CLOSE
QUEEN ST.
Elm Tree Park
Burtree Park
Viklea Lodge
LITHGO CL.
HORNBY CL.
COWLEY CL.
WAINWRIGHT CLOSE
Wainwright Wlk.
LAWSON RD.
LAWSON ROAD
CLIFFE CT.
STAINCLIFFE RD.
NORTH RD.
THE GREEN
GREEN TER.
Saffron Walk
Bolton Gro
BOLTON GRO.
SEATON CAREW
BRIGANDINE CL.
BRIGANDINE
GLENTOWER
GILLPARK GRO.
GLAISDALE GRO.
STATION LANE
VICTORIA
BELGRAVE CT.
Lib.
Seaton Carew Park
Pav.
Major Cooper Ct.
ALLENDALE ST.
BERWICK ST.
CARLISLE ST.
FARNDALE ROAD
DANBY GRO.
BYLAND GRO.
STAMMORE GRO.
GROVE
CHARLES ST.
ASH-BURN ST.
Proctor's Ct.
Bowl. Grn.
Tennis Courts
CASTLETON ROAD
GREENHOW GRO.
STOKESLEY
BRISDALE GRO.
ELIZABETH WAY
GROVE
Seaton Carew
Sch.
Cem.
CHURCH ST.
Caravan Park
South Shelter
North Shelter
CRAWFORD STREET
GROSMONT ROAD
SWAINBY ROAD
Playing Fields
WRAY CT.
RECTORY WY.
RUSWARP GRO.
DEANE GDS.
REGAL CL.
Club House
Sewage Works
GOATHLAND DR.
EGTON DR.
INGLBY RD.
Brompton Walk
Seaton Carew Nrsy. Sch.
Community Centres
GRACE CL.
THE LINKS
THE WICKETS
THE ASHES
Meadowfield Court
Pav.
Cricket Ground
Sports Ground
BILSDALE ROAD
KILDALE
WESTERDALE
COMMONDALE DR.
ROXBY CL.
LINGDALE
BILSDALE RD.
PAVILION CL.
HEADINGLEY CT.
VICKERS LA.
HAWKER CL.
AVRO GS.
SARO PL.
HANDLEY CL.
LANE
LAND WY.
33
SEATON CAREW GOLF COURSE

A
B
C
34
435
530
29
28
1
2
3
4
5
Sprucely Plantation
Carr Wood
Knotty Hill
Club House
Golf Driving Range
Dogkennel Plantation
Knotty Hill Plantation
KNOTTY HILL GOLF COURSE
Green Knowles
Low Hardwick
South Durham Hunt Kennels
Brick Kiln Plantation
Pheasant Plantation
Hardwick Hall
HARDWICK HALL COUNTRY PARK
Temple (Ruin)
Serpentine Lake
Hardwick Park Visitor Cen.
P
Brakes Farm
DURHAM ROAD
A177
SEDGEFIELD
HARDWICK PARK
Sedgefield Showground
Pav.
Cricket Ground
Sands Hall Roundabout
STATION ROAD
A689
SANDY BANK
West Lodge
East Lodge
Home Farm
Sands Hall
Bath Plantation
Sands Farm
SEDGEFIELD RACE COURSE
Grandstands
Stables
OLD
WELLGARTH M.
DURHAM ROAD
TOWN
Turnpike
FARFIELD MNR.
MEADOW
CUNNINGHAM CT.
NEVILLE
H
KERR
CR.
DRIVE
MILBOURNE CT.
MITFORD CT.
WOLFE CT.
WALLINGTON DR.
MATFEN CT.
BELSAY CT.
NORTH PARK ROAD
HARDWICK
BOYNE CT.
PARK LANE
ROAD WEST
WEST PARK VW.
TOWN FARM CT.
DUNELM CT.
LAMBTON CRES.
STATION
QUEENS DRIVE
CLAREMONT GR.
HASLEDON GR.
Play Field
HORNBY AV.
WAY
MELGROVE
HADLEIGH CL.
The Willows
SPRING

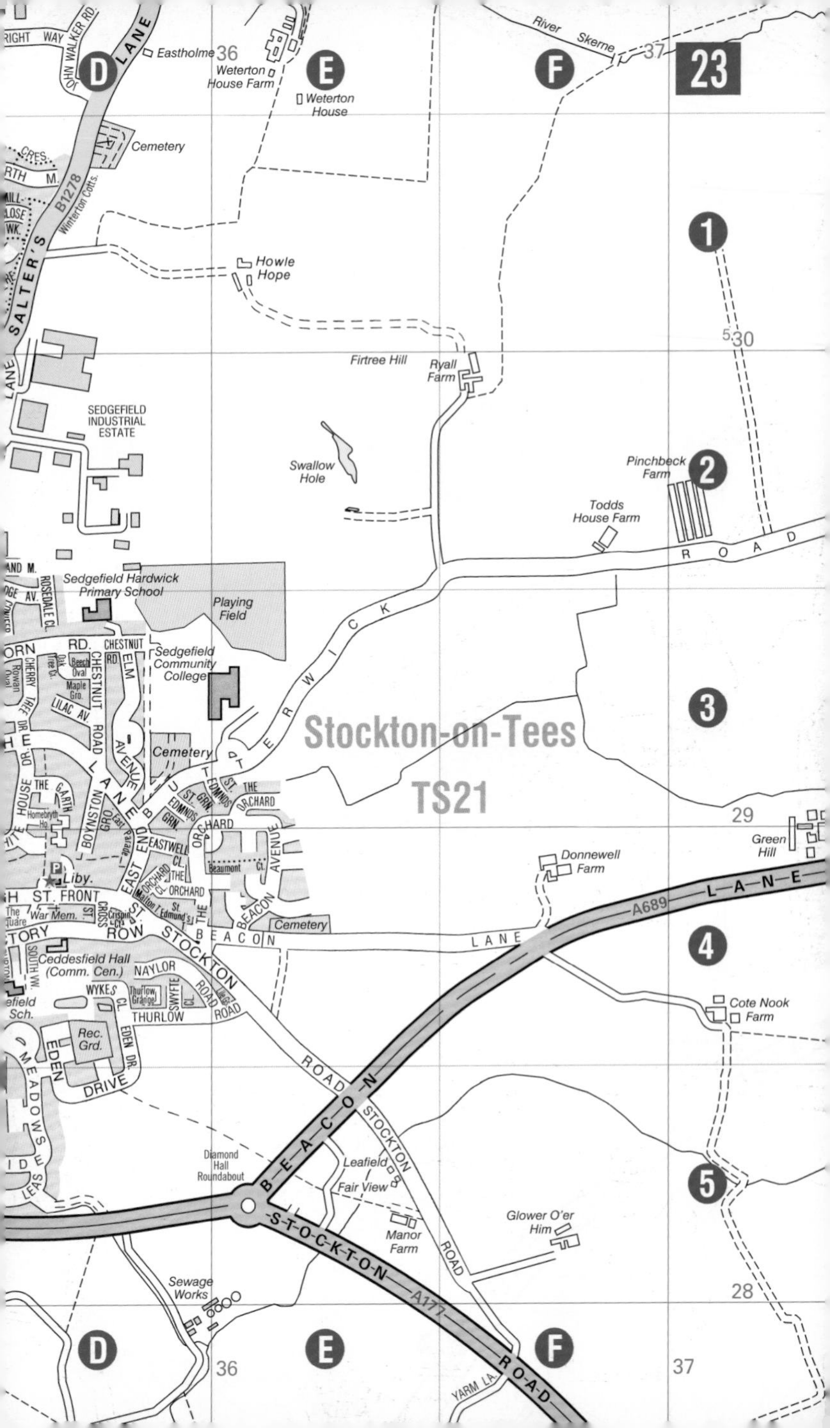
Stockton-on-Tees
TS21
D
E
F
1
2
3
4
5
36
37
30
29
28
River Skerne
Eastholme
Weterton House Farm
Weterton House
Cemetery
Howle Hope
Firtree Hill
Ryall Farm
SEDGEFIELD INDUSTRIAL ESTATE
Swallow Hole
Pinchbeck Farm
Todds House Farm
Sedgefield Hardwick Primary School
Playing Field
Sedgefield Community College
Cemetery
Donnewell Farm
Green Hill
Cote Nook Farm
Liby.
War Mem.
Ceddesfield Hall (Comm. Cen.)
Rec. Grd.
Diamond Hall Roundabout
Leafield
Fair View
Manor Farm
Glower O'er Him
Sewage Works
SALTER'S LANE
B1278
Winterton Cotts.
JOHN WALKER RD.
WRIGHT WAY
RTH M.
CRES.
BUTTERWICK ROAD
A689
LANE
BEACON LANE
STOCKTON ROAD
A177
BEACON
STOCKTON
YARM LA.
ST. FRONT
ROW
CROSS
EAST END
THE ORCHARD
ORCHARD
AVENUE
Beaumont Ct.
EASTWELL CL.
ST. EDMONDS GRN.
THE ORCHARD
CHESTNUT RD.
CHESTNUT ROAD
ELM AVENUE
LILAC AV.
CHERRY TREE DR.
Rowan Oval
Maple Gro.
Beech Oval
Oak Tree Cl.
HAWTHORN RD.
ROSEDALE CL.
BOYNSTON GRO
East Parade
THE GARTH
Homebryth Ho.
HOUSE DR.
Crispin Ct.
Malton T.
St. Edmund's T.
THE BEACON
Cemetery
NAYLOR
WYKES CL.
Thurlow Grange
SWYFTE CL.
THURLOW ROAD
EDEN DR.
EDEN DRIVE
MEADOWS
LEAS
SOUTH VW.
Sch.

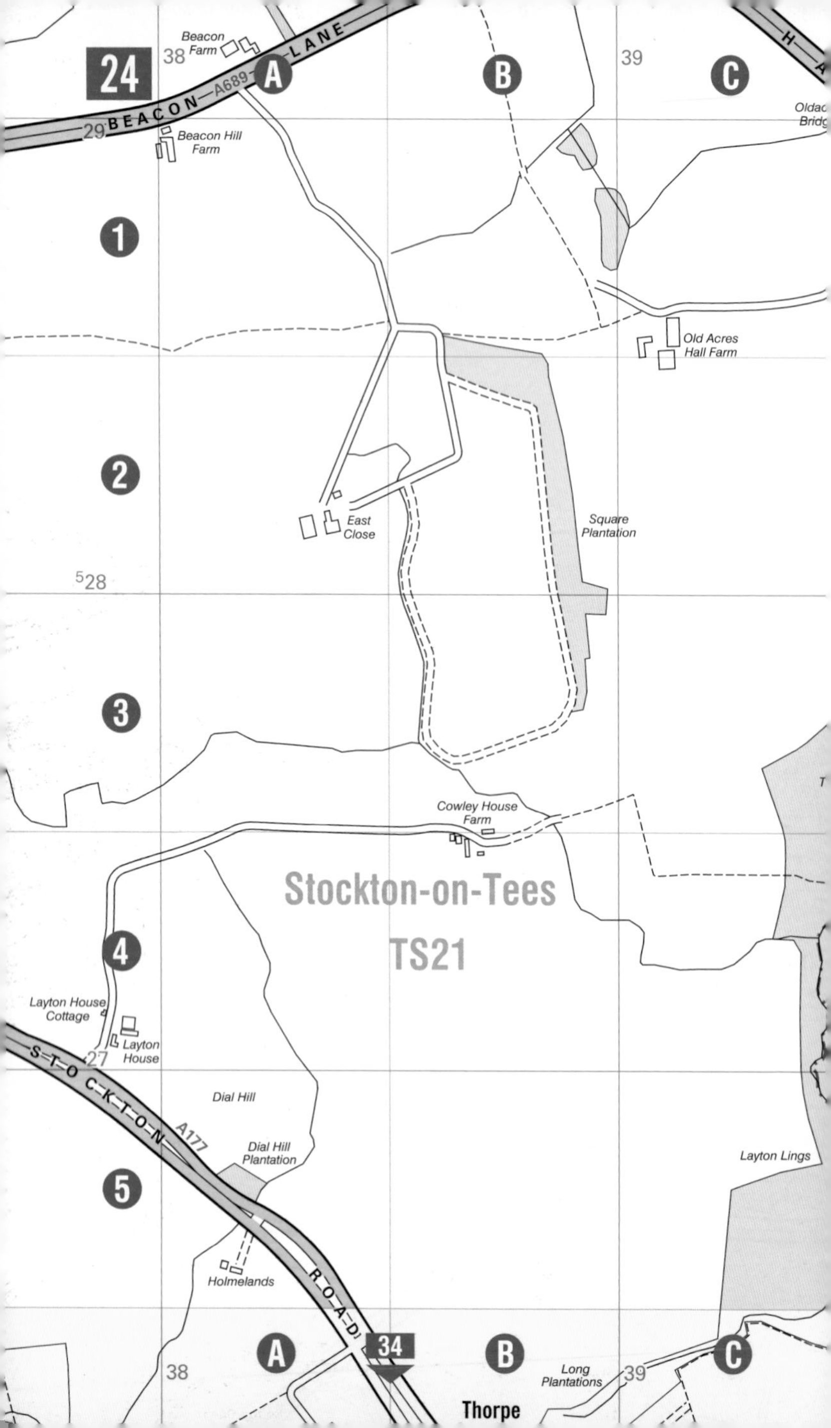
BEACON LANE
A689
Beacon Farm
Beacon Hill Farm
Old Acres Hall Farm
East Close
Square Plantation
Cowley House Farm
Stockton-on-Tees
TS21
Layton House Cottage
Layton House
Dial Hill
Dial Hill Plantation
STOCKTON ROAD
A177
Holmelands
Layton Lings
Long Plantations
Thorpe
34
A
B
C
1
2
3
4
5
38
39
29
528
27

25
D
E
F
440
41
Middle Swainston
29
High Swainston
HARTLEPOOL ROAD
A689
Newlands
Tilery Cottage
Middle Swainston Plantation
Station Cottages
Battle-stations
Station House
Tilery Wood
DURHAM
HARTLEPOOL
Billingham
TS22
Sluice
528
1
2
3
4
5
BRIERLEY DRIVE
Cockpit
DRIVE
DURHAM
STOCKTON-ON-TEES
Brierley Wood
BLACK
BLACK SQUARES
BLACK SQUARES DRIVE
WOOD
WYNYARD WOODS
SAVILLE
CAWTHORNE PL.
MAYNARD GRO.
26
SWAINSTON CL.
WYNYARD WOODS
GUNNERS
THE PLANTATIONS
HOLDER
DRIVE
THE RACECOURSE
BRIERLEY
BRIERLEY WOOD
Seaham New Plantation
27
THE NURSERY
DRIVE
Woodend Farm
35
BRIERLEY
Brierley
Spring Bank

A
B
C
1
2
3
4
5
41
442
29
528
27
Middle Swainston
Newton Hanzard Plantations
Middle Swainston Plantation
DURHAM
HARTLEPOOL
Black Moor Plantation
Newton Hanzard Plantation
NEWTON HANZARD LONG DRIVE
Thunderbuck Drive
Sluice
HARTLEPOOL ROAD
A689
Newton Hanzard Beck
SWEET PEA CL.
SUMMER
LOVE LANE
HEATHER CL.
ORCHID CL.
LILY POT CL.
BUTTERCUP AV.
LAVENDER AV.
HONEYPOT CL.
BUTTERCUP
LANE
SNOWDROP AV.
NEWTON HANZARD SHORT DRIVE
THE MEADOWS
Forester's Lodge Roundabout
Forester's Lodge
MANOR FIELDS
GLEDSTONE
WYNYARD
SAVILLE CL.
CAWTHORNE PL.
ESHTON
DELAMERE
WOODS
BLACK
WOOD
BLACK SQUARES
25
MAYNARD GRO.
SWAINSTON CL.
BLACK SQUARES DRIVE
GUNNERS VALE
THE PLANTATIONS
HOLDERNESSE
SHEEPDENE
AMERSTON
SWANCER CT.
BUTTERWICK GRO.
HARESTONES
NURSERY DRIVE
Sylvan M.
SPRING BANK
WOOD PDK.
TILERY WOOD GN.
HORSE SHOE POND
WOODSIDE
THE STABLES
Salter House Wood
North Lodges
BRIERLEY DR.
BRIERLEY DR.
Rose Cottage
SALTER
HARRISON CT.
WOODEND CT.
Salter Houses
GRANARY
THE
WYNYARD
WYNYARD VILLAGE
THE AVENUE
PARK AV.
THE OVAL
CASTLEREAGH
Seaham New Plantation
THE RACECOURSE
Fanny's Glen
Black Corner Plantation
BRIERLEY
Brierley
Spring Bank
The Paddocks
THE
36

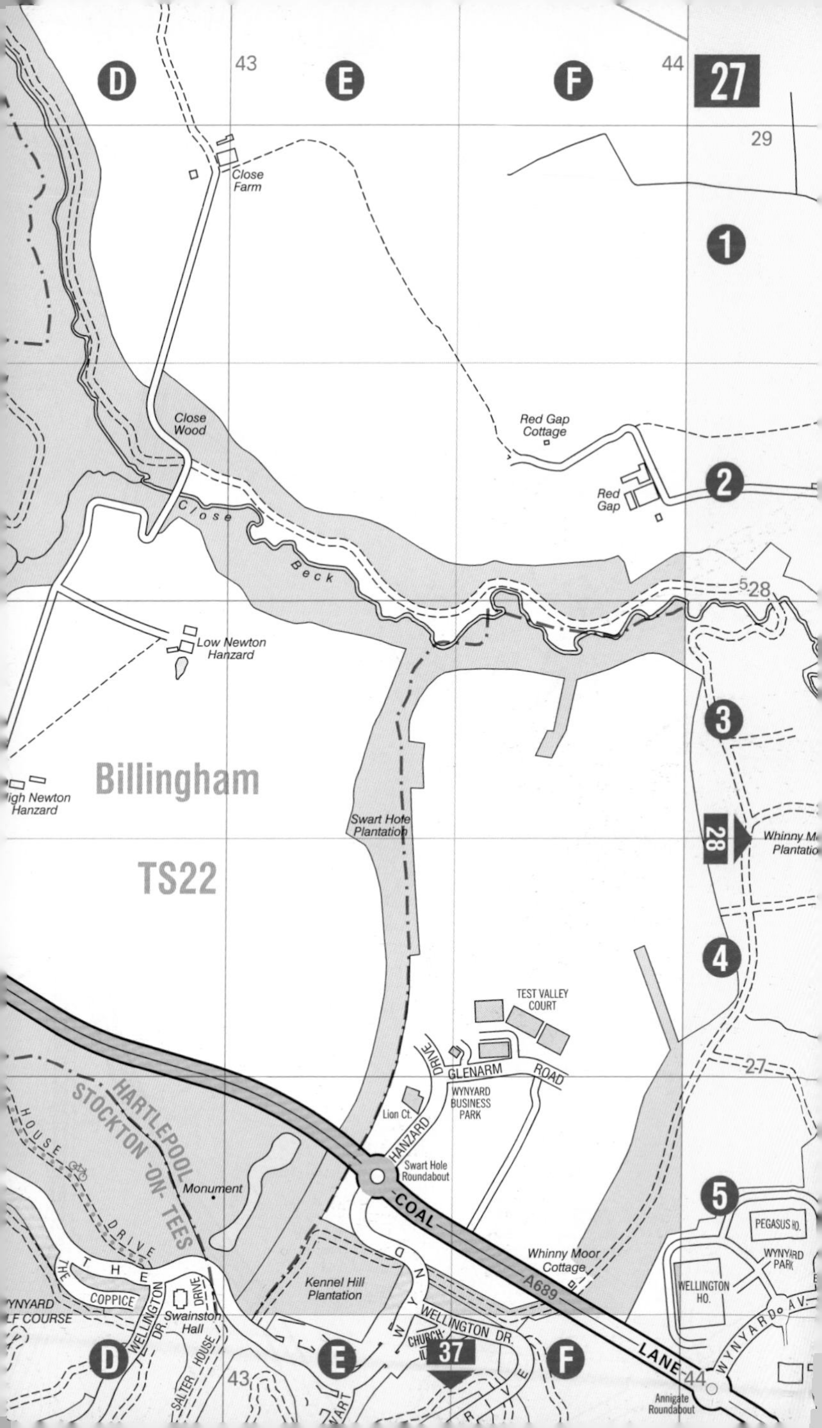
D
E
F
43
44
29
1
2
3
4
5
Close Farm
Close Wood
Close Beck
Red Gap Cottage
Red Gap
28
Low Newton Hanzard
Billingham
High Newton Hanzard
TS22
Swart Hole Plantation
28
Whinny Moor Plantation
TEST VALLEY COURT
DRIVE
GLENARM ROAD
WYNYARD BUSINESS PARK
Lion Ct.
HANZARD
Swart Hole Roundabout
27
HARTLEPOOL
STOCKTON -ON- TEES
HOUSE
DRIVE
THE
Monument
COAL
A689
LANE
Whinny Moor Cottage
Kennel Hill Plantation
PEGASUS HO.
WYNYARD PARK
WELLINGTON HO.
WYNYARD AV.
THE COPPICE
WELLINGTON DR.
DRIVE
Swainston Hall
WYNYARD GOLF COURSE
SALTER
HOUSE
WELLINGTON DR.
CHURCH
37
DRIVE
Annigate Roundabout
44
43

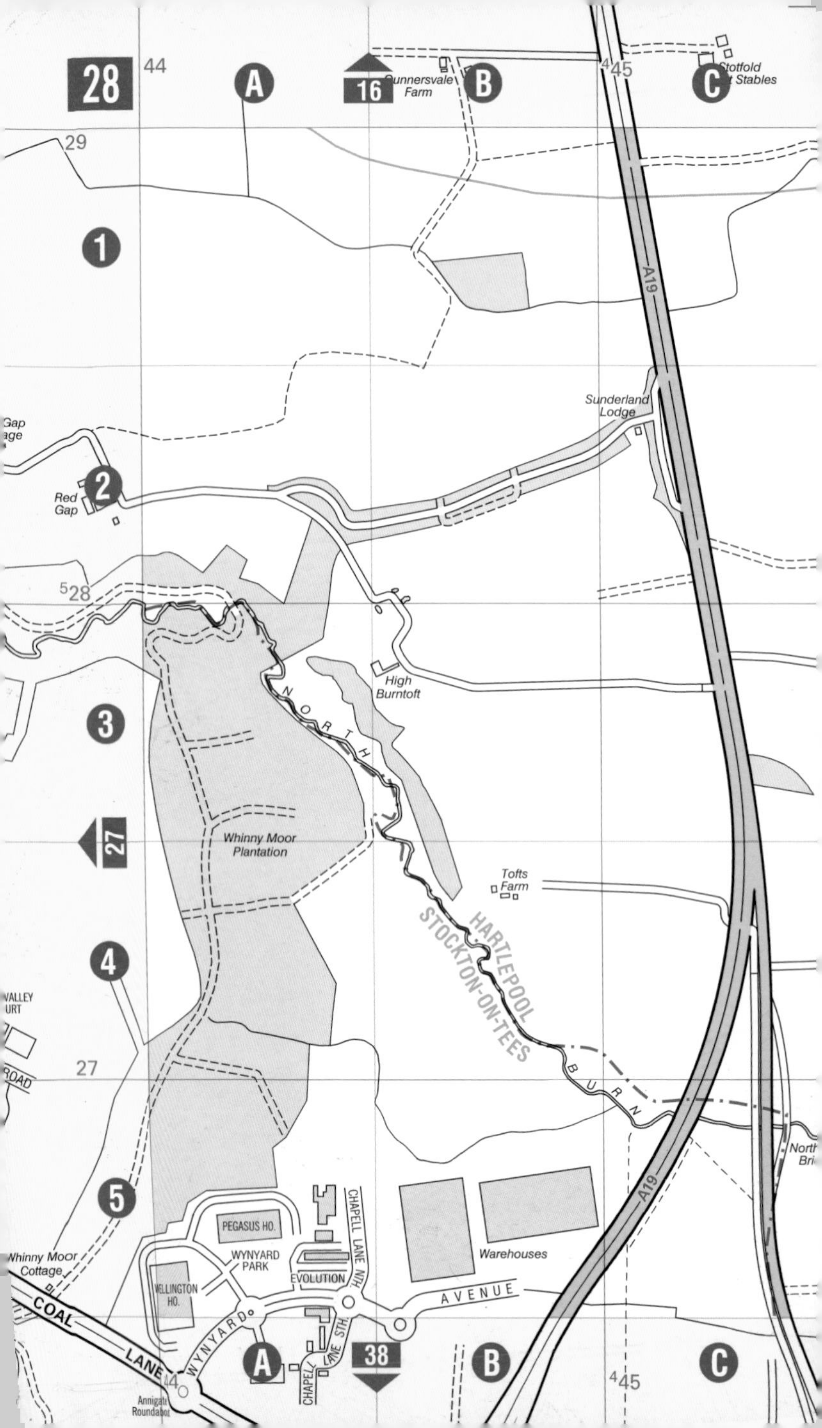

28
44
A
16
B
445
C
29
1
A19
Sunderland Lodge
2
Red Gap
528
3
High Burntoft
NORTH BURN
27
Whinny Moor Plantation
Tofts Farm
HARTLEPOOL
STOCKTON-ON-TEES
4
27
5
PEGASUS HO.
CHAPELL LANE NTH.
WYNYARD PARK
EVOLUTION
Warehouses
A19
Whinny Moor Cottage
AVENUE
WYNYARD
COAL LANE
CHAPELL LANE STH.
A
38
B
C
44
445

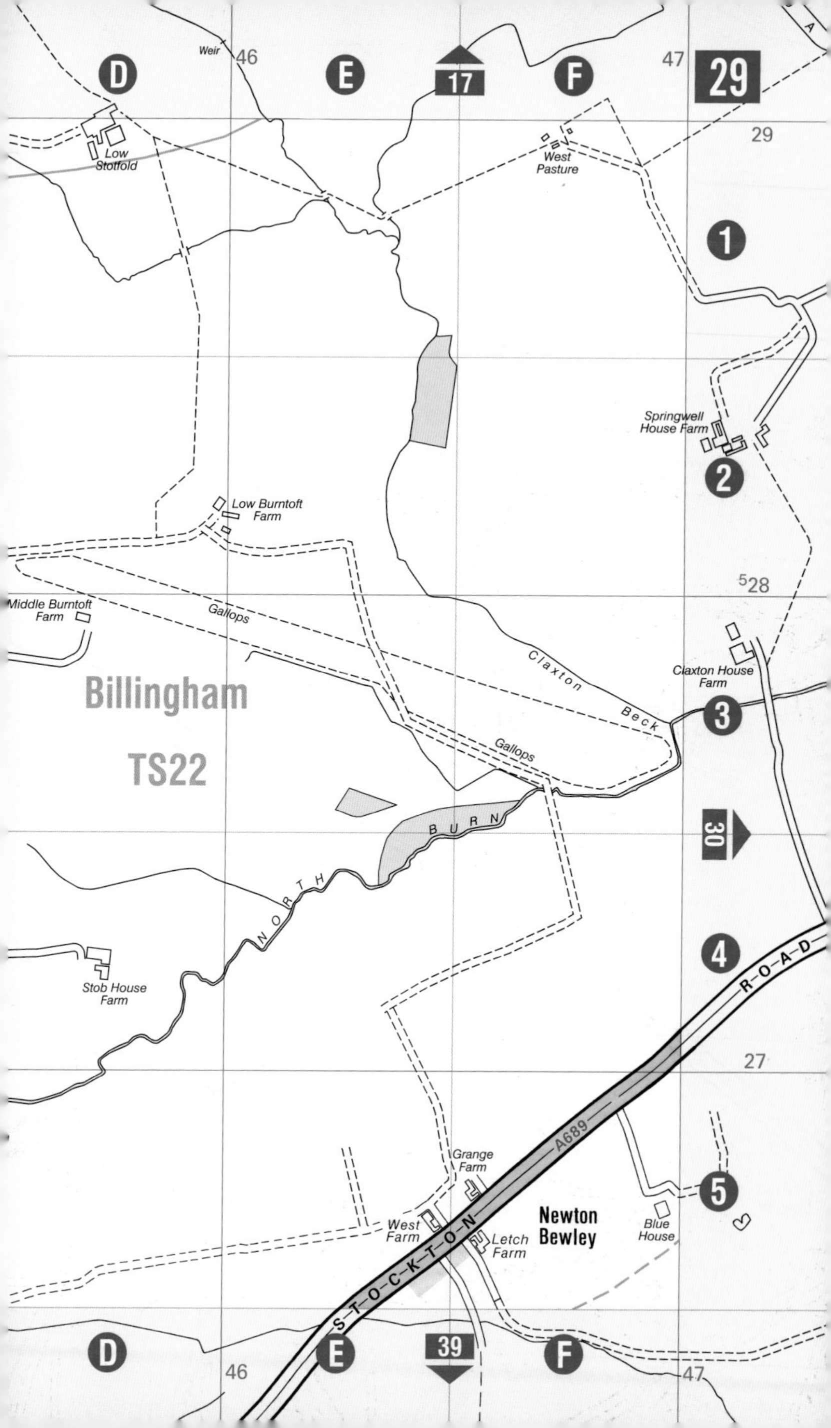
29
17
D
E
F
46
47
Weir
Low Stotfold
West Pasture
1
Springwell House Farm
2
Low Burntoft Farm
Middle Burntoft Farm
Gallops
Claxton Beck
528
Claxton House Farm
3
Billingham
TS22
Gallops
NORTH BURN
30
4
Stob House Farm
ROAD
27
A689
Grange Farm
5
West Farm
STOCKTON
Letch Farm
Newton Bewley
Blue House
39
D
E
F
46
47

30
House
DALTON
18
A
B
C
47
48
29
West Pasture
Greatham
1
2
3
4
5
TS22
BACK
Springwell House Farm
Claxton Grange Cottages
Claxton Grange
Claxton Farm
528
Billingham
Claxton
Claxton House Farm
LANE
ROAD
OLD
29
Claxton Bridge
Claxton
A689
North Close Farm
STOCKTON
27
TS23
Beck
Field House Farm
Newton Bewley
Blue House
Claxton
Beck
40
A
B
C
47
48

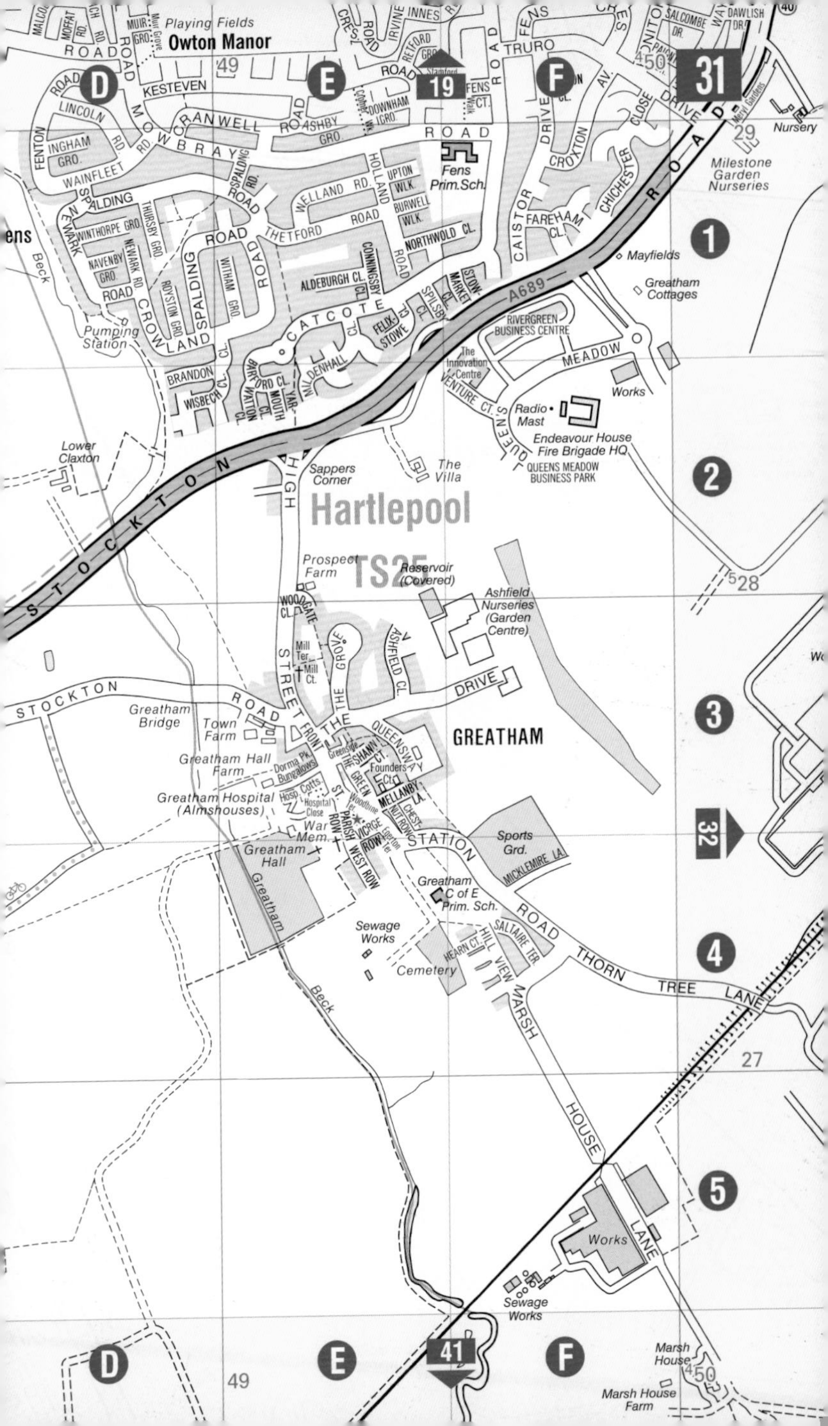
31
Owton Manor
Playing Fields
D
E
F
19
41
32
1
2
3
4
5
49
450
29
28
27
Hartlepool
TS25
GREATHAM
STOCKTON ROAD
A689
MOWBRAY ROAD
CRANWELL ROAD
KESTEVEN ROAD
TRURO
FENS
CATCOTE ROAD
THETFORD ROAD
SPALDING ROAD
CROWLAND ROAD
WAINFLEET RD.
LINCOLN RD.
INGHAM GRO.
FENTON ROAD
NEWARK
WINTHORPE GRO.
NAVENBY GRO.
NEWARK RD.
THURSBY GRO.
ROYSTON GRO.
WITHAM GRO.
BRANDON
WISBECH CL.
WELLAND RD.
HOLLAND ROAD
UPTON WLK.
BURWELL WLK.
NORTHWOLD CL.
CONINGSBY CL.
ALDEBURGH CL.
FELIXSTOWE CL.
MILDENHALL CL.
SPILSBY CL.
STOWMARKET CL.
ASHBY GRO.
DOWNHAM GRO.
CAISTOR DRIVE
CROXTON AV.
FAREHAM CL.
CHICHESTER CLOSE
DRIVE
DAWLISH DR.
SALCOMBE DR.
Fens Prim.Sch.
Milestone Garden Nurseries
Nursery
Mayfields
Greatham Cottages
RIVERGREEN BUSINESS CENTRE
The Innovation Centre
VENTURE CT.
MEADOW
QUEENS
Works
Radio Mast
Endeavour House Fire Brigade HQ
QUEENS MEADOW BUSINESS PARK
Lower Claxton
Pumping Station
Sappers Corner
The Villa
HIGH STREET
FRONT
Prospect Farm
Reservoir (Covered)
Ashfield Nurseries (Garden Centre)
WOODGATE CL.
Mill Ter.
Mill Ct.
THE GROVE
ASHFIELD CL.
DRIVE
QUEENSWAY
Greatham Bridge
Town Farm
Greatham Hall Farm
Greatham Hospital (Almshouses)
Dorma Pk. Bungalows
Hosp. Cotts.
Hospital Close
War Mem.
Greatham Hall
THE GREEN
Founders Ct.
MELLANBY LA.
PARISH ROW
WEST ROW
STATION ROAD
Sports Grd.
MICKLEMIRE LA.
Greatham C of E Prim. Sch.
Sewage Works
Cemetery
HEARN CT.
HILL VIEW
SALTAIRE TER.
THORN TREE LANE
MARSH HOUSE LANE
Greatham Beck
Works
Sewage Works
Marsh House
Marsh House Farm

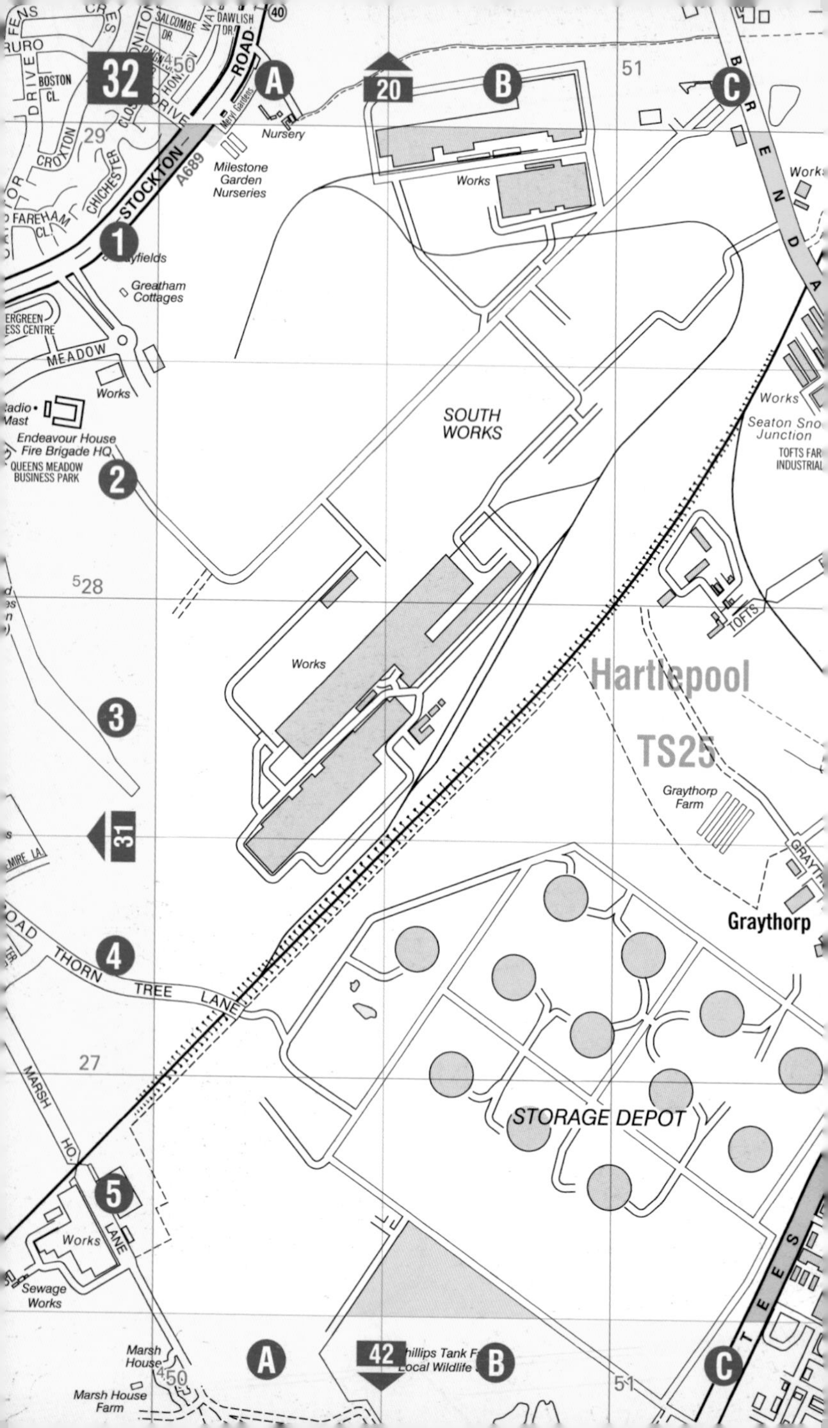

A
B
C
20
51
29
STOCKTON ROAD
A689
DAWLISH DR.
SALCOMBE DR.
BOSTON CL.
CROXTON
CHICHESTER CLOSE
FAREHAM CL.
TRURO DRIVE
Meryl Gardens
Nursery
Milestone Garden Nurseries
Works
Greatham Cottages
MEADOW
Works
Radio Mast
Endeavour House Fire Brigade HQ
QUEENS MEADOW BUSINESS PARK
SOUTH WORKS
BRENDA
Works
Seaton Snook Junction
TOFTS FARM INDUSTRIAL
528
Works
TOFTS
Hartlepool
TS25
Graythorp Farm
Graythorp
31
THORN TREE LANE
27
MARSH HOUSE LANE
STORAGE DEPOT
Works
Sewage Works
Marsh House
Marsh House Farm
450
42
Local Wildlife
TEES
51
1
2
3
4
5

Seaton Carew Nrsy. Sch.
Community Centre
GRACE CL.
THE LINKS
THE WICKETS
Meadowfield Court
Pav.
Cricket Ground
Sports Ground
21
BILSDALE
BILSDALE RD.
WESTERDALE
COMMONDALE
WESTDALE
ROXBY CL.
LINGDALE
DR.
PAVILION CL.
HEADINGLEY CT.
DINGLEY
VICKERS
VICKERS LA.
HAWKER CL.
AVRO GS.
SARO PL.
HANDLEY CL.
LANE
DE HAVILAND WY.
D
E
F
53
52
29
28
27
SEATON CAREW GOLF COURSE
1
2
3
4
5
TOFTS FARM EAST INDUSTRIAL ESTATE
JD Sports Domes
The Mayfair Centre
TOFTS ROAD
TOFTS ROAD EAST
HUNTER HOUSE INDUSTRIAL ESTATE
EAST
A178
ROAD
Seaton Snook
Seaton Common
Dunn's Hill
WEST
B1277
STEPHENSON INDUSTRIAL ESTATE
Works
TEES BAY BUSINESS PARK
Sewage Works
TEES ROAD
WORKS ROAD
Radio Mast
Seaton Snook
Playing Field
Teesmouth Field Study Centre
Cricket Grd.
Hartlepool Power Station Visitor Centre
Works
Works
THORP EST.
ROAD
A178
Works
Sewage Works
Able Seaton Port
Works
Power Station
Dry Dock
Reservoir
Seaton on Tees Channel Back Light
Reservoir
Seaton on Tees Channel Front Light
Works
SEATON ON TEES CHANNEL
HARTLEPOOL
STOCKTON-ON-TEES
Seaton Snook Wharf Light
43
Greenabella Marsh (Nature Reserve)

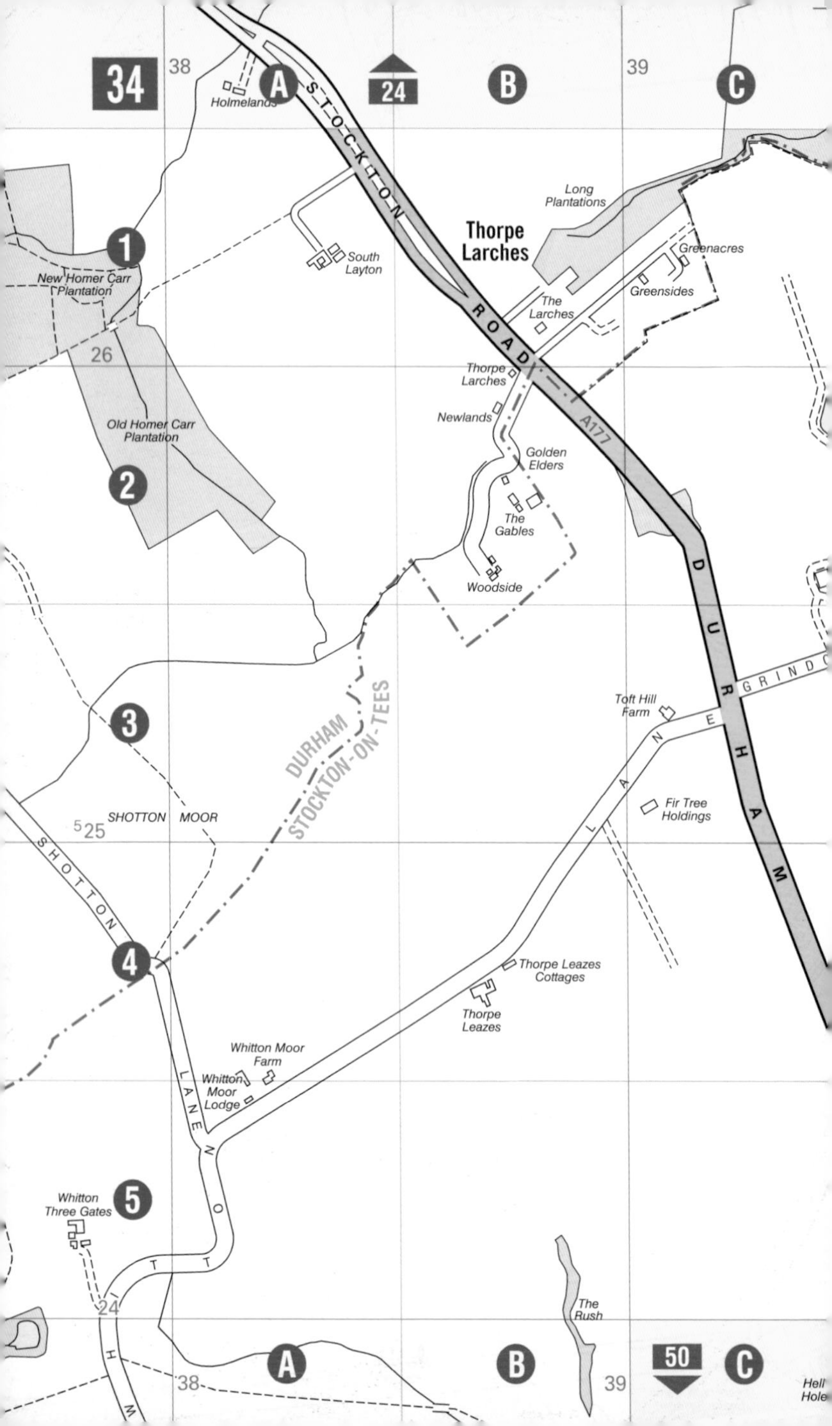
38
A
24
B
39
C
Holmelands
STOCKTON ROAD
South Layton
Thorpe Larches
Long Plantations
Greenacres
Greensides
The Larches
1
New Homer Carr Plantation
26
Thorpe Larches
Newlands
A177
Old Homer Carr Plantation
Golden Elders
2
The Gables
Woodside
DURHAM
STOCKTON-ON-TEES
GRINDON
Toft Hill Farm
3
DURHAM
LANE
Fir Tree Holdings
SHOTTON MOOR
25
SHOTTON
4
Thorpe Leazes Cottages
Thorpe Leazes
Whitton Moor Farm
Whitton Moor Lodge
LANE
NOTT
5
Whitton Three Gates
The Rush
24
A
B
50
C
38
39
Hell Hole

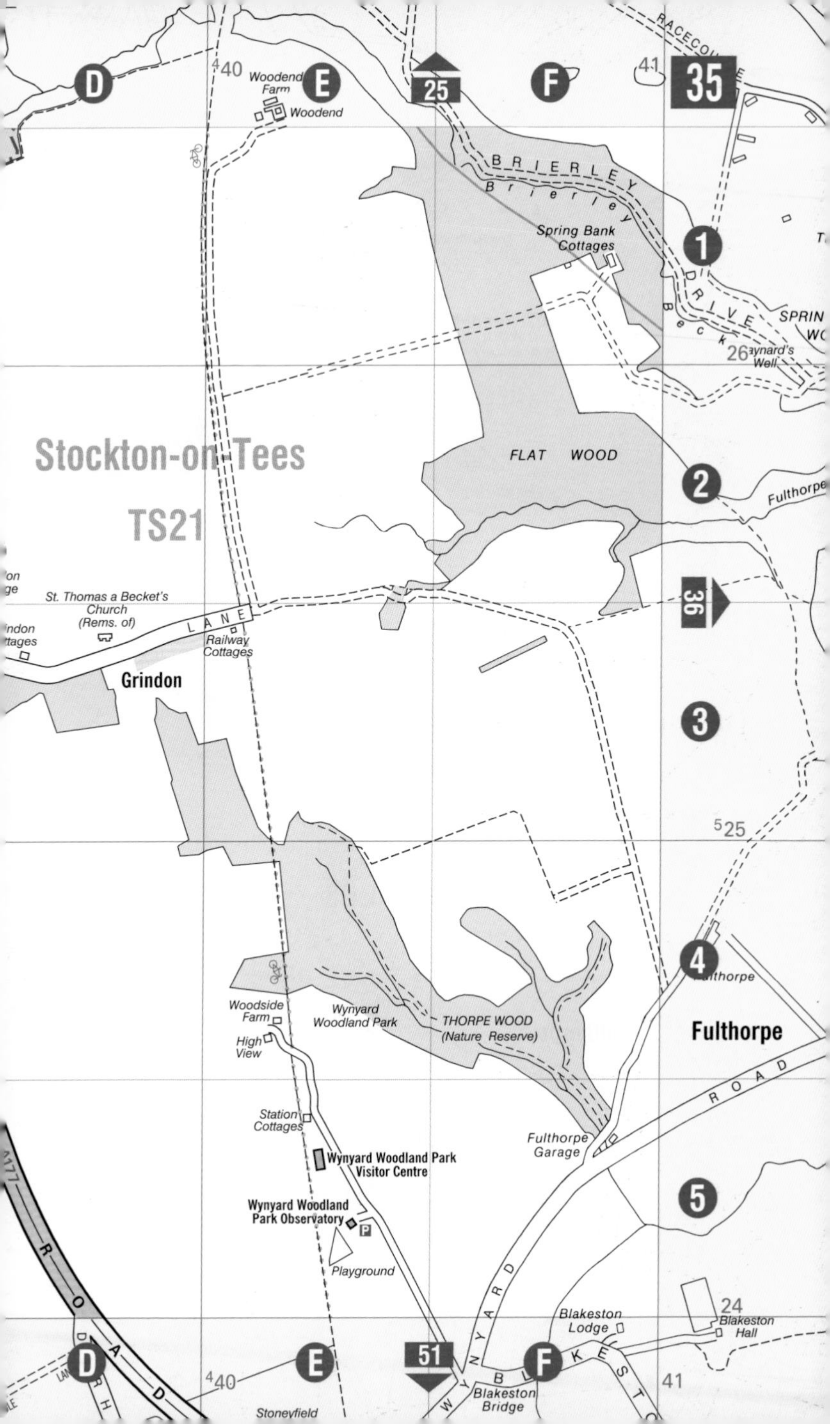
35
25
36
51
D
E
F
1
2
3
4
5
440
41
525
26
24
Stockton-on-Tees
TS21
RACECOURSE
Woodend Farm
Woodend
BRIERLEY
Brierley
Beck
DRIVE
Spring Bank Cottages
SPRIN
Wynyard's Well
FLAT WOOD
Fulthorpe
St. Thomas a Becket's Church (Rems. of)
LANE
Railway Cottages
Grindon
Fulthorpe
Woodside Farm
High View
Wynyard Woodland Park
THORPE WOOD (Nature Reserve)
Station Cottages
Wynyard Woodland Park Visitor Centre
Wynyard Woodland Park Observatory
P
Playground
Fulthorpe Garage
ROAD
WYNYARD
Blakeston Lodge
Blakeston Hall
BLAKESTON
Blakeston Bridge
ROAD
Stoneyfield

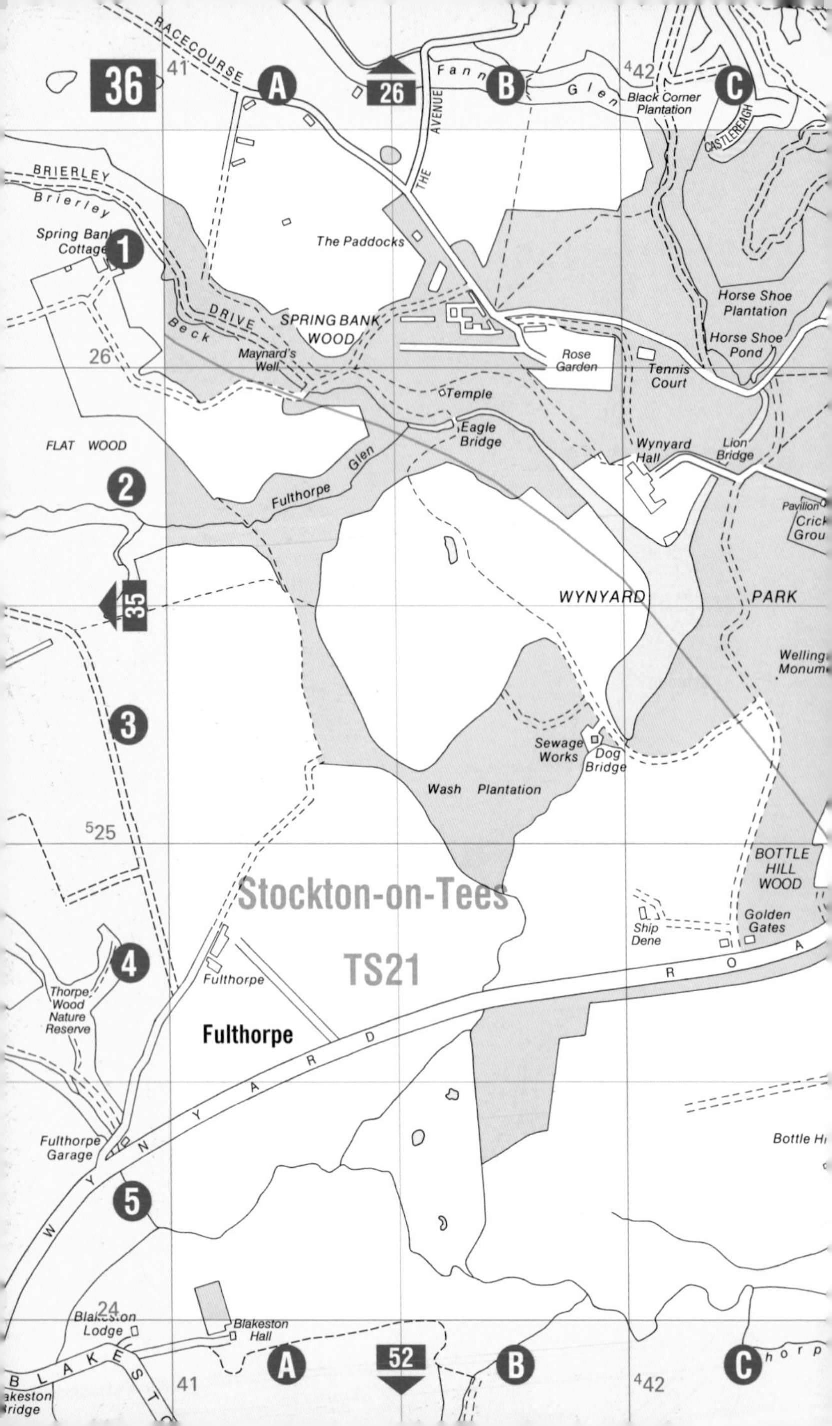
36
41
RACECOURSE
A
26
Fann
B
Glen
442
Black Corner Plantation
C
CASTLEREAGH
THE AVENUE
BRIERLEY
Brierley
Spring Bank Cottage
1
The Paddocks
Horse Shoe Plantation
DRIVE
Beck
SPRING BANK WOOD
Horse Shoe Pond
Maynard's Well
Rose Garden
Tennis Court
26
Temple
Eagle Bridge
FLAT WOOD
Wynyard Hall
Lion Bridge
2
Fulthorpe Glen
Pavilion
WYNYARD
PARK
35
Wellin
3
Sewage Works
Dog Bridge
Wash Plantation
525
BOTTLE HILL WOOD
Stockton-on-Tees
Golden Gates
Ship Dene
4
TS21
Thorpe Wood Nature Reserve
Fulthorpe
Fulthorpe
WYNYARD ROAD
Fulthorpe Garage
Bottle Hi
5
24
Blakeston Lodge
Blakeston Hall
BLAKESTO
A
52
B
C
41
442
Blakeston Bridge

37
27
38
53
D
E
F
43
44
26
25
24
1
2
3
4
5
THE DRIVE
COPPICE
WYNYARD GOLF COURSE
Swainston Hall
DRIVE
HOUSE DRIVE
Kennel Hill Plantation
Whinny Moor
COAL LANE
A689
PEGASUS HO.
WYNYARD BUSINESS PARK
WYNYARD AV.
Annigate Roundabout
WELLINGTON DR.
CHURCHILL CL.
WYNYARD VILLAGE
WELLINGTON
MOUNTSTEWART
DRIVE
VANE CL.
RUDD CL.
SALTER
GROVE
FULTHORPE
TEMPEST CT.
DAVISON CL.
ANNIGATE CL.
EAGLE BRIDGE CT.
LION BRIDGE CL.
FORESTERS CL.
BURNTOFT
EMBLETON GRO.
EMBLETON
Club House
Driving Range
WYNYARD GOLF COURSE
Swancar Pond
Cowbridge Beck
Parkside Manor
Billingham
Warren Farm
Mickel Hill
Warren Lodge
ROAD
WYNYARD ROAD
SANDY LANE
Bradley Farm
Aranvale
Nursery
Bottle Hill Cottage
TS22
DIVERSION
Corner's Plantation
Hurle House
Wilmire House
WEST
EDEN WAY
RIBBLE CL.
LOWTHER CL.
WOLVISTON
White House Farm
CALDER CL.
SEVERN CL.
A19
ASHCOMBE CL.
DR.
HAZELMERE CL.
LENHAM CL.
HAWKSTONE CL.
DRIVE
GLENFALL CL.
CHILCROFT CL.
TROON CL.
GANTON
GLEN EAGLES
BILLINGHAM
SKRIPKA
DALBY CL.
WYKEHAM CL.
SKRIPKA
BICKLEY CL.
KIELDER CL.
Thornley Hill
Wolviston Mill
Viewly Hill

38
28
37
54
A
B
C
1
2
3
4
5
Whinny Moor Cottage
PEGASUS HO.
WYNYARD BUSINESS PARK
WELLINGTON HO.
EVOLUTION
CHAPELL LANE
CHAPELL LANE STH.
Warehouses
WYNYARD AVENUE
COAL LANE
A689
Annigate Roundabout
A19
Wolviston Services
Wolviston Interchange
Coal Lane Roundabout
STOCKTON-ON-TEES
HARTLEPOOL
DIVERSION
Wolviston
The Ashes
MORELAND CL.
THE POPLARS
THE PIPPINS
SUNDERLAND RD.
WEST
Sundial M.
DURHAM ROAD
Green Farm Cl.
THOMPSONS CL.
Sch.
LAX CT.
CHURCH RW.
MUSVE
The Park
HIGH ST.
The Green
Billingham
Cowbridge Beck
Garth End
MANOR CT.
Grange View
MANOR CL.
Warren Farm
Mickel Hill
WYNYARD ROAD
HALL FARM CL.
LANE
Bradley Farm
SANDY LANE
Nursery
MILL LANE
TS22
Wilmire House
WOLVISTON ROAD
Northfield School & Sports College
St.Paul's RC Prim.Sch.
WEST THAMES ROAD
BARKSTON CL.
White House Farm
EDEN WAY
RIBBLE CL.
LOWTHER CL.
HUMBER GRO.
CLYDE GDNS.
CALDER CL.
WOLVISTON
SEVERN CT.
SEVERN GRO.
LIVERTON CRES.
PICTON AV.
AVENUE
ELTON RD.
THAMES RD.
Comm. Cen.
MATLOCK GDS.
Rec. Grd.
CARLTON AVENUE
ASHCOMBE CL.
WHITEHOUSE DRIVE
AVON GRO.
RUDSTON
Prior's Mill CE Prim. Sch.
HAZELMERE CL.
LENHAM CL.
CAYTON DRIVE
EMBLETON
CARLTON
Playgrd.
BRAEMAR
GLAMIS RD.
GUILDFORD RD.
KINGS RD.
HAWKSTONE CL.
BURNISTON DRIVE
ASTON RD.
CLIFTON
MIDDLETON AV.
STAINTON
BELMONT AV.
CHATSWORTH GDNS.
QUEENS DR.
GLENFALL CL.
KNAPTON
GANTON CL.
TANTON GRO.
BARTON CRES.
NEWTON GRO.
MONKS-EATON DR.
CHILCROFT CL.
TROON CL.
GLEN EAGLES CL.
SANDY
Wolviston Ct.
Prim. Sch.
CRANSTOCK CL.
SKRIPKA
HARTON AV.
GROSVENOR ROAD
GROSMONT DR.
COULTON GRO.
ORTON GRO.
BROUGHTON
THORNTON CR.
CASTLETON DR.
BUXTON GDNS.
JUBILEE GROVE
DALBY CL.
BICKLEY CL.
WYKEHAM CL.
SKRIPKA
KIELDER CL.
FLIXTON GRO.
WHORLTON R.
MURTON GRO.
NORTHFIELD RD.
WEBSTER RD.
PORLOCK RD.
LUTTON CRES.
LANGTON AV.
WILMIRE RD.
CAMBRIAN RD.
BILLINGHAM
MARTON
ROAD
DRIVE
IVESTON GRO.
LANE
Club House
ROSEBERY
26
25
24
44
45
BILLINGHAM GOLF COURSE

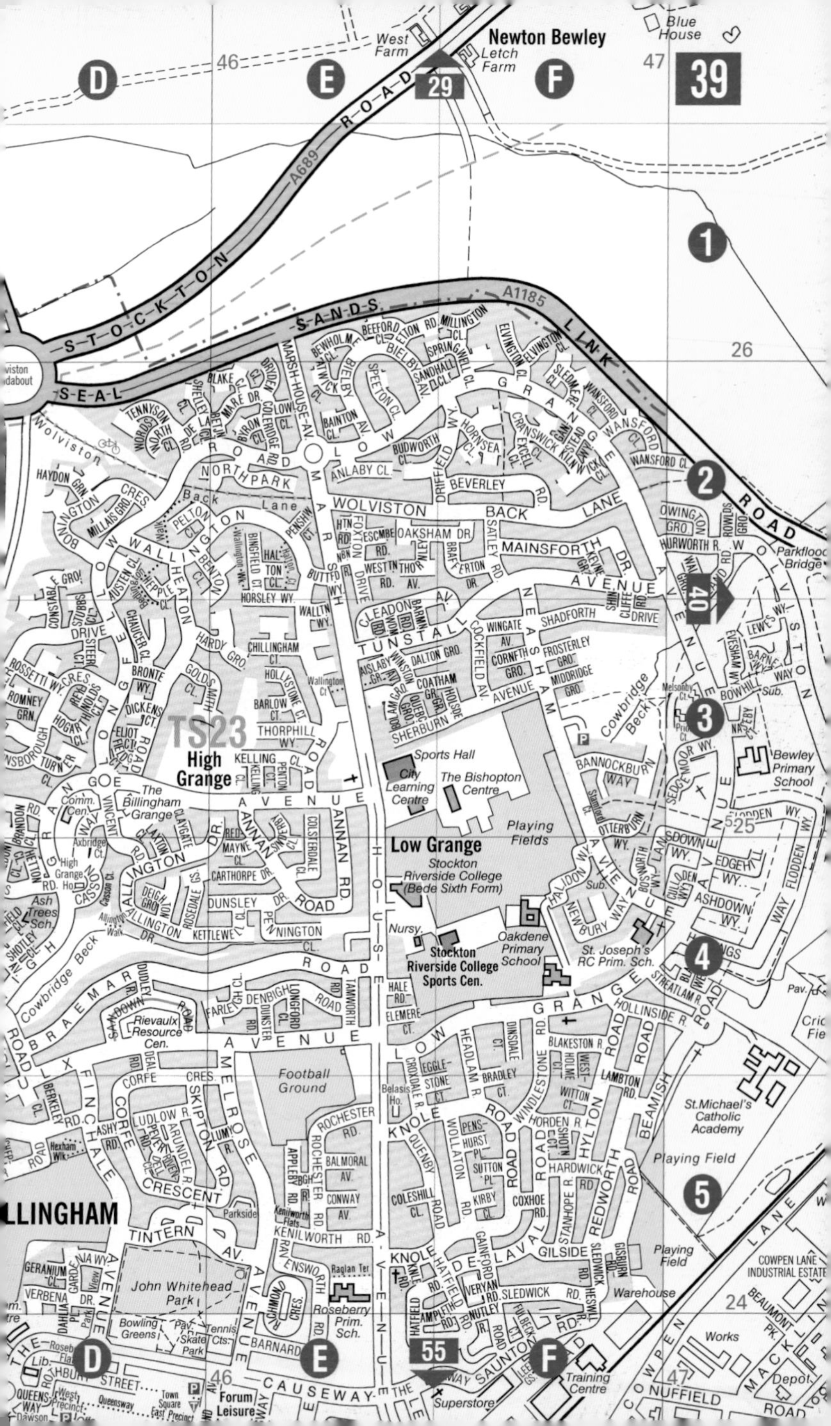
Newton Bewley
West Farm
Letch Farm
Blue House
29
STOCKTON ROAD
A689
SEAL SANDS LINK
A1185
WOLVISTON ROAD
40
55
TS23
High Grange
Low Grange
BILLINGHAM
Parkflood Bridge
Sports Hall
City Learning Centre
The Bishopton Centre
Playing Fields
Stockton Riverside College (Bede Sixth Form)
Nursy.
Stockton Riverside College Sports Cen.
Oakdene Primary School
St. Joseph's RC Prim. Sch.
Bewley Primary School
The Billingham Grange
Comm. Cen.
High Grange Ho.
Ash Trees Sch.
Cowbridge Beck
Rievaulx Resource Cen.
Football Ground
Belasis Ho.
St.Michael's Catholic Academy
Playing Field
COWPEN LANE INDUSTRIAL ESTATE
Warehouse
Works
Depot
Training Centre
Superstore
John Whitehead Park
Bowling Greens
Tennis Cts.
Skate Park
Roseberry Prim. Sch.
Raglan Ter
Parkside
Forum Leisure
Town Square
East Precinct
West Precinct
WOLVISTON BACK LANE
MAINSFORTH DR.
TUNSTALL AVENUE
NEASHAM AVENUE
GRANGE AVENUE
ANNAN RD.
MARSH HOUSE AVENUE
BRAEMAR ROAD
FINCHALE AVENUE
MELROSE AVENUE
KNOLE ROAD
LOW GRANGE AVENUE
CAUSEWAY
COWPEN LANE
NUFFIELD ROAD
MACKLIN AVENUE
BEAUMONT PK.
TINTERN AV.
KENILWORTH RD.
ROCHESTER RD.
HYLTON ROAD
REDWORTH ROAD
LAMBTON RD.
BEAMISH ROAD
DE LAVAL ROAD
HOLLINSIDE R.
WALLINGTON ROAD
NORTHPARK
ALLINGTON DR.
PENNINGTON CL.
D
E
F
1
2
3
4
5
46
47
26
25
24

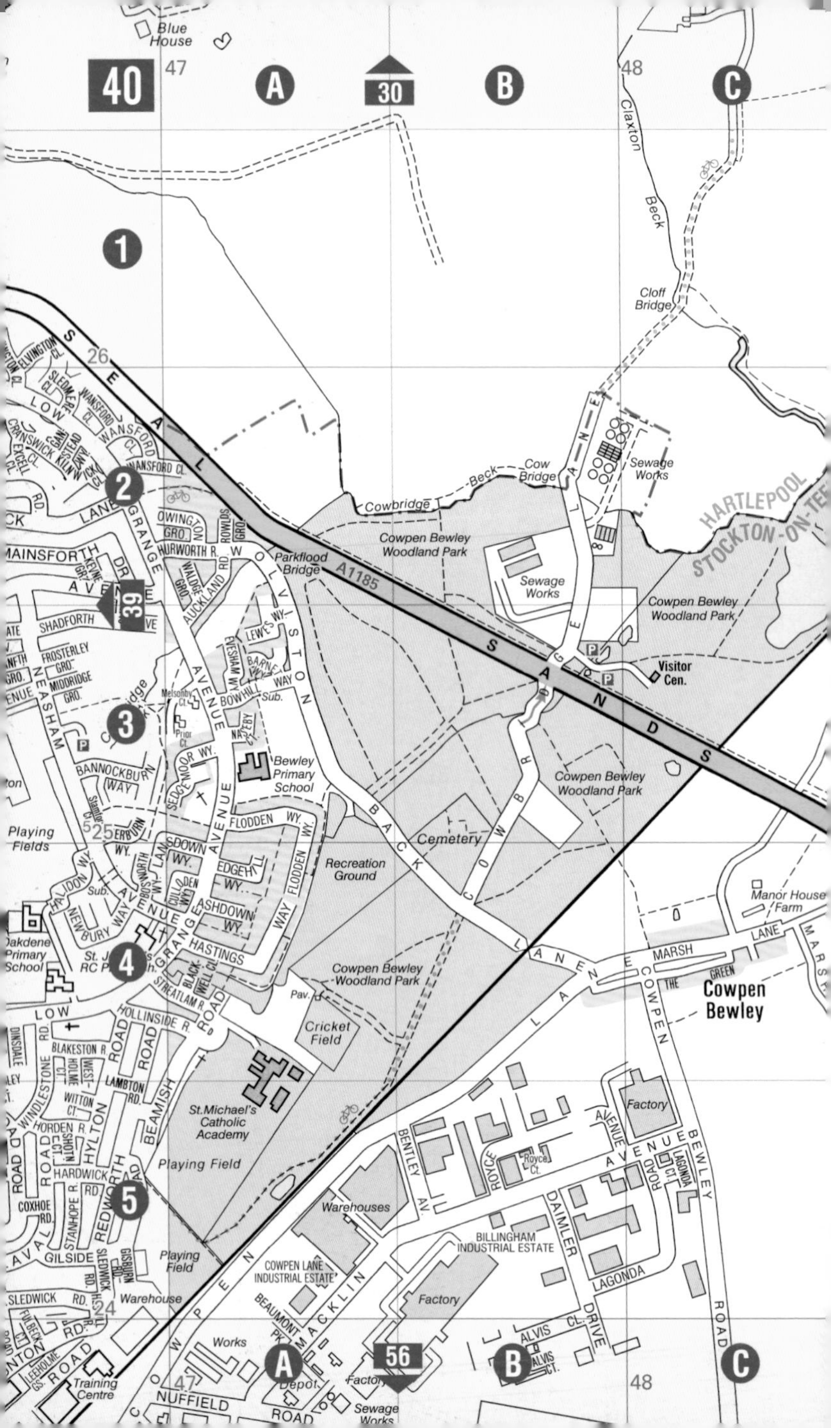
Blue House
47
A
30
B
48
C
1
2
3
4
5
26
25
24
Claxton Beck
Cloff Bridge
Cow Bridge
Beck
Sewage Works
HARTLEPOOL
STOCKTON-ON-TEES
Cowbridge
Cowpen Bewley Woodland Park
Parkflood Bridge
A1185
SEAL SANDS
Visitor Cen.
Cowpen Bewley Woodland Park
ELVINGTON CL.
SLEDMERE CL.
LOW
WANSFORD CL.
CRANSWICK CL.
EXCELL CL.
KILNWICK CL.
WANSFORD CL.
LANE
GRANGE
OWINGTON GRO.
ROWLDS GRO.
HURWORTH R.
WOLVISTON
MAINSFORTH
DR.
AVENUE
KEVINE GRO.
WALDGE GRO.
AUCKLAND RD.
39
SHADFORTH
LEWES WY.
EVESHAM WY.
BARNET PKWY.
FROSTERLEY GRO.
MIDDRIDGE GRO.
NEASHAM
BOWHILL WAY
Sub.
Melsonby Cl.
Prior Ct.
NASEBY CT.
Bewley Primary School
BANNOCKBURN WAY
SEDGEMOOR WY.
FLODDEN WY.
BACK LANE
Cemetery
COWBRIDGE LANE
Cowpen Bewley Woodland Park
Playing Fields
LANSDOWN WY.
EDGEHILL WY.
Recreation Ground
HALIDON WY.
Sub.
NEWBURY WAY
BOSWORTH WY.
CULLODEN WY.
ASHDOWN WY.
FLODDEN WAY
Dakdene Primary School
St. J... RC P... ch.
HASTINGS
BLACKWELL CL.
STREATLAM R.
Manor House Farm
MARSH LANE
THE GREEN
COWPEN LANE
Cowpen Bewley
Cowpen Bewley Woodland Park
Pav.
Cricket Field
LOW
HOLLINSIDE R.
DINSDALE RD.
BLAKESTON R.
HOLME CT.
WEST- CT.
LAMBTON RD.
WITTON CT.
WINDLESTONE
HORDEN R.
SHOTON CT.
HYLTON
BEAMISH
ROAD
ROAD
St.Michael's Catholic Academy
Factory
BENTLEY AV.
ROYCE
Royce Ct.
AVENUE
COWPEN BEWLEY ROAD
HARDWICK
REDWORTH ROAD
Playing Field
COXHOE RD.
STANHOPE R.
Warehouses
DAIMLER DRIVE
LAGONDA CT.
BILLINGHAM INDUSTRIAL ESTATE
GILSIDE
SLEDWICK RD.
GISBURN RD.
Playing Field
COWPEN LANE INDUSTRIAL ESTATE
LAGONDA
SLEDWICK RD.
Warehouse
MACKLIN
BEAUMONT PK.
Factory
ALVIS CL.
ALVIS CT.
FULBECK CT.
LEEHOLME GS.
ROAD
Training Centre
Works
56
Depot
Factory
Sewage Works
NUFFIELD ROAD

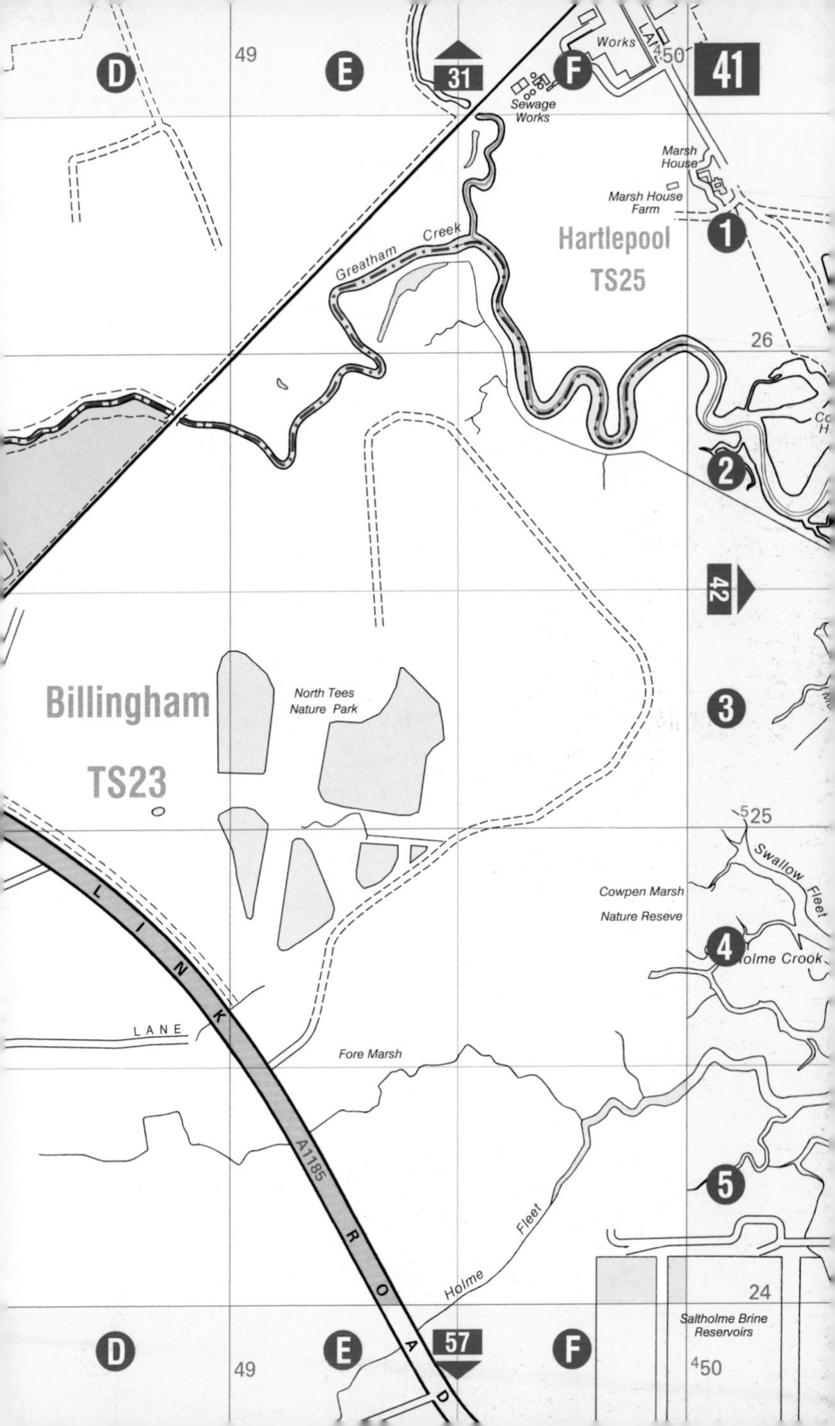

41
31
42
57
D
E
F
49
450
26
525
24
Works
LANE
Sewage Works
Marsh House
Marsh House Farm
Hartlepool TS25
Greatham Creek
Billingham TS23
North Tees Nature Park
Cowpen Marsh Nature Reseve
Swallow Fleet
Fore Marsh
LANE
LINK ROAD
A1185
Holme Fleet
Saltholme Brine Reservoirs
1
2
3
4
5

Works
450
A
32
B
51
C
Marsh House
Marsh House Farm
Phillips Tank Farm
Local Wildlife Site
1
26
Hartlepool
Saltern Wetlands
TS25
Cote Hill
2
TEES ROAD
A178
Greatham Creek
41
Greatham Creek Bridge
3
Mucky Fleet
Brine Field
525
P
Rough Marsh
Swallow Fleet
Billingham
Cowpen Marsh
Nature Reseve
4
Holme Crook
TS23
Holme Fleet
SEATON CAREW ROAD
A178
5
24
Saltholme Brine Reservoirs
A
58
B
C
450
51

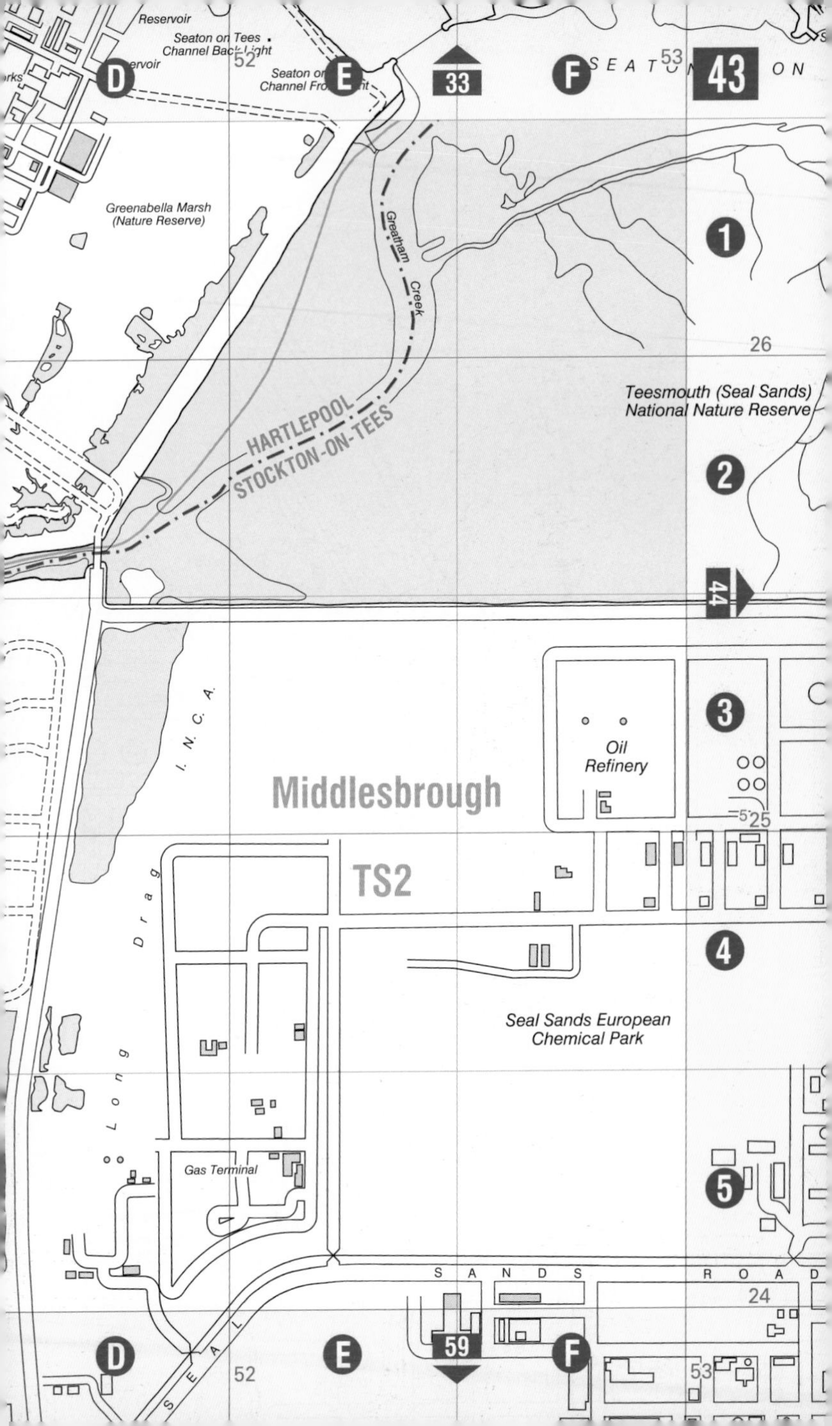
Reservoir
Seaton on Tees Channel Back Light
Seaton on Tees Channel Front Light
Greenabella Marsh (Nature Reserve)
Greatham Creek
HARTLEPOOL
STOCKTON-ON-TEES
SEATON ON
Teesmouth (Seal Sands) National Nature Reserve
I. N. C. A.
Middlesbrough
Oil Refinery
TS2
Long Drag
Seal Sands European Chemical Park
Gas Terminal
SANDS ROAD
SEAL
33
44
59
D
E
F
1
2
3
4
5
52
53
26
25
24

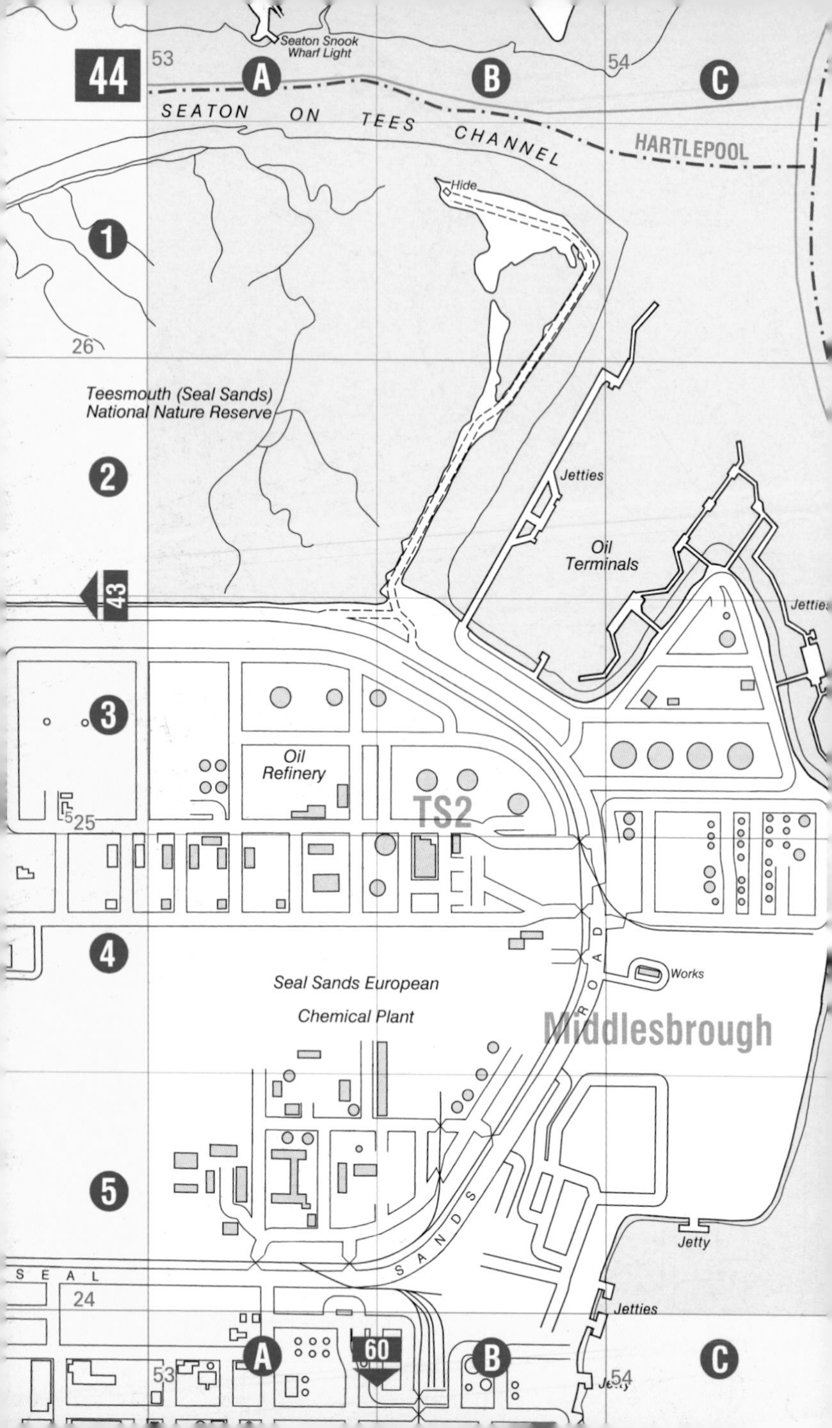
Seaton Snook
Wharf Light
53
54
A
B
C
SEATON ON TEES CHANNEL
HARTLEPOOL
Hide
1
26
Teesmouth (Seal Sands)
National Nature Reserve
2
Jetties
Oil
Terminals
43
Jetties
3
Oil
Refinery
TS2
25
4
Works
Seal Sands European
Chemical Plant
ROAD
Middlesbrough
5
SANDS
Jetty
SEAL
24
Jetties
60
A
B
C
53
54

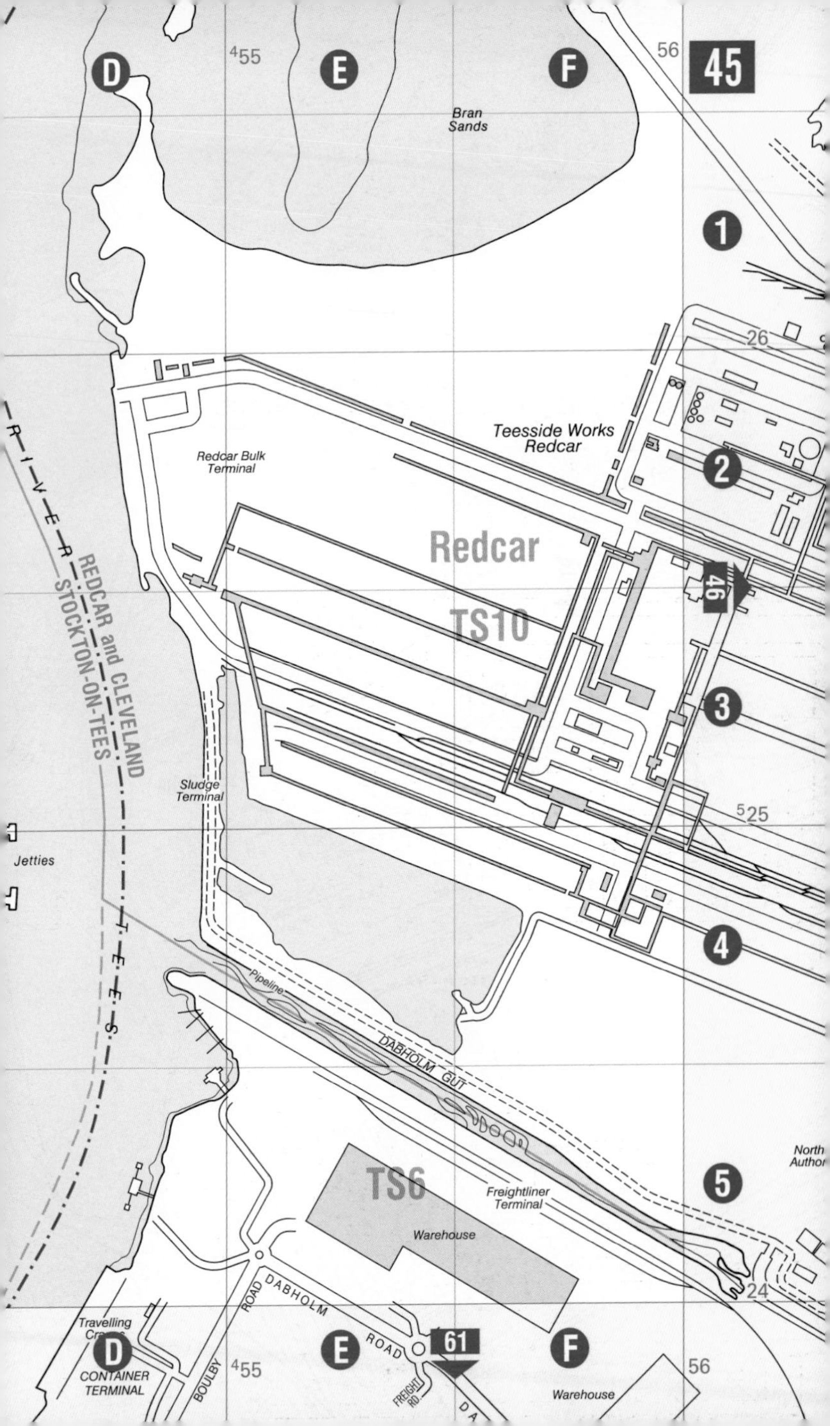
D
E
F
455
56
Bran Sands
1
26
Teesside Works Redcar
2
Redcar Bulk Terminal
Redcar
TS10
46
3
RIVER TEES
REDCAR and CLEVELAND
STOCKTON-ON-TEES
Sludge Terminal
525
Jetties
4
Pipeline
DABHOLM GUT
North Author
5
TS6
Freightliner Terminal
Warehouse
24
DABHOLM ROAD
BOULBY ROAD
Travelling Cranes
CONTAINER TERMINAL
FREIGHT RD.
61
Warehouse

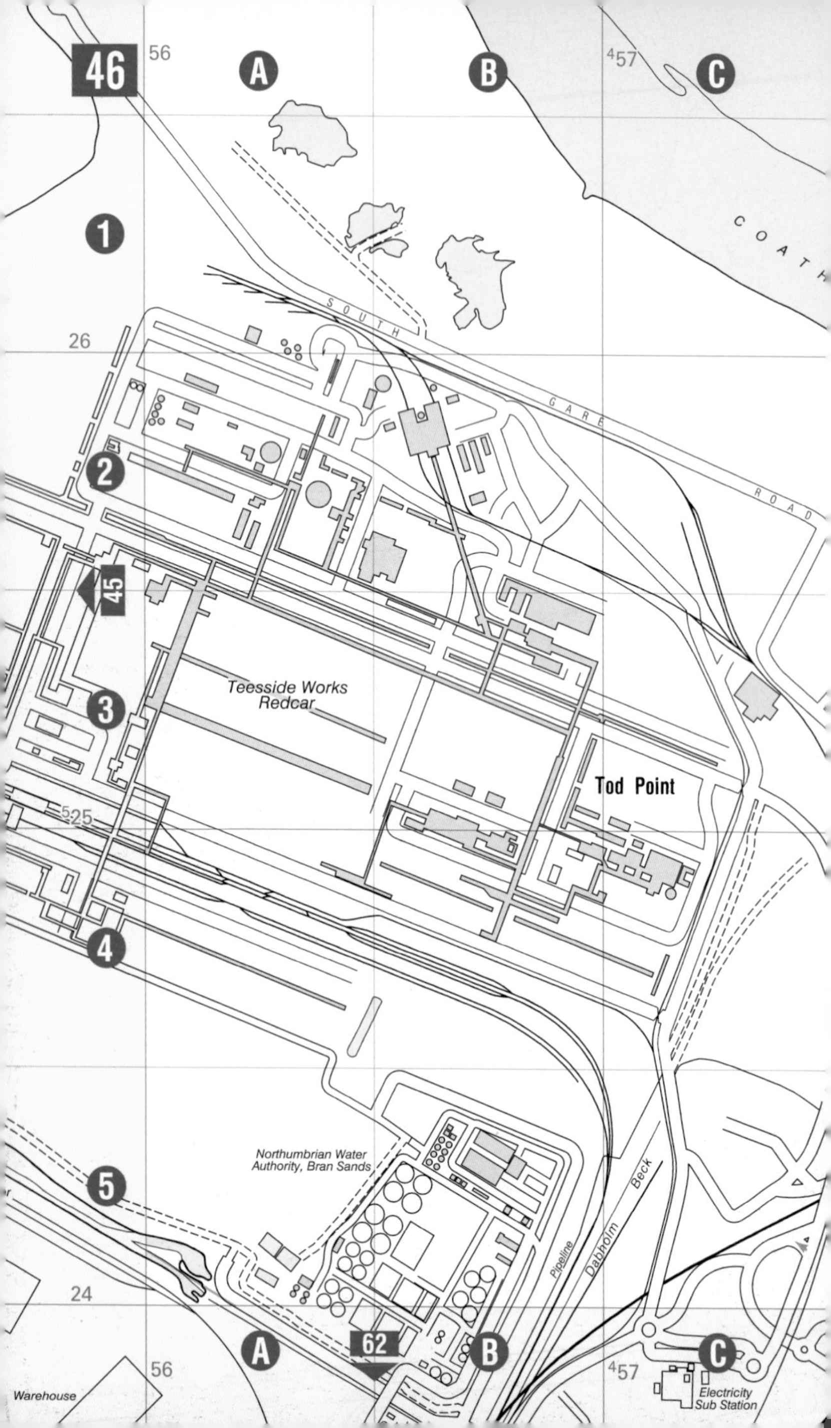
56
A
B
457
C
1
COATH
SOUTH
GARE
ROAD
26
2
45
3
Teesside Works
Redcar
Tod Point
525
4
Northumbrian Water
Authority, Bran Sands
5
Pipeline
Dabholm
Beck
24
A
62
B
C
56
457
Warehouse
Electricity
Sub Station

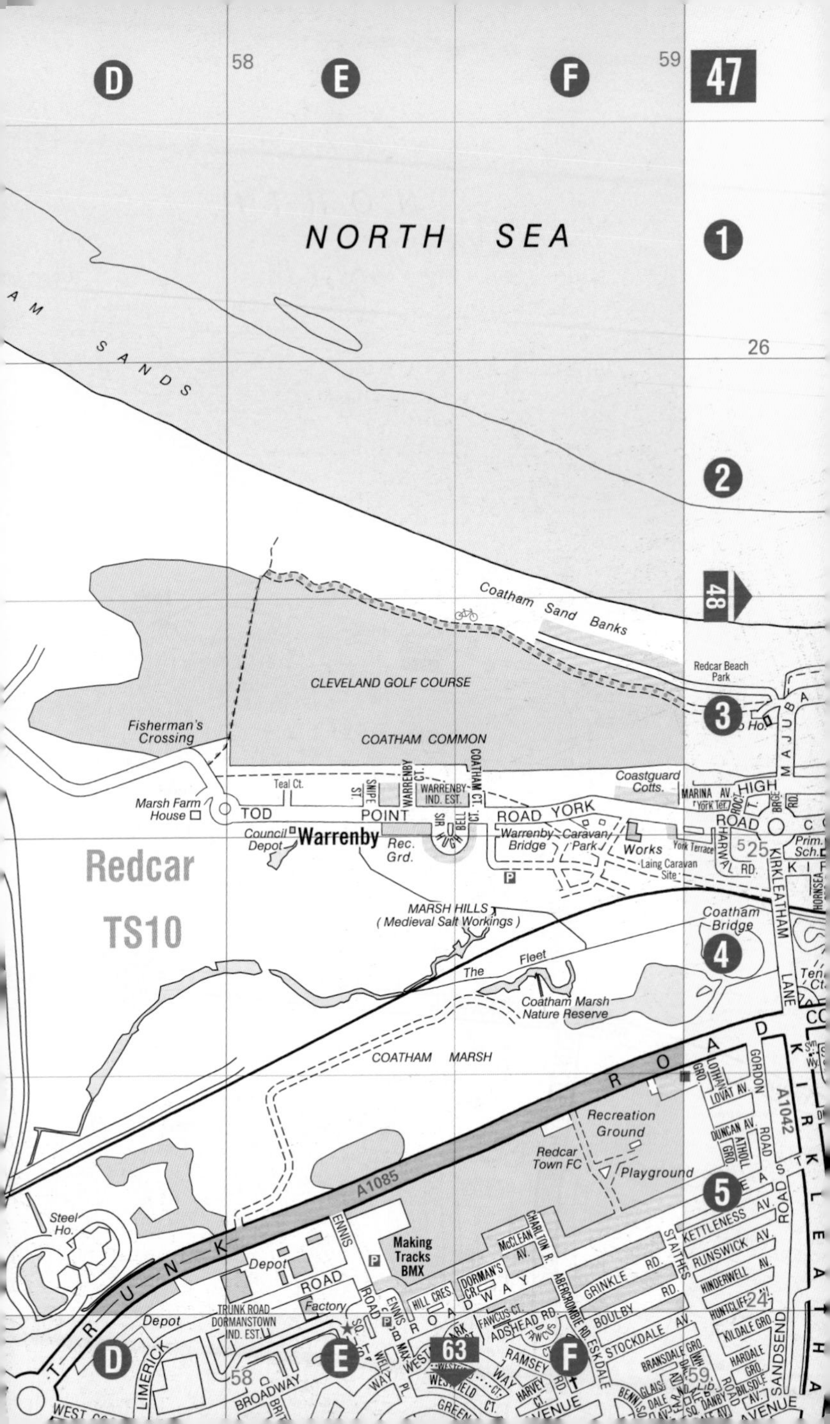
D
58
E
F
59
NORTH SEA
1
26
SANDS
2
48
Coatham Sand Banks
CLEVELAND GOLF COURSE
Redcar Beach Park
3
Fisherman's Crossing
COATHAM COMMON
Coastguard Cotts.
Teal Ct.
SNIPE ST.
WARRENBY CT.
WARRENBY IND. EST.
COATHAM CT.
Marsh Farm House
TOD POINT ROAD
YORK ROAD
HIGH
MARINA AV.
York Ter.
MAJUBA
Council Depot
Warrenby
Rec. Grd.
SIR HUGH BELL CT.
Warrenby Bridge
Caravan Park
Works
York Terrace
HARWAL RD.
Laing Caravan Site
KIRKLEATHAM
Prim. Sch.
HORNSEA
Redcar
TS10
MARSH HILLS
(Medieval Salt Workings)
Coatham Bridge
4
The Fleet
Coatham Marsh Nature Reserve
LANE
COATHAM MARSH
ROAD
LOTHIAN GRO.
LOVAT AV.
GORDON
A1042
KIRKLEATHAM
Recreation Ground
DUNCAN AV.
ATHOLL GRO.
Redcar Town FC
Playground
A1085
5
Steel Ho.
ENNIS
Making Tracks BMX
McCLEAN AV.
CHARLTON R.
STAITHES
KETTLENESS AV.
RUNSWICK AV.
HINDERWELL AV.
TRUNK
Depot
ROAD
GRINKLE RD.
Factory
DORMAN'S CR.
HILL CRES.
BROADWAY
ABERCROMBIE RD.
BOULBY RD.
HUNTCLIFF AV.
24
TRUNK ROAD DORMANSTOWN IND. EST.
Depot
FAWCUS CT.
ADSHEAD RD.
STOCKDALE AV.
KILDALE GRO.
LIMERICK
63
RAMSEY
ESKDALE
BRANSDALE GRO.
HARDALE GRO.
SANDSEND
WESTFIELD
HARVEY CT.
BROADWAY
AVENUE
WEST

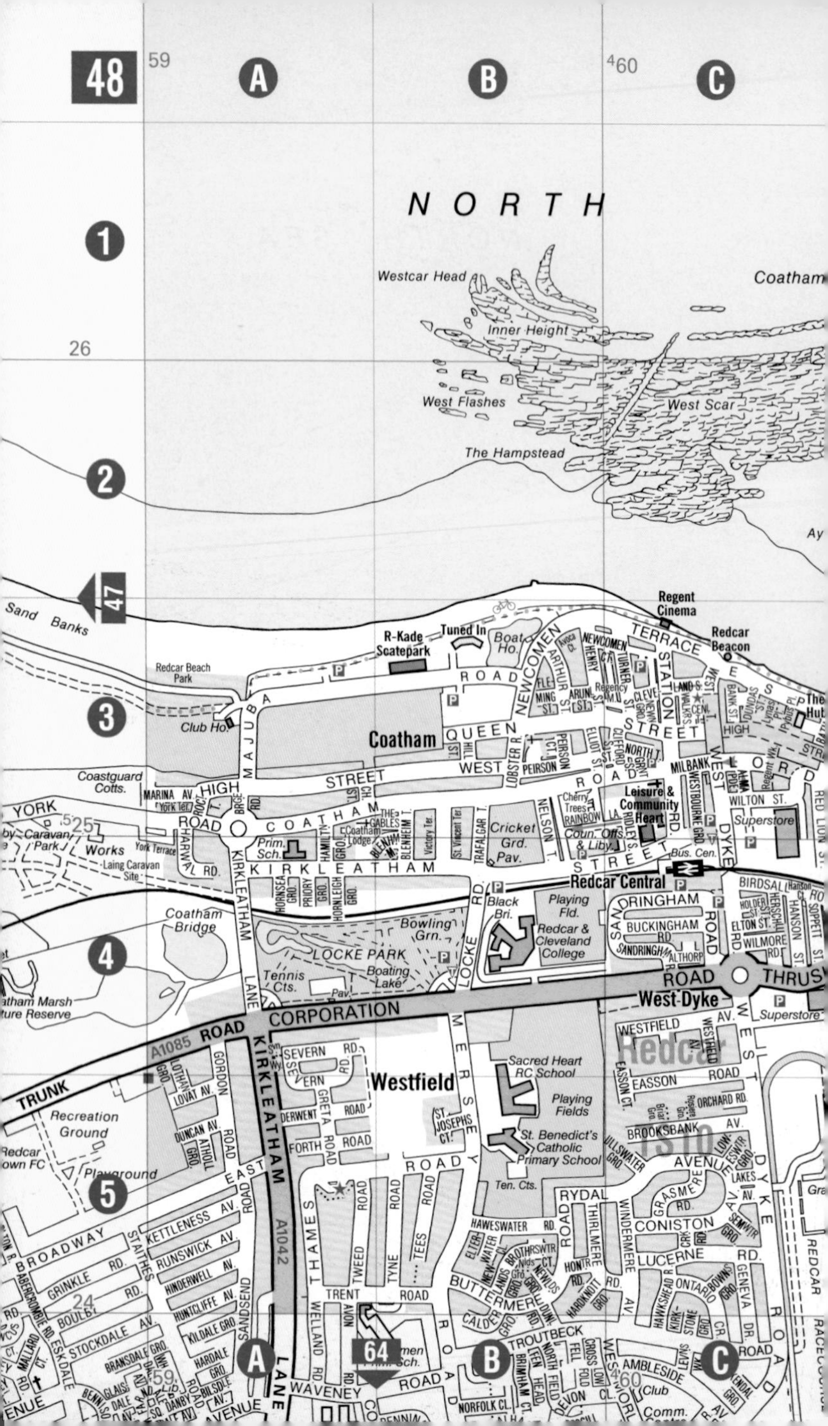

59
A
B
460
C
1
2
3
4
5
26
25
24
NORTH
Westcar Head
Inner Height
West Flashes
The Hampstead
West Scar
Coatham
Ay
47
Sand Banks
Redcar Beach Park
Club Ho.
Coastguard Cotts.
R-Kade Scatepark
Tuned In
Boat Ho.
Regent Cinema
Redcar Beacon
The Hub
TERRACE
ROAD
MAJUBA
NEWCOMEN
ARTHUR ST.
HENRY
TURNER
STATION
Coatham
QUEEN
STREET
WEST
HIGH
HIGH STREET
MARINA AV.
York Ter.
YORK ROAD
COATHAM
KIRKLEATHAM
Caravan Park
Works
York Terrace
Laing Caravan Site
HARWAL RD.
Prim. Sch.
Coatham Lodge
THE GABLES
BLENHEIM T.
Victory Ter.
St. Vincent Ter.
TRAFALGAR T.
Cricket Grd. Pav.
NELSON T.
Cherry Trees
RAINBOW LA.
Leisure & Community Heart
Coun. Offs. & Liby.
MILBANK
WESTBOURNE GRO.
WILTON ST.
Superstore
Bus. Cen.
DYKE
RED LION
Redcar Central
HORNSEA GRO.
PRIORY GRO.
HORNLEIGH GRO.
Coatham Bridge
Bowling Grn.
LOCKE PARK
Tennis Cts.
Boating Lake
Pav.
LOCKE RD.
Black Bri.
Playing Fld.
Redcar & Cleveland College
SANDRINGHAM
BUCKINGHAM
ALTHORP
ROAD
BIRDSALL
HOLDER ST.
ELTON ST.
WILMORE RD.
HANSON ST.
SOPPETT ST.
THRUS
West Dyke
Superstore
atham Marsh
ture Reserve
LANE
CORPORATION
ROAD
A1085
TRUNK
KIRKLEATHAM
A1042
SEVERN RD.
Westfield
DERWENT
GRETA
FORTH
ROAD
MERSEY
ST. JOSEPHS CT.
Sacred Heart RC School
Playing Fields
St. Benedict's Catholic Primary School
Ten. Cts.
WESTFIELD AV.
Redcar
EASSON CT.
EASSON ROAD
ORCHARD RD.
BROOKSBANK AV.
TS10
ULLSWATER GRO.
AVENUE
GRASMERE RD.
LAKES AV.
CONISTON
LUCERNE
RD.
GENEVA DR.
ONTARIO
BOWNESS
HAWKSHEAD R.
KIRKSTONE
REDCAR
ROAD
Recreation Ground
Redcar Town FC
Playground
LOTHIAN GRO.
LOVAT AV.
GORDON
DUNCAN AV.
ATHOLL GRO.
EAST
BROADWAY
STAITHES
KETTLENESS AV.
RUNSWICK AV.
HINDERWELL AV.
HUNTCLIFFE AV.
KILDALE GRO.
GRINKLE RD.
BOULBY
STOCKDALE AV.
ESKDALE
ABERCROMBIE RD.
MALLARD
BRANSDALE GRO.
HARDALE GRO.
SANDSEND
THAMES ROAD
TWEED
TYNE
TEES
TRENT ROAD
WELLAND RD.
AVON
64
Prim. Sch.
WAVENEY
RYDAL
HAWESWATER RD.
THIRLMERE
WINDERMERE
BUTTERMERE
CALDER GRO.
TROUTBECK
NORFOLK CL.
DEVON
AMBLESIDE
Club
Comm.
KENDAL GRO.
AVENUE
LANE

D
E
F
61
62
1
2
3
4
5
26
525
24
SEA
Salt Scar
Off Height
Inner Height
Luff Way
ocks
The Islands
High Stone
Hole
Laid
The Flashes
East Scar
Stokesley Scar
Redcar Rocks
Redcar
REDCAR
Slipway
Sands
Mus.
GRANVILLE TERRACE
STREET
Redcar Bus. Sta.
HIGH
CHARLES ST.
CHARLOTTE ST.
ALFRED ST.
MURIEL ST.
Caroline M.
DENE GRO.
REDCAR
Sch.
WILLIAM ST.
GOSFORTH
Dobson Ter.
STANLEY GRO.
FISHERMANS SQ.
SOUTH TER.
Pine Cl.
ELM RD.
BEECH AV.
LIME RD.
PARK AVENUE
COAST ROAD
A1085
ROAD
REDCAR LANE
AVENUE
STANLEY GRO.
LABURNUM ROAD
CEDAR GRO.
LIME
THE CRESCENT
Zetland Park
Bowl. Gn.
Ten. Cts.
The Stray
POPLAR GR.
HAZEL GR.
SYCAMORE RD.
SOUTHAMPTON
FITZWILLIAM S
YEOMAN S
OLIVER ST.
GEORGE
LAWRENCE S
LUMLEY
ROAD
ASKE ROAD
STABLE M.
Ings Mews
INGS ROAD
THE FURLONGS
Redcar Cemetery
ST. PETER'S GRO.
ST. JOHN'S GRO.
THE CHASE
QUEENSLAND AV.
VICTORIA AV.
ST. THOMAS GRO.
THWAITES LA.
Cemetery
B1269
Bowling Greens
Redcar Borough Park Bowling Club
Borough Park
Tennis Cts.
GREENLANDS RD.
WARDMAN CR.
MALCOLM GRO.
BOROUGH ROAD
RICHMOND
RABY
STIRLING
BARNARD GRO.
PEMBROKE
Redcar East
LILAC GROVE
THE WILLOWS
OAK ROAD
HAWTHORN
HOLLIES
CHESTNUT AV.
THE LARCHS
WALNUT
Sch.
GROVE
HAMPTON GRO.
CYPRESS ROAD
LAUREL R.
ROAD
Lily Parks
Promenade
The Stray
A1085
SALISBURY GRO.
ELY CR.
WELLS GRO.
Mill Howle
CHESTER ROAD
Ings Farm Prim. Sc
65
CONWAY RD.
WINDSOR RD.
ST. MARGARET'S GRO.
WARWICK
CASTLE ROAD
ZETLAND
CANTERBURY
RIPON
DURHAM R.
WHITBY CR.
RD.
NOTHM
ROAD
LANE

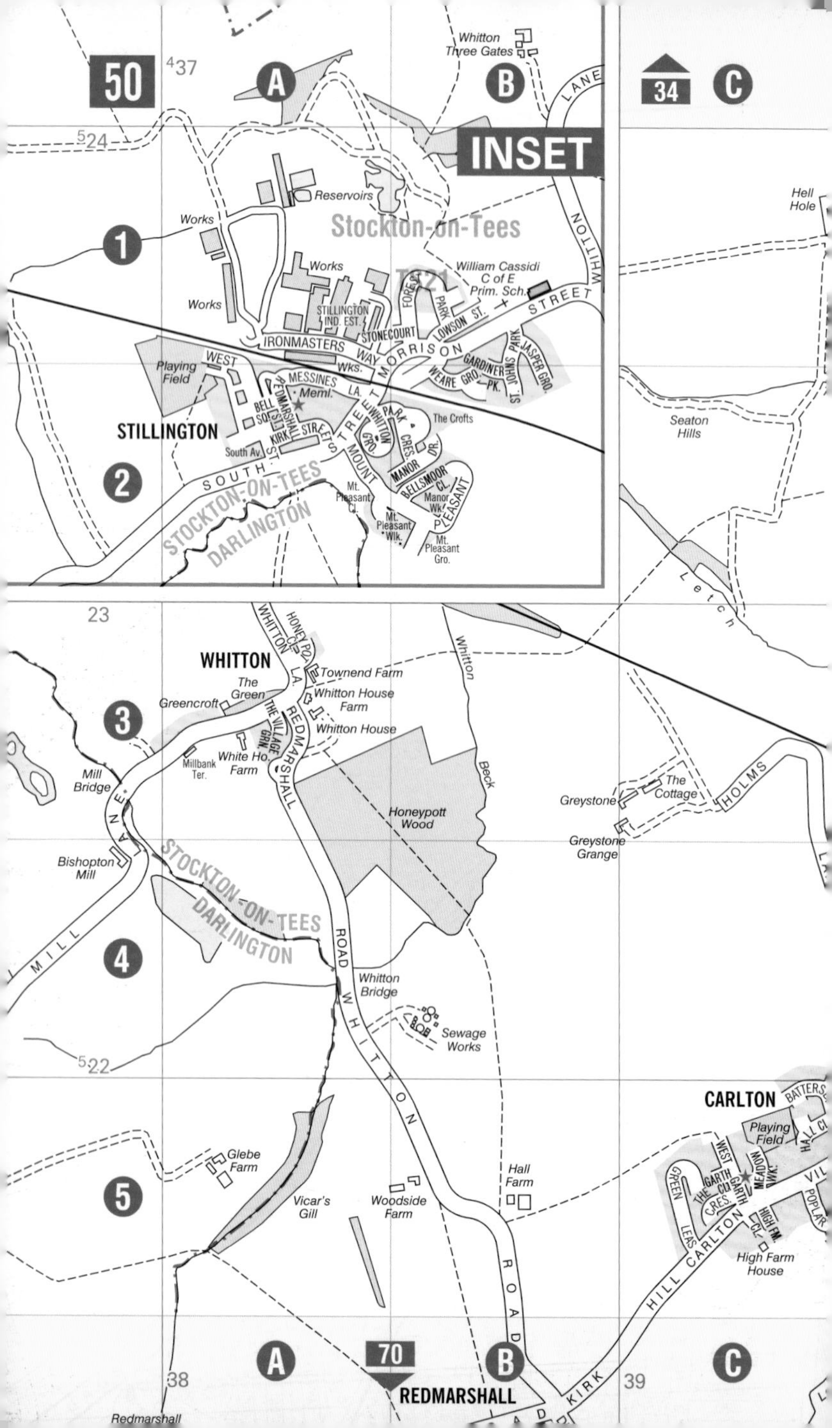
INSET
34
A
B
C
1
2
3
4
5
437
524
23
522
38
39
Whitton Three Gates
Reservoirs
Stockton-on-Tees
Works
Works
Works
William Cassidi C of E Prim. Sch.
STILLINGTON IND. EST.
STONECOURT
IRONMASTERS WAY
MORRISON STREET
WHITTON LANE
FOREST
PARK
LOWSON ST.
GARDINER GRO.
WEARE GRO.
ST. JOHNS PARK
PK.
JASPER GRO.
Playing Field
WEST
Wks.
MESSINES LA.
REDMARSHALL ST.
Meml.
BELL SQ.
KIRK STREET
STILLINGTON
South Av.
SOUTH ST.
WHITTON GRO.
PARK CRES.
The Crofts
MOUNT
MANOR DR.
BELLSMOOR CL.
Manor Wk.
PLEASANT
Mt. Pleasant Cl.
Mt. Pleasant Wlk.
Mt. Pleasant Gro.
STOCKTON-ON-TEES
DARLINGTON
Hell Hole
Seaton Hills
Letch
WHITTON
HONEY POT CL.
WHITTON LA.
Townend Farm
Whitton House Farm
Whitton House
The Green
Greencroft
THE VILLAGE GRN.
REDMARSHALL
Millbank Ter.
White Ho. Farm
Whitton Beck
Mill Bridge
LANE
Honeypott Wood
Greystone
The Cottage
HOLMS
Greystone Grange
Bishopton Mill
STOCKTON-ON-TEES
DARLINGTON
MILL
ROAD
Whitton Bridge
Sewage Works
WHITTON
CARLTON
BATTERS
Playing Field
HALL CL.
WEST GARTH
THE GARTH CL.
CRES.
MEADOW WK.
GREEN LEAS
HIGH FM. CL.
POPLAR
Glebe Farm
Hall Farm
Vicar's Gill
Woodside Farm
ROAD
HILL CARLTON
High Farm House
KIRK
70
REDMARSHALL
Redmarshall

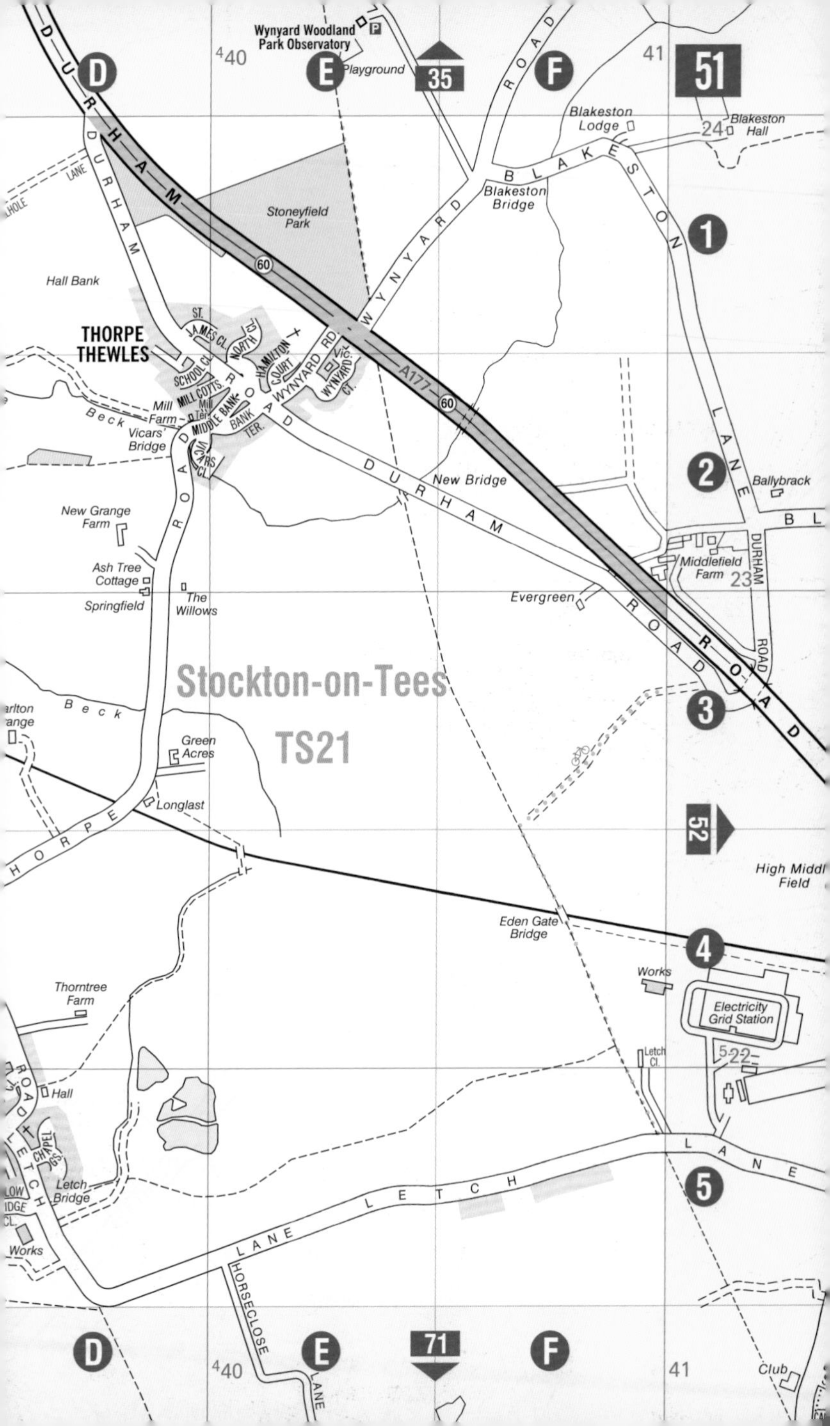
51
Wynyard Woodland Park Observatory
Playground
35
D
E
F
440
41
Blakeston Lodge
Blakeston Hall
24
BLAKESTON LANE
Blakeston Bridge
WYNYARD ROAD
DURHAM ROAD
Stoneyfield Park
Hall Bank
THORPE THEWLES
ST. JAMES CL.
NORTH CL.
HAMILTON COURT
SCHOOL CL.
MILL COTTS.
Mill Ter.
MIDDLE BANK
BANK TER.
WYNYARD RD.
Vic.
WYNYARD CT.
VICARS CL.
Mill Farm
Vicars' Bridge
Beck
A177
60
New Bridge
Ballybrack
Middlefield Farm
23
Evergreen
New Grange Farm
Ash Tree Cottage
Springfield
The Willows
Stockton-on-Tees
TS21
Green Acres
Longlast
THORPE ROAD
1
2
3
4
5
52
High Middl Field
Eden Gate Bridge
Works
Electricity Grid Station
22
Letch Cl.
Thorntree Farm
Hall
CHAPEL GS.
Letch Bridge
Works
LETCH LANE
HORSECLOSE LANE
71
Club

A
B
C
36
41
42
Blakeston Hall
Blakeston Lodge
Thorpe
TS21
Low Middlefield Farm
West Newlands Farm
Thorney Farm
Ballybrack
BLAKESTON LANE
BLAKESTON
Coppice Farm
DURHAM ROAD
Middlefield Farm
Evergreen
Stockton-on-Tees
A177
Howden Lodge
Howden Hall
High Middle Field
Exercise4less
Superstore
Works
Club
Depot
Summerville Farm
Electricity Grid Station
Letch Cl.
Horse & Jockey Roundabout
LETCH LANE
HARROWGATE LANE
Stockton Lodge
Hardwick
KNOWLE
PIPER ROAD
EDISON DR.
EBCHESTER CL.
RENVYLE AVENUE
ROSSLARE
RUDYARD
INGLETON
Ray Ct.
STEPHENSON
GEORGE
51
72
1
2
3
4
5

Thornley Hill
43
44
D
E
F
37
Billingham
TS22
BILLINGHAM DIVERSION
24
Beck
Wolviston Mill
Viewly Hill
1
2
3
4
5
Newclose Farm
Billingham Beck
Gravel H Farm
Riflebutts Farm
NORTON GOLF COURSE
Club House
Brookdale Farm
Golf Course
Brookfield
Calf Fallow Farm
All Weather Sports Pitch
Tennis Cts.
Sports Pitch
TS20
Hornleys
White House Plantation
Norton East Junction
Norton West Junction
Cricket Ground Club
Bowling Grn.
Pav.
Norton Sports Complex
Crooksbarn Prim. Sch.
Tinkers Yd. Pocket Pk.
54
WESTMINSTER OVAL
ST. STEPHENS CL.
FULMAR
STATION ROAD
NORTHUMBERLAND GRO.
CUMBERLAND GRO.
COUNTISBURY RD.
LYNMOUTH RD.
SYON GDNS.
KENLEY GDS.
CHELSEA GDNS.
B1274
Norton Junction Cotts.
TEES HOSPITAL
Glebe
The Education Centre
HENSLEY CT.
WOLSEY DR.
MAPLETON DRIVE
WHINFLOWER DRIVE
FOSTON CL.
BRAMBLING CL.
ASHTON ROAD
KINDERTON GROVE
FULTHORPE
THE RING ROAD
A1027
The Glebe Prim. Sch.
PULFORD RD.
SALTNEY ROAD
WEAVERHAM ROAD
ROSENEATH AV.
ROSTREVOR AVENUE
ROMFORD ROAD
ROTHBURY ROAD
REDBROOK AVENUE
Redbrook Villas
Rec. Grd.
ROCHESTER RD.
RADSTOCK AV.
Comm. Cen.
Red House
TS19
Frederick Nattrass Prim. Acad.
DARLINGTON LANE
LEVEN ROAD
SWALE ROAD
RAGWORTH LANE
OAKWELL GS.
Sch.
Recreation Grd
NORTON AV.
73

38
53
74
A
B
C
1
2
3
4
5
BILLINGHAM GOLF COURSE
TS22
TS20
Stockton-on-Tees
BILLINGHAM DIVERSION
A19
Billingham Beck Valley Country Park
Crooksbarn
Norton
Norton Junction
Newclose Farm
Gravel Hole Farm
Riflebutts Farm
Gravel Hole Nature Reserve
Calf Fallow Farm
All Weather Sports Pitch
Tennis Cts.
Bowling Grn.
Cricket Ground
Club
Crooksbarn Prim. Sch.
Tinkers Yd. Pocket Pk.
Norton Sports Complex
The Education Centre
Club House
Northfield House
The Lodge
Visitors Cen.
Picnic Area
Northcote Hill Farm
Playing Fields
Red Ho. Sch.
Comm. Cen.
Recreation Grd.
Frederick Nattrass Prim. Acad.
Billingham Bottoms Interchange
THE RING
A1027
JUNCTION ROAD
B1274
HIGH ST.
THE GREEN
BILLINGHAM RD.
A139
BILLINGHAM ROAD BR.
STATION ROAD
SANDY LANE
MARTON ROAD
WHITEHOUSE DR.
NORTON AV.
LEVEN ROAD
DARLINGTON LANE
Subway
Billingham Beck

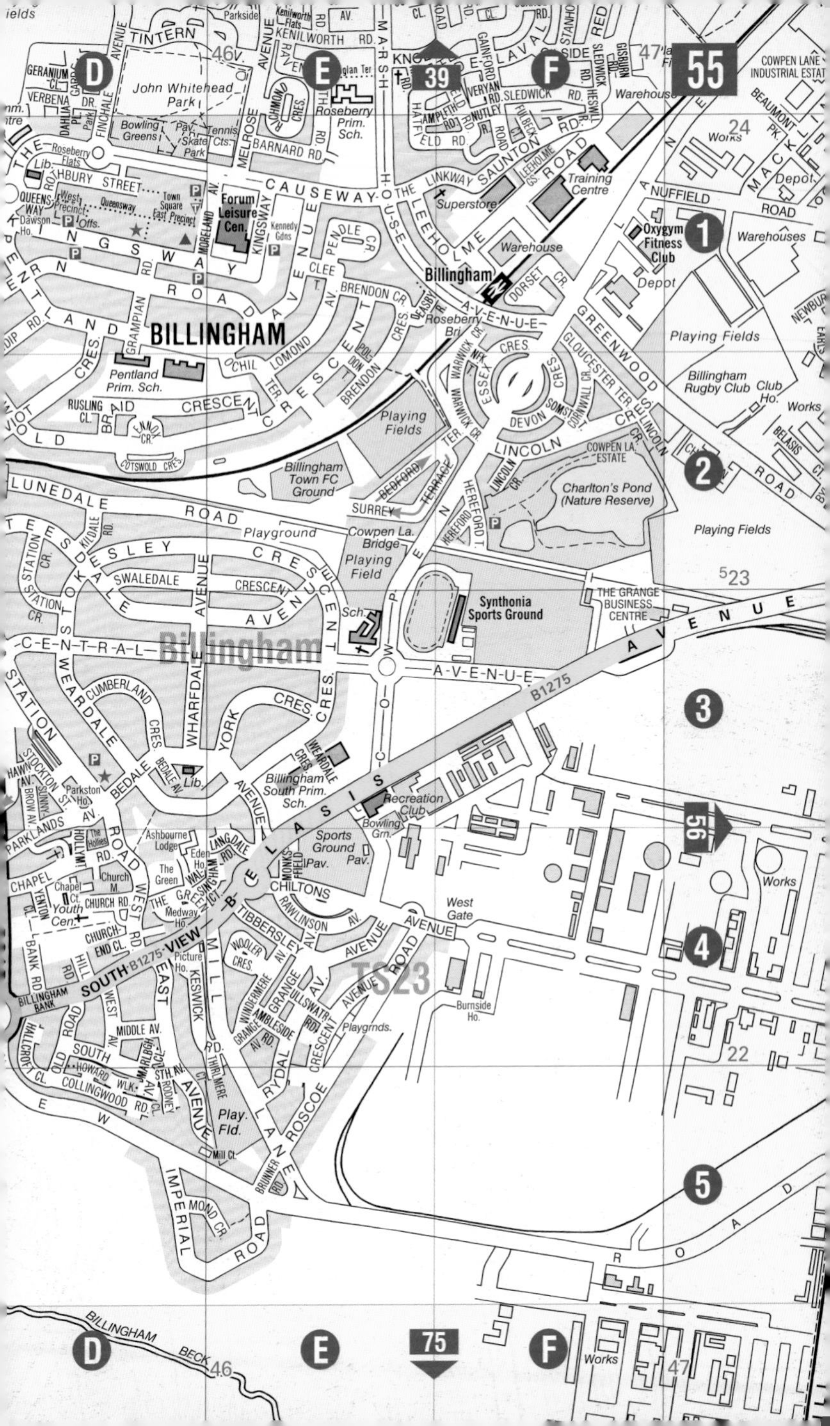

BILLINGHAM
Billingham
TS23
B1275
D
E
F
1
2
3
4
5
39
56
75
46
47
24
23
22
John Whitehead Park
Bowling Greens
Tennis Cts.
Skate Park
Pav.
TINTERN AVENUE
Parkside
Kenilworth Flats
KENILWORTH RD.
AV.
GERANIUM CL.
VERBENA DR.
DAHLIA
FINCHALE
MELROSE AVENUE
RICHMOND CRES.
Roseberry Prim. Sch.
BARNARD RD.
MARSH HOUSE AVENUE
KNOWLES
LAVAL
GAINFORD
VERYAN
SLEDWICK RD.
NUTLEY
HATFIELD RD.
FULBECK
HESWALL
GISBURN RD.
SIDE
Warehouse
COWPEN LANE INDUSTRIAL ESTATE
BEAUMONT PK.
MACKLIN
Works
Depot
NUFFIELD ROAD
Warehouses
Oxygym Fitness Club
SAUNTON ROAD
LEEHOLME GS.
Training Centre
THE LINKWAY
Superstore
LEEHOLME
Warehouse
Billingham
DORSET CR.
CAUSEWAY
THE CAUSEWAY
Roseberry Flats
Lib.
ROXBURY STREET
QUEENSWAY
West Precinct
Queensway
Town Square
East Precinct
Dawson Ho.
Offs.
Forum Leisure Cen.
MORELAND AV.
KINGSWAY
Kennedy Gdns
KINGSWAY
PENDLE CR.
CLEE AV.
BRENDON CR.
DEASBY
Roseberry Bri.
RD.
PENTLAND ROAD
GRAMPIAN RD.
BILLINGHAM
Pentland Prim. Sch.
CHILTERN
LOMOND CRES.
POLDEN
BRENDON CRES.
CRESCENT
RUSLING CL.
BRAID CRESCENT
LENNOX CR.
COTSWOLD CRES.
CHEVIOT
WOLD
Playing Fields
WARWICK CR.
ESSEX CRES.
DEVON CRES.
SOMERSET
CORNWALL CR.
GLOUCESTER TER.
GREENWOOD
Playing Fields
Billingham Rugby Club
Club Ho.
Works
NEWBURN
BELASIS CT.
ROAD
LINCOLN CRES.
LINCOLN
LINCOLN CR.
COWPEN LA. ESTATE
Charlton's Pond (Nature Reserve)
Playing Fields
Billingham Town FC Ground
BEDFORD TERRACE
SURREY
HEREFORD T.
LUNEDALE ROAD
TEESDALE
KILDALE RD.
Playground
Cowpen La. Bridge
Playing Field
STATION CR.
STOKESLEY CRESCENT
SWALEDALE CRESCENT
AVENUE
Sch.
Synthonia Sports Ground
THE GRANGE BUSINESS CENTRE
AVENUE
CENTRAL AVENUE
PENTWOOD
STATION
WEARDALE
CUMBERLAND CRES.
WHARFDALE
YORK CRES.
BEDALE AV.
Lib.
WEARDALE CRES.
Billingham South Prim. Sch.
BELASIS AVENUE
Recreation Club
Bowling Grn.
Sports Ground
Pav.
STOCKTON ST.
SUNNY BROW AV.
PARKLANDS AV.
Parkston Ho.
BEDALE
The Hollies
ROAD
Ashbourne Lodge
Eden Ho.
LANGDALE RD.
MONKS FIELD
CHAPEL RD.
Chapel Ct.
Church
CHURCH RD.
The Green
WALSINGHAM CT.
THE GREEN
Youth Cen.
Medway Ho.
CHILTONS AV.
RAWLINSON AV.
TIBBERSLEY AV.
AVENUE
West Gate
AVENUE
ROAD
CHURCH END CL.
BANK RD.
HILL RD.
SOUTH VIEW
Picture Ho.
KESWICK
MILL LANE
WOOLER CRES.
WINDERMERE AV.
GRANGE AV.
ULLSWATER RD.
AVENUE
Burnside Ho.
BILLINGHAM BANK
WEST ROAD
EAST
OLD ROAD
MIDDLE AV.
SOUTH
HOWARD WLK.
MARLBOROUGH AV.
STH. AV.
RODNEY CL.
HALCROFT CL.
COLLINGWOOD RD.
AMBLESIDE RD.
RYDAL
CRESCENT
Playgrnds.
THIRLMERE
AVENUE
Play. Fld.
Mill Ct.
ROSCOE
LANE
BRUNNER RD.
IMPERIAL
MOND CR.
ROAD
ROAD
BILLINGHAM BECK
Works

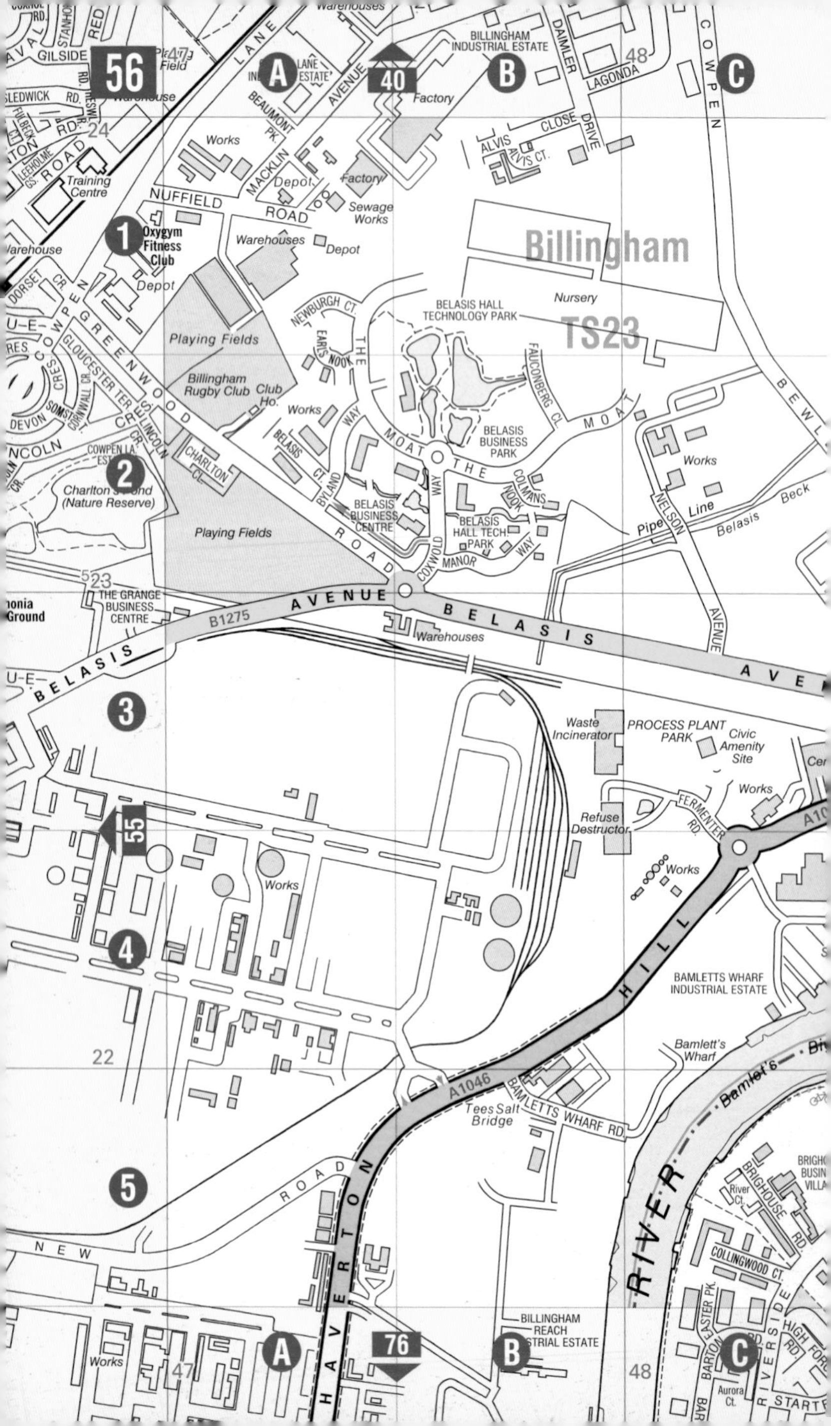

56
A
B
C
1
2
3
4
5
40
55
76
47
48
24
23
22
Billingham
TS23
BILLINGHAM INDUSTRIAL ESTATE
Factory
Works
Training Centre
NUFFIELD ROAD
Oxygym Fitness Club
Depot
Sewage Works
Warehouses
Warehouse
Playing Fields
Billingham Rugby Club
Club Ho.
Charlton's Pond (Nature Reserve)
BELASIS HALL TECHNOLOGY PARK
Nursery
BELASIS BUSINESS PARK
BELASIS BUSINESS CENTRE
BELASIS HALL TECH. PARK
THE GRANGE BUSINESS CENTRE
B1275
BELASIS AVENUE
COWPEN LANE
GREENWOOD ROAD
THE MOAT
Waste Incinerator
PROCESS PLANT PARK
Civic Amenity Site
Refuse Destructor
FERMENTER RD.
BAMLETTS WHARF INDUSTRIAL ESTATE
Bamlett's Wharf
Tees Salt Bridge
BAMLETTS WHARF RD.
A1046
HAVERTON HILL
NEW ROAD
RIVER
BILLINGHAM REACH INDUSTRIAL ESTATE
COLLINGWOOD CT.
BRIGHOUSE RD.
RIVERSIDE
Aurora Ct.
River Ct.
BARTON
EASTER PK.
Pipe Line
Belasis Beck
NELSON AVENUE

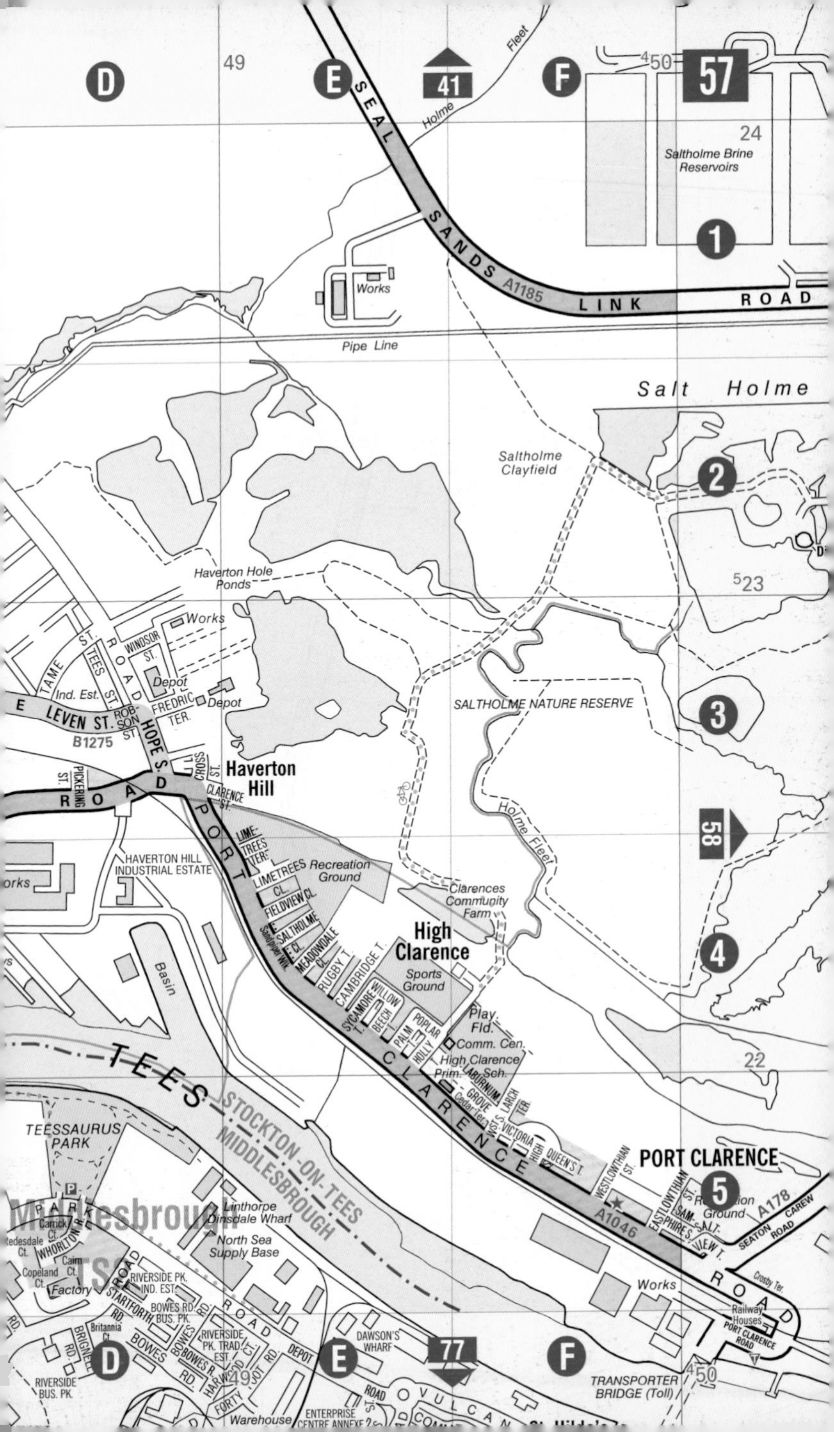
D
49
E
41
F
450
Fleet
Holme
SEAL SANDS LINK ROAD
A1185
24
Saltholme Brine Reservoirs
1
Works
Pipe Line
Salt Holme
Saltholme Clayfield
2
523
Haverton Hole Ponds
Works
WINDSOR ST.
TAME ST.
TEES ST.
ROAD
Ind. Est.
Depot
Depot
FREDRIC TER.
ROBSON ST.
LEVEN ST.
B1275
HOPE S.
CROSS ST.
SALTHOLME NATURE RESERVE
3
Haverton Hill
CLARENCE ST.
PICKERING ST.
ROAD
PORT CLARENCE ROAD
Holme Fleet
58
LIMETREES TER.
HAVERTON HILL INDUSTRIAL ESTATE
Works
LIMETREES CL.
FIELDVIEW CL.
Recreation Ground
Clarences Community Farm
SALTHOLME CL.
Sandpiper Wlk.
MEADOWDALE CL.
High Clarence
RUGBY T.
CAMBRIDGE T.
4
Sports Ground
Basin
SYCAMORE T.
WILLOW
BEECH
PALM
POPLAR
HOLLY
Play. Fld.
Comm. Cen.
High Clarence Prim. Sch.
LABURNUM
GROVE
Cedar Ter.
LARCH
TER.
W. ST.
VICTORIA
HIGH
QUEEN'S T.
22
TEES
STOCKTON-ON-TEES
MIDDLESBROUGH
TEESSAURUS PARK
P
PARK
Middlesbrough
Carrick Ct.
WHORLTON
Redesdale Ct.
Cairn Ct.
Copeland Ct.
Factory
Linthorpe Dinsdale Wharf
North Sea Supply Base
RIVERSIDE PK. IND. EST.
STARTFORTH RD.
BOWES RD. BUS. PK.
WESTLOWTHIAN ST.
PORT CLARENCE
5
EASTLOWTHIAN ST.
SAMPHIRES
SALTVIEW T.
Recreation Ground
A178
SEATON CAREW ROAD
A1046
Crosby Ter.
Works
ROAD
Railway Houses
PORT CLARENCE ROAD
Britannia Ct.
BRIGNELL RD.
D
BOWES
BOWES RD.
RIVERSIDE PK. TRAD. EST.
ROAD
DEPOT
E
DAWSON'S WHARF
77
F
RIVERSIDE BUS. PK.
HARWOOD CT.
49
FORTY
FOOT RD.
Warehouse
ENTERPRISE CENTRE ANNEXE
ROAD
VULCAN
TRANSPORTER BRIDGE (Toll)
450

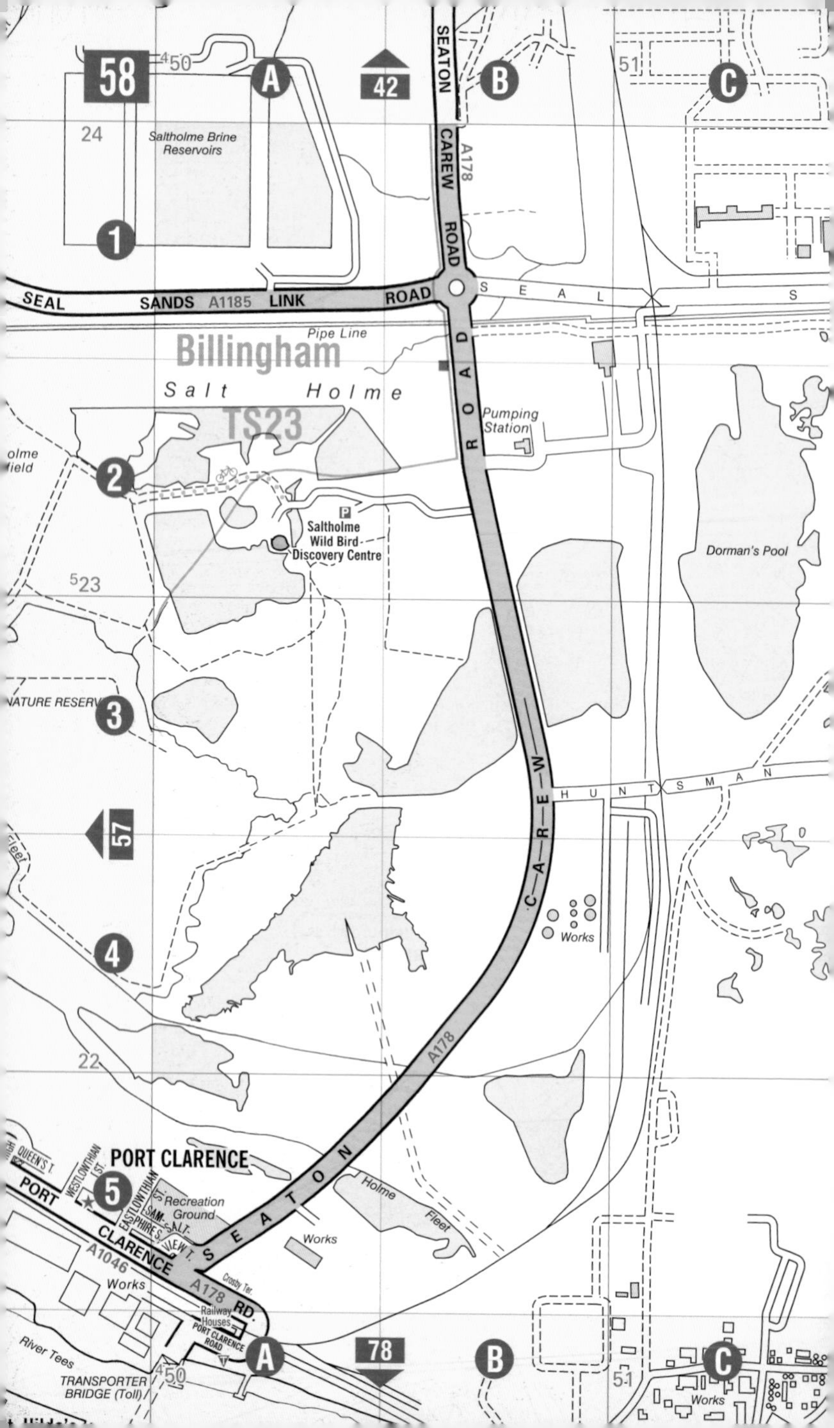
58
42
57
78
A
B
C
1
2
3
4
5
450
451
24
523
22
Saltholme Brine Reservoirs
SEATON
CAREW ROAD
A178
SEAL SANDS A1185 LINK ROAD
SEAL S
Pipe Line
Billingham
Salt Holme
TS23
Pumping Station
Saltholme Wild Bird Discovery Centre
Dorman's Pool
NATURE RESERV
HUNTSMAN
CAREW
Works
SEATON
PORT CLARENCE
Recreation Ground
Holme Fleet
PORT CLARENCE
A1046
A178 RD.
Crosby Ter.
Railway Houses
PORT CLARENCE ROAD
River Tees
TRANSPORTER BRIDGE (Toll)

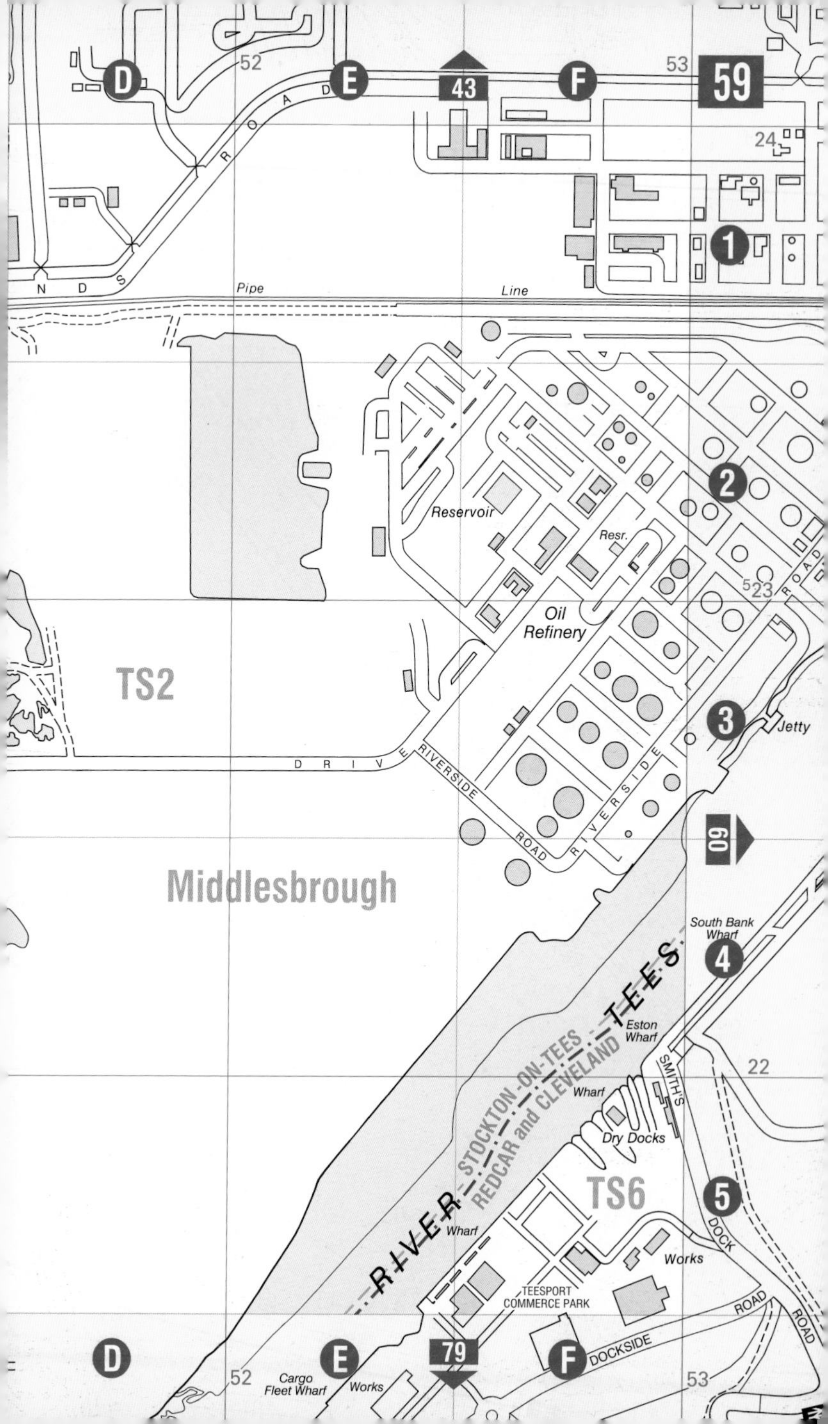

59
43
D
E
F
52
53
24
1
ROAD
Pipe Line
2
Reservoir
Resr.
Oil Refinery
ROAD
23
TS2
3
Jetty
DRIVE
RIVERSIDE ROAD
RIVERSIDE
60
Middlesbrough
South Bank Wharf
4
RIVER TEES
STOCKTON-ON-TEES
REDCAR and CLEVELAND
Eston Wharf
22
SMITH'S
Wharf
Dry Docks
TS6
5
DOCK ROAD
Wharf
Works
TEESPORT COMMERCE PARK
ROAD
DOCKSIDE
79
D
E
F
Cargo Fleet Wharf
Works
52
53

60
53
A
44
B
C
54
Jetty
Jetties
Jetty
24
1
Oil
Refinery
ROAD
Jetty
TS2
STOCKTON-ON-TEES
REDCAR and CLEVELAND
TEES
TEESPORT
TEES
2
Resr.
23
Jetty
3
Jetty
RIVERSIDE
RIVER
59
Works
Middlesbrough
South Bank
Wharf
4
Slag Tip
Eston
Wharf
22
SMITH'S
Wharf
Dry Docks
5
DOCK
Works
Works
ROAD
ROAD
DOCKSIDE
A
80
Works
B
C
53
54
BOYLE

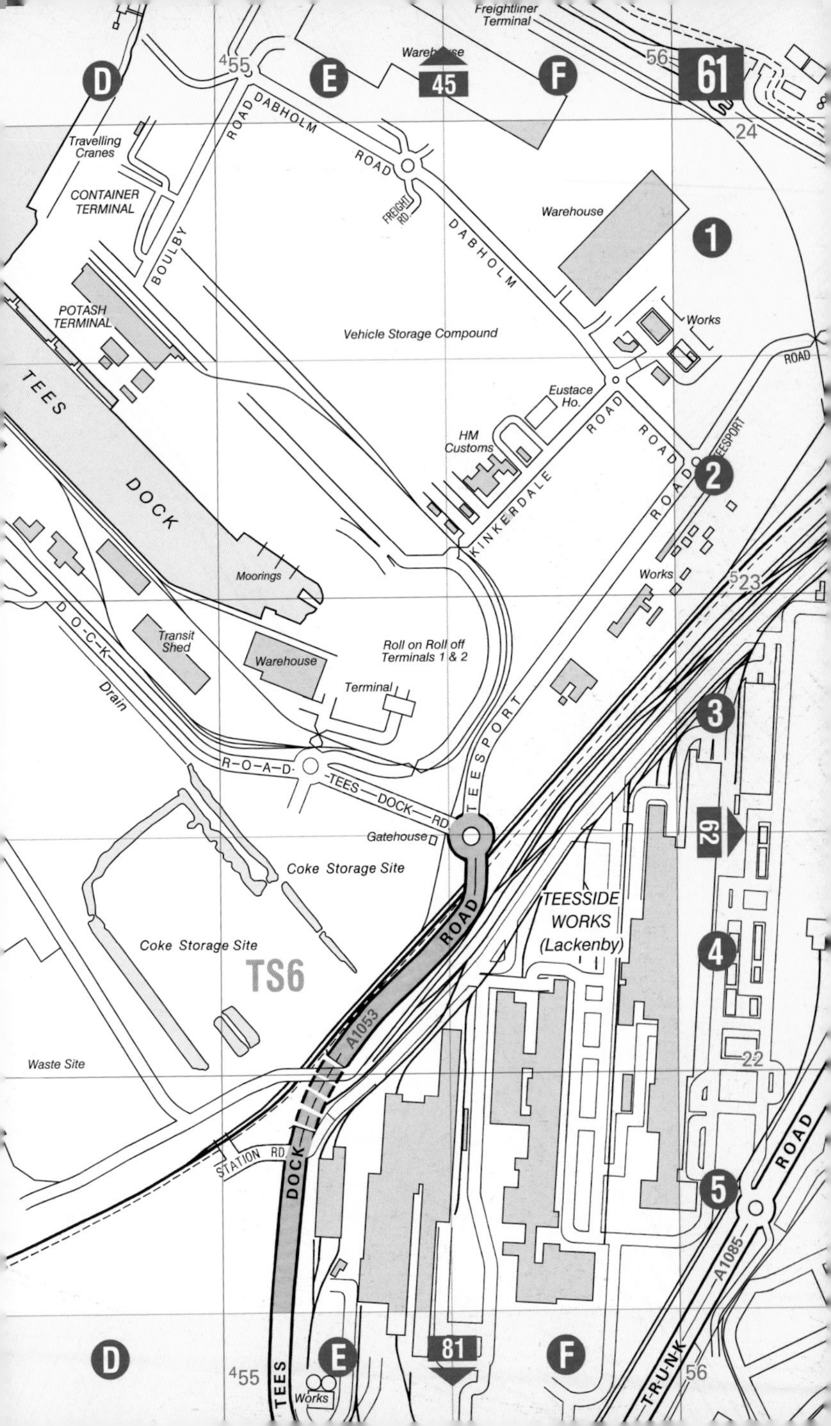

Freightliner Terminal
Warehouse
45
61
56
24
455
D
E
F
DABHOLM ROAD
BOULBY ROAD
FREIGHT RD.
Travelling Cranes
CONTAINER TERMINAL
Warehouse
1
Works
Vehicle Storage Compound
POTASH TERMINAL
TEES DOCK
Eustace Ho.
HM Customs
KINKERDALE ROAD
TEESPORT ROAD
2
Works
523
Moorings
DOCK Drain
Transit Shed
Warehouse
Roll on Roll off Terminals 1 & 2
Terminal
3
ROAD TEES DOCK RD
Gatehouse
62
Coke Storage Site
Coke Storage Site
TS6
TEESSIDE WORKS (Lackenby)
4
A1053
22
Waste Site
STATION RD
DOCK ROAD
5
A1085
TRUNK ROAD
81
TEES
Works
56

62
46
61
82
A
B
C
1
2
3
4
5
56
457
24
523
22
British Steel Redcar
Electricity Sub Station
Pipeline
Dabholm
Gatehouse
Warehouse
DABHOLM
Works
Eustace Ho.
ROAD
TEESPORT
ROAD
Dabholm Beck
The Mill Race
Middlesbrough
TS6
A1085
Lord
Dabholm Beck
TEESIDE WORKS (Lackenby)
FREIGHTLINER DEPOT
TRUNK
Tanks
Sub Station

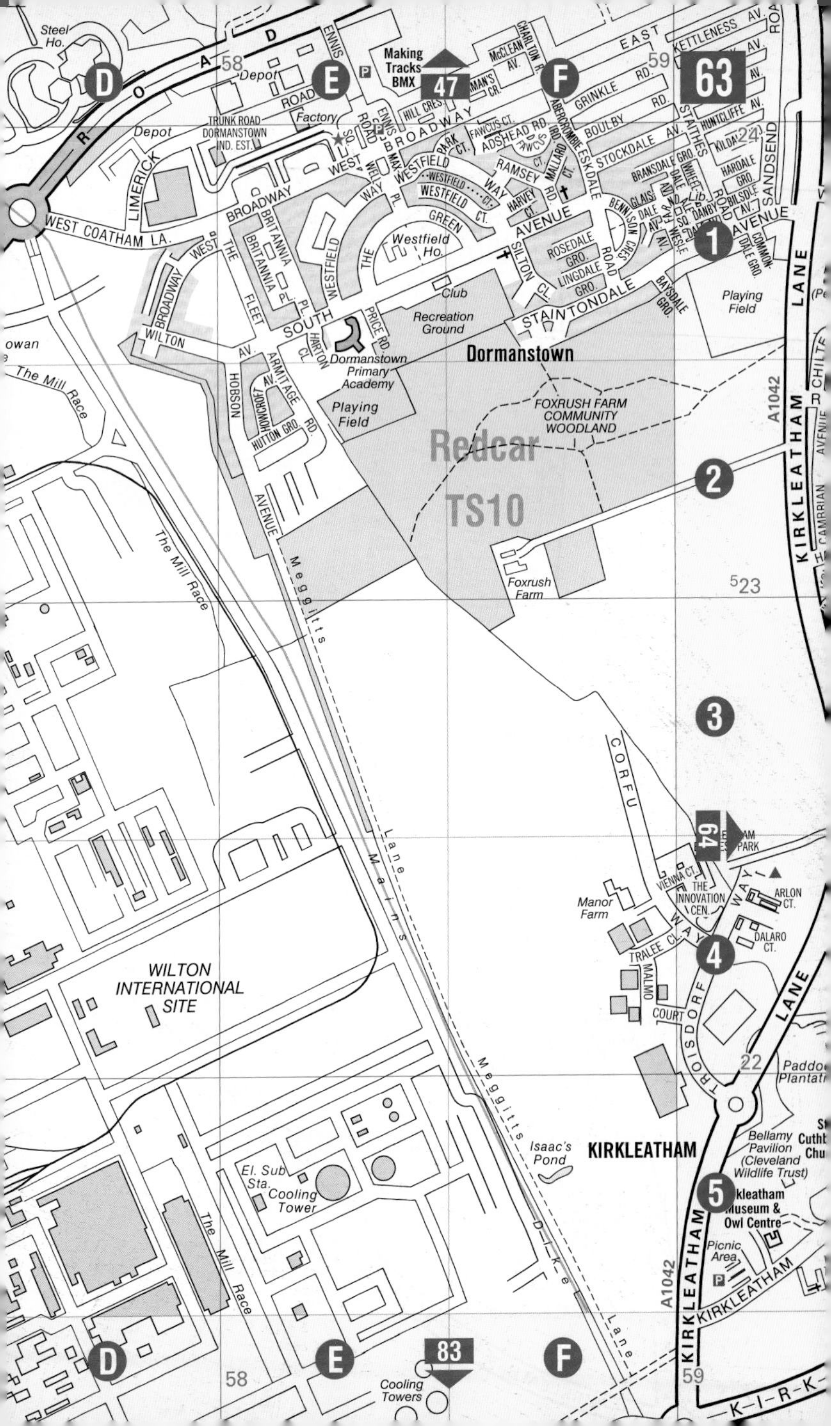
63
47
64
83
D
E
F
1
2
3
4
5
58
59
523
24
22
Dormanstown
Redcar
TS10
KIRKLEATHAM
WILTON INTERNATIONAL SITE
Steel Ho.
Depot
Making Tracks BMX
Factory
TRUNK ROAD DORMANSTOWN IND. EST.
TRUNK ROAD
EAST
KETTLENESS AV.
McCLEAN AV.
CHARLTON R.
GRINKLE RD.
BOULBY RD.
STAITHES
HUNTCLIFFE AV.
KILDALE
STOCKDALE AV.
SANDSEND
HARDALE GRO.
BRANSDALE GRO.
BROADWAY
WEST
ENNIS SQ.
ENNIS ROAD
HILL CRES.
PARK CT.
FAWCUS CT.
ADSHEAD RD.
ABERCROMBIE RD.
ESKDALE
MALLARD CT.
RAMSEY
WESTFIELD
WESTFIELD WAY
WESTFIELD CT.
WESTFIELD GREEN
HARVEY CT.
AVENUE
BENNISON CRES.
DANBY
ROSEDALE GRO.
LINGDALE GRO.
ROAD
SILTON CL.
STAINTONDALE
BAYSDALE GRO.
COMMONDALE GRO.
Playing Field
LIMERICK
WEST COATHAM LA.
BRITANNIA
BRITANNIA PL.
THE FLEET
WESTFIELD
THE
Westfield Ho.
Club
Recreation Ground
SOUTH
PRICE RD.
HARTON CL.
Dormanstown Primary Academy
Playing Field
WILTON AV.
HOBSON
HOWCROFT AV.
ARMITAGE RD.
HUTTON GRO.
AVENUE
FOXRUSH FARM COMMUNITY WOODLAND
Foxrush Farm
The Mill Race
Meggitts Lane
Mains Dike
Meggitts Lane
A1042
KIRKLEATHAM LANE
CORFU
VIENNA CT.
THE INNOVATION CEN.
WAY
ARLON CT.
DALARO CT.
Manor Farm
TRALEE CL.
MALMO COURT
TROISDORF
LANE
Isaac's Pond
Bellamy Pavilion (Cleveland Wildlife Trust)
Kirkleatham Museum & Owl Centre
Picnic Area
KIRKLEATHAM
El. Sub Sta.
Cooling Tower
Cooling Towers
The Mill Race
K-I-R-K-

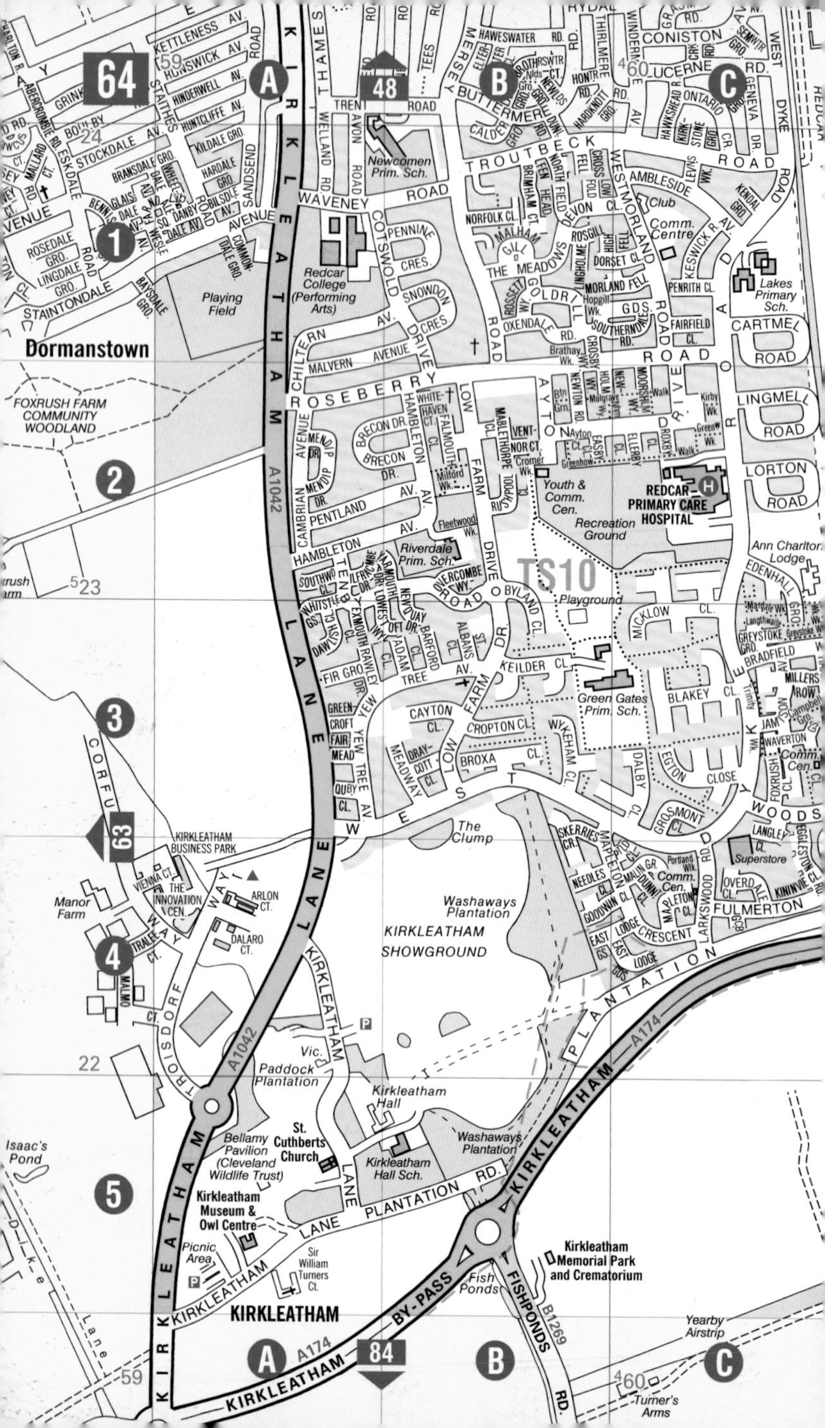

A
B
C
48
Dormanstown
FOXRUSH FARM COMMUNITY WOODLAND
KETTLENESS AV.
RUNSWICK AV.
HINDERWELL AV.
HUNTCLIFFE AV.
STAITHES
GRINKLE
BOULBY
STOCKDALE AV.
ESKDALE
ABERCROMBIE RD.
MALLARD CT.
KILDALE GRO.
HARDALE GRO.
BRANSDALE GRO.
BILSDALE AV.
SANDSEND
AVENUE
ROSEDALE GRO.
LINGDALE GRO.
STAINTONDALE
BAYSDALE GRO.
COMMONDALE GRO.
Playing Field
THAMES
TRENT
ROAD
WELLAND RD.
AVON ROAD
TEES
Newcomen Prim. Sch.
WAVENEY ROAD
Redcar College (Performing Arts)
PENNINE CRES.
COTSWOLD
SNOWDON CRES.
DRIVE
CHILTERN AV.
MALVERN AVENUE
ROSEBERRY
HAWESWATER RD.
MERSEY
BUTTERMERE
CALDER GRO.
THIRLMERE
WINDERMERE
CONISTON RD.
ULLSWATER
LUCERNE RD.
ONTARIO
GENEVA
HAWKSHEAD RD.
KIRKSTONE GRO.
DYKE
TROUTBECK ROAD
WESTMORLAND
AMBLESIDE
Club
Comm. Centre
KESWICK AV.
KENDAL GRO.
Lakes Primary Sch.
NORFOLK CL.
MALHAM
THE MEADOWS
DEVON CL.
ROSGILL
DORSET CL.
MORLAND FELL
PENRITH CL.
GOLDRILL
OXENDALE RD.
SOUTHERNDALE RD.
FAIRFIELD CL.
CARTMEL ROAD
ROAD
LINGMELL ROAD
LORTON ROAD
AYTON DRIVE
Youth & Comm. Cen.
REDCAR PRIMARY CARE HOSPITAL
Recreation Ground
Ann Charlton Lodge
TS10
Playground
MICKLOW CL.
EDENHALL GRO.
GREYSTOKE GRO.
BRADFIELD
MILLERSROW
BLAKEY CL.
Green Gates Prim. Sch.
KEILDER CL.
WYKEHAM CL.
DALBY CL.
EGTON CLOSE
GROSMONT CL.
WOODS
LANGLEY CL.
Superstore
OVERDALE CL.
FULMERTON
CRESCENT
LARKSWOOD RD.
BRECON DR.
HAMBLETON AV.
PENTLAND AV.
CAMBRIAN AVENUE
MENDIP DR.
LOW FARM DRIVE
Riverdale Prim. Sch.
OVERCOMBE WY.
ROAD
BYLAND CL.
CAYTON CL.
CROPTON CL.
BROXA CL.
DRAYCOTT CL.
MEADWAY
YEW TREE AV.
FIR GRO.
TREE AV.
WEST
The Clump
KIRKLEATHAM LANE
A1042
CORFU
63
KIRKLEATHAM BUSINESS PARK
VIENNA CT.
THE INNOVATION CEN.
ARLON CT.
DALARO CT.
WAY
TRALEE CT.
MALMO CT.
TROISDORF
Manor Farm
Washaways Plantation
KIRKLEATHAM SHOWGROUND
SKERRIES CR.
NEEDLES CL.
GOODWIN CL.
EAST LODGE GS.
LODGE CRESCENT
Comm. Cen.
PLANTATION
A174
KIRKLEATHAM
Vic.
Paddock Plantation
Kirkleatham Hall
St. Cuthberts Church
Bellamy Pavilion (Cleveland Wildlife Trust)
Kirkleatham Hall Sch.
Washaways Plantation
PLANTATION RD.
LANE
Kirkleatham Museum & Owl Centre
Picnic Area
Sir William Turners Ct.
KIRKLEATHAM
Isaac's Pond
Dike Lane
BY-PASS
Fish Ponds
FISHPONDS RD.
B1269
Kirkleatham Memorial Park and Crematorium
Yearby Airstrip
Turner's Arms
84
1
2
3
4
5
22
23
24
59
60

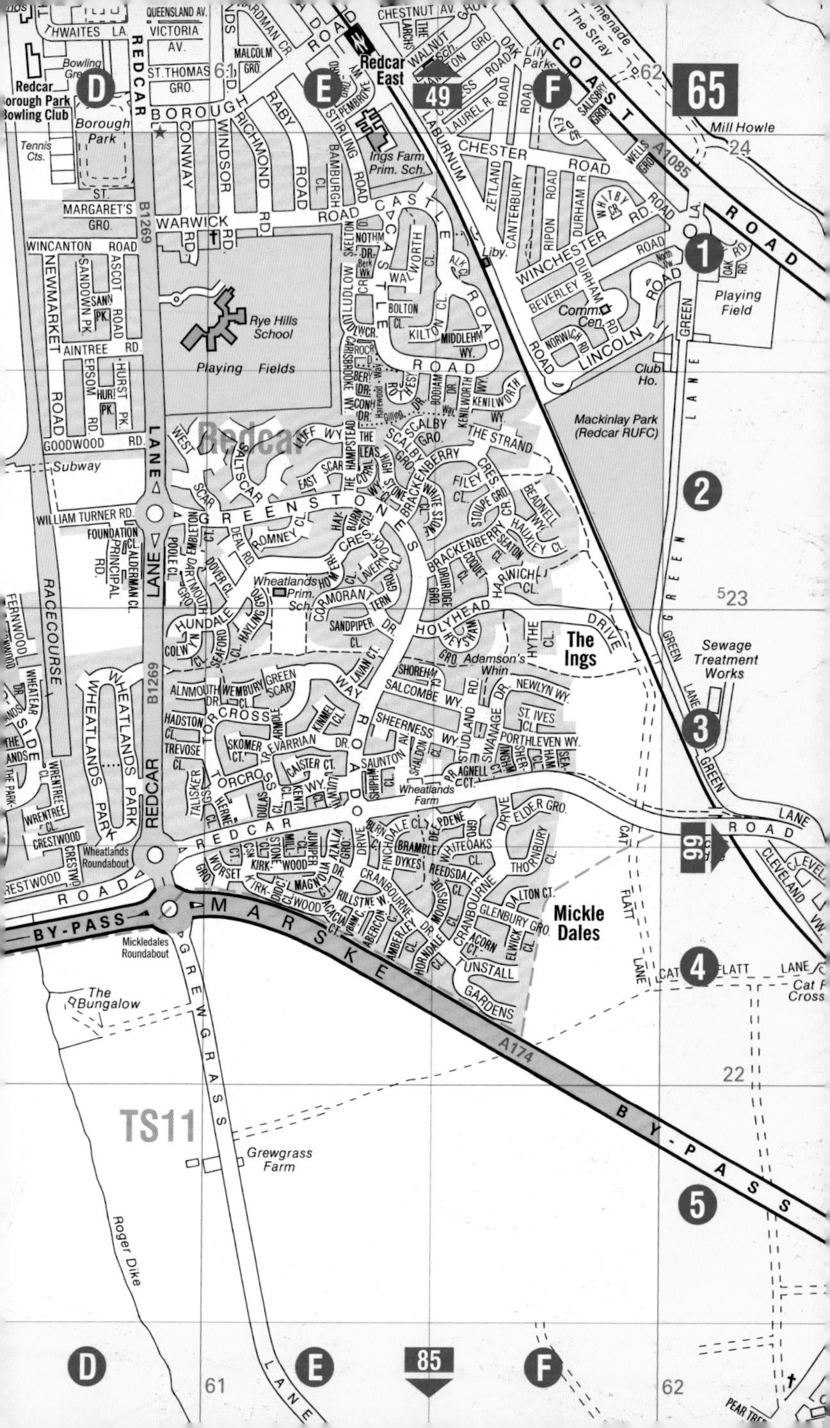

QUEENSLAND AV.
VICTORIA AV.
THWAITES LA.
ST. THOMAS GRO.
MALCOLM GRO.
CHESTNUT AV.
WALNUT
Redcar East
49
Lily Parks
The Stray
62
Mill Howle
24
D
E
F
Redcar Borough Park Bowling Club
Bowling Grn.
Borough Park
Tennis Cts.
BOROUGH
RICHMOND
WINDSOR
CONWAY
RABY
STIRLING ROAD
BAMBURGH CL.
PEMBROKE WY.
Ings Farm Prim. Sch.
LABURNUM
CHESTER ROAD
ZETLAND
CANTERBURY
RIPON ROAD
DURHAM R.
WHITBY CR.
WINCHESTER RD.
COAST ROAD
A1085
WELLS GRO.
SALISBURY GRO.
ELY CR.
ST. MARGARET'S GRO.
WARWICK RD.
B1269
WINCANTON ROAD
NEWMARKET ROAD
ASCOT ROAD
SANDOWN PK.
AINTREE RD.
EPSOM RD.
HURST PK.
GOODWOOD RD.
Rye Hills School
Playing Fields
CASTLE ROAD
SKELTON
NOTHM DR.
WALWORTH CL.
BOLTON CL.
KILTON CL.
MIDDLEHM WY.
LUDLOW
CARISBROOKE WY.
BODIAM DR.
KENILWORTH WY.
Liby.
BEVERLEY
DURHAM RD.
Comm. Cen.
NORWICH RD.
LINCOLN ROAD
Club Ho.
Playing Field
GREEN LANE
Mackinlay Park (Redcar RUFC)
1
2
3
4
5
Redcar
Subway
WEST
SALTSCAR
LUFF WY
EAST SCAR
THE HAMPSTEAD
THE LEAS
SCALBY GRO.
BRACKENBERRY
THE STRAND
FILEY CL.
HIGH STONE
WHITE STONES
STOUPE GRO.
BEADNELL WY.
HAUXLEY CL.
GREENSTONES
WILLIAM TURNER RD.
FOUNDATION
ALDERMAN CL.
PRINCIPAL RD.
LANE
REDCAR
POOLE CL.
EMBLETON
DARTMOUTH GRO.
DOVER CL.
DEAL RD.
ROMNEY CL.
HOWFIELD CRES.
LAVERNOCK
TERN GRO.
CORMORANT
Wheatlands Prim. Sch.
SEATON
HARWICH CL.
DRURIDGE GRO.
COQUET
523
RACECOURSE
FERNWOOD
HUNDALE
COLWYN CL.
SEAFORD
HAYLING GRO.
SANDPIPER CL.
HOLYHEAD DR.
HEYSHAM
HYTHE CL.
DRIVE
The Ings
Adamson's Whin
Sewage Treatment Works
WHEATEAR
WHEATLANDS PARK
ALNMOUTH DR.
WEMBURY
GREEN SCAR
LAVAN CT.
SHOREHM CL.
SALCOMBE WY.
NEWLYN WY.
HADSTON CL.
TORCROSS
KINMEL CL.
TREVOSE CL.
SKOMER CT.
TREVARRIAN DR.
SHEERNESS WY.
STUDLAND RD.
SWANAGE DR.
ST. IVES CL.
PORTHLEVEN WY.
TALISKER
TORCROSS
CAISTER CT.
SAUNTON
SHALDON CL.
AGNELL CT.
Wheatlands Farm
WRENTREE CL.
CRESTWOOD
Wheatlands Roundabout
REDCAR ROAD
JUNIPER CL.
AZALIA GRO.
FINCHDALE CL.
DEEPDENE GRO.
ELDER GRO.
BRAMBLE
WHITEOAKS CL.
THORNBURY CL.
WORSET
KIRKSTONE
MILLWOOD
MAGNOLIA
CRANBOURNE
DYKES
REEDSDALE
DALTON CT.
GLENBURY GRO.
ACORN CT.
ELWICK CL.
TUNSTALL GARDENS
Mickle Dales
CAT FLATT LANE
Cat Flatt Cross
ROAD
LANE
99
CLEVELAND VW.
BY-PASS
MARSKE
A174
Mickledales Roundabout
The Bungalow
GREWGRASS LANE
22
TS11
Grewgrass Farm
Roger Dike
85
61
62
PEAR TREE

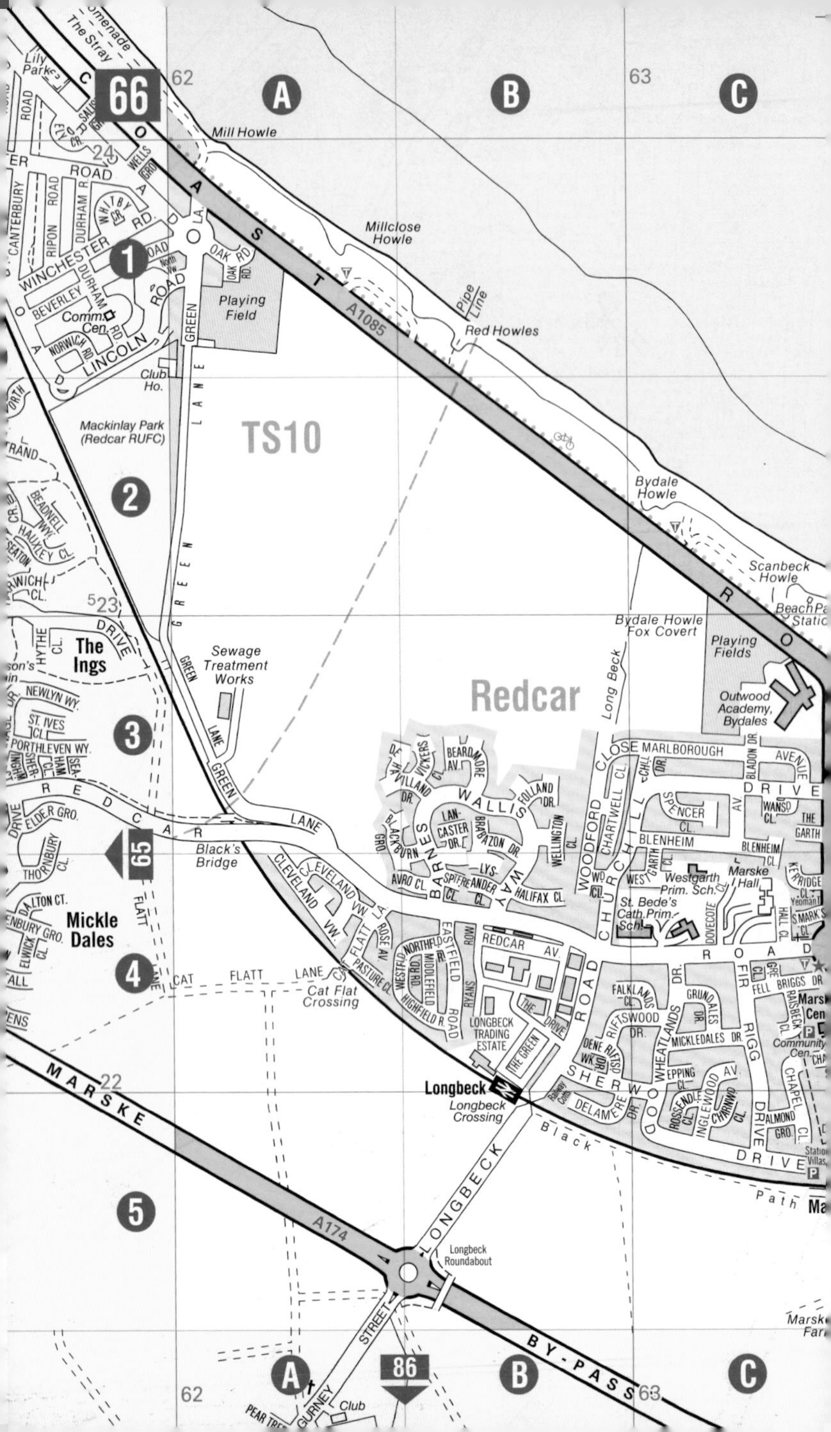
66
62
63
A
B
C
1
2
3
4
5
TS10
Redcar
Mill Howle
Millclose Howle
Pipe Line
Red Howles
Bydale Howle
Scanbeck Howle
Bydale Howle Fox Covert
Playing Field
Playing Fields
Outwood Academy, Bydales
Westgarth Prim. Sch.
St. Bede's Cath. Prim. Schl.
Marske Hall
Mackinlay Park (Redcar RUFC)
Club Ho.
Comm. Cen.
Sewage Treatment Works
The Ings
Mickle Dales
Black's Bridge
Cat Flat Crossing
Longbeck
Longbeck Crossing
Longbeck Roundabout
LONGBECK TRADING ESTATE
Long Beck
COAST ROAD
A1085
A174
MARSKE BY-PASS
GREEN LANE
REDCAR LANE
CAT FLATT LANE
LONGBECK
STREET
GURNEY
WINCHESTER ROAD
LINCOLN ROAD
DURHAM RD.
BEVERLEY
NORWICH RD.
CANTERBURY
RIPON ROAD
WHITBY CR.
OAK RD.
WELLS GRO.
North Vw.
CLEVELAND VW.
CLEVELAND
FLATT LA.
ROSE AV.
PASTURE CL.
WESTFLD. RD.
NORTHFLD. RI.
MIDDLEFIELD
EASTFIELD ROAD
HIGHFIELD R.
RYANS ROW
REDCAR AV.
THE DRIVE
THE GREEN
ROAD
WALLIS WAY
BARNES
DE HAVILLAND DR.
VICKERS CL.
BEARDMORE AV.
FOLLAND DR.
LANCASTER DR.
BRABAZON DR.
BLACKBURN GRO.
WELLINGTON CL.
AVRO CL.
SPITFIRE CL.
LYSANDER CL.
HALIFAX CL.
WOODFORD CLOSE
CHARTWELL CL.
CHURCHILL DRIVE
MARLBOROUGH
BLENHEIM
BLENHEIM CL.
SPENCER CL.
WESTGARTH CL.
DOVECOTE CL.
BLADON DR.
AVENUE
WANSD. CL.
THE GARTH
KERRIDGE CL.
HALL CL.
ST. MARK'S CL.
FALKLANDS CL.
RIFTSWOOD DR.
DENE RIFTSWOOD
WK. DR.
WHEATLANDS DR.
GRUNDALES DR.
MICKLEDALES DR.
FIR RIGG DRIVE
EPPING CL.
ROSSENDALE CL.
INGLEWOOD AV.
CHARNWD. CL.
SHERWOOD DRIVE
DELAMERE DR.
Railway Cotts.
ALMOND GRO.
CHAPEL CL.
FELL BRIGGS DR.
RAISBECK CL.
GREEN CL.
Community Cen.
Station Villas
Black Path
Beach Pa. Static.
DRIVE
NEWLYN WY.
ST. IVES CL.
PORTHLEVEN WY.
SEA-
HYTHE CL.
ELDER GRO.
THORNBURY CL.
DALTON CT.
ELWICK CL.
BEADNELL WY.
HAUXLEY CL.
SEATON
CR.
23
24
22
65
86
The Stray
Lily Parks
ELY CR.
SALISBURY
Marske Farm
Club
PEAR TREE

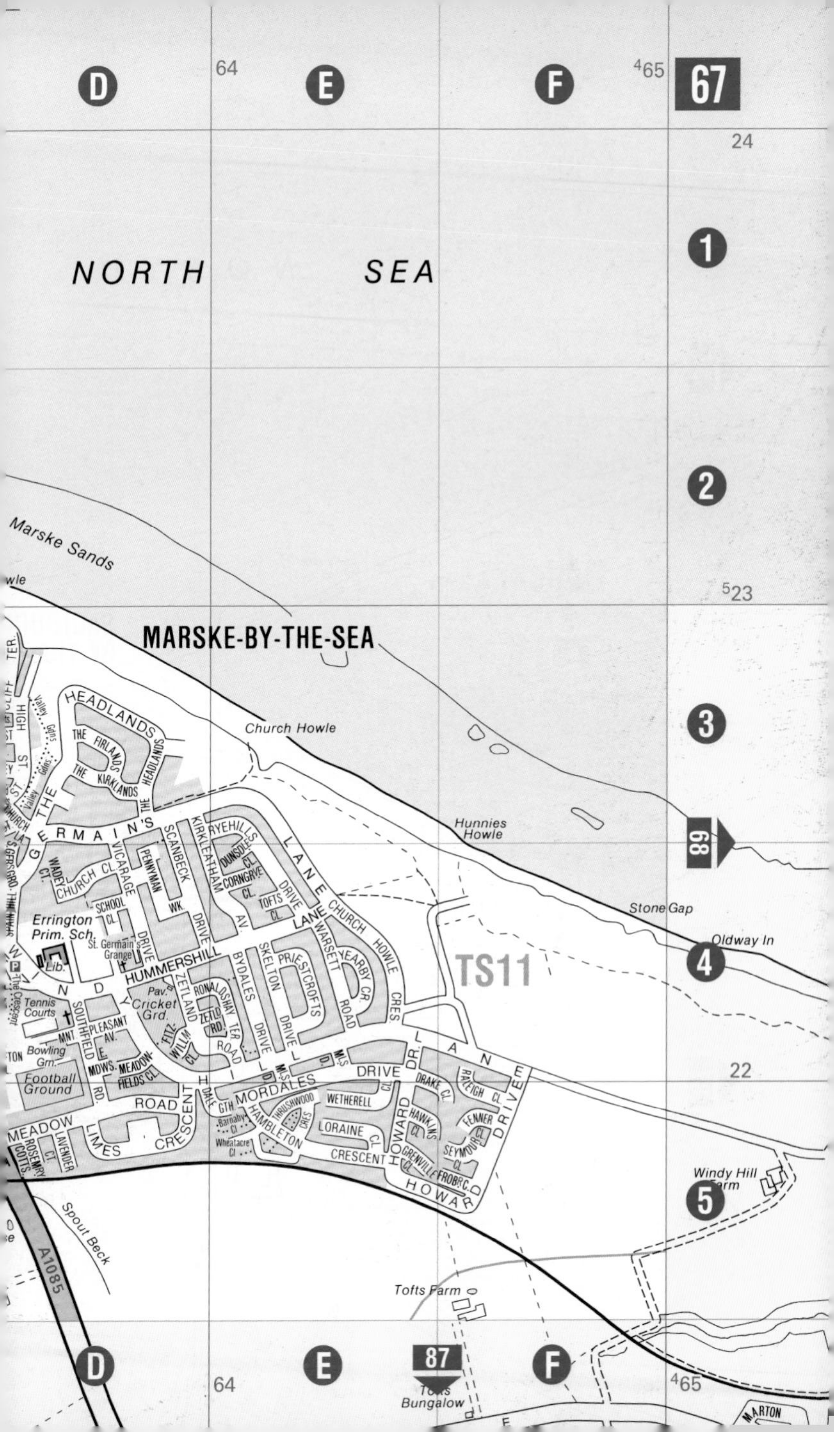
D
E
F
64
465
24
1
2
3
4
5
523
22
NORTH SEA
Marske Sands
MARSKE-BY-THE-SEA
Church Howle
Hunnies Howle
Stone Gap
Oldway In
TS11
68
HEADLANDS
THE FIRLANDS
THE KIRKLANDS
THE HEADLANDS
ST. GERMAIN'S
SCANBECK WK.
KIRKLEATHAM DRIVE
RYEHILLS LANE
DUNSDALE CL.
CORNGRAVE CL.
TOFTS CL.
DRIVE
CHURCH HOWLE CRES.
WARSETT ROAD
YEARBY CR.
PRIESTCROFTS DRIVE
SKELTON DRIVE
BYDALES DRIVE
RONALDSHAY TER.
ZETLAND
HUMMERSHILL LANE
PENNYMAN
VICARAGE DRIVE
CHURCH CL.
WADE CT.
SCHOOL CL.
Errington Prim. Sch.
St. Germain's Grange
Lib.
WINDY HILL LANE
Tennis Courts
Pav.
Cricket Grd.
FITZ-WILLM CL.
SOUTHFIELD RD.
PLEASANT AV.
E. MDWS.
MEADOW-FIELDS CL.
Bowling Grn.
Football Ground
ROAD
MEADOW
ROSEMARY COTTS.
LAVENDER CT.
LIMES CRESCENT
CRESCENT
DALE GTH.
MORDALES DRIVE
HAMBLETON CRES.
THRUSHWOOD
Barnaby Cl
Wheatacre Cl
WETHERELL CL.
LORAINE CL.
CRESCENT
HOWARD DR.
HOWARD DRIVE
DRAKE CL.
RALEIGH CL.
HAWKINS CL.
FENNER CL.
SEYMOUR CL.
GRENVILLE CL.
FROBR.C.
HIGH ST.
Valley Gdns.
CHURCH ST.
The Crescent
Windy Hill Farm
Spout Beck
A1085
Tofts Farm
Tofts Bungalow
87
MARTON

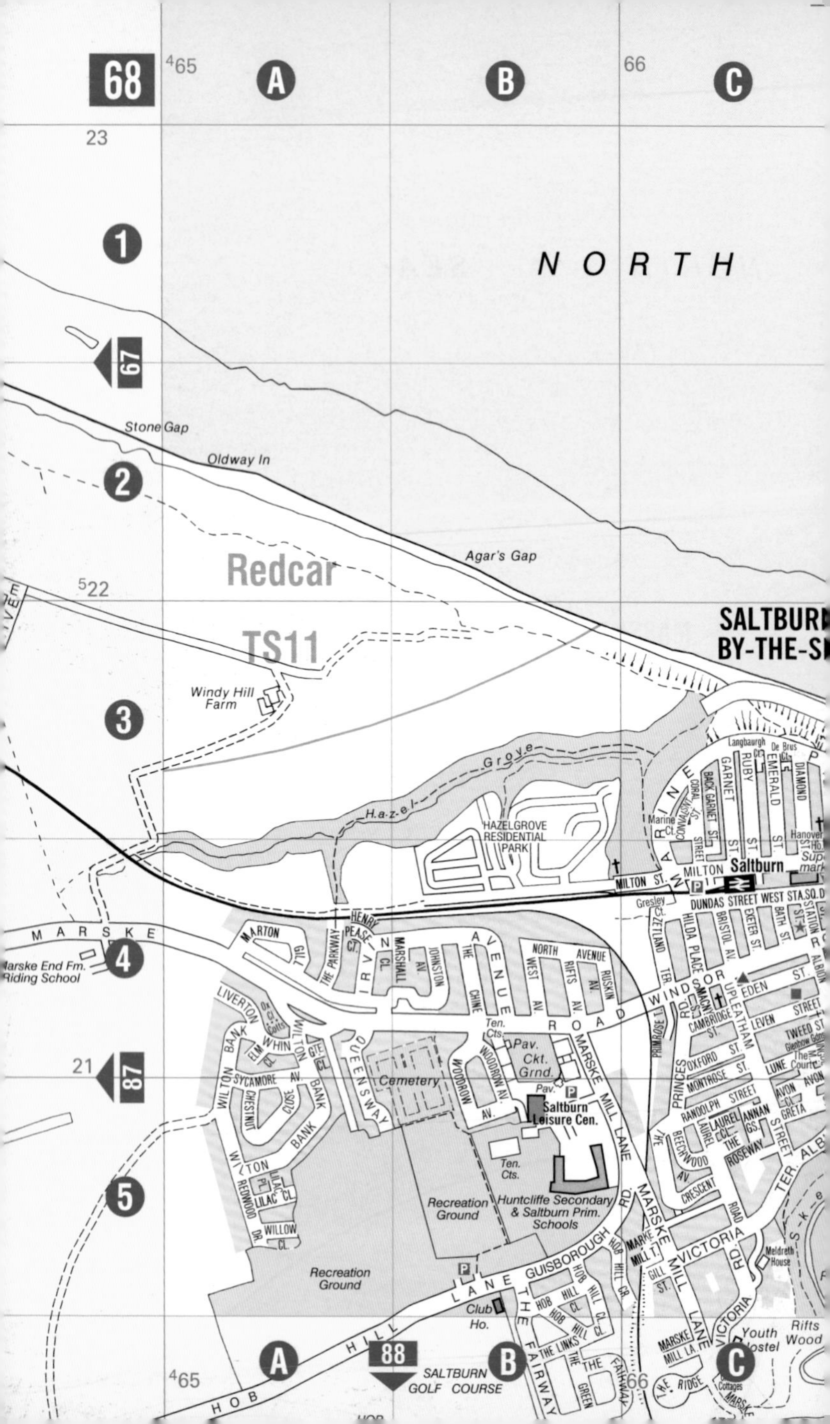

465
A
B
66
C
23
1
NORTH
67
Stone Gap
Oldway In
2
Agar's Gap
Redcar
522
TS11
SALTBURN
BY-THE-S
Windy Hill Farm
3
Grove
Hazel
HAZELGROVE RESIDENTIAL PARK
Langbaugh Ct.
De Brus Ct.
RUBY
EMERALD
DIAMOND
GARNET
BACK GARNET ST.
CORAL ST.
CONNAUGHT CT.
MARINE
Marine Ct.
STREET
ST.
Hanover Ho.
Super mark
MILTON ST.
MILTON
Saltburn
Gresley Ct.
DUNDAS STREET WEST
STA.SQ.
STATION ST.
BATH ST.
EXETER ST.
BRISTOL AV.
HILDA PLACE
ZETLAND TER.
ALBION
MARSKE
HENRY PEASE CT.
MARTON GILL
THE PARKWAY
IRVIN
MARSHALL CL.
JOHNSTON AV.
THE CHINE
AVENUE
NORTH AVENUE
WEST AV.
RIFTS AV.
RUSKIN AV.
4
Marske End Fm. Riding School
WINDSOR
ROAD
PRIMROSE
RD.
MACNAY ST.
UPLEATHAM
EDEN ST.
CAMBRIDGE ST.
LEVEN
STREET
TWEED ST.
Glenbow Gdns.
LIVERTON
Ox Cl.
Colts
WHIN
WILTON
ELM
BANK
GTE. CL.
QUEENSWAY
Ten. Cts.
Pav.
Ckt. Grnd.
MARSKE MILL LANE
OXFORD ST.
MONTROSE ST.
PRINCES
LUNE
The Court
21
87
SYCAMORE AV.
CHESTNUT
CLOSE
Cemetery
WOODROW
WOODROW AV.
AV.
Saltburn Leisure Cen.
RANDOLPH STREET
AVON CL.
AVON
GRETA
LAUREL
LAUREL CL.
ANNAN GS.
THE ROSEWAY
STREET
BEECHWOOD AV.
CRESCENT
THE
WILTON
REDWOOD DR.
PL.
LILAC
LILAC CL.
WILLOW CL.
Ten. Cts.
5
Recreation Ground
Huntcliffe Secondary & Saltburn Prim. Schools
RD.
ALB
TER.
ROAD
GUISBOROUGH
HOB HILL CR.
MARSKE MILL T.
VICTORIA
RD.
Meldreth House
Recreation Ground
LANE
HOB HILL CL.
Club Ho.
GILL ST.
MARSKE MILL LANE
VICTORIA
Youth Hostel
Rifts Wood
HILL
88
HOB HILL CL.
THE LINKS
THE FAIRWAY
THE GREEN
THE
FAIRWAY
MARSKE MILL LA.
THE RIDGE
Cottages
MARSKE
A
B
C
465
66
SALTBURN GOLF COURSE
HOB

D
67
E
F
68
23
1
SEA
Stone Ridge
2
22
Saltburn Scar
Penny Hole
Saltburn Pier
PROMENADE
Saltburn Sands
Saltburn Cliff Lift
3
ROAD
SALTBURN
North Bank
Alexandra Ho.
Hotel
Cat Nab
Mill Farm
Saltburn Miniature Railway
Coastguard Cottages
Landgates
Brough Cott.
Brough House Farm
Old Saltburn
Bandstand
Little
Dale
SALTBURN
BANK
4
Cliffden Ct.
White House Wood
White House
Saltburn
Saltburn Valley Woodland Centre
21
Old Rigg Wood
Play. Flds.
Darn
Bottle
Saltburn-by-the-Sea
Tommy Nook Wood
Lum Hole Plantation
5
TS12
Barnes Farm
Lum Hole
Gill
The Coach House
Saltburn Grange
LANE
Saltburn Gill Nature Reserve
ROAD
Green Acres
D
E
89
F
67
68
Playing Fields
MARSHALL
Wood
Benson Banks

Vicar's Gill
Woodside Farm
50
38
39
A
B
C
High Farm House
HIGH FM. CL.
HILL CARLTON
LEAS
CRES.
WHITTON RD.
KIRK
REDMARSHALL
ROAD
DROVERS LA.
Redmarshall Bridge
1
Karamea
REDMARSHALL
CHURCH LANE
FERGUSON WY.
DERWENT CL.
RYDAL WY.
CONISTN CR.
WINDERMERE AV.
Mainside
High Farm
Church Farm Flats
The Mains
The Garth
21
Letch
High View
Hill House Farm
2
Gately Moor Reservoir
Reservoir
3
STOCKTON-ON-TEES
DARLINGTON
20
TS21
4
Ox Eye Farm
Whispers
Hill View
Longhirst
LANE
BACK
Delholme Farm
Gooseberry Farm
5
Whinney Hill
Sunnyfield Stud
19
Ox Hill Farm
Sandyleas Plantation Farm
DARLINGTON
SANDY LEAS LA.
94
A
B
C
38
39
ine Acres Nurseries
Depot
The
Sandyleas

Stockton-on-Tees
TS19
Bishopsgarth
Elton Park
D
E
F
1
2
3
4
5
51
72
95
440
41
21
20
19
LETCH LANE
HORSECLOSE LANE
Works
Bridge
California
Club
Bishopsgarth School
& Comm. Cen.
East View Reservoir (Covered)
East View
Coalgarth House
REDMARSHALL ROAD
Two Mile House Farm
Grassy Nook Farm
Ouston Moor House
Ouston Moor Farm
Elton Lane Farm
DARLINGTON ROAD
YARM BACK LANE
BACK LANE
Elton Lane Gdns.
Bishopsgarth Cottages
Bishopsgarth
HARROWGATE LANE
BISHOPTON ROAD
WIMPOLE ROAD
CARDINAL GRO.
ABBOTS WY.
ABBEY CL.
ARMADALE CL.
BARRHEAD CL.
Playing Field
KIRKWALL CL.
LERWICK CL.
CULROSS GRO.
CROXTON CL.
LEONARD
ULLAPOOL CL.
ROPNER
FAIRBURN CL.
FAIRVILLE RD.
FAIRSTONE AV.
FAIRTHORN AV.
GRANGEVILLE AV.
ROSS GRO.
BROOKFIELD ROAD
LIMBRICK
WEST
SCALBY GROVE
SADBERGE
KNAYTON GRO.
MUKER GRO.
HAYLING WY.
GREENFIELDS WY.
LYNDON
TYRONE RD.
MARIA DR.
SHANNON CR.
KENVILLE GRO.
THE CLOISTERS
CATHEDRAL DR.
BISHOPS WY
DALE CL.
TOVIL CL.
MOWBRAY GRO.
MITFORD
LEAM
DRIVE
NORTON
MALTON
POWBN CL.
BONDNE GRO.
THE WYNDE
Briard Wk.
GUNNERSIDE
MCALTON

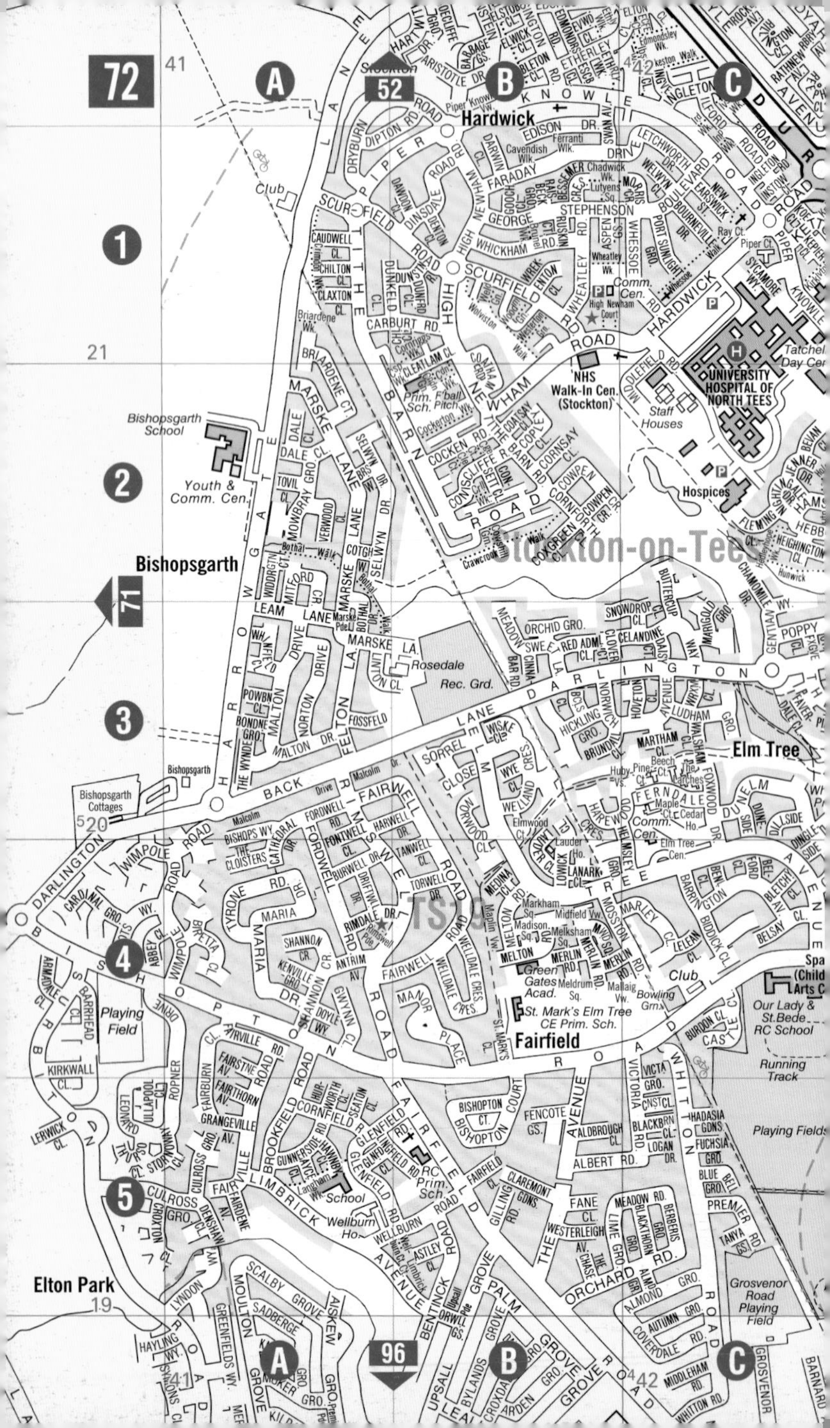
Hardwick
Stockton 52
Bishopsgarth
71
Bishopsgarth School
Youth & Comm. Cen.
Bishopsgarth Cottages
Stockton-on-Tees
UNIVERSITY HOSPITAL OF NORTH TEES
NHS Walk-In Cen. (Stockton)
Staff Houses
Hospices
Tatchell Day Cen.
Rosedale Rec. Grd.
Elm Tree
Ferndale Comm. Cen.
Elm Tree Cen.
TS19
Fairfield
Green Gates Acad.
St. Mark's Elm Tree CE Prim. Sch.
Our Lady & St.Bede RC School
Running Track
Playing Fields
Playing Field
RC Prim. Sch.
School
Wellburn Ho.
Grosvenor Road Playing Field
Elton Park
96
HARDWICK ROAD
DARLINGTON LANE
DARLINGTON ROAD
DARLINGTON BACK LANE
HARROWGATE LANE
BISHOPTON ROAD
MARSKE LANE
BARN LANE
NEWHAM WAY
HIGH NEWHAM ROAD
SCURFIELD ROAD
PIPER KNOWLE ROAD
ELM TREE AVENUE
FAIRWELL ROAD
FAIRFIELD ROAD
LIMBRICK AVENUE
WHITTON ROAD
DURHAM ROAD
BISHOPTON COURT
THE AVENUE
VICTORIA AVENUE
ORCHARD ROAD
Club
Bowling Grn.
Comm. Cen.
A
B
C
1
2
3
4
5
41
42
21
20
19

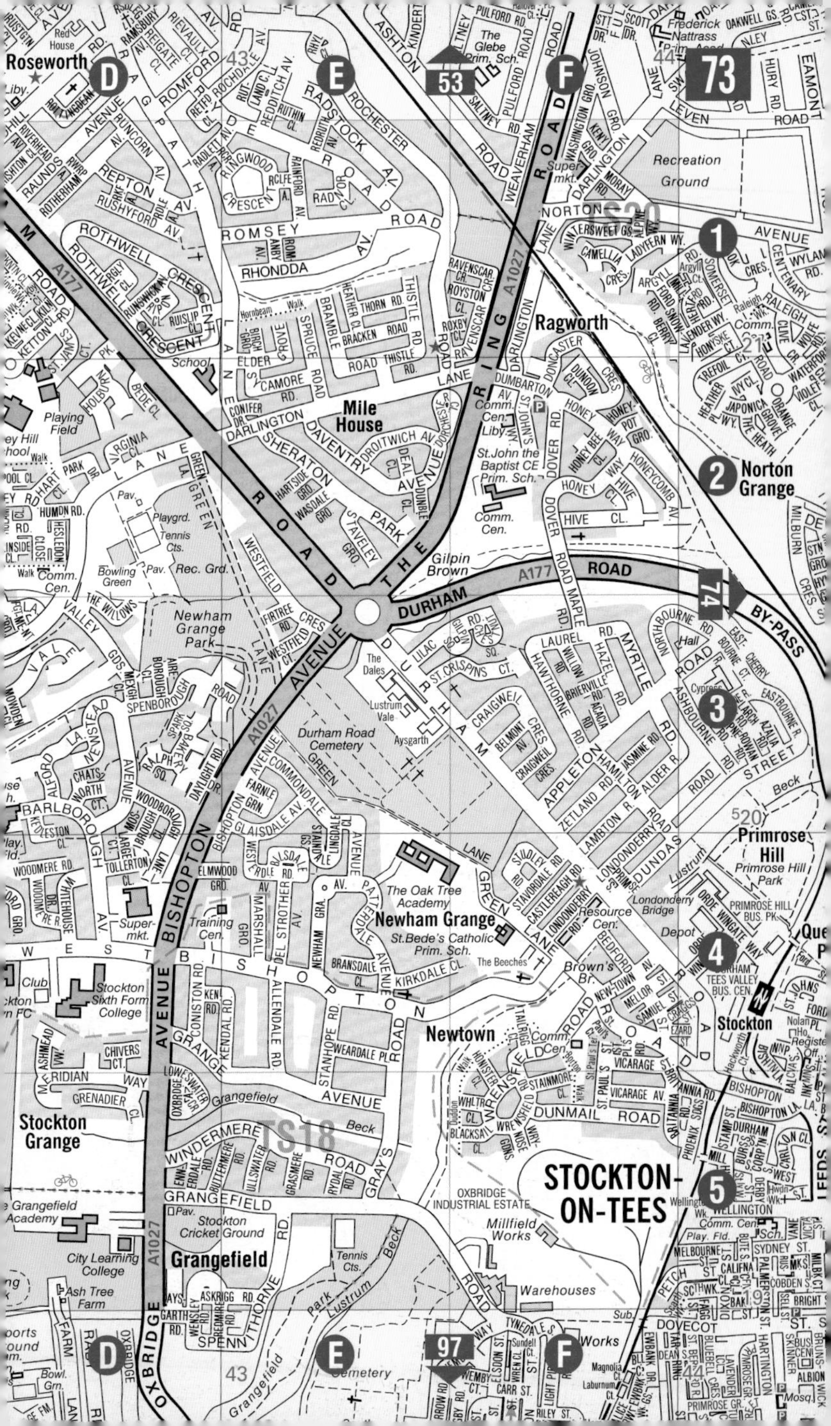
73
53
74
97
D
E
F
1
2
3
4
5
43
44
Roseworth
Red House
Liby.
The Glebe Prim. Sch.
Frederick Nattrass Prim. Acad.
Recreation Ground
TS20
Ragworth
Norton Grange
Mile House
School
Playing Field
St.John the Baptist CE Prim. Sch.
Comm. Cen.
Gilpin Brown
DURHAM ROAD
A177
BY-PASS
THE RING ROAD
A1027
Pav.
Playgrd.
Tennis Cts.
Bowling Green
Rec. Grd.
Newham Grange Park
The Dales
Lustrum Vale
Aysgarth
Durham Road Cemetery
The Oak Tree Academy
Newham Grange
St.Bede's Catholic Prim. Sch.
The Beeches
Resource Cen.
Londonderry Bridge
Depot
Primrose Hill
Primrose Hill Park
PRIMROSE HILL BUS. PK.
DURHAM TEES VALLEY BUS. CEN.
Stockton
Brown's Br.
Newtown
Training Cen.
Super-mkt.
Club
Stockton Sixth Form College
Stockton Grange
TS18
Grangefield Beck
Grangefield Academy
City Learning College
Ash Tree Farm
Stockton Cricket Ground
Grangefield
Tennis Cts.
OXBRIDGE INDUSTRIAL ESTATE
Millfield Works
Warehouses
STOCKTON-ON-TEES
Works
Cemetery
BISHOPTON AVENUE
OXBRIDGE AVENUE
BISHOPTON ROAD
DARLINGTON LANE
NORTON AVENUE
WEST AVENUE

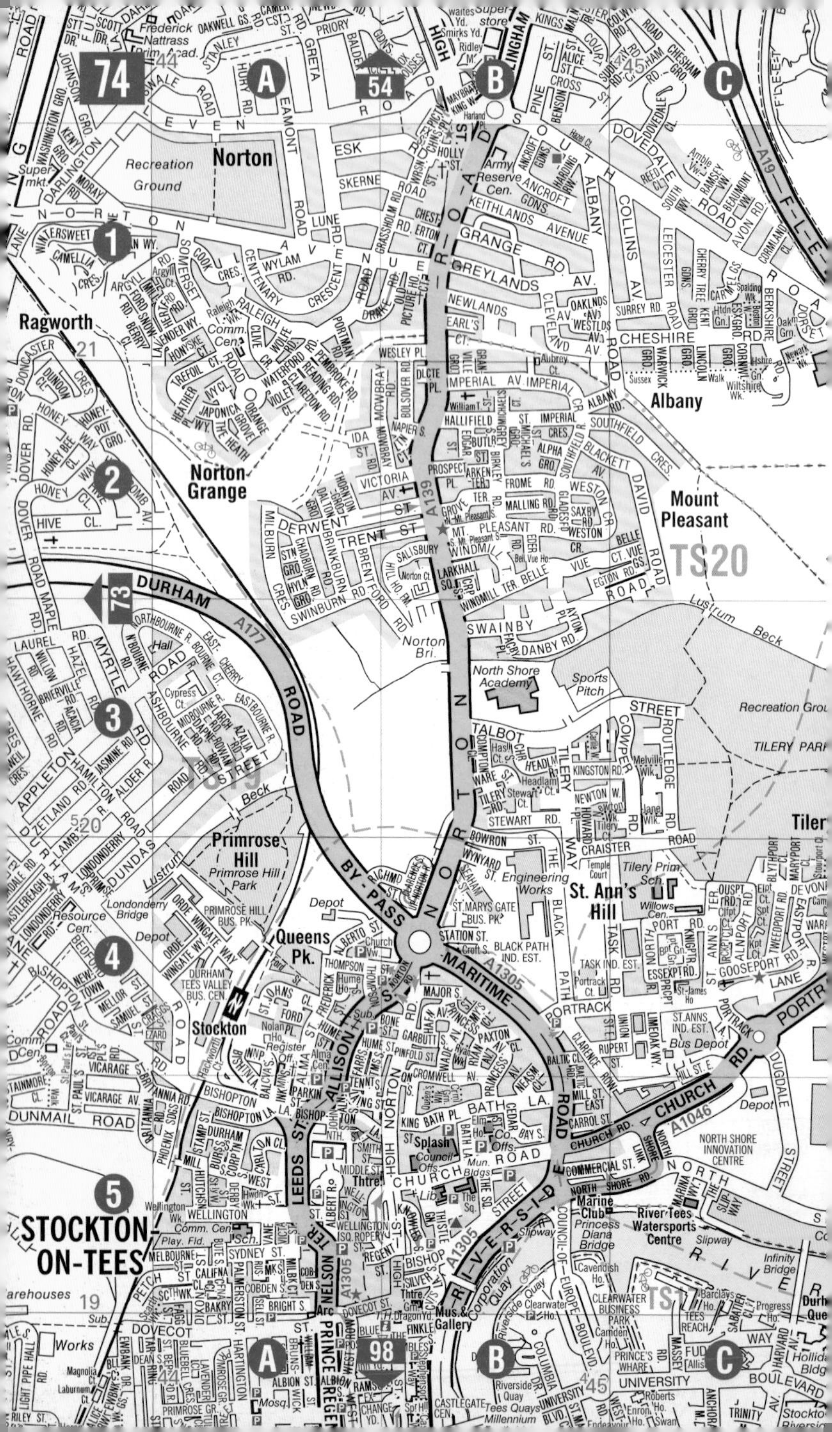
74
54
73
98
A
B
C
1
2
3
4
5
Norton
Recreation Ground
Ragworth
Norton Grange
Albany
Mount Pleasant
TS20
TS19
Primrose Hill
Primrose Hill Park
Queens Pk.
St. Ann's Hill
STOCKTON-ON-TEES
Stockton
North Shore Academy
Sports Pitch
Recreation Ground
TILERY PARK
NORTON ROAD
DURHAM ROAD
BY-PASS
A177
A139
A1305
A1046
A19
MARITIME
RIVERSIDE
CHURCH RD.
LEVEN ROAD
NORTON AVENUE
DARLINGTON LANE
SOUTH ROAD
FLEET
Lustrum Beck
River Tees Watersports Centre
Princess Diana Bridge
Infinity Bridge
Splash
Mus.& Gallery
Durham Tees Valley Bus. Cen.
North Shore Innovation Centre
Engineering Works
Black Path Ind. Est.
Task Ind. Est.
St. Anns Ind. Est.
Bus Depot
Depot
Corporation Quay
Riverside Quay
Clearwater Business Park
University
Castlegate Cen.
Tees Quays Millennium

D
E
55
F
IMPERIAL ROAD
RICHMOND CRES.
46
47
Billingham
TS23
Works
BILLINGHAM BECK
1
Norton Bottoms
Norton Com. Sch.
21
CASSEL CT.
A1046
HAVERTON HILL RD.
Works
BRIDGE ROAD
Billingham Beck Bri.
2
Portrack Interchange
Stockton-on-Tees
HMP HOLME HOUSE
PORTRACK BACK LANE
CHELTENHAM
Clip n Climb
Fun Shack
PORTRACK TRADE PK.
PORTRACK INTERCHANGE BUSINESS PARK
PORTRACK INTERCHANGE RETAIL PK.
A19
76
DRIVE
ASCOT ROAD
AINTREE RD.
TEES (NEWPORT) BRIDGE APPROACH ROAD
A1032
TEES VIADUCT
LUSTRUM RETAIL PARK
AVENUE
3
WETHERBY CL.
SEDGEFIELD WY.
MANDALE CT.
Portrack Bri.
LUSTRUM AVENUE
PENNINE AVENUE
Hugo Ct.
TEES WAY
ARKGROVE INDUSTRIAL ESTATE
HOLME HOUSE RD.
Superstore
A1046
PORTRACK LANE
PORTRACK LA.
PORTRACK IND. EST.
520
NORTH TEES INDUSTRIAL ESTATE
ROSS ROAD
QUEENSPORT CL.
KINGSPORT CL.
LAMPORT CL.
ROMAX IND. UNITS
PORTRACK RETAIL PARK
BLUE HOUSE POINT ROAD
PORTRACK INDUSTRIAL ESTATE
Lustrum Beck
WALTON ST.
Walton Ct.
MANDALE RETAIL PARK
SOUTHSIDE RETAIL PARK
BLUE HOUSE POINT RD.
PORTRACK GRANGE CL.
GRANGE ROAD
4
Portrack
Warehouse
CROFTON WAY
MARSTON AV.
MARSTON ROAD
Superstore
Marston Ct.
GREATHAM
CRIMDON
BECK CL.
NORTH BURN CL.
DEEPDALE AVENUE
TS18
Caravan & Camping Site
Portrack Marsh Nature Reserve
Warehouse
Works
Sewage Works
CLEVELAND IND. EST.
Crofton Ct.
Maize Beck Wk.
HORDENBURN CL.
SLEIGHTHOLME CL.
HUDESHOPE CL.
Wks.
Warehouse
MALLEABLE WAY
ROAD
DEEPDALE AV.
HARWOOD CT.
WHITEWATER WY.
STOCKTON-ON-TEES
MIDDLESBROUGH
Jetty
ROAD
David Lloyd Leisure
TEES BARRAGE WAY
5
Point
BROOKBY CT.
ROLLESBY WY.
FOSTON WY.
GRAINTON CT.
LAURELWOOD RD.
RIVERTON CFT.
Ten.Cts.
Tees Barrage International White Water Centre
White Water Course
MAZE PARK
Blue Ho. Point
TEES
University Campus, Stockton
Wolfson Research Institute
Tees Barrage
NAVIGATION WAY
MAZE LANE
19
99
THE DRIVE
Ebsworth Building
Playgrd.
46
47
STOCKTON

A
B
C
56
47
48
21
20
19
75
100
1
2
3
4
5
HAVERTON HILL ROAD
A1046
BILLINGHAM REACH INDUSTRIAL ESTATE
RIVER TEES
Billingham
TS23
Works
Wharf
Billingham Reach
CASSEL CT.
STOCKTON-ON-TEES
MIDDLESBROUGH
Portrack Interchange
TEES (NEWPORT) BRIDGE APPROACH ROAD
TEES VIADUCT
A19
A1032
DRIVE
PORTRACK LA.
LUSTRUM RETAIL PARK
AVENUE
NEVILLE RD.
PENNINE AVENUE
Hugo Ct.
TEES WAY
NORTH TEES INDUSTRIAL ESTATE
Stockton-on-Tees
TS18
Lustrum Beck
POINT ROAD
Sewage Works
Marsh Reserve
Jetty
View Point
MAZE PARK
STOCKTON ROAD
T.A. Cen.
TEES (NEWPORT) BRIDGE
Warehouse
Wks.
CANNON ST.
IRON
AYRESOME RD.
EDITH ST.
LETITIA ST.
LETITIA IND. EST.
NEWPORT RD.
NEWPORT ROAD
B6541
WEST AIDAN
BISHOP ST.
CORDER RD.
ARNCLIFFE RD.
ROAD
AIDAN CT.
LANE
BEDE CT.
DUNSTABLE RD.
Macmillan Academy
Goals Soccer Centre
All Weather Pitches
CONNAUGHT CL.
DUNLANE
Playing Fields
NORTHERN ROUTE
A66
LIVERTON AV.
BARNABY AV.
ASHLING WY.
LANE
WEST
ACKLAM A1032 RD.
AYRESOME GRN. LA.
Archibald Prim. Sch.
WEST LANE HOSPITAL
LINTHORPE CEMETERY
CRATHNE
ROAD
MALDON
HEYWOOD ST.
Laycock Gdns.
CARLOW
MEATH
LONGFORD
WICKLOW
DONEGL RT.
Comm. Cen.
AYRESOME
CLOU
Newport
NEWPORT
Superstore
LAMPORT ST.
PARLIAMENT
LAYCOCK ST.
MILLS ST.
STREET
CANNON
PUNCH ST.
PEARSON ST.
Gasholder Station
MASTERS WAY
PARK WAY
South West Ironmasters Park
Metz Bridge Caravan Site
Marsh Works
RIVERSIDE PARK
HOLWICK RD.
INTELECT CT.
RALEIGH CT.
SIMCOX CT.
DRAKE CT.
ROMALD RD.
BRITANNIA BUSINESS PARK
RIVERSIDE BUSINESS PARK
BARTON RD.
EASTER PK.
Aurora Ct.
HIGH FORCE RD.
STARTFORTH
EGGLESTON CT.
River Ct.

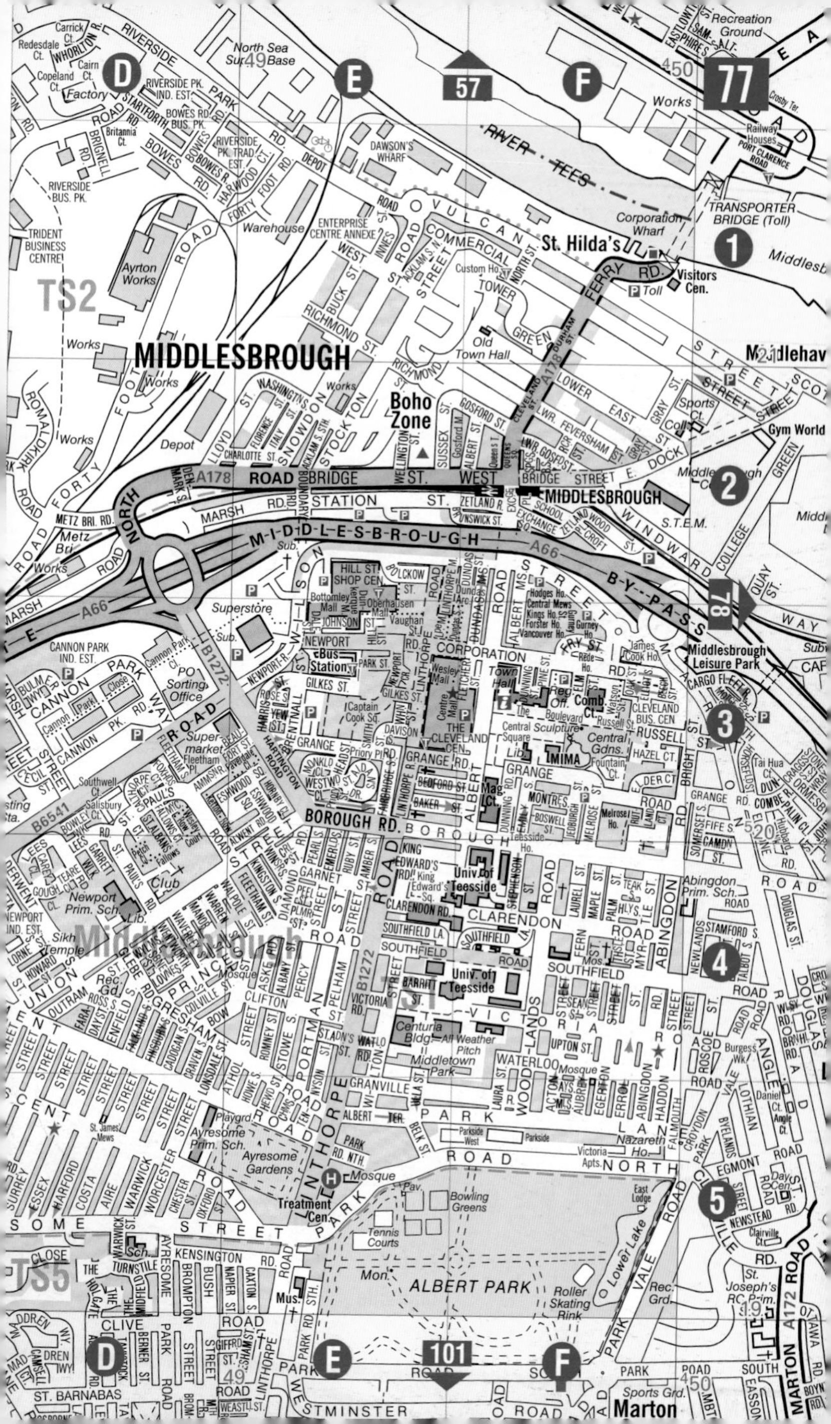
77
57
78
101
D
E
F
1
2
3
4
5
MIDDLESBROUGH
TS2
TS1
TS5
RIVER TEES
Recreation Ground
Works
North Sea Supply Base
Riverside Park
Riverside Pk. Ind. Est.
Bowes Rd. Bus. Pk.
Riverside Pk. Trad. Est.
Riverside Bus. Pk.
Trident Business Centre
Ayrton Works
Dawson's Wharf
Enterprise Centre Annexe
Warehouse
Corporation Wharf
St. Hilda's
Transporter Bridge (Toll)
Visitors Cen.
Toll
Custom Ho.
Old Town Hall
Boho Zone
Railway Houses
Port Clarence Road
Sports Ct.
Gym World
Middlesbrough College
S.T.E.M.
Middlesbrough Leisure Park
Metz Bri.
Superstore
Cannon Park Ind. Est.
PO Sorting Office
Hill St. Shop Cen.
Bottomley Mall
Oberhausen Mall
Bus Station
Captain Cook Sq.
Wesley Mall
Centre Mall
The Cleveland Cen.
Town Hall
Reg. Off.
Comb. Ct.
Cleveland Bus. Cen.
Central Square
Central Gdns.
MIMA
Lib.
Mag. Ct.
Teesside Ho.
Univ. of Teesside
King Edward's Sq.
Centuria Bldg.
All Weather Pitch
Middletown Park
Newport Prim. Sch.
Sikh Temple
Mosque
Ayresome Prim. Sch.
Ayresome Gardens
Treatment Cen.
Bowling Greens
Tennis Courts
ALBERT PARK
Lower Lake
Roller Skating Rink
Mus.
East Lodge
Nazareth Ho.
Victoria Apts.
Abingdon Prim. Sch.
St. Joseph's RC Prim.
Sports Grd.
Marton
A178
A66
B1272
B6541
A172
MIDDLESBROUGH BY-PASS
ROAD BRIDGE ST. WEST
STATION ST.
MARSH RD.
BOROUGH RD.
CORPORATION RD.
GRANGE RD.
CLARENDON RD.
SOUTHFIELD RD.
VICTORIA RD.
PARK RD. NORTH
PARK VALE ROAD
AYRESOME STREET
LINTHORPE ROAD
WESTMINSTER ROAD
MARTON ROAD
PRINCES RD.
NEWPORT RD.
CANNON PARK WAY
WOODLANDS ROAD
ABINGDON ROAD
ALBERT ROAD
FERRY RD.
COMMERCIAL STREET
VULCAN ST.
DOCK STREET
WINDWARD WAY
CARGO FLEET RD.
PARK LANE
PARK ROAD SOUTH
CLIVE ROAD
ST. BARNABAS ROAD
KENSINGTON RD.

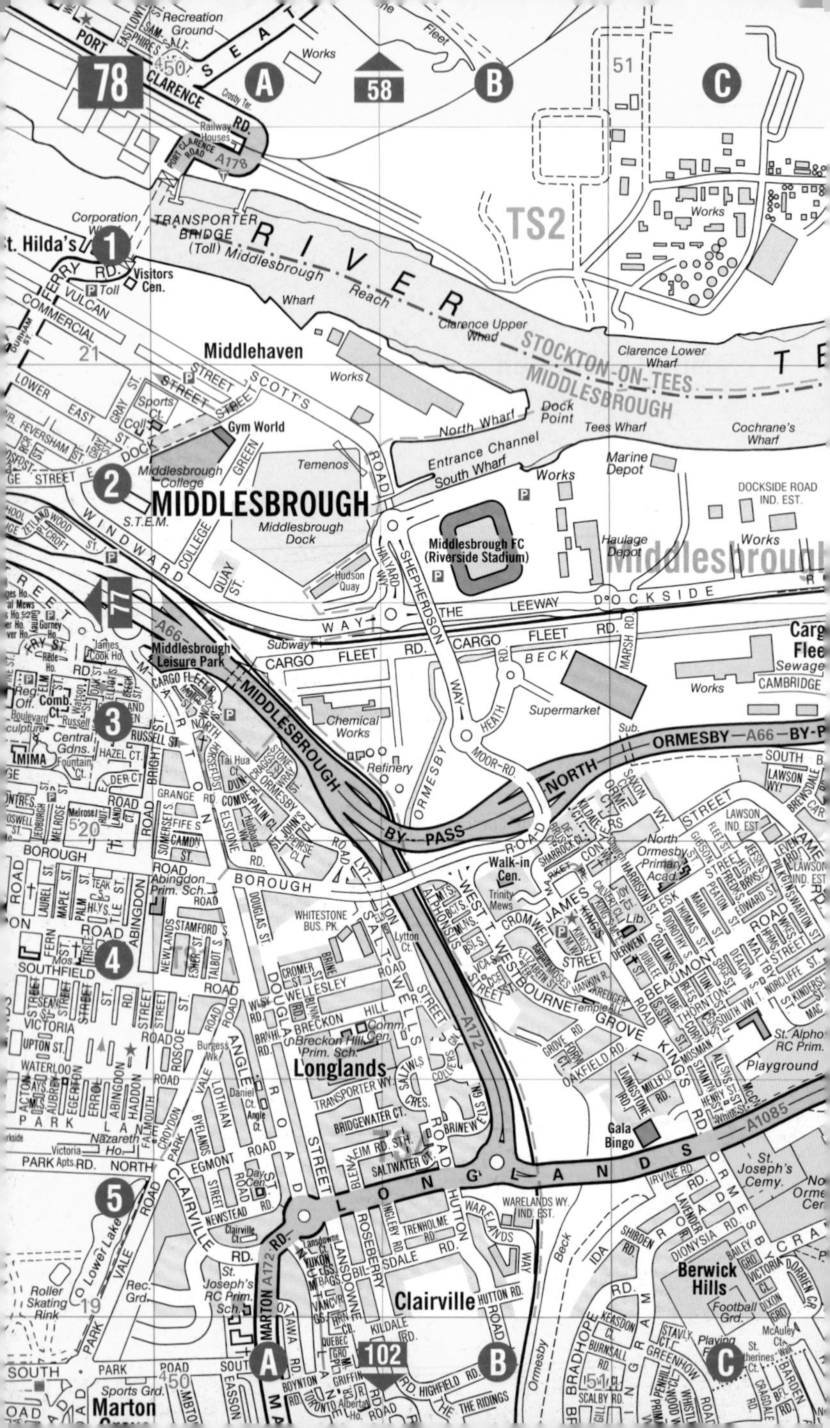
78
58
77
102
A
B
C
1
2
3
4
5
TS2
RIVER TEES
Middlesbrough Reach
TRANSPORTER BRIDGE (Toll)
Corporation Wharf
Clarence Upper Wharf
Clarence Lower Wharf
STOCKTON-ON-TEES
MIDDLESBROUGH
Dock Point
Tees Wharf
Cochrane's Wharf
North Wharf
Entrance Channel
South Wharf
Marine Depot
DOCKSIDE ROAD IND. EST.
Haulage Depot
Middlesbrough FC (Riverside Stadium)
MIDDLESBROUGH
Middlehaven
Middlesbrough Dock
Middlesbrough College
S.T.E.M.
Gym World
Temenos
Hudson Quay
Visitors Cen.
Recreation Ground
Railway Houses
PORT CLARENCE RD.
A178
St. Hilda's
FERRY RD.
VULCAN
COMMERCIAL
LOWER EAST ST.
SCOTT'S
DOCK STREET
WINDWARD WAY
COLLEGE
QUAY ST.
HALYARD WAY
SHEPHERDSON WAY
THE LEEWAY
DOCKSIDE RD.
CARGO FLEET RD.
BECK
MARSH RD.
Supermarket
Chemical Works
Refinery
Middlesbrough Leisure Park
MIDDLESBROUGH BY-PASS
A66
NORTH ORMESBY BY-PASS
CAMBRIDGE
Sewage
Works
Central Gdns.
MIMA
Comb. Ct.
BOROUGH ROAD
GRANGE RD.
Walk-in Cen.
North Ormesby Primary Acad.
Trinity Mews
LAWSON IND. EST.
St. Alphonsus RC Prim.
Playground
WHITESTONE BUS. PK.
Longlands
Breckon Hill Prim. Sch.
Comm. Cen.
Abingdon Prim. Sch.
A172
LONGLANDS RD.
A1085
Gala Bingo
St. Joseph's Cemy.
WARELANDS WY. IND. EST.
Berwick Hills
Football Grd.
Clairville
HUTTON RD.
MARTON RD.
St. Joseph's RC Prim. Sch.
Rec. Grd.
Lower Lake
Roller Skating Rink
PARK VALE RD.
SOUTHFIELD
VICTORIA
PARK LANE
PARK RD. NORTH
Victoria Apts.
Nazareth Ho.
SOUTH
Sports Grd.
Marton
ORMESBY RD.
Ormesby Beck
THE RIDINGS
HIGHFIELD RD.
Playing Fd.
450
51
21
19
20

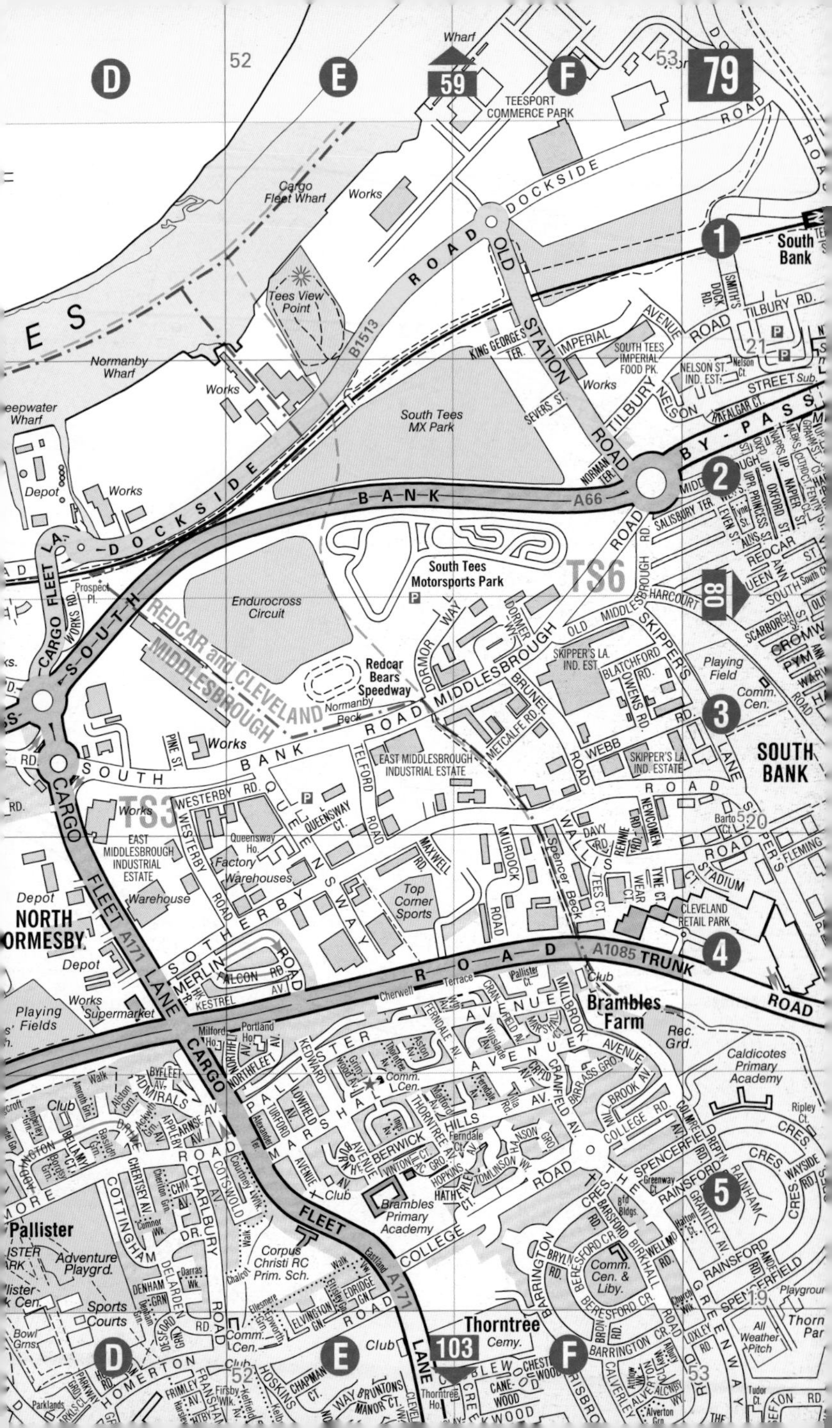
D
52
E
Wharf
59
F
53
TEESPORT COMMERCE PARK
ROAD
DOCKSIDE
Cargo Fleet Wharf
Works
1
South Bank
ROAD
OLD
Tees View Point
B1513
SMITH'S DOCK RD.
TILBURY RD.
ROAD
AVENUE
KING GEORGES TER.
IMPERIAL
STATION
SOUTH TEES IMPERIAL FOOD PK.
Normanby Wharf
Works
Deepwater Wharf
NELSON ST. IND. EST.
Nelson Ct.
STREET
South Tees MX Park
SEVERS ST.
TILBURY
NELSON
TRAFALGAR CT.
BY-PASS
ROAD
NORMAN TER.
2
Depot
Works
DOCKSIDE
BANK
A66
SALISBURY TER.
LEVEN ST.
PRINCESS ST.
OXFORD ST.
NAPIER ST.
REDCAR
ROAD
South Tees Motorsports Park
TS6
CARGO FLEET LA.
WORKS RD.
Prospect Pl.
Endurocross Circuit
HARCOURT
80
SOUTH
SCARBOROUGH ST.
CROMWELL
PYM
SOUTH
REDCAR and CLEVELAND
MIDDLESBROUGH
DORMOR WAY
DORMER WY.
OLD MIDDLESBROUGH
SKIPPER'S
Playing Field
Comm. Cen.
SKIPPER'S LA. IND. EST.
BLATCHFORD RD.
OWENS RD.
Redcar Bears Speedway
Normanby Beck
ROAD
MIDDLESBROUGH
BRUNEL
3
METCALFE RD.
WEBB
LANE
SOUTH BANK
PINE ST.
Works
ROAD
SKIPPER'S LA. IND. ESTATE
SOUTH BANK
EAST MIDDLESBROUGH INDUSTRIAL ESTATE
TELFORD ROAD
RD.
CARGO
TS3
WESTERBY RD.
QUEENSWAY CT.
Works
ROAD
NEWCOMEN RD.
Barton Ct.
20
EAST MIDDLESBROUGH INDUSTRIAL ESTATE
WESTERBY ROAD
Queensway Ho.
Factory
Warehouses
MAXWELL RD.
MURDOCK ROAD
WALLIS
DAVY RD.
RENNIE RD.
Spencer Beck
ROAD
STADIUM
FLEMING
Depot
NORTH ORMESBY
FLEET
Warehouse
SOTHERBY
QUEENSWAY
Top Corner Sports
TEES CT.
WEAR CT.
TYNE CT.
CLEVELAND RETAIL PARK
4
Depot
A171
LANE
MERLIN
FALCON RD.
ROAD
ROAD
A1085 TRUNK
Club
Pallister Ct.
Terrace
Cherwell
KESTREL
AV.
AVENUE
MILLBROOK
Brambles Farm
ROAD
Playing Fields
Works
Supermarket
Milford Ho.
Portland Ho.
NORTHFLEET AV.
KEDWARD
PALLISTER
Rec. Grd.
Caldicotes Primary Academy
CARGO
Comm. Cen.
AVENUE
AVENUE
ADMIRALS
AV.
BYFLEET AV.
Club
MARSHALL
THORNTREE AV.
HILLS
CRANFIELD AV.
BARRASS GRO.
MILLBROOK AV.
COLLEGE RD.
Ripley Ct.
CRES.
COLLEGE
RD.
BERWICK
HILLS
ROAD
THE
SPENCERFIELD
RAINSFORD
RAINHAM
WAYSIDE RD.
CRES.
5
DRIVE
ROAD
CHARLBURY
COTSWOLD
COTTINGHAM
Club
Brambles Primary Academy
TOMLINSON WY.
HATHERLEY CT.
CRES.
BARSFORD RD.
GRANTLEY AV.
Pallister
Adventure Playgrd.
DELARDEN
FLEET
COLLEGE
Corpus Christi RC Prim. Sch.
A171
BARRINGTON RD.
Comm. Cen. & Liby.
BIRKHALL RD.
RAINSFORD
SPENCERFIELD
Playground
19
Sports Courts
DENHAM GRN.
ROAD
ROAD
GREENWAY
Thorntree
Thorntree Par
All Weather Pitch
D
Comm. Cen.
E
Club
103
LANE
Cemy.
F
BARRINGTON CR.
53
HOMERTON
52
HOSKINS
CHAPMAN CT.
BRUNTONS MANOR CT.
Thorntree Ho.
CANEWOOD
CHESTERWOOD
CALVERLEY
LOXLEY RD.
Tudor Ct.
RD.
Parklands

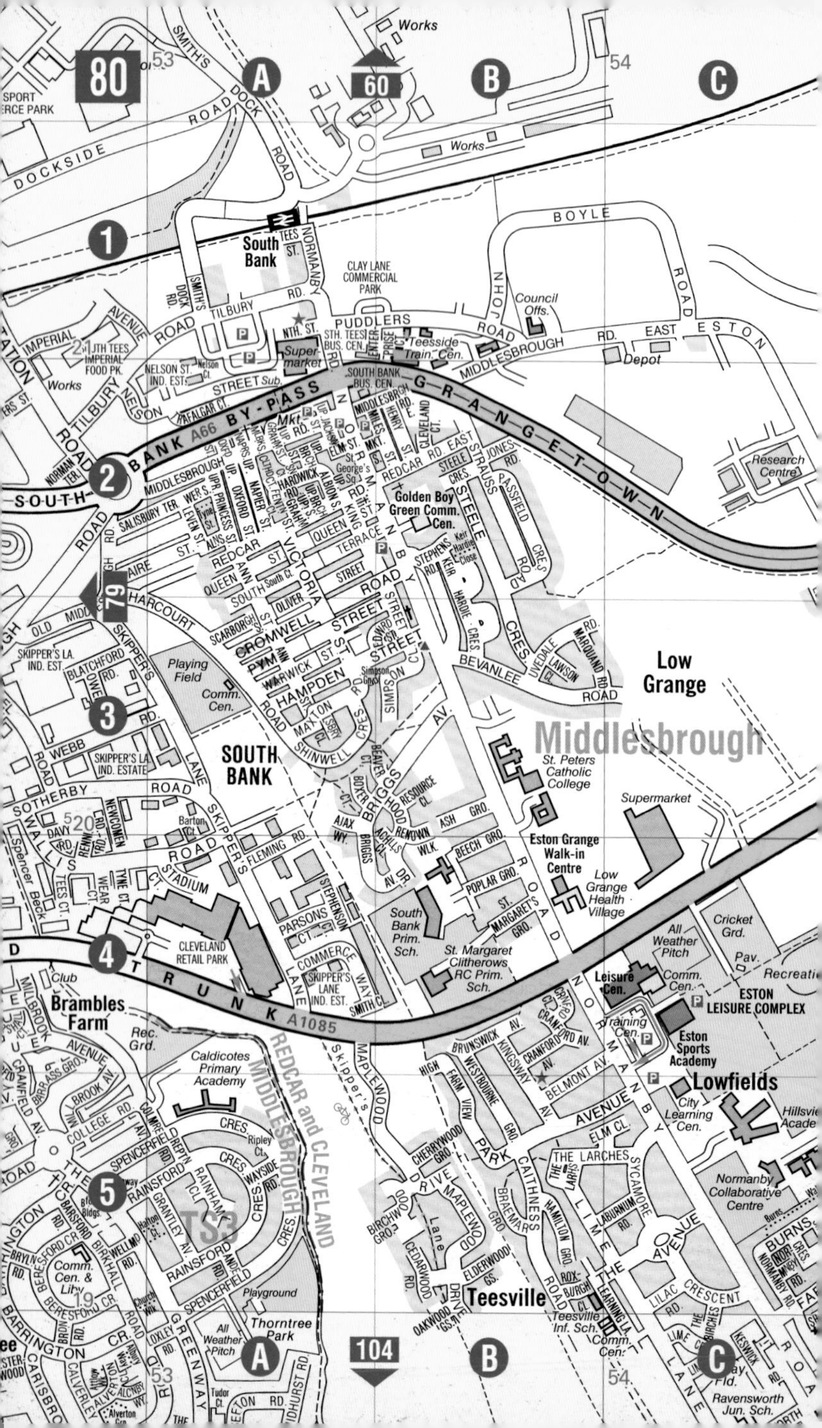

53
54
A
B
C
60
Works
SMITH'S DOCK ROAD
DOCKSIDE
SPORT
ERCE PARK
1
2
3
4
5
South Bank
TEES ST.
NORMANBY
BOYLE ROAD
CLAY LANE COMMERCIAL PARK
JOHN
Council Offs.
SMITH'S DOCK RD.
TILBURY
PUDDLERS ROAD
NTH. ST.
STH. TEES BUS. CEN.
ENTERPRISE CT.
Teesside Train. Cen.
MIDDLESBROUGH RD. EAST
ESTON
Depot
IMPERIAL AVENUE
STH TEES IMPERIAL FOOD PK.
Works
NELSON ST. IND. EST.
Nelson Ct.
Super-market
STREET
Sub.
SOUTH BANK BUS. CEN.
GRANGETOWN
BANK A66 BY-PASS
TILBURY ROAD
TRAFALGAR CT.
Mkt.
MIDDLESBROUGH
HENRY RD.
CLEVELAND CT.
REDCAR RD. EAST
STEELE CRES.
STRAUSS
JONES RD.
PASSFIELD CRES.
Research Centre
NORMAN TER.
SOUTH
ROAD
SALISBURY TER.
LEVEN ST.
UPR. PRINCESS ST.
OXFORD ST.
NAPIER ST.
HARDWICK ST.
ALBION ST.
St. George's Sq.
KING ST.
Golden Boy Green Comm. Cen.
STEPHENS RD.
KEIR HARDIE CRES.
Keir Hardie Close
REDCAR ST.
QUEEN ST.
VICTORIA
TERRACE
NORMANBY
AIRE ST.
ANN ST.
SOUTH ST.
OLIVER
STREET
ROAD
79
HARCOURT
OLD MIDD
SKIPPER'S
SCARBOROUGH ST.
CROMWELL STREET
PYM
ANN
WARWICK ST.
STREET
EDWARD ST.
BEVANLEE
UVEDALE
LAWSON CL.
MARQUAND RD.
Low Grange
ROAD
SKIPPER'S LA. IND. EST.
BLATCHFORD RD.
OWEN
Playing Field
Comm. Cen.
HAMPDEN
Simpson Gro.
SIMPSON
MAXTON
SHINWELL CRES.
AV.
Middlesbrough
St. Peters Catholic College
WEBB RD.
SKIPPER'S LA. IND. ESTATE
SOUTH BANK
LANE
BEAVER CT.
BOXER CT.
BRIGGS
HOOD CL.
RESOURCE CL.
SOTHERBY ROAD
WALLIS
NEWCOMEN
DAVY RD.
Barton Ct.
AJAX WY.
RENOWN WLK.
ASH GRO.
Supermarket
20
Spencer Beck
TEES CT.
WEAR CT.
TYNE CT.
STADIUM CT.
SKIPPER'S ROAD
FLEMING RD.
STEPHENSON
PARSONS CT.
ACHILLS CL.
AV.
DR.
BEECH GRO.
POPLAR GRO.
ST. MARGARET'S GRO.
Eston Grange Walk-in Centre
Low Grange Health Village
South Bank Prim. Sch.
Cricket Grd.
All Weather Pitch
Pav.
Recreati
CLEVELAND RETAIL PARK
TRUNK A1085
COMMERCE WAY
SKIPPER'S LANE IND. EST.
SMITH CL.
St. Margaret Clitherows RC Prim. Sch.
Leisure Cen.
Comm. Cen.
ESTON LEISURE COMPLEX
Club
Brambles Farm
MILLBROOK AVENUE
Rec. Grd.
REDCAR and CLEVELAND
MIDDLESBROUGH
Skipper's
MAPLEWOOD
CRANFORD CL.
CRANFORD AV.
BRUNSWICK AV.
KINGSWAY
WESTBOURNE GRO.
HIGH FARM VIEW
BELMONT AV.
Training Cen.
Eston Sports Academy
Lowfields
CRANFIELD AV.
BARRASS GRO.
BROOK AV.
COLLEGE RD.
Caldicotes Primary Academy
COLMERE AV.
SPENCERFIELD
CRES.
Ripley Ct.
PARK
AVENUE
ELM CL.
City Learning Cen.
Hillsvie Acade
THE
CHERRYWOOD GRO.
DRIVE
MAPLEWOOD
THE LARCHES
SYCAMORE
CAITHNESS
RAINSFORD
REPTON
RAINHAM CL.
WAYSIDE RD.
TS3
BIRCHWOOD GRO.
Lane
BRAEMAR
HAMILTON GRO.
LIME
LABURNUM RD.
Normanby Collaborative Centre
BURNS CRES.
BARRINGTON CR.
BARSFORD CR.
BERESFORD CR.
BIRKHALL
WELLMD
GRANTLEY AV.
Halton Ct.
RAINSFORD
ANDE
ELDERWOOD GS.
THE AVENUE
Comm. Cen. & Liby.
19
Church Wlk.
ROAD
SPENCERFIELD
Playground
CEDARWOOD RD.
DRIVE
Teesville
ROXBURGH CL.
LEARNING LA.
LILAC CRESCENT
THE BIRCHES
Thorntree Park
OAKWOOD GS.
Teesville Inf. Sch.
Comm. Cen.
LIME CR.
KESWICK
BARRINGTON CR.
CARISBRO
CALVERLEY
ALVERTON
ALCNBY WY.
GREENWAY
LOXLEY RD.
All Weather Pitch
104
WIDHURST RD.
Tudor Ct.
EFTON RD.
LANE
Play Fld.
Ravensworth Jun. Sch.
Alverton Gro.

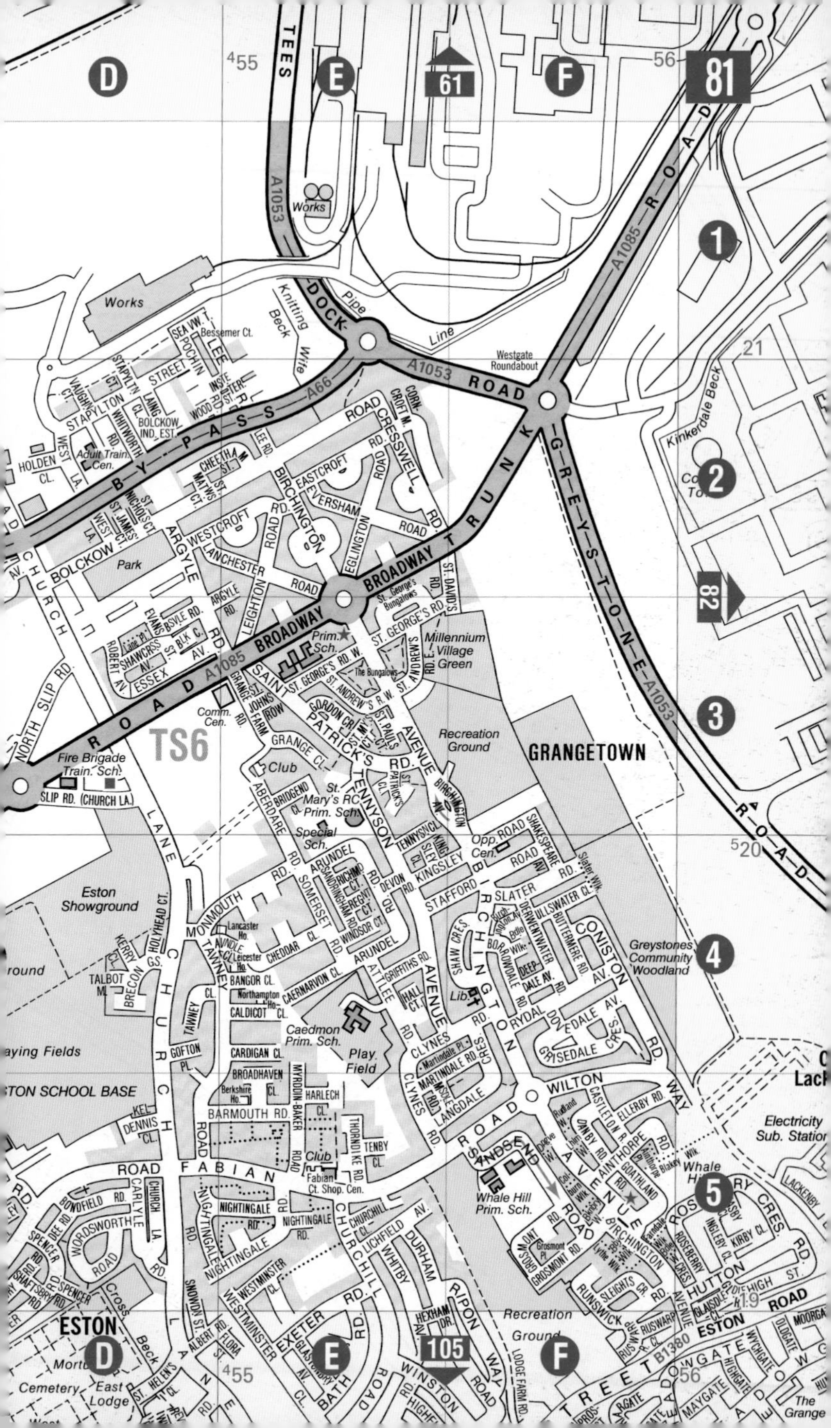
D
E
F
455
56
61
TEES
A1053
Works
DOCK-
Knitting Beck
Wife
Pipe
Line
Westgate Roundabout
A1053 ROAD
A1085 ROAD
TRUNK
GREYSTONE
A66
BY-PASS
1
2
3
4
5
21
520
419
Kinkerdale Beck
82
Works
Bessemer Ct.
SEA VW. T.
POCHIN
LEE
STREET
STAPYLTN CT.
VAUGHN CT.
STAPYLTON
LAING CL.
WHITWORTH RD.
BOLCKOW IND. EST.
WOOD
INSTE RD.
STERL ST.
LEE RD.
HOLDEN CL.
WEST LA.
Adult Train. Cen.
CHEETHAM ST.
MATWS CT.
ST. NICHOLS CT.
ST. JAMES CT.
WEST LA.
BOLCKOW
Park
ARGYLE RD.
WESTCROFT
LANCHESTER
LEIGHTON
ROAD
CORN-CROFT M.
CRESSWELL RD.
EASTCROFT
EVERSHAM
BIRCHINGTON
EGLINTON
ROAD
BROADWAY
St. George's Bungalows
ST. DAVID'S RD.
ST. GEORGE'S RD.
Millennium Village Green
ST. ANDREW'S RD. E.
The Bungalows
ST. GEORGE'S RD. W.
ST. ANDREW'S R. W.
ARGYLE RD.
EVANS
BSVLE RD.
B'LK C.
Lane Pl.
SHAWCRSS AV.
ROBERT AV.
ESSEX AV.
Prim. Sch.
SAINT
ST. JOHNS ROW
GRANGE FARM RD.
GORDON CR.
ST. MTS CT.
ST. PAULS CT.
PATRICK'S RD.
AVENUE
Recreation Ground
GRANGETOWN
Comm. Cen.
TS6
NORTH SLIP RD.
CHURCH
Fire Brigade Train. Sch.
SLIP RD. (CHURCH LA.)
GRANGE CL.
Club
ABERDARE RD.
BRIDGEND CL.
St. Mary's RC Prim. Sch.
TENNYSON
ST. PATRICKS CL.
BIRCHINGTON AV.
Special Sch.
TENNYSN CL.
KINGSLEY
LANE
Opp. Cen.
ROAD
SHAKESPEARE AV.
Slater Wlk.
ARUNDEL
SOMERSET
SANDRINGHAM RD.
RICHMD CT.
REGNT CT.
WINDSOR CT.
DEVON RD.
RD.
STAFFORD
SLATER
BIRCHINGTON
DERWENTWATER
ULLSWATER CL.
BUTTERMERE RD.
CONISTON AV.
Eston Showground
MONMOUTH
Lancaster Ho.
AVNDLE CL.
Leicester Ho.
TAWNEY
CHEDDAR CL.
ARUNDEL
ATTLEE
GRIFFITHS RD.
AVENUE
SHAW CRES.
Birch Ington AV.
Bdle Wlk.
BORROWDALE RD.
DEEPDALE AV.
Greystones Community Woodland
KERRY CL.
HOLYHEAD CT.
BRECON GS.
TALBOT M.
BANGOR CL.
Northampton Ho.
CAERNARVON CL.
HALL CT.
Lib.
RYDAL
EDALE AV.
DON
WAY
Playing Fields
TAWNEY CL.
CALDICOT CL.
Caedmon Prim. Sch.
Play. Field
CLYNES
Martindale Pl.
MARTINDALE RD.
CRES.
GRISEDALE CRES.
GOFTON PL.
CARDIGAN CL.
BROADHAVEN CL.
MYRDDIN-BAKER ROAD
HARLECH CL.
ESTON SCHOOL BASE
Berkshire Ho.
CLYNES RD.
LANGDALE
WILTON
CASTLETON R.
ELLERBY RD.
Electricity Sub. Station
KEL
DENNIS CL.
BARMOUTH RD.
THORNDIKE RD.
TENBY CL.
SANDSEND
Rudland W.
DANBY RD.
Liverton W.
Club
ROAD
FABIAN
Fabian Ct. Shop. Cen.
AINTHORPE
Aislaby Wlk.
Blakey Wlk.
Whale Hill
LACKENBY
GOATHLAND RD.
Whale Hill Prim. Sch.
ROSEBERRY CRES.
INGLEBY CL.
KIRBY CL.
CARLYLE RD.
BOWDFIELD RD.
CHURCH LA.
NIGHTINGALE
NIGHTINGALE RD.
CHURCHILL CL.
LICHFIELD AV.
DURHAM
GROSMONT RD.
Grosmont Pl.
BIRCHINGTON
Lythe Wlk.
Farndale Wlk.
ROSEBERRY CRES.
HUTTON
HIGH ST.
WORDSWORTH ROAD
SPENCER
DEE RD.
SHAFTSBRY RD.
WESTMINSTER
CHURCHILL
WHITBY
RIPON WAY
SLEIGHTS CR.
RUNSWICK AVENUE
ESTON
Cross Beck
SNOWDN ST.
ALBERT RD.
FLORA
EXETER RD.
HEXHAM DR.
Recreation Ground
RUSWARP CL.
B1380
ESTON
ROAD
105
MEADOWGATE
WYCHGATE
OLDGATE
MOORGA
Mortuary
Cemetery
East Lodge
ST. HELEN'S CL.
GLASTONBURY AV.
BATH
WINSTON
LODGE FARM RD.
STREET
MAYGATE
HIGHGATE
The Grange

A
B
C
62
56
457
1
2
3
4
5
81
106
21
520
19
TRUNK ROAD
A1085
GREYSTONE ROAD
A1053
Electricity Sub Station
Tanks
WILTON WORKS
Kinkerdale Beck
Cooling Tower
Cooling Tower
Cooling Towers
Power Station
Middlesbrough
TS6
Kettle
Beck
PASTURE LANE
LAZENBY
KINGS CL.
LILAC CL.
QUEEN ST.
NORTH
CHAPEL ST.
GRANGE
PARRINGTON PLACE
GRANGE EST.
ESTATE
LANE
Wilton Prim. S & Lib
HIGH
Turner Ter.
Farrier M.
WILTON
GREEN
ESTON ROAD
LACKENBY RD.
CHESTNUT CL.
A174
Playing Field
Reservoir
Greystones Roundabout
Reservoir
LAZENBY BANK ROAD
Agar's Gill
Old Lackenby
High Farm Cottage
Electricity Sub. Station
LACKENBY LANE
CROW
Old Hall Farm
Rosedene Farm
LACKENBY
SOUTH LACKENBY LANE
LANE
B1380
ROAD
California
Greystones Community Woodland
Whale Hill
SHAKESPEARE AV.
RD.
Slater Wlk.
ULLSWATER CL.
DERWENTWATER
BUTTERMERE RD.
CONISTON AV.
EDALE AV.
GRISEDALE CRES.
RD.
WILTON WAY
CASTLETON R.
ELLERBY RD.
DANBY RD.
AINTHORPE
Blakey Wlk.
AVENUE
ROAD
BIRCHINGTON
ROSEBERRY CRES.
ROSEBERRY
EASBY CL.
INGLEBY CL.
KIRBY CL.
RD.
HUTTON
HIGH ST.
GROSMONT RD.
RUNSWICK
RUSWARP
AVENUE
MOORGATE
MEADOWGATE
SOUTHGATE
HUNTERSGATE
SUNNYGATE
HIGH STREET
ESTON
MEADOWGATE
MAYGATE
HIGHGATE
WYCHGATE
The Grange
Recreation Ground

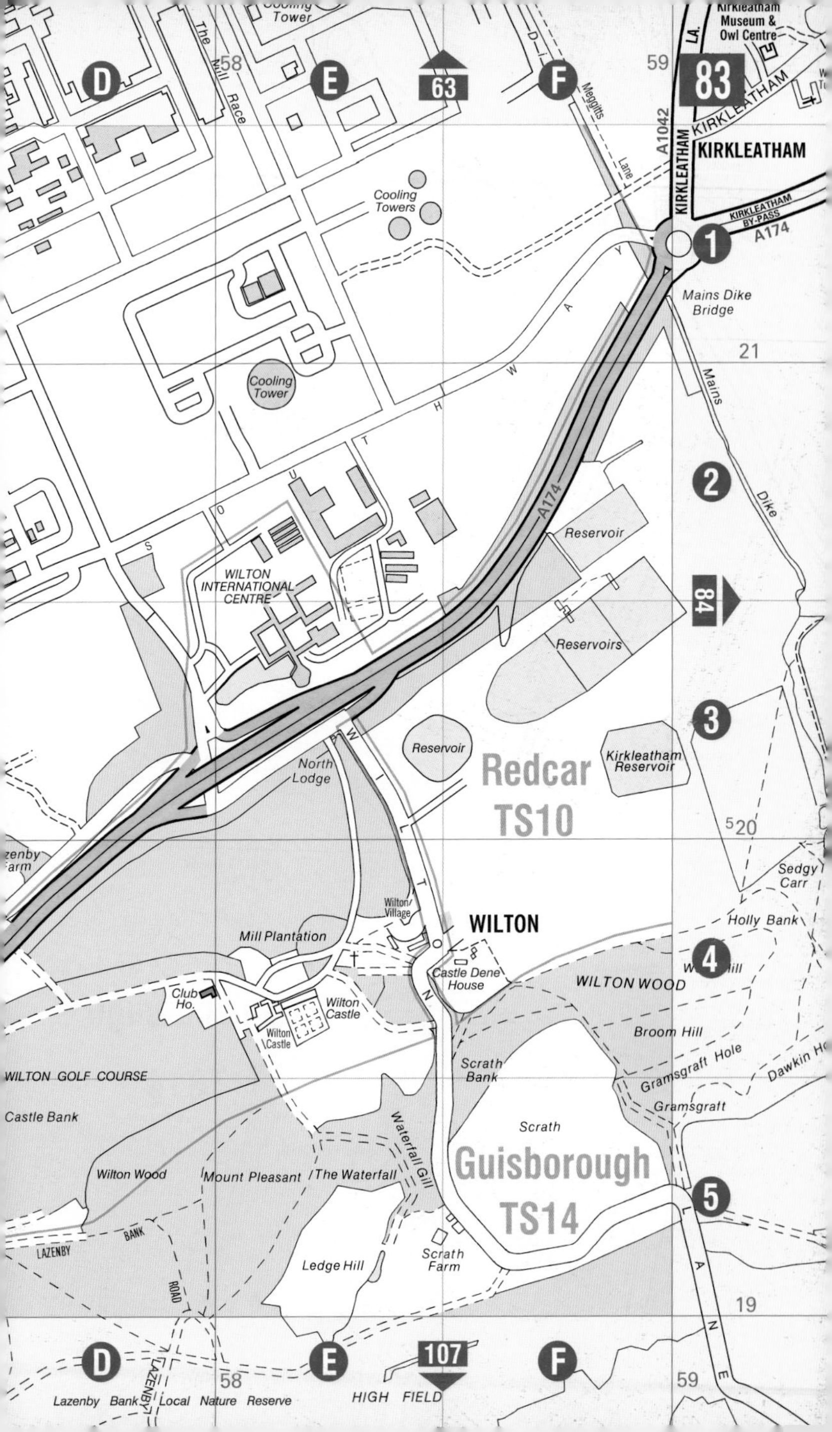
83
63
107
84
D
E
F
58
59
21
20
19
1
2
3
4
5
Kirkleatham Museum & Owl Centre
KIRKLEATHAM
KIRKLEATHAM LA.
A1042
KIRKLEATHAM BY-PASS
A174
Meggitts Lane
The Mill Race
Cooling Tower
Cooling Towers
Mains Dike Bridge
Mains Dike
SOUTH WAY
WILTON INTERNATIONAL CENTRE
Reservoir
Reservoirs
Kirkleatham Reservoir
Redcar TS10
North Lodge
WILTON LANE
Lazenby Farm
Sedgy Carr
Holly Bank
Wilton Village
WILTON
Mill Plantation
Castle Dene House
WILTON WOOD
Club Ho.
Wilton Castle
Broom Hill
Scrath Bank
Gramsgraft Hole
Dawkin Ho
Gramsgraft
WILTON GOLF COURSE
Castle Bank
Scrath
Guisborough TS14
Waterfall Gill
Wilton Wood
Mount Pleasant
The Waterfall
LAZENBY BANK ROAD
Ledge Hill
Scrath Farm
LAZENBY
Lazenby Bank Local Nature Reserve
HIGH FIELD

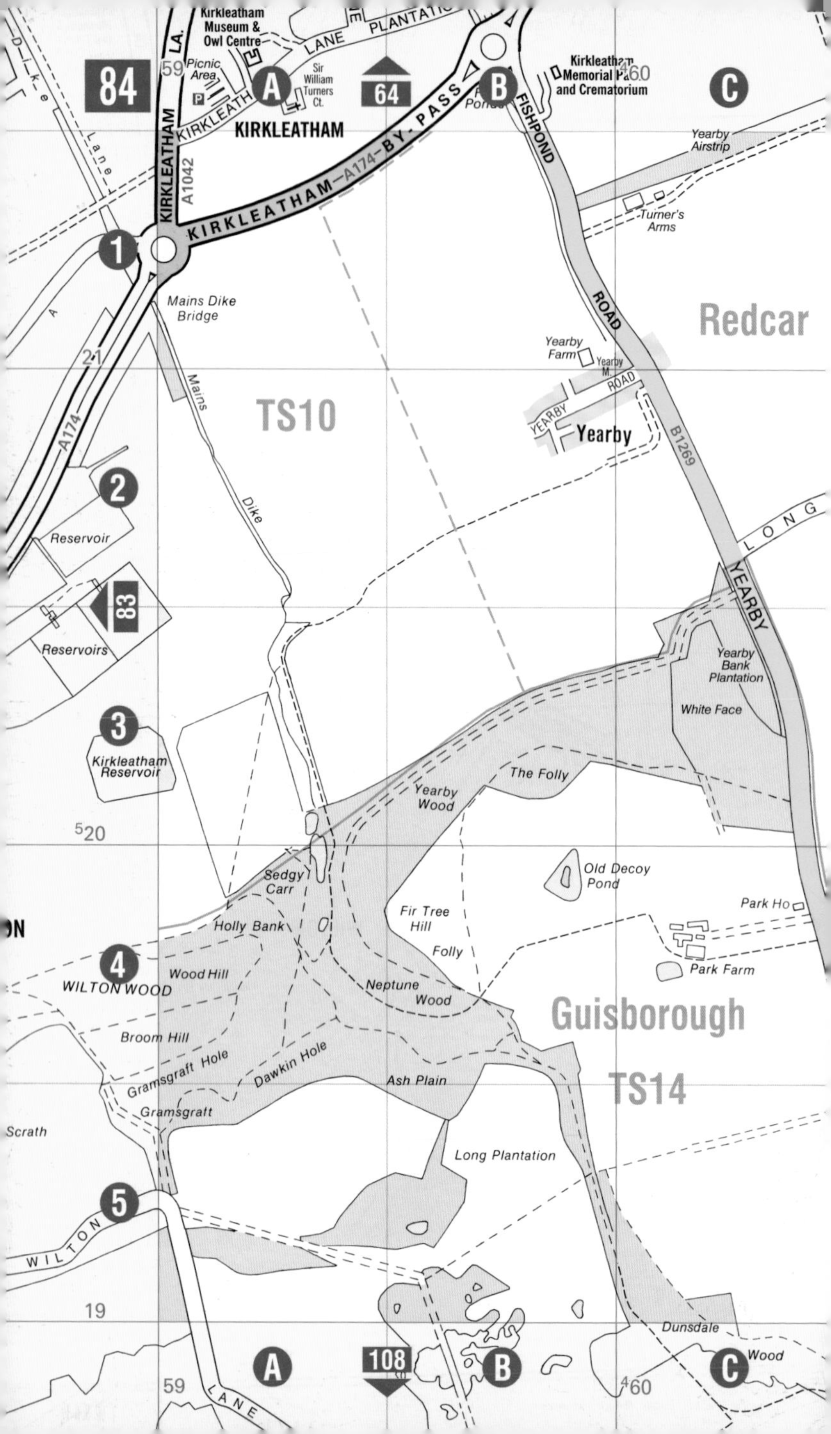
Kirkleatham Museum & Owl Centre
LANE PLANTATION
Picnic Area
Sir William Turners Ct.
KIRKLEATHAM
KIRKLEATHAM LA.
A1042
KIRKLEATHAM—A174—BY-PASS
Kirkleatham Memorial Park and Crematorium
FISHPOND ROAD
Dike Lane
Yearby Airstrip
Turner's Arms
Mains Dike Bridge
Mains Dike
A174
TS10
Redcar
Yearby Farm
YEARBY ROAD
Yearby
B1269
LONG
YEARBY
Reservoir
Reservoirs
Kirkleatham Reservoir
Yearby Bank Plantation
White Face
The Folly
Yearby Wood
Old Decoy Pond
Sedgy Carr
Holly Bank
Fir Tree Hill
Folly
Park Ho
Park Farm
Wood Hill
WILTON WOOD
Neptune Wood
Guisborough
Broom Hill
Gramsgraft Hole
Dawkin Hole
Ash Plain
TS14
Gramsgraft
Scrath
Long Plantation
WILTON
LANE
Dunsdale Wood
ON
59
460
21
520
19
1 2 3 4 5
A B C
64
83
108

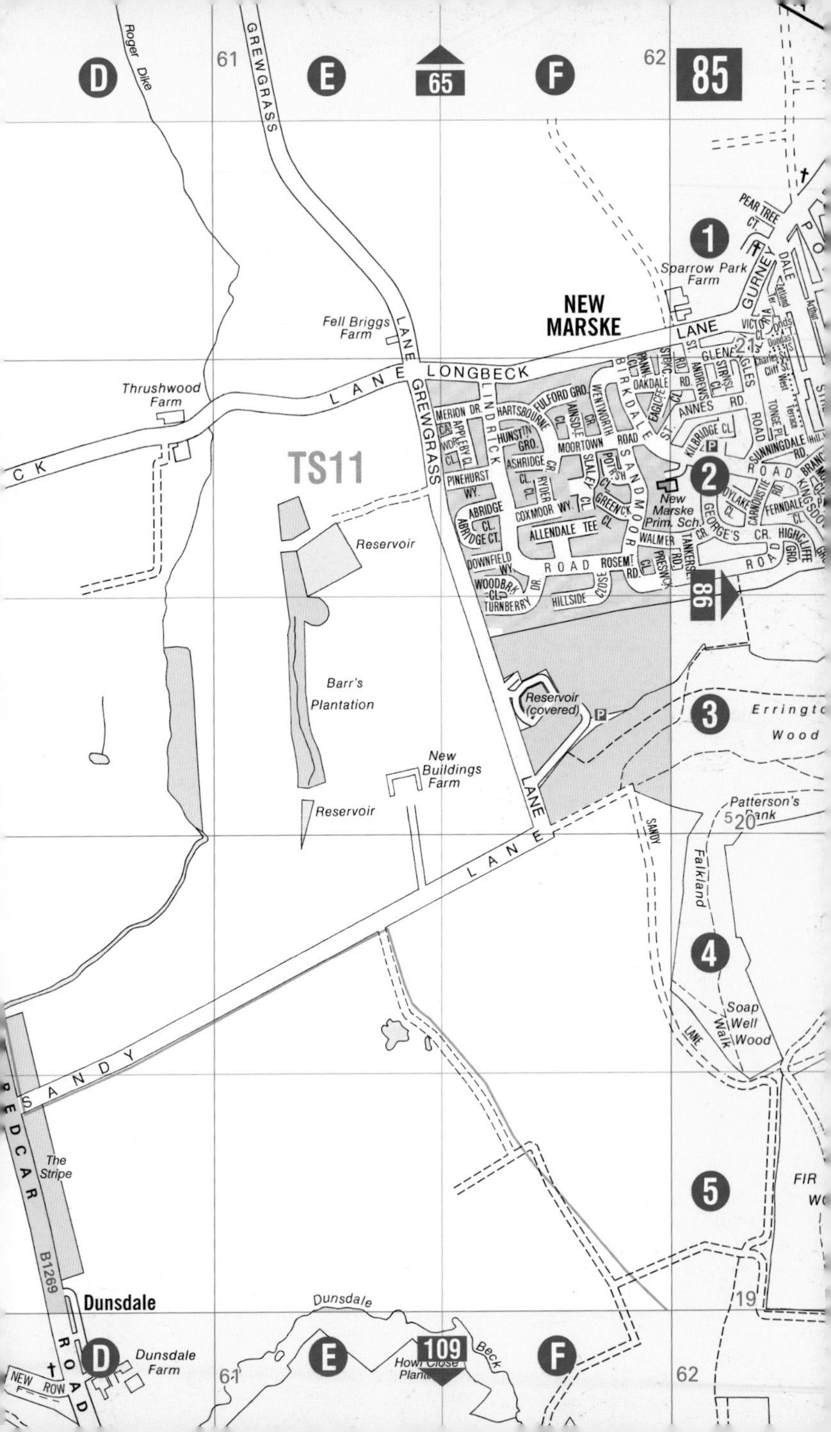
D
E
F
61
62
65
NEW MARSKE
TS11
Roger Dike
GREWGRASS LANE
LONGBECK LANE
Fell Briggs Farm
Thrushwood Farm
Sparrow Park Farm
Reservoir
Barr's Plantation
Reservoir (covered)
New Buildings Farm
Errington Wood
Patterson's Bank
Falkland
Soap Well Wood
Walk
SANDY LANE
REDCAR ROAD
B1269
The Stripe
Dunsdale
Dunsdale Farm
Dunsdale Beck
NEW ROW
New Marske Prim. Sch.
GURNEY
PEAR TREE CT.
BIRKDALE
SANDMOOR ROAD
MOORTOWN ROAD
LINDRICK
WENTWORTH CR.
FULFORD GRO.
HARTSBOURNE
MERION DR.
PINEHURST WY.
ABRIDGE CL.
ABRIDGE CT.
COXMOOR WY.
ALLENDALE TEE
DOWNFIELD WY.
WOODBRK CL.
TURNBERRY DR.
HILLSIDE
CLOSE
ROSEMT. RD.
WALMER
PRESWCK CL.
TANKERSL.
ST. GEORGE'S CR.
ST. ANNES RD.
ST. ANDREWS CL.
KILBRIDGE CL.
SUNNINGDALE RD.
OAKDALE RD.
GLENEAGLES
TONGE PL.
HIGHCLIFFE GRO.
FERNDALE CL.
CARNOUSTIE
ASHRIDGE CL.
RYDER CL.
SLALEY CL.
GREENCK CL.
HUNSTN. GRO.
APPLEBY CL.
86
1
2
3
4
5
20
21
19
FIR W
109
Howl Close Plant.

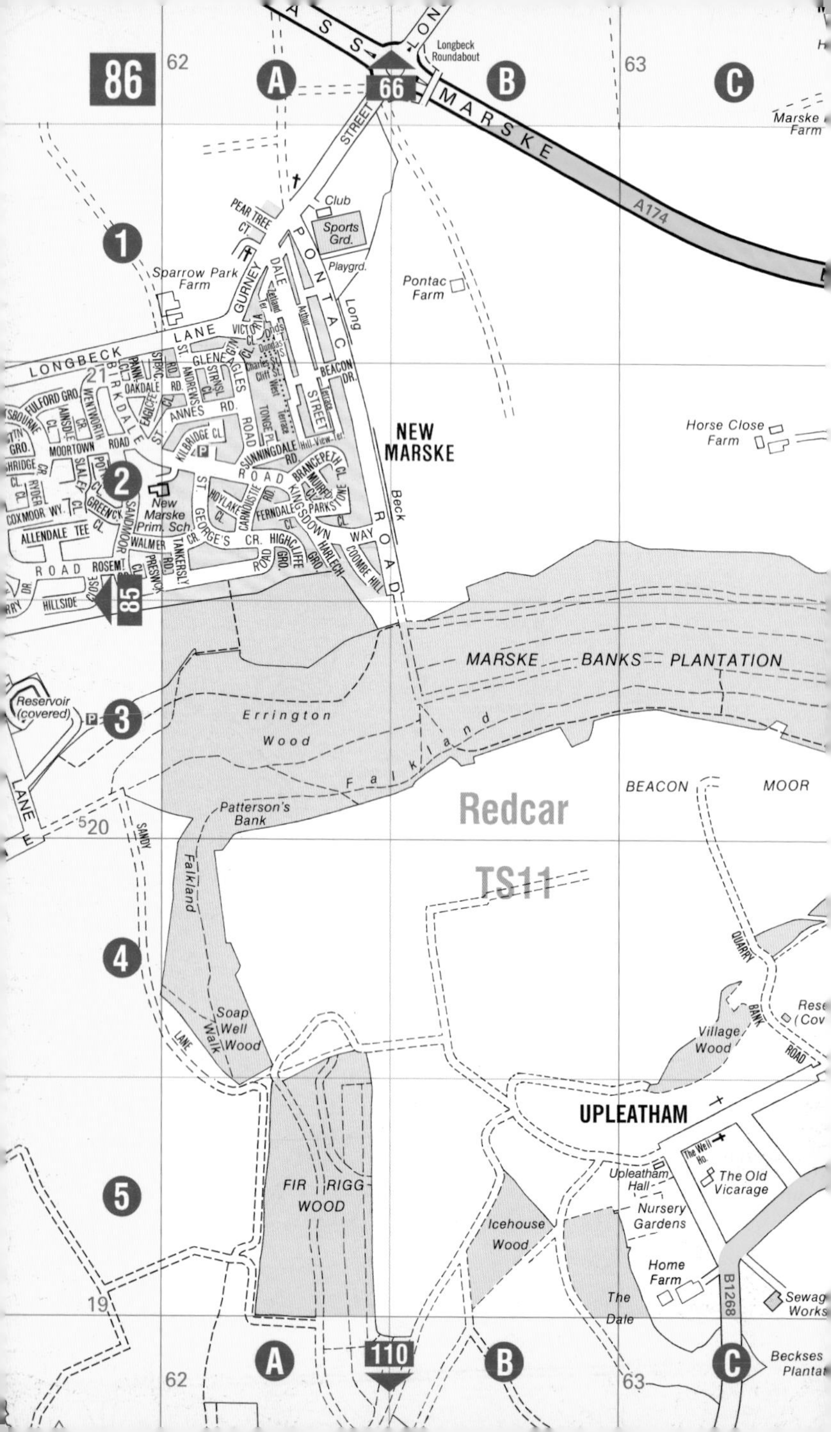
62
63
A
B
C
1
2
3
4
5
21
20
19
66
85
110
Longbeck Roundabout
MARSKE
A174
Marske Farm
STREET
Club
Sports Grd.
Playgrd.
PEAR TREE CT.
Sparrow Park Farm
GURNEY
DALE
PONTAC
Long
Pontac Farm
LANE
LONGBECK
BIRKDALE
VICTORIA
BEACON DR.
STREET
Terrace
NEW MARSKE
Horse Close Farm
FULFORD GRO.
WENTWORTH
OAKDALE
GLENEAGLES
ANDREWS
ANNES RD.
TONGE PL.
MOORTOWN
ROAD
KILBRIDGE CL.
SUNNINGDALE RD.
BRANCEPETH CL.
PARKSTONE
SLALEY
ROAD
New Marske Prim. Sch.
HOYLAKE CL.
CARNOUSTIE
FERNDALE
KINGSDOWN
Beck
COXMOOR WY.
ALLENDALE TEE
SANDMOOR
WALMER
ST. GEORGE'S CR.
HIGHCLIFFE GRO.
WAY
COOMBE HILL
HARLECH
ROAD
ROSEM
CLOSE
PRESWICK
TANKERSLY
HILLSIDE
MARSKE BANKS PLANTATION
Reservoir (covered)
Errington Wood
Falkland
LANE
SANDY
Patterson's Bank
BEACON MOOR
Redcar
TS11
Falkland
QUARRY
BANK
ROAD
Rese (Cov
Soap Well Wood
Walk
Village Wood
UPLEATHAM
FIR RIGG WOOD
Upleatham Hall
The Well Ho.
The Old Vicarage
Nursery Gardens
Icehouse Wood
Home Farm
The Dale
B1268
Sewag Works
Beckses Plantat

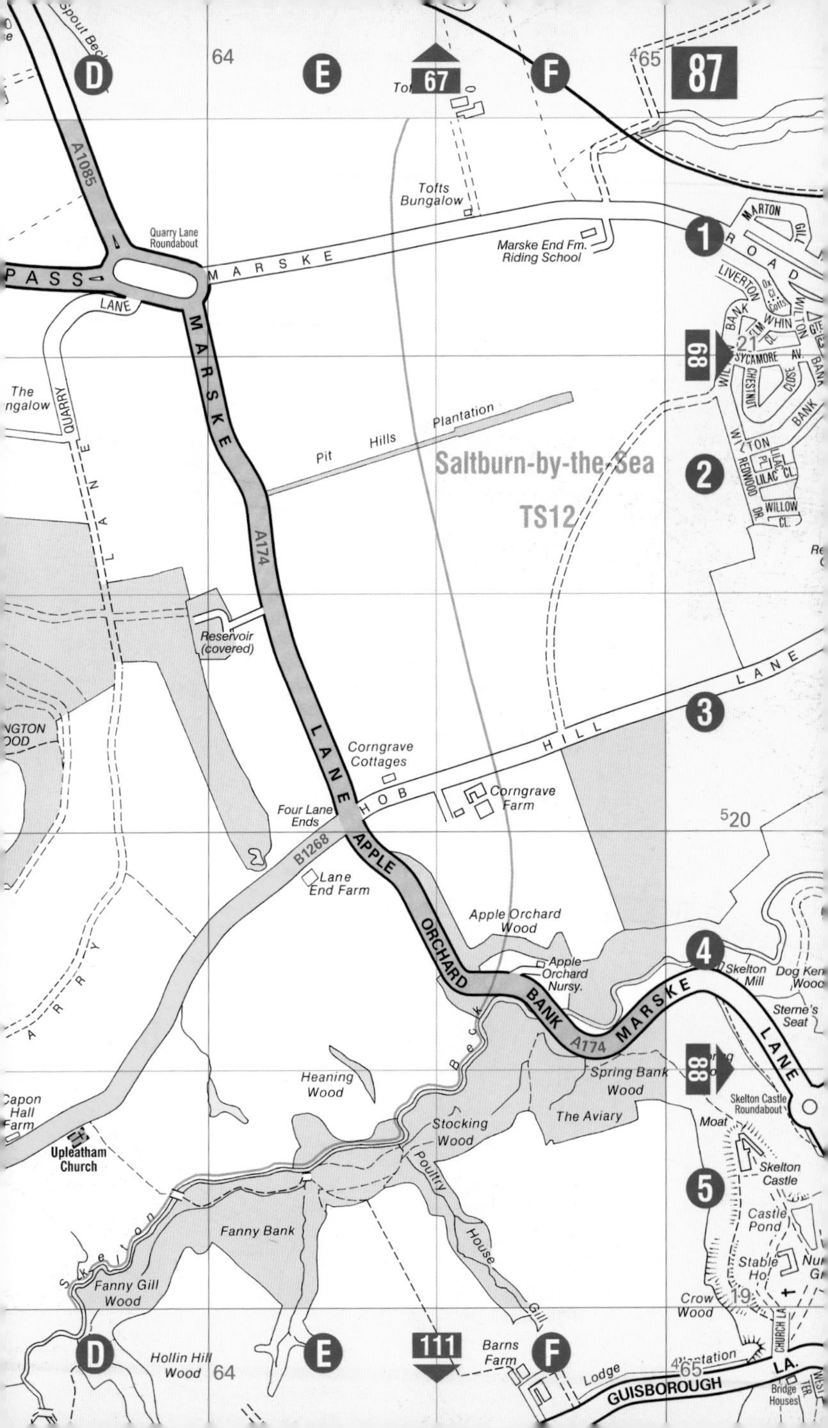
64
465
D
E
F
67
Tofts Bungalow
A1085
Quarry Lane Roundabout
PASS
LANE
MARSKE
Marske End Fm. Riding School
MARTON ROAD
1
LIVERTON
Ox Cl. Cotts.
BANK
WHIN
ELM CL.
WILTON
89
21
SYCAMORE AV.
CHESTNUT
CLOSE
BANK
The Bungalow
QUARRY
LANE
Pit Hills Plantation
Saltburn-by-the-Sea
TS12
WILTON PL.
LILAC
LILAC CL.
REDWOOD DR.
WILLOW CL.
2
A174
Reservoir (covered)
LANE
3
HILL
HOB
Corngrave Cottages
Corngrave Farm
Four Lane Ends
520
B1268
APPLE
Lane End Farm
ORCHARD
Apple Orchard Wood
Apple Orchard Nursy.
BANK
A174
MARSKE
LANE
4
Skelton Mill
Dog Kennel Wood
Sterne's Seat
Beck
Heaning Wood
Spring Bank Wood
88
Skelton Castle Roundabout
The Aviary
Stocking Wood
Capon Hall Farm
Upleatham Church
Moat
Skelton Castle
5
Poultry House Gill
Fanny Bank
Castle Pond
Stable Ho.
Skelton
Fanny Gill Wood
Crow Wood
19
CHURCH LA.
D
E
111
F
Barns Farm
Hollin Hill Wood
64
465
Lodge
GUISBOROUGH LA.
Bridge Houses
WEST TER.

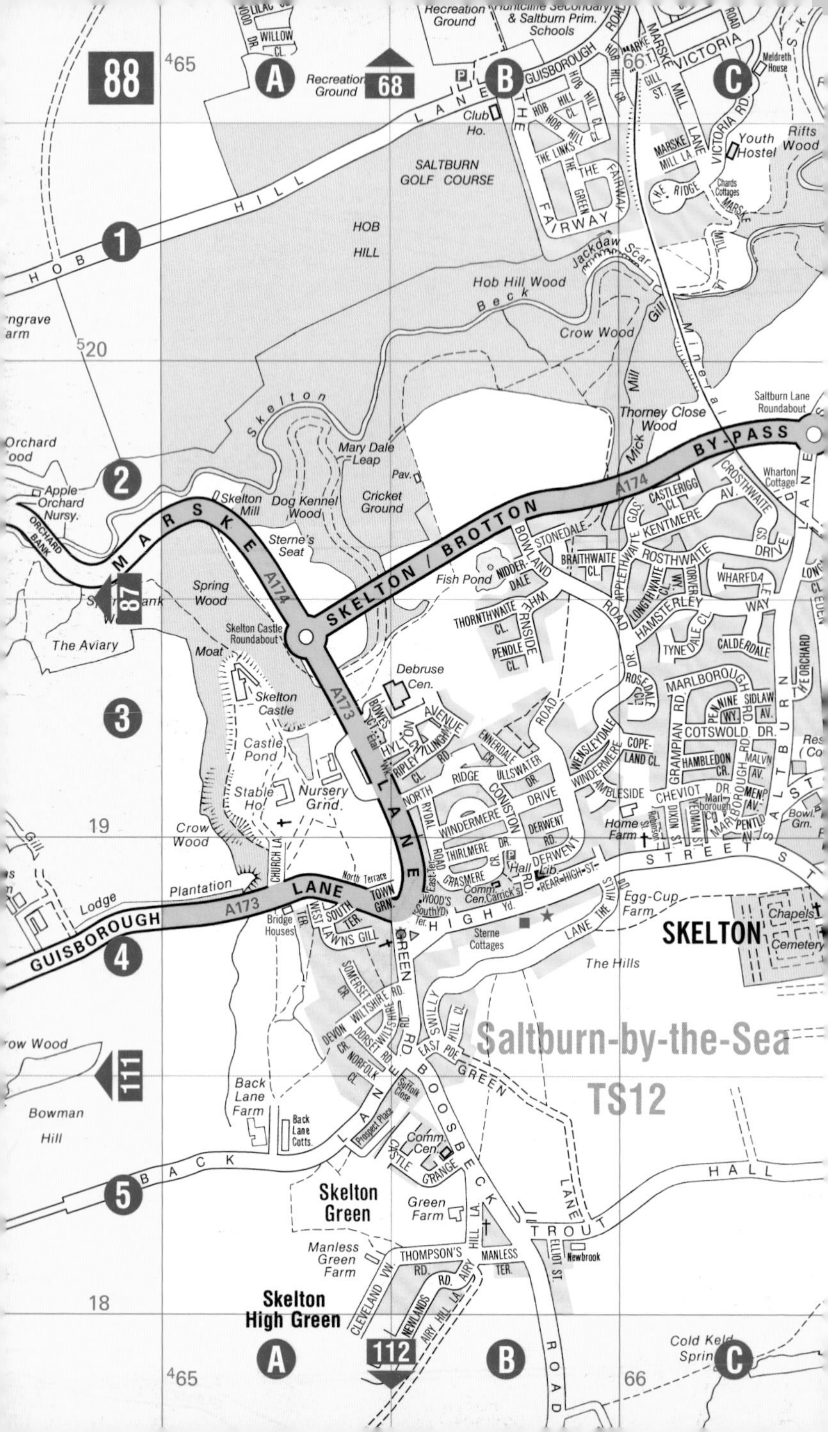
A
B
C
1
2
3
4
5
465
66
520
19
18
68
87
111
112
Recreation Ground
Huntcliffe Secondary & Saltburn Prim. Schools
WILLOW CL.
HOB HILL LANE
GUISBOROUGH ROAD
MARSKE MILL LANE
VICTORIA RD.
Meldreth House
Youth Hostel
Rifts Wood
Chards Cottages
THE RIDGE
Club Ho.
SALTBURN GOLF COURSE
HOB HILL
HOB HILL CL.
THE LINKS
THE GREEN
THE FAIRWAY
Jackdaw Scar
Hob Hill Wood
Skelton Beck
Crow Wood
Mill Gill
Mineral
Thorney Close Wood
Mick Mill
Saltburn Lane Roundabout
SKELTON / BROTTON BY-PASS
A174
Wharton Cottage
Orchard Wood
Apple Orchard Nursy.
ORCHARD BANK
MARSKE LANE
Skelton Mill
Dog Kennel Wood
Mary Dale Leap
Pav.
Cricket Ground
Sterne's Seat
Spring Wood
Spring Bank Wood
The Aviary
Skelton Castle Roundabout
Moat
Skelton Castle
Castle Pond
Stable Ho.
Nursery Grnd.
Crow Wood
CHURCH LA.
Plantation
Lodge
GUISBOROUGH LANE
A173
North Terrace
TOWN GRN.
Bridge Houses
SOUTH TER.
WEST TER.
LAWNS GILL
GREEN
HIGH ST.
Sterne Cottages
Debruse Cen.
BOWES CT.
HYLTON AVENUE
ILLINGHAM
RIPLEY CL.
ENNERDALE CR.
ULLSWATER DR.
NORTH RIDGE
CONISTON DRIVE
RYDAL ROAD
WINDERMERE
THIRLMERE DR.
GRASMERE CR.
DERWENT RD.
Hall
Lib.
Comm. Cen.
Carrick's Yd.
REAR HIGH ST.
Fish Pond
NIDDERDALE
BOWLAND ROAD
STONEDALE
THORNTHWAITE CL.
FERNSIDE
PENDLE CL.
CASTLERIGG CL.
KENTMERE
CROSTHWAITE AV.
BRAITHWAITE CL.
APPLETHWAITE GDS.
ROSTHWAITE
LONGTHWAITE CL.
TORVER WY.
WHARFDALE
HAMSTERLEY WAY
TYNEDALE CL.
CALDERDALE
ROSEDALE CL.
WENSLEYDALE
WINDERMERE
AMBLESIDE
COPELAND CL.
GRAMPIAN RD.
MARLBOROUGH RD.
PENNINE WY.
SIDLAW AV.
COTSWOLD DR.
HAMBLEDON CR.
CHEVIOT DR.
MALVN AV.
MENP AV.
PENTLD AV.
DIXON ST.
YEOMAN ST.
Robinson St.
Home Farm
Bowl. Grn.
SALTBURN LANE
THE ORCHARD
LONG CL.
EDEN
DRIVE
Egg-Cup Farm
THE HILLS LANE
SKELTON
Chapels
Cemetery
The Hills
Saltburn-by-the-Sea
TS12
SOMERSET CR.
WILTSHIRE RD.
DEVON CR.
DORSET RD.
NORFOLK CL.
SWILLY HILL CL.
EAST PDE.
GREEN
BOOSBECK RD.
Suffolk Close
Prospect Place
Back Lane Farm
Back Lane Cotts.
BACK LANE
Comm. Cen.
CASTLE GRANGE
Skelton Green
Green Farm
HALL LANE
TROUT
ELLIOT ST.
Newbrook
HILL LA.
MANLESS TER.
Manless Green Farm
THOMPSON'S RD.
CLEVELAND VW.
NEWLANDS RD.
AIRY HILL LA.
Skelton High Green
Bowman Hill
Cold Keld Spring
ROAD

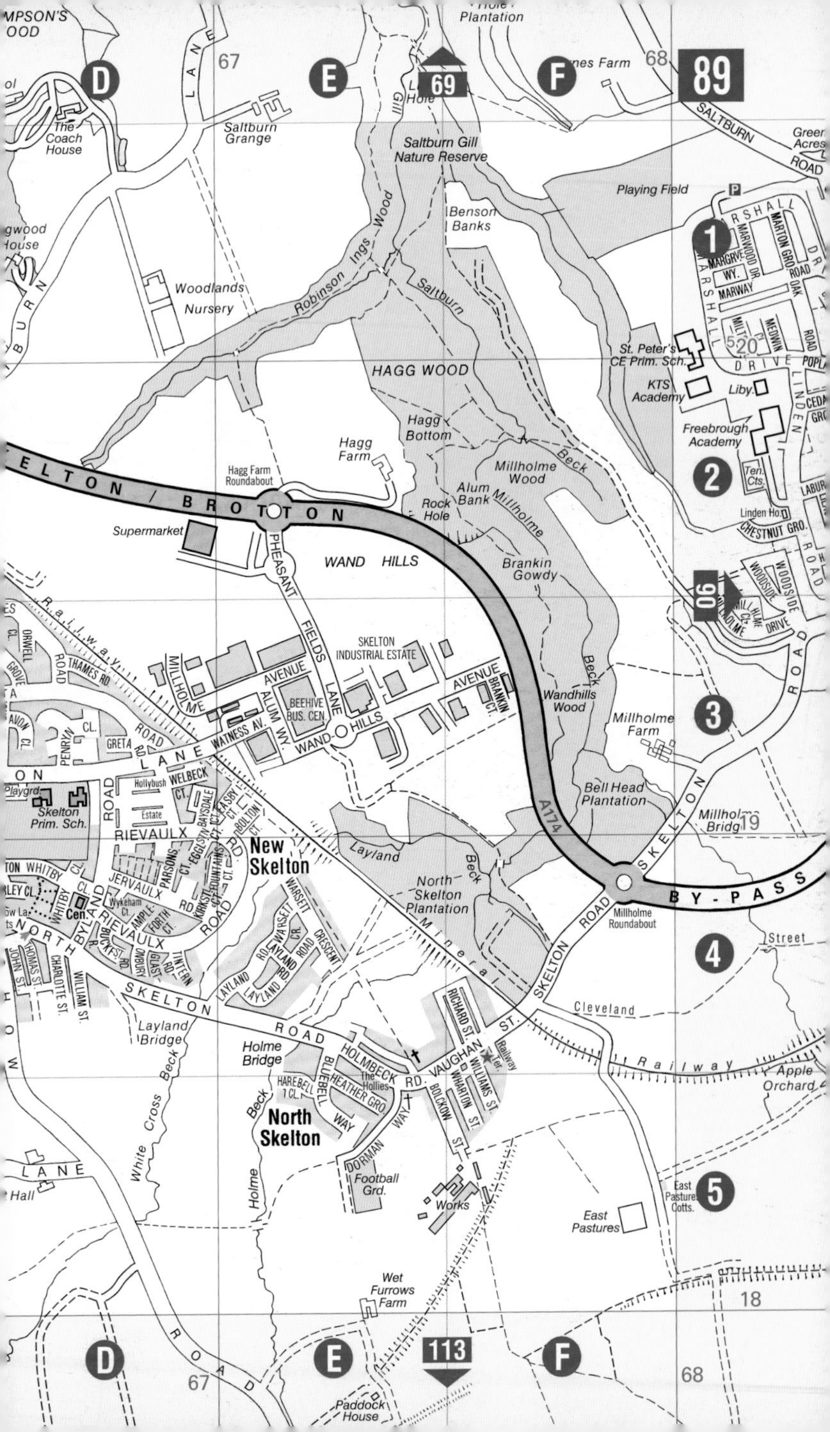

Saltburn Grange
The Coach House
Saltburn Gill Nature Reserve
Playing Field
Benson Banks
Robinson Ings Wood
Saltburn
Woodlands Nursery
HAGG WOOD
St. Peter's CE Prim. Sch.
KTS Academy
Liby.
Freebrough Academy
Hagg Bottom
Hagg Farm
Hagg Farm Roundabout
Millholme Wood
Beck
Alum Bank
Millholme
Rock Hole
Supermarket
SKELTON / BROTTON
WAND HILLS
Brankin Gowdy
PHEASANT FIELDS LANE
SKELTON INDUSTRIAL ESTATE
BEEHIVE BUS. CEN.
WAND-HILLS
AVENUE
MILLHOLME
ALUM WY.
WATNESS AV.
BRANKIN CT.
Wandhills Wood
Millholme Farm
Bell Head Plantation
A174
Millholme Bridge
Millholme Roundabout
BY-PASS
SKELTON ROAD
Railway
THAMES RD
ORWELL
GROVE
PENRYN
CL.
GRETA RD.
AVON CL.
LANE
Playgrd.
Skelton Prim. Sch.
Hollybush Estate
WELBECK CT.
RIEVAULX
New Skelton
Layland
North Skelton Plantation
Mineral
JERVAULX
PARSONS CT.
BAYSDALE CT.
FOUNTAINS CT.
Wykeham CT.
AMPLE CT.
FORTH CT.
BUCKFST. RD.
ONBURY
GLAST. RD.
TINTERN
WHITBY CL.
Cen.
BYLAND R.
NORTH
THOMAS ST.
JOHN ST.
CHARLOTTE ST.
WILLIAM ST.
SKELTON ROAD
WARSETT CRESCENT
LAYLAND RD
Layland Bridge
Holme Bridge
HOLMBECK RD.
The Hollies
HAREBELL CL.
BLUEBELL WAY
HEATHER GRO.
North Skelton
DORMAN WAY
BOLCKOW ST.
VAUGHAN ST.
RICHARD ST.
WILLIAMS ST.
WHARTON ST.
Railway Ter.
Cleveland Street
Railway
Apple Orchard
White Cross Beck
Holme Beck
Football Grd.
Works
East Pastures
East Pastures Cotts.
Wet Furrows Farm
Paddock House
LANE
Hall
ROAD
67
68
18
19
20
69
90
113
D
E
F
1
2
3
4
5

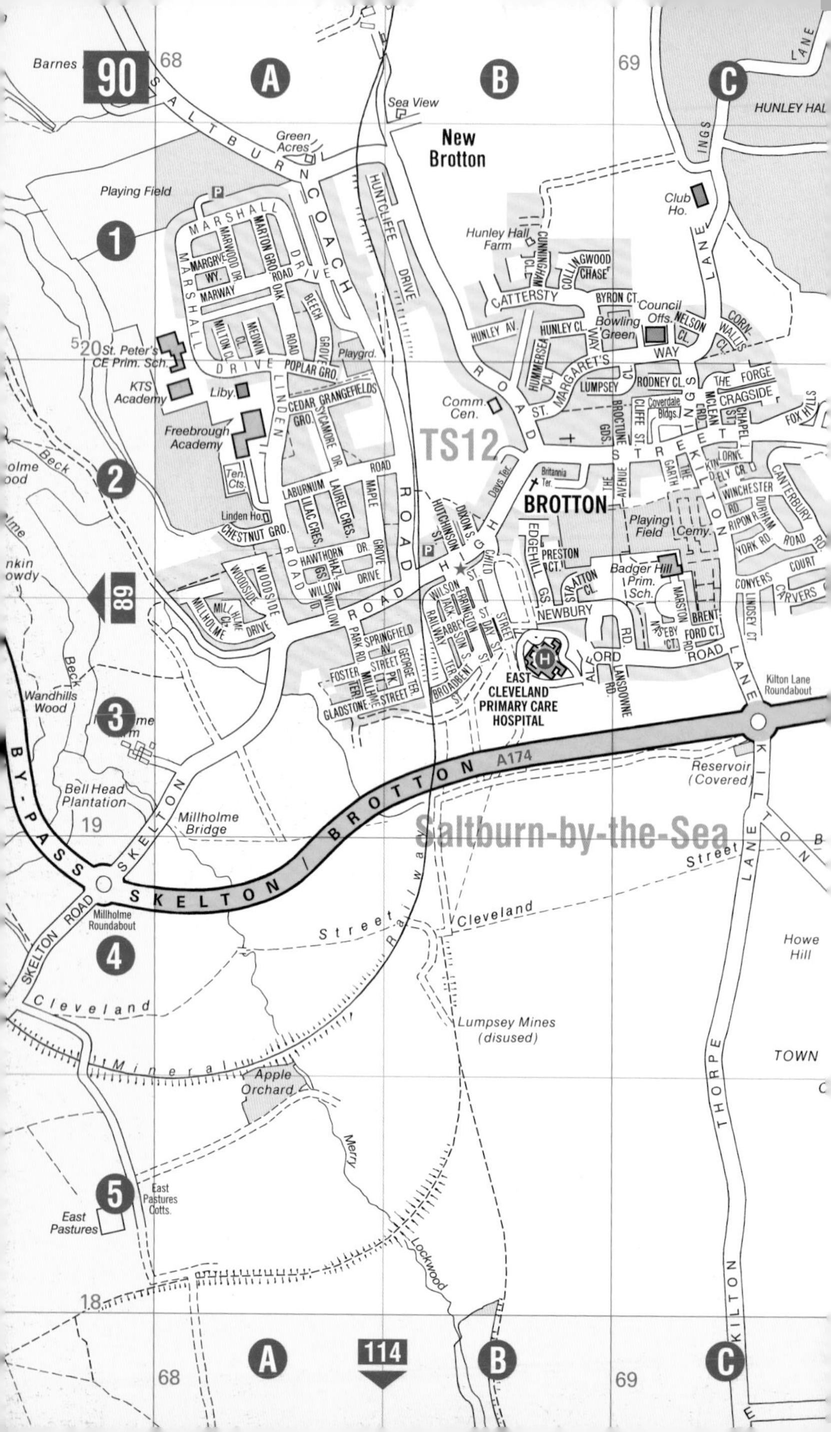
90
68
69
A
B
C
1
2
3
4
5
Barnes
SALTBURN ROAD
Sea View
Green Acres
New Brotton
HUNLEY HALL
INGS LANE
Club Ho.
Playing Field
MARSHALL DRIVE
MARGRAVE WY.
MARWOOD DR.
MARTON GRO.
OAK ROAD
MARWAY
COACH ROAD
HUNTCLIFFE DRIVE
Hunley Hall Farm
CUNNINGHAM CL.
COLLINGWOOD CHASE
CATTERSTY
BYRON CT.
Council Offs.
Bowling Green
NELSON CL.
CORNWALLIS CL.
HUNLEY AV.
HUNLEY CL.
WAY
BEECH GROVE
MILTON CL.
MEDWIN CL.
Playgrd.
St. Peter's CE Prim. Sch.
POPLAR GRO.
LINDEN ROAD
KTS Academy
Liby.
CEDAR GRO.
GRANGEFIELDS
SYCAMORE DR.
Comm. Cen.
HUMMERSEA CL.
ST. MARGARET'S WAY
LUMPSEY CL.
RODNEY CL.
THE FORGE
CRAGSIDE
FOX HILLS
Coverdale Bldgs.
BROCTUNE GDS.
CLIFFE ST.
MCLEAN CRD.
CHAPEL ST.
Freebrough Academy
TS12
Britannia Ter.
BROTTON
THE AVENUE
THE GARTH
KILTON LANE
LORNE
KTN. CT.
ELY CR.
CANTERBURY
WINCHESTER RD.
Ten. Cts.
LABURNUM
LILAC CRES.
LAUREL CRES.
MAPLE GROVE
Linden Ho.
CHESTNUT GRO.
HUTCHINSON ST.
DIXON'S
Days Ter.
HIGH STREET
CHILD ST.
EDGEHILL GS.
PRESTON CT.
Playing Field
Cemy.
DURHAM ROAD
RIPON RD.
YORK RD.
COURT
Badger Hill Prim. Sch.
HAWTHORN DR.
HAZEL GS.
WILLOW DRIVE
WOODSIDE
MILLHOLME CT.
MILLHOLME DRIVE
WILSON ST.
JACK.
ERRINGTON ST.
RAILWAY
STRATTON CL.
NEWBURY RD.
MARSTON
BRENT
CONYERS
LINDSEY CT.
CARVERS
ABBEY ST.
SON S.
DAY ST.
PARK RD.
SPRINGFIELD AV.
GEORGE TER.
ALFORD ROAD
LANSDOWNE RD.
MASEBY CT.
FORD CT.
FOSTER TER.
MILLHOLME PK.
STREET
BROADBENT ST.
EAST CLEVELAND PRIMARY CARE HOSPITAL
Kilton Lane Roundabout
GLADSTONE STREET
A174
Reservoir (Covered)
Wandhills Wood
Beck
Holme Wood
Bell Head Plantation
19
20
Millholme Bridge
SKELTON ROAD
BROTTON / SKELTON BY-PASS
Saltburn-by-the-Sea
Cleveland Street
Railway
Howe Hill
Millholme Roundabout
Lumpsey Mines (disused)
TOWN
Mineral
Apple Orchard
Merry
THORPE LANE
East Pastures Cotts.
East Pastures
Lockwood
18
114
89

D
E
F
470
71
OLF COURSE
Cattersty Gill
Mineral Railway
Low Farm
Reservoir
1
TS13
520
Skinningrove Bank
Gripps Farm
STEEL WORKS
Works
2
BROTTON ROAD
Cragghall Roundabout
BY-PASS
BROTTON
A174 Railway Cotts.
ROAD
92
CLIFF TERRACE
MARINE
HIGH ST.
New Grove Ter.
Larvik Ct.
The Sq.
ROAD
HUTTON ST.
Ridley Ter.
New Company Row
GROVE
Primrose Hill
PRIMROSE HILL
Railway Cotts.
Rockcliffe Vw.
KENT
RAWLSN
BOULBY RD.
WESTRAY ST.
PLEASANT
BECK
Cleveland Ironstone Museum
Tyreman Ct.
Cotts.
3
Craggs Hall
Low Craggs Hall
CARLIN PK.
CLIFFE AVENUE
GLADSTONE STREET
CORONATION ST.
QUEEN
GROSVENOR TERRACE
IRENE
Belle Vue Ter.
ST.
MUNIEL
MAYNARD
FRONT ST.
DIXON ST.
Wesley Ter.
MOUNT
LOFTUS
CARLIN HOW
Viaduct
Works
19
Mill
Kilton Mill Bridge
Deepdale Wood
Street
Maynard Foundry
KILTON LA.
Bowling Green
Pav.
Football Ground
Playgrd.
Playing Field
MILLBANK
BECK
Whitecliff Cotts.
4
CRAGGS HILL
MILL LANE
SKINNINGROVE
BANK
ST. HILDA'S T.
VALLEY
HARTGTN ST.
HIGH ST.
COWSCOTE
END
LANE
BRAYGATE
Whitecliff Wood Nature Reserve
White Cliff
5
Kilton
Kilton Hall
Patten Bank Beck
Petch Bridge
Playgrd.
MINERS GTH.
IRONSTONE WY.
CLEVELAND ST.
GRAHAM ST.
18
LIVERTON
Liverton Mines
115
KILTON
Hill Wood
Cock Shots
LEVELAND ST.
SCHOOL LANE
PECTEN CT.
St. Helens Wlk.
Cricket

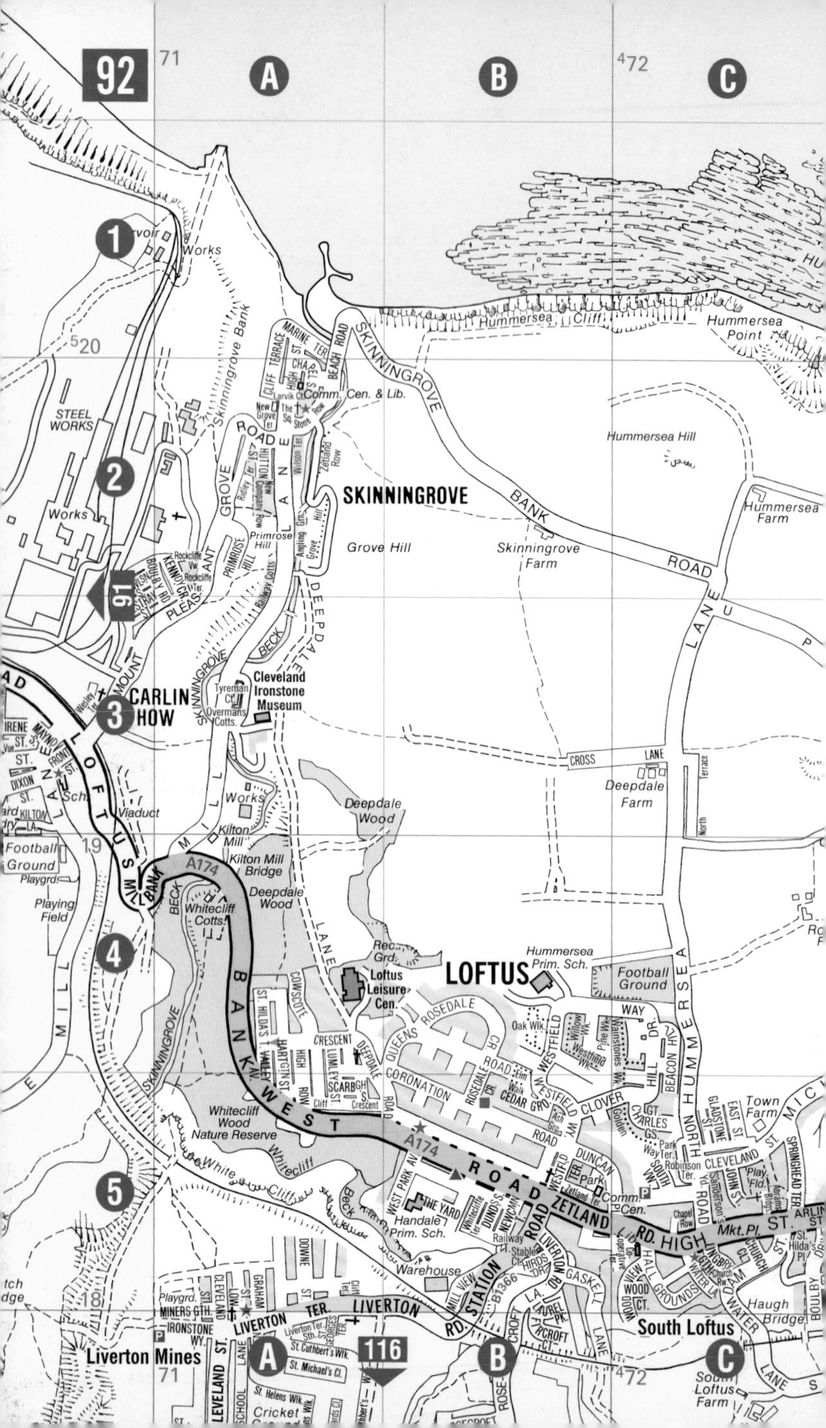
71
A
B
472
C
Works
520
STEEL WORKS
Works
Skinningrove Bank
Hummersea Cliff
Hummersea Point
SKINNINGROVE
Comm. Cen. & Lib.
Hummersea Hill
SKINNINGROVE BANK ROAD
Hummersea Farm
Grove Hill
Skinningrove Farm
Primrose Hill
91
CARLIN HOW
Cleveland Ironstone Museum
Tyreman Ct.
Overmans Cotts.
CROSS LANE
Deepdale Farm
North Terrace
Deepdale Wood
Works
Kilton Mill
Viaduct
Football Ground
Playgrd.
Playing Field
Kilton Mill Bridge
Deepdale Wood
Whitecliff Cotts.
A174
MILL BANK
DEEPDALE LANE
Rec. Grd.
Loftus Leisure Cen.
LOFTUS
Hummersea Prim. Sch.
Football Ground
HUMMERSEA LANE
WEST BANK AV.
Whitecliff Wood Nature Reserve
White Cliff
Town Farm
ZETLAND ROAD
Handale Prim. Sch.
THE YARD
Warehouse
Comm. Cen.
HIGH ST.
Mkt. Pl.
STATION RD.
B1366
LIVERTON RD.
Playgrd.
MINERS GTH.
IRONSTONE WY.
LIVERTON TER.
Liverton Mines
South Loftus
Haugh Bridge
South Loftus Farm
116
A
B
C
71
472
18
19

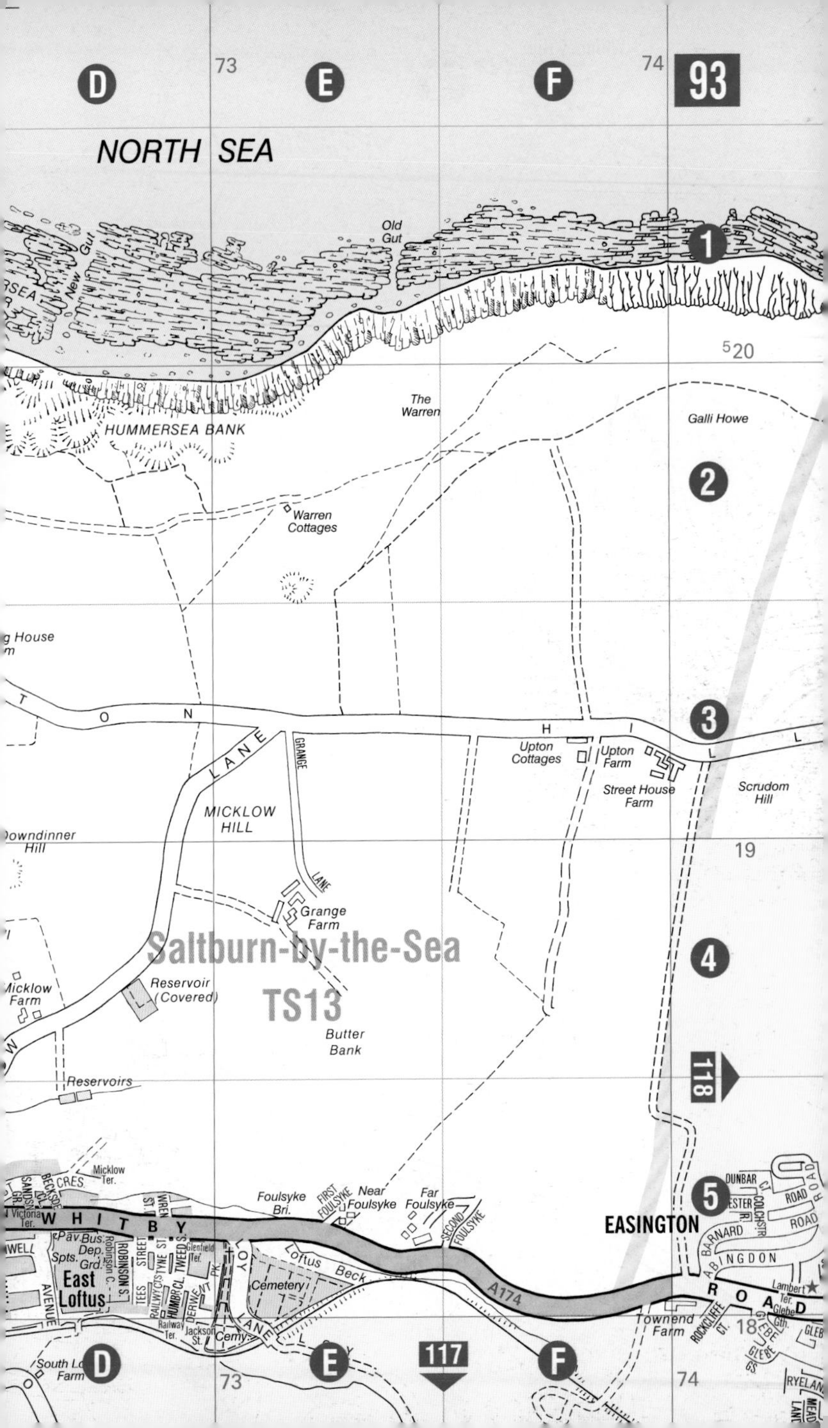
D
73
E
F
74
NORTH SEA
Old Gut
New Gut
1
The Warren
HUMMERSEA BANK
Galli Howe
2
Warren Cottages
g House
Upton Cottages
Upton Farm
Street House Farm
Scrudom Hill
3
GRANGE
LANE
MICKLOW HILL
Downdinner Hill
19
Grange Farm
Saltburn-by-the-Sea
TS13
4
Micklow Farm
Reservoir (Covered)
Butter Bank
Reservoirs
Micklow Ter.
CRES.
Foulsyke Bri.
FIRST FOULSYKE
Near Foulsyke
Far Foulsyke
SECOND FOULSYKE
5
EASINGTON
DUNBAR CT.
COLCHSTR
ROAD
BARNARD
ABINGDON
WHITBY
East Loftus
Cemetery
Loftus Beck
A174
Cemy.
Railway Ter.
Jackson St.
Townend Farm
ROAD
Lambert Ter.
Glebe Gth.
GLEBE
ROCKCLIFFE CT.
18
South Lo Farm
RYELAN

118
117

94
Whinney Hill
38
A
B
C
39
70
Stud
LANE
BACK
Ox Hill Farm
19
Sandyleas Plantation Farm
Cliffolgwen
Nine Acres Nurseries
The Hermitage
The Bungalow
Depot
Sandyleas Plantations
Elton Moor Farm (Field Sports Ce
DARLINGTON
1
Elton Home Park
SANDY
2
Sandy Lees Farm
18
LEAS
BACK
Larberry Pastures
3
Gas Valve Compound
TS21
Fir Tree House
Viewley Hill Farm
4
LANE
17
LANE
ROAD
DARLINGTON
5
A66
ROAD
Mount Pleasant Cottage
Sewage Works
LONG NEWTON
Long Newton House
WHITE HOUSE CFT.
BAL
CFT.
St. Mary's C of E Prim. Sch.
Comm. Cen.
STOCKTON
THE STRAY
THE CLOSE
CHASE
RECTORY
DARLINGTON
GRASS CFT.
CASTLE
Rec. Grd.
124
THE GREEN LA.
WAY
WILLOW
ODLAND
Parkside
Gate
Church Vw.
FAIRVIEW
The Bungalows
BURT
WOOD CT.

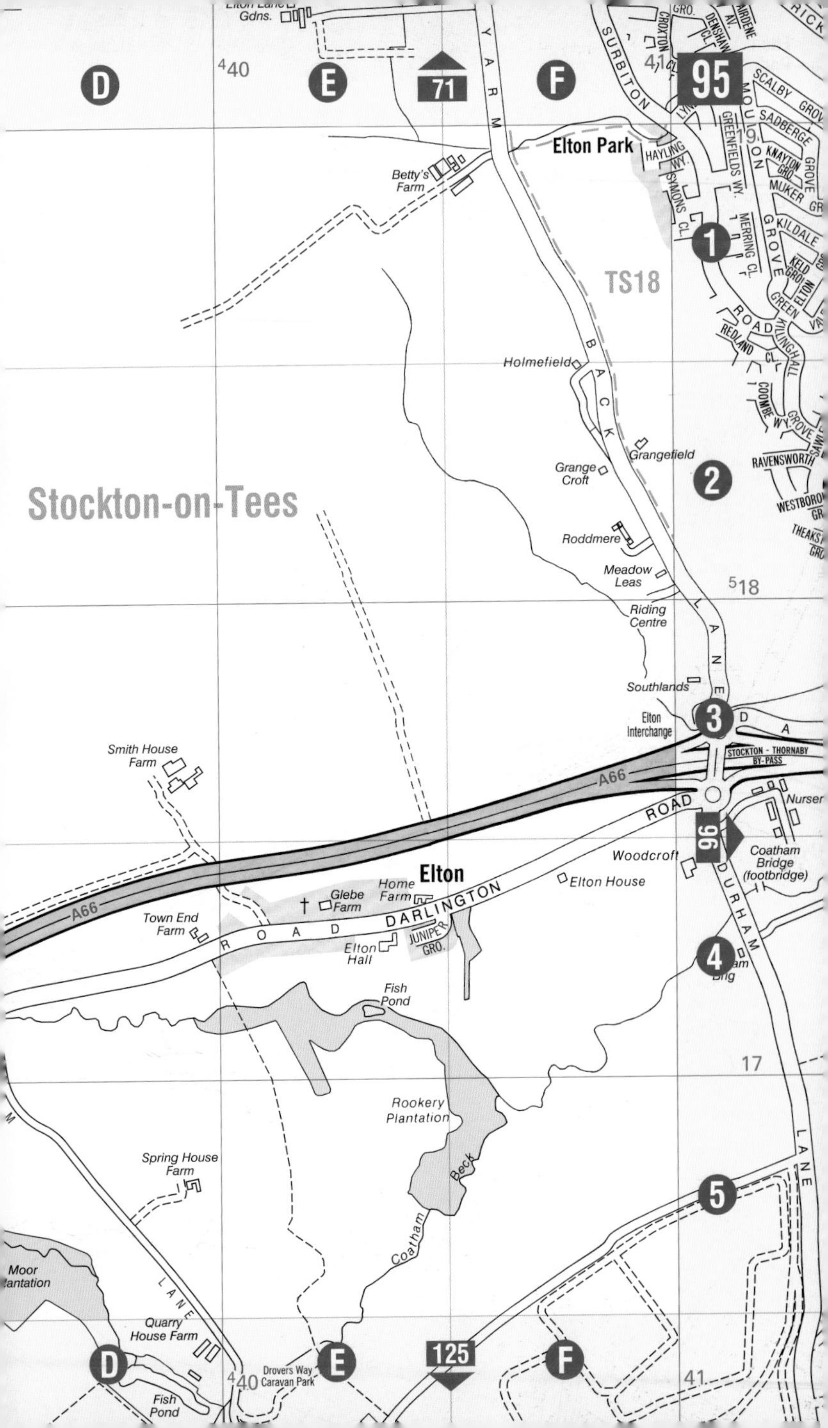
D
E
F
440
41
71
Elton Lane Gdns.
YARM
SURBITON
CROXTON
DENSHAW AV.
AIRDENE
GRO.
CL.
SCALBY GROVE
SADBERGE
MOULTON
GREENFIELDS WY.
19
Elton Park
HAYLING WY.
SIMONS CL.
KNAYTON GRO.
MUKER
GROVE
MERRING CL.
KILDALE
KELD GRO.
ELTON
GREEN
ROAD
KILLINGHALL
REDLAND
CL.
COOMBE WY.
GROVE
RAVENSWORTH
WESTBOROUGH
THEAKSTON GRO.
Betty's Farm
TS18
1
2
3
4
5
Holmefield
BACK LANE
Grangefield
Grange Croft
Stockton-on-Tees
Roddmere
Meadow Leas
518
Riding Centre
Southlands
Elton Interchange
A66
STOCKTON - THORNABY BY-PASS
Smith House Farm
ROAD
96
Nursery
Coatham Bridge (footbridge)
Woodcroft
Elton
Elton House
DURHAM
Home Farm
Glebe Farm
DARLINGTON
Town End Farm
ROAD
JUNIPER GRO.
Elton Hall
Fish Pond
17
Rookery Plantation
Spring House Farm
Beck
Coatham
LANE
Moor Plantation
LANE
Quarry House Farm
Fish Pond
Drovers Way Caravan Park
125

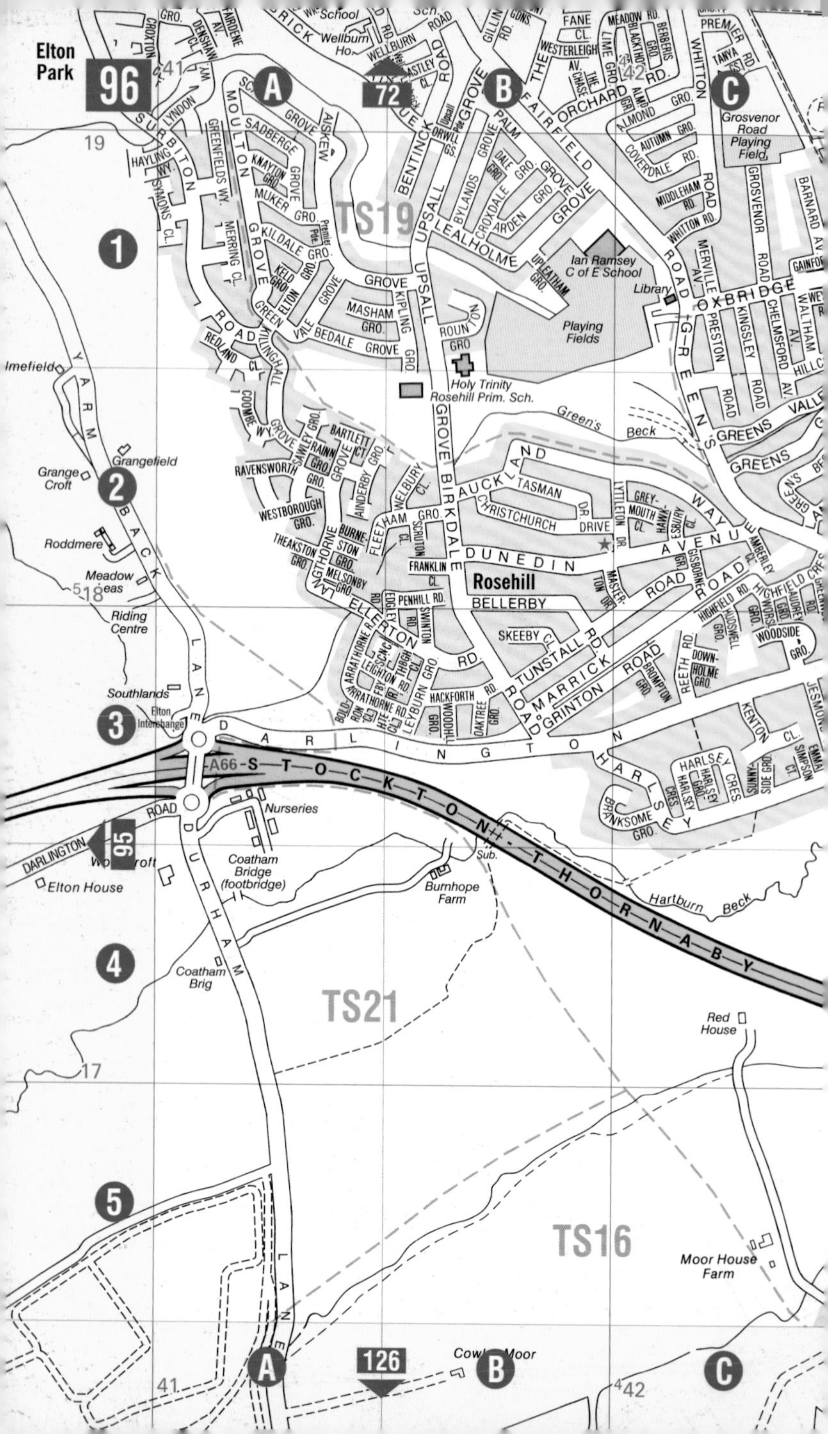
A
B
C
1
2
3
4
5
72
95
126
TS19
TS21
TS16
Rosehill
Ian Ramsey C of E School
Library
Playing Fields
Grosvenor Road Playing Field
Holy Trinity Rosehill Prim. Sch.
Wellburn Ho.
School
Green's Beck
Hartburn Beck
Imefield
Grangefield
Grange Croft
Roddmere
Meadow Leas
Riding Centre
Southlands
Elton Interchange
Nurseries
Coatham Bridge (footbridge)
Burnhope Farm
Sub.
Elton House
Coatham Brig
Red House
Moor House Farm
Cowley Moor
A66 STOCKTON - THORNABY ROAD
DARLINGTON ROAD
DURHAM LANE
YARM BACK LANE
SURBITON ROAD
MOULTON GROVE
UPSALL GROVE
BIRKDALE ROAD
FAIRFIELD ROAD
HARTBURN LANE
GREENS LANE
GREENS VALLEY
AUCKLAND WAY
DUNEDIN AVENUE
ELLERTON RD.
TUNSTALL RD.
MARRICK ROAD
GRINTON ROAD
HARLSEY CRES.
GREENSIDE
OXBRIDGE
19
18
17
41
42

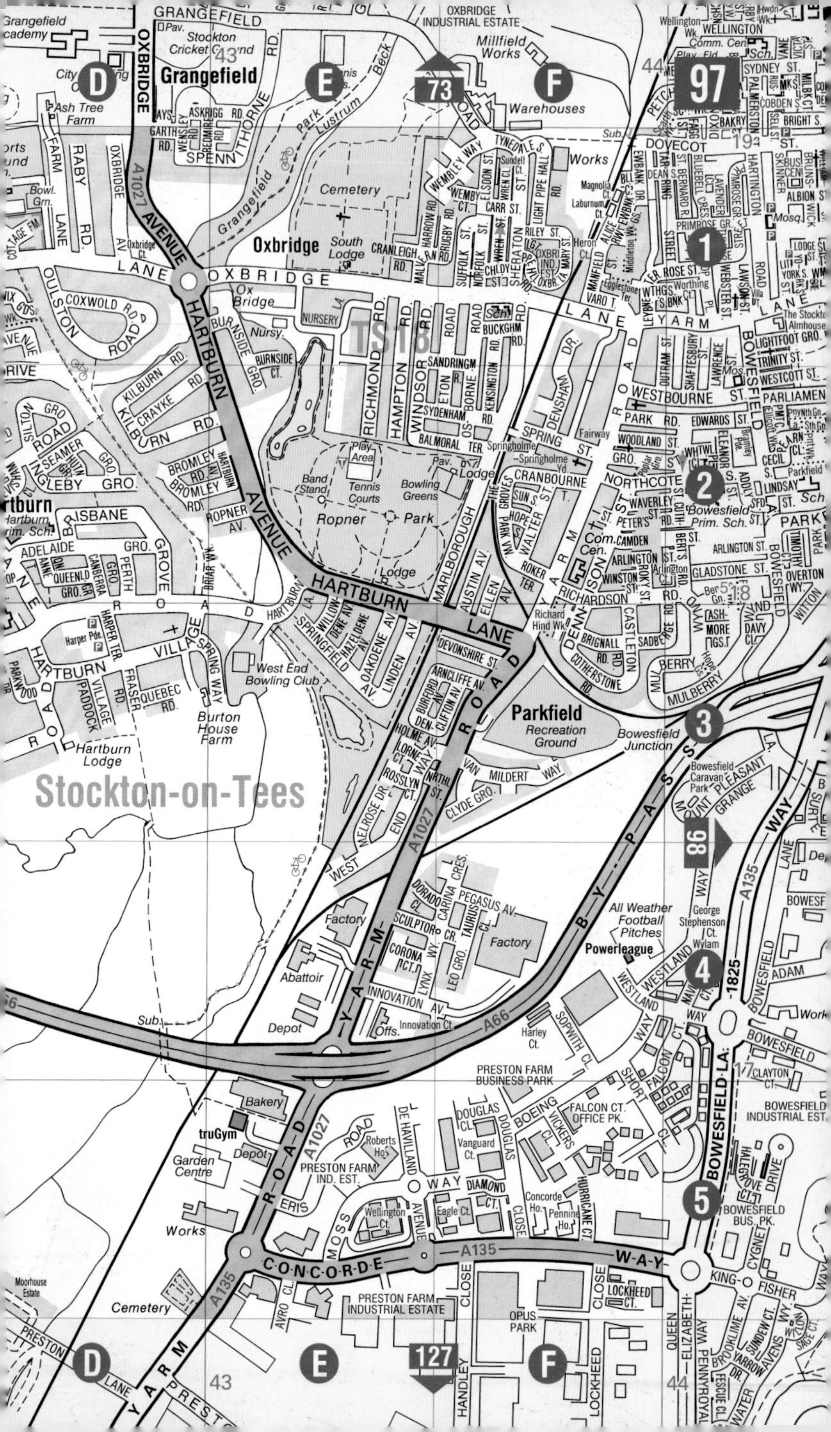
GRANGEFIELD
OXBRIDGE INDUSTRIAL ESTATE
Grangefield Academy
Stockton Cricket Ground
Grangefield
Millfield Works
73
Warehouses
D
E
F
44
43
Ash Tree Farm
RABY RD.
OXBRIDGE AV.
OXBRIDGE AVENUE
A1027
ASKRIGG RD.
SPENNITHORNE RD.
Grangefield Park
Lustrum Beck
Cemetery
South Lodge
Oxbridge
CRANLEIGH RD.
WEMBLEY WAY
TYNEDALE ST.
Works
Magnolia Ct.
Laburnum Ct.
Heron Ct.
DOVECOT ST.
EWBANK DR.
BLUEBELL CRES.
LAVENDER
HARTINGTON RD.
ALBION ST.
PRIMROSE GR.
SYDNEY ST.
PALMERSTON ST.
COBDEN ST.
BRIGHT ST.
WELLINGTON
Wellington Wk.
Comm. Cen.
Play Fld.
SKINNER ST.
BRUNSWICK ST.
Mosq.
Oxbridge Ct.
BOWL. GRN.
COTTAGE FM.
FARM LANE
OXBRIDGE LANE
OXBRIDGE
Ox Bridge
WREN ST.
SHERATON ST.
RILEY ST.
MARY ST.
CARR ST.
SUFFOLK ST.
NORFOLK ST.
RUGBY RD.
HARROW RD.
MALVERN RD.
LIGHT PIPE HALL RD.
MANFIELD ST.
ALICE ST.
VARO T.
ROSE ST.
Worthing Ct.
WEBSTER ST.
LAWSON ST.
Eaglestone Ter.
YARM LANE
COXWOLD RD.
OULSTON ROAD
HARTBURN AVENUE
BURNSIDE GRO.
BURNSIDE CT.
Nursy.
NURSERY LA.
TS18
RICHMOND RD.
HAMPTON RD.
WINDSOR RD.
SANDRINGM.
ETON RD.
OSBORNE RD.
KENSINGTON RD.
BUCKGHM RD.
SYDENHAM RD.
BALMORAL TER.
DENSHAM DR.
Fairway
SPRING ST.
Springholme
Springholme Yd.
OUTRAM ST.
SHAFTESBURY ST.
LAWRENCE ST.
BOWESFIELD LANE
LIGHTFOOT GRO.
TRINITY ST.
WESTCOTT ST.
WESTBOURNE ST.
PARLIAMENT
The Stockton Almshouse
PARK RD.
EDWARDS ST.
WOODLAND ST.
ELEANOR ST.
CECIL ST.
Parkfield
DRIVE
KILBURN RD.
CRAYKE RD.
SILTON GRO.
SEAMER GRO.
INGLEBY GRO.
BROMLEY RD.
ROPNER AV.
Play Area
Band Stand
Tennis Courts
Bowling Greens
Pav.
Lodge
Ropner Park
MARLBOROUGH ROAD
CRANBOURNE T.
NORTHCOTE ST.
WAVERLEY
ST. PETER'S RD.
Bowesfield Prim. Sch.
LINDSAY ST.
PARK
Hartburn
Hartburn Prim. Sch.
BRISBANE GRO.
ADELAIDE GRO.
QUEENLD.
CANBERRA
PERTH GRO.
GROVE ROAD
HARTBURN LA.
HARTBURN LANE
AUSTIN AV.
ELLEN AV.
WALTER ST.
PARK VW.
THE GROVES
ROKER TER.
Com. Cen.
CAMDEN
ARLINGTON ST.
WINSTON
GLADSTONE ST.
OVERTON WY.
TIMOTHY CT.
RICHARDSON RD.
Ber. Gn.
WITTON
Richard Hind Wk.
DENNISON ST.
BRIGNALL RD.
CASTLETON
SADBERGE
ASHMORE GS.
DAVY CL.
COTHERSTONE RD.
MULBERRY
Harper Pde.
HARPER TER.
VILLAGE
SPRING WAY
BRIAR WK.
HARTBURN
WILLOW DENE AV.
HAZELDENE AV.
OAKDENE AV.
LINDEN AV.
SPRINGFIELD AV.
DEVONSHIRE ST.
ARNCLIFFE AV.
BURFORD AV.
CLIFTON AV.
HARTBURN VILLAGE
PADDOCK
FRASER RD.
QUEBEC RD.
West End Bowling Club
Burton House Farm
Parkfield Recreation Ground
Bowesfield Junction
Hartburn Lodge
HOLME AV.
LORNE CT.
LORNE WAY
ROSSLYN CT.
NRTHL ST.
VAN MILDERT WAY
CLYDE GRO.
Bowesfield Caravan Park
MOUNT PLEASANT GRANGE
Stockton-on-Tees
MELROSE DR.
END
WEST
A1027
BY PASS
98
A135
WAY
LANE
BOWESF.
DORADO CL.
CARINA CRES.
PEGASUS AV.
SCULPTOR CR.
TAURUS CL.
CORONA CT.
Factory
All Weather Football Pitches
George Stephenson Ct.
Wylam
Powerleague
WESTLAND WAY
BOWESFIELD
ADAM
Works
Abattoir
Depot
LYNX WY.
LEO GRO.
INNOVATION AV.
Innovation Ct.
Offs.
A66
Harley Ct.
SOPWITH CL.
SHORT CL.
FALCON CT.
Sub.
PRESTON FARM BUSINESS PARK
Bakery
truGym
Garden Centre
Depot
DE HAVILLAND AVENUE
Roberts Ho.
PRESTON FARM IND. EST.
DOUGLAS CL.
DOUGLAS CLOSE
Vanguard Ct.
BOEING WAY
VICKERS CL.
FALCON CT. OFFICE PK.
HURRICANE CT.
DIAMOND CT.
Concorde Ho.
Pennine Ho.
BOWESFIELD LA.
1825
CLAYTON CT.
BOWESFIELD INDUSTRIAL EST.
HALEGROVE DRIVE
BOWESFIELD BUS. PK.
ERIS
MOSS
Wellington Ct.
Eagle Ct.
Works
CONCORDE WAY
A135
AVRO CL.
PRESTON FARM INDUSTRIAL ESTATE
CLOSE
LOCKHEED CT.
OPUS PARK
KINGFISHER
CYGNET
Moorhouse Estate
Cemetery
PRESTON LANE
YARM ROAD
127
HANDLEY CLOSE
LOCKHEED
QUEEN ELIZABETH WAY
PENNYROYAL
BROOKLIME AV.
YARROW DR.
SUNDEW CT.
AVENS WY.
WATER
FESCUE CL.
SAGE CT.
1
2
3
4
5

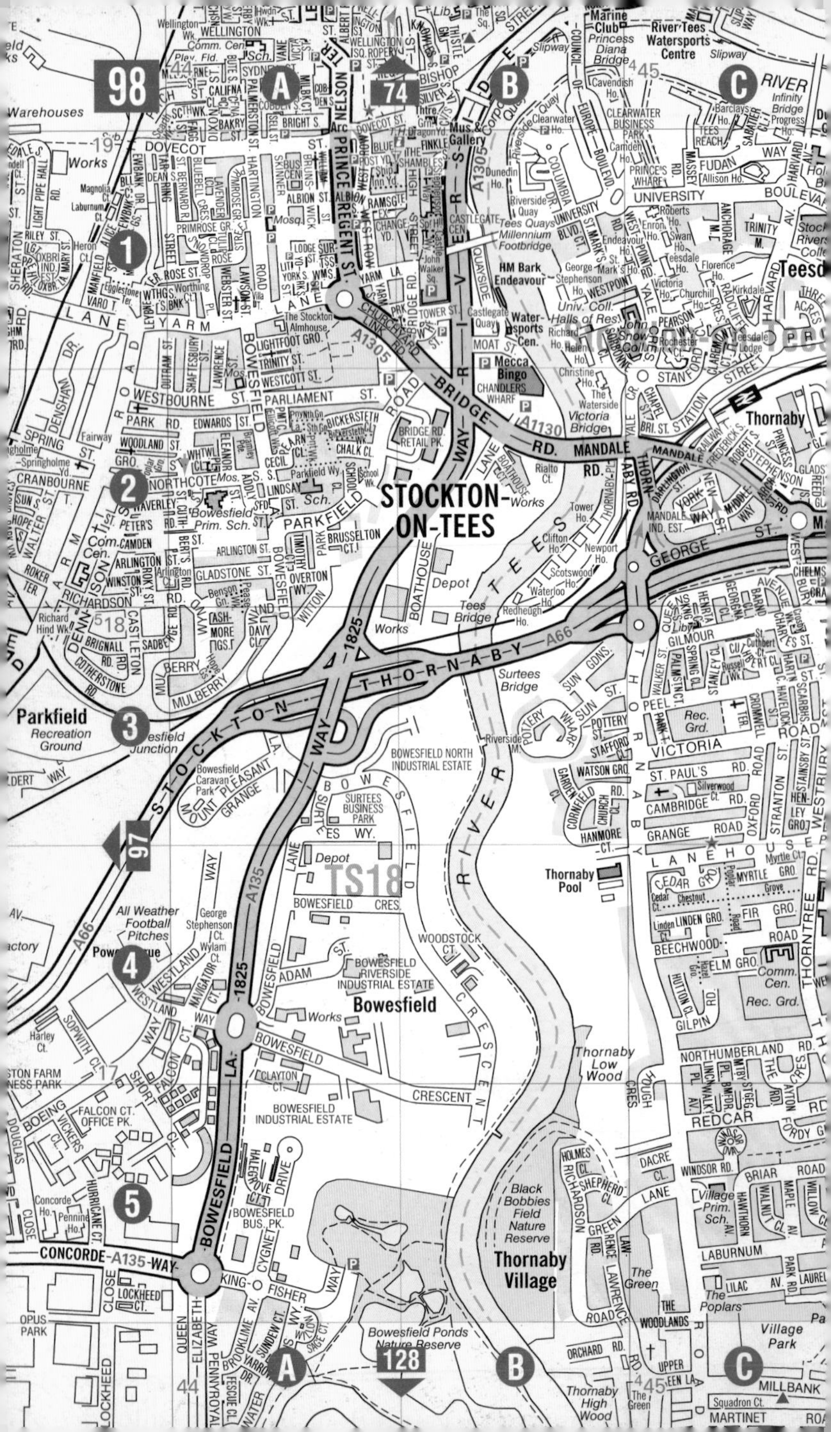
98
74
97
128
A
B
C
1
2
3
4
5
44
45
18
17
19
STOCKTON-ON-TEES
TS18
Bowesfield
Thornaby Village
Parkfield Recreation Ground
Bowesfield Junction
Thornaby
Teesdale
Warehouses
Works
DOVECOT ST.
WELLINGTON ST.
YARM LANE
YARM ROAD
PRINCE REGENT ST.
WEST ROW
HIGH STREET
BRIDGE RD.
RIVERSIDE
BISHOP ST.
FINKLE ST.
THE SHAMBLES
CHURCH ROAD
CASTLEGATE CEN.
Mus.& Gallery
Arc
The Stockton Almhouse
LIGHTFOOT GRO.
TRINITY ST.
WESTCOTT ST.
PARLIAMENT ST.
WESTBOURNE ST.
PARK RD.
EDWARDS ST.
WOODLAND ST.
NORTHCOTE ST.
WAVERLEY TER.
PETER'S
Com. Cen.
CAMDEN
ARLINGTON ST.
WINSTON ST.
RICHARDSON RD.
GLADSTONE ST.
BOWESFIELD LA.
PARKFIELD RD.
BRUSSELTON CT.
TIMOTHY CT.
OVERTON WY.
WITTON
BOATHOUSE LANE
Depot
Tees Bridge
Works
Bowesfield Prim. Sch.
Parkfield Wy.
BICKERSTETH CL.
CHALK CL.
BRIDGE RD. RETAIL PK.
BRIDGE RD.
A1305
A1130
A66
A135
1825
STOCKTON-THORNABY WAY
RIVER TEES
Tees Quays Millennium Footbridge
HM Bark Endeavour
Water-sports Cen.
Castlegate Quay
MOAT ST.
Mecca Bingo
CHANDLERS WHARF
Victoria Bridge
MANDALE RD.
THORNABY RD.
Rialto Ct.
Tower Ho.
Clifton Ho.
Newport Ho.
Scotswood Ho.
Waterloo Ho.
Redheugh Ho.
Surtees Bridge
Riverside M.
Marine Club
Princess Diana Bridge
River Tees Watersports Centre
Slipway
COUNCIL OF EUROPE BOULEVD.
Cavendish Ho.
CLEARWATER BUSINESS PARK
Camden Ho.
Columbia Dr.
Riverside Quay
Clearwater Ho.
Dunedin Ho.
UNIVERSITY BOULEVARD
UNIVERSITY BLVD.
ST. MARK'S CT.
WESTPOINT RD.
YALE CRES.
Endeavour Ho.
George Stephenson Ho.
Univ. Coll.
Halls of Res.
John Snow Coll.
Richard Ho.
Helen Ho.
Christine Ho.
The Waterside Ho.
Roberts Ho.
Enron Ho.
Swan Ho.
Teesdale Ho.
Victoria Ho.
Churchill Ho.
PEARSON WY.
Rochester Ct.
Florence Ho.
Kirkdale Ho.
Teesdale Lodge
ANCHORAGE M.
TRINITY M.
HARVARD AV.
THREE ACRES
CLAREMONT CT.
RADCLIFFE CRES.
STANFORD CT.
CHAPEL ST.
BRI. ST.
STATION STREET
PRINCE'S WHARF
MASSEY RD.
FUDAN WAY
Allison Ho.
Barclays Ho.
TEES REACH
SABATIER CL.
Progress Ho.
Infinity Bridge
RIVER
RAILWAY T.
FREDERICK S.
ROBERTS S.
STEPHENSON ST.
PRINCESS
DARLINGTON ST.
YORK WAY
NEW ST.
MIDDLE WAY
MANDALE IND. EST.
GEORGE ST.
QUEENS
HENRIETTA ST.
GEORGINA CL.
BARNARD CL.
AVENUE
CHARLES ST.
GILMOUR
SPRING CL.
PALMIST CT.
CUTHBERT CL.
WALKER ST.
PEEL ST.
SUN ST.
POTTERY WHARF
Rec. Grd.
VICTORIA
ST. PAUL'S RD.
CAMBRIDGE RD.
GRANGE ROAD
LANEHOUSE RD.
OXFORD RD.
STRANTON ST.
STAINSBY ST.
WESTBURY ST.
WATSON GRO.
CORNFIELD RD.
CHURCH RD.
HANMORE CT.
GARDEN CL.
Thornaby Pool
CEDAR GRO.
MYRTLE GRO.
Chestnut Grove
FIR GRO.
LINDEN GRO.
BEECHWOOD ROAD
ELM GRO.
HUTTON CL.
GILPIN RD.
Comm. Cen.
Rec. Grd.
THORNTREE RD.
NORTHUMBERLAND RD.
THE AYTON CRES.
REDCAR RD.
FORDY GRO.
WINDSOR RD.
BRIAR ROAD
WALNUT CL.
MAPLE AV.
WILLOW
Village Prim. Sch.
HAWTHORN AV.
LABURNUM
LILAC AV.
LAUREL
The Poplars
Village Park
MILLBANK
Squadron Ct.
MARTINET ROAD
HOUGH CRES.
DACRE CL.
GREEN LANE
HOLMES CL.
RICHARDSON
SHEPHERD CL.
LAWRENCE ROAD
The Green
THE WOODLANDS
ORCHARD RD.
UPPER GREEN LA.
Thornaby High Wood
Thornaby Low Wood
Black Bobbies Field Nature Reserve
Bowesfield Ponds Nature Reserve
BOWESFIELD NORTH INDUSTRIAL ESTATE
SURTEES BUSINESS PARK
SURTEES WY.
Depot
BOWESFIELD CRES.
WOODSTOCK CT.
BOWESFIELD RIVERSIDE INDUSTRIAL ESTATE
ADAM ST.
BOWESFIELD CRESCENT
CLAYTON CT.
BOWESFIELD INDUSTRIAL ESTATE
HALEGROVE CT.
DRIVE
BOWESFIELD BUS. PK.
CYGNET WAY
KINGFISHER WAY
SWAN WY.
BROOKLIME AV.
SUNDEW CT.
SAGE CT.
YARROW DR.
FESCUE CL.
WATER
PENNYROYAL
QUEEN ELIZABETH WAY
CONCORDE-A135-WAY
LOCKHEED CT.
LOCKHEED
OPUS PARK
CLOSE
Concorde Ho.
Pennine Ho.
HURRICANE CT.
BOEING
VICKERS CL.
FALCON CT. OFFICE PK.
FALCON CT.
SHORT
DOUGLAS CLOSE
SOPWITH CL.
Harley Ct.
STON FARM NESS PARK
WESTLAND WAY
NAVIGATOR CT.
George Stephenson Ct.
Wylam Ct.
All Weather Football Pitches
Actory
MOUNT PLEASANT GRANGE
Bowesfield Caravan Park
ELDERT WAY
MULBERRY
CASTLETON
BRIGNALL RD.
COTHERSTONE RD.
SADBERGE
ASHMORE GS.
DAVY CL.
Richard Hind Wk.
ROKER TER.
DENNISON
SPRING ST.
CRANBOURNE
SUN S.
HOPE
WALTER
Springholme Yd.
Fairway
DENSHAM DR.
SHERATON
RILEY ST.
LIGHT PIPE HALL RD.
MANFIELD
Heron Ct.
Magnolia Ct.
Laburnum Ct.
EWBANK DR.
ROSE ST.
WEBSTER ST.
LAWSON ST.
Worthing Ct.
PRIMROSE GR.
LAVENDER
HARTINGTON
ALBION ST.
RAMSGATE
Mosq.
SKINNER
BRUNSWICK
Bus Cen.
WILLIAM ST.
BRIGHT S.
COBDEN S.
PALMERSTON ST.
Comm. Cen.
Plev. Fld.
Sch.
SYDNEY ST.
Wellington Wk.
TOWER ST.
YARM LA.
Thtre.
Mosq.
Sch.

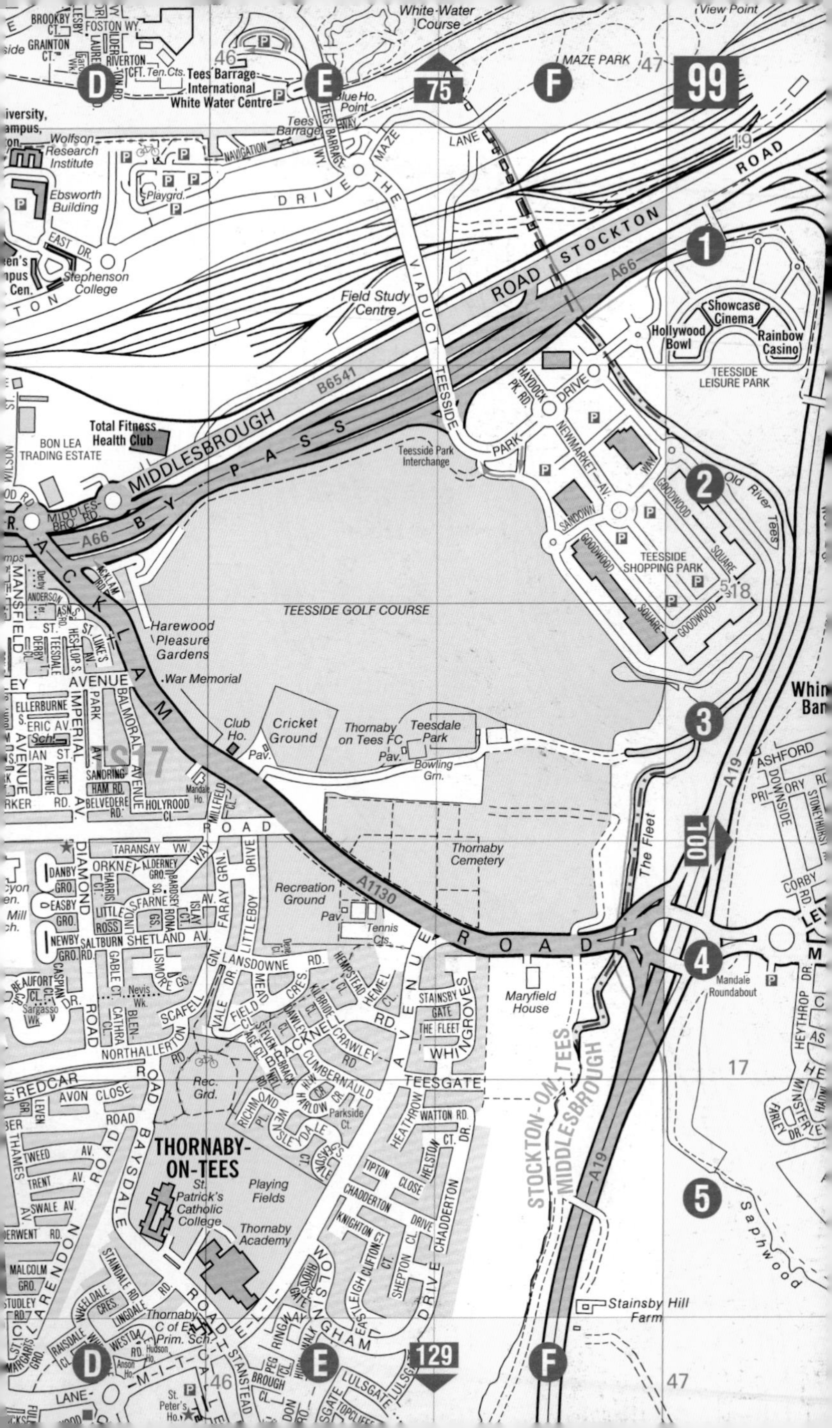
White Water Course
View Point
MAZE PARK
46
47
75
D
E
F
BROOKBY CT.
FOSTON WY.
GRAINTON CT.
RIVERTON
Ten.Cts.
Tees Barrage International White Water Centre
Blue Ho. Point
Tees Barrage
TEES BARRAGE WY.
TEES WAY
MAZE LANE
University, Campus
Wolfson Research Institute
NAVIGATION
Playgrd.
Ebsworth Building
DRIVE
EAST DR.
Stephenson College
THE VIADUCT
TEESSIDE
STOCKTON ROAD
A66
Field Study Centre
19
1
Showcase Cinema
Hollywood Bowl
Rainbow Casino
TEESSIDE LEISURE PARK
HAYDOCK PK. RD.
DRIVE
B6541
Total Fitness Health Club
BON LEA TRADING ESTATE
MIDDLESBROUGH ROAD
BY PASS
Teesside Park Interchange
PARK
NEWMARKET AV.
WAY
2
Old River Tees
GOODWOOD
SANDOWN
GOODWOOD SQUARE
TEESSIDE SHOPPING PARK
18
MIDDLESBRO' RD.
A66
ACKLAM ROAD
ACKLAM RD.
MANSFIELD AV.
DERBY CL.
ANDERSON
TEESDALE
ST. LUKE'S AV.
HESLOP S.
TEESSIDE GOLF COURSE
Harewood Pleasure Gardens
War Memorial
AVENUE
IMPERIAL AVENUE
PARK AV.
BALMORAL AVENUE
ELLERBURNE S.
ERIC AV.
Schl.
IAN ST.
TS17
Club Ho.
Pav.
Cricket Ground
Thornaby on Tees FC
Pav.
Teesdale Park
Bowling Grn.
Whinfield Bank
3
ASHFORD
DOWNSIDE
PRIORY
STONEHURST
A19
SANDRINGHAM RD.
BELVEDERE RD.
HOLYROOD CL.
Mandale Ho.
MILLFIELD CL.
ROAD
100
The Fleet
TARANSAY VW.
DIAMOND
DANBY GRO.
ORKNEY
ALDERNEY GRO.
HARRIS CT.
BARDSEY SQ.
WAY
FARAY GRN.
DRIVE
Thornaby Cemetery
EASBY GRO.
FARNE
RONA
ISLAY CT.
LITTLEBOY
Recreation Ground
A1130
CORBY RD.
LITTLE ROSS
Pav.
Tennis Cts.
NEWBY GRO.
SALTBURN RD.
SHETLAND AV.
ROAD
4
Mandale Roundabout
BEAUFORT CL.
CASPIAN DR.
GABLE CT.
LISMORE GS.
LANSDOWNE RD.
HEMPSTEAD CL.
HEMEL CL.
Maryfield House
Sargasso Wk.
Nevis Wk.
BLEN.
CATHRA CL.
SCAFELL
VALE DR.
FIELD CL.
MEAD CRES.
KILBRIDE CL.
STAINSBY GATE
THE FLEET
WHINGROVES
HEYTHROP DR.
ROAD
NORTHALLERTON RD.
BRACKNELL RD.
CRAWLEY RD.
CUMBERNAULD
AVENUE
TEESGATE
STOCKTON-ON-TEES
MIDDLESBROUGH
17
REDCAR
AVON CLOSE
ROAD
Rec. Grd.
RICHMOND PL.
WENSLEYDALE CT.
HARLOW CR.
Parkside Ct.
HEATHROW
WATTON RD.
HELSTON CT.
DR.
FARLEY DR.
MINSTER
THAMES
TWEED AV.
TRENT AV.
SWALE AV.
BAYSDALE
THORNABY-ON-TEES
St. Patrick's Catholic College
Playing Fields
TIPTON CLOSE
CHADDERTON
A19
5
Saphwood
DERWENT RD.
CLARENDON ROAD
MALCOLM GRO.
Thornaby Academy
KNIGHTON CT.
CLIFTON CT.
SHEPTON CL.
CHADDERTON DRIVE
STAINDALE RD.
WHEELDALE CRES.
LINGDALE
STUDLEY RD.
Thornaby C of E Prim. Sch.
MITCHELL
ROAD
RINGWAY
WALK
WOLSINGHAM
EASTLEIGH
Stainsby Hill Farm
ST. MARGARETS GRO.
RAISDALE CL.
WESTDALE RD.
Anson Ho.
Hudson Ho.
STANSTEAD
129
LANE
St. Peter's Ho.
46
BROUGH CL.
LULSGATE
47

View Point
MAZE PARK
76
Goals Soccer Centre
All Weather Pitches
Macmillan Academy
Archibald Prim. Sch.
Playing Fields
STOCKTON ROAD
B6541
A66
NORTHERN ROUTE
A66
A19
A1032
LIVERTON AV.
AYRESOME
WEST LANE
WEST LANE HOSPITAL
LINTHORPE CEM
Showcase Cinema
Hollywood Bowl
Rainbow Casino
TEESSIDE LEISURE PARK
Stockton-on-Tees TS17
HAYDOCK PK. RD.
DRIVE
NEWMARKET AV.
SANDOWN
GOODWOOD
TEESSIDE SHOPPING PARK
GOODWOOD SQUARE
Old River Tees
STOCKTON-ON-TEES
MIDDLESBROUGH
MALDON ROAD
NORTHERN
MATTISON AV.
SPRINGFIELD ROAD
Pond
HARELLS RD.
BURLAM
HENLEY RD.
Thornberry Ct.
WESTBOURNE ROAD
HAMBLEDON
OXFORD
BARKER RD.
WHINNEY BANKS ROAD
ST. FRANCIS CL.
WEATHERHEAD AVENUE
FAIRFIELD AV.
CAMBRIDGE ROAD
STAINSBY ROAD
Comm. Cen.
Whinney Banks
Whinney Banks Prim. Schs. (Oaktree Cen.)
ACKLAM ROAD
THORNFIELD ROAD
S5
HARROW
ASHFORD AV.
FAKENHAM AV.
CRESCENT
PRICE AV.
PANNELL AV.
LEVICK
A1130
CROFT AVENUE
GREEN
Acklam
Acklam Park
Middlesbrough Cricket & Rugby
BUTTERMERE AV.
Lib.
ULLSWATER
CONISTON
HEATHER DR.
ACKLAM RD.
Maryfield House
Mandale Roundabout
MANDALE ROAD
A1130
CHALFORD OAKS DRIVE
ASTERLEY DRIVE
HEYTHROP DRIVE
RUSKIN AVENUE
Acklam Ct.
Anchorage M.
CHURCH
Acorn Cen.
Acklam Grange School
Playing Fields
Saphwood
The Fleet
99
Stainsby Hill Farm
YEARBY CL.
TRIMDON AVENUE
KADER AVENUE
130
West Plantation
Beck
Sub.
1
2
3
4
5
A
B
C
47
48
17
18
19

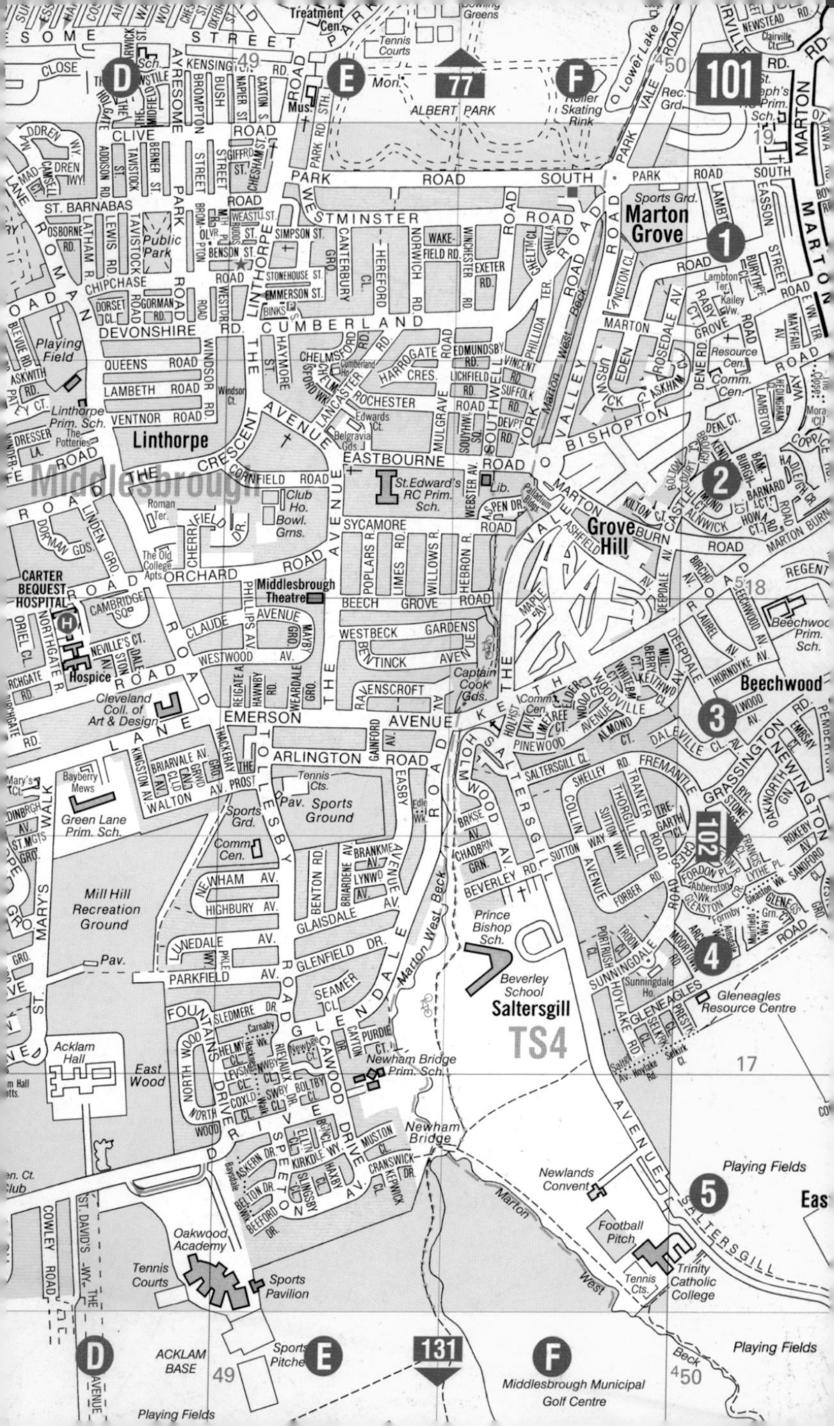
101
77
131
102
D
E
F
1
2
3
4
5
49
450
19
17
518
ALBERT PARK
Mon.
Mus.
Tennis Courts
Treatment Cen.
Bowling Greens
Roller Skating Rink
Rec. Grd.
Lower Lake
SOMERSET STREET
CLOSE
KENSINGTON RD.
AYRESOME
BROMPTON
BUSH
NAPIER ST.
CAXTON ST.
PARK ROAD SOUTH
PARK RD. NTH.
CLIVE ROAD
ADDISON RD.
TAVISTOCK ST.
BERNER ST.
PARK ROAD
STREET
CHESHAM ST.
GIFFORD ST.
ST. BARNABAS ROAD
OSBORNE RD.
LATHAM R.
LEWIS RD.
Public Park
BENSON ST.
SIMPSON ST.
STONEHOUSE ST.
EMMERSON ST.
WESTMINSTER ROAD
CANTERBURY GRO.
HEREFORD CL.
NORWICH RD.
WAKEFIELD RD.
WINCHESTER RD.
EXETER RD.
CHELTENHAM
ROMAN ROAD
CHIPCHASE ROAD
DORSET CL.
GORMAN RD.
DEVONSHIRE RD.
LINTHORPE ROAD
CUMBERLAND ROAD
Playing Field
QUEENS ROAD
LAMBETH ROAD
VENTNOR ROAD
WINDSOR RD.
Windsor Ct.
THE AVENUE
HAYMORE ST.
CHELMSFORD RD.
HARROGATE CRES.
EDMUNDSBY RD.
VINCENT RD.
LICHFIELD RD.
SUFFOLK RD.
ROCHESTER
LANCASTER RD.
MULGRAVE ROAD
SOUTHWELL RD.
YORK RD.
Marton West Beck
VALLEY ROAD
Linthorpe Prim. Sch.
Linthorpe
The Potteries
DRESSER LA.
THE CRESCENT
Middlesbrough
CORNFIELD ROAD
EASTBOURNE ROAD
St.Edward's RC Prim. Sch.
Lib.
WEBSTER AV.
ASPEN DR.
Club Ho.
Bowl. Grns.
Roman Ter.
CHERRYFIELD DR.
DORMAN GDS.
LINDEN GRO.
The Old College Apts.
ORCHARD ROAD
SYCAMORE ROAD
POPLARS R.
LIMES RD.
WILLOWS R.
HEBRON R.
CARTER BEQUEST HOSPITAL
CAMBRIDGE SQ.
Middlesbrough Theatre
BEECH GROVE ROAD
PHILLIPS AV.
AVENUE GRO.
MAYBY GRO.
CLAUDE
WESTBECK GARDENS
BENTINCK AVENUE
Captain Cook Gds.
RAVENSCROFT AV.
WESTWOOD AV.
REIGATE AV.
HAWNBY RD.
WEARDALE GRO.
NEVILLE'S CT.
Hospice
NORTHGATE R.
ORIEL CL.
Cleveland Coll. of Art & Design
GREEN LANE
EMERSON AVENUE
ARLINGTON ROAD
TOLLESBY ROAD
HACKERAY
GAINFORD AV.
EASBY
KINGSTON AV.
BRIARVALE AV.
WALTON AV.
PROST
Bayberry Mews
Green Lane Prim. Sch.
Tennis Cts.
Pav.
Sports Ground
Sports Grd.
Comm. Cen.
NEWHAM AV.
HIGHBURY AV.
BENTON RD.
BRIARDENE AV.
BRANKSOME AV.
GLAISDALE AV.
GLENFIELD DR.
LUNEDALE AV.
PARKFIELD AV.
Mill Hill Recreation Ground
Pav.
MARY'S WALK
SEAMER CL.
FOUNTAINS DRIVE
SLEDMERE DR.
NORTH WOOD
GLENDALE
CAWOOD DR.
PURDIE CT.
CAYTON DR.
RIEVAULX DR.
Newham Bridge Prim. Sch.
Newham Bridge
Acklam Hall
East Wood
DRIVE
SPEETON AV.
MUSTON CL.
CRANSWICK
KEPWICK DR.
ASKERN DR.
BELTON DR.
BEEFORD GR.
KIRKDALE WY.
SLINGSBY CL.
HAXBY CL.
ELLTON CL.
COWLEY ROAD
ST. DAVID'S WY.
THE AVENUE
Oakwood Academy
Tennis Courts
Sports Pavilion
Sports Pitches
ACKLAM BASE
Playing Fields
Middlesbrough Municipal Golf Centre
Marton West Beck
Newlands Convent
Football Pitch
Tennis Cts.
Trinity Catholic College
SALTERSGILL AVENUE
Playing Fields
Saltersgill
TS4
Beverley School
Prince Bishop Sch.
BEVERLEY RD.
CHADBRN GRN.
HOLMWOOD AV.
SALTERSGILL CL.
KEITH ROAD
THE VALE
PINEWOOD
ALMOND CT.
WOODVILLE AVENUE
Comm. Cen.
SHELLEY RD.
COLLIN AVENUE
SUTTON WAY
THORGILL CL.
TRANTER ROAD
FREMANTLE
GRASSINGTON RD.
OAKWORTH GN.
NEWINGTON
FORBER RD.
PORTRUSH CL.
TROON CL.
SUNNINGDALE
Sunningdale Ho.
HOYLAKE RD.
GLENEAGLES
Gleneagles Resource Centre
PRESTWICK
SELKIRK CL.
MOORTOWN RD.
Marton Grove
Sports Grd.
LAMBTON
EASSON STREET
MARTON ROAD
ROSEDALE AV.
EDEN
URSWICK CL.
ASKHAM CL.
MARTON GROVE ROAD
DENE RD.
Resource Cen.
Comm. Cen.
MAYFAIR AV.
BISHOPTON ROAD
DEAL CT.
BOLTON
KENDAL
BAMBURGH
BARNARD CT.
HADLEIGH CR.
ALNWICK
KILTON CT.
MARTON BURN ROAD
Grove Hill
ASHFIELD AV.
MAPLE AV.
DEEPDALE AV.
BIRCHO AV.
LAUREL AV.
BEECHWOOD AV.
Beechwood Prim. Sch.
Beechwood
THORNDYKE AV.
REGENT
DALEVILLE CL.
MULBERRY CT.
KEITHWOOD CL.
ROKEBY AV.
SANDFORD
GLENEGLES

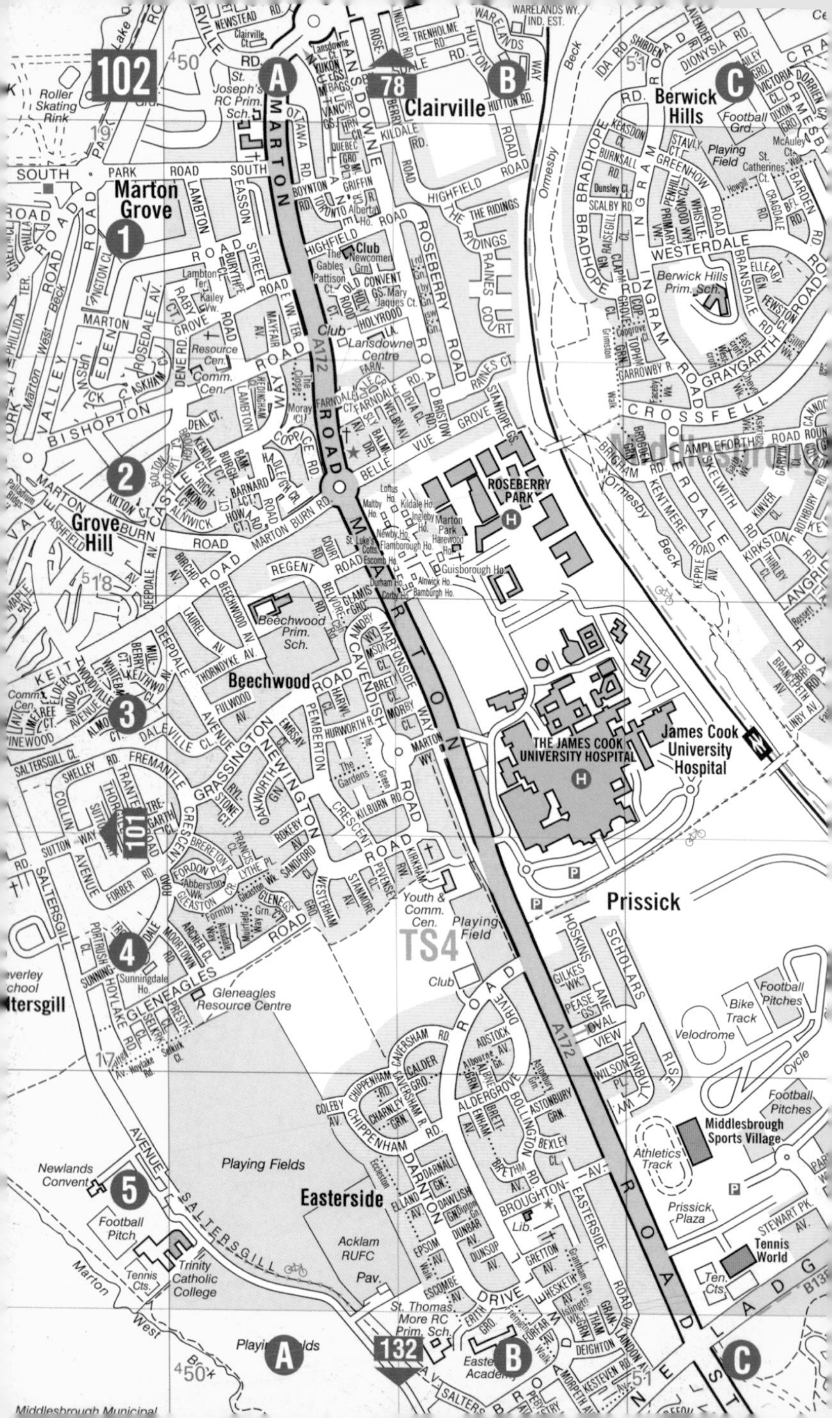

A
B
C
78
Clairville
Berwick Hills
Marton Grove
Grove Hill
Beechwood
Prissick
Easterside
TS4
1
2
3
4
5
101
132
Roller Skating Rink
St. Joseph's RC Prim. Sch.
WARELANDS WY. IND. EST.
NEWSTEAD RD.
MARTON ROAD
A172
LANSDOWNE ROAD
KILDALE RD.
HIGHFIELD ROAD
THE RIDINGS
RAINES COURT
ROSEBERRY ROAD
SOUTH PARK ROAD
LAMBTON ROAD
EASSON STREET
Ormesby Beck
BRADHOPE RD.
INGRAM ROAD
GREENHOW ROAD
WESTERDALE
Berwick Hills Prim. Sch.
Football Grd.
Playing Field
St. Catherines Ct.
BRANSDALE RD.
GRAYGARTH ROAD
CROSSFELL ROAD
Middlesbrough
KEPPLE AV.
KIRKSTONE RD.
Club
Lansdowne Centre
Resource Cen.
Comm. Cen.
BISHOPTON ROAD
MARTON BURN RD.
BELLE VUE GROVE
ROSEBERRY PARK
REGENT
Beechwood Prim. Sch.
THORNDYKE AV.
CAVENDISH ROAD
THE JAMES COOK UNIVERSITY HOSPITAL
James Cook University Hospital
GRASSINGTON CRESCENT
NEWINGTON ROAD
FREMANTLE
SALTERSGILL AVENUE
Youth & Comm. Cen.
Playing Field
GLENEAGLES ROAD
Gleneagles Resource Centre
HOYLAKE RD.
Football Pitches
Bike Track
Velodrome
Middlesbrough Sports Village
Athletics Track
Prissick Plaza
Tennis World
STEWART PK. AV.
CHIPPENHAM RD.
CAVERSHAM RD.
ALDERGROVE
BOLLINGTON RD.
BROUGHTON AV.
EASTERSIDE ROAD
Lib.
Playing Fields
Acklam RUFC
Pav.
Newlands Convent
Football Pitch
Trinity Catholic College
Tennis Cts.
Marton West Beck
St. Thomas More RC Prim. Sch.
Easterside Academy
Playing Fields
LADGATE LANE
B1380
Middlesbrough Municipal

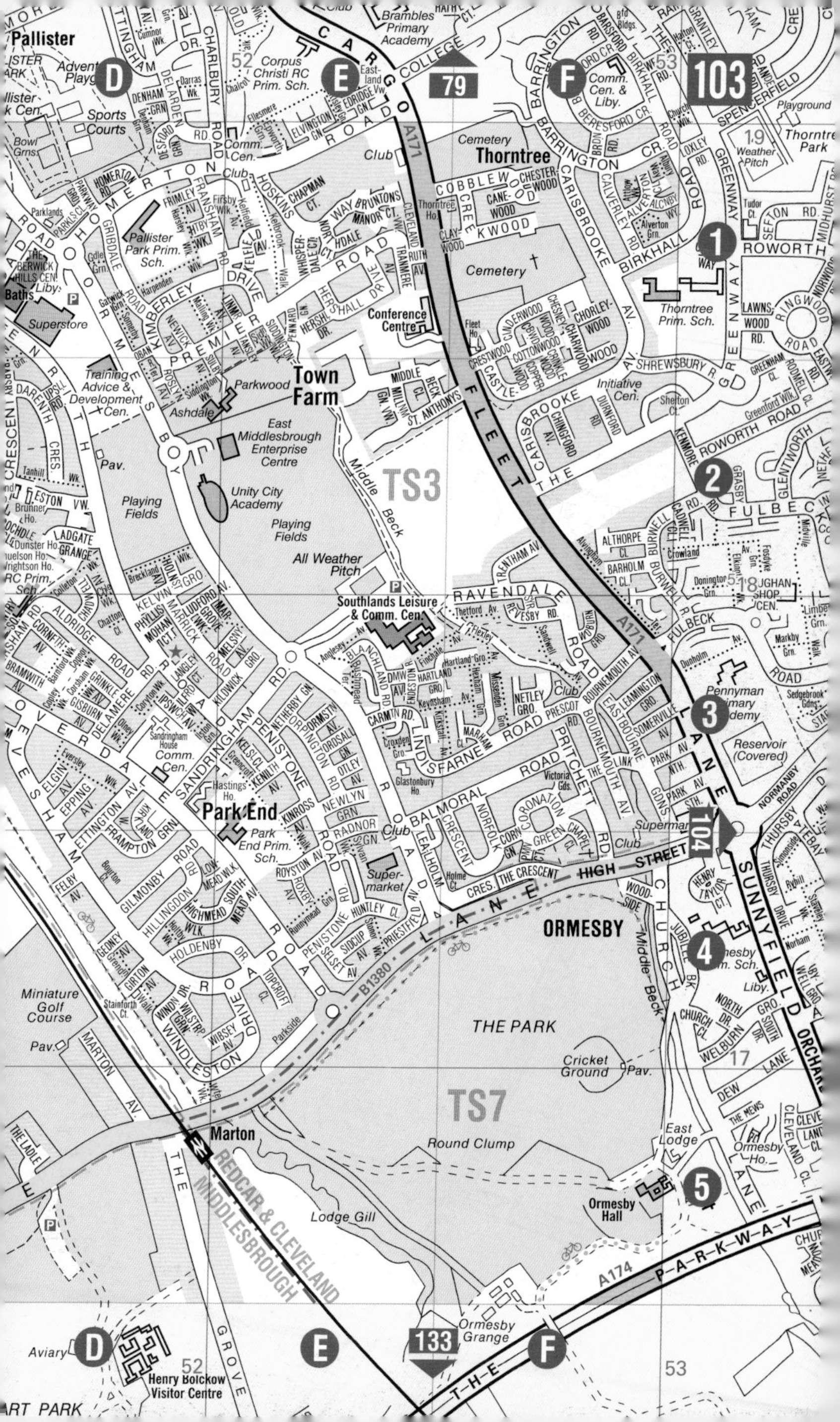
Pallister
Adventure Playground
Sports Courts
Bowl Grns.
Brambles Primary Academy
Corpus Christi RC Prim. Sch.
Comm. Cen. & Liby.
79
Cemetery
Thorntree
Thorntree Park
Weather Pitch
Playground
CARGO FLEET
COLLEGE ROAD
A171
HOMERTON ROAD
BARRINGTON CR.
CARISBROOKE AV.
BIRKHALL ROAD
ROWORTH ROAD
SPENCERFIELD
GREENWAY
Pallister Park Prim. Sch.
Superstore
Baths
Training Advice & Development Cen.
Parkwood
Ashdale
Town Farm
Conference Centre
East Middlesbrough Enterprise Centre
Unity City Academy
Playing Fields
All Weather Pitch
Southlands Leisure & Comm. Cen.
TS3
Thorntree Prim. Sch.
Initiative Cen.
Pennyman Primary Academy
Reservoir (Covered)
FULBECK ROAD
RAVENDALE ROAD
PREMIER ROAD
KIMBERLEY
SANDRINGHAM RD.
PENISTONE ROAD
BALMORAL ROAD
LINDISFARNE ROAD
PRESCOT ROAD
Sandringham House Comm. Cen.
Park End
Park End Prim. Sch.
Supermarket
Club
104
HIGH STREET
LANE
B1380
SUNNYFIELD
ORMESBY
Ormesby Prim. Sch.
Liby.
Middle Beck
THE PARK
Cricket Ground
Pav.
TS7
Round Clump
East Lodge
Ormesby Hall
Ormesby Ho.
Lodge Gill
Miniature Golf Course
Marton
REDCAR & CLEVELAND
MIDDLESBROUGH
A174
THE PARKWAY
133
Ormesby Grange
Aviary
Henry Bolckow Visitor Centre
ART PARK
THE GROVE
MARTON AV.
D
E
F
52
53
1
2
3
4
5
17
18
19

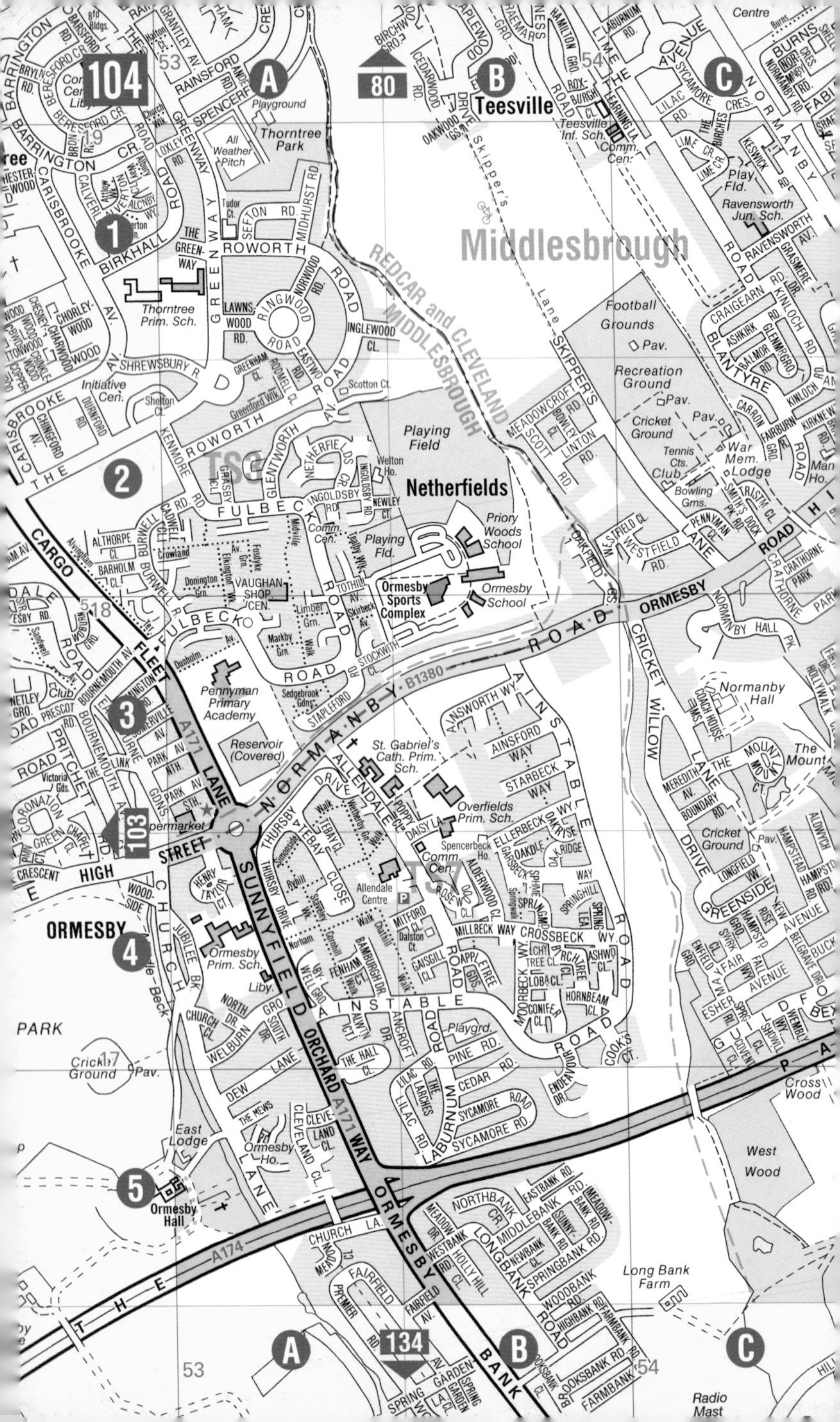

80
A
B
C
Teesville
Middlesbrough
Netherfields
ORMESBY
Thorntree Park
All Weather Pitch
Playground
Thorntree Prim. Sch.
Teesville Inf. Sch.
Comm. Cen.
Play Fld.
Ravensworth Jun. Sch.
Football Grounds
Recreation Ground
Cricket Ground
Tennis Cts.
Club
Bowling Grns.
War Mem. Lodge
Man Ho.
Pav.
Playing Field
Playing Fld.
Priory Woods School
Ormesby Sports Complex
Ormesby School
Welton Ho.
Scotton Ct.
Initiative Cen.
VAUGHAN SHOP. CEN.
Pennyman Primary Academy
Reservoir (Covered)
St. Gabriel's Cath. Prim. Sch.
Overfields Prim. Sch.
Spencerbeck Ho.
Allendale Centre
Ormesby Prim. Sch.
Liby.
Normanby Hall
The Mount
Supermarket
Cricket Ground
East Lodge
Ormesby Ho.
Ormesby Hall
PARK
Cross Wood
West Wood
Long Bank Farm
Radio Mast
REDCAR and CLEVELAND
MIDDLESBROUGH
TS3
TS7
A171
A174
B1380
1
2
3
4
5
53
54
18
17
19
103
134
BARRINGTON RD.
BARRINGTON CR.
CARISBROOKE AV.
BIRKHALL ROAD
GREENWAY
THE GREENWAY
ROWORTH ROAD
SEFTON RD.
MIDHURST RD.
RINGWOOD ROAD
NORWOOD
LAWNS WOOD RD.
INGLEWOOD CL.
SHREWSBURY R.
KENMORE
FULBECK ROAD
GLENTWORTH
NETHERFIELDS CR.
INGOLDSBY RD.
NEWLEY CT.
ALTHORPE CL.
BARHOLM CL.
BURWELL RD.
CARGO FLEET LANE
SKIPPER'S LANE
Skipper's Lane
MEADOWCROFT
SCOTT CL.
LINTON RD.
OAKFIELD CL.
WESTFIELD CL.
WESTFIELD RD.
PENNYMAN LANE
ORMESBY ROAD
NORMANBY ROAD
BLANTYRE RD.
KINLOCH RD.
CARRON
FAIRBURN
CRAIGEARN RD.
RAVENSWORTH AV.
THE AVENUE
LIME RD.
LILAC
SYCAMORE
THE BIRCHES
NORMANBY HALL PK.
CRICKET WILLOW LANE
CRATHORNE PARK
NORMANBY ROAD
AINSWORTH WY.
AINSFORD WAY
STARBECK WAY
AINSTABLE ROAD
ALLENDALE
DAISY LA.
ELLERBECK WY.
OAKRISE
OAKRIDGE
CROSSBECK WY.
MILLBECK WAY
HORNBEAM CL.
CONIFER CL.
COOK'S CT.
ENDEAVOUR DR.
THURSBY DRIVE
TEBAY CL.
CLOSE
MITFORD
FENHAM
BAMBURGH DR.
ANCROFT DR.
PINE RD.
CEDAR RD.
SYCAMORE ROAD
SYCAMORE RD.
LABURNUM RD.
LILAC RD.
THE LARCHES
THE HALL CL.
HIGH STREET
SUNNYFIELD
ORCHARD WAY
JUBILEE BK.
CHURCH LANE
CHURCH CL.
WELBURN
DEW LANE
THE MEWS
CLEVELAND CL.
CLEVE-LAND CL.
ORMESBY BANK
NORTHBANK CR.
EASTBANK RD.
MIDDLEBANK RD.
LONGBANK ROAD
SPRINGBANK RD.
WOODBANK RD.
HIGHBANK RD.
BROOKSBANK RD.
FARMBANK RD.
FAIRFIELD AV.
PREMIER RD.
SPRING GARDEN LA.
THE PARKWAY
MEREDITH AV.
BOUNDARY RD.
GREENSIDE
LONGFIELD
AVENUE
BELGRAVE DR.
MAYFAIR AV.
GUILDFORD
ESHER
CORONATION
PRITCHETT ROAD
BOURNEMOUTH AV.
PRESCOT RD.
CRESCENT
ORMESBY CRESCENT

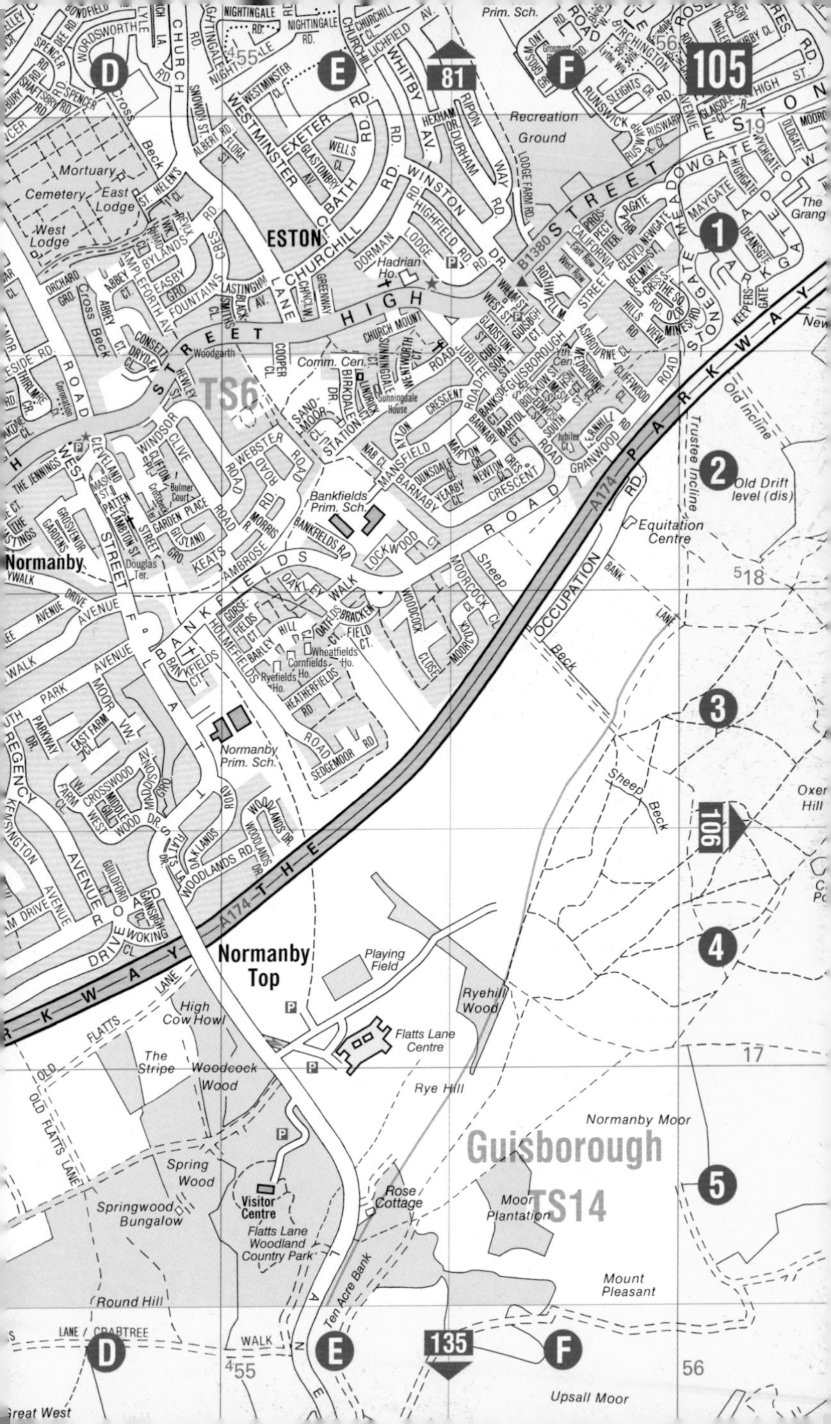
ESTON
Normanby
Normanby Top
TS6
Guisborough
TS14
HIGH STREET
B1380
ESTON
A174
THE PARKWAY
Recreation Ground
Cemetery
Mortuary
East Lodge
West Lodge
Hadrian Ho.
Comm. Cen.
Sunningdale House
Bankfields Prim. Sch.
Normanby Prim. Sch.
Bulmer Court
Douglas Ter.
Woodgarth
Yth. Cen.
Jubilee Ct.
Equitation Centre
Old Drift level (dis)
Old Incline
Trustee Incline
Sheep Beck
Wheatfields Ho.
Cornfields Ho.
Ryefields Ho.
Playing Field
Ryehill Wood
Flatts Lane Centre
Rye Hill
High Cow Howl
The Stripe
Woodcock Wood
Spring Wood
Springwood Bungalow
Visitor Centre
Flatts Lane Woodland Country Park
Rose Cottage
Ten Acre Bank
Normanby Moor
Moor Plantation
Mount Pleasant
Round Hill
Upsall Moor
Great West
Oxen Hill
Prim. Sch.
CHURCH LANE
WESTMINSTER RD.
CHURCHILL RD.
WHITBY AV.
OCCUPATION RD.
BANK LANE
FLATTS LANE
OLD FLATTS LANE
CRABTREE WALK
BANKFIELDS ROAD
FLATTS LANE
CLEVELAND STREET
D
E
F
D
E
F
1
2
3
4
5
81
106
135
455
455
56
56
518
519
17

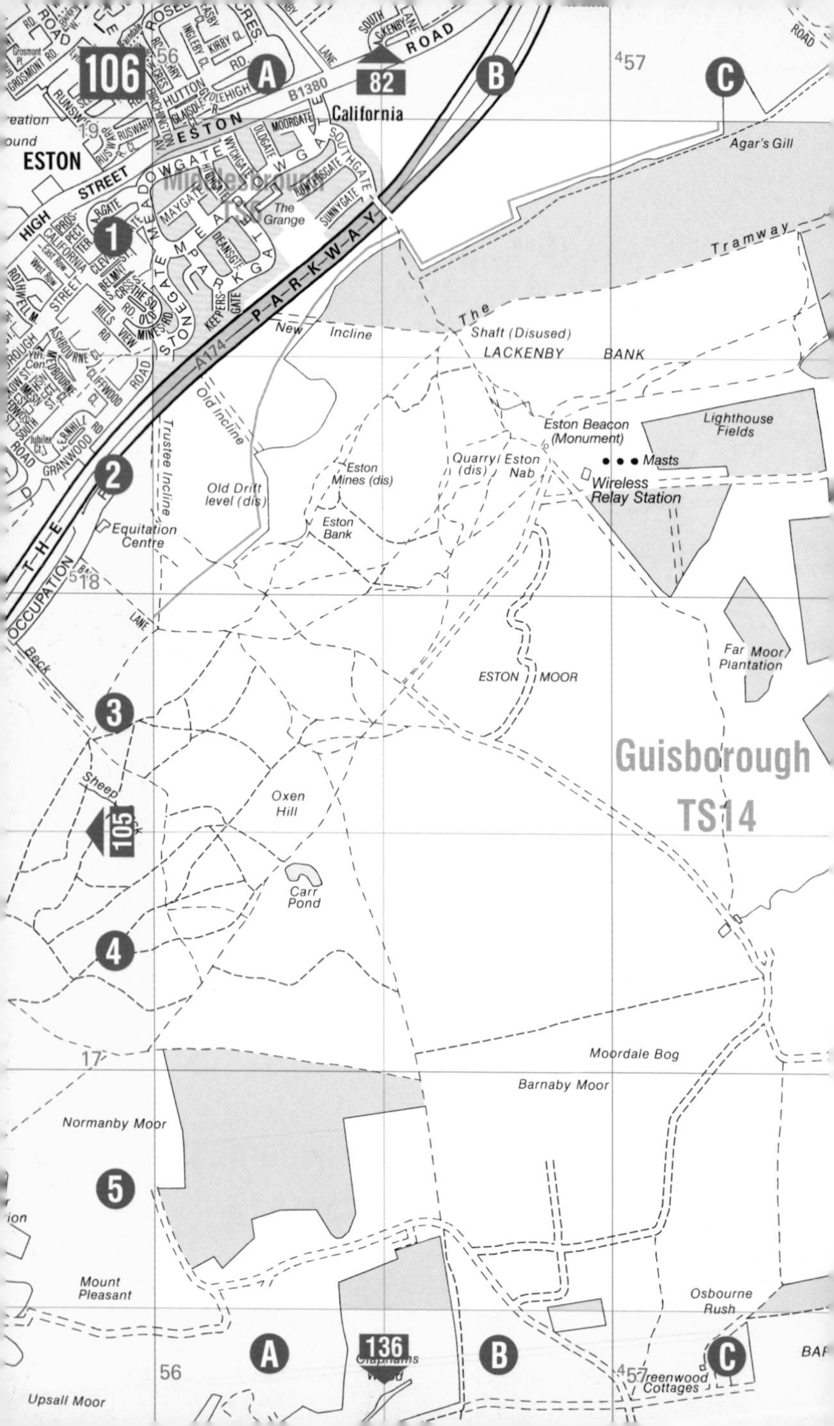
106
82
105
136
A
B
C
1
2
3
4
5
ESTON
HIGH STREET
California
B1380
ROAD
Middlesbrough TS6
The Grange
THE PARKWAY
A174
OCCUPATION LANE
Agar's Gill
Tramway
The New Incline
Shaft (Disused)
LACKENBY BANK
Old Incline
Trustee Incline
Old Drift level (dis)
Eston Mines (dis)
Eston Bank
Quarry (dis)
Eston Nab
Eston Beacon (Monument)
Masts
Wireless Relay Station
Lighthouse Fields
Far Moor Plantation
ESTON MOOR
Guisborough TS14
Equitation Centre
Beck
Sheep
Oxen Hill
Carr Pond
Moordale Bog
Barnaby Moor
Normanby Moor
Mount Pleasant
Osbourne Rush
Greenwood Cottages
Upsall Moor
MEADOWGATE
STONEGATE
PARKGATE
MAYGATE
DEANSGATE
KEEPERS GATE
HIGHGATE
WYCHGATE
OLDGATE
MOORGATE
SOUTHGATE
SUNNYGATE
RUNSWICK
RUSWARP
BIRCHINGTON AV.
HUTTON
GLAISDALE
INGLEBY CL.
KIRBY CL.
CALIFORNIA
STREET
ROTHWELL M.
ASHBOURNE CL.
MELBOURNE
CLIFFWOOD CL.
GRANWOOD RD.
FERNHILL
Jubilee Ct.
HILLS RD.
VIEW
MINES RD.
OLD
THE SQ.
BELMONT
CLEVE ST.
PROSPECT TER.
GROSMONT RD.
Grosmont Pl.
SOUTH LANE
LACKENBY
ROAD
19
18
17
56
457

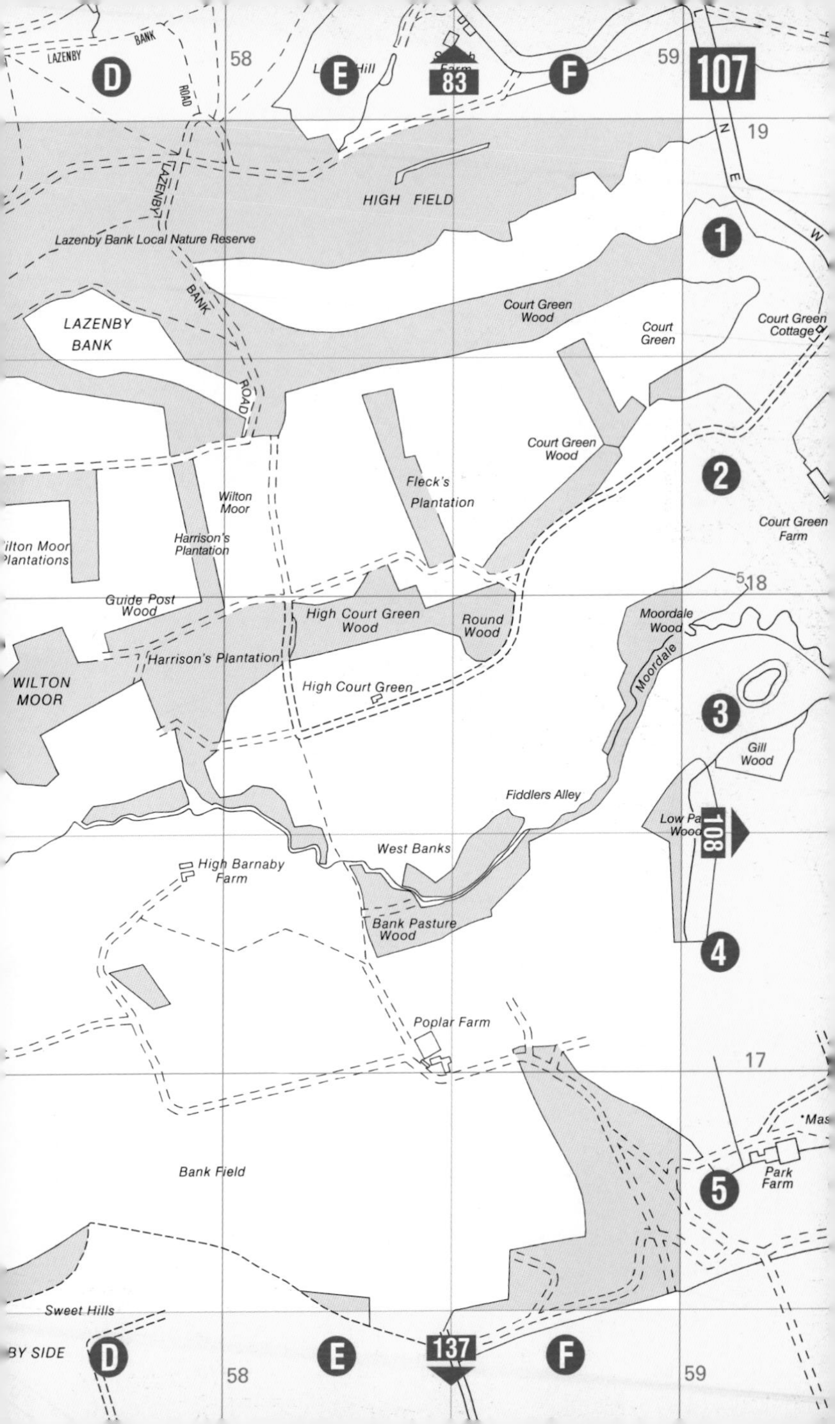
LAZENBY
BANK
ROAD
58
59
D
E
F
83
19
HIGH FIELD
LAZENBY
Lazenby Bank Local Nature Reserve
BANK
LAZENBY BANK
Court Green Wood
Court Green
Court Green Cottage
ROAD
Fleck's Plantation
Court Green Wood
Wilton Moor
Harrison's Plantation
Court Green Farm
Guide Post Wood
High Court Green Wood
Round Wood
18
Moordale Wood
Moordale
Harrison's Plantation
WILTON MOOR
High Court Green
1
2
3
4
5
Gill Wood
Fiddlers Alley
108
West Banks
High Barnaby Farm
Bank Pasture Wood
Poplar Farm
17
Park Farm
Bank Field
Sweet Hills
BY SIDE
D
E
137
F
58
59

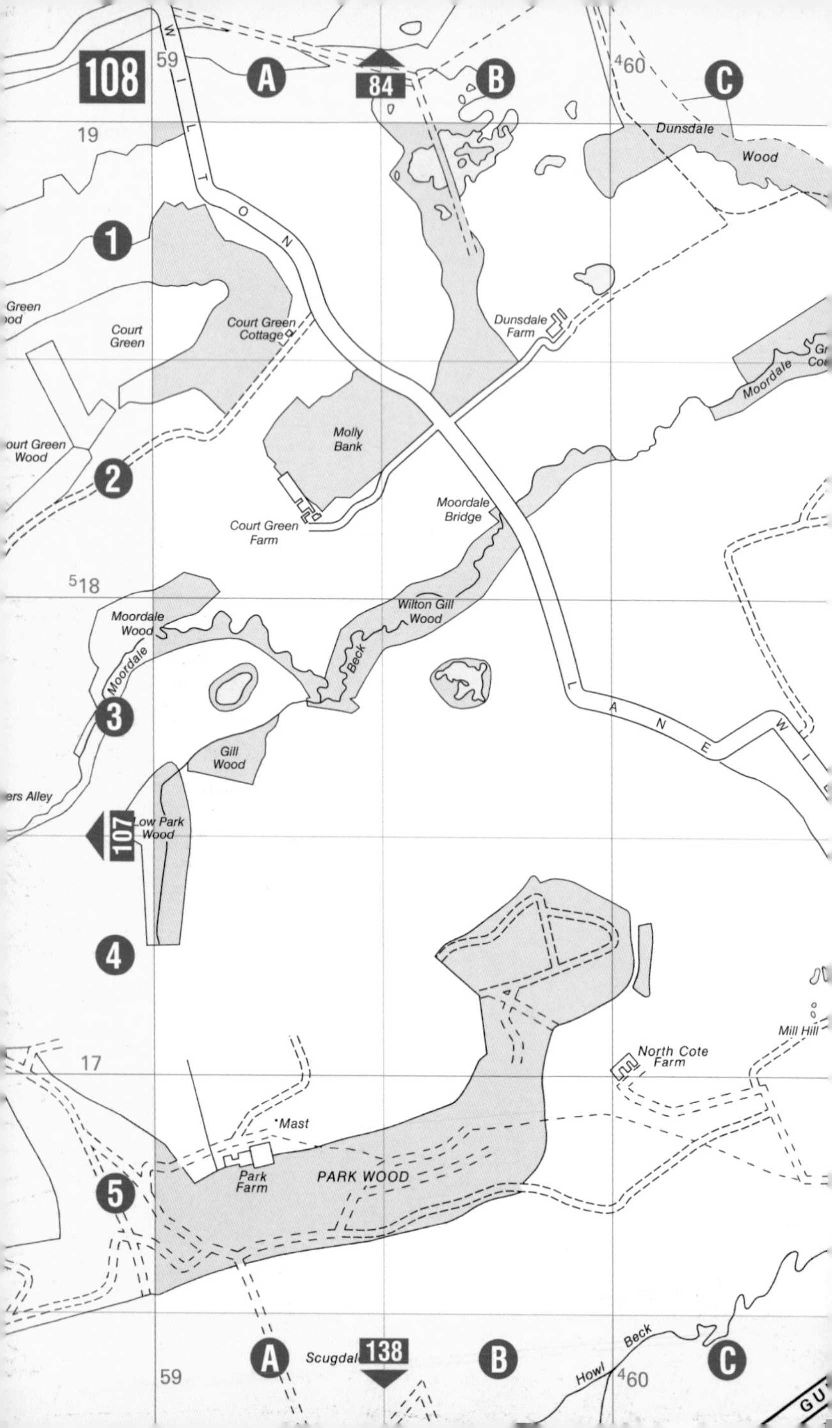
59
A
84
B
4 60
C
19
Dunsdale
Wood
WILTON
1
Green
Wood
Court
Green
Court Green
Cottage
Dunsdale
Farm
Moordale
Court Green
Wood
2
Molly
Bank
Moordale
Bridge
Court Green
Farm
5 18
Moordale
Wood
Wilton Gill
Wood
Beck
Moordale
3
LANE
Gill
Wood
ers Alley
107
Low Park
Wood
4
Mill Hill
North Cote
Farm
17
Mast
Park
Farm
PARK WOOD
5
A
Scugdale
138
B
Beck
Howl
C
59
4 60

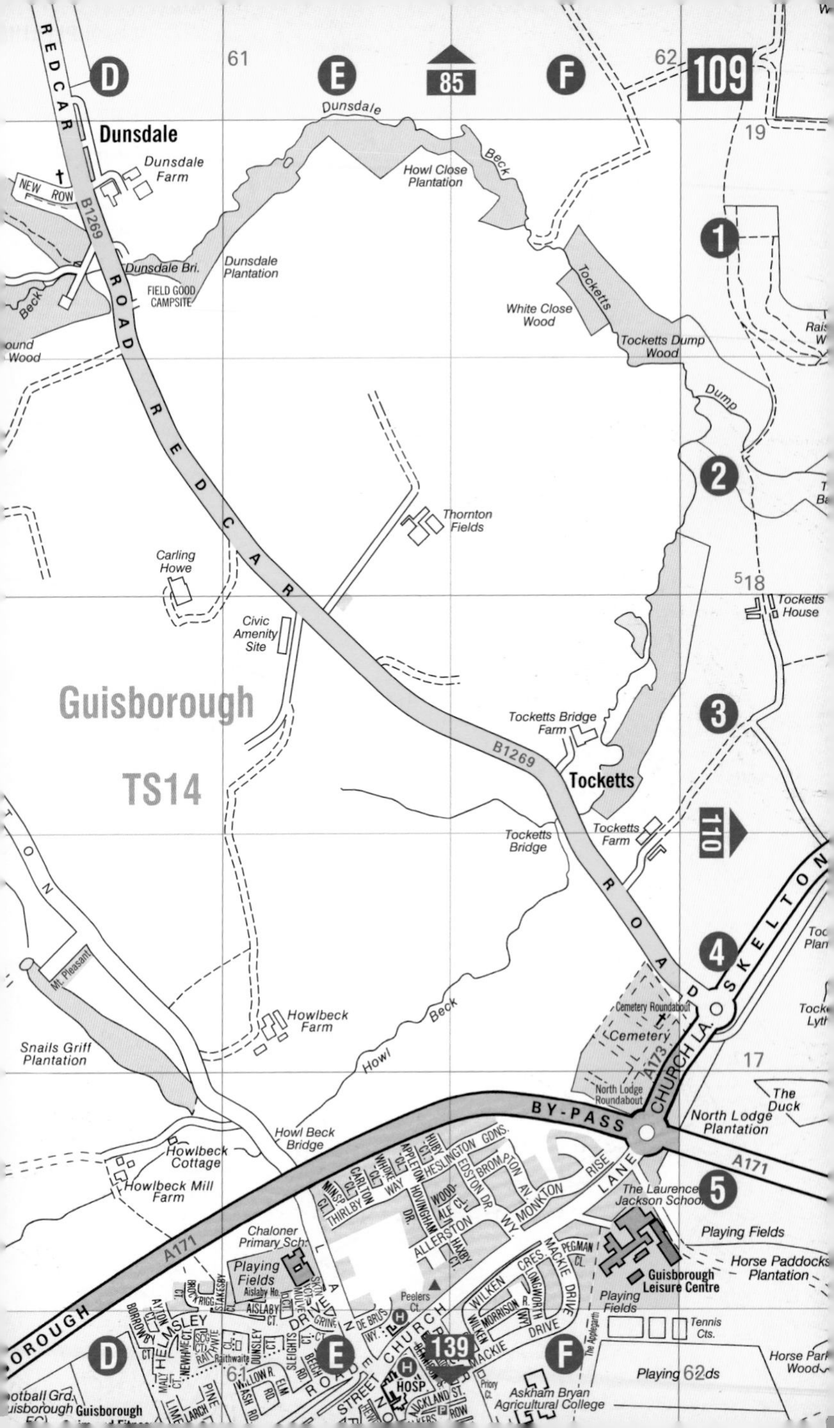

109
85
D
E
F
61
62
19
18
17
1
2
3
4
5
110
139
Dunsdale
Dunsdale Farm
Dunsdale Beck
Howl Close Plantation
NEW ROW
B1269
REDCAR ROAD
Dunsdale Bri.
Dunsdale Plantation
FIELD GOOD CAMPSITE
Beck
Tocketts
White Close Wood
Tocketts Dump Wood
Dump
Thornton Fields
Carling Howe
Civic Amenity Site
Guisborough
TS14
Tocketts House
Tocketts Bridge Farm
Tocketts
Tocketts Farm
Tocketts Bridge
Mt. Pleasant
Snails Griff Plantation
Howlbeck Farm
Howl Beck
Cemetery Roundabout
Cemetery
A173
CHURCH LA.
SKELTON
North Lodge Roundabout
BY-PASS
The Duck
North Lodge Plantation
A171
Howl Beck Bridge
Howlbeck Cottage
Howlbeck Mill Farm
The Laurence Jackson School
Playing Fields
Horse Paddocks Plantation
Guisborough Leisure Centre
Tennis Cts.
Horse Park Wood
Askham Bryan Agricultural College
Chaloner Primary Sch.
Peelers Ct.
HOSP.
Priory Ct.
GUISBOROUGH
Guisborough
HESLINGTON GDNS.
BROMPTON AV.
MONKTON RISE
LANE
ALLERSTON
WILKEN CRES.
LONGWORTH
MACKIE DRIVE
PEGMAN CL.
MORRISON R.
CHURCH
ROAD
STREET
HELMSLEY
LARCH
PINE
ELM
ASH RD.
WILLOW R.
DUNSLEY
SLEIGHTS
AISLABY CT.
Aislaby Ho.
STAKESBY
THIRLBY
CARLTON CL.
HOVINGHAM DR.
WOODALE CL.
EDSTON DR.
HUBY CT.
APPLETON

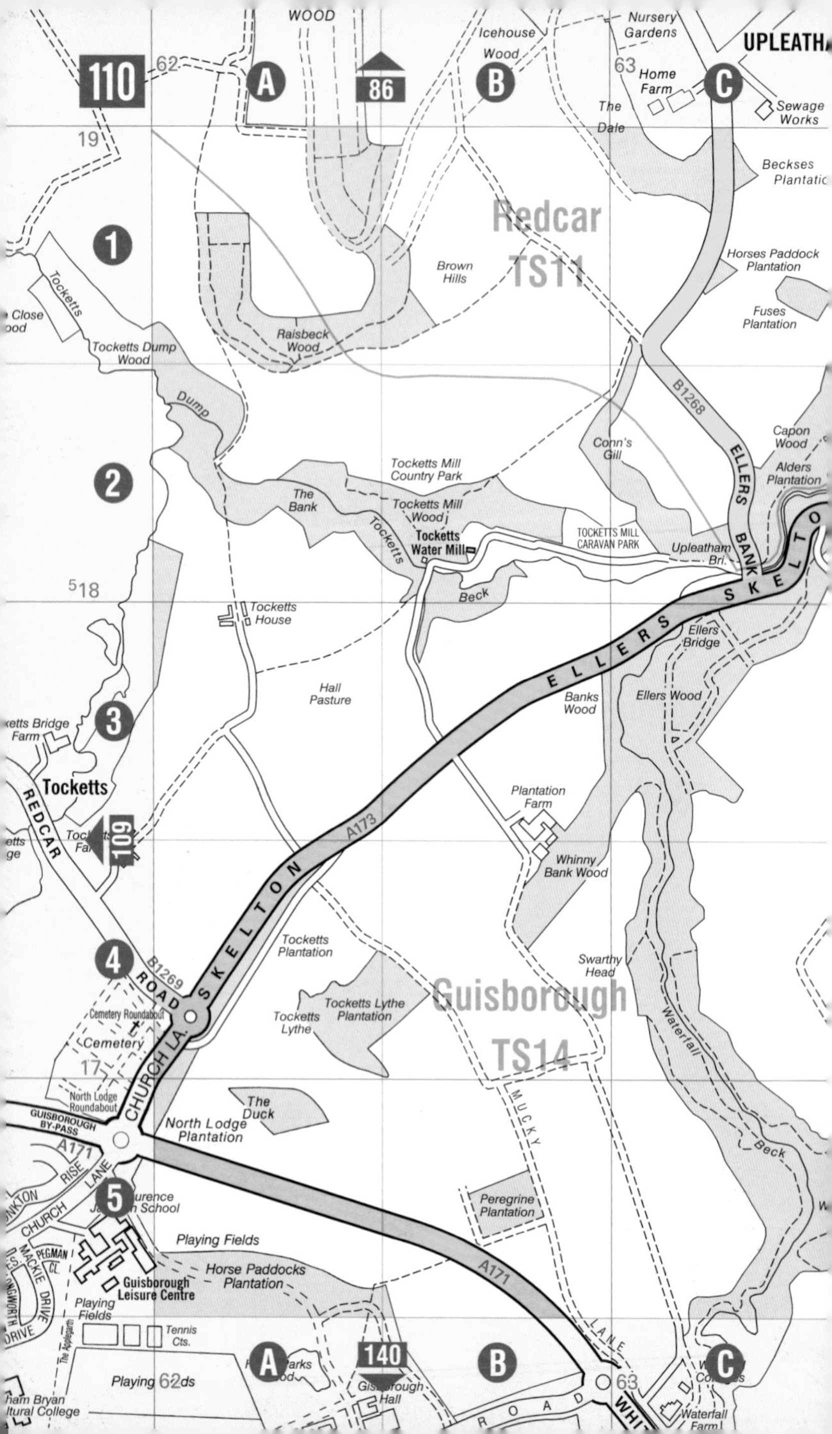

110
86
109
140
A
B
C
1
2
3
4
5
62
63
19
18
17
UPLEATHAM
WOOD
Icehouse Wood
Nursery Gardens
Home Farm
The Dale
Sewage Works
Beckses Plantation
Redcar TS11
Brown Hills
Raisbeck Wood
Horses Paddock Plantation
Fuses Plantation
Tocketts
Tocketts Dump Wood
Dump
B1268
ELLERS BANK
Capon Wood
Alders Plantation
Conn's Gill
Tocketts Mill Country Park
The Bank
Tocketts Mill Wood
Tocketts Water Mill
TOCKETTS MILL CARAVAN PARK
Upleatham Bri.
Beck
Tocketts House
SKELTON
ELLERS
Ellers Bridge
Hall Pasture
Banks Wood
Ellers Wood
Tocketts
REDCAR
Plantation Farm
A173
Whinny Bank Wood
Tocketts Plantation
Swarthy Head
B1269
ROAD
Tocketts Lythe Plantation
Tocketts Lythe
Guisborough TS14
Waterfall
Cemetery Roundabout
Cemetery
CHURCH LA.
North Lodge Roundabout
GUISBOROUGH BY-PASS
A171
The Duck
North Lodge Plantation
MUCKY
RISE
LANE
CHURCH
Beck
Peregrine Plantation
Playing Fields
PEGMAN CL.
MACKIE DRIVE
DRIVE
Guisborough Leisure Centre
Horse Paddocks Plantation
A171
Playing Fields
Tennis Cts.
The Applegarth
LANE
Playing Fields
Gisborough Hall
ROAD
Waterfall Farm

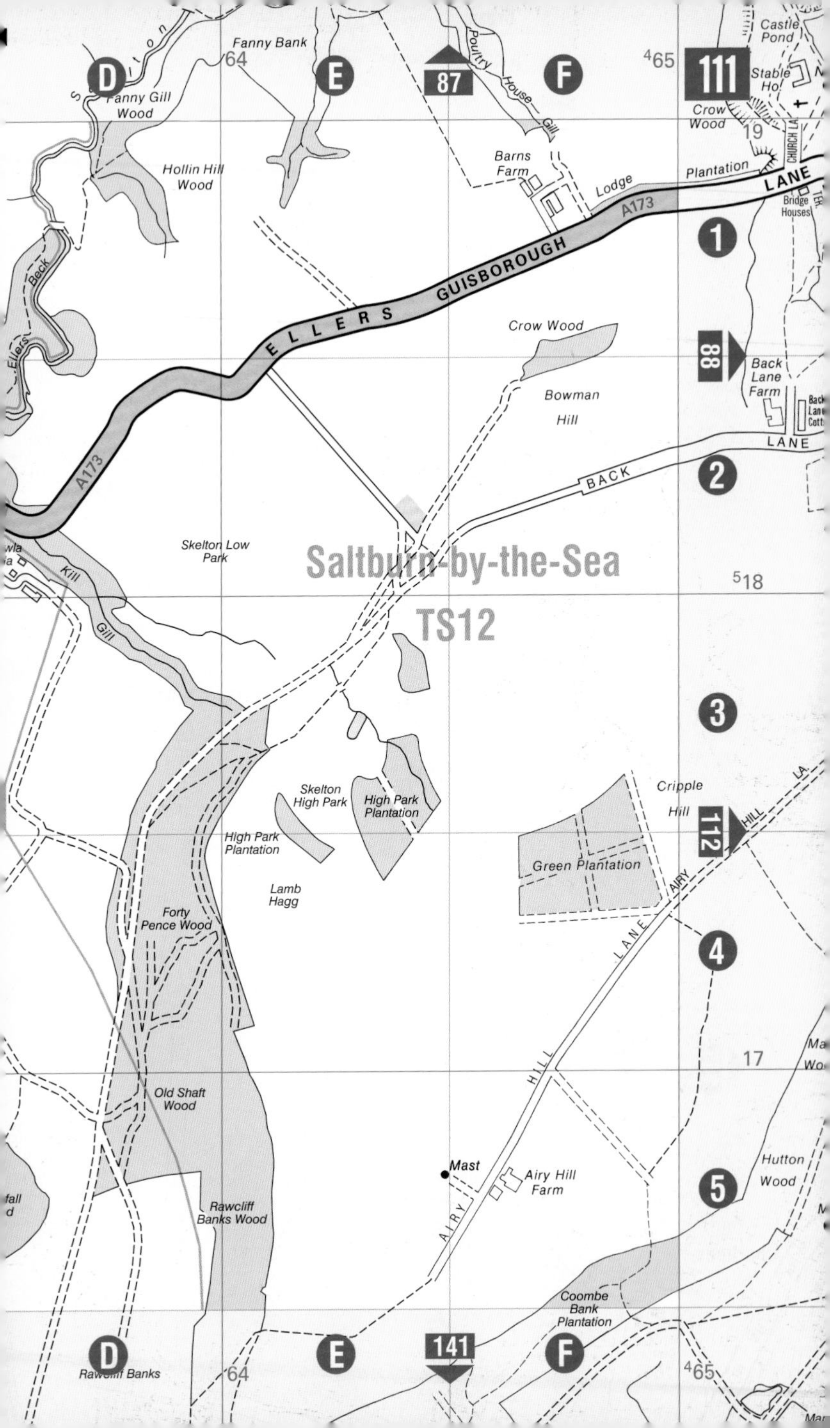
111
87
88
112
141
D
E
F
1
2
3
4
5
64
465
518
19
17
Saltburn-by-the-Sea
TS12
Fanny Bank
Fanny Gill Wood
Hollin Hill Wood
Poultry House Gill
Barns Farm
Lodge
Plantation
Castle Pond
Stable Ho
Crow Wood
CHURCH LA
LANE
A173
Bridge Houses
ELLERS GUISBOROUGH
Ellers Beck
Crow Wood
Bowman Hill
Back Lane Farm
BACK LANE
Skelton Low Park
Kill Gill
Skelton High Park
High Park Plantation
High Park Plantation
Lamb Hagg
Cripple Hill
Green Plantation
AIRY HILL LA
AIRY HILL LANE
Forty Pence Wood
Old Shaft Wood
Mast
Airy Hill Farm
Rawcliff Banks Wood
Hutton Wood
Coombe Bank Plantation
Rawcliff Banks

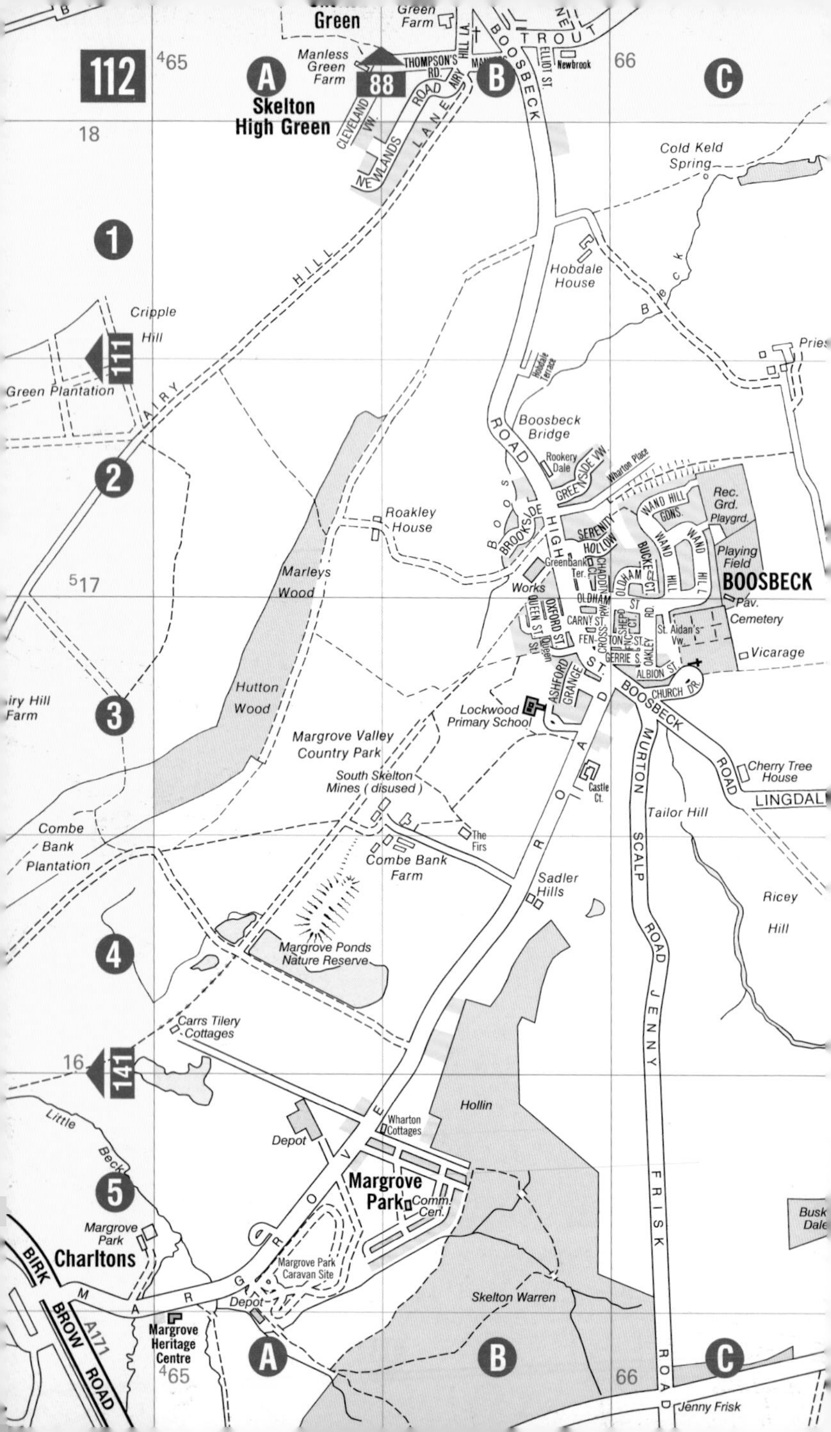
Green
Green Farm
TROUT
Manless Green Farm
THOMPSON'S RD.
88
MANLESS
ELLIOT ST.
Newbrook
465
66
A
B
C
Skelton High Green
CLEVELAND VW.
ROAD
AIRY
HILL LA.
BOOSBECK
18
NEWLANDS LANE
Cold Keld Spring
1
HILL
Hobdale House
Beck
Cripple Hill
111
Green Plantation
AIRY
Hobdale Terrace
Pries
Boosbeck Bridge
ROAD
2
Rookery Dale
GREENSIDE VW.
Wharton Place
Roakley House
Boos
BROOKSIDE
HIGH
SERENITY
HOLLOW
WAND HILL GDNS.
Rec. Grd.
Playgrd.
Playing Field
Marleys Wood
517
Greenbank Ter.
Works
CHADDIN CL.
OLDHAM CT.
BUCKE CL.
WAND HILL
BOOSBECK
OLDHAM
QUEEN ST.
OXFORD ST.
CARNY ST.
FEN-TON
CROSS RW.
SHEPD CT.
ST.
RD.
OAKLEY
Pav.
Cemetery
St. Aidan's Vw.
Vicarage
GERRIE S.
ALBION ST.
Queen St.
ST.
Airy Hill Farm
Hutton Wood
3
ASHFORD
GRANGE
BOOSBECK
CHURCH DR.
Lockwood Primary School
Margrove Valley Country Park
MURTON
ROAD
Cherry Tree House
South Skelton Mines (disused)
Castle Ct.
LINGDALE
Tailor Hill
Combe Bank Plantation
The Firs
Combe Bank Farm
Sadler Hills
SCALP
Ricey Hill
4
Margrove Ponds Nature Reserve
ROAD
JENNY
Carrs Tilery Cottages
16
141
Hollin
Little Beck
Depot
Wharton Cottages
FRISK
5
Margrove Park
Comm. Cen.
Busk Dale
Margrove Park
Charltons
Margrove Park Caravan Site
BIRK BROW ROAD
A171
MARGROVE
Depot
Skelton Warren
Margrove Heritage Centre
465
66
ROAD
Jenny Frisk

113
89
114
D
E
F
1
2
3
4
5
67
68
18
17
16
Works
East Pastures
Cotts.
Wet Furrows Farm
STANGHOW
Paddock House
Gallops
Hill Croft
Saltburn-by-the-Sea
TS12
CLAPHOW RESERVOIR
CLAPHOW WHIN
Green Hills Farm
Groundhills Farm
Claphow
LANE
LINGDALE
Depot
Moorcock Row
HIGH ROAD
Recreation Ground
BARMET IND. EST.
KILTON
BELLWOOD AV.
WILKINSON ST.
WILSON ST.
Lingdale Head
Ricey Park
Eskdale Ter.
Rosedale Gds.
LINGDALE IND. EST.
Farndale Gardens
Prospect Pl.
AVON CT.
MEADOW DALE CT.
Hall
Meml.
STONEHOUSE IND. EST.
Whitwell Pl.
LITTLE MOORSHOLM LANE
KILTON LA.
PROSPECT
SANDHME
CATHERINE S.
PEASE ST.
COCKBURN
KIRKBRI
DAVISON
CEDARHURST
DR.
BEECHCROFT CL.
Dale Ter.
Lingdale Prim. Sch.
ROAD
Football Ground
WINDSOR DR.
SANDRINGHAM
BALMORAL
Little Moorsholm
Cricket Field
Pav.
Well Farm
Great C Hi
Low House
Stanghow House
Hun
STANGHOW ROAD
LOW STANGHOW
Seaton Hill House
Seaton Hill
Seaton Ter.
Stanghow
Stanghow Ridge
Butts Hill

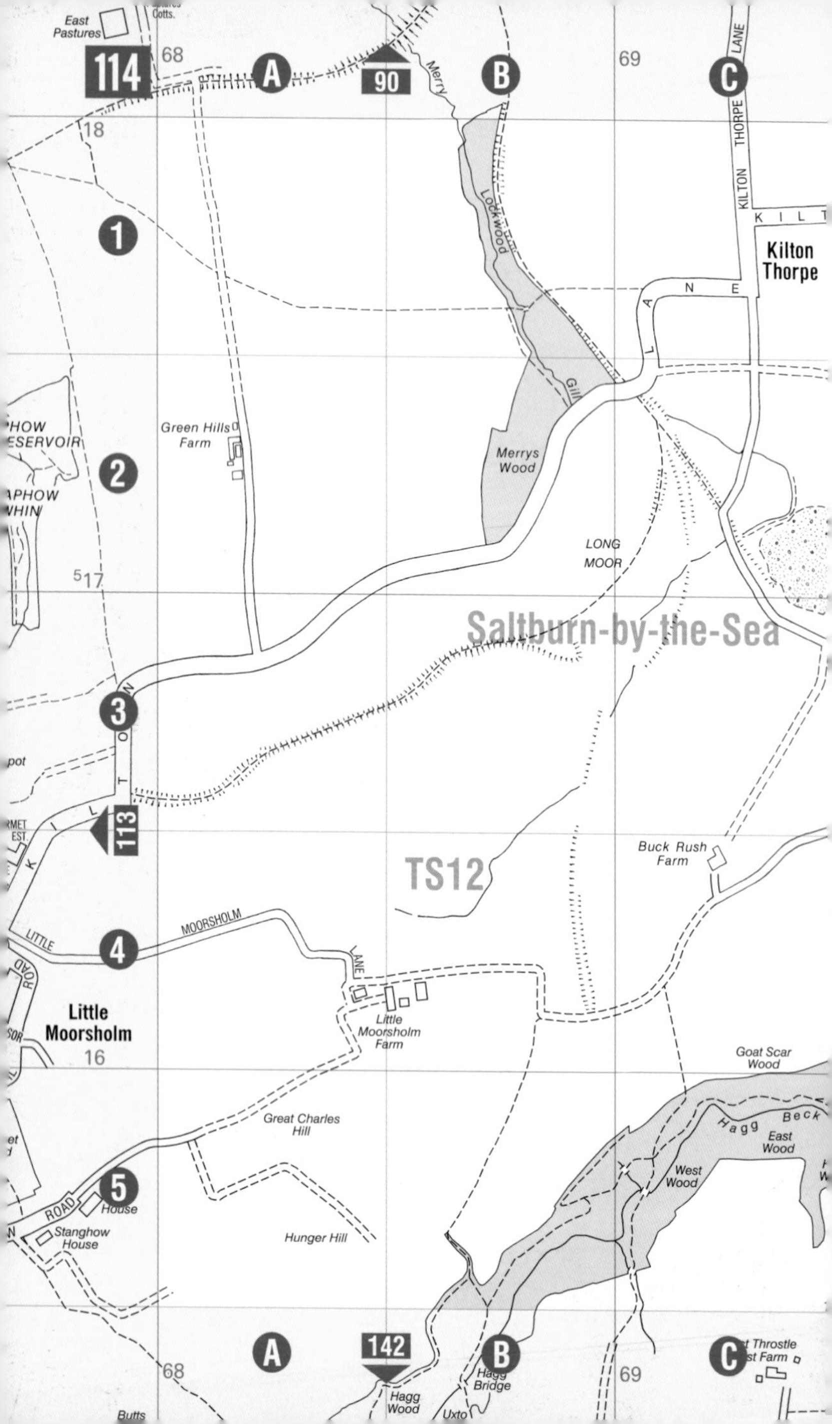
East Pastures
Cotts.
114
68
69
A
B
C
90
Merry
KILTON THORPE LANE
KILT
Kilton Thorpe
LANE
18
1
Lockwood
Gill
Green Hills Farm
Merrys Wood
PHOW
ESERVOIR
2
APHOW
WHIN
LONG MOOR
517
Saltburn-by-the-Sea
3
KILTON
pot
113
TS12
Buck Rush Farm
4
LITTLE
MOORSHOLM
LANE
ROAD
Little Moorsholm
Little Moorsholm Farm
16
Goat Scar Wood
Great Charles Hill
Hagg Beck
East Wood
West Wood
5
ROAD
House
Stanghow House
Hunger Hill
142
Hagg Bridge
Hagg Wood
Uxto
Butts
Throstle
Farm

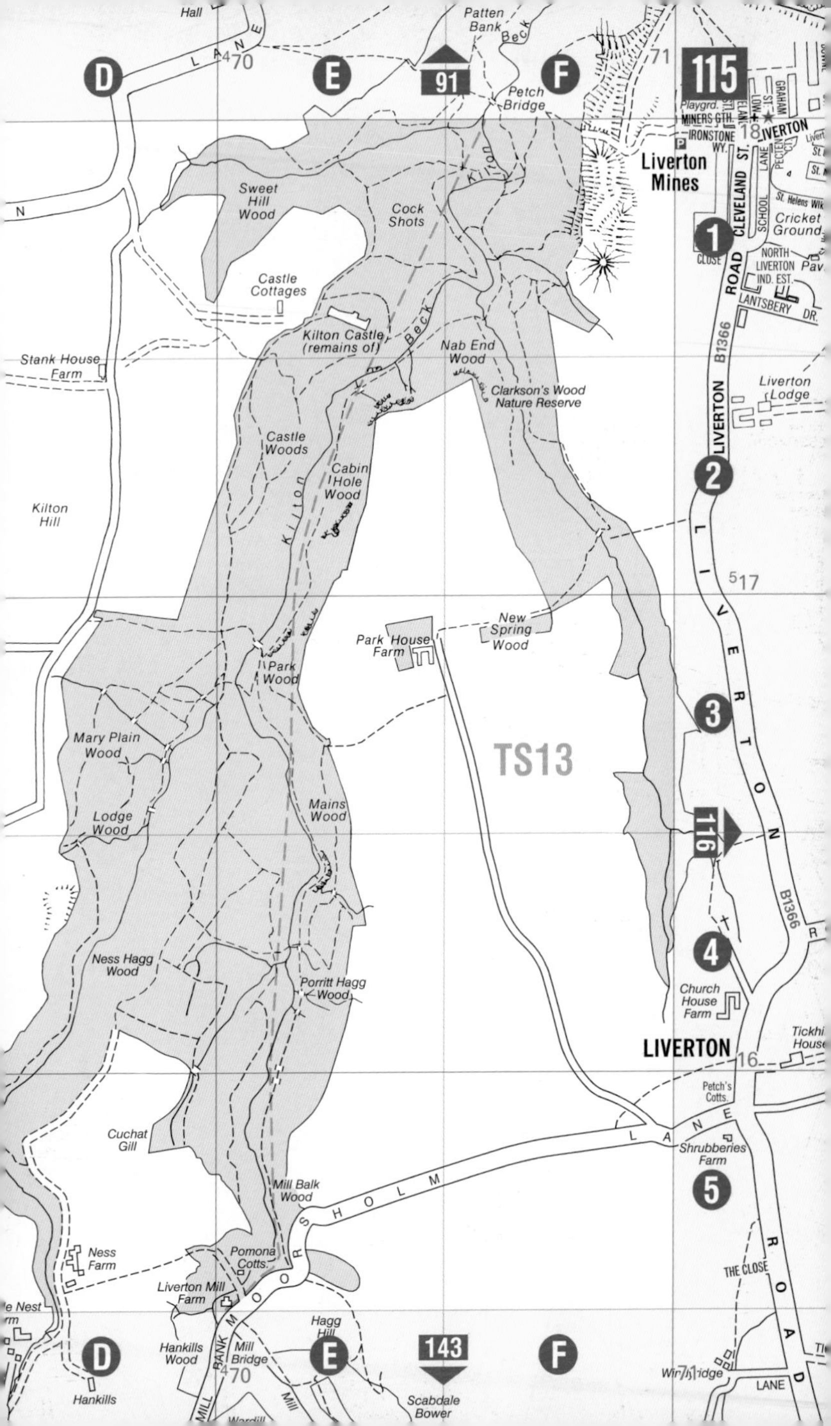

115
91
143
116
D
E
F
1
2
3
4
5
Hall
Patten Bank
Beck
Petch Bridge
Playgrd.
MINERS GTH.
IRONSTONE WY.
Liverton Mines
CLEVELAND ST.
SCHOOL LANE
GRAHAM ST.
LIVERTON
St. Helens Wlk
Cricket Ground
NORTH LIVERTON IND. EST.
LANTSBERY DR.
LIVERTON ROAD
B1366
Liverton Lodge
Sweet Hill Wood
Cock Shots
Kilton Beck
Castle Cottages
Kilton Castle (remains of)
Nab End Wood
Clarkson's Wood Nature Reserve
Stank House Farm
Castle Woods
Cabin Hole Wood
Kilton Hill
Park House Farm
New Spring Wood
Park Wood
Mary Plain Wood
Lodge Wood
TS13
Mains Wood
Ness Hagg Wood
Porritt Hagg Wood
Church House Farm
LIVERTON
Tickhill House
Petch's Cotts.
Shrubberies Farm
Cuchat Gill
Mill Balk Wood
MOORSHOLM LANE
Ness Farm
Pomona Cotts.
Liverton Mill Farm
THE CLOSE
Hagg Hill
Hankills Wood
Mill Bridge
MILL BANK
Hankills
Scabdale Bower
LANE
470
471
517
16
18

A
B
C
1
2
3
4
5
92
115
71
18
17
16
472
LOFTUS
South Loftus
Liverton Mines
LIVERTON
Handale Prim. Sch.
Warehouse
THE YARD
ZETLAND
HIGH ST.
Mkt. Pl.
Chapel Row
Comm. Cen.
St. Hilda's Pl.
CHURCH CT.
WATER LA.
HALL GROUNDS
WOOD VIEW
WOOD CT.
GASKELL LANE
LIVERTON RD.
HIRDS DR.
Railway Stables
MILL VIEW
STA. RD.
LAUREL PK.
FIRCROFT CT.
ROSECROFT LA.
Haugh Bridge
WATER LANE
South Loftus Farm
West Field Farm
Playgrd.
MINERS GTH.
IRONSTONE WY.
CLEVELAND ST.
LOW ST.
LIVERTON TER.
Liverton Ter. Sth.
ST. GEORGES TER.
St. Cuthbert's Wlk.
St. Michael's Cl.
St. Helens Wlk.
St. Leonards Cl.
St. Cuthbert's Walk
Cricket Ground
Pav.
ST. MARTINS CLOSE
SCHOOL LANE
CLEVELAND ROAD
NORTH LIVERTON IND. EST.
LANTSBERY DR.
B1366
ROSECROFT AV.
St. Joseph's RC Prim. Sch.
Playing Field
Waytail Beck
HILLCREST DR.
Rosecroft Wood
Liverton Lodge
LIVERTON ROAD
ROSECROFT LANE
Rosecroft
Middle Gill
Loftus Wood
Waytail Slack
Waytail Gate
Blue House
Elsie Wath
Church House Farm
Tickhill House
Petch's Cotts.
MOORHOLM LANE
Shrubberies Farm
Handale Bank
Handale Bank Fm.
THE CLOSE
Tick Hills
Windyridge
TICK HILLS LANE
LIVERTON LA.
Handale

WHITBY ROAD
A174
93
74
East Loftus
Victoria Ter.
Pav.
Bus. Dep.
Spts.
ROBINSON ST.
STREET
TYNE ST.
TWEED S.
TEES
RAILWAY COTTS.
HUMBER CL.
DERWENT
73
LOY LANE
Cemetery
Cemy.
Jackson St.
Railway Ter.
Loftus Beck
Bri.
Foulsyke
SECOND FOULSYKE
Townend Farm
ROCKCLIFFE CT.
GLEBE
Glebe Gth.
Lambert Ter.
BARNARD
ROAD
DON
18
EASINGTON
RYELANDS
MEADOWLANDS CL.
Easington Tunnel
Ryelands Pk. Fm.
South Loftus Farm
SOUTH TOWN LANE
118
Reservoir (Covered)
Saltburn-by-the-Sea
TS13
517
Highfields Farm
Holywell Farm
Lane Farm
Three Neuks
Gother Hill
Square Plantation
Warren House
The Warren
Handale Wood
16
Grinkle Park Cottages
Grinkle Park Farm
SNIPE LANE
Handale Abbey
Handale
NORTH YORK MOORS NATIONAL PARK
North Plantation
Grinkle Park
Fishpond Wood
HANDALE HO. RD.
GRINKLE LANE
The Lodge
Fish Pond
South Plantation
D
E
F
1
2
3
4
5

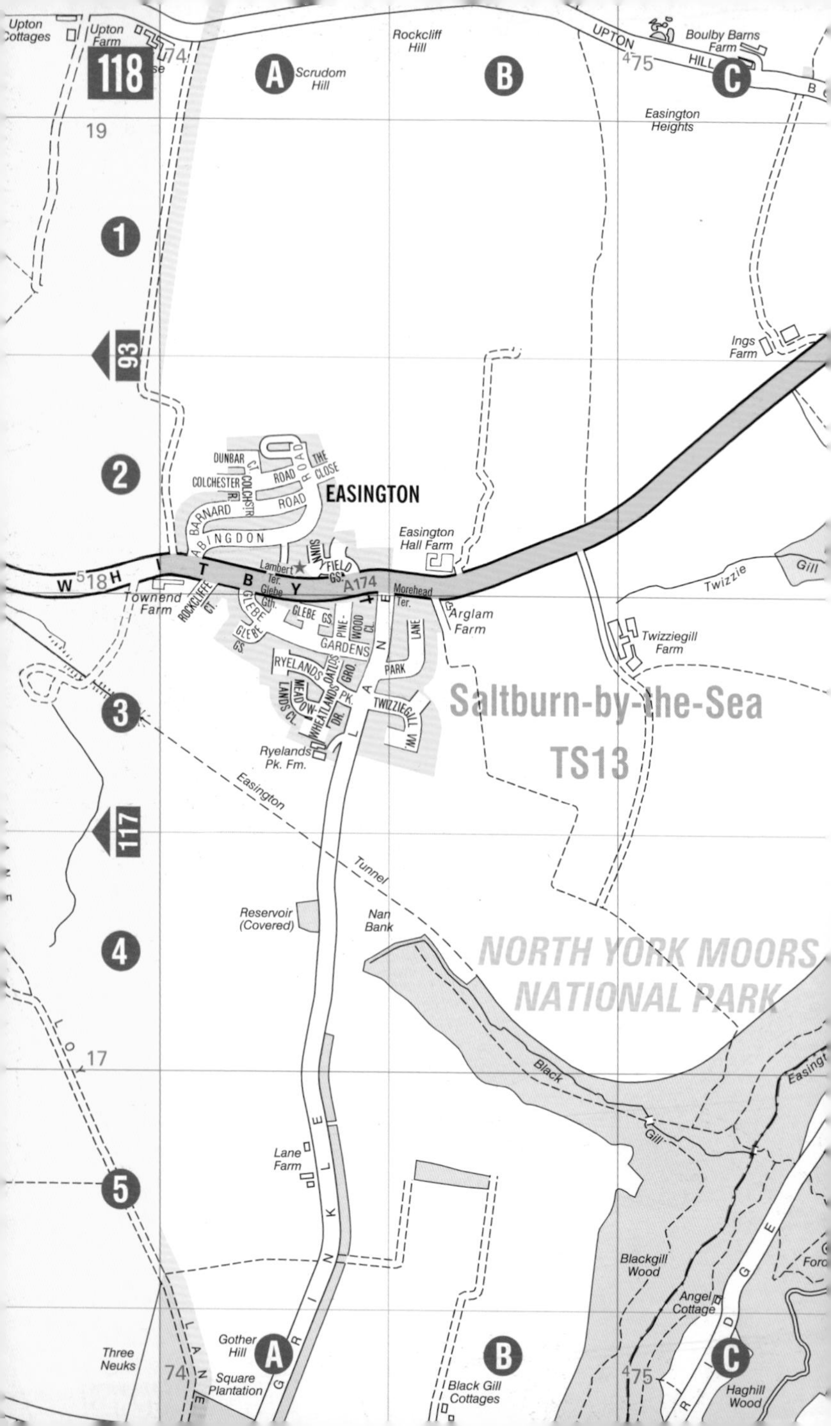

118
93
117
Upton Cottages
Upton Farm
Rockcliff Hill
Scrudom Hill
UPTON HILL
Boulby Barns Farm
Easington Heights
Ings Farm
EASINGTON
DUNBAR CT.
COLCHESTER RD.
COLCHESTER RD.
ROAD
BARNARD
ABINGDON
THE CLOSE
SUNNYFIELD GS.
Lambert Ter.
Glebe Gth.
GLEBE
GLEBE GS.
ROCKCLIFFE CT.
WHITBY
A174
Morehead Ter.
Easington Hall Farm
Townend Farm
Arglam Farm
Twizzie Gill
Twizziegill Farm
PINEWOOD CL.
GARDENS
RYELANDS
OATLDS. GRO.
MEADOWLANDS CL.
WHEATLANDS DR.
PK.
PARK LANE
TWIZZIEGILL VW.
Ryelands Pk. Fm.
Saltburn-by-the-Sea
TS13
Easington Tunnel
Reservoir (Covered)
Nan Bank
NORTH YORK MOORS
NATIONAL PARK
Black Gill
Lane Farm
GRINKLE LANE
LONG LANE
Blackgill Wood
Angel Cottage
RIDGE
Gother Hill
Three Neuks
Square Plantation
Black Gill Cottages
Haghill Wood
A
B
C
1
2
3
4
5
19
17
474
475
518

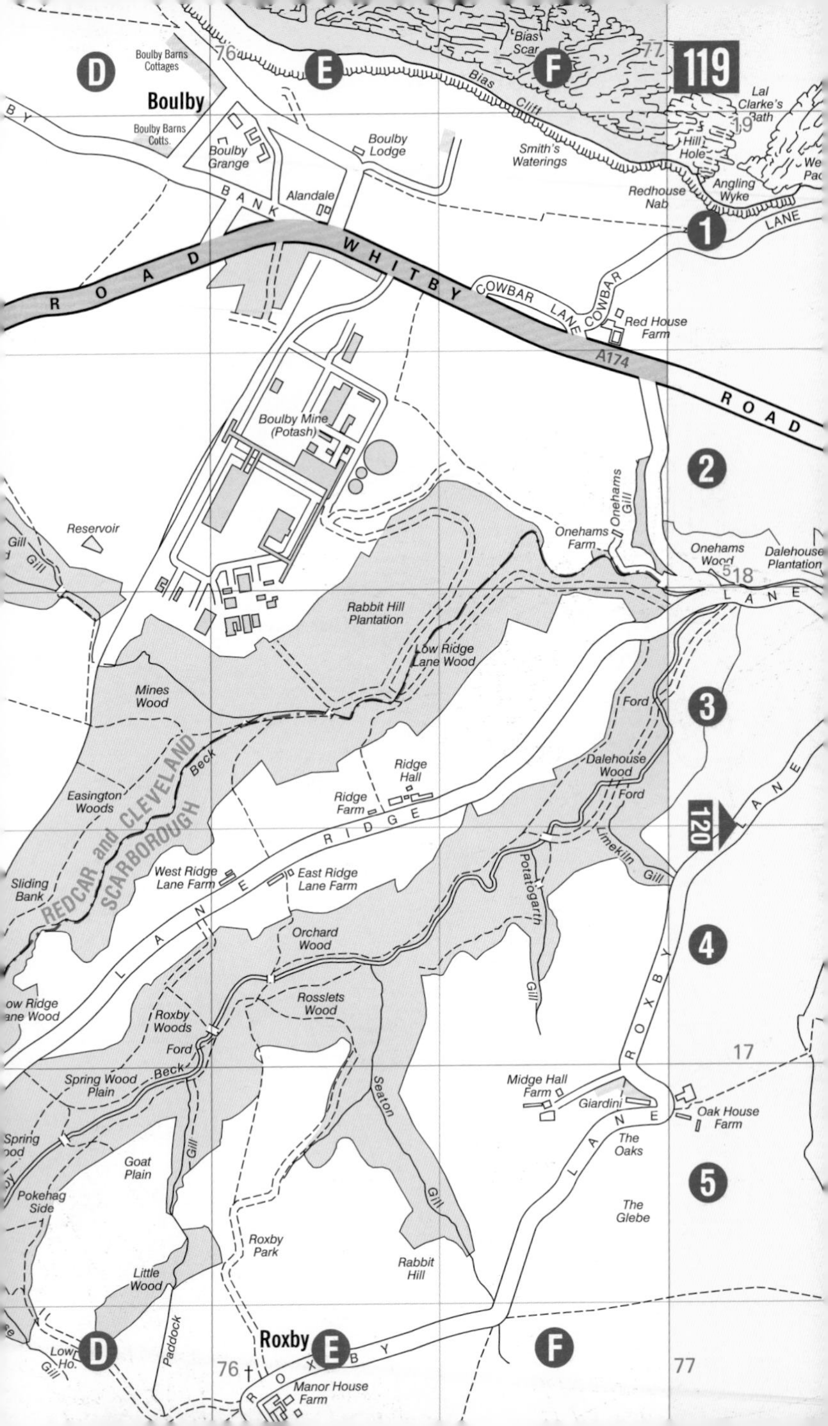
D
E
F
1
2
3
4
5
76
77
19
18
17
Boulby
Boulby Barns Cottages
Boulby Barns Cotts.
Boulby Grange
Boulby Lodge
Alandale
BANK
Bias Scar
Bias Cliff
Smith's Waterings
Lal Clarke's Bath
Hill Hole
Angling Wyke
Redhouse Nab
LANE
WHITBY ROAD
COWBAR LANE
COWBAR
Red House Farm
A174
ROAD
Boulby Mine (Potash)
Reservoir
Gill
Onehams Gill
Onehams Farm
Onehams Wood
Dalehouse Plantation
LANE
Rabbit Hill Plantation
Low Ridge Lane Wood
Mines Wood
Ford
REDCAR and CLEVELAND
SCARBOROUGH
Beck
Easington Woods
Ridge Hall
Ridge Farm
RIDGE
Dalehouse Wood
Ford
120
LANE
Limekiln Gill
Sliding Bank
West Ridge Lane Farm
East Ridge Lane Farm
Potatogarth
LANE
Orchard Wood
Gill
Low Ridge Lane Wood
Rosslets Wood
Roxby Woods
ROXBY
Ford
Spring Wood Plain
Beck
Seaton
Midge Hall Farm
Giardini
Oak House Farm
LANE
The Oaks
Spring Wood
Goat Plain
Gill
Gill
Pokehag Side
The Glebe
Roxby Park
Rabbit Hill
Little Wood
Paddock
Roxby
ROXBY
Low Ho.
Gill
Manor House Farm

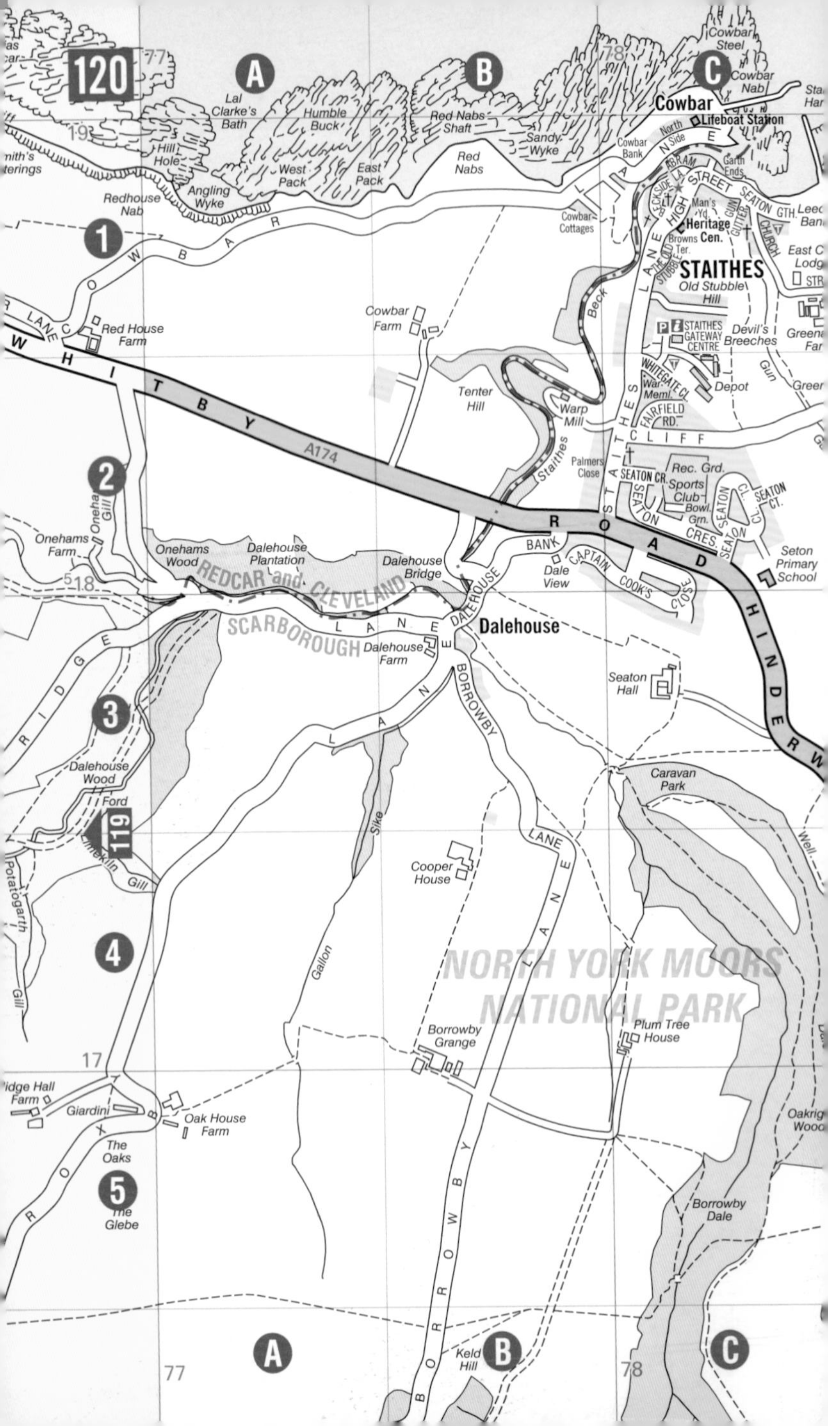

Lal Clarke's Bath
Humble Buck
Red Nabs Shaft
Sandy Wyke
Cowbar Steel
Cowbar Nab
Cowbar
Lifeboat Station
Hill Hole
West Pack
East Pack
Red Nabs
Angling Wyke
Redhouse Nab
Cowbar Bank
North Side
Garth Ends
Cowbar Cottages
Man's Yd.
Heritage Cen.
Browns Ter.
STAITHES
Old Stubble Hill
HIGH STREET
SEATON GTH.
CHURCH
East Cliff Lodge
COWBAR LANE
Red House Farm
Cowbar Farm
STAITHES GATEWAY CENTRE
Devil's Breeches
WHITEGATE CL.
War Meml.
Depot
FAIRFIELD RD.
CLIFF
WHITBY ROAD
A174
Tenter Hill
Warp Mill
Beck
Staithes
Palmers Close
STAITHES LANE
SEATON CR.
Rec. Grd.
Sports Club
Bowl. Grn.
SEATON CRES.
SEATON CL.
SEATON CT.
Seton Primary School
Onehams Gill
Onehams Farm
Onehams Wood
Dalehouse Plantation
Dalehouse Bridge
REDCAR and CLEVELAND
BANK
Dale View
CAPTAIN COOK'S CLOSE
SCARBOROUGH LANE
DALEHOUSE
Dalehouse
Dalehouse Farm
HINDERWELL
RIDGE
Seaton Hall
Caravan Park
Dalehouse Wood
Ford
119
Limekiln Gill
Potatogarth Gill
Sike
BORROWBY LANE
Cooper House
Gallon
NORTH YORK MOORS NATIONAL PARK
Borrowby Grange
Plum Tree House
Well
Oakridge Wood
Ridge Hall Farm
Giardini
Oak House Farm
The Oaks
The Glebe
ROXBY
Borrowby Dale
Keld Hill
A
B
C
1
2
3
4
5
77
78
19
18
17

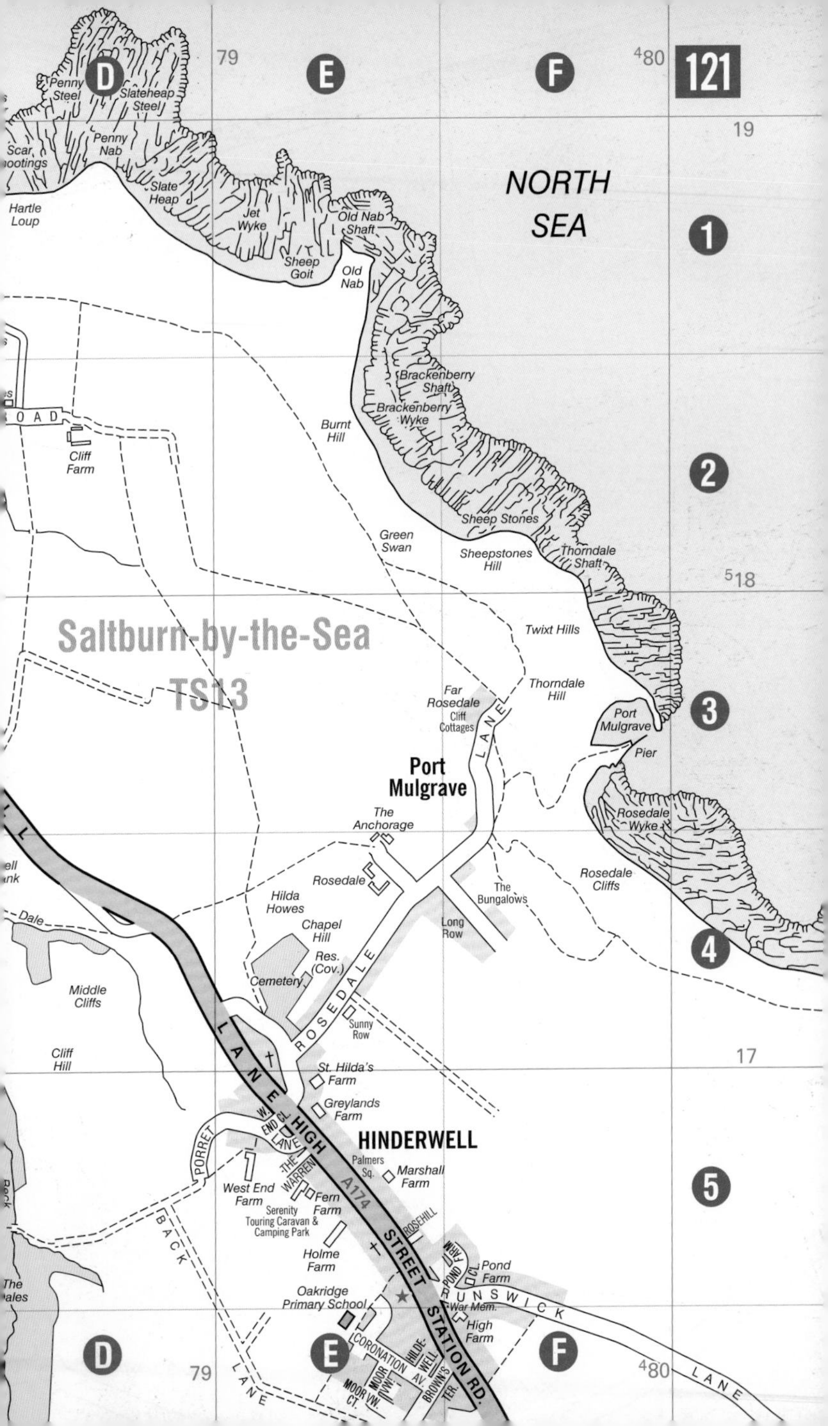

79
4 80
19
5 18
17
D
E
F
1
2
3
4
5
NORTH SEA
Penny Steel
Slateheap Steel
Penny Nab
Scar
Hartle Loup
Slate Heap
Jet Wyke
Sheep Goit
Old Nab Shaft
Old Nab
Brackenberry Shaft
Brackenberry Wyke
Burnt Hill
ROAD
Cliff Farm
Green Swan
Sheep Stones
Sheepstones Hill
Thorndale Shaft
Twixt Hills
Saltburn-by-the-Sea
TS13
Far Rosedale
Cliff Cottages
LANE
Thorndale Hill
Port Mulgrave
Pier
Port Mulgrave
Rosedale Wyke
The Anchorage
Rosedale
Hilda Howes
Chapel Hill
The Bungalows
Long Row
Rosedale Cliffs
Dale
Middle Cliffs
Res. (Cov.)
Cemetery
ROSEDALE
Sunny Row
Cliff Hill
LANE
St. Hilda's Farm
Greylands Farm
HIGH
W. END CL.
LANE
PORRET
HINDERWELL
THE WARREN
Palmers Sq.
Marshall Farm
A174
West End Farm
Fern Farm
Serenity Touring Caravan & Camping Park
ROSEHILL
BACK
Holme Farm
STREET
POND FARM
CL.
Pond Farm
The
RUNSWICK
Oakridge Primary School
War Mem.
High Farm
STATION RD.
CORONATION AV.
HILDEWELL
MOOR VW.
MOOR CT.
BROWN'S TER.
LANE
LANE

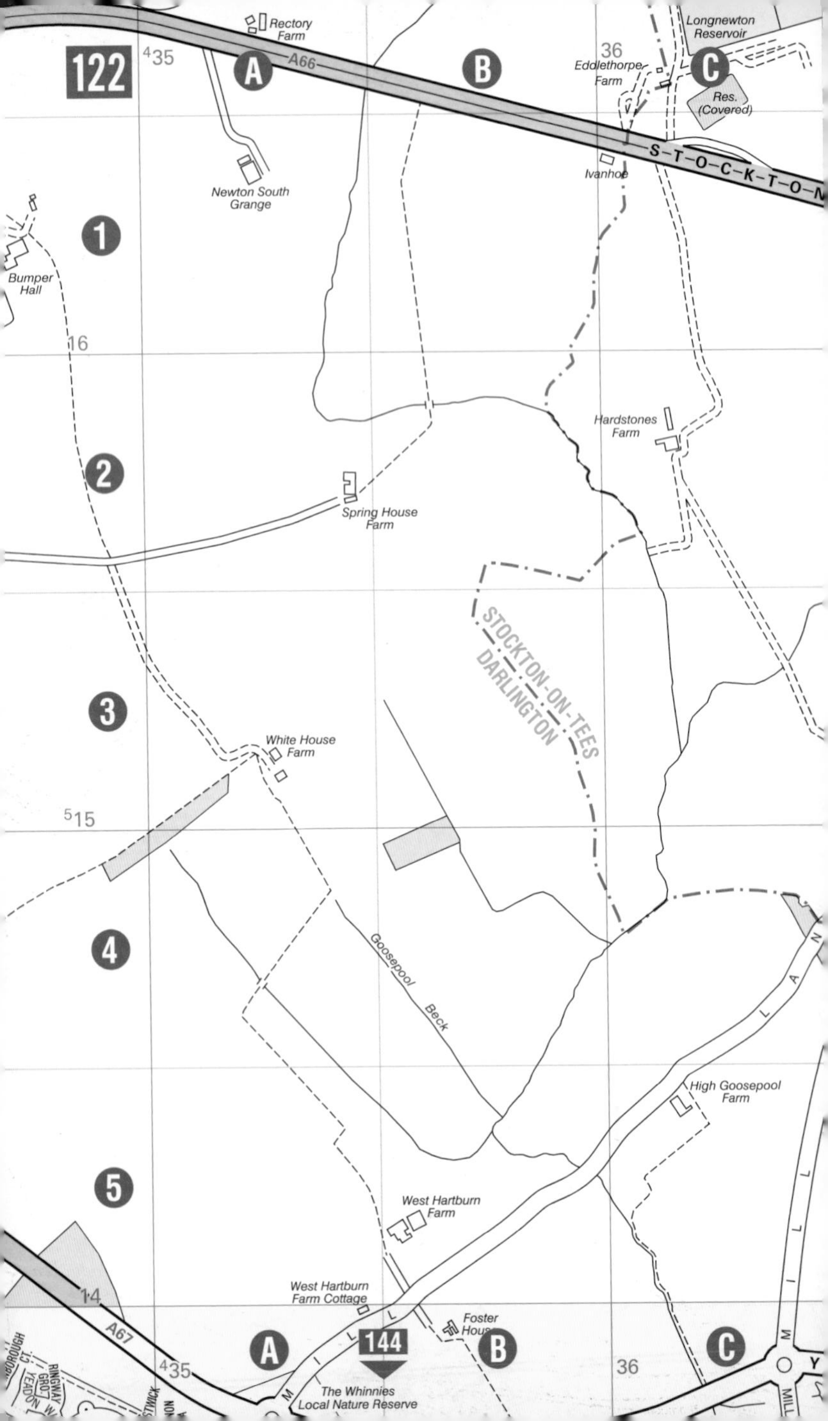

122
435
A
A66
Rectory Farm
B
Longnewton Reservoir
36
Eddlethorpe Farm
C
Res. (Covered)
S-T-O-C-K-T-O-N
Ivanhoe
Newton South Grange
1
Bumper Hall
16
2
Hardstones Farm
Spring House Farm
STOCKTON-ON-TEES
DARLINGTON
3
White House Farm
515
4
Goosepool Beck
L A N E
High Goosepool Farm
5
West Hartburn Farm
14
A67
West Hartburn Farm Cottage
Foster
144
A
B
C
435
36
The Whinnies Local Nature Reserve
M I L L
M I L L

123
Hang Thorn Farm
Fairfields Bungalow
D
E
F
37
38
STOCKTON ROAD
A66
R-O-A-D
Long Newton House
St. Mary's C of E Prim. Sch.
Comm. C
WILLOW CHASE
THE CLOSE
THE STRAY
THE GREEN
RECTORY LA.
WOODLAND
Parkside
WAY
BURN ROAD
Manor Gate
VANE CT.
DARLINGTON DR.
THE YEW WK.
DARLINGTON LANE
Stockton-on-Tees
TS21
LONG NEWTON
West End Farm
FAIRFIELDS CL.
16
Middle Town Farm
MILL LANE
Londonderry Cottage
Darlington
DL2
124
Mill Hill Farm
Lyndale
West Moor
Beck
15
Burnwood
West Gate Fox Covert
Westgate Farm
Long Plantation
Sewage Works
Goosepool Beck
Low Goosepool Farm
Teesside Airport
145
A67
ROAD
14
Thornburn
1
2
3
4
5

STOCKTON ROAD
38
A
B
C
94
Long Newton House
St. Mary's C of E Prim. Sch.
Comm. Cen.
Mount Pleasant Cottage
Sewage Works
39
WHITE HOUSE CFT.
Rec. Grd.
RECTORY LA.
THE GREEN
THE STRAY
THE CLOSE
CHASE
WILLOW
VANE CT.
THE YEW WK.
WOODLAND
Parkside
WAY
FAIRVIEW
CASTLEREAGH CL.
GRASS CFT.
The Bungalows
Church Vw.
BURNWOOD CT.
Manor Gate
ALONBY CT.
DARLINGTON LANE
FARFIELDS CL.
LONG NEWTON
LONG NEWTON
TS21
16
Middle Town Farm
Coatham
Burnwood Bridge
Burn Wood
Beck
Burnwood
123
1
2
3
4
5
515
Beck
Eastgate Farm
Burn Wood
Call Hill
Darlington DL2
A67
YARM ROAD
CARTER'S LANE
East Brocks Farm
14
146
West Brocks Farm
Aislaby Grange

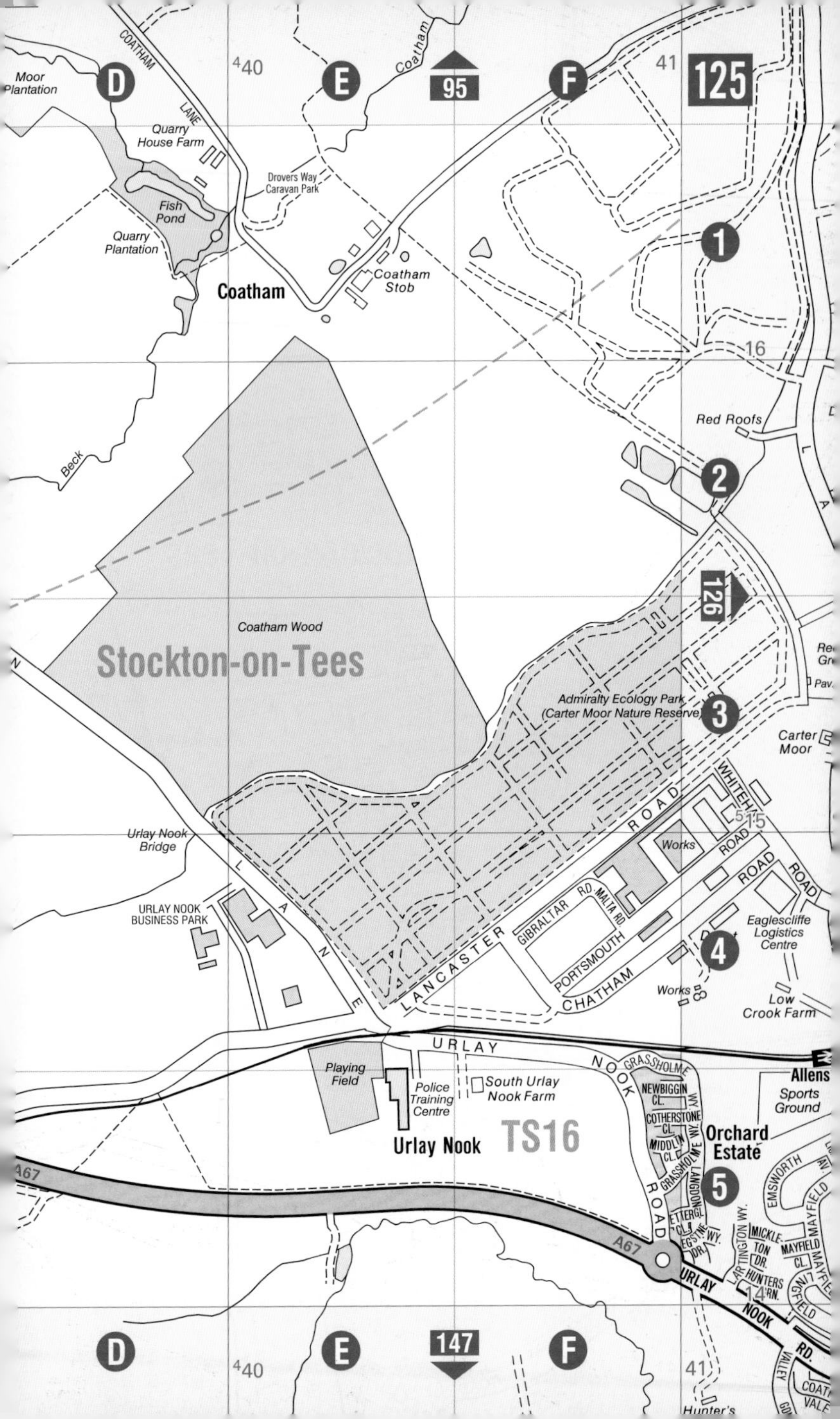
D
E
F
440
41
95
126
147
Moor Plantation
COATHAM LANE
Quarry House Farm
Fish Pond
Quarry Plantation
Drovers Way Caravan Park
Coatham
Coatham Stob
Coatham
Beck
16
Red Roofs
1
2
3
4
5
Stockton-on-Tees
Coatham Wood
Admiralty Ecology Park (Carter Moor Nature Reserve)
Carter Moor
Pav.
Urlay Nook Bridge
URLAY NOOK BUSINESS PARK
LANE
LANCASTER ROAD
WHITEHOUSE ROAD
ROAD
Works
515
GIBRALTAR RD.
MALTA RD.
PORTSMOUTH
CHATHAM
Eaglescliffe Logistics Centre
Works
Low Crook Farm
URLAY NOOK ROAD
GRASSHOLME
NEWBIGGIN CL.
COTHERSTONE CL.
MIDDLETON CL.
GRASSHOLME WY.
LANGDON
Playing Field
Police Training Centre
South Urlay Nook Farm
Urlay Nook
TS16
Allens
Sports Ground
Orchard Estate
EMSWORTH
MAYFIELD AV.
MAYFIELD CL.
MICKLETON DR.
HUNTERS GRN.
LARTINGTON WY.
A67
URLAY NOOK RD.
14
VALLEY
Hunter's

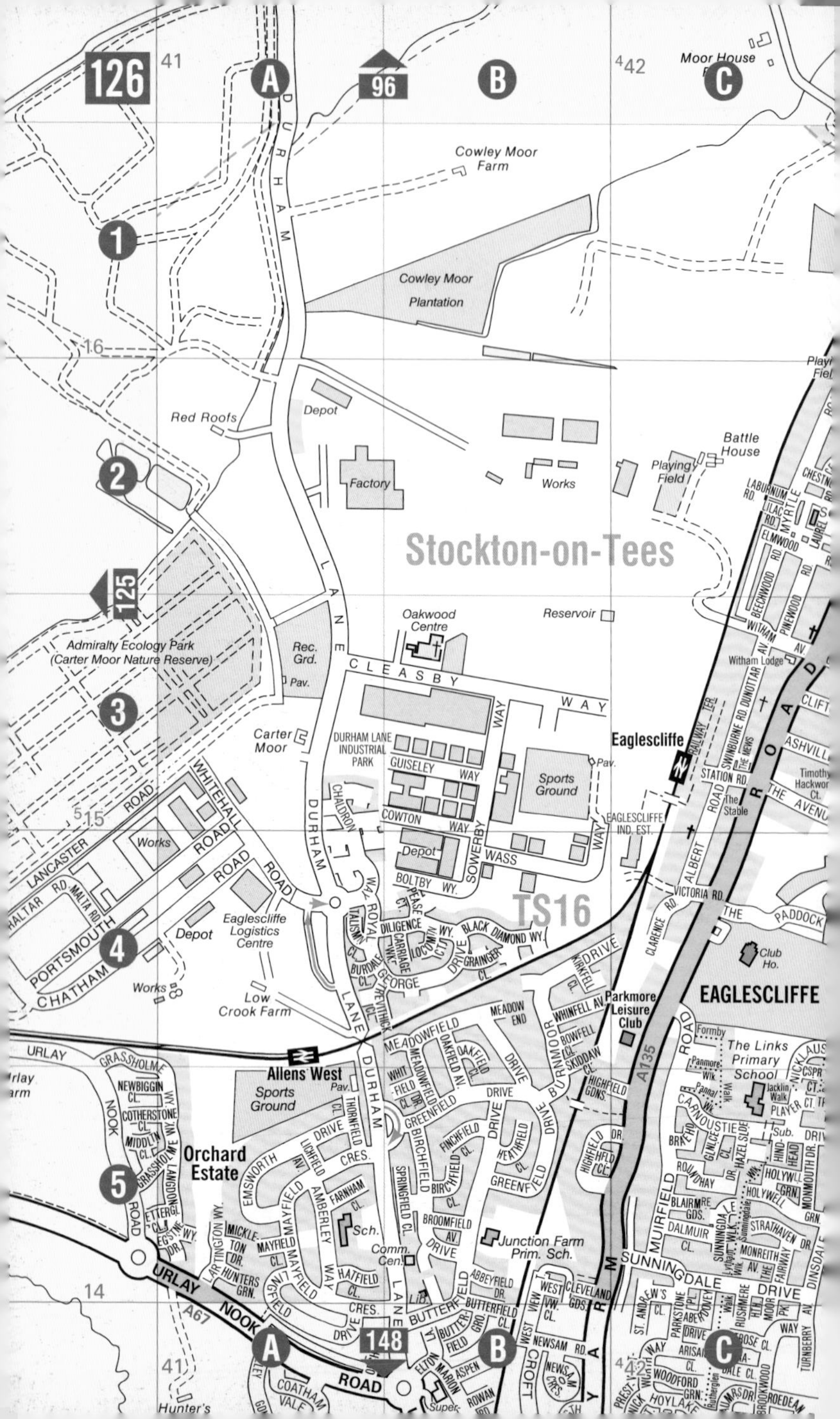

126
41
A
96
B
442
Moor House
C
Cowley Moor Farm
DURHAM
1
Cowley Moor Plantation
16
Red Roofs
Depot
2
Factory
Works
Playing Field
Battle House
Stockton-on-Tees
125
LANE
Oakwood Centre
Reservoir
Admiralty Ecology Park (Carter Moor Nature Reserve)
Rec. Grd.
Pav.
CLEASBY WAY
3
Carter Moor
DURHAM LANE INDUSTRIAL PARK
GUISELEY WAY
COWTON WAY
SOWERBY WAY
Sports Ground
Eaglescliffe
EAGLESCLIFFE IND. EST.
WHITEHALL ROAD
LANCASTER ROAD
Works
CHALDRON
Depot
WASS WAY
BOLTBY WY.
TS16
GIBRALTAR RD.
MALTA RD.
PORTSMOUTH ROAD
4
Depot
Eaglescliffe Logistics Centre
ROYAL WAY
TALISMAN CL.
DILIGENCE
CARRIAGE WK.
LOCOMOTION CT.
BLACK DIAMOND WY.
GRAINGER CL.
GEORGE DRIVE
BURDALE CL.
TREVITHICK CL.
PEASE CT.
CHATHAM ROAD
Works
Low Crook Farm
URLAY
GRASSHOLME WY.
NEWBIGGIN CL.
COTHERSTONE CL.
MIDDLIN CL.
NOOK ROAD
Allens West
Sports Ground
Pav.
Orchard Estate
THORNFIELD CL.
EMSWORTH
LICHFIELD AV.
DRIVE
CRES.
5
GRASSHOLME WY.
LANGDON
ETTERGILL
EGGLESTONE DR.
LARTINGTON WY.
MICKLETON DR.
MAYFIELD
AMBERLEY WAY
FARNHAM
Sch.
HUNTERS GRN.
HATFIELD CL.
URLAY NOOK ROAD
A67
14
CRES.
DRIVE
A
148
41
Hunter's
COATHAM VALE
ROAD
MEADOWFIELD
OAKFIELD AV.
OAKFIELD CL.
WHITFIELD DR.
GREENFIELD
DRIVE
BIRCHFIELD
FINCHFIELD CL.
HEATHFIELD CL.
GREENFIELD
SPRINGFIELD CL.
BIRCHFIELD CL.
BROOMFIELD AV.
DRIVE
Junction Farm Prim. Sch.
Comm. Cen.
Lib.
ABBEYFIELD DR.
BUTTERFIELD
BUTTERFIELD GRO.
ELTON
MARION
ASPEN
ROWAN
Super-
B
WEST VIEW
WEST VW. CL.
CROFT
NEWSAM RD.
NEWSAM CRES.
CLEVELAND GDS.
MEADOW END
BURNMOOR DRIVE
WHINFELL AV.
BOWFELL CL.
SKIDDAW CL.
KIRKFELL CL.
DRIVE
HIGHFIELD GDNS.
HIGHFIELD DR.
HFLD CL.
Parkmore Leisure Club
YARM ROAD
A135
CLARENCE RD.
VICTORIA RD.
ALBERT ROAD
RAILWAY TER.
STATION RD.
SWINBURNE RD.
THE MEWS
The Stable
DUNOTTAR AV.
Witham Lodge
WITHAM AV.
BEECHWOOD RD.
PINEWOOD RD.
ELMWOOD
LILAC RD.
LABURNUM RD.
MYRTLE
LAUREL
CHESTNUT
ROAD
CLIFTON
ASHVILLE
Timothy Hackworth Ct.
THE AVENUE
THE PADDOCK
Club Ho.
EAGLESCLIFFE
ROAD
Formby
The Links Primary School
Panmore Wlk.
Pannal Wk.
Walk
Jacklin Walk
PLAYER CT.
NICKLAUS CT.
CARNOUSTIE
BRAEHEAD
GLENEAGLES
HAZELSLADE
HINDHEAD
HOLYWELL GRN.
HOLYWELL
MONMOUTH DR.
Sub.
ROUNDHAY
MUIRFIELD
BLAIRMORE GDS.
DALMUIR CL.
SUNNINGDALE WLK.
STRATHAVEN DR.
MONREITH AV.
THE FAIRWAY
SUNNINGDALE DRIVE
DINSDALE
ST. ANDREW'S CL.
PARKSTONE PL.
ABERDOVEY DRIVE
RUSHMERE
MOOR PK.
WAY
TURNBERRY AV.
ARISAIG
MONTROSE CL.
C
442
WOODFORD GRN.
HOYLAKE
PRESTWICK
ROEDEAN
BROOKWOOD

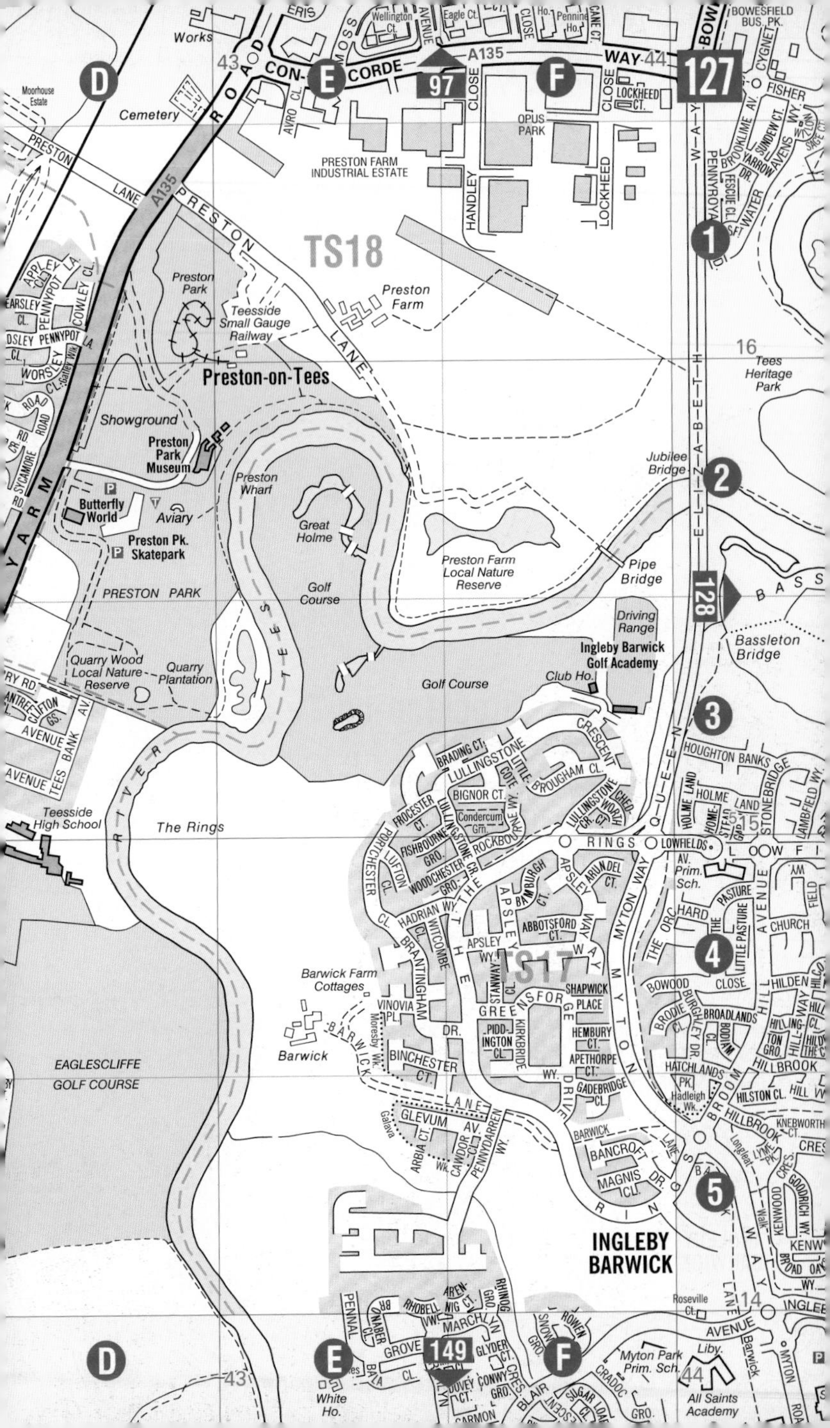
127
97
128
149
D
E
F
1
2
3
4
5
43
44
16
15
14
TS18
TS17
Works
Moorhouse Estate
Cemetery
CONCORDE WAY
A135
YARM ROAD
PRESTON LANE
Wellington Ct.
Eagle Ct.
Pennine Ho.
BOWESFIELD BUS. PK.
LOCKHEED CT.
OPUS PARK
PRESTON FARM INDUSTRIAL ESTATE
HANDLEY CLOSE
LOCKHEED CLOSE
AVRO CL.
Preston Park
Teesside Small Gauge Railway
Preston Farm
Preston-on-Tees
Showground
Preston Park Museum
Butterfly World
Aviary
Preston Pk. Skatepark
PRESTON PARK
Preston Wharf
Great Holme
Golf Course
Preston Farm Local Nature Reserve
Jubilee Bridge
Pipe Bridge
ELIZABETH WAY
Tees Heritage Park
Bassleton Bridge
Driving Range
Ingleby Barwick Golf Academy
Club Ho.
Quarry Wood Local Nature Reserve
Quarry Plantation
RIVER TEES
The Rings
Teesside High School
EAGLESCLIFFE GOLF COURSE
QUEEN ELIZABETH WAY
HOUGHTON BANKS
LULLINGSTONE CRESCENT
BROUGHAM CL.
BIGNOR CT.
FISHBOURNE GRO.
PORTCHESTER CL.
HADRIAN WY.
RINGS
LOWFIELDS AV.
Prim. Sch.
MYTON WAY
APSLEY WAY
ABBOTSFORD CT.
BRANTINGHAM
WITCOMBE
GREENSFORGE DRIVE
Barwick Farm Cottages
Barwick
BARWICK LANE
VINOVIA PL.
BINCHESTER CT.
GLEVUM AV.
BANCROFT DR.
MAGNIS CL.
THE RINGS
BROOM HILL AVENUE
HILLBROOK
INGLEBY BARWICK
Roseville Ct.
AVENUE
Myton Park Prim. Sch.
Liby.
All Saints Academy
White Ho.
GROVE
BLAIR

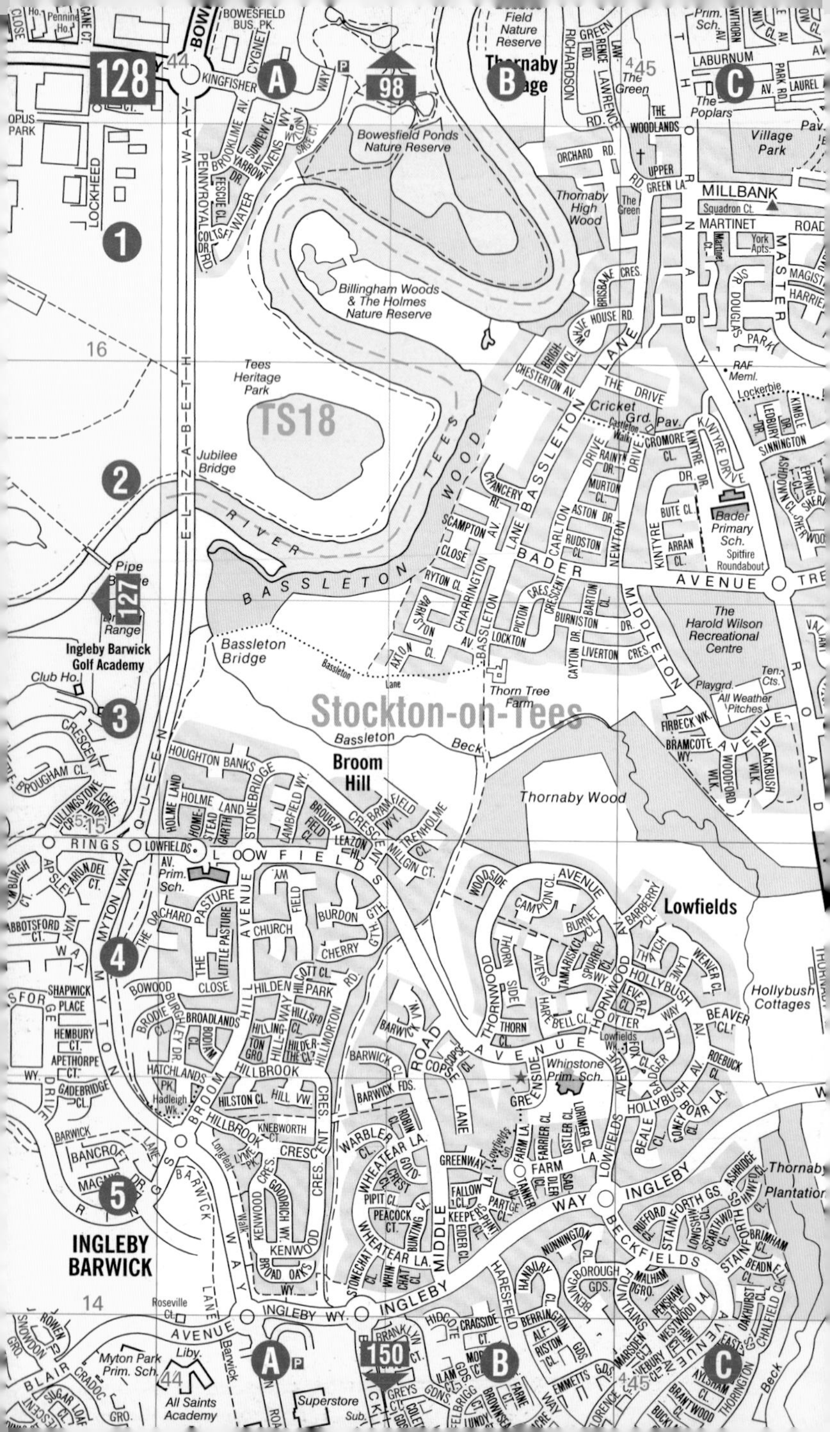
128
98
127
150
A
B
C
1
2
3
4
5
44
45
16
15
14
TS18
Stockton-on-Tees
BOWESFIELD BUS. PK.
OPUS PARK
LOCKHEED
KINGFISHER
CYGNET
Field Nature Reserve
Thornaby Village
RICHARDSON RD.
GREEN RD.
LAWRENCE
The Green
THE WOODLANDS
LABURNUM AV.
The Poplars
Village Park
Prim. Sch.
Bowesfield Ponds Nature Reserve
BROOKLIME AV.
SUNDEW CT.
YARROW DR.
PENNYROYAL
FESCUE CL.
WATER AVENS WY.
COLTSFT. DR.
ORCHARD RD.
UPPER GREEN LA.
Thornaby High Wood
MILLBANK
Squadron Ct.
MARTINET ROAD
York Apts.
SIR DOUGLAS PARK
MASTER
Billingham Woods & The Holmes Nature Reserve
BRISBANE CRES.
WHITE HOUSE RD.
BRIGHTON CL.
CHESTERTON AV.
THE DRIVE
RAF Meml.
Lockerbie
LEDBURY DR.
KIMBLE DR.
SINNINGTON
Tees Heritage Park
Jubilee Bridge
RIVER TEES
BASSLETON WOOD
Cricket Grd. Pav.
Castleton Walk
CROMORE CL.
KINTYRE DR.
KINTYRE DRIVE
RAINTN DR.
MURTON CL.
ASTON DR.
CHANCERY RI.
SCAMPTON AV.
CLOSE
CHARRINGTON
BASSLETON LANE
CARLTON DRIVE
NEWTON DRIVE
RUDSTON CL.
BUTE CL.
ARRAN CL.
Bader Primary Sch.
Spitfire Roundabout
BADER AVENUE
RYTON CL.
OAKS CL.
CRESCENT
PICTON CRES.
BARTON CL.
BURNISTON DR.
MIDDLETON
LOCKTON
LIVERTON CRES.
CAYTON DR.
AXTON CL.
The Harold Wilson Recreational Centre
Pipe Bridge
Driving Range
Ingleby Barwick Golf Academy
Club Ho.
Bassleton Bridge
Bassleton Lane
Thorn Tree Farm
Ten. Cts.
Playgrd.
All Weather Pitches
FIRBECK WK.
BRAMCOTE WY.
AVENUE
WOODFORD WLK.
BLACKBUSH WLK.
Bassleton Beck
Broom Hill
Thornaby Wood
ELIZABETH WAY
QUEEN
CRESCENT
BROUGHAM CL.
LULLINGSTONE CR.
HOUGHTON BANKS
HOLME LAND
HOMESTEAD GARTH
STONEBRIDGE
LAMBFIELD WY.
BROUGH FIELD CL.
BRAMFIELD WY.
LEAZON HL.
TRENHOLME CL.
MILLGIN CT.
RINGS
LOWFIELDS AV.
LOWFIELDS
Prim. Sch.
APSLEY WAY
ARUNDEL CT.
ABBOTSFORD CT.
MYTON WAY
PASTURE
THE ORCHARD
LITTLE PASTURE
CHURCH
FIELD WY.
BURDON GTH.
CHERRY GTH.
WOODSIDE
CAMPION CL.
AVENUE
BURNET CL.
BARBERRY
Lowfields
THORNWOOD
TAMARISK CL.
SPURREY CL.
THATCH
WEAVER CL.
HOLLYBUSH LANE
Hollybush Cottages
BOWOOD
CLOSE
HILDEN PARK
HILCOTT CL.
SHAPWICK PLACE
HEMBURY CT.
APETHORPE CT.
GADEBRIDGE CL.
BRODIE CL.
BURGHLEY DR.
BROADLANDS
BODIAM CL.
HILLSFD CL.
HILLING TON GRO.
HILLMORTON
HILDERTHE CL.
HATCHLANDS PK.
HILLBROOK
Hadleigh Wk.
HILSTON CL.
HILL VW.
BARWICK WY.
BARWICK CL.
BARWICK FDS.
ROAD
COPSE CL.
THORN SIDE
THORN CL.
HAREBELL CL.
LEVERET CL.
OTTER WAY
Lowfields Wk.
FOX CL.
BADGER LA.
BEAVER CL.
ROEBUCK CL.
GREENSIDE
Whinstone Prim. Sch.
HOLLYBUSH AV.
BOAR LA.
CONEY CL.
BEALE CL.
BARWICK LANE
BANCROFT
MAGNA DR.
INGLEBY BARWICK
KNEBWORTH CT.
HILLBROOK CRESCENT
Longleat Walk
LYME PK.
KENWOOD CRES.
GOODRICH WY.
KENWOOD
BROAD OAKS
WARBLER CL.
ROBIN CL.
WHEATEAR LA.
GOLDCREST
PIPIT CL.
PEACOCK CT.
BUNTING CL.
STONECHAT CL.
WHINCHAT CL.
GREENWAY
LANE
MIDDLE
Lowfields Gn.
FARM LA.
FARRIER CL.
OSTLER CL.
LORIMER CL.
FARM LA.
SADDLER CL.
TANNER CL.
FALLOW CL.
KEEPERS LA.
EIDER CL.
PARTGE CL.
INGLEBY WAY
BECKFIELDS AVENUE
RUFFORD CL.
STAINFORTH GS.
ASHRIDGE
HAWFOLD
Thornaby Plantation
LONGSHAW CL.
SCARTHWD CL.
BRIMHAM CL.
BEADNELL CL.
NUNNINGTON CL.
HANBURY CL.
BENINGBOROUGH GDS.
MALHAM GRO.
FOUNTAINS
PENSHAW CL.
WESTWOOD LA.
OAKHURST CL.
CHALFIELD CL.
HARESFIELD WAY
BERRINGTON GDS.
ALFRISTON CL.
INGLEBY WY.
Roseville Ct.
AVENUE
ROWEN CL.
SNOWDON GRO.
BLAIR
CRADOC GRO.
SUGAR LOAF
Myton Park Prim. Sch.
Liby.
All Saints Academy
Barwick
Superstore
Sub.
HIDCOTE
CRAGSIDE CT.
BRANKLYN CT.
ILAM GDS.
GREYS GDNS.
ELBRIGG
BROWNSEA
FARNE CT.
EMMETTS GDS.
MARSDEN CL.
AVEBURY CL.
AYLSHAM CL.
BRANTWOOD CL.
THORINGTON GS.
Beck

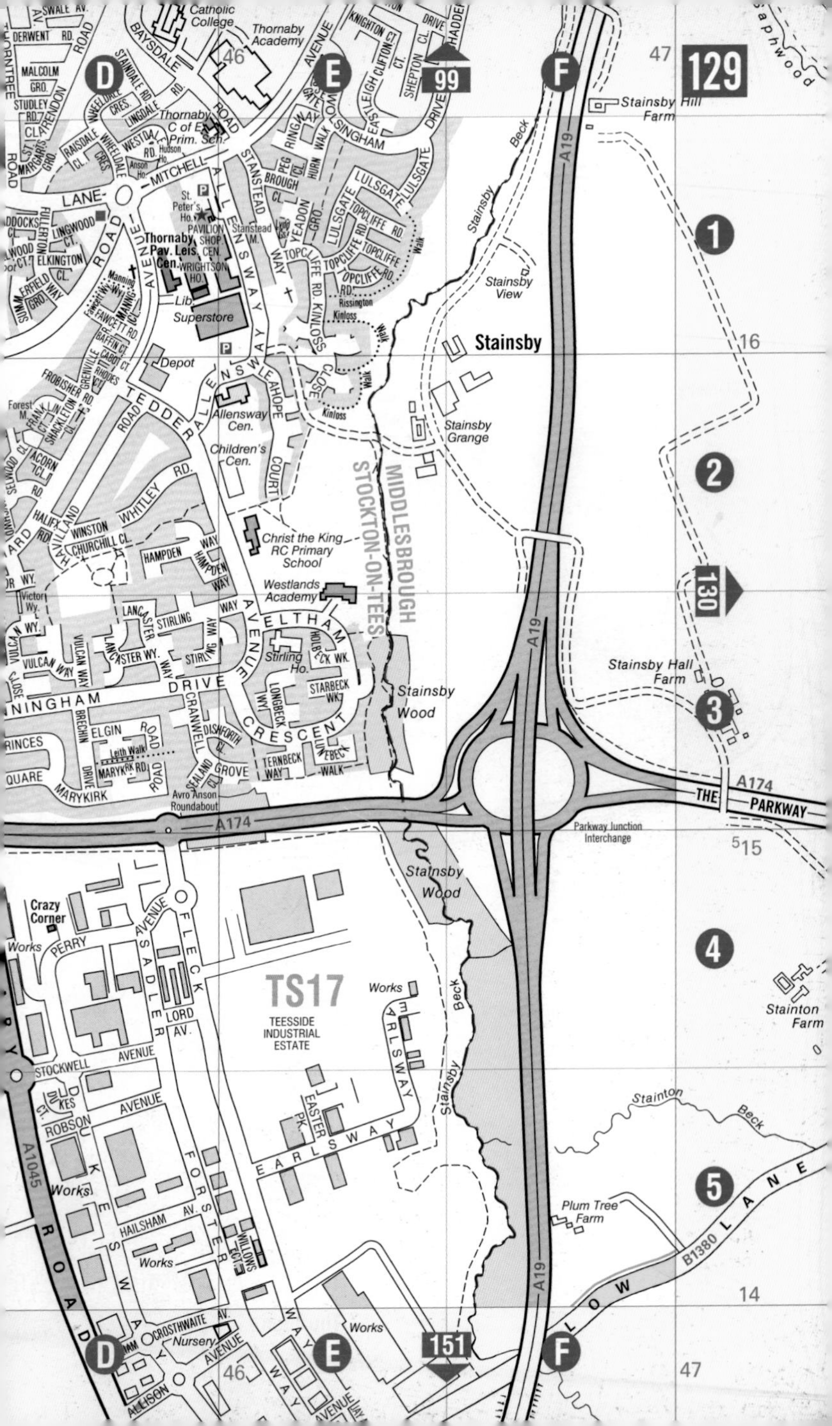

Catholic College
Thornaby Academy
Thornaby C of E Prim. Sch.
St. Peter's Ho.
Thornaby Pav. Leis. Cen.
Pavilion Shop. Cen.
Wrightson Ho.
Stanstead M.
Lib.
Superstore
Depot
Allensway Cen.
Children's Cen.
Christ the King RC Primary School
Westlands Academy
Stirling Ho.
Stainsby Hill Farm
Stainsby Beck
Stainsby View
Stainsby
Stainsby Grange
Stainsby Wood
Stainsby Hall Farm
STOCKTON-ON-TEES
MIDDLESBROUGH
A19
A174
THE PARKWAY
Parkway Junction Interchange
Avro Anson Roundabout
Crazy Corner
TS17
TEESSIDE INDUSTRIAL ESTATE
Works
Stainton Farm
Stainton Beck
Plum Tree Farm
LOW LANE
B1380
A1045
Nursery
MITCHELL AVENUE
LANE
ALLENSWAY
TEDDER ROAD
WHITLEY RD.
WINSTON CHURCHILL CL.
HAMPDEN WAY
LANCASTER WY.
STIRLING WAY
VULCAN WAY
FELTHAM AVENUE
FELTHAM CRESCENT
HOLBECK WK.
STARBECK WK.
LONGBECK WY.
TERNBECK WAY
LINBECK WALK
DRIVE
CRANWELL GROVE
DISHFORTH CL.
SEALAND CL.
BRECHIN DRIVE
ELGIN ROAD
MARYKIRK RD.
Leith Walk
PRINCES SQUARE
STANSTEAD WAY
TOPCLIFFE RD.
LULSGATE
KINLOSS CLOSE
Rissington Rd.
YEADON GRO.
BROUGH CL.
PEG CL.
RINGWAY
HURN WALK
WOLSINGHAM
EASTLEIGH CT.
CLIFTON CT.
SHEPTON CL.
KNIGHTON CT.
STAINDALE RD.
BAYSDALE ROAD
WHEELDALE CRES.
LINGDALE
WESTDALE RD.
RAISDALE CL.
CLARENDON ROAD
FULLERTON RD.
LINGWOOD CT.
ELKINGTON CL.
FAWCETT RD.
BAFFIN CT.
CABOT CT.
RHODES CT.
FROBISHER RD.
GRENVILLE RD.
SHACKLETON CL.
HALIFAX RD.
HAVILLAND RD.
ACORN CL.
FLECK WAY
PERRY AVENUE
SADLER AVENUE
LORD AV.
STOCKWELL AVENUE
ROBSON AVENUE
DUKES WAY
FORSTER
HAILSHAM AV.
WILLOWS CT.
CROSTHWAITE AV.
ALLISON AVENUE
EARLSWAY
EASTER PK.
Forest M.
47
46
16
515
14
1
2
3
4
5
D
E
F
99
130
151

47
48
A
B
C
1
2
3
4
5
16
15
14
100
129
152
Stainsby Hill Farm
Stainsby
Stainsby Hall Farm
Parkway Junction Interchange
A19
West Plantation
Acklam Whin
Saphwood Beck
Playing Fields
YEARBY
MOSSWOOD CRES.
CL.
KADER
AVENUE
ELWICK
WALWORTH GRO.
DINSDALE AV.
CASSOP GRO.
RAINTON AV.
STAINDROP DRIVE
ACKLAM
HALL
BEWLEY GRO.
CORNSAY CL.
HONISTER
WTN CL.
Sub.
Kader Prim. Sch.
Kader Cotts.
Playgrd.
Blue Bell Beck
TRIMDON
NEWFIELD CR.
HUMWICK
AVENUE
WELLSPRING CL.
WELLS SPRING
Kader Pde.
SWAINSTON CL.
Brafferton
BRUSSELTON
Hartburn
TAYLOR CL.
SHERBURN CL.
Walk
THROCKLEY AV.
DAKENSHAW DR.
KIMMERTON
HESLEDEN
CL.
BENRIDGE CL.
EARLSDON
CARLBURY AV.
RAISBY CL.
HALLGARTH CL.
PARTRIDGE AV.
FORCETT CL.
MERRINGTON AV.
FAVERDALE AV.
GILSLAND CL.
DENTON CL.
FOXBERRY AV.
RICKNALL CL.
Stotfold Wk.
AVENUE
Acklam Whin Prim. Sch.
TS5
RAVENSDALE
GELTSDALE
MARTINDALE
RUNSWICK AV.
RUNSWICK AVENUE
ROAD
COTHERSTONE DR.
GATENBY DR.
SEDGEFIELD RD.
GRISEDALE CL.
TOPCLIFFE DR.
CURTHWAITE
BALDOON
BASSENTHWAITE
St.Clare's RC Prim. Sch.
MALLTRAETH SANDS
Brackenthwaite
MERSEHEAD SANDS
SANDS
GORE SANDS
Stonedale Wk.
WARDALE AV.
TINDLE WK.
ROSTWTE
Thornthwaite
BANK SDS.
LUCE SANDS
DORNOCH SDS.
GALLOWAY SDS.
BLACK SDS.
WIGTN SEA
GAYTON SDS.
EASTHAM SDS.
Dundon Sands
Fiske Ct.
RAWCLIFFE AV.
ALDWARK CL.
BROOKFIELD
AYLTON
CRADLEY
PAUNTLEY DR.
HUSTLER RD.
OVAL
DRIVE
MALVERN
WELNO
MEADOW
HAMPSTEAD WY.
SALIS CL.
JOCELYN WAY
BARON CL.
Saphwood Wk.
JACK SIMON WAY
LORD CL.
LORD CLOSE
HOLT CL.
B1380
LOW LANE
THE A174
Stockton-on-Tees
TS17
Stainton Interchange
LYNMOUTH CL.
HEMLINGTON
ST. AUSTELL CL.
STAINTON
PEXTON
CAWTHORN
SPAUNTON
BRISCOE
FEN MOOR
SKIPLAM CL.
LOCKTON CL.
GIRRICK CL.
Hotel
Stainton Vale Farm
BUTTERCUP GRO.
BRAMBLE CL.
STRAIT
ROSE COTTAGE GDS.
HIGH RIFTS
SEVERS DR.
PENNYMAN WAY
CHAPELGARTH
WHINSTONE DR.
FAWCETT AV.
ROSEBERRY DR.
QUARRY DR.
PRIORY DR.
MELDYKE LA.
THE DR.
HOLLY LA.
Vernon Cl.
VERNON CT.
GREENACRES
BROAD CL.
ROWAN GRO.
Five Acres
THE WYND
Kelgate Ter.
CHURCH CL.
HEMLINGTON ROAD
STAINTON
GLEBE GDS.
COBBLESTONE CL.
CEDARWOOD
Stainton Beck
Plum Tree Farm
LOW
Upper Farm
Thornton
Stainton Ho.
Kell Gate Bri.
ROAD
THORNTON CL.
THORNTON VALE
Thornton Cotts.

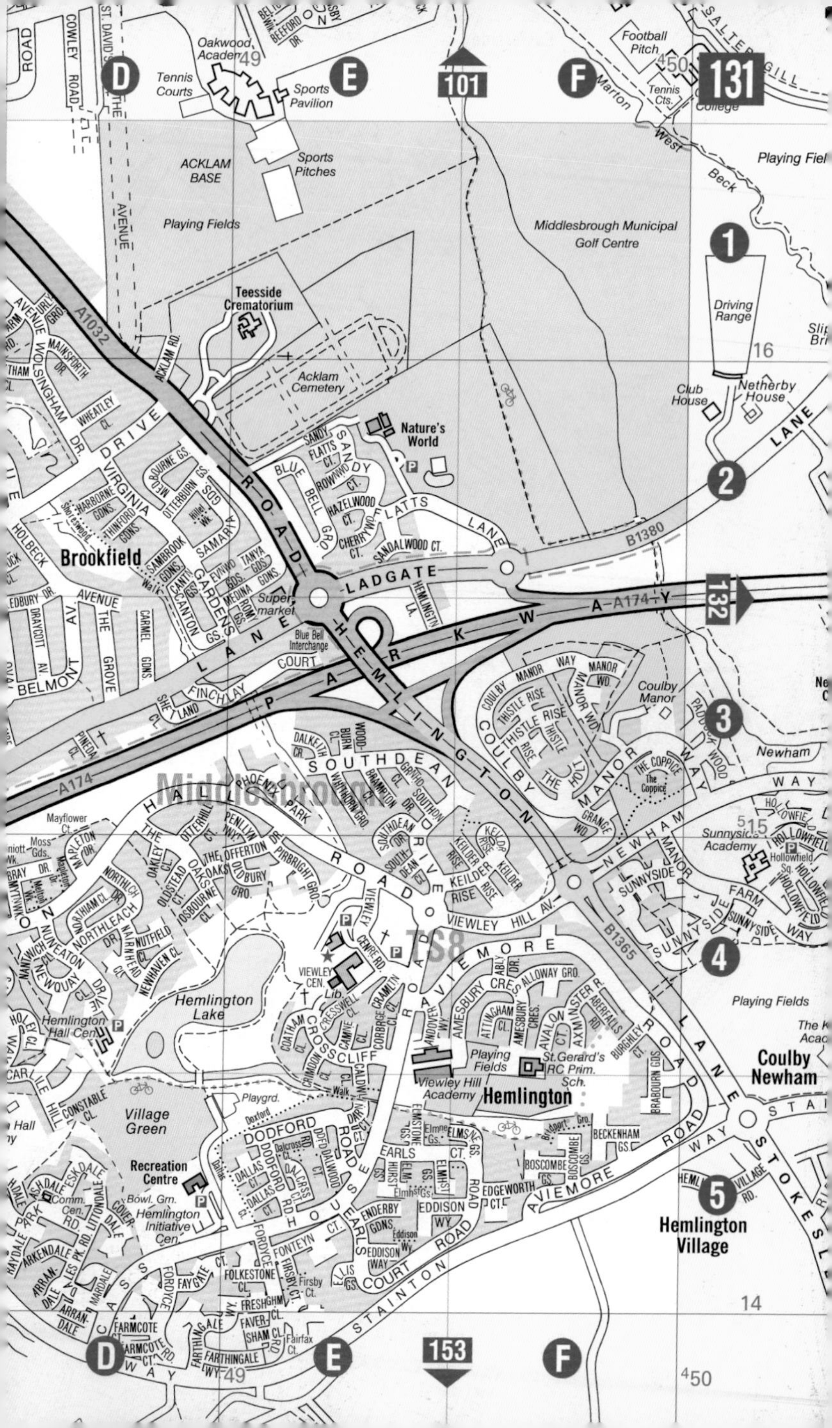
101
153
132
D
E
F
1
2
3
4
5
Oakwood Academy
Tennis Courts
Sports Pavilion
Sports Pitches
ACKLAM BASE
Playing Fields
Football Pitch
Tennis Cts.
College
Marton West Beck
Middlesbrough Municipal Golf Centre
Driving Range
Club House
Netherby House
Teesside Crematorium
Acklam Cemetery
Nature's World
Brookfield
Supermarket
Blue Bell Interchange
LADGATE LANE
HEMLINGTON LANE
PARKWAY
A1032
A174
B1380
B1365
Coulby Manor
Newham
Sunnyside Academy
Middlesbrough
TS8
Hemlington Lake
Hemlington Hall Cen.
Village Green
Recreation Centre
Bowl. Grn.
Hemlington Initiative Cen.
Viewley Cen.
Lib.
Viewley Hill Academy
Hemlington
St.Gerard's RC Prim. Sch.
Playing Fields
Coulby Newham
Hemlington Village
STAINTON WAY
STOKESLEY ROAD
ACKLAM RD.
VIRGINIA GARDENS
HALL DRIVE
SOUTHDEAN DRIVE
VIEWLEY HILL AV.
AVIEMORE ROAD
DODFORD ROAD
HOUSE ROAD
COURT ROAD
CASS WAY
COULBY MANOR WAY
NEWHAM WAY
HOLLOWFIELD
SUNNYSIDE FARM WAY
MANOR WD.
THISTLE RISE
THE HOLT
THE COPPICE
PADDOCK WOOD
KEILDER RISE
BELMONT AV.
THE GROVE
FINCHLAY COURT
PHOENIX PARK
NUNEATON DRIVE
NORTHLEACH DR.
CROSSCLIFF
EARLS
FOLKESTONE CL.
FARMCOTE CT.
FARTHINGALE WY.
ARRANDALE
ESKDALE
LITTONDALE
16
14
449
450
515

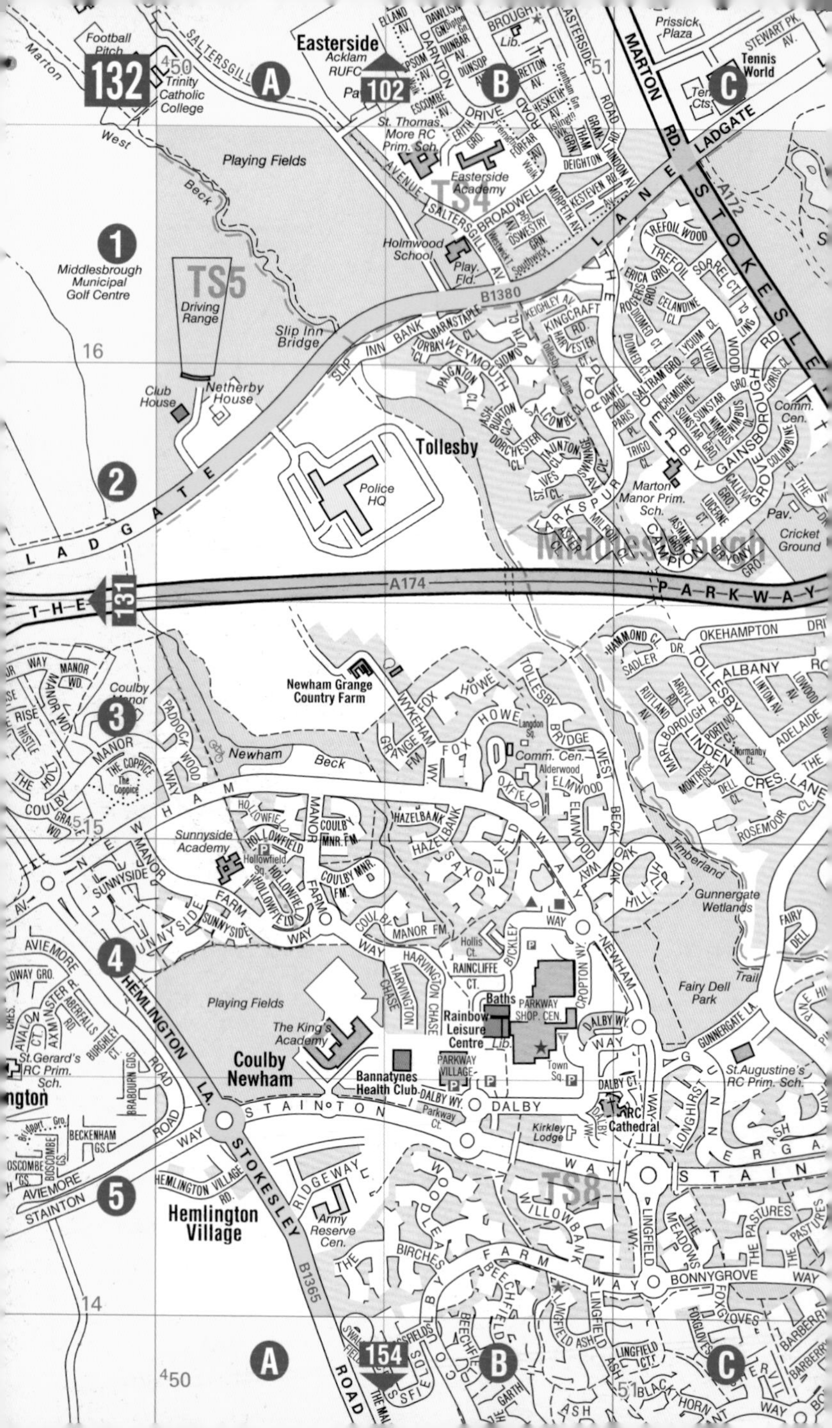

132
102
131
154
A
B
C
1
2
3
4
5
Easterside
Acklam RUFC
Football Pitch
Trinity Catholic College
Saltersgill
Marton West Beck
Playing Fields
St. Thomas More RC Prim. Sch.
Easterside Academy
TS4
Holmwood School
Play. Fld.
Lib.
Prissick Plaza
Tennis World
Ten. Cts.
Marton Rd.
Ladgate Lane
Stokesley Rd.
A172
B1380
Middlesbrough Municipal Golf Centre
TS5
Driving Range
Slip Inn Bridge
Club House
Netherby House
Police HQ
Tollesby
Marton Manor Prim. Sch.
Comm. Cen.
Cricket Ground
Pav.
Middlesbrough
A174
The Parkway
Newham Grange Country Farm
Coulby Manor
Newham Beck
Sunnyside Academy
Hollowfield Sq.
Langdon Sq.
Alderwood
Timberland
Gunnergate Wetlands
Fairy Dell Park
Trail
Hollis Ct.
Raincliffe Ct.
Baths
Rainbow Leisure Centre
Parkway Shop. Cen.
Town Sq.
Playing Fields
The King's Academy
Coulby Newham
Bannatynes Health Club
Parkway Village
Parkway Ct.
Kirkley Lodge
RC Cathedral
St.Augustine's RC Prim. Sch.
St.Gerard's RC Prim. Sch.
Hemlington Lane
Stainton Way
Stokesley Road
B1365
Hemlington Village
Army Reserve Cen.
TS8
Willowbank
Farm Way
Lingfield
Bonnygrove Way
The Pastures
The Meadows
Foxgloves
Gunnergate La.
Okehampton Dr.
Tollesby Rd.
Marlborough Rd.
Linden Cres.
Rosemoor Cl.
Newham Way
Dalby Way
Oxfield Way
Saxonfield
Elmwood
Beck Way
Oak Hill
Ridgeway
Woodleas
The Birches
Beechfield
Ashfield
Blackthorn
16
15
14
450
51

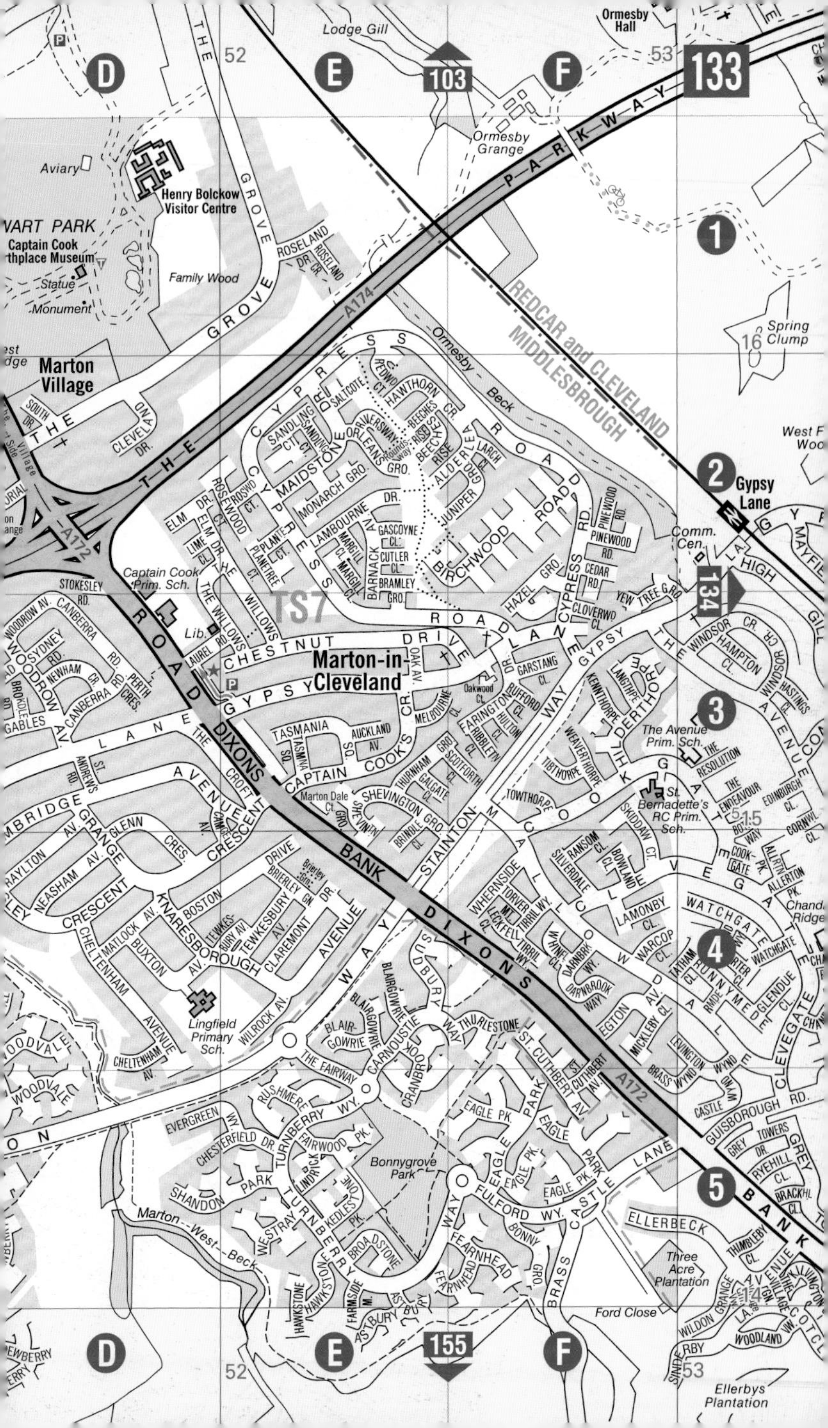
Lodge Gill
Ormesby Hall
103
52
53
D
E
F
1
2
3
4
5
Aviary
Henry Bolckow Visitor Centre
Captain Cook Birthplace Museum
Statue
Monument
Family Wood
Ormesby Grange
PARKWAY
A174
THE GROVE
ROSELAND DR.
ROSELAND CR.
REDCAR and CLEVELAND
MIDDLESBROUGH
Ormesby Beck
Spring Clump
16
Marton Village
West Wood
Gypsy Lane
Comm. Cen.
134
CYPRESS DR.
CYPRESS ROAD
SALTCOTE
HAWTHORN CR.
SANDLING CT.
MAIDSTONE DR.
ORLEANS GRO.
RIVERSWAY
BEECHES RISE
ALDERLEA
LARCH CL.
JUNIPER GRO.
MONARCH GRO.
LAMBOURNE DR.
GASCOYNE CL.
CUTLER CL.
BRAMLEY GRO.
BARNACK AV.
MARGILL CL.
BIRCHWOOD ROAD
PINEWOOD RD.
CEDAR RD.
HAZEL GRO.
YEW TREE GRO.
CLOVERWD CL.
CYPRESS RD.
ELM DR.
ROSEWOOD CT.
LIME CL.
PLANETREE CT.
THE WILLOWS
A172
STOKESLEY RD.
Captain Cook Prim. Sch.
Lib.
TS7
LAUREL RD.
CHESTNUT DRIVE
OAK AV.
Marton-in-Cleveland
GYPSY LANE
Oakwood Ct.
GARSTANG CL.
RUFFORD CL.
HULTON CL.
FARINGTON CL.
RIBBLETN CL.
THE WINDSOR
HAMPTON CL.
WINDSOR CR.
HASTINGS CL.
THE AVENUE
The Avenue Prim. Sch.
THE RESOLUTION
THE ENDEAVOUR
EDINBURGH CL.
CORNWALL CL.
COOK GATE
ALLERTON PK.
St. Bernadette's RC Prim. Sch.
KENNTHORPE
LANGTHORPE
HILDERTHORPE
WEAVERTHORPE
TIBTHORPE
TOWTHORPE
WOODROW AV.
CANBERRA RD.
SYDNEY RD.
NEWHAM CR.
PERTH CRES.
BROOKDALE
GABLES
LANE
ST. ANDREWS RD.
THE CROFT
DIXONS BANK
ROAD
TASMANIA SQ.
AUCKLAND AV.
CAPTAIN COOK'S CR.
MELBOURNE CL.
THURNHAM GRO.
SCOTFORTH CL.
GALGATE CL.
SHEVINGTON GRO.
Marton Dale Ct.
BRINDLE CL.
STAINTON WAY
MALLOWDALE
SKIDDAW CT.
RANSOM CL.
BOWLAND CL.
SILVERDALE
WHERNSIDE
TORVER
TIRRIL WY.
LECKFELL
LAMONBY CL.
CLEVEGATE
WATCHGATE
RUNNYMEDE
GLENDUE CL.
WARCOP CL.
TATHAM CL.
DARNBROOK WAY
EGTON AV.
MICKLEBY CL.
LEVINGTON WYND
BRASS WYND
CASTLE WYND
GUISBOROUGH RD.
GREY TOWERS DR.
RYEHILL CL.
BRACKHL CL.
Chandlers Ridge
CAMBRIDGE AVENUE
GRANGE AV.
GLENN CRES.
CRESCENT
HAYLTON AV.
NEASHAM AV.
KNARESBOROUGH
BOSTON DRIVE
BRIERLEY GN.
Brierley Grn.
TEWKESBURY AV.
CLAREMONT AV.
AVENUE
MATLOCK AV.
BUXTON AV.
CHELTENHAM AVENUE
CHELTENHAM AV.
Lingfield Primary Sch.
WILROCK AV.
WAY
SUDBURY WAY
BLAIRGOWRIE
CARNOUSTIE
THURLESTONE
ST. CUTHBERT AV.
THE FAIRWAY
CRANBROOK
WOODVALE
EVERGREEN WY.
RUSHMERE
TURNBERRY WY.
CHESTERFIELD DR.
FAIRWOOD PK.
LINDRICK
Bonnygrove Park
EAGLE PK.
EAGLE PARK
CASTLE LANE
FULFORD WY.
BONNY GRO.
BRASS
SHANDON PARK
KEDLESTONE PK.
WESTRAY
BROADSTONE
HAWKSTONE
FEARNHEAD
FARMSIDE M.
ASTBURY
Marton West Beck
ELLERBECK
THIMBLEBY CL.
Three Acre Plantation
Ford Close
WILDON GRANGE
WOODLAND VW.
Ellerbys Plantation
155
NEWBERRY

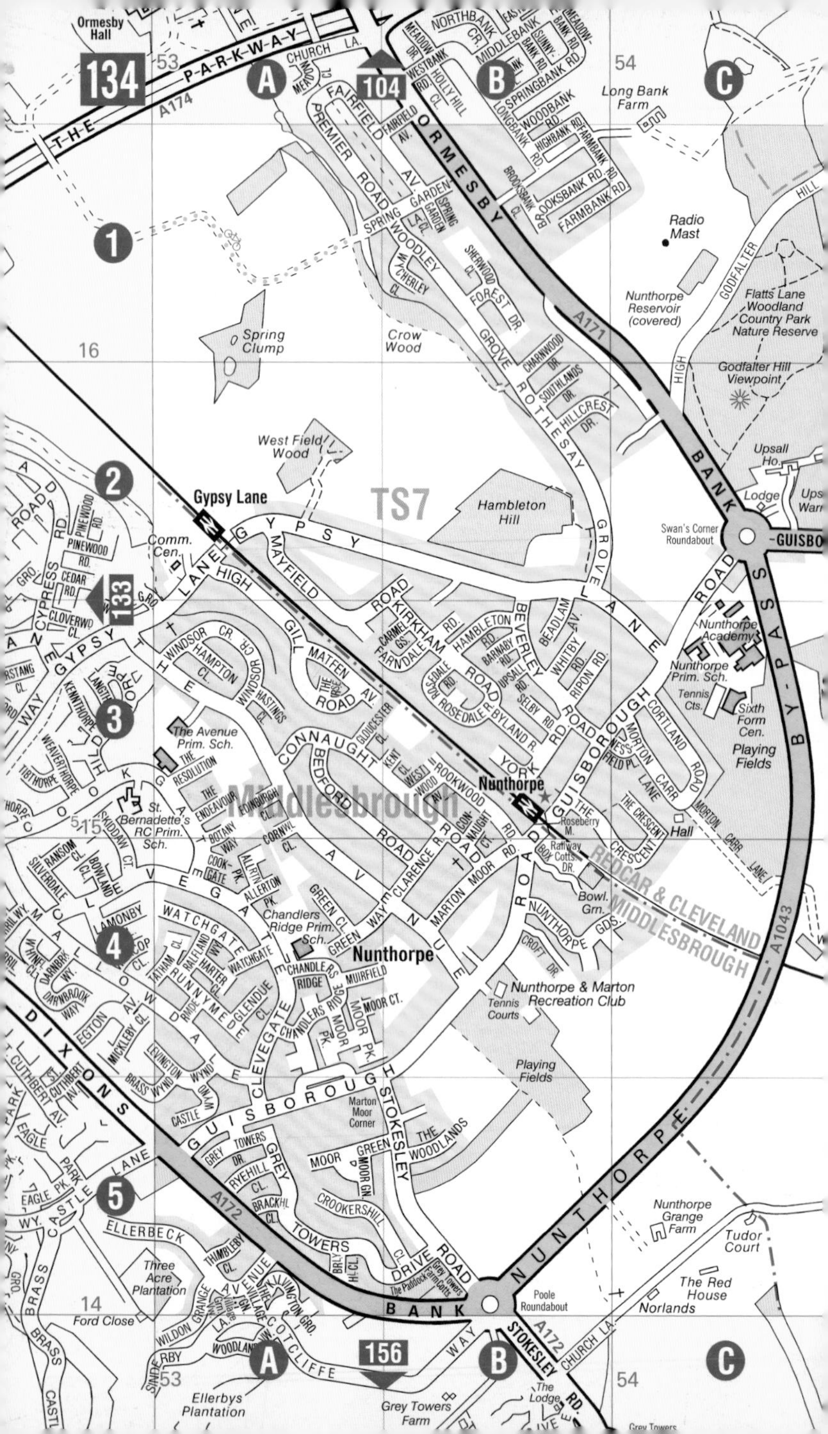
Ormesby Hall
THE PARKWAY
A174
CHURCH LA.
104
NORTHBANK CR.
MIDDLEBANK
MEADOW DR.
WESTBANK RD.
HOLLY HILL CL.
SPRINGBANK RD.
WOODBANK RD.
HIGHBANK RD.
FARMBANK RD.
BROOKSBANK RD.
LONGBANK RD.
Long Bank Farm
FAIRFIELD AV.
PREMIER ROAD
SPRING GARDEN
SPRING GARDEN CL.
WOODLEY GROVE
WYCHERLEY CL.
ORMESBY BANK
A171
SHERWOOD CL.
FOREST DR.
Radio Mast
Nunthorpe Reservoir (covered)
GODFALTER HILL
HIGH
Flatts Lane Woodland Country Park Nature Reserve
Godfalter Hill Viewpoint
Spring Clump
Crow Wood
16
CHARNWOOD DR.
SOUTHLANDS DR.
HILLCREST DR.
ROTHESAY GROVE
West Field Wood
Hambleton Hill
TS7
Upsall Ho.
Lodge
Swan's Corner Roundabout
GUISBOROUGH
Gypsy Lane
GYPSY LANE
GROVE LANE
Comm. Cen.
PINEWOOD RD.
CEDAR RD.
CYPRESS RD.
CLOVERWD CL.
133
MAYFIELD ROAD
HIGH GILL ROAD
KIRKHAM ROAD
HAMBLETON RD.
BEVERLEY ROAD
BEADLAM AV.
WHITBY RD.
RIPON RD.
BARNABY RD.
UPSALL RD.
SELBY RD.
BYLAND R.
ROSEDALE RD.
FARNDALE RD.
CARMEL GS.
Nunthorpe Academy
Nunthorpe Prim. Sch.
Tennis Cts.
Sixth Form Cen.
Playing Fields
BY-PASS
GUISBOROUGH ROAD
CORTLAND ROAD
MORTON CARR LANE
THE CRESCENT
Hall
WINDSOR CR.
HAMPTON CL.
HASTINGS CL.
MATFEN AV.
THE AVENUE
The Avenue Prim. Sch.
CONNAUGHT ROAD
BEDFORD ROAD
GLOUCESTER CL.
KENT CL.
WESTWOOD AV.
ROOKWOOD ROAD
YORK RD.
Nunthorpe
Roseberry M.
Railway Cotts. DR.
Middlesbrough
THE RESOLUTION
THE ENDEAVOUR
EDINBURGH
BOTANY WAY
COOK GATE
CORNWL CL.
CLARENCE R.
CONNAUGHT CT.
MARTON MOOR RD.
St. Bernadette's RC Prim. Sch.
SKIDDAW CT.
RANSOM CL.
BOWLAND CL.
SILVERDALE
ALLERTON PK.
Chandlers Ridge Prim. Sch.
GREEN CL.
GREEN WAY
Bowl. Grn.
NUNTHORPE GDS.
CROFT DR.
REDCAR & CLEVELAND
MIDDLESBROUGH
A1043
LAMONBY
WATCHGATE
RALFLAND WY.
HARTER CL.
TATHAM CL.
RUNNYMEDE
GLENDUE CL.
CHANDLERS RIDGE
MUIRFIELD
MOOR CT.
MOOR PK.
Nunthorpe & Marton Recreation Club
Tennis Courts
Playing Fields
DIXONS
DARNBROOK WAY
EGTON AV.
MICKLEBY CL.
LEVINGTON WYND
BRASS WYND
CASTLE
CLEVEGATE
GUISBOROUGH ROAD
STOKESLEY ROAD
Marton Moor Corner
THE WOODLANDS
MOOR GREEN
MOOR GN.
CROOKERSHILL
GREY TOWERS DR.
RYEHILL CL.
BRACKHL CL.
TOWERS DRIVE
A172
ST. CUTHBERT AV.
EAGLE PARK
EAGLE PK.
CASTLE LANE
ELLERBECK
THIMBLEBY CL.
Three Acre Plantation
NUNTHORPE
Nunthorpe Grange Farm
Tudor Court
The Red House
Norlands
Poole Roundabout
BANK
14
Ford Close
WILDON GRANGE
THE VILLAGE
COTCLIFFE
WOODLAND
156
WAY
STOKESLEY RD.
CHURCH LA.
53
54
Ellerbys Plantation
Grey Towers Farm
The Lodge

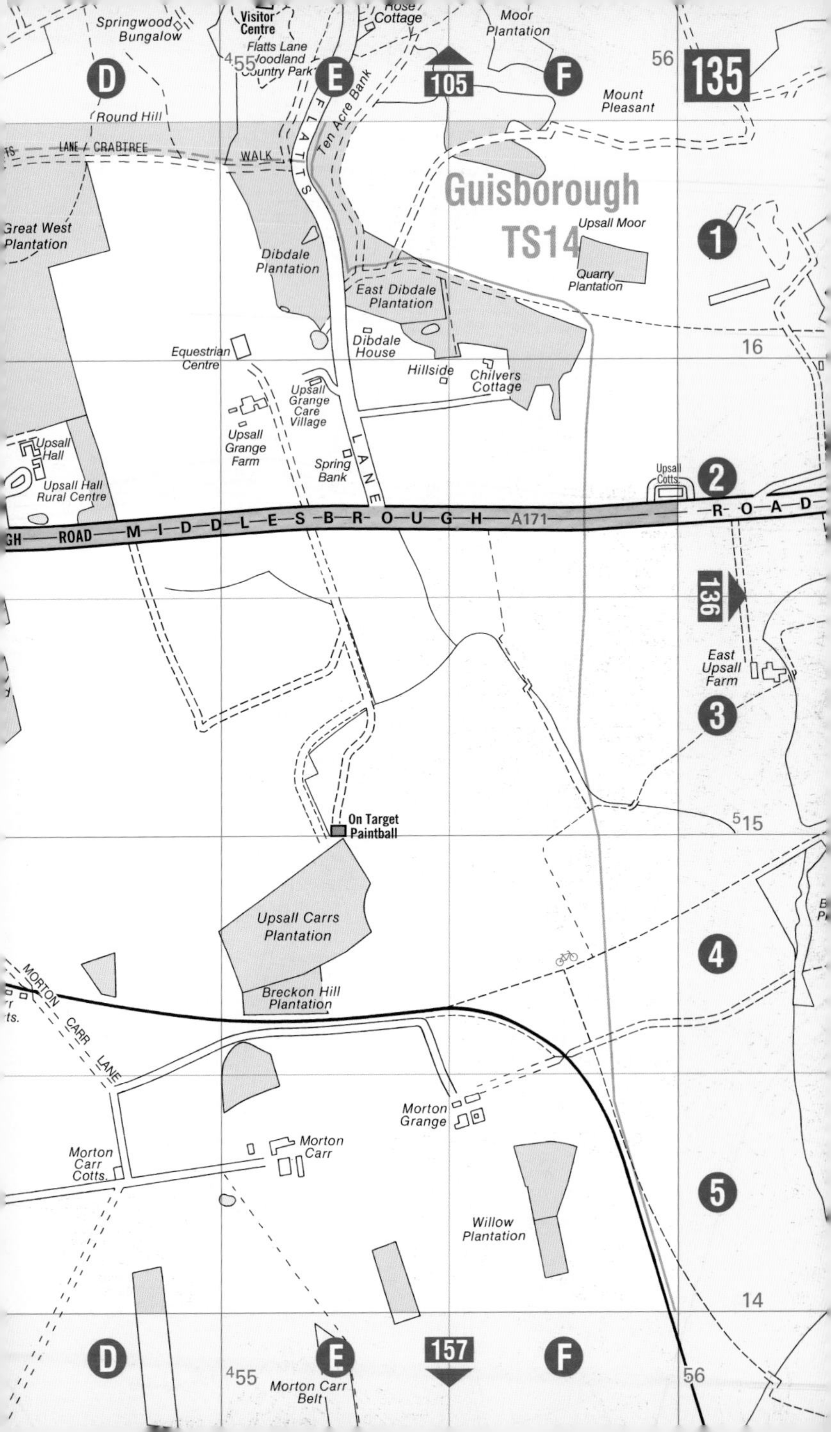
135
Springwood Bungalow
Visitor Centre
Flatts Lane Woodland Country Park
Rose Cottage
Moor Plantation
455
56
105
D
E
F
Round Hill
Mount Pleasant
LANE / CRABTREE WALK
FLATTS LANE
Ten Acre Bank
Guisborough
TS14
Upsall Moor
Quarry Plantation
Great West Plantation
Dibdale Plantation
East Dibdale Plantation
Dibdale House
Equestrian Centre
Hillside
Chilvers Cottage
16
Upsall Grange Care Village
Upsall Grange Farm
Spring Bank
Upsall Hall
Upsall Hall Rural Centre
Upsall Cotts.
ROAD MIDDLESBROUGH A171 ROAD
1
2
3
4
5
136
East Upsall Farm
On Target Paintball
515
Upsall Carrs Plantation
Breckon Hill Plantation
MORTON CARR LANE
Morton Grange
Morton Carr
Morton Carr Cotts.
Willow Plantation
14
157
Morton Carr Belt

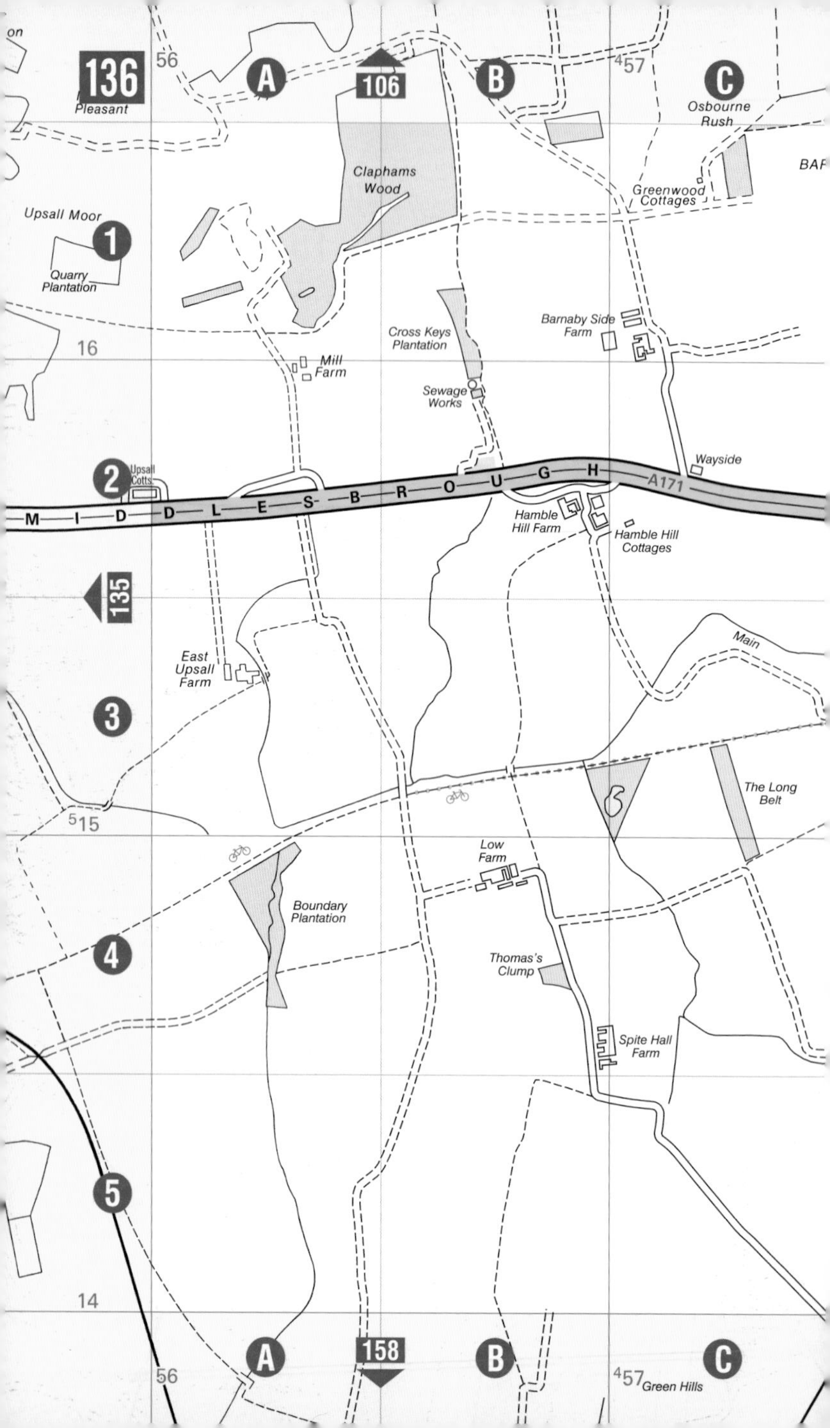
136
106
158
135
A
B
C
1
2
3
4
5
56
457
16
515
14
on
Pleasant
Osbourne Rush
BAR
Claphams Wood
Upsall Moor
Quarry Plantation
Greenwood Cottages
Barnaby Side Farm
Cross Keys Plantation
Mill Farm
Sewage Works
Wayside
Upsall Cotts
M-I-D-D-L-E-S-B-R-O-U-G-H
A171
Hamble Hill Farm
Hamble Hill Cottages
Main
East Upsall Farm
The Long Belt
Low Farm
Boundary Plantation
Thomas's Clump
Spite Hall Farm
Green Hills

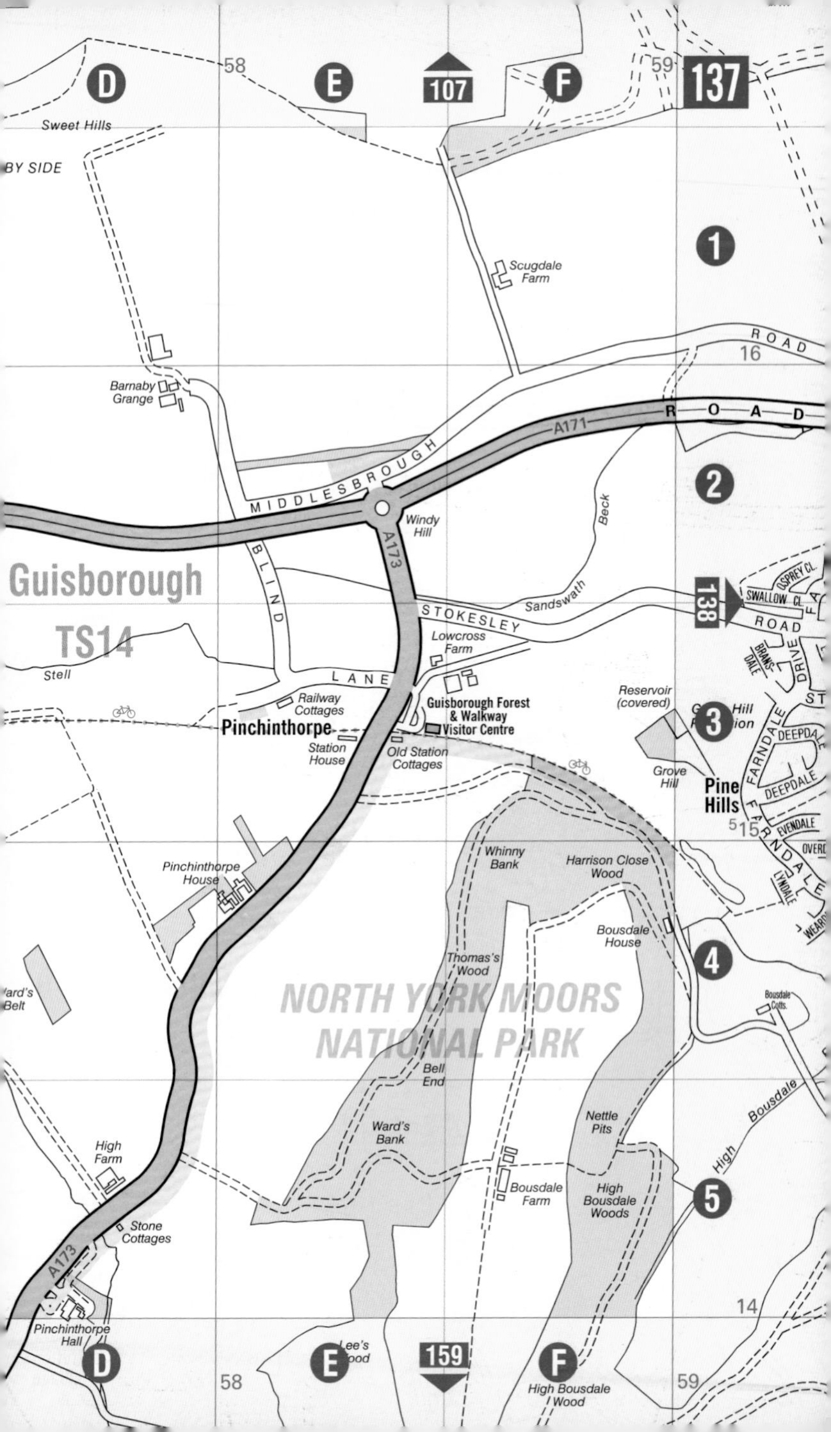

D
E
F
107
58
59
Sweet Hills
BY SIDE
Scugdale Farm
1
ROAD
16
Barnaby Grange
A171
ROAD
MIDDLESBROUGH
2
Windy Hill
A173
Beck
Guisborough
TS14
BLIND
Sandswath
STOKESLEY
ROAD
138
OSPREY CL.
SWALLOW CL.
BRANSDALE
DRIVE
Lowcross Farm
Stell
LANE
Railway Cottages
Guisborough Forest & Walkway Visitor Centre
Reservoir (covered)
3
Pinchinthorpe
Station House
Old Station Cottages
FARNDALE
DEEPDALE
DEEPDALE
Grove Hill
Pine Hills
15
EVENDALE
Whinny Bank
Harrison Close Wood
OVERDALE
LYNDALE
Pinchinthorpe House
Bousdale House
WEARDALE
4
Thomas's Wood
NORTH YORK MOORS NATIONAL PARK
Bousdale Cotts.
Ward's Belt
Bell End
Bousdale
Nettle Pits
High
Ward's Bank
High Farm
Bousdale Farm
High Bousdale Woods
5
Stone Cottages
A173
14
Pinchinthorpe Hall
Lee's Wood
159
High Bousdale Wood

138
108
137
A
B
C
1
2
3
4
5
59
460
16
515
14
Scugdale Close
Howl Beck
Holmes Bridge
Sewage Works
Wood House
Sandswath Bridge
Woodhouse Roundabout
MIDDLESBROUGH ROAD
MIDDLESBROUGH ROAD A171
GUISBOROUGH ROAD
King Play
Chapel Beck
Galley Hill
The Knoll
Chapel Beck Bri.
Westmead
Newstead
Sandswath Beck
STOKESLEY ROAD
Galley Hill Prim. Sch.
Comm. Cen.
Shop. Cen.
St. Paulinus Cath. Prim. Sch.
Reservoir (covered)
Grove Hill Plantation
Grove Hill
Pine Hills
Harrison Close Wood
Bousdale House
Hutton Beck
Highcliffe Primary School
Guisborough
TS14
Hutton Gate
Waterfall
Pease Ct.
Hutton Hall
Lowcross Gate
Bousdale Cotts.
High Bousdale Beck
Home Farm
Nettle Pits
High Bousdale Wood
Bousdale Farm
Hutton Lowcross Woods
Hall Heads
Blue Lake
Blue Lake Wood
Reed's Wood
NORTH YORK
High Bank Bottom
Hutton Village
HUTTON VILLAGE ROAD
HUTTON LANE
PARK
GUISBOROUGH ROAD
FALCON WAY
STAINDALE DRIVE
FARNDALE DRIVE
ROSEDALE DRIVE
THE AVENUE
CAMPION DRIVE
ST. LEONARDS ROAD
THAMES AV.
TIDKIN LA.
LOWCROSS AV.
WOODHOUSE ROAD

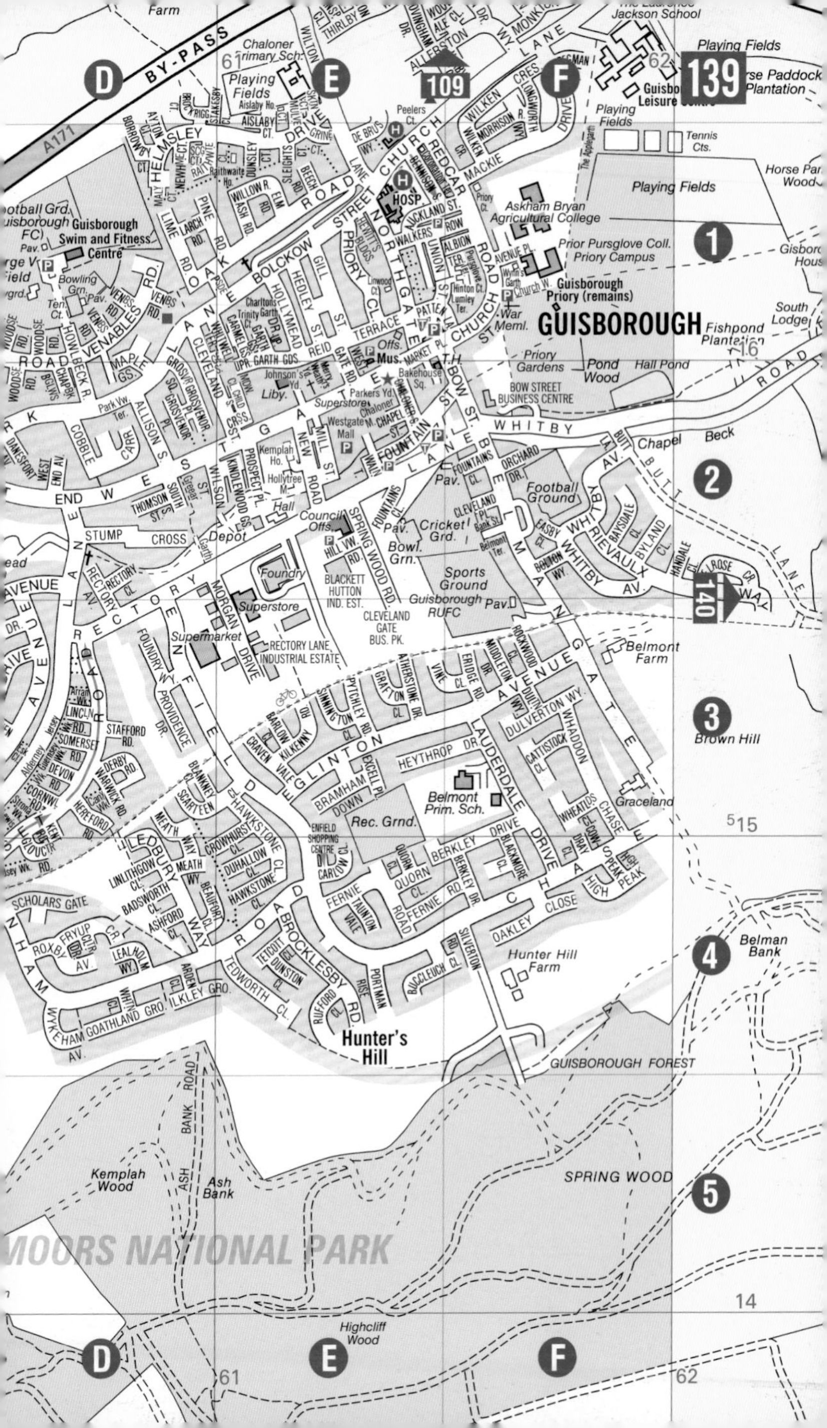

139
D
E
F
1
2
3
4
5
109
140
61
62
16
15
14
GUISBOROUGH
A171
BY-PASS
Chaloner Primary Sch.
Playing Fields
Playing Fields
Playing Fields
Horse Paddock Plantation
Guisborough Leisure Centre
Tennis Cts.
Horse Park Wood
Askham Bryan Agricultural College
Prior Pursglove Coll. Priory Campus
Guisborough Priory (remains)
War Meml.
South Lodge
Fishpond Plantation
Priory Gardens
Pond Wood
Hall Pond
BOW STREET BUSINESS CENTRE
HOSP.
Peelers Ct.
Guisborough Swim and Fitness Centre
Bowling Grn.
Mus.
T.H.
Bakehouse Sq.
Liby.
Superstore
Westgate Mall
Kemplah Ho.
Hollytree M.
Hall
Council Offs.
Depot
Foundry
Superstore
Supermarket
RECTORY LANE INDUSTRIAL ESTATE
BLACKETT HUTTON IND. EST.
CLEVELAND GATE BUS. PK.
Cricket Grd.
Bowl. Grn.
Sports Ground
Guisborough RUFC
Football Ground
Chapel Beck
Belmont Farm
Brown Hill
Graceland
Belmont Prim. Sch.
Rec. Grnd.
ENFIELD SHOPPING CENTRE
Hunter Hill Farm
Hunter's Hill
Belman Bank
GUISBOROUGH FOREST
SPRING WOOD
Kemplah Wood
Ash Bank
MOORS NATIONAL PARK
Highcliff Wood
WESTGATE
NORTHGATE
BOLCKOW ROAD
CHURCH STREET
WHITBY LANE
BELMANGATE
RECTORY LANE
ENFIELD ROAD
AVENUE
BROCKLESBY RD.
LAUDERDALE DRIVE
CHASE CLOSE
EGLINTON
STUMP CROSS
PARK LANE
WEST END
ASH BANK ROAD

The Laurence Jackson School
Playing Fields
Horse Paddocks Plantation
110
Peregrine Plantation
MUCKY LANE
63
62
A
B
C
Guisborough Leisure Centre
Playing Fields
Tennis Cts.
Horse Parks Wood
A171
Waterfall Cottages
Waterfall Farm
Playing Fields
Gisborough Hall
WHITBY
ROAD
Prior Pursglove Coll. Priory Campus
Gisborough House
Guisborough Priory (remains)
South Lodge
Fishpond Plantation
16
Priory Gardens
Pond Wood
Hall Pond
ROAD FANCY
Little Waterfall Farm
WHITBY
Chapel Beck
BUTTS LA.
Football Ground
Foxdale Farm
BUTT LA.
WHITBY AV.
EASBY CL.
RIEVAULX
BAYSDALE CL.
BYLAND CL.
HANDALE CL.
MELROSE CR.
WAY
BOLTON WY.
WHITBY
139
Belmont Farm
Guisborough
TS14
Brown Hill
WHADDON
CATTISTOCK CL.
Cow Pasture Hill
Graceland
15
DRIVE
HIGH PEAK
CLOSE
West Banks
Belman Bank
GUISBOROUGH WOODS
GUISBOROUGH FOREST
SPRING WOOD
14
1
2
3
4
5
Westworth Wood

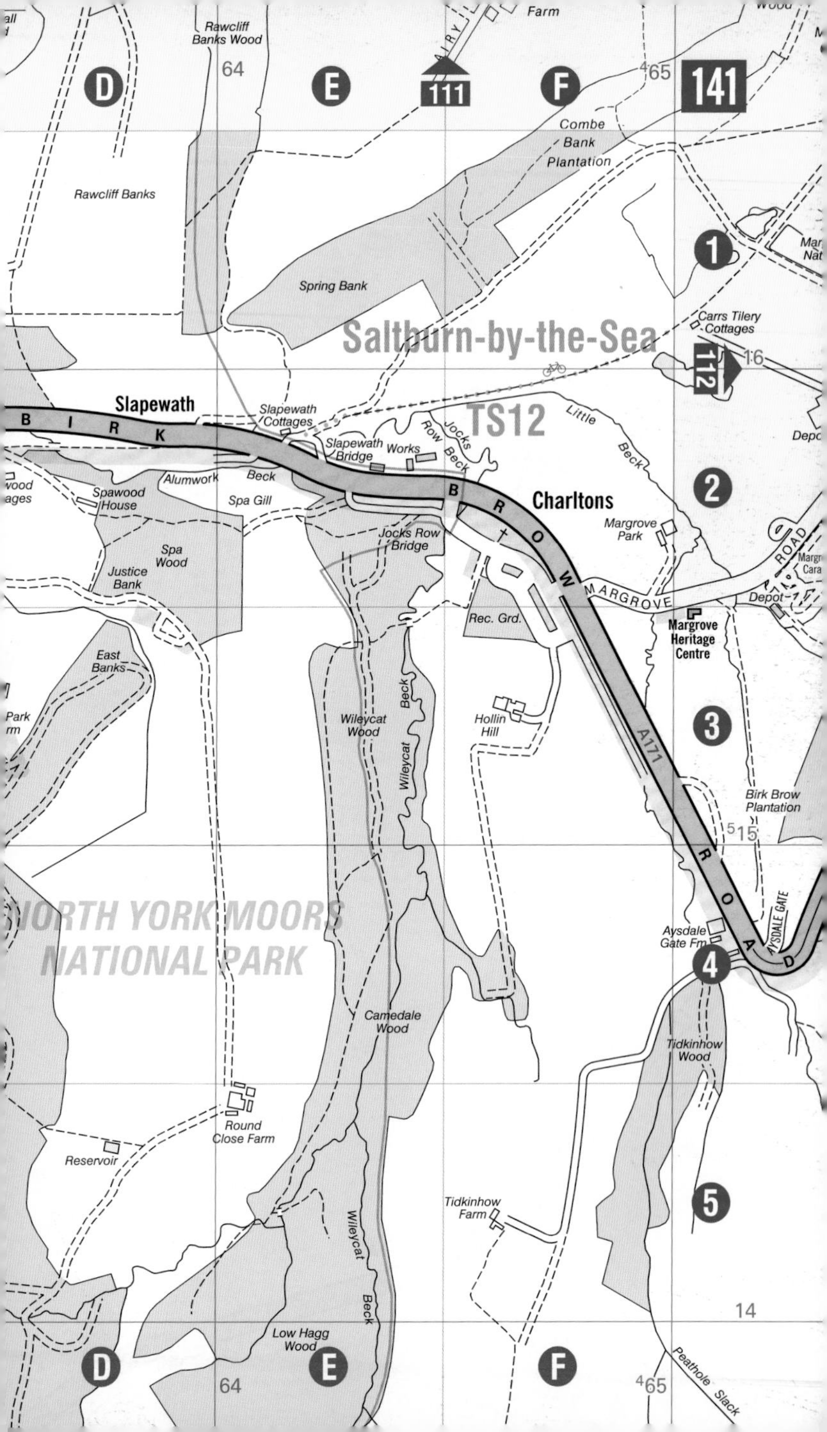
141
Rawcliff Banks Wood
Farm
AIRY
111
64
465
D
E
F
Combe Bank Plantation
Rawcliff Banks
1
Spring Bank
Carrs Tilery Cottages
Saltburn-by-the-Sea
112
16
Slapewath
Slapewath Cottages
TS12
Little Beck
Jocks Row Beck
Slapewath Bridge
Works
BIRK BROW
Alumwork
Beck
Spawood House
Spa Gill
Charltons
2
Margrove Park
Jocks Row Bridge
Spa Wood
Justice Bank
MARGROVE ROAD
Depot
Rec. Grd.
Margrove Heritage Centre
East Banks
Park
Wileycat Wood
Beck
Hollin Hill
3
Wileycat
A171
Birk Brow Plantation
515
NORTH YORK MOORS NATIONAL PARK
ROAD
AYSDALE GATE
Aysdale Gate Fm
4
Camedale Wood
Tidkinhow Wood
Round Close Farm
Reservoir
5
Tidkinhow Farm
Wileycat
Beck
14
Low Hagg Wood
Peathole Slack

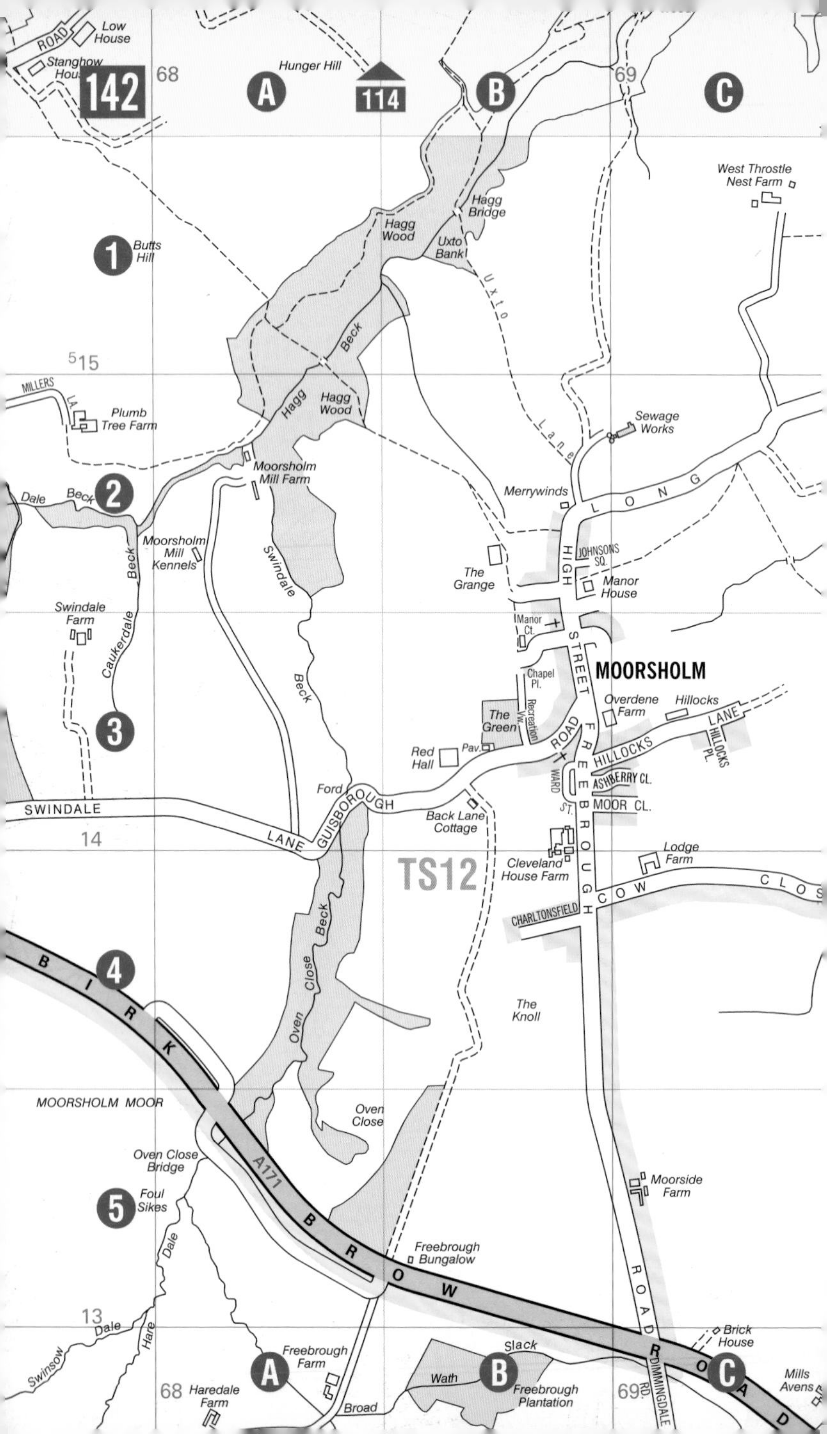
ROAD
Low House
Stanghow House
68
A
Hunger Hill
114
B
69
C
West Throstle Nest Farm
Hagg Bridge
Hagg Wood
Uxto Bank
Uxto Lane
1
Butts Hill
Hagg Beck
515
MILLERS LA.
Plumb Tree Farm
Hagg Wood
Sewage Works
Moorsholm Mill Farm
2
Dale Beck
Merrywinds
LONG
Moorsholm Mill Kennels
Swindale
The Grange
HIGH
JOHNSONS SQ.
Manor House
Caukerdale Beck
Swindale Farm
Manor Ct.
STREET
MOORSHOLM
Chapel Pl.
Beck
Overdene Farm
Hillocks
3
The Green
Recreation Vw.
Red Hall
Pav.
ROAD
HILLOCKS LANE
HILLOCKS PL.
FREEBROUGH
WARD ST.
ASHBERRY CL.
MOOR CL.
Ford
GUISBOROUGH
SWINDALE LANE
Back Lane Cottage
14
TS12
Cleveland House Farm
Lodge Farm
COW CLOSE
CHARLTONSFIELD
Oven Close Beck
4
BIRK BROW
The Knoll
MOORSHOLM MOOR
Oven Close
Oven Close Bridge
A171
5
Foul Sikes
Moorside Farm
Dale
Freebrough Bungalow
ROAD
13
Dale
Hare
Swinsow
Brick House
Slack
Freebrough Farm
A
Wath
B
Freebrough Plantation
C
Mills Avens
68
Haredale Farm
Broad
69
RD.
DIMMINGDALE

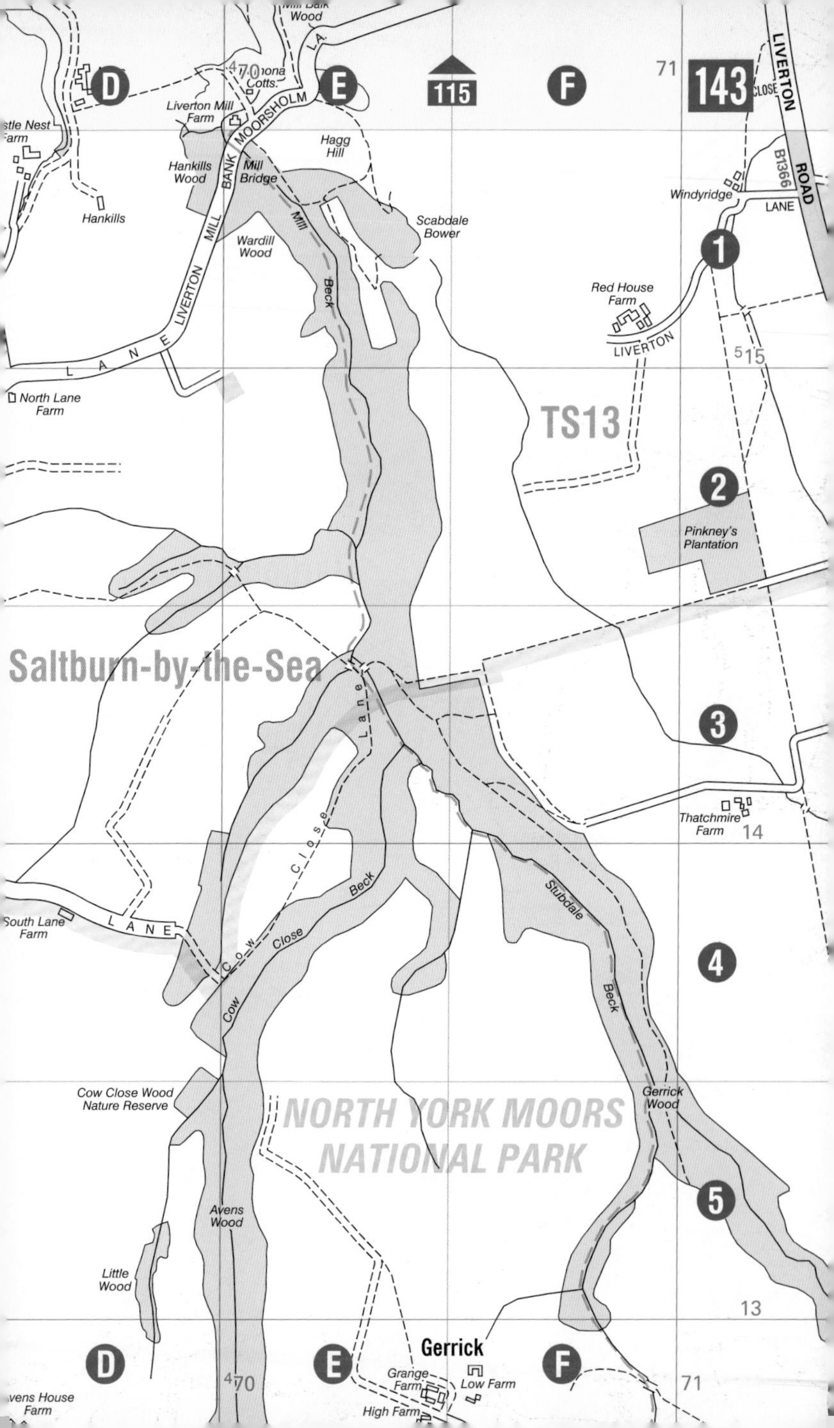
Mill Bank Wood
470
Ramona Cotts.
LA.
D
E
115
F
71
LIVERTON
CLOSE
stle Nest Farm
Liverton Mill Farm
MOORSHOLM
BANK
MILL
LIVERTON
LANE
Hagg Hill
Hankills Wood
Mill Bridge
B1366
ROAD
Windyridge
LANE
Hankills
Scabdale Bower
Wardill Wood
Mill
Beck
1
Red House Farm
LIVERTON
515
North Lane Farm
TS13
2
Pinkney's Plantation
Saltburn-by-the-Sea
Lane
3
Cow Close
Thatchmire Farm
14
Beck
Stubdale
South Lane Farm
LANE
Close
Cow
Cow
4
Beck
Gerrick Wood
Cow Close Wood Nature Reserve
NORTH YORK MOORS
NATIONAL PARK
5
Avens Wood
Little Wood
13
Gerrick
D
E
F
470
Grange Farm
Low Farm
71
vens House Farm
High Farm

435
A
122
B
36
C
West Hartburn Farm
West Hartburn Farm Cottage
LANE
14
Foster House
MILL
A67
The Whinnies Local Nature Reserve
RINGWAY
GRO.
YEADON
WLK.
WOOLSINGTON
ROW
HEATHROW CL.
WOODLANDS GN.
PRESTWICK CT.
SHANNON LEA
STANSTED GRO.
MANSTON CT.
THE BEECHES
ACORN CL.
Swain Ct.
DRIVE
Killinghall Row
YARM ROAD
Playground
ALEXANDRIA
VIRGINIA ESTATE
DENVER DR.
THE SPINNEY
FAIRFAX
WASHINGTON
ROAD
DRIVE
AVENUE
Oak Tree
ST. GEORGE
THE OAKS
OAKTREE CL.
CLOSE
OAK TREE
THE CRESCENT
ASHDALE CL.
Oaktree Farm
Depot
MIDDLETON ST. GEORGE
THE WATERSIDE
Middleton Woods
Middleton Hall
The Lodge
High Scrog Farm
PINE TREE GRO.
Darlington
513
DL2
Robinson's Plantation
MIDDLETON
ST. MARGARETS CL.
ST. ANNES GS.
COATHAM AV.
DESMOND RD.
Oaklands Farm
Byers End
High Meadows
THE PADDOCK
CEDAR GRO.
ROPNER GDS.
Village Farm
Middleton One Row
LANE
CHURCH LA.
THE
Devonport Gds.
THE OAKLANDS
ARCHER RD.
EAST VW.
HILL RISE
Tower Hill
RIVER TEES
The Green
FRONT
White House
DARLINGTON
HAMBLETON
12
Sewage Works
5
Masarak
Poltalloch Lodge
Over Dinsdale Grange
Over Dinsdale Hall
Grange Cottage
Ivy Cottages
The Farmhous
West Middleton Farm
Inte
Fire
1
2
3
4

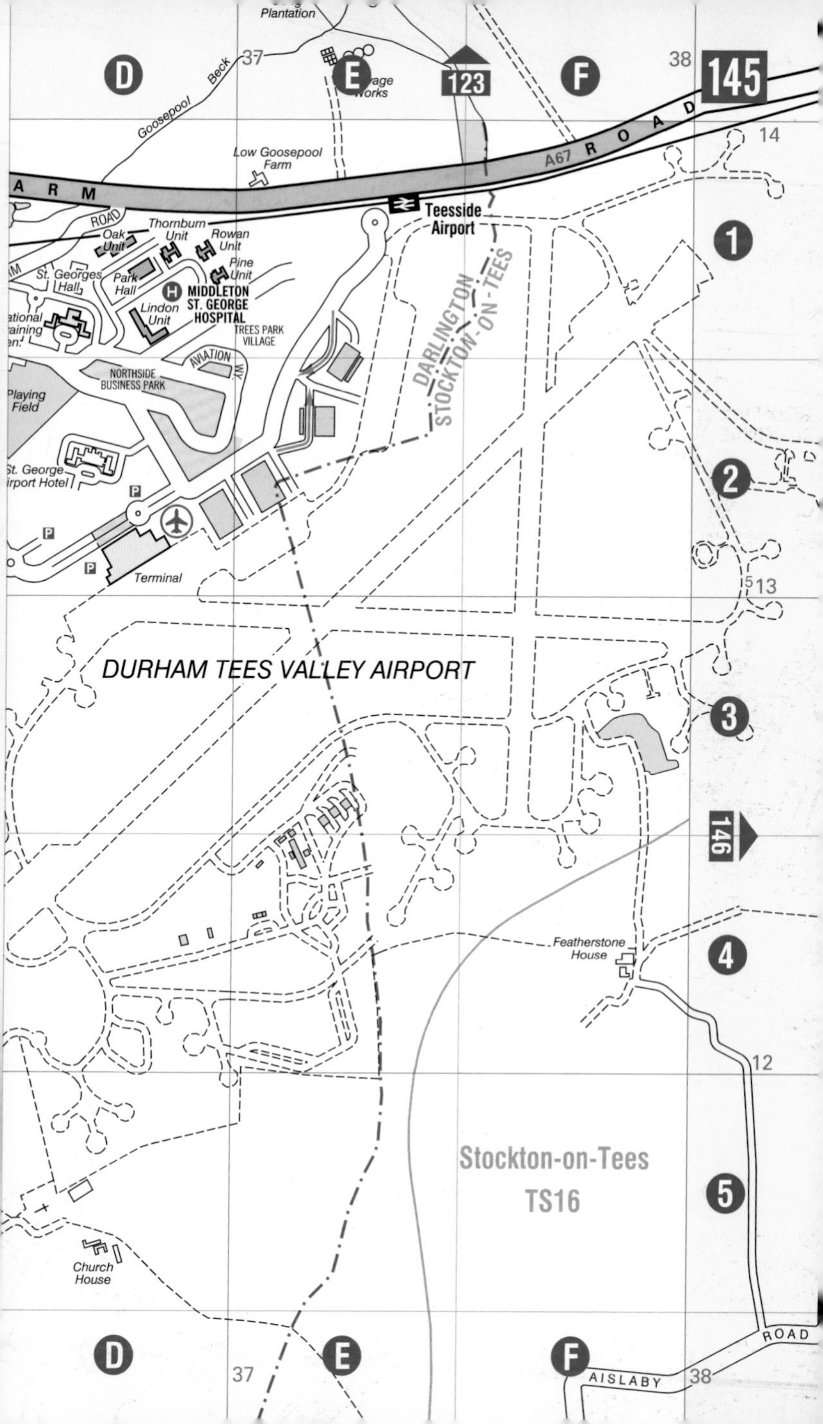
Plantation
D
E
F
37
38
123
Beck
Goosepool
Sewage Works
A67 ROAD
ARM
ROAD
Low Goosepool Farm
14
Teesside Airport
Thornburn Unit
Oak Unit
Rowan Unit
Pine Unit
St. Georges Hall
Park Hall
MIDDLETON ST. GEORGE HOSPITAL
Lindon Unit
TREES PARK VILLAGE
ational raining en.
AVIATION WY.
NORTHSIDE BUSINESS PARK
Playing Field
DARLINGTON
STOCKTON-ON-TEES
St. George Airport Hotel
P
Terminal
1
2
3
4
5
13
DURHAM TEES VALLEY AIRPORT
146
Featherstone House
12
Stockton-on-Tees
TS16
Church House
D
E
F
37
38
ROAD
AISLABY

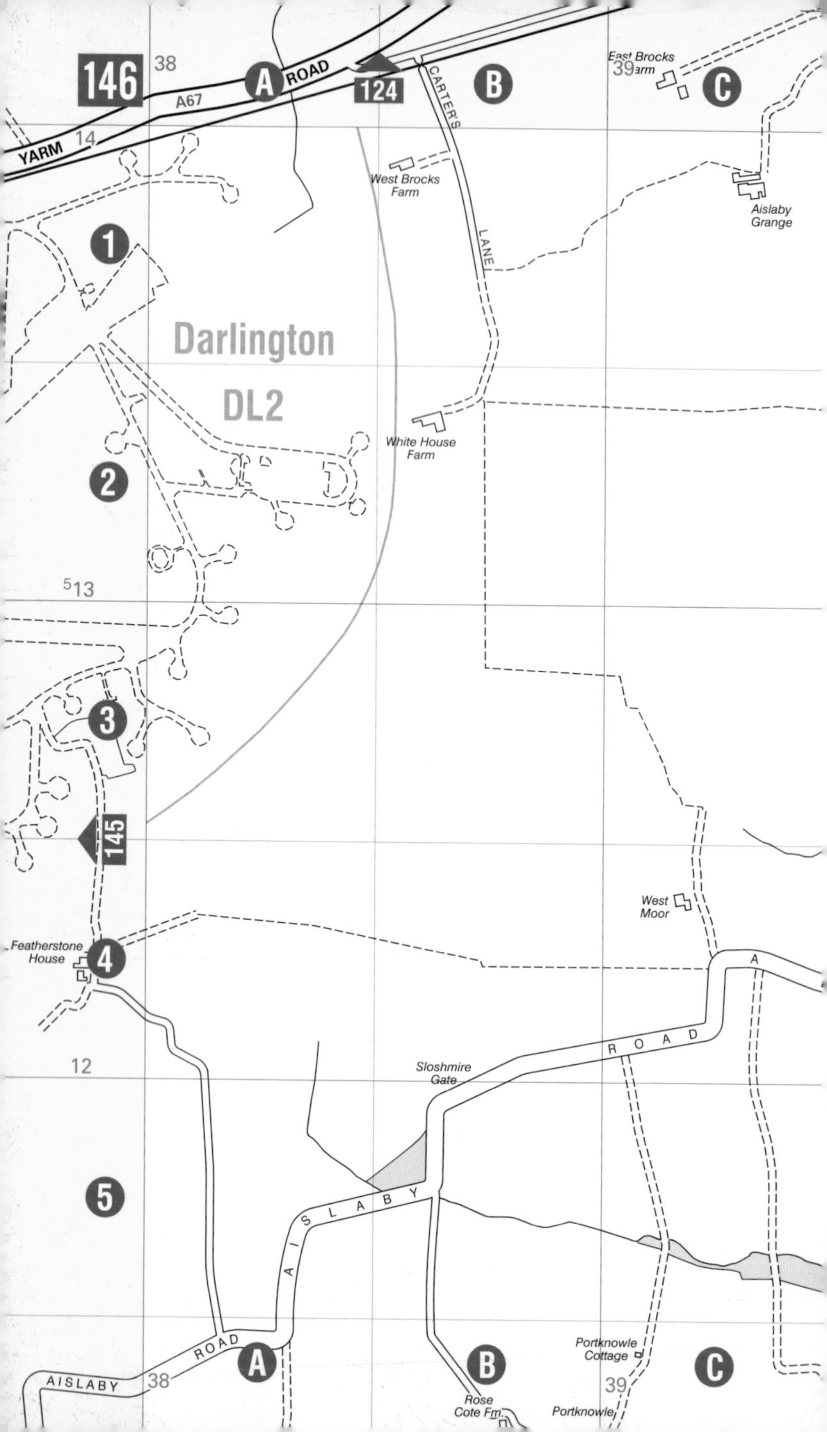

38
A
ROAD
A67
124
CARTER'S
LANE
B
East Brocks Farm
39
C
YARM
14
West Brocks Farm
Aislaby Grange
1
Darlington
DL2
White House Farm
2
513
3
145
West Moor
Featherstone House
4
A
ROAD
12
Sloshmire Gate
5
AISLABY
ROAD
AISLABY
38
A
B
C
Portknowle Cottage
39
Rose Cote Fm.
Portknowle

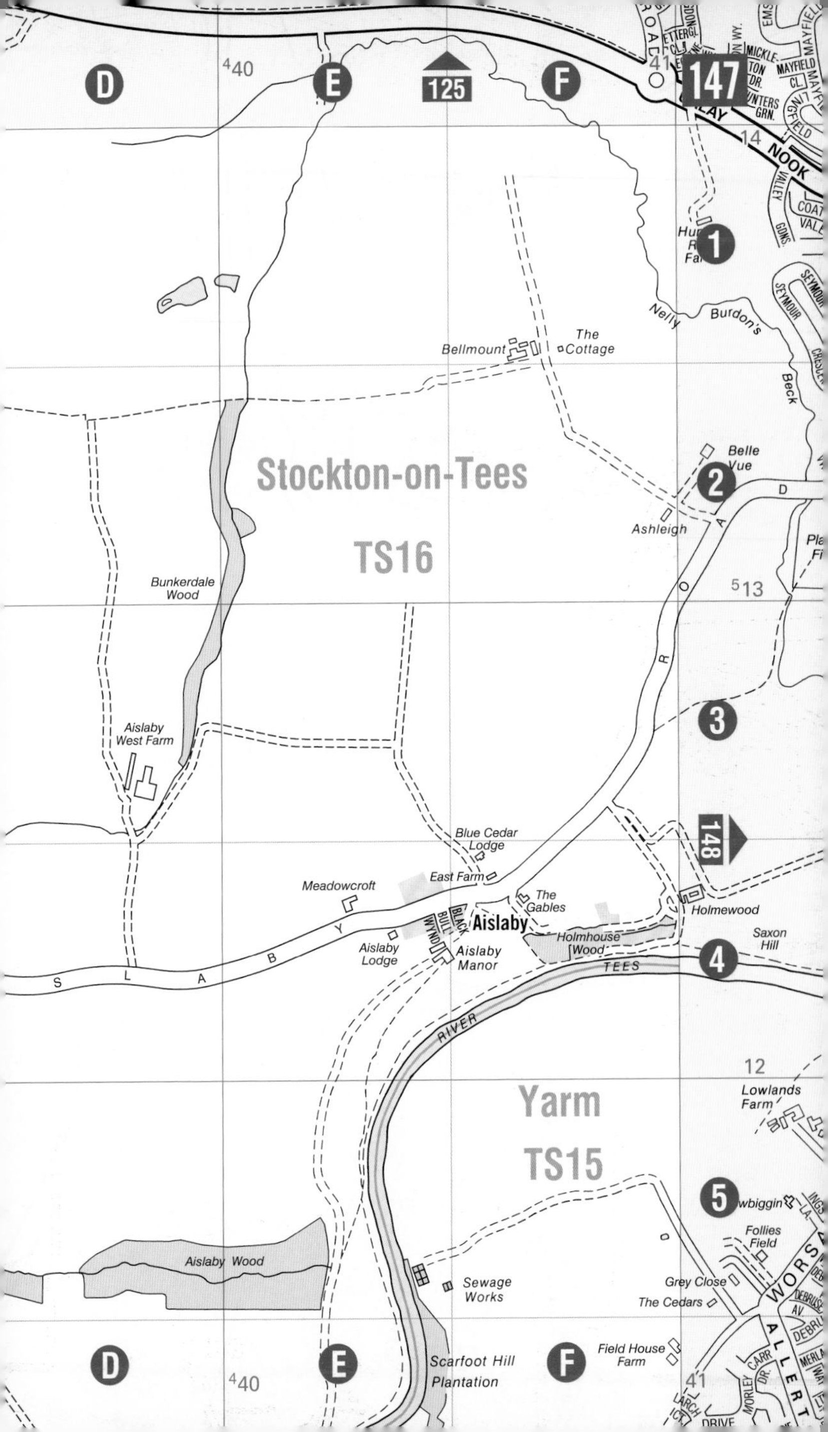

D
E
F
440
125
147
1
2
3
4
5
148
14
41
513
12
Stockton-on-Tees
TS16
Yarm
TS15
Bellmount
The Cottage
Nelly Burdon's Beck
Belle Vue
Ashleigh
Bunkerdale Wood
Aislaby West Farm
Blue Cedar Lodge
East Farm
Meadowcroft
The Gables
Aislaby
BLACK BULL WYND
Aislaby Lodge
Aislaby Manor
Holmhouse Wood
Holmewood
Saxon Hill
SLAISBY ROAD
RIVER TEES
Lowlands Farm
Follies Field
Grey Close
The Cedars
Field House Farm
Aislaby Wood
Sewage Works
Scarfoot Hill Plantation
MAYFIELD
MICKLETON DR.
HUNTERS GRN.
NOOK
VALLEY GDNS.
SEYMOUR
ALLERTON
WORSALL
CARR
MORLEY
LARCH CT.
DRIVE
DEBRUSE AV.

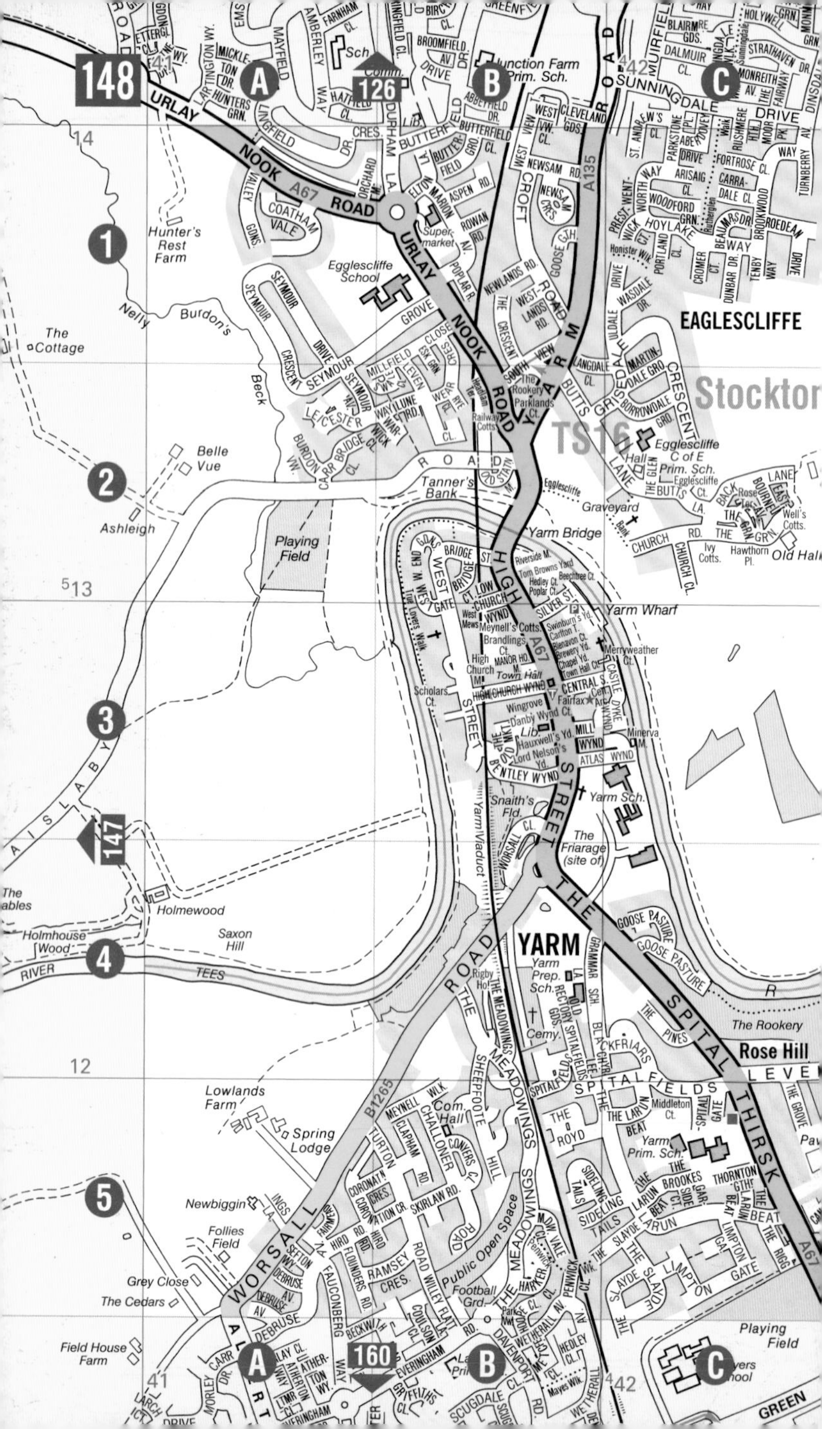

A
B
C
126
160
147
1
2
3
4
5
41
42
14
13
12
URLAY NOOK ROAD
A67
Junction Farm Prim. Sch.
Sch.
Comm.
Lib.
Super-market
Egglescliffe School
Hunter's Rest Farm
Nelly Burdon's Beck
The Cottage
Belle Vue
Ashleigh
Playing Field
Tanner's Bank
Yarm Bridge
Egglescliffe Graveyard
Egglescliffe C of E Prim. Sch.
EAGLESCLIFFE
Stockton
TS16
YARM ROAD
A135
HIGH STREET
Yarm Wharf
Town Hall
Yarm Sch.
The Friarage (site of)
Snaith's Fld.
Yarm Viaduct
THE SPITAL
THIRSK
AISLABY
Holmewood
Holmhouse Wood
Saxon Hill
RIVER TEES
YARM
Yarm Prep. Sch.
Cemy.
The Rookery
Rose Hill
LEVEN
Lowlands Farm
Spring Lodge
B1265
WORSALL ROAD
Newbiggin
Follies Field
Grey Close
The Cedars
Field House Farm
Com. Hall
Public Open Space
Football Grd.
Yarm Prim. Sch.
Playing Field
Old Hall
Ivy Cotts.
Hawthorn Pl.
Well's Cotts.
SEYMOUR DRIVE
LEICESTER
CARR BRIDGE CL.
SUNNINGDALE DRIVE
MUIRFIELD
MEADOWINGS
SPITALFIELDS
LARUN BEAT
THE SLAYDE
LIMPTON GATE
GREEN

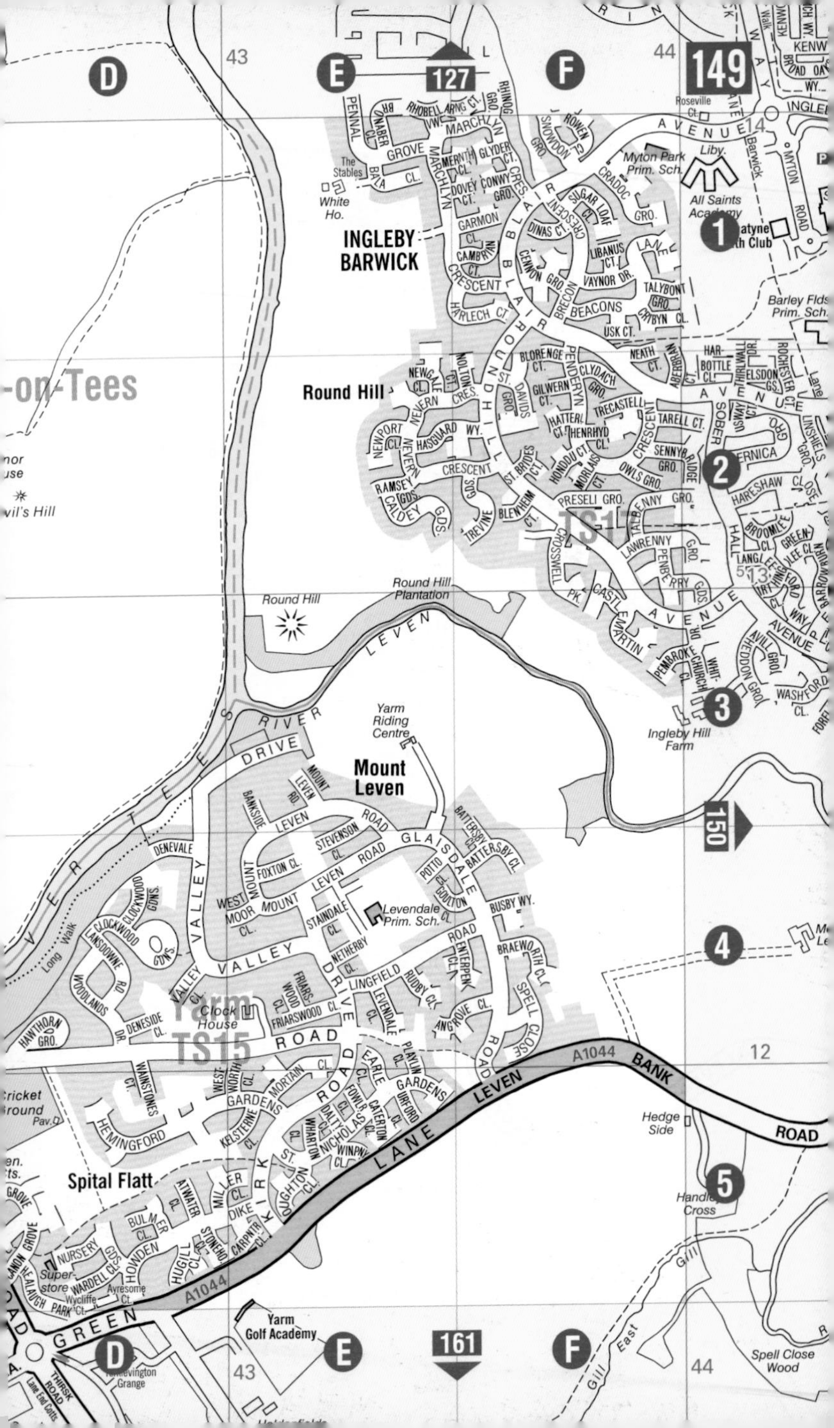
D
E
F
43
44
127
INGLEBY BARWICK
Round Hill
Round Hill
Round Hill Plantation
-on-Tees
RIVER LEVEN
RIVER TEES
Yarm Riding Centre
Mount Leven
Ingleby Hill Farm
150
1
2
3
4
5
14
13
12
TS17
TS15
Yarm
Clock House
Myton Park Prim. Sch.
All Saints Academy
Liby.
Roseville Ct.
Barley Flds Prim. Sch.
The Stables
White Ho.
AVENUE
BLAIR
CRESCENT
ROUNDHILL
SOBER HALL AVENUE
MYTON ROAD
Barwick Walk
GROVE
MARCHLYN
MARCHLYN CRES.
PENNAL
BRONABER CL.
RHOBELL
ARNG CT.
RHINOG GRO.
SNOWDON GRO.
ROWEN
GLYDER CT.
MERNTH CL.
DOVEY CT.
CONWY GRO.
BALA CL.
GARMON CL.
CAMBRIAN CT.
HARLECH CT.
CRADOC GRO.
SUGAR LOAF CT.
DINAS CT.
LIBANUS CT.
CENNON GRO.
VAYNOR DR.
TALYBONT GRO.
CRIBYN CL.
BRECON
BEACONS
USK CT.
NEATH CT.
ABERBRAN CT.
HAR-BOTTLE CL.
THIRLWALL DR.
ROCHESTER CT.
ELSDON GS.
BLORENGE CT.
PENDERYN
CLYDACH GRO.
GILWERN CT.
ST. DAVIDS GRO.
NEWGALE CL.
NOLTON CT.
NEVERN CRES.
NEWPORT CL.
HASGUARD WY.
NEVERN CRESCENT
RAMSEY GDS.
CALDEY GDS.
TREVINE
BLEWHEIM CT.
ST. BRIDES CT.
HATTERL CT.
HENRHYD CL.
TRECASTELL
MORLAIS CT.
HONDDU CT.
TARELL CT.
SENNYBRIDGE GRO.
OWLS GRO.
PRESELI GRO.
TALBENNY GRO.
LAWRENNY GRO.
PENBERRY GDS.
CROSSWELL PK.
CASTLE MARTIN
PEMBROKE DR.
CHURCH
WHIT-
USWAY CT.
OGMORE GRO.
ERNICA
HARESHAW CLOSE
LINSHIELS GRO.
BROOMLEE CL.
GREEN LEE CL.
LANGLEEFORD WAY
IRTHING CL.
BARROWBURN
HEDDON GRO.
AVILL GRO.
WASHFORD CL.
BATTERSBY CL.
BATTERSBY CL.
DRIVE
MOUNT LEVEN RD.
BANKSIDE
LEVEN
ROAD
STEVENSON CL.
GLAISDALE ROAD
DENEVALE
FOXTON CL.
WEST MOOR CL.
MOUNT
MOUNT LEVEN ROAD
POTTO CL.
GOULTON CL.
BUSBY WY.
Levendale Prim. Sch.
STAINDALE CL.
NETHERBY CL.
VALLEY
VALLEY DRIVE
CLOCKWOOD GDNS.
CLOCKWOOD GDNS.
LANSDOWNE RD.
WOODLANDS DR.
VALLEY CL.
FRIARSWOOD CL.
FRIARSWOOD CL.
LINGFIELD CL.
LEVENDALE
RUDBY CL.
ENTERPEN CL.
BRAEWORTH CL.
SPELL CLOSE
ANGROVE CL.
HAWTHORN GRO.
DENESIDE CL.
ROAD
Long Walk
A1044
LEVEN BANK ROAD
LEVEN LANE
Hedge Side
Handley Cross
WAINSTONES CT.
WESTWORTH CL.
GARDENS
MORTAIN CL.
EARLE CL.
PLAYLIN CL.
GARDENS
URFORD
HEMINGFORD
KELSTERNE CL.
FOWLR CL.
DALTY CL.
CATERTON CL.
WHARTON CL.
NICHOLAS CL.
WINPNY CL.
ST.
KIRK
DOUGHTON CL.
Spital Flatt
ATWATER CL.
MILLER CL.
DIKE
CARPNTR CL.
STONEHO CL.
HUGILL CL.
BULMER CL.
NURSERY GDS.
HOWDEN
WARDELL CL.
CANON GROVE
HEALAUGH PARK
Super-store
Wycliffe Ct.
Ayresome Ct.
GREEN ROAD
THIRSK ROAD
Lane End Cotts.
Kirklevington Grange
Cricket Ground
Pav.
GROVE
Yarm Golf Academy
161
East Gill
Gill
Spell Close Wood
Devil's Hill

INGLEBY BARWICK
Stockton-on-Tees
TS17
Beckfields
Sober Hall
High Leven
Leven Bridge
Little Maltby
128
149
162
A
B
C
1
2
3
4
5
44
45
14
13
12
Roseville Ct.
Myton Park Prim. Sch.
Liby.
All Saints Academy
Bannatyne Health Club
Superstore
Sub.
Romano Park
Barley Flds. Prim. Sch.
St.Therese of Lisieux Prim. Sch.
Comm. Cen.
Beckfields Cen.
Grosvenor Ct.
Ingleby Hill Farm
Leven View Residential Park
The Old Mill
Ingleby Mill Prim. Sch.
Leven Bridge Mill (disused)
Leven Holmes
Mount Leven
Roslin
Hedge Side
Handley Cross
Leven Bridge Plantation
Spell Wood
Crow Wood
Bassleton Beck
INGLEBY WAY
INGLEBY AVENUE
BARWICK WAY
BECKFIELDS AVENUE
BARWICK LANE
MYTON ROAD
SOBER HALL AVENUE
PENNINE WAY
LOW LANE
ROAD
LEVEN BANK
A1044
HILTON LANE
RIVER LEVEN
East Gill
BRIDGEWATER
PRIORWOOD
SIMONSIDE
DUNMOOR GRO.
BERNICA
HARESHAW CLOSE
KIRKNEWTON DRIVE
ROTHBURY CL.
REGENCY PARK
WINDMILL WY.
ROUNDHILL
CROSSWELL PK.
CASTLE MARTIN
BLAIR AVENUE
BEACONS
VAYNOR DR.
TALYBONT GRO.
USK CT.
PRESELI GRO.
LAWRENNY
PEMBROKE DR.
WASHFORD CL.
SELWORTHY
HAWKRIDGE CL.
DULVERTON
LUCCOMBE
WATERSMEET CL.
ACORN BANK
THORINGTON
AYLSHAM CL.
BRANTWOOD CL.
BUCKLAND CL.
CHARTWELL CL.
EMMETTS GDS.
FLORENCE CT.
NUNNINGTON
HANBURY CL.
HARESFIELD
BERRINGTON
ALFRISTON CL.
STONEACRE AV.
SALTRAM CL.
FELBRIGG GDS.
COLETON GDS.
UPTON CT.
BRANKLYN
HIDCOTE
CRAGSIDE CT.
MORVILLE CT.
MELFORD GRO.
CLAYDON GRO.
PETWORTH CR.
ICKWORTH CT.
ROWALLANE GS.
SPRINGHILL GRO.
JOWLETTS CT.
RAINHAM
STROME CL.
BROOK CL.
WELL GARDENS
PEACOCK CT.
BUNTING CL.
KEEPERS CL.
EIDER CL.
KENWOOD
MYTON WY.
STAINFORTH
MALHAM GRO.
PENSHAW CL.
WESTWOOD LA.
AVEBURY CL.
MARSDEN CL.
EASTBURY GARDENS
CHALFIELD CL.
OAKHURST
BRIMHAM CL.
RUFFORD CL.
BENINGBOROUGH GDS.
FOUNTAINS

Plum Tree Farm
129
151
HAILSHAM AV.
SADLER
FLECK
Works
DUKESWAY
CROSTHWAITE AV.
FORSTER
Nursery
AVENUE
WILLIAM
ALLISON
WAY
JAY AV.
Ingleby Manor Sch.
Factory
THORNABY ROAD
A1045
LOW LANE
B1380
A19
MIDDLESBROUGH
STOCKTON-ON-TEES
BEECH GROVE
WILLOWS AV.
MALTBY
Maltby
DUNSMORE CL.
OXHILL CL.
PENNYMAN GN.
HIGH
ROGER LANE
Homefield Farm
Pav.
ancis Park
tby Ckt. Club)
altby
m
A1044
Hazel Grove
Thorn
Farr
Maltby Farm
Middlesbrough
TS8
Oaklands Farm
Garthorne House
Woodcote
Maltby Grange
152
White House Farm
Yarm
TS15
Red Hill
Hilton Fishing Lakes
Hilton House
YARM
HILTON
Greenfield
Hilton House Farm
MANOR DR.
163
MOORBERRIES
FALCON
SEAMER ROAD
Fir Tree
D
E
F
1
2
3
4
5
46
47
14
13
12

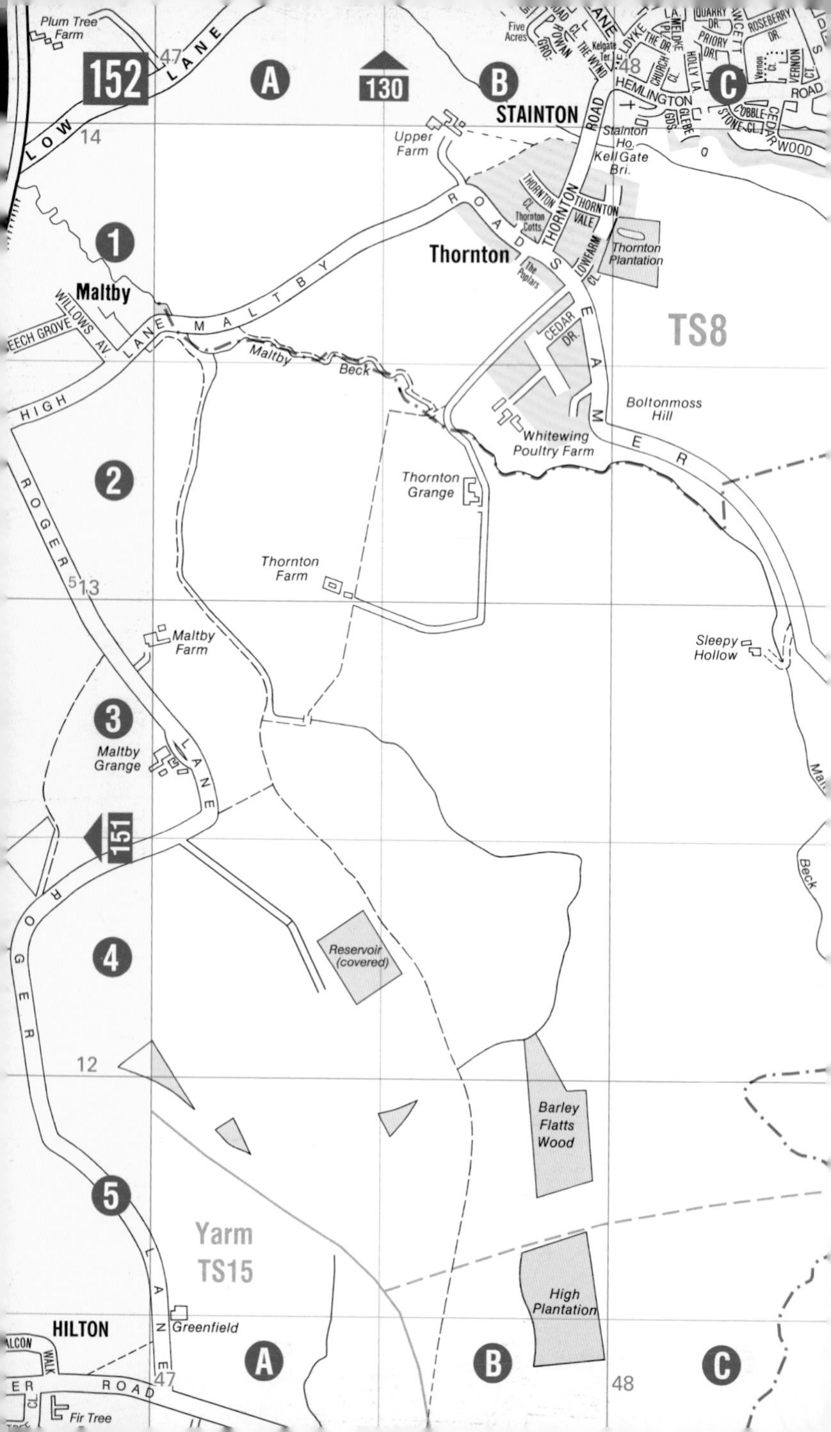
152
130
151
A
B
C
1
2
3
4
5
Plum Tree Farm
LOW LANE
47
14
STAINTON
Five Acres
ROWAN GRO.
THE WYND
Kelgate Ter.
LA.
QUARRY DR.
ROSEBERRY DR.
PRIORY DR.
THE DR.
MELDKE
CHURCH CL.
HOLLY LA.
Vernon Ct.
VERNON CT.
ROAD
48
HEMLINGTON
GLEBE GDS.
COBBLE-STONE CL.
CEDARWOOD
Upper Farm
Stainton Ho.
Kell Gate Bri.
THORNTON CL.
Thornton Cotts
THORNTON
THORNTON VALE
LOWFARM CL.
Thornton Plantation
Thornton
The Poplars
MALTBY ROAD
STAINTON ROAD
Maltby
WILLOWS AV.
BEECH GROVE
HIGH LANE
TS8
CEDAR DR.
Maltby Beck
Boltonmoss Hill
Whitewing Poultry Farm
Thornton Grange
Thornton Farm
ROGER LANE
13
Maltby Farm
Sleepy Hollow
Maltby Grange
Beck
Reservoir (covered)
12
Barley Flatts Wood
Yarm TS15
High Plantation
Greenfield
HILTON
FALCON WALK
ROAD
47
48
Fir Tree

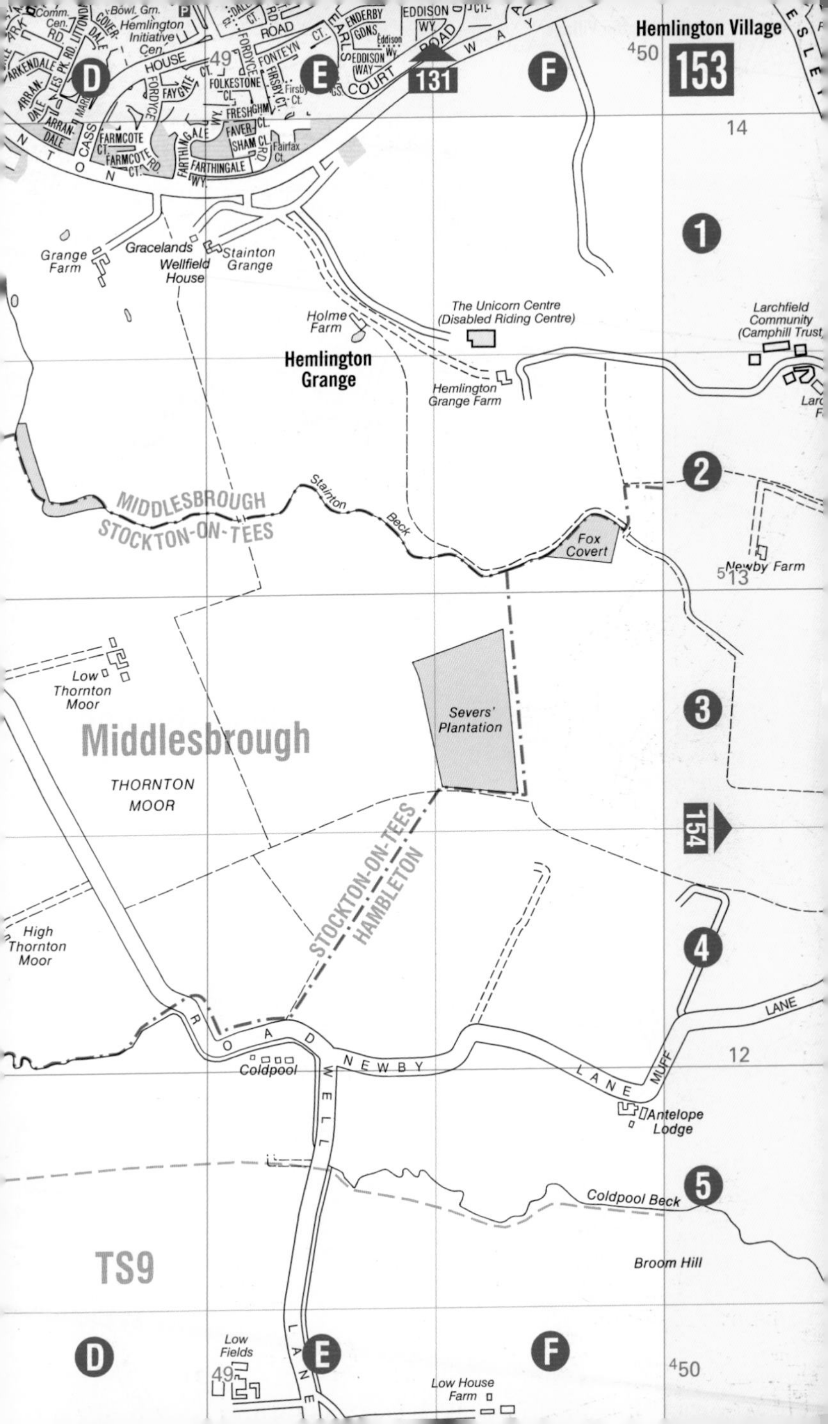
Hemlington Grange
Middlesbrough
TS9
MIDDLESBROUGH
STOCKTON-ON-TEES
STOCKTON-ON-TEES
HAMBLETON
THORNTON MOOR
Low Thornton Moor
High Thornton Moor
Grange Farm
Gracelands
Wellfield House
Stainton Grange
Holme Farm
The Unicorn Centre (Disabled Riding Centre)
Hemlington Grange Farm
Larchfield Community (Camphill Trust)
Stainton Beck
Fox Covert
Newby Farm
Severs' Plantation
Coldpool
NEWBY ROAD
WELL LANE
MUFF LANE
LANE
Antelope Lodge
Coldpool Beck
Broom Hill
Low Fields
Low House Farm
HEMLINGTON
HOUSE ROAD
EARLS COURT ROAD
WAY
Hemlington Initiative Cen.
Comm. Cen.
Bowl. Grn.
FARMCOTE CT.
FARMCOTE CT.
FARTHINGALE WY.
FARTHINGALE WY.
FAVERSHAM CL.
FOLKESTONE CL.
FRESHAM CL.
FAYGATE CT.
FORDYCE RD.
FONTEYN CT.
FIRSBY CT.
Firsby Ct.
Fairfax Ct.
ENDERBY GDNS.
EDDISON WY.
EDDISON WAY
Eddison Wy.
ARRANDALE
ARKENDALE
CASS
131
154
D E F
1 2 3 4 5
49
450
14
13
12
513

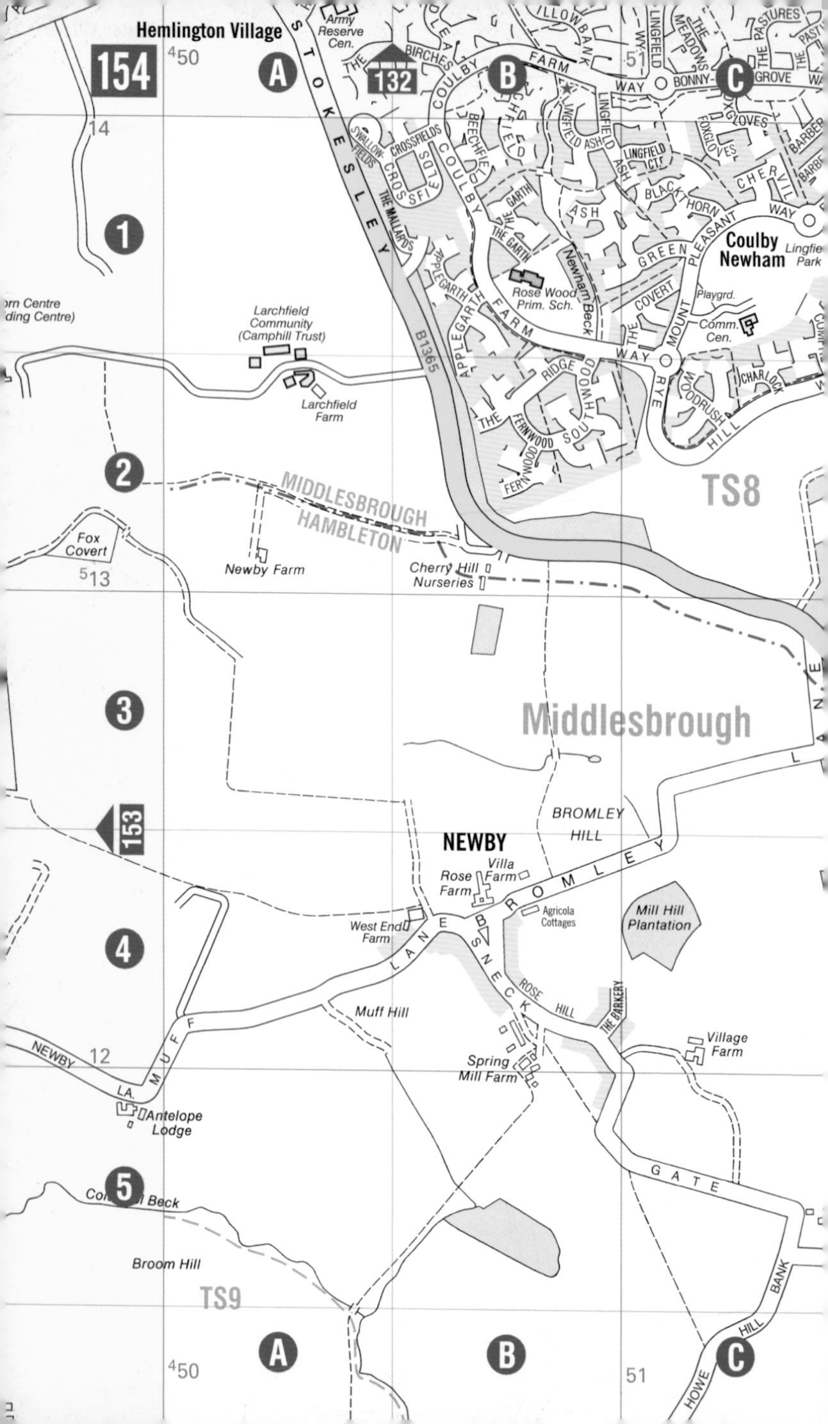
Hemlington Village
154
450
A
B
C
132
14
1
2
3
4
5
153
Army Reserve Cen.
THE BIRCHES
COULBY FARM WAY
LINGFIELD
THE MEADOWS
THE PASTURES
BONNY GROVE
FOXGLOVES
BARBERRY
SWALLOWFIELDS
CROSSFIELDS
THE MALLARDS
STOKESLEY
BEECHFIELD
LINGFIELD ASH
LINGFIELD CT.
THE GARTH
BLACKTHORN
CHERVIL WAY
PLEASANT
GREEN
ASH
Coulby Newham
Lingfield Park
Rose Wood Prim. Sch.
Newham Beck
APPLEGARTH
THE COVERT
MOUNT
Playgrd.
Comm. Cen.
RIDGE
SOUTHWOOD
THE FERNWOOD
RYE
WOODRUSH HILL
CHARLOCK
B1365
Larchfield Community (Camphill Trust)
Larchfield Farm
TS8
MIDDLESBROUGH
HAMBLETON
Fox Covert
513
Newby Farm
Cherry Hill Nurseries
Middlesbrough
BROMLEY HILL
NEWBY
Villa Farm
Rose Farm
BROMLEY LANE
Agricola Cottages
Mill Hill Plantation
West End Farm
SNECK
ROSE HILL
THE BAKERY
Muff Hill
Village Farm
Spring Mill Farm
NEWBY LA.
MUFF
12
Antelope Lodge
Broom Hill
TS9
GATE
HILL BANK
HOWE
51

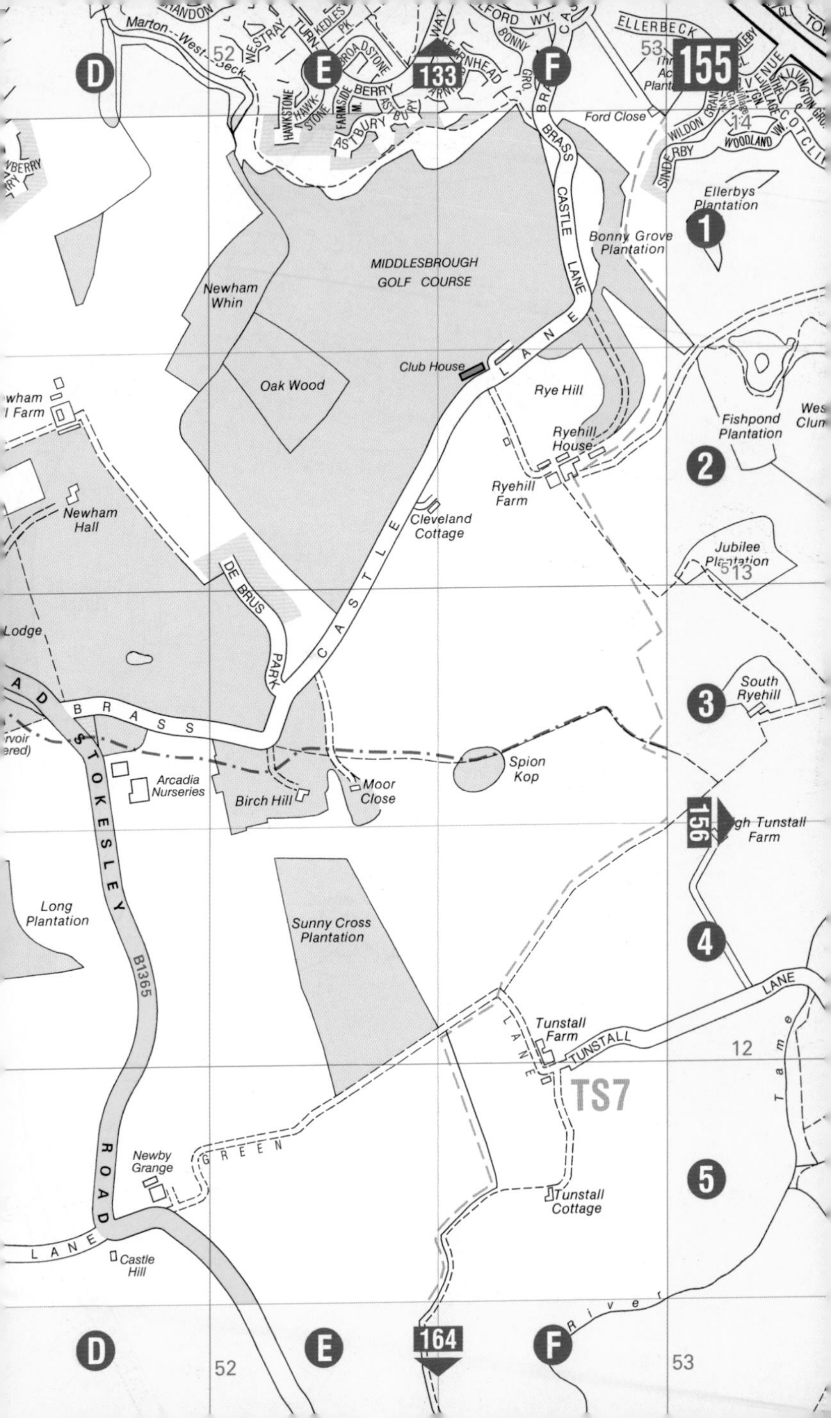

D
E
F
52
53
133
Marton West Beck
WESTRAY
TURN
KEDLES PK.
BROADSTONE
BERRY
HAWKSTONE
HAWKSTONE
FARMSIDE M.
ASTBURY
ASTBURY
FERNHEAD
ELLERBECK
Ford Close
Ellerbys Plantation
1
Bonny Grove Plantation
BRASS CASTLE LANE
MIDDLESBROUGH GOLF COURSE
Newham Whin
Oak Wood
Club House
Rye Hill
Ryehill House
Ryehill Farm
Fishpond Plantation
2
Newham Hall
Cleveland Cottage
Jubilee Plantation
13
DE BRUS PARK
CASTLE
Lodge
South Ryehill
3
BRASS
Spion Kop
Arcadia Nurseries
Birch Hill
Moor Close
156
High Tunstall Farm
STOKESLEY
Long Plantation
Sunny Cross Plantation
4
B1365
Tunstall Farm
TUNSTALL LANE
LANE
12
TS7
Tame
GREEN
Newby Grange
ROAD
5
Tunstall Cottage
LANE
Castle Hill
River
D
E
164
F
52
53

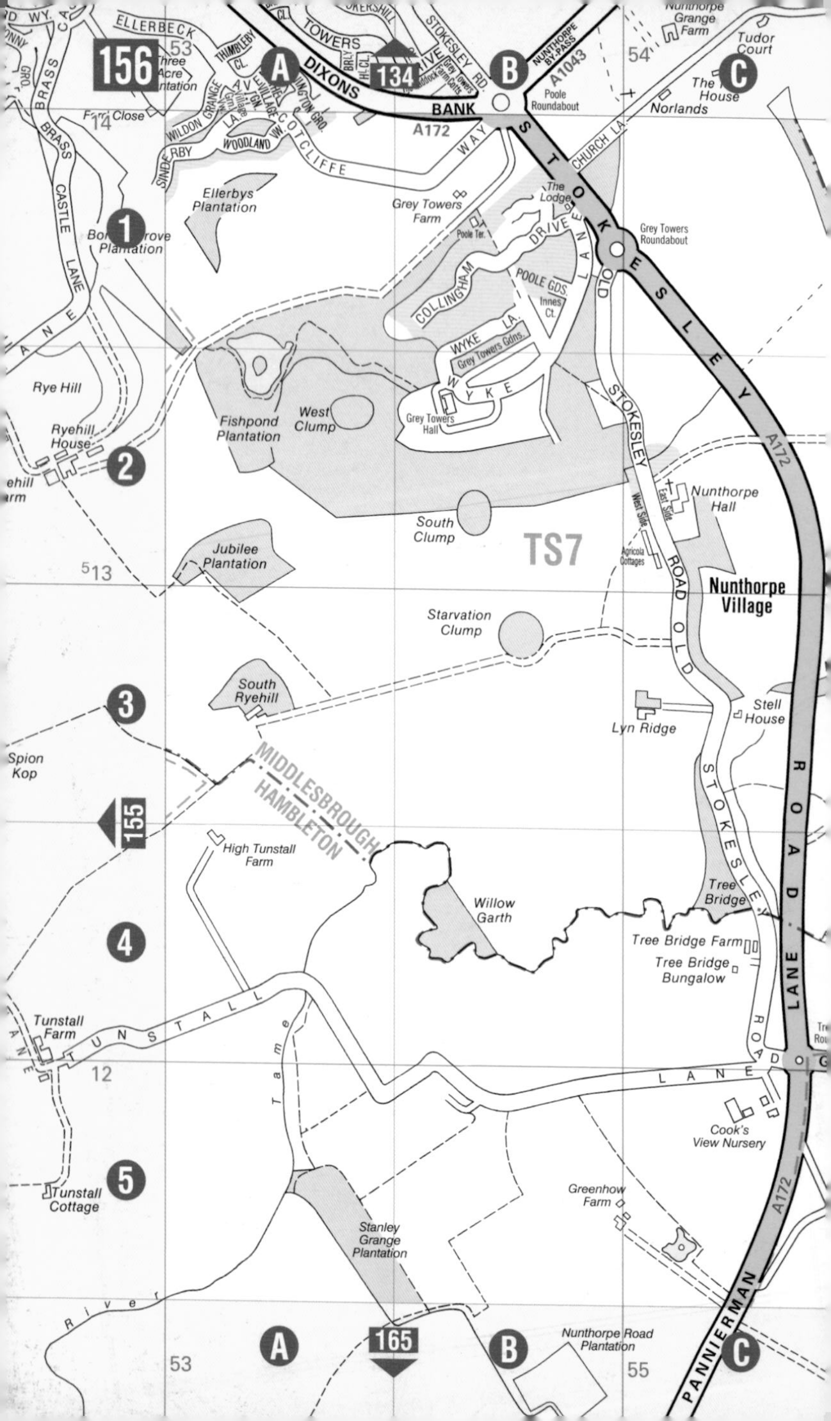

A
B
C
1
2
3
4
5
53
54
55
14
13
12
134
155
165
ELLERBECK
Three Acre Plantation
THIMBLEBY CL.
TOWERS
DIXONS
BANK
A172
STOKESLEY RD.
NUNTHORPE BY-PASS
A1043
Poole Roundabout
Nunthorpe Grange Farm
Tudor Court
Norlands
BRASS CASTLE LANE
Farm Close
WILDON GRANGE
WOODLAND
SINDERBY
COTCLIFFE WAY
CHURCH LA.
Ellerbys Plantation
Grey Towers Farm
Poole Ter.
The Lodge
Grey Towers Roundabout
STOKESLEY ROAD
COLLINGHAM DRIVE
POOLE GDS.
Innes Ct.
WYKE LA.
Grey Towers Gdns.
WYKE
OLD LANE
Grey Towers Hall
Rye Hill
Ryehill House
Fishpond Plantation
West Clump
South Clump
TS7
STOKESLEY
West Side
East Side
Nunthorpe Hall
Agricola Cottages
ROAD OLD
Nunthorpe Village
Jubilee Plantation
Starvation Clump
South Ryehill
Lyn Ridge
Stell House
Spion Kop
MIDDLESBROUGH
HAMBLETON
High Tunstall Farm
STOKESLEY
Willow Garth
Tree Bridge
Tree Bridge Farm
Tree Bridge Bungalow
ROAD
LANE
Tunstall Farm
TUNSTALL
Tame
Cook's View Nursery
Tunstall Cottage
Greenhow Farm
Stanley Grange Plantation
River
PANNIERMAN
Nunthorpe Road Plantation

157
Willow Plantation
455
D
E
135
F
56
14
Morton Carr Belt
Stell
1
Nunthorpe
Eastfield Farm
MIDDLESBROUGH
REDCAR and CLEVELAND
Main Stell
2
513
Stell
Middlesbrough
3
Quarry Hill
158
Round Hill
4
Langbaugh Quarry (disused)
Whinstone View Farm
Langbaugh Ridge
Lodges
Whinstone View Camping & Caravan Site
12
EAT AYTON ROAD
B1292
TS9
Langbaugh
5
Langbaugh Cottage
Langbaugh Hall
Langbaugh Grange
Langbaugh Farm
Langbaugh Ridge
NEWTON
GUISBOROUGH A173 RD.
D
E
166
F
454
56

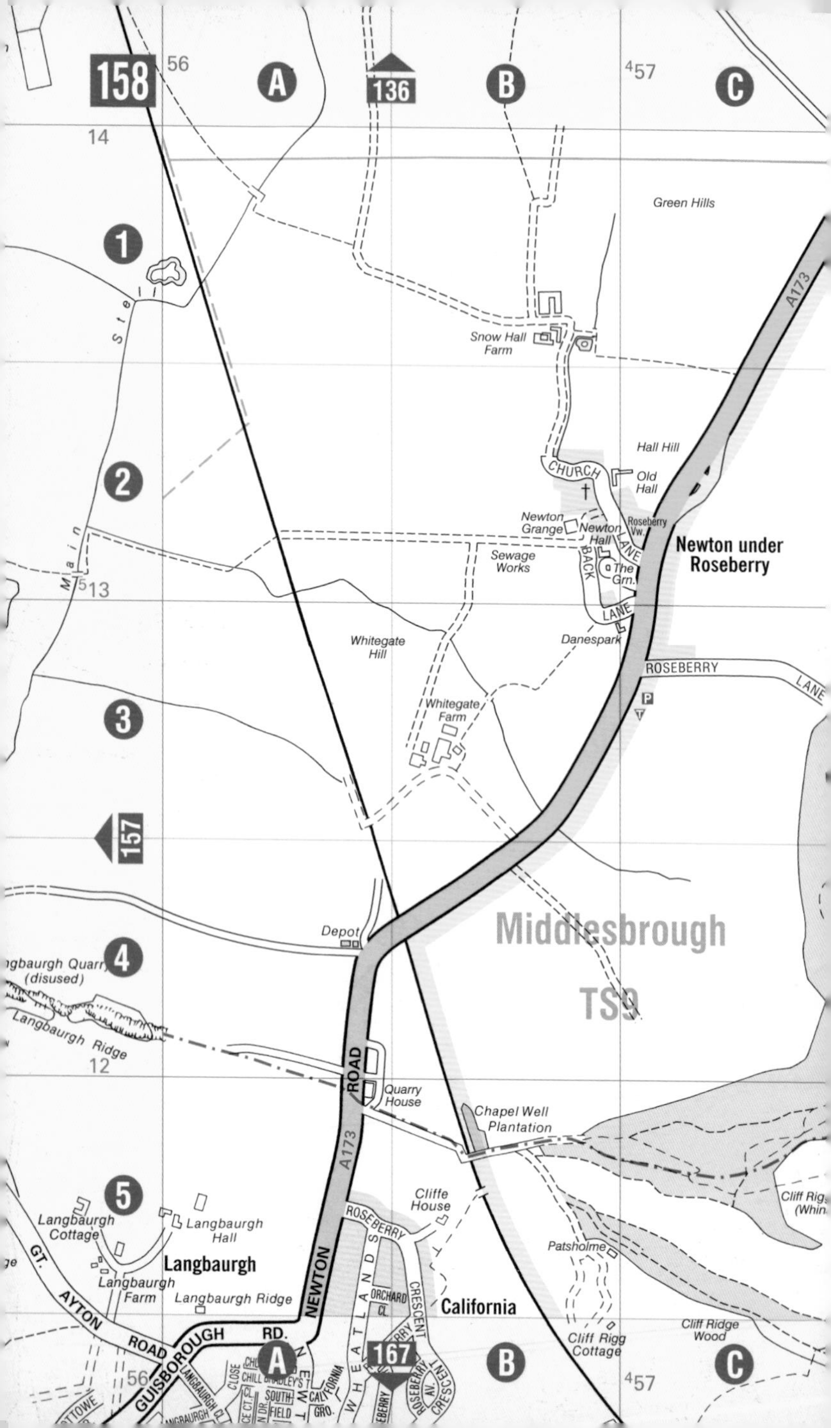
158
56
A
136
B
457
C
14
Green Hills
1
Ste
Snow Hall Farm
A173
Hall Hill
2
CHURCH
Old Hall
Newton Grange
Newton Hall
Roseberry Vw.
LANE
Newton under Roseberry
Sewage Works
BACK
The Grn.
Main
513
LANE
Danespark
Whitegate Hill
ROSEBERRY
LANE
Whitegate Farm
3
157
Depot
Middlesbrough
4
gbaugh Quarry (disused)
TS9
Langbaugh Ridge
12
ROAD
Quarry House
Chapel Well Plantation
A173
5
Cliffe House
Cliff Rigg (Whin
Langbaugh Cottage
Langbaugh Hall
ROSEBERRY
Patsholme
Langbaugh
Langbaugh Farm
Langbaugh Ridge
NEWTON
WHEATLANDS
ORCHARD CL.
CRESCENT
California
Cliff Ridge Wood
GT. AYTON ROAD
GUISBOROUGH RD.
Cliff Rigg Cottage
A
167
B
C
56
457
LANGBAURGH CL.
CLOSE
CHILL
BRADLEY'S
SOUTH FIELD
CALIFORNIA
GRO.
ROSEBERRY AV.
CRESCENT

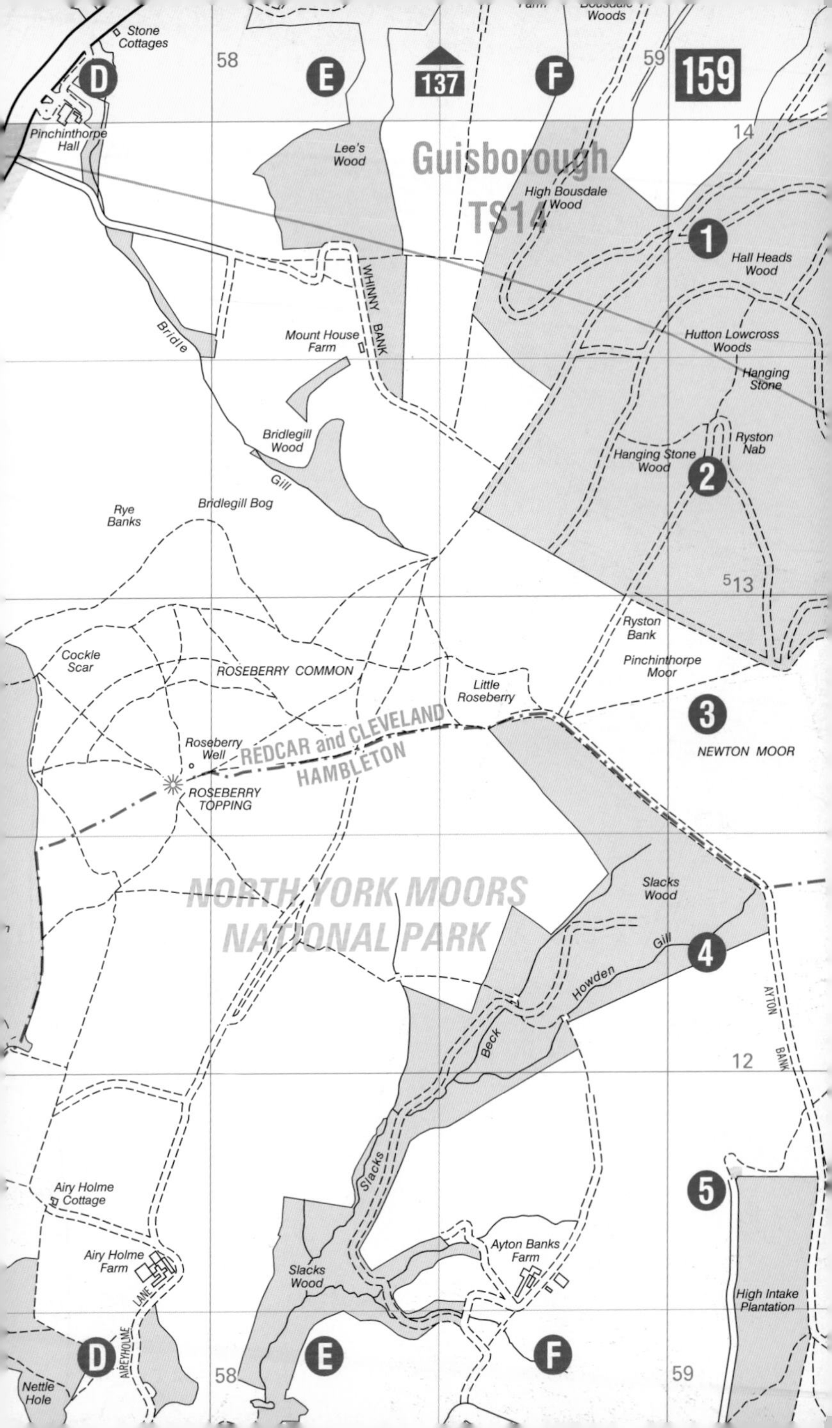

Stone Cottages
58
D
E
137
F
Woods
59
14
Pinchinthorpe Hall
Lee's Wood
Guisborough TS14
High Bousdale Wood
1
Hall Heads Wood
WHINNY BANK
Bridle
Mount House Farm
Hutton Lowcross Woods
Hanging Stone
Bridlegill Wood
Ryston Nab
Hanging Stone Wood
2
Gill
Rye Banks
Bridlegill Bog
513
Ryston Bank
Cockle Scar
ROSEBERRY COMMON
Pinchinthorpe Moor
Little Roseberry
3
REDCAR and CLEVELAND
HAMBLETON
NEWTON MOOR
Roseberry Well
ROSEBERRY TOPPING
Slacks Wood
NORTH YORK MOORS NATIONAL PARK
Gill
4
Howden
AYTON BANK
Beck
12
Slacks
5
Airy Holme Cottage
Airy Holme Farm
Ayton Banks Farm
Slacks Wood
High Intake Plantation
LANE
AIREYHOLME
D
E
F
58
59
Nettle Hole

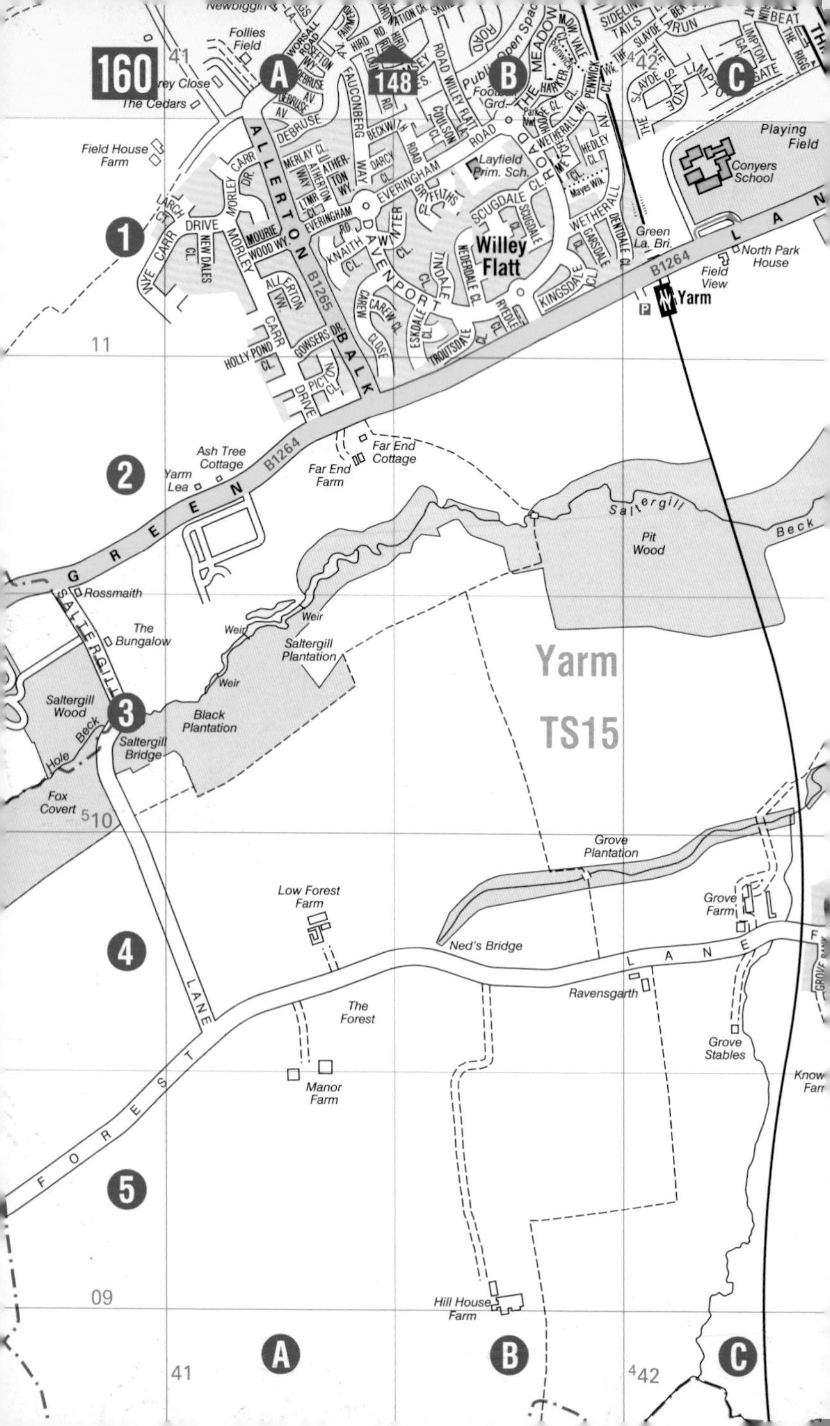
148
Follies Field
The Cedars
Field House Farm
Playing Field
Conyers School
Layfield Prim. Sch.
Willey Flatt
Public Open Space
Footb. Grd.
ALLERTON BALK
B1265
B1264
GREEN LANE
Green La. Bri.
North Park House
Field View
Yarm
Ash Tree Cottage
Yarm Lea
Far End Cottage
Far End Farm
Saltergill Beck
Pit Wood
Rossmaith
The Bungalow
Weir
Saltergill Plantation
Black Plantation
Saltergill Wood
Saltergill Bridge
Hole Beck
Fox Covert
Yarm
TS15
Grove Plantation
Grove Farm
Low Forest Farm
Ned's Bridge
LANE
Ravensgarth
The Forest
Grove Stables
FOREST LANE
Manor Farm
Hill House Farm
A
B
C
1
2
3
4
5
41
42
11
10
09

149
161
162
D
E
F
1
2
3
4
5
11
10
09
43
44
Handley Cross
LANE
GREEN
A1044
THIRSK
ROAD
A67
Super-store
NURSERY
BULMER CL.
HUGILL CL.
STONEHO.
DIKE
Ayresome Ct.
Wycliffe Ct.
Yarm Golf Academy
Kirklevington Grange
Lane End Cotts.
Holdenfields
HMP KIRKLEVINGTON GRANGE
East
Gill
West
Spell Close Wood
The Lodge
HALL DR.
Wood Croft
Chamarel
Kirklevington Hall Farm
Spell Close Farm
KIRKLEVINGTON
Kirklevington Hall
Toft Hill
Waterfall
Waterfall
KIRKLEVINGTON
JASMINE FLDS.
SPRINGFIELD GR.
GROVE
BIRCH CL.
BRAESIDE
PENDERS LA.
LANE
LEVINGTON CT.
TOWN END CL.
Vic.
PUMP LA.
WESTLANDS
THE GREEN
HALL MOOR CL.
STRATHMORE DR.
MANOR GTH.
School
MOOR CL.
ST. MARTIN'S WAY
Fir Tree Farm
Field House Farm
A79
LONG LANE

162
Handley Cross
Leven Bridge Plantation
150
A
B
C
44
445
LEVEN
RIVER
Gill East Gill
Spell Close Wood
Red Hall Wood
Crow Wood
Leven Close Farm
1
11
Stockdale Wood
Spell Close Farm
2
Red Hall Farm
The Cottage
RED HALL LANE
Toft Hill
Ravenscar Wood
161
Yarm
TS15
A19
White Hall Farm
3
510
Crossfield House Farm
4
Fir Tree Farm
Field House Farm
Subway
Old Crow Wood
Weary Bank Wood
5
Eller Wood
North Holme Wood
09
Hunter Banks Wood
A
B
C
44
445
Coalpit Wood
Red Scar
A67

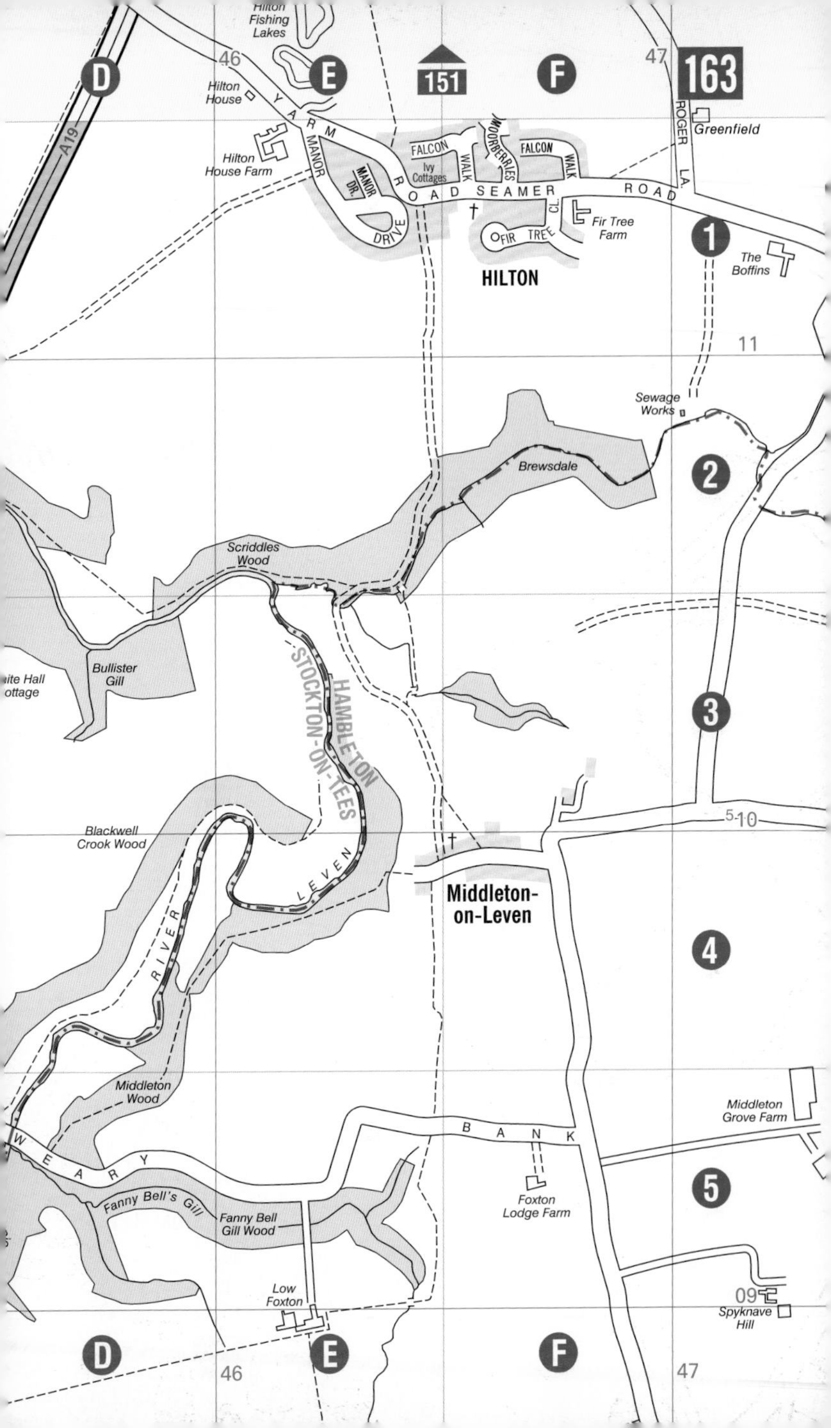
Hilton Fishing Lakes
151
D
E
F
46
47
Hilton House
YARM ROAD
A19
MANOR DRIVE
MANOR DR.
Hilton House Farm
FALCON WALK
Ivy Cottages
MOORBERRIES
SEAMER ROAD
ROGER LA.
Greenfield
FIR TREE CL.
Fir Tree Farm
HILTON
1
The Boffins
11
Sewage Works
2
Brewsdale
Scriddles Wood
Bullister Gill
ite Hall
ottage
STOCKTON-ON-TEES
HAMBLETON
3
Blackwell Crook Wood
RIVER LEVEN
10
Middleton-on-Leven
4
Middleton Wood
Middleton Grove Farm
WEARY BANK
5
Fanny Bell's Gill
Fanny Bell Gill Wood
Foxton Lodge Farm
Low Foxton
09
Spyknave Hill
D
E
F
46
47

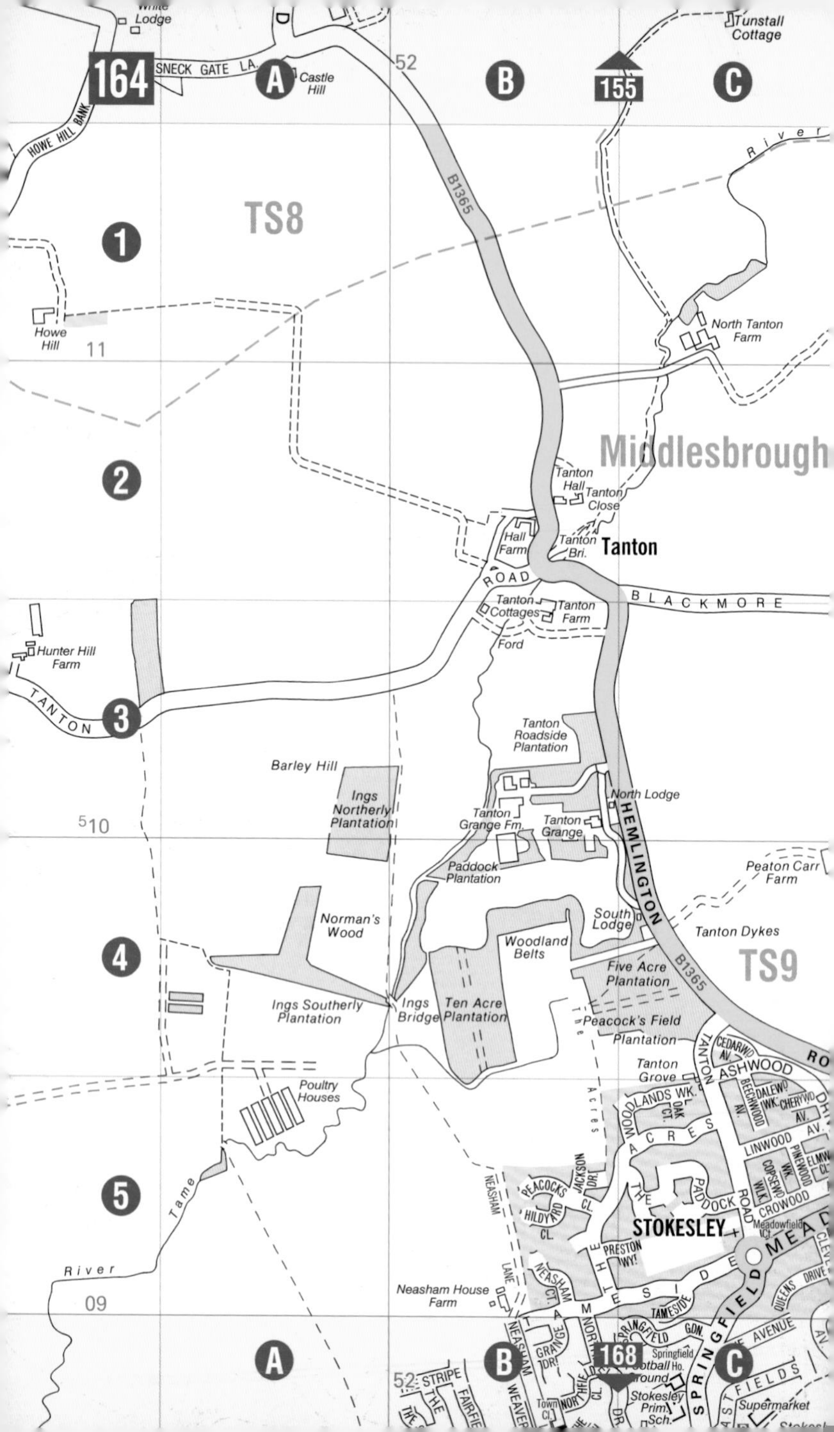
164
SNECK GATE LA.
Castle Hill
White Lodge
HOWE HILL BANK
52
155
Tunstall Cottage
A
B
C
B1365
TS8
River
1
Howe Hill
11
North Tanton Farm
Middlesbrough
2
Tanton Hall
Tanton Close
Hall Farm
Tanton Bri.
Tanton
ROAD
BLACKMORE
Tanton Cottages
Tanton Farm
Ford
Hunter Hill Farm
TANTON
3
Tanton Roadside Plantation
Barley Hill
Ings Northerly Plantation
North Lodge
Tanton Grange Fm.
Tanton Grange
HEMLINGTON
510
Paddock Plantation
Peaton Carr Farm
Norman's Wood
South Lodge
Tanton Dykes
4
Woodland Belts
Five Acre Plantation
TS9
Ings Southerly Plantation
Ings Bridge
Ten Acre Plantation
Peacock's Field Plantation
The Acres
Poultry Houses
Tanton Grove
TANTON
CEDARWD AV.
ASHWOOD
BEECHWOOD AV.
DALEWD WK.
CHERYWD AV.
WOODLANDS WK.
OAK CT.
ACRES
LINWOOD AV.
JACKSON DR.
NEASHAM
PEACOCKS
HILDYARD CL.
JACKSON CL.
THE PADDOCK
ROAD
COPSEWD WLK.
PINEWOOD WK.
ELMWD CL.
CROWOOD
5
Tame
STOKESLEY
Meadowfield Ct.
PRESTON WY.
MEADE
SPRINGFIELD
NEASHAM CT.
LANE
River
09
Neasham House Farm
TAMESIDE
QUEENS DRIVE
GRANGE DR.
NORTHFIELD CL.
SPRINGFIELD GDN.
168
Springfield Ho.
Football Ground
Stokesley Prim. Sch.
AVENUE
FIELDS
Supermarket
STRIPE
FAIRFIELD
WEAVER
Town Cl.
52
A
B
C

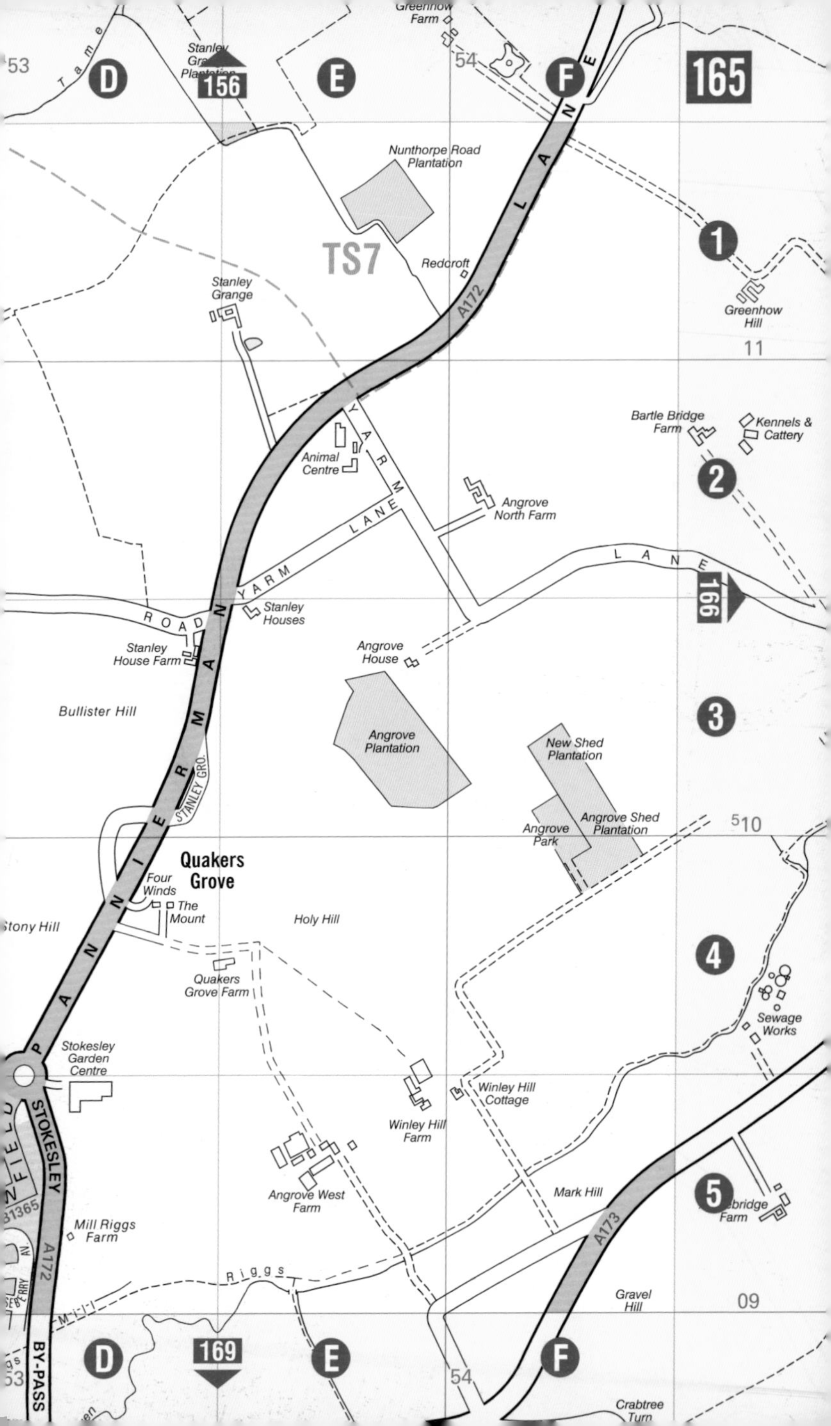
Greenhow Farm
Stanley Grange Plantation
156
Tame
53
D
E
F
54
LANE
Nunthorpe Road Plantation
TS7
Redcroft
A172
Stanley Grange
1
Greenhow Hill
11
Bartle Bridge Farm
Kennels & Cattery
2
YARM
Animal Centre
Angrove North Farm
YARM LANE
LANE
166
ROAD
Stanley Houses
Stanley House Farm
Angrove House
Bullister Hill
3
Angrove Plantation
New Shed Plantation
STANLEY GRO.
Angrove Shed Plantation
Angrove Park
510
PANNIERMAN
Quakers Grove
Four Winds
The Mount
Stony Hill
Holy Hill
4
Quakers Grove Farm
Sewage Works
Stokesley Garden Centre
Winley Hill Cottage
Winley Hill Farm
FIELD
STOKESLEY
5
Angrove West Farm
Mark Hill
A173
B1365
Mill Riggs Farm
A172
Riggs
Mill
Gravel Hill
09
BY-PASS
169
Crabtree Turn

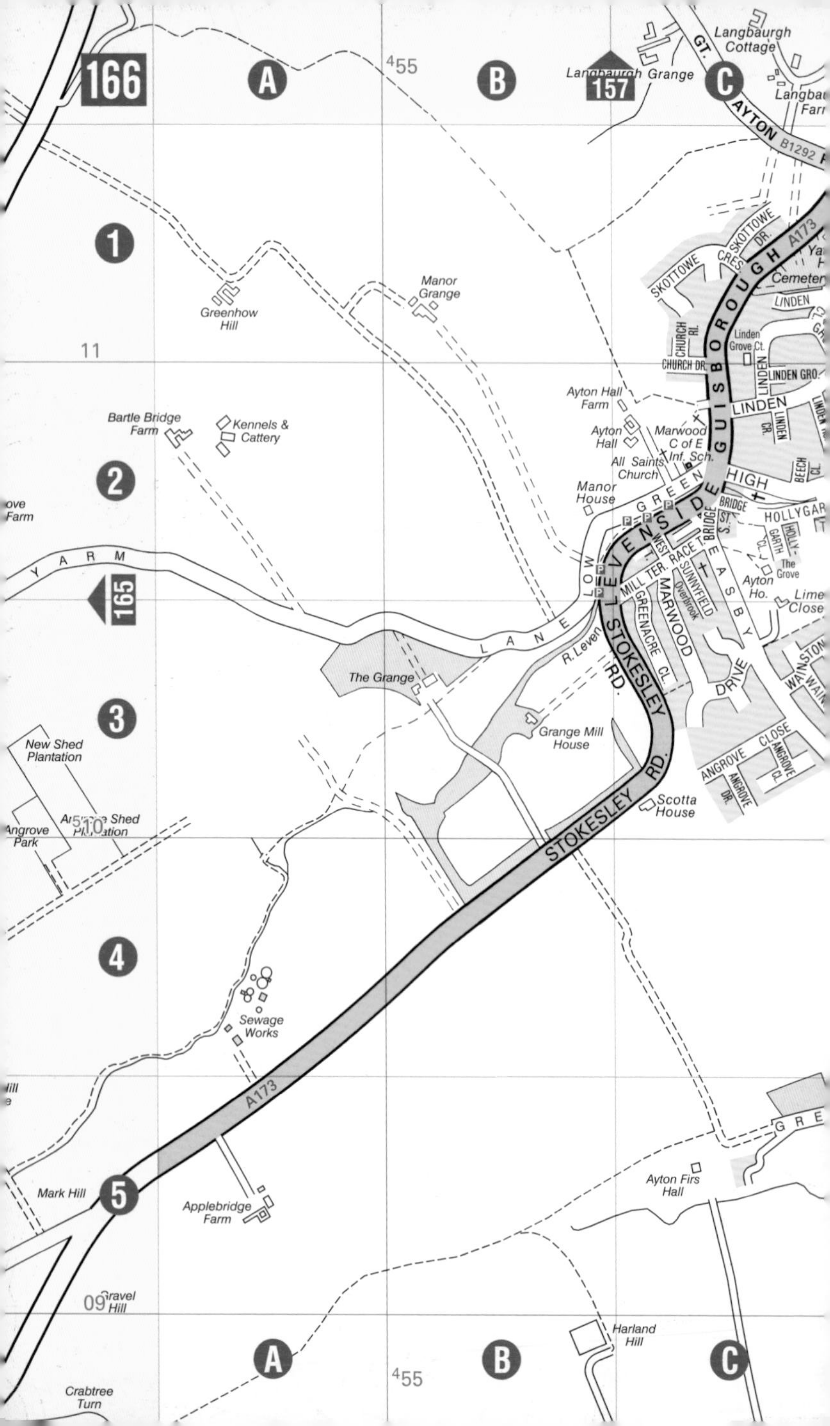

166
A
B
C
455
157
Langbaurgh Cottage
Langbaurgh Grange
GT. AYTON B1292
1
2
3
4
5
11
510
09
Greenhow Hill
Manor Grange
Bartle Bridge Farm
Kennels & Cattery
YARM LANE
165
The Grange
Grange Mill House
R. Leven
LOW GREEN
Manor House
Ayton Hall Farm
Ayton Hall
All Saints Church
Marwood C of E Inf. Sch.
SKOTTOWE
SKOTTOWE CRES.
SKOTTOWE DR.
GUISBOROUGH A173
Cemetery
LINDEN
Linden Grove Ct.
LINDEN GRO.
CHURCH RI.
CHURCH DR.
LINDEN CR.
BEECH CL.
HIGH
BRIDGE
BRIDGE ST.
HOLLYGARTH
HOLLY-GARTH
WEST TER.
MILL TER.
RACE T.
LEVENSIDE
SUNNYFIELD
Overbrook
MARWOOD
GREENACRE CL.
EASBY
MARWOOD DRIVE
The Grove
Ayton Ho.
Lime Close
WAINSTONE
STOKESLEY RD.
ANGROVE CLOSE
ANGROVE CL.
ANGROVE DR.
Scotta House
New Shed Plantation
Angrove Park
Angrove Shed Plantation
Sewage Works
A173
Mark Hill
Applebridge Farm
Ayton Firs Hall
GREEN
Gravel Hill
Harland Hill
Crabtree Turn

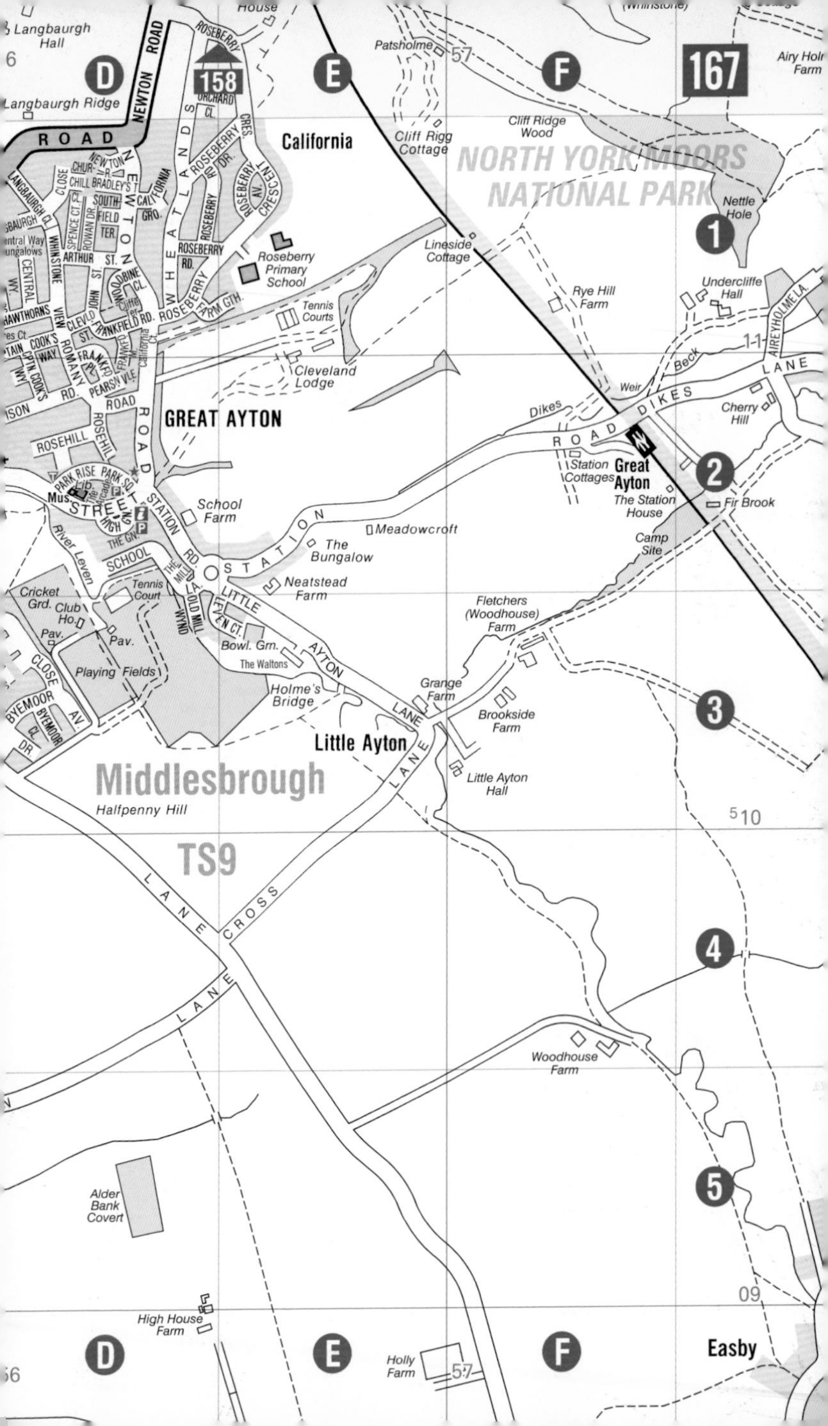
167
158
D
E
F
Langbaugh Hall
Langbaugh Ridge
NEWTON ROAD
ROAD
ROSEBERRY
ORCHARD
California
NORTH YORK MOORS NATIONAL PARK
Patsholme
Cliff Rigg Cottage
Cliff Ridge Wood
Airy Holme Farm
Nettle Hole
1
Roseberry Primary School
Tennis Courts
Lineside Cottage
Rye Hill Farm
Undercliffe Hall
AIREYHOLME LA.
Beck
LANE
Weir
Cleveland Lodge
GREAT AYTON
Dikes
DIKES
ROAD
Cherry Hill
Station Cottages
Great Ayton
The Station House
2
Fir Brook
Camp Site
School Farm
STATION
STREET
HIGH
Mus.
Lib.
The Arcade
PARK RISE
PARK SQ.
ROSEHILL
River Leven
Meadowcroft
The Bungalow
Neatstead Farm
SCHOOL
THE GN.
Cricket Grd.
Club Ho.
Pav.
Tennis Court
Playing Fields
LITTLE
AYTON
LANE
Bowl. Grn.
The Waltons
Holme's Bridge
Fletchers (Woodhouse) Farm
Grange Farm
Brookside Farm
3
Little Ayton
Little Ayton Hall
CLOSE
BYEMOOR
Middlesbrough
Halfpenny Hill
TS9
CROSS
LANE
4
Woodhouse Farm
5
Alder Bank Covert
High House Farm
Holly Farm
57
09
510
Easby

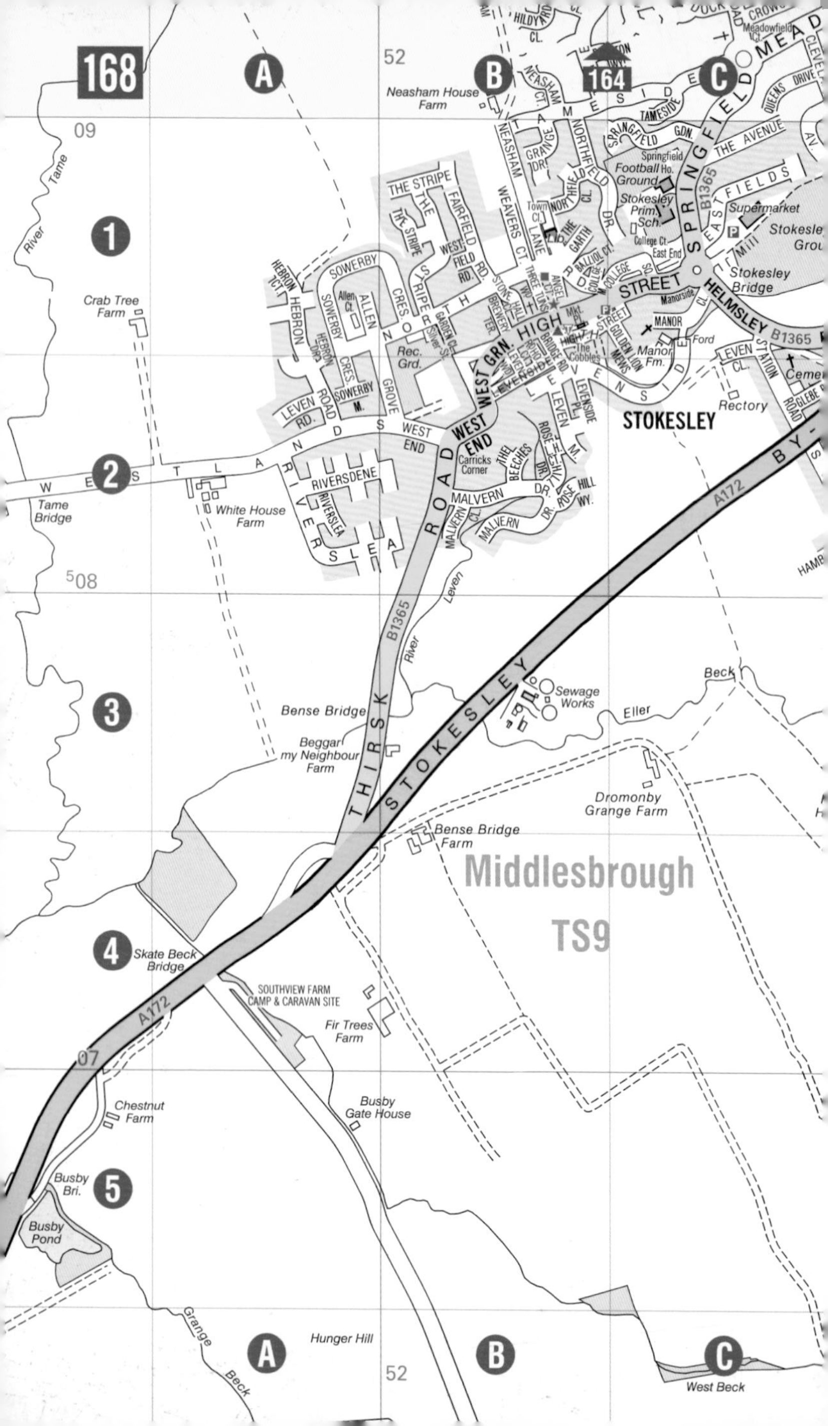
164
A
B
C
52
09
1
2
3
4
5
508
07
River Tame
Neasham House Farm
Crab Tree Farm
WEST LANDS
Tame Bridge
White House Farm
HILDYARD CL.
NEASHAM CT.
TAMESIDE
NEASHAM LANE
GRANGE DR.
NORTHFIELD
NORTHFIELD CL.
NORTHFIELD DR.
SPRINGFIELD
SPRINGFIELD GDN.
Meadowfield Ct.
THE AVENUE
QUEENS DRIVE
Springfield Ho.
Football Ground
Stokesley Prim. Sch.
College Ct.
East End
B1365
EAST FIELDS
Supermarket
Stokesley Bridge
HELMSLEY
THE STRIPE
FAIRFIELD RD.
WESTFIELD RD.
WEAVERS CT.
Town Cl.
Lib.
THE GARTH
BALLIOL CT.
COLLEGE SQ.
STREET
HIGH
THREE TUNS WD.
ANGEL CT.
Mkt. Pl.
Manorside
MANOR
Manor Fm.
Ford
LEVEN CL.
STATION ROAD
GLEBE
Cemetery
Rectory
STOKESLEY
HEBRON
HEBRON CT.
HEBRON ORD.
SOWERBY
SOWERBY CRES.
SOWERBY M.
Allen Ct.
ALLEN
CRES.
GARDEN CL.
Silver St.
NORTH RD.
Rec. Grd.
GROVE
WEST GRN.
STONE HALL
BREWERY TER.
LEVENSIDE
BRIDGE RD.
The Cobbles
GOLDEN LION MEWS
LEVEN RD.
LEVEN ROAD
WEST END
Carricks Corner
THE BEECHES
ROSE H. DR.
ROSE HILL WY.
MALVERN DR.
MALVERN CL.
RIVERSDENE
RIVERSLEA
ROAD
BY-PASS
A172
STOKESLEY
THIRSK
River Leven
Bense Bridge
Beggar my Neighbour Farm
Sewage Works
Eller Beck
Dromonby Grange Farm
Bense Bridge Farm
Middlesbrough
TS9
Skate Beck Bridge
SOUTHVIEW FARM CAMP & CARAVAN SITE
Fir Trees Farm
Chestnut Farm
Busby Gate House
Busby Bri.
Busby Pond
Grange Beck
Hunger Hill
West Beck
HAMB

Angrove West Farm
Mill Riggs Farm
Applebridge Farm
165
Riggs
Mill
D
E
F
53
54
09
08
07
STOKESLEY BY-PASS
A172
Gravel Hill
River Leven
Crabtree Turn
A173
AYTON RD.
Prospect Farm
Prospect House
Kirkby School Farm
Stokesley Golf Course
Cricket Ground
Homestead
The Rakish
Pav.
Bowl. Grn.
Tennis Court
Villa Farm
BROUGHTON RD
Football Pitch
Driving Range
Stokesley Leisure Cen.
Swimming Pool
Club Ho.
Broughton Bridge Beck
Stokesley School
The Oaks
B1257
Playing Fields
The Bungalow
Ings
Cleveland Nurseries
MILLENNIUM CT.
WAY
Broughton Bridge
Kirby Bridge
WAINSTONES CT.
MT. PLEASANT WY.
Field House
Beck
TERRY DICKEN IND. EST.
WESTON CT.
STOKESLEY INDUSTRIAL PARK
Broughton Bridge Farm
ELLERBECK
ELLERBECK WY.
ROSEBERRY CT.
ROSEDALE COURT
BURDON
Creyke Nest Farm
STATION ROAD
Kirby Bridge
Ings Farm
INGS LANE
Station Cottages
STATION ROAD INDUSTRIAL ESTATE
Jubilee House
Sewage Works
Broughton Beck
Railway Bridge Farm
INGS BACK LANE
KIRKBY LANE
The Bungalow
Wainstones
Greencroft
Kirkby Lane Farm
HALLGARTH
HIGH ST.
MANOR GRO.
ROSEGARTH CT.
ROSEWORTH
Tennis Cts.
Pav.
Ckt. Grd.
GREAT BROUGHTON
LOWCROSS DR.
THE DORKINGS
KIRKBY LANE
INGLEBY RD.
The Grange
1
2
3
4
5

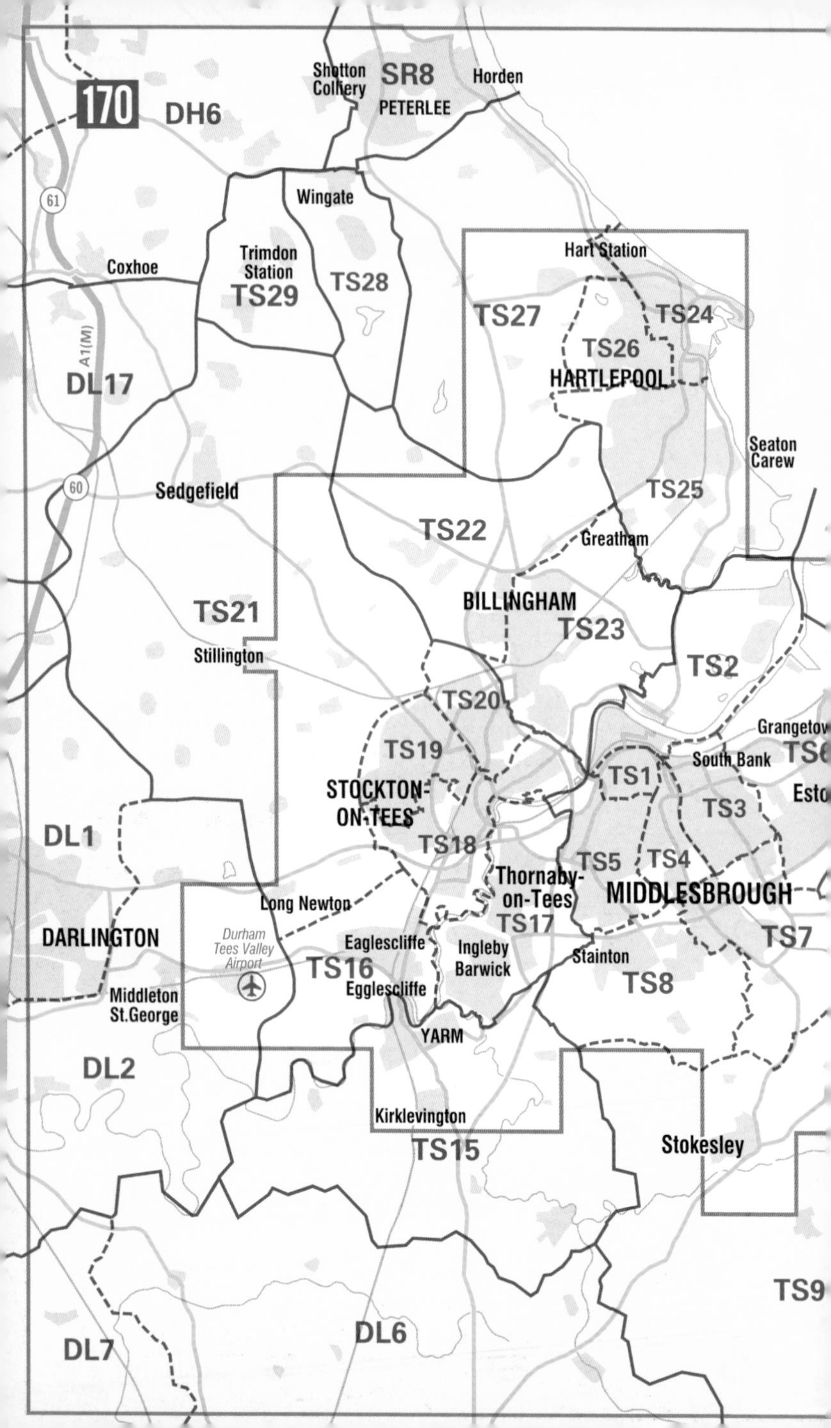
170
DH6
Shotton Colliery
SR8
PETERLEE
Horden
61
Wingate
Trimdon Station
TS29
TS28
Coxhoe
A1(M)
DL17
Hart Station
TS27
TS24
TS26
HARTLEPOOL
Seaton Carew
60
Sedgefield
TS25
TS22
Greatham
BILLINGHAM
TS23
TS21
Stillington
TS2
TS20
Grangetov
TS19
South Bank
TS6
TS1
STOCKTON-ON-TEES
Esto
TS3
DL1
TS18
TS5
TS4
Thornaby-on-Tees
MIDDLESBROUGH
Long Newton
TS17
DARLINGTON
Durham Tees Valley Airport
Eaglescliffe
Ingleby Barwick
TS7
Stainton
TS16
Egglescliffe
TS8
Middleton St.George
YARM
DL2
Kirklevington
TS15
Stokesley
TS9
DL6
DL7

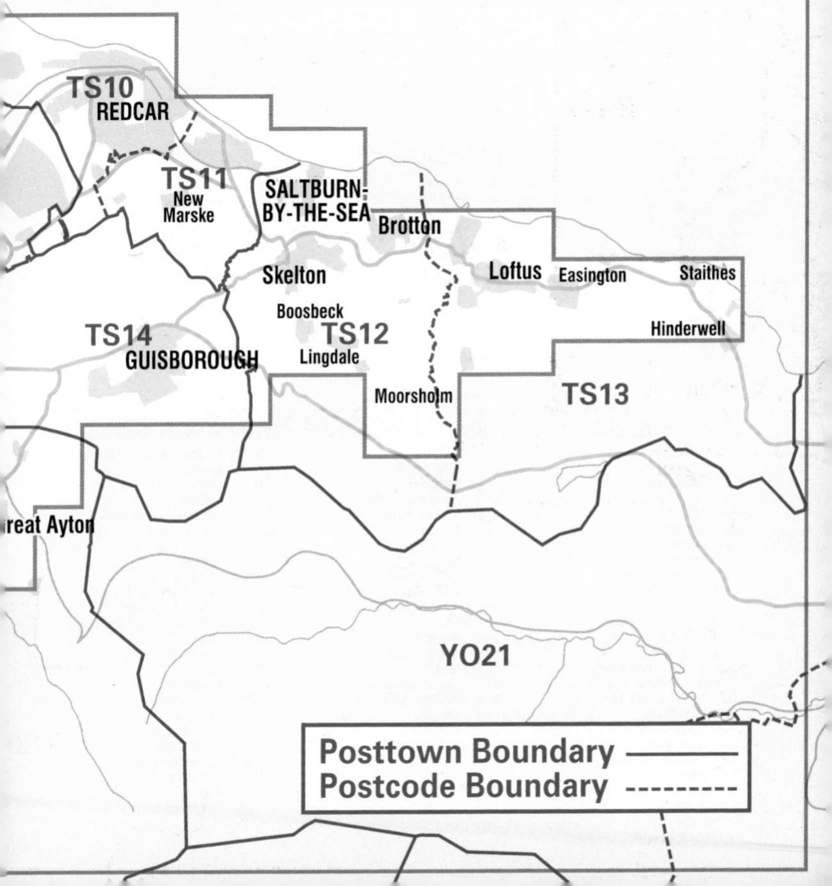
TS10
REDCAR
TS11
New Marske
SALTBURN-BY-THE-SEA
Brotton
Skelton
Loftus
Easington
Staithes
Boosbeck
TS12
Lingdale
Hinderwell
TS14
GUISBOROUGH
Moorsholm
TS13
reat Ayton
YO21
Posttown Boundary
Postcode Boundary

INDEX

Including Streets, Places & Areas, Industrial Estates,
Selected Flats & Walkways, Service Areas, Stations and Selected Places of Interest.

HOW TO USE THIS INDEX

1. Each street name is followed by its Postcode District, then by its Locality abbreviation(s) and then by its map reference; e.g. **Abingdon Rd.** TS1: Midd . . . .5F **77** is in the TS1 Postcode District and the Middlesbrough Locality and is to be found in square 5F on page **77**. The page number is shown in bold type.

2. A strict alphabetical order is followed in which Av., Rd., St., etc. (though abbreviated) are read in full and as part of the street name; e.g. **Black Wood** appears after **Blackwell Cl.** but before **Blackwood Cl.**

3. Streets and a selection of flats and walkways that cannot be shown on the mapping, appear in the index with the thoroughfare to which they are connected shown in brackets;
e.g. **Admiral Ho.** *TS24: H'pool . . . .3D **15** (off Admiral Way)*

4. Addresses that are in more than one part are referred to as not continuous.

5. Places and areas are shown in the index in **BLUE TYPE** and the map reference is to the actual map square in which the town centre or area is located and not to the place name shown on the map; e.g. **BECKFIELDS 2B 150**

6. An example of a selected place of interest is **Captain Cook Birthplace Mus. 1D 133**

7. Examples of stations are:
Allens West Station (Rail) . . . .4A 126; Redcar Bus Station 3D 49

8. Junction names and Service Areas are shown in the index in **BOLD CAPITAL TYPE**; e.g. **NORTON JUNC 3B 54**

GENERAL ABBREVIATIONS

All. : Alley
App. : Approach
Arc. : Arcade
Av. : Avenue
Bk. : Back
Blvd. : Boulevard
Bri. : Bridge
Bldgs. : Buildings
Bungs. : Bungalows
Bus. : Business
Cvn. : Caravan
Cen. : Centre
Chu. : Church
Cl. : Close
Cnr. : Corner
Cott. : Cottage
Cotts. : Cottages
Ct. : Court
Cres. : Crescent
Cft. : Croft
Dr. : Drive
E. : East
Ent. : Enterprise
Est. : Estate
Fld. : Field
Flds. : Fields
Gdn. : Garden
Gdns. : Gardens
Gth. : Garth
Ga. : Gate
Gt. : Great
Grn. : Green
Gro. : Grove
Hgts. : Heights
Ho. : House
Ho's. : Houses
Ind. : Industrial
Info. : Information
Intl. : International
Junc. : Junction
La. : Lane
Lit. : Little
Lwr. : Lower
Mnr. : Manor
Mdw. : Meadow
Mdws. : Meadows
M. : Mews
Mt. : Mount
Mus. : Museum
Nth. : North
Pde. : Parade
Pk. : Park
Pl. : Place
Pct. : Precinct
Prom. : Promenade
Ri. : Rise
Rd. : Road
Rdbt. : Roundabout
Shop. : Shopping
Sth. : South
Sq. : Square
St. : Street
Ter. : Terrace
Twr. : Tower
Trad. : Trading
Up. : Upper
Va. : Vale
Vw. : View
Vs. : Villas
Vis. : Visitors
Wlk. : Walk
W. : West
Yd. : Yard

LOCALITY ABBREVIATIONS

Ais : **Aislaby**
Bill : **Billingham**
Bis : **Bishopton**
Boo : **Boosbeck**
Borr : **Borrowby**
Boul : **Boulby**
Bri : **Brierton**
Brot : **Brotton**
Carl H : **Carlin How**
Carlt : **Carlton**
Cast E : **Castle Eden**
Cast : **Castlelevington**
Char : **Charltons**
Clax : **Claxton**
Coul N : **Coulby Newham**
Cowp B : **Cowpen Bewley**
Dalt P : **Dalton Piercy**
Dun : **Dunsdale**
Eag : **Eaglescliffe**
Eas : **Easington**
Egg : **Egglescliffe**
Elt : **Elton**
Elw : **Elwick**
Est : **Eston**
Fish : **Fishburn**
Gran : **Grangetown**
Gt A : **Great Ayton**
Gt Bro : **Great Broughton**
Gt Bus : **Great Busby**
Grea : **Greatham**
Guis : **Guisborough**
Hart : **Hart**
H'pool : **Hartlepool**
Hem : **Hemlington**
High L : **High Leven**
Hilt : **Hilton**
Hind : **Hinderwell**
Ing B : **Ingleby Barwick**
Kirkb : **Kirkby**
K'ham : **Kirkleatham**
K'ton : **Kirklevington**
Laze : **Lazenby**
Ling : **Lingdale**
L Ayt : **Little Ayton**
Live : **Liverton**
Loft : **Loftus**
Long N : **Long Newton**
Malt : **Maltby**
Marsk S : **Marske-by-the-Sea**
Mart : **Marton**
Midd : **Middlesbrough**
Mid R : **Middleton One Row**
Mid L : **Middleton-on-Leven**
Mid G : **Middleton St George**
Moor : **Moorsholm**
Newb : **Newby**
N Mar : **New Marske**
News : **Newsham**
Newt B : **Newton Bewley**
Newt R : **Newton under Roseberry**
Norm : **Normanby**
N Orm : **North Ormesby**
Nort : **Norton**
Nun : **Nunthorpe**
Old L : **Old Lackenby**
Orm : **Ormesby**
Pin : **Pinchinthorpe**
Port C : **Port Clarence**
Port M : **Port Mulgrave**
Prest T : **Preston-on-Tees**
Redc : **Redcar**
Redm : **Redmarshall**

Rox : **Roxby**
Sadb : **Sadberge**
Salt : **Saltburn-by-the-Sea**
Seal S : **Seal Sands**
Seam : **Seamer**
Seat C : **Seaton Carew**
Sed : **Sedgefield**
Sher : **Sheraton**
Skel : **Skelton**
Skin : **Skinningrove**
Slape : **Slapewath**
S Ban : **South Bank**
Stain : **Stainton**
Stait : **Staithes**
Stil : **Stillington**
Stock T : **Stockton-on-Tees**
Stokes : **Stokesley**
Thorn T : **Thornaby-on-Tees**
Thornt : **Thornton**
Thorpe L : **Thorpe Larches**
Thorpe T : **Thorpe Thewles**
Upleat : **Upleatham**
Whinn H : **Whinney Hill**
Whit : **Whitton**
Wilt : **Wilton**
Wolv : **Wolviston**
Wyn : **Wynyard**
Yarm : **Yarm**
Year : **Yearby**

A

Abberley Dr. TS8: Hem 4F **131**
Abberston Wlk. TS4: Midd. . . . 4A **102**
Abbey Cl. TS19: Stock T 4F **71**
Abbey Ct. TS6: Norm. 1D **105**
Abbeyfield Dr. TS16: Eag. 5B **126**
Abbeygate TS5: Midd 5B **76**
Abbey St. TS12: Brot. 3B **90**
TS24: H'pool. 1F **15**
Abbotsford Ct. TS17: Ing B . . . 4F **127**
Abbotsford Rd. TS5: Midd 3B **100**
Abbots Lea TS27: Dalt P 1E **17**
Abbots Way TS19: Stock T. 4F **71**
Abdale Av. TS5: Midd 3B **100**
Abdiel Ct. TS24: H'pool 5C **8**
Abdiel Ho. TS24: H'pool 2D **15**
Aberbran Ct. TS17: Ing B. 2F **149**
Abercorn Cl. TS10: Redc 4E **65**
Abercrombie Rd.
TS10: Redc. 5F **47**
Aberdare Rd. TS6: Gran. 3E **81**
Aberdeen Rd. TS25: H'pool. . . . 3A **20**
Aberdovey Dr. TS16: Eag. 1C **148**
Aberfalls Rd. TS8: Hem 4F **131**
Abigail Wlk. TS24: H'pool 2B **14**
Abingdon Rd. TS1: Midd 5F **77**
TS13: Eas. 2A **118**
Abram La. TS13: Stait 1C **120**
Abrams Bldgs. TS13: Loft 5C **92**
Abridge Cl. TS11: N Mar 2F **85**
Acacia Ct. TS10: Redc 4E **65**
Acacia Rd. TS19: Stock T 3F **73**
Acclom St. TS24: H'pool 1A **14**
Achilles Cl. TS6: S Ban 4B **80**
ACKLAM 4C **100**
Acklam Ct. TS5: Midd 5C **100**
Acklam Hall Cotts.
TS5: Midd 5D **101**
Acklam Rd. TS5: Midd. 3B **100**
TS17: Thorn T 2D **99**
Acklam St. Nth. TS2: Midd 1E **77**
Acklam St. Sth. TS2: Midd 2E **77**
Ackworth Grn. TS3: Midd 5D **79**
Acorn Bank TS17: Ing B. 2B **150**
Acorn Cl. DL2: Mid G. 1A **144**
TS17: Thorn T 2D **129**
Acorn Ct. TS10: Redc. 4F **65**
Acres, The TS9: Stokes 4B **164**
(not continuous)
Acton St. TS1: Midd 5F **77**
Adam Cl. TS10: Redc. 3B **64**
Adam St. TS18: Stock T. 4A **98**
Adcott Rd. TS5: Midd. 5C **100**
Adderley St. TS18: Stock T 2A **98**
Addington Dr. TS3: Midd. 5D **79**
Addison Rd. TS5: Midd 1D **101**
TS9: Gt A. 2D **167**
TS24: H'pool 2B **14**
Adelaide Gro. TS18: Stock T. . . 2D **97**
Adelaide Pl. TS11: Marsk S . . . 4C **66**
Adelaide Rd. TS7: Mart. 3C **132**
Adlington Rd. TS24: H'pool. . . . 2B **14**
Admiral Ho. *TS24: H'pool 3D 15*
(off Admiral Way)
Admirals Av. TS3: Midd. 5D **79**
Admiralty Ecology Pk.
(Carter Moor Nature Reserve)
. . . . 3F 125
Admiral Way TS24: H'pool 3D **15**
Adshead Rd. TS10: Redc 1F **63**
Adstock Av. TS4: Midd. 4B **102**
Agricola Cotts. TS7: Nun. 2C **156**
TS8: Newb 4B **154**
Aidan Ct. TS5: Midd 5C **76**
Ainderby Gro. TS18: Stock T. . . 2A **96**
Ainderby Wlk. TS24: H'pool 5B **8**
Ainderby Way TS4: Midd 3A **102**
Ainsdale Cl. TS11: N Mar 2F **85**
Ainsdale Way TS4: Midd 4A **102**
Ainsford Way TS7: Orm. 3B **104**
Ainsley St. TS25: H'pool 5D **15**
Ainstable Rd. TS7: Orm. 4A **104**
Ainsworth Way TS7: Orm 3B **104**
Ainthorpe Pl. TS6: Est 5F **81**
Ainthorpe Rd. TS6: Est. 5F **81**
Aintree Rd. TS10: Redc. 1D **65**
TS18: Stock T. 3F **75**
Airdrie Gro. TS25: H'pool. 3F **19**
Aireborough Cl.
TS19: Stock T 3D **73**
Aire St. TS1: Midd. 5D **77**
Aireyholme La.
TS9: Gt A . . . . . 5D **159** & 1F **167**
Airy Hill La.
TS12: Boo, Skel 5F **111**
Aiskew Gro. TS19: Stock T 5A **72**
AISLABY 4F **147**
Aislaby Ct. TS14: Guis. 5E **109**
Aislaby Gro. TS23: Bill. 3E **39**
Aislaby Ho. TS14: Guis 5E **109**
Aislaby Rd.
TS16: Ais, News 5F **145**
Ajax Way TS6: S Ban. 3A **80**
Alan St. TS6: S Ban 2A **80**
ALBANY 1B **74**
Albany Ct. TS26: H'pool. 3A **14**
Albany Rd. TS7: Mart 3C **132**
TS20: Nort 1B **74**
Albany St. TS1: Midd. 4E **77**
Alberta Ho. TS4: Midd 1A **102**
Albert M. TS1: Midd. 3F **77**
Alberto St. TS18: Stock T 4A **74**
Albert Rd. TS1: Midd 3F **77**
TS6: Est 1D **105**
TS16: Eag. 4C **126**
TS18: Stock T 5A **74**
TS19: Stock T 5B **72**
Albert St. TS2: Midd. 2F **77**
TS24: H'pool 4C **14**
Albert Ter. TS1: Midd. 5E **77**
Albion St. TS12: Boo 3C **112**
TS18: Stock T 1A **98**
(not continuous)
Albion Ter. TS12: Salt 4C **68**
TS14: Guis 1F **139**
TS24: H'pool. 2F **15**
Albourne Grn. TS4: Midd. 4B **102**
Albury Way TS3: Midd 1F **103**
Alconbury Way TS3: Midd 1F **103**
Aldbrough Cl. TS19: Stock T . . . 5B **72**
Aldeburgh Cl. TS25: H'pool. . . . 1E **31**
Aldenham Rd. TS14: Guis 4C **138**
Aldergrove Dr. TS4: Midd 5B **102**
Alderlea TS7: Mart. 2E **133**
Alderman Cl. TS10: Redc 2D **65**
Alderney Gro.
TS17: Thorn T 4D **99**
Alderney Wlk. TS14: Guis 3D **139**
Alder Rd. TS19: Stock T. 3F **73**
Alderson St. TS26: H'pool 4A **14**
Alderwood TS8: Coul N 3B **132**
Alderwood Cl. TS7: Orm 4B **104**
TS27: H'pool 2C **6**
Aldridge Rd. TS3: Midd. 3D **103**
Aldwark Cl. TS5: Midd. 3C **130**
Aldwych Cl. TS6: Norm 3C **104**
Alexander Ter. TS3: Midd 5E **79**
Alexandra Ho. TS12: Salt 3D **69**
Alexandria Dr. DL2: Mid G . . . 1B **144**
Alford Ct. TS25: H'pool 4A **20**
Alford La. TS19: Stock T. 3D **73**
Alford Rd. TS12: Brot 3B **90**
Alfred St. TS10: Redc 3D **49**
TS24: H'pool. 5F **9**
Alfriston Cl. TS17: Ing B 1B **150**
Alice Row TS18: Stock T 1F **97**
Alice St. TS20: Nort. 5B **54**
Allen Ct. TS9: Stokes. 1A **168**
Allendale Cen. TS7: Orm. 4A **104**
Allendale Rd. TS7: Orm 3A **104**
TS18: Stock T. 4E **73**
TS23: Bill 2C **54**
Allendale St. TS25: Seat C 4E **21**
Allendale Tee TS11: N Mar 2F **85**
Allen Gro. TS9: Stokes 1A **168**
Allensway TS17: Thorn T. 1E **129**
Allens West Station (Rail) . . . 4A **126**
Allerford Cl. TS17: Ing B. 3A **150**
Allerston Way TS14: Guis 5E **109**
Allerton Balk TS15: Yarm 1A **160**
Allerton Cl. TS24: H'pool. 1B **14**
Allerton Pk. TS7: Nun 4A **134**
Allerton Vw. TS15: Yarm 1A **160**
Alliance St. TS24: H'pool. 5F **9**
Allington Dr. TS23: Bill 4D **39**
Allington Wlk. TS23: Bill. 4D **39**
Allinson St. TS3: N Orm 4C **78**
Allison Av. TS17: Thorn T 1D **151**
Allison Ho. TS17: Thorn T. 1C **98**
Allison Pl. TS24: H'pool. 5E **9**
Allison St. TS14: Guis 2D **139**
TS18: Stock T 5A **74**
Alloa Gro. TS25: H'pool. 3A **20**
Alloway Gro. TS8: Hem 4F **131**
Alma Cen. TS18: Stock T. 4A **74**
Alma Pde. TS10: Redc. 3C **48**
Alma St. TS18: Stock T 4A **74**
TS26: H'pool. 3F **13**
(not continuous)
Almond Ct. TS4: Midd 3F **101**
Almond Gro. TS11: Marsk S . . . 5C **66**
TS19: Stock T 5C **72**
Alness Gro. TS25: H'pool 3A **20**
Alnmouth Dr. TS10: Redc 3D **65**
Alnport Rd. TS18: Stock T. 4C **74**
Alnwick Cl. TS10: Redc 1F **65**
TS27: H'pool 3C **6**
Alnwick Ct. TS4: Midd 2A **102**
Alnwick Gro. TS20: Nort 4A **54**
Alnwick Ho. TS4: Midd 2B **102**
Alonby Ct. TS21: Long N. 1A **124**
Alpha Gro. TS20: Nort. 2B **74**
Alphonsus St. TS3: N Orm. 4B **78**
Alpine Way TS20: Nort. 1F **73**
Alston Grn. TS3: Midd. 5D **79**
Alston St. TS26: H'pool 5B **14**
Althorp TS10: Redc 4C **48**
Althorpe Cl. TS3: Midd. 2F **103**
Alton Rd. TS5: Midd 1B **100**
Alum Way TS12: Skel. 3E **89**
Alva Gro. TS25: H'pool 3A **20**

Alverstone Av. TS25: H'pool . . . 1B **20**
Alverton Cl. TS3: Midd . . . 1F **103**
Alverton Grn. TS3: Midd . . . 1F **103**
Alvingham Ter. TS3: Midd . . . 2F **103**
Alvis Cl. TS23: Bill . . . 1B **56**
Alvis Ct. TS23: Bill . . . 1B **56**
Alwent Rd. TS1: Midd . . . 3E **77**
Alwin Cl. TS17: Ing B . . . 2B **150**
Alwinton Ct. TS7: Orm . . . 4A **104**
Amberley Cl. TS10: Redc . . . 4E **65**
TS18: Stock T . . . 2C **96**
Amberley Grn. TS3: Midd . . . 5D **79**
Amberley Way TS16: Eag . . . 5A **126**
Amber St. TS1: Midd . . . 4E **77**
TS12: Salt . . . 3D **69**
Amberton Rd. TS24: H'pool . . . 1B **14**
Amberwood Cl. TS27: H'pool . . . 2C **6**
Amberwood Wlk.
*TS27: H'pool . . . 2C **6***
(off Amberwood Cl.)
Amble Cl. TS26: H'pool . . . 3D **13**
Amble Ct. TS26: H'pool . . . 5F **13**
Ambleside TS12: Skel . . . 3B **88**
Ambleside Av. TS10: Redc . . . 1C **64**
Ambleside Gro. TS5: Midd . . . 4C **100**
Ambleside Rd. TS6: Norm . . . 2C **104**
TS23: Bill . . . 4E **55**
Amble Vw. TS20: Nort . . . 1C **74**
Ambrose Rd. TS6: Est . . . 2E **105**
Amersham Rd. TS3: Midd . . . 3D **103**
Amerston TS22: Wyn . . . 4B **26**
Amesbury Cres. TS8: Hem . . . 4F **131**
Ammerston Rd. TS1: Midd . . . 3D **77**
Ampleforth Av. TS6: Est . . . 1D **105**
Ampleforth Ct. TS12: Skel . . . 4D **89**
Ampleforth Rd. TS3: Midd . . . 2C **102**
TS23: Bill . . . 1E **55**
Amroth Grn. TS3: Midd . . . 5D **79**
Anchorage M. TS5: Midd . . . 5C **100**
TS17: Thorn T . . . 1C **98**
Anchor Ct. TS24: H'pool . . . 1F **15**
Anchor Ho. TS24: H'pool . . . 3D **15**
Anchor Retail Pk.
TS24: H'pool . . . 2B **14**
Ancroft Dr. TS7: Orm . . . 4A **104**
Ancroft Gdns. TS20: Nort . . . 1B **74**
Anderson Rd. TS17: Thorn T . . . 2D **99**
Anderson St. TS17: Thorn T . . . 3D **99**
Andover Way TS8: Hem . . . 4E **131**
Andrew Pl. TS24: H'pool . . . 4C **14**
Andrew St. TS24: H'pool . . . 4C **14**
Angel Ct. TS9: Stokes . . . 1B **168**
Angle Ct. TS4: Midd . . . 5A **78**
Anglesey Av. TS3: Midd . . . 3E **103**
Anglesey Gro. TS26: H'pool . . . 5E **7**
Anglesey Wlk. *TS14: Guis . . . 3D **139***
(off Dorset Rd.)
Angle St. TS4: Midd . . . 4A **78**
Angling Grn. TS13: Skin . . . 2A **92**
Angrove Cl. TS9: Gt A . . . 3C **166**
TS15: Yarm . . . 4E **149**
Angrove Dr. TS9: Gt A . . . 3C **166**
Angus St. *TS26: H'pool . . . 3A **14***
(off Brook St.)
Anlaby Cl. TS23: Bill . . . 2E **39**
Anna Ct. *TS26: H'pool . . . 5A **14***
(off Flaxton St.)
Annandale Cres. TS24: H'pool . . . 3F **7**
Annan Gdns. TS12: Salt . . . 5C **68**
Annan Rd. TS23: Bill . . . 3E **39**
Ann Crooks Way TS24: H'pool . . . 5F **9**
Annfield Cl. TS23: Bill . . . 4D **39**
Annie St. TS1: Midd . . . 4C **76**
Annigate Cl. TS22: Wyn . . . 2E **37**
ANNIGATE RDBT. . . . 1F **37**
Ann St. TS6: S Ban . . . 2A **80**
Ansdale Rd. TS3: Midd . . . 5A **80**
Anson Ho. TS17: Thorn T . . . 1D **129**
Anstey Ho. TS20: Nort . . . 5A **54**
Antrim Av. TS19: Stock T . . . 4A **72**
Apethorpe Ct. TS17: Ing B . . . 4F **127**
Appleby Av. TS3: Midd . . . 5D **79**
Appleby Cl. TS11: N Mar . . . 2F **85**
Appleby Gro. TS24: H'pool . . . 1B **14**
Appleby Rd. TS23: Bill . . . 5E **39**
Applegarth TS8: Coul N . . . 1B **154**
Applegarth, The TS14: Guis . . . 1F **139**
Apple Orchard Bank
TS11: Skel, Upleat . . . 4E **87**
TS12: Skel . . . 4E **87**
Applethwaite Gdns.
TS12: Skel . . . 2C **88**
Appleton Cl. TS14: Guis . . . 5E **109**
Appleton Rd. TS5: Midd . . . 3B **100**
TS19: Stock T . . . 3F **73**
Appletree Gdns. TS7: Orm . . . 4B **104**
Applewood Cl. TS27: H'pool . . . 2B **6**
Appley Cl. TS16: Prest T . . . 1D **127**
Apsley St. TS1: Midd . . . 5F **77**
Apsley Way TS17: Ing B . . . 4F **127**
Arabella Cl. TS24: H'pool . . . 5E **9**
Arabella St. TS24: H'pool . . . 5E **9**
Arbia Ct. TS17: Ing B . . . 5E **127**
Arbroath Gro. TS25: H'pool . . . 3F **19**
Arc . . . 5A 74
Arcade, The TS9: Gt A . . . 2D **167**
Arch Ct. TS24: H'pool . . . 5C **8**
Archer Cl. TS4: Midd . . . 4A **102**
Archer Rd. DL2: Mid R . . . 4A **144**
Archer St. TS17: Thorn T . . . 2C **98**
TS24: H'pool . . . 3C **14**
Arden Cl. TS14: Guis . . . 4D **139**
Arden Gro. TS19: Stock T . . . 1B **96**
Ardrossan Ct. TS25: H'pool . . . 3A **20**
Ardrossan Rd. TS25: H'pool . . . 3A **20**
Arennig Ct. TS17: Ing B . . . 5F **127**
Argory, The TS17: Ing B . . . 1B **150**
Argyle Rd. TS6: Gran . . . 2D **81**
Argyll Ct. TS20: Nort . . . 1A **74**
Argyll Rd. TS7: Mart . . . 3C **132**
TS20: Nort . . . 1F **73**
TS25: H'pool . . . 3A **20**
Arisaig Cl. TS16: Eag . . . 1C **148**
Aristotle Dr. TS19: Stock T . . . 5B **52**
Arkendale TS8: Hem . . . 5D **131**
Arken Ter. TS20: Nort . . . 2B **74**
Arkgrove Ho. TS24: H'pool . . . 2D **15**
Arkgrove Ind. Est.
TS18: Stock T . . . 3D **75**
Arkley Cres. TS24: H'pool . . . 4A **8**
Ark Royal Cl. TS25: Seat C . . . 3D **21**
Arlington Ct. TS18: Stock T . . . 2F **97**
Arlington Rd. TS5: Midd . . . 3E **101**
Arlington St. TS13: Loft . . . 5C **92**
TS18: Stock T . . . 2F **97**
(not continuous)
Arlon Ct. TS10: K'ham . . . 4A **64**
Armadale TS10: Redc . . . 3E **65**
Armadale Cl. TS19: Stock T . . . 4F **71**
Armadale Gro. TS25: H'pool . . . 3F **19**
Armitage Rd. TS10: Redc . . . 2E **63**
Arncliffe Av. TS18: Stock T . . . 3F **97**
Arncliffe Gdns. TS26: H'pool . . . 4A **14**
Arncliffe Rd. TS5: Midd . . . 5B **76**
Arnold Gro. TS25: H'pool . . . 2E **19**
Arnside Av. TS3: Midd . . . 5D **79**
Arran Cl. TS17: Thorn T . . . 2C **128**
Arrandale TS8: Hem . . . 1D **153**
Arran Gro. TS25: H'pool . . . 3A **20**
Arran Wlk. TS14: Guis . . . 3D **139**
Arrathorne Rd.
TS18: Stock T . . . 3A **96**
Arthur St. TS9: Gt A . . . 1D **167**
TS10: Redc . . . 3B **48**
Arthur Ter. TS11: N Mar . . . 1A **86**
Arundel Ct. TS17: Ing B . . . 4F **127**
Arundel Grn. TS3: Midd . . . 5D **79**
Arundel Rd. TS6: Gran . . . 4E **81**
TS23: Bill . . . 5D **39**
Arundel St. TS10: Redc . . . 3B **48**
Ascot Dr. TS18: Stock T . . . 3F **75**
Ascot Rd. TS10: Redc . . . 1D **65**
Ash Bank Rd. TS14: Guis . . . 5D **139**
Ashberry Cl. TS12: Moor . . . 3B **142**
Ashbourne Cl. TS6: Est . . . 1F **105**
Ashbourne Lodge TS23: Bill . . . 4D **55**
Ashbourne Rd.
TS19: Stock T . . . 3A **74**
Ashbrooke Way TS5: Midd . . . 1B **100**
Ashburn St. TS25: Seat C . . . 4E **21**
Ashburton Cl. TS8: Midd . . . 2B **132**
Ashby Gro. TS25: H'pool . . . 1E **31**
Ashby Rd. TS23: Bill . . . 5D **39**
Ashcombe Cl. TS22: Bill . . . 4A **38**
Ashdale TS8: Hem . . . 5D **131**
Ashdale Cl. DL2: Mid G . . . 2C **144**
Ashdown Cl.
TS17: Thorn T . . . 2C **128**
Ashdown Way TS23: Bill . . . 4A **40**
Ashes, The TS22: Wolv . . . 2C **38**
TS25: Seat C . . . 5E **21**
Ashfield Av. TS4: Midd . . . 2F **101**
Ashfield Caravan Pk.
TS27: Dalt P . . . 5A **12**
Ashfield Cl. TS25: Grea . . . 3E **31**
Ashford Av. TS5: Midd . . . 3A **100**
Ashford Cl. TS14: Guis . . . 4D **139**
Ashford Grange
TS12: Boo . . . 3B **112**
Ash Grn. TS8: Coul N . . . 1B **154**
Ash Gro. TS6: S Ban . . . 3B **80**
TS13: Loft . . . 5B **92**
TS15: K'ton . . . 4C **160**
Ashgrove Av. TS25: H'pool . . . 1B **20**
Ashgrove Pl. TS25: H'pool . . . 1B **20**
Ash Hill TS8: Coul N . . . 5C **132**
Ashkirk Rd. TS6: Norm . . . 1C **104**
Ashley Gdns. TS24: H'pool . . . 1F **13**
Ashling Way TS5: Midd . . . 1C **100**
Ashmead Vw. TS18: Stock T . . . 4D **73**
Ashmore Gdns.
TS18: Stock T . . . 3A **98**
Ashridge Cl. TS11: N Mar . . . 2F **85**
TS17: Ing B . . . 5C **128**
Ash Rd. TS14: Guis . . . 1E **139**
Ashton Rd. TS20: Nort . . . 5E **53**
Ash Tree Grn. TS21: Carlt . . . 5C **50**
Ash Vale Holiday Pk.
TS27: H'pool . . . 2B **6**
Ashville Av. TS16: Prest T . . . 3C **126**
TS20: Nort . . . 4F **53**
Ashwood Cl. TS7: Orm . . . 4B **104**
TS27: H'pool . . . 2C **6**
Ashwood Dr. TS9: Stokes . . . 4C **164**
Askern Dr. TS5: Midd . . . 5E **101**
Aske Rd. TS1: Midd . . . 4E **77**
TS10: Redc . . . 4D **49**
Askewdale TS14: Guis . . . 3A **138**
Askham Cl. TS4: Midd . . . 2F **101**
Askrigg Rd. TS18: Stock T . . . 5D **73**
Askrigg Wlk. TS3: Midd . . . 2C **102**
Askwith Rd. TS5: Midd . . . 2D **101**
Aspen Dr. TS5: Midd . . . 2F **101**
Aspen Gdns.
TS19: Stock T . . . 1B **72**
Aspen Rd. TS16: Eag . . . 1B **148**
Astbury TS8: Mart . . . 1E **155**
Aster Cl. TS7: Mart . . . 2B **132**
Asterley Dr. TS5: Midd . . . 4A **100**
Astley Cl. TS19: Stock T . . . 5B **72**
Aston Av. TS3: Midd . . . 4E **79**
Astonbury Grn. TS4: Midd . . . 4B **102**
Aston Dr. TS17: Thorn T . . . 2B **128**
Aston Rd. TS22: Bill . . . 5B **38**
Atherstone Dr. TS14: Guis . . . 3E **139**
Atherton Way TS15: Yarm . . . 1A **160**
Atholl Gro. TS10: Redc . . . 5A **48**
TS25: H'pool . . . 3A **20**
Athol St. TS1: Midd . . . 5E **77**
Atkinson Ct. TS24: H'pool . . . 3A **8**
Atkinson Ind. Est.
TS25: H'pool . . . 5C **14**
Atlantic Cres. TS17: Thorn T . . . 4D **99**
Atlas Wynd TS15: Yarm . . . 3B **148**
Attingham Cl. TS8: Hem . . . 4F **131**
Attlee Rd. TS6: Gran . . . 4E **81**
Attlow Wlk. TS3: Midd . . . 1F **103**
Atwater Cl. TS15: Yarm . . . 5D **149**
Atwick Cl. TS23: Bill . . . 2E **39**

Aubrey Ct. TS20: Nort 1B **74**
Aubrey St. TS1: Midd 5F **77**
Auckland Av. TS7: Mart 3E **133**
Auckland Rd. TS23: Bill 3A **40**
Auckland St. TS14: Guis 1E **139**
Auckland Way
TS18: Stock T 2B **96**
TS26: H'pool 4C **12**
Audrey Gro. TS18: Stock T 2C **96**
Aurora Ct. TS2: Midd 1C **76**
Austen Cl. TS23: Bill 2D **39**
Austin Av. TS18: Stock T 2F **97**
Autumn Gro. TS19: Stock T 1C **96**
Avalon Ct. TS8: Hem 4F **131**
Avebury Cl. TS17: Ing B 1C **150**
Avens Way TS17: Ing B 4B **128**
Avenue, The TS5: Midd 5D **101**
(St David's Way)
TS5: Midd 2E **101**
(Windsor Ct.)
TS6: Norm 5C **80**
TS7: Nun 3F **133**
TS9: Stokes 1C **168**
TS10: Redc 4D **49**
TS12: Brot 2C **90**
TS14: Guis 3B **138**
TS16: Prest T 3C **126**
TS17: Thorn T 3D **99**
TS19: Stock T 5B **72**
(not continuous)
TS22: Wyn 1B **36**
Avenue Pl. TS14: Guis 1F **139**
Avenue Rd. TS24: H'pool 3B **14**
Aviation Way DL2: Mid G 2D **145**
Aviemore Rd. TS8: Hem 4E **131**
Avill Gro. TS17: Ing B 3A **150**
Avoca Ct. TS10: Redc 3B **48**
Avon Cl. TS12: Salt 5C **68**
TS12: Skel 3D **89**
TS17: Thorn T 5D **99**
Avon Ct. TS12: Ling 4E **113**
Avondale Cl. TS6: Est 4E **81**
Avondale Gdns.
TS24: H'pool 1A **14**
Avon Dr. TS14: Guis 3C **138**
Avon Gro. TS22: Bill 4A **38**
Avon Rd. TS10: Redc 1A **64**
TS20: Nort 1C **74**
Avon St. TS12: Salt 4C **68**
AVRO ANSON RDBT. **3D 129**
Avro Cl. TS11: Marsk S 4B **66**
TS18: Stock T 5E **97**
Avro Gdns. TS25: Seat C 1D **33**
Axbridge Ct. TS23: Bill 4D **39**
Axminster Rd. TS8: Hem 4F **131**
Axton Cl. TS17: Thorn T 3B **128**
Aycliffe Cl.
TS19: Stock T 5A **72**
Aycliffe Rd. TS7: Mart 3C **132**
Aylsham Cl. TS17: Ing B 1C **150**
Aylton Dr. TS5: Midd 3C **130**
Ayresome Ct. TS15: Yarm 5D **149**
Ayresome Grange Rd.
TS5: Midd 5C **76**
Ayresome Grn. La.
TS5: Midd 5C **76**
Ayresome Pk. Rd.
TS5: Midd 5D **77**
Ayresome Rd. TS5: Midd 4B **76**
Ayresome St. TS1: Midd 5C **76**
Ayr Gro. TS25: H'pool 3A **20**
Aysdale Ga. TS12: Char 4F **141**
Aysgarth TS19: Stock T 3E **73**
Aysgarth Rd. TS5: Midd 2C **100**
TS18: Stock T 5D **73**
Ayton Bank TS9: Gt A 4F **159**
Ayton Ct. TS10: Redc 2B **64**
TS14: Guis 1D **139**
Ayton Cres. TS6: Est 2E **105**
Ayton Dr. TS10: Redc 2B **64**
Ayton Pl. TS20: Nort 3B **74**
Ayton Rd. TS9: Stokes 1D **169**
TS17: Thorn T 5C **98**
Azalia Gro. TS10: Redc 4E **65**
Azalia Rd. TS19: Stock T 3A **74**

B

Babbage Gdns.
TS19: Stock T 5B **52**
Bk. Amber St. TS12: Salt 3D **69**
Bk. Garnet St. TS12: Salt 3C **68**
Back La. TS9: Gt Bro 5F **169**
TS9: Newt R 2B **158**
TS12: Skel 2F **111**
TS13: Hind 5D **121**
TS16: Egg 2C **148**
TS21: Long N 3A **94**
(not continuous)
Back La. Cotts. TS12: Skel 5A **88**
Bk. Throston St.
*TS24: H'pool 1F **15***
(off Throston St.)
Bk. Turner St. *TS10: Redc 3C **48***
(off Newcomen Ct.)
Bacon Wlk. TS25: H'pool 2D **19**
Baden St. TS26: H'pool 5A **14**
Bader Av. TS17: Thorn T 2B **128**
Badger La. TS17: Ing B 4C **128**
Badminton Av. TS12: Skel 4C **88**
Badsworth Cl. TS14: Guis 4D **139**
Baffin Ct. TS17: Thorn T 1D **129**
Bailey Gro. TS3: Midd 5C **78**
Bailey St. TS26: H'pool 4B **14**
Bainton Cl. TS23: Bill 2E **39**
Baird Ho. *TS17: Thorn T 1D **129***
(off Lingwood Ct.)
Bakehouse Sq. TS14: Guis . . . 2E **139**
Baker Cl. TS27: H'pool 3D **7**
Bakers Ct. TS24: H'pool 5B **8**
Baker St. TS1: Midd 3E **77**
Bakery Dr. TS19: Stock T 3D **73**
Bakery Ho. *TS19: Stock T 3D **73***
(off Daylight Rd.)
Bakery St. TS18: Stock T 5A **74**
Balaclava St. TS18: Stock T . . . 5A **74**
Bala Cl. TS17: Ing B 1E **149**
Balcary Ct. TS25: H'pool 4F **19**
Balcary Gro. TS25: H'pool 4F **19**
Balder Rd. TS20: Nort 5A **54**
Baldoon Sands TS5: Midd 2B **130**
Balfour Ter. TS5: Midd 3B **100**
Baliol Cft. TS21: Long N 5A **94**
Ballater Gro. TS25: H'pool 4A **20**
Balliol Ct. TS9: Stokes 1B **168**
Balmoral Av. TS17: Thorn T . . . 3D **99**
TS23: Bill 5E **39**
Balmoral Ct. TS25: H'pool 4A **20**
Balmoral Dr. TS4: Midd 2A **102**
Balmoral Rd. TS3: Midd 3E **103**
TS12: Ling 5F **113**
TS25: H'pool 4F **19**
Balmoral Ter. *TS12: Salt 4D **69***
(off Cleveland St.)
TS18: Stock T 2E **97**
Balmor Rd. TS6: Norm 2C **104**
Baltic Cl. TS18: Stock T 4B **74**
Baltic Rd. TS18: Stock T 4B **74**
Baltic St. TS25: H'pool 5C **14**
Bamburgh Cl. TS10: Redc 1E **65**
Bamburgh Ct. TS4: Midd 2A **102**
TS17: Ing B 4F **127**
TS27: H'pool 3D **7**
Bamburgh Dr. TS7: Orm 4A **104**
Bamburgh Ho. TS4: Midd 2B **102**
Bamburgh Rd. TS27: H'pool 3D **7**
Bamford Rd. TS17: Thorn T 5C **98**
Bamletts Wharf Ind. Est.
TS23: Bill 4C **56**
Bamletts Wharf Rd.
TS23: Bill 5B **56**
Banbury Gro. TS5: Midd 5B **100**
Bancroft Dr. TS17: Ing B 5F **127**
Banff Gro. TS25: H'pool 4A **20**
Bangor Cl. TS6: Est 4E **81**
Bangor St. TS26: H'pool 5A **14**
Bankfields Ct. TS6: Est 3D **105**
Bankfields Rd. TS6: Est 3D **105**
Bank La. TS6: Est 2F **105**
Bank Rd. TS23: Bill 4D **55**
Bank Sands TS5: Midd 3B **130**
Bankside TS15: Yarm 3E **149**
Bankside Ct. TS6: Est 2F **105**
Bankston Cl. TS26: H'pool 2C **12**
Bank St. TS10: Redc 3C **48**
TS14: Guis 2F **139**
Bank Ter. TS21: Thorpe T 2E **51**
Bannatyne Health Club
Coulby Newham 4A 132
Stockton-on-Tees 1A 150
Bannockburn Way TS23: Bill . . . 3F **39**
Baptist St. TS24: H'pool 1F **15**
Barbara Mann Ct.
TS26: H'pool 3A **14**
Barberry TS8: Coul N 1C **154**
(not continuous)
Barberry Cl. TS17: Ing B 4C **128**
Barbers Yd. TS13: Stait 1C **120**
Barclays Ho. TS17: Thorn T . . . 5C **74**
Barden Rd. TS3: Midd 1C **102**
Bardsey Sq. TS17: Thorn T 4D **99**
Bardsey Wlk. TS14: Guis 4D **139**
Bardsley Cl. TS16: Prest T . . . 1D **127**
Barford Cl. TS10: Redc 3B **64**
TS20: Nort 4E **53**
TS25: H'pool 2E **31**
Bargate TS3: N Orm 4B **78**
Barholm Cl. TS3: Midd 2F **103**
Barker Rd. TS5: Midd 2C **100**
TS17: Thorn T 3D **99**
Barkers Pl. TS24: H'pool 1F **15**
Barkery, The TS8: Newb 4B **154**
Barkston Av.
TS17: Thorn T 3B **128**
Barkston Cl. TS22: Bill 4B **38**
Barlborough Av.
TS19: Stock T 3D **73**
Barle Cl. TS17: Ing B 3B **150**
Barley Cl. TS26: H'pool 2E **13**
Barley Hill Cl. TS6: Est 3E **105**
Barlow Cl. TS14: Guis 3E **139**
Barlow Ct. TS23: Bill 3E **39**
Barmet Ind. Est. TS12: Ling . . . 3F **113**
Barmoor Gro. TS20: Nort 3A **54**
Barmouth Rd. TS6: Est 5E **81**
Barmpton Rd. TS23: Bill 3E **39**
Barnaby Av. TS5: Midd 5C **76**
Barnaby Cl. TS11: Marsk S 5E **67**
Barnaby Cres. TS6: Est 2E **105**
Barnaby Pl. TS14: Guis 2C **138**
Barnaby Rd. TS7: Nun 3B **134**
Barnack Av. TS7: Mart 2E **133**
Barnard Av. TS19: Stock T 1C **96**
Barnard Cl. TS17: Thorn T 2C **98**
Barnard Ct. TS4: Midd 2A **102**
Barnard Gallery 5B 74
Barnard Gro. TS10: Redc 5E **49**
TS24: H'pool 2D **7**
Barnard Rd. TS13: Eas 2A **118**
TS23: Bill 1E **55**
Barnes Ct. TS24: H'pool 3E **7**
Barnes Wallis Way
TS11: Marsk S 4B **66**
Barnet Way TS23: Bill 3A **40**
Barnford Wlk. TS3: Midd 3D **103**
Barnstaple Cl. TS8: Midd 1B **132**
Baronport Grn.
TS18: Stock T 4C **74**
Barra Gro. TS25: H'pool 4A **20**
Barrass Gro. TS3: Midd 5F **79**
Barras Sq. *TS13: Stait 1C **120***
(off High St.)
Barras Way TS19: Stock T 2A **72**
Barrhead Cl. TS19: Stock T 4F **71**
Barrington Av.
TS19: Stock T 4C **72**
Barrington Cres. TS3: Midd 5F **79**
Barritt St. TS1: Midd 4E **77**

Barrowburn Grn.
TS17: Ing B 3A **150**
Barsby Grn. TS3: Midd 2C **102**
Barsford Rd. TS3: Midd 5F **79**
Bartol Ct. TS6: Est 2F **105**
Barton Av. TS25: H'pool. 1A **20**
Barton Cl. TS5: Midd 3C **130**
TS17: Thorn T 3B **128**
Barton Ct. TS6: S Ban 3A **80**
Barton Cres. TS22: Bill 5B **38**
Barton Rd. TS2: Midd 1C **76**
Bartram Ct. TS27: H'pool. 2C **6**
Barwick Cl. TS17: Ing B 4A **128**
Barwick Flds. TS17: Ing B. . . . 5A **128**
Barwick La. TS15: High L 3B **150**
TS17: Ing B, High L 5F **127**
(not continuous)
Barwick Vw. TS17: Ing B. 4B **128**
Barwick Way TS17: Ing B 1A **150**
Basildon Grn. TS3: Midd. 5D **79**
Basil St. TS3: N Orm 4B **78**
Bassenthwaite TS5: Midd 2B **130**
Bassleton Ct.
*TS17: Thorn T 2B **128***
(off Newton Dr.)
Bassleton La.
TS17: Thorn T 3A **128**
(not continuous)
Bathgate Ter. TS24: H'pool 5B **14**
Bath La. TS18: Stock T 5B **74**
Bath Pl. TS18: Stock T. 5B **74**
Bath Rd. TS6: Est. 1E **105**
Bath St. TS10: Redc. 3C **48**
TS12: Salt 4C **68**
Bath Ter. TS24: H'pool 1F **15**
Battersby Cl. TS15: Yarm. 3F **149**
Battersby Grn. TS21: Carlt. 5C **50**
BATTLE-STATIONS 2E 25
Bayberry M. TS5: Midd 3D **101**
Baysdale Cl. TS14: Guis 2F **139**
Baysdale Ct. TS12: Skel 3D **89**
Baysdale Gro. TS10: Redc. 1F **63**
Baysdale Rd. TS17: Thorn T . . . 5D **99**
Baysdale Wlk. TS5: Midd 5E **101**
TS6: Est 5F **81**
Bay St. TS18: Stock T 5B **74**
Beachfield Dr. TS25: H'pool . . . 1A **20**
Beach Rd. TS13: Skin 2A **92**
Beacon Av. TS21: Sed 4E **23**
Beacon Dr. TS11: N Mar 2A **86**
Beacon Hill TS13: Loft. 5C **92**
Beacon La.
TS21: Sed . . . . . . 4E **23** & 1A **24**
Beaconsfield Rd. TS20: Nort. . . 4B **54**
Beaconsfield Sq.
TS24: H'pool. 5F **9**
Beaconsfield St. TS24: H'pool. . . 5F **9**
Beacons La. TS17: Ing B 1F **149**
Beacon St. TS24: H'pool 5F **9**
Beadlam Av. TS7: Nun. 3B **134**
Beadnall Ho.
*TS17: Thorn T 1D **129***
(off Lingwood Ct.)
Beadnell Cl. TS17: Ing B. 5C **128**
Beadnell Way TS10: Redc 2F **65**
Beadon Gro. TS5: Midd 1B **100**
Beale Cl. TS17: Ing B 5C **128**
Beamish Rd. TS23: Bill 5F **39**
Beardmore Av.
TS11: Marsk S 3B **66**
Beath Gro. TS25: H'pool 4A **20**
Beaufort Cl. TS14: Guis. 4D **139**
TS17: Thorn T 4D **99**
Beaufort St. TS1: Midd 3E **77**
Beauly Gro. TS25: H'pool 4A **20**
Beaumaris Dr. TS16: Eag 1C **148**
Beaumont Ct. TS21: Sed 4E **23**
Beaumont Pk. TS23: Bill 5A **40**
Beaumont Rd. TS3: N Orm 4C **78**
Beaumont Vw. TS20: Nort. 1C **74**
Beaver Cl. TS17: Ing B 4C **128**
Beaver Ct. TS6: S Ban. 3B **80**
Beccles Cl. TS19: Stock T 3B **72**
Beckenham Gdns.
TS8: Hem 5F **131**
BECKFIELDS 2B 150
Beckfields Av. TS17: Ing B . . . 5C **128**
Beckfields Cen.
TS17: Ing B 1C **150**
Beckside TS13: Stait 1C **120**
Beckside Cl. TS13: Loft. 5D **93**
Beckston Cl. TS26: H'pool. 3C **12**
Beckwith Rd. TS15: Yarm 1A **160**
Bedale Av. TS23: Bill. 3D **55**
Bedale Cl. TS25: H'pool 5C **20**
Bedale Gro. TS19: Stock T 1A **96**
Bede Cl. TS19: Stock T. 2D **73**
Bede Ct. TS5: Midd 5C **76**
Bede Gro. TS25: H'pool 1F **19**
Bedford Rd. TS7: Nun 3A **134**
Bedford St. TS1: Midd 3E **77**
TS19: Stock T. 4F **73**
TS24: H'pool. 1F **15**
Bedford Ter. TS23: Bill. 2E **55**
Bedlington Wlk. TS23: Bill 2D **39**
(not continuous)
Beech Av. TS10: Redc 4E **49**
Beech Cl. TS9: Gt A. 2C **166**
Beech Ct. TS19: Stock T 3C **72**
Beechcroft Cl. TS12: Ling 4E **113**
Beeches, The DL2: Mid G 1A **144**
TS9: Stokes 2B **168**
TS19: Stock T. 4F **73**
TS23: Bill 2C **54**
Beeches Ri. TS7: Mart. 2E **133**
Beechfield TS8: Coul N 5B **132**
(not continuous)
Beech Gro. TS6: S Ban 4B **80**
TS8: Malt 1F **151**
TS12: Brot 1A **90**
Beech Gro. Rd. TS5: Midd. . . . 3E **101**
Beech Oval TS21: Sed. 3D **23**
Beech Rd. TS14: Guis 1E **139**
Beech St. TS1: Midd 3F **77**
Beech Ter. TS2: Port C. 4E **57**
Beechtree Ct. TS15: Yarm 2B **148**
BEECHWOOD 3A 102
Beechwood Av. TS4: Midd. . . . 2A **102**
TS9: Stokes 5C **164**
TS12: Salt 5C **68**
Beechwood Rd.
TS16: Prest T. 3C **126**
TS17: Thorn T 4C **98**
Beeford Cl. TS23: Bill. 1E **39**
Beeford Dr. TS5: Midd 5E **101**
Beehive Bus. Cen.
TS12: Skel 3E **89**
Belasis Av. TS23: Bill. 4E **55**
Belasis Bus. Cen. TS23: Bill . . . 2A **56**
Belasis Ct. TS23: Bill. 2A **56**
Belasis Hall Technology Pk.
TS23: Bill 2B **56**
(Manor Way)
TS23: Bill 1B **56**
(The Moat)
Belasis Ho. TS23: Bill 5E **39**
Belford Cl. TS19: Stock T 4C **72**
Belgrave Ct. TS25: Seat C 4E **21**
Belgrave Dr. TS6: Norm 4C **104**
Belgravia Gdns. TS5: Midd . . . 2E **101**
Belk Cl. TS6: Gran. 3D **81**
Belk St. TS1: Midd. 5E **77**
TS24: H'pool 2B **14**
Bellamy Ct. TS3: Midd 5D **79**
Bellasis Gro. TS27: H'pool 3D **7**
Bell Cl. TS18: Stock T 1F **97**
Bellerby Rd. TS18: Stock T. . . . 2B **96**
BELLEVUE 1B 20
Belle Vue Ct. TS20: Nort 2B **74**
Belle Vue Gdns.
TS20: Nort 2C **74**
Belle Vue Gro. TS4: Midd 2A **102**
Belle Vue Rd. TS5: Midd. 1D **101**
Belle Vue Sports Cen.. . . . . 1B 20
Belle Vue Ter. TS13: Carl H 3F **91**
Belle Vue Way TS25: H'pool . . . 5B **14**
Bellows Burn La.
TS27: Cast E 1A **4**
Bellsmoor Cl. TS21: Stil 2B **50**
Bell Sq. TS21: Stil 2A **50**
Bell St. TS5: Midd 5C **76**
Bell Vue Ho. TS20: Nort 2B **74**
Bellwood Av. TS12: Ling 4D **113**
Belmangate TS14: Guis 2F **139**
Belmont Av. TS5: Midd 3D **131**
TS6: S Ban. 5B **80**
TS19: Stock T. 3F **73**
TS22: Bill 5C **38**
Belmont Gdns. TS26: H'pool . . . 4F **13**
Belmont St. TS6: Est 1F **105**
Belmont Ter. TS14: Guis 2F **139**
Belsay Cl. TS19: Stock T. 4C **72**
Belsay Ct. TS21: Sed. 3C **22**
Belton Dr. TS5: Midd 5E **101**
Belvedere Rd. TS4: Midd 2A **102**
TS17: Thorn T 3D **99**
Benedict St. TS3: N Orm 4B **78**
Beningborough Gdns.
TS17: Ing B 5B **128**
Benmore Rd. TS25: H'pool 4F **19**
Bennett Rd. TS25: H'pool 1E **19**
Bennison Cres. TS10: Redc 1F **63**
Bennison St. TS14: Guis 1E **139**
Benridge Cl. TS5: Midd 1B **130**
Benson Grn. TS18: Stock T 2A **98**
Benson St. TS5: Midd 1D **101**
TS20: Nort 5B **54**
TS26: H'pool 4A **14**
Bentick St. TS26: H'pool 3A **14**
Bentinck Av. TS5: Midd 3E **101**
Bentinck Rd. TS19: Stock T. . . . 1B **96**
Bentley Av. TS23: Bill 5B **40**
Bentley St. TS26: H'pool 4A **14**
Bentley Wynd TS15: Yarm. . . . 3B **148**
Benton Cl. TS23: Bill 2D **39**
Benton Rd. TS5: Midd 4E **101**
Benwell Cl. TS19: Stock T. 4C **72**
Berberis Gro. TS19: Stock T . . . 5C **72**
Beresford Bldgs. TS3: Midd. . . . 5F **79**
Beresford Cres. TS3: Midd. 5F **79**
Berkeley Av. TS25: H'pool. 5A **20**
Berkeley Cl. TS23: Bill. 5D **39**
Berkley Dr. TS10: Redc 2E **65**
TS14: Guis 4F **139**
Berkshire Ho. TS6: Est. 5E **81**
Berkshire Rd. TS20: Nort 1C **74**
Bernaldby Av. TS14: Guis 3C **138**
Berner St. TS5: Midd. 1D **101**
Bernica Gro. TS17: Ing B. 2A **150**
Berrington Gdns.
TS17: Ing B 1B **150**
Bertha St. TS24: H'pool. 5C **14**
Berwick Gro. TS20: Nort 4A **54**
BERWICK HILLS 1C 102
Berwick Hills Av. TS3: Midd . . . 5E **79**
Berwick Hills Cen., The
TS3: Midd 1D **103**
Berwick St. TS25: Seat C. 4E **21**
Berwick Wlk. TS10: Redc 1E **65**
Bessemer Ct. TS6: Gran 1D **81**
Bessemer Cres.
TS19: Stock T 1B **72**
Bethune Rd. TS5: Midd 1B **100**
Betjeman Cl. TS23: Bill 2E **39**
Bevan Cl. TS19: Stock T 2C **72**
Bevanlee Rd. TS6: S Ban 3B **80**
Beverley Rd. TS4: Midd. 4F **101**
TS7: Nun 3B **134**
TS10: Redc. 1F **65**
TS23: Bill 2F **39**
Bewholme Cl. TS23: Bill 1E **39**
Bewley Gro. TS5: Midd 5C **100**
Bexley Cl. TS4: Midd. 5B **102**
Bexley Dr. TS6: Norm 4C **104**
TS25: H'pool 2B **20**
Bickersteth Cl.
TS18: Stock T 2A **98**
Bickersteth Wlk.
TS18: Stock T 2A **98**

Bickley Cl. TS22: Bill 5A **38**
Bickley Way TS8: Coul N 4B **132**
Biddick Cl. TS19: Stock T 4C **72**
Bielby Av. TS23: Bill. 1E **39**
Biggin Cl. TS5: Midd 5E **101**
Bignor Ct. TS17: Ing B 3F **127**
BILLINGHAM 1D **55**
Billingham Bank TS23: Bill 4D **55**
Billingham Beck Ecology Pk.
Vis. Cen. 3C **54**
Billingham Beck Valley Country Pk.
. . . . 3C **54**
BILLINGHAM BOTTOMS
INTERCHANGE **5C 54**
Billingham Diversion
TS20: Bill, Nort. 1A **54**
TS22: Bill, Wolv 5A **38**
Billingham Golf Course 1B **54**
Billingham Ind. Est.
TS23: Bill 5B **40**
Billingham Reach Ind. Est.
TS23: Bill 1B **76**
Billingham Rd. TS20: Nort 5B **54**
(not continuous)
Billingham Rd. Bri.
TS20: Nort 5C **54**
TS23: Bill 5C **54**
Billingham Station (Rail). 1F **55**
Billingham Woods
& The Holmes Nature Reserve
. . . . 1A **128**
Bilsdale Av. TS10: Redc 1A **64**
Bilsdale Rd. TS4: Midd 5A **78**
TS19: Stock T. 4E **73**
TS25: Seat C 5D **21**
Binchester Ct. TS17: Ing B . . . 4E **127**
Bingfield Ct. TS23: Bill. 2E **39**
Binks St. TS5: Midd 1E **101**
Birch Cl. TS15: K'ton 4D **161**
Birches, The TS6: Norm 1C **104**
TS8: Coul N 5A **132**
Birchfield Cl. TS16: Eag 5B **126**
Birchfield Dr. TS16: Eag 5B **126**
Birchgate Rd. TS5: Midd 3D **101**
Birch Gro. TS19: Stock T 1E **73**
Birchill Gdns. TS26: H'pool 2E **13**
Birchington Av.
TS6: Est, Gran 2E **81**
Birchtree Cl. TS7: Orm 4B **104**
Birch Wlk. TS24: H'pool 1A **14**
Birchwood Av. TS4: Midd 2A **102**
Birchwood Gro. TS6: Norm 5B **80**
Birchwood Rd. TS7: Mart. 2E **133**
Birdsall Brow TS20: Nort 4F **53**
Birdsall Row TS10: Redc. 4C **48**
Biretta Cl. TS19: Stock T 4A **72**
Birk Brow Rd. TS12: Char 2D **141**
TS12: Moor 4A **142**
TS14: Slape 2D **141**
Birkdale Cl. TS27: H'pool 2C **6**
Birkdale Dr. TS6: Est 2E **105**
Birkdale Rd. TS11: N Mar 2F **85**
TS18: Stock T 2B **96**
Birkhall Rd. TS3: Midd. 5F **79**
Birkley Rd. TS20: Nort. 2B **74**
Birtley Av. TS5: Midd. 1C **130**
Bisham Av. TS5: Midd 2C **100**
BISHOP CUTHBERT 5D **7**
BISHOPSGARTH. 3A **72**
Bishopsgarth TS19: Stock T . . . 3A **72**
Bishopsgarth Cotts.
TS19: Stock T. 3F **71**
Bishops Mill TS20: Nort 4B **54**
Bishop St. TS5: Midd. 5B **76**
TS18: Stock T 5B **74**
Bishops Way TS19: Stock T. . . . 3A **72**
Bishopton Av. TS19: Stock T . . . 4D **73**
Bishopton Ct. TS19: Stock T . . . 5B **72**
Bishopton La. TS18: Stock T. . . 5A **74**
(not continuous)
Bishopton Rd. TS4: Midd. 2F **101**
TS18: Stock T 4D **73**
TS19: Stock T 4D **73**
Bishopton Rd. W.
TS19: Stock T. 4F **71**
Blackberry Apartments
TS26: H'pool *4E 7*
(off Merlin Way)
Black Bobbies Field Nature Reserve
. . . . 5B **98**
Black Bull Wynd TS16: Ais. . . . 4F **147**
Blackburn Cl. TS19: Stock T . . . 5C **72**
Blackburn Gro.
TS11: Marsk S 3A **66**
Blackbush Wlk.
TS17: Thorn T 3C **128**
Black Diamond Way
TS16: Eag. 4B **126**
Blackett Av. TS20: Nort 2B **74**
Blackett Hutton Ind. Est.
TS14: Guis 2E **139**
Blackfriars TS15: Yarm 4B **148**
Blackhall Sands
TS5: Midd 3B **130**
Blackmore Cl. TS14: Guis 4F **139**
Blackmore Rd.
TS9: Gt A, Stokes. 2C **164**
Blackmore Wlk.
TS25: H'pool 2D **19**
Black Path TS11: Marsk S 5B **66**
Black Path, The TS20: Nort. . . . 4B **74**
Black Path Ind. Est.
TS20: Nort 4B **74**
Blacksail Cl. TS19: Stock T 5F **73**
Blacksmiths Cl. TS6: Est 1E **105**
Black Squares Dr.
TS22: Wyn 4E **25**
Blackthorn TS8: Coul N 1C **154**
Blackthorn Cl. TS10: Redc. 3E **65**
Blackthorn Gro.
TS19: Stock T 5C **72**
Blackton Rd. TS26: H'pool. 3C **12**
Blackwell Cl. TS23: Bill. 4A **40**
Black Wood TS22: Wyn 3F **25**
Blackwood Cl. TS27: H'pool 2C **6**
Bladon Dr. TS11: Marsk S 3C **66**
Blair Av. TS17: Ing B 1F **149**
Blairgowrie TS8: Mart 4E **133**
(not continuous)
Blairgowrie Gro.
TS25: H'pool. 4F **19**
Blairmore Gdns. TS16: Eag . . . 5C **126**
Blaise Gdn. Village
TS26: H'pool 3D **13**
Blake Cl. TS23: Bill 2E **39**
Blakelock Gdns.
TS25: H'pool 5A **14**
Blakelock Rd. TS25: H'pool 1F **19**
Blakeston Ct. TS19: Stock T . . . 4D **53**
Blakeston La. TS19: Stock T. . . 2A **52**
TS21: Stock T, Thorpe T . . . 1F **51**
Blakeston Rd. TS23: Bill 4F **39**
Blake St. TS26: H'pool. 2A **14**
Blake Wlk. TS26: H'pool 2A **14**
Blakey Cl. TS10: Redc. 3C **64**
Blakey Wlk. TS6: Est 5F **81**
Blanchland Rd. TS3: Midd. . . . 3E **103**
Blandford Cl. TS20: Nort 4B **54**
Blankney Cl. TS14: Guis 3D **139**
Blantyre Gro. TS25: H'pool 4A **20**
Blantyre Rd. TS6: Norm 1C **104**
Blatchford Rd. TS6: S Ban 3F **79**
Blenavon Ct. TS15: Yarm. 3B **148**
Blencathra Cl.
TS17: Thorn T 4D **99**
Blenheim Av. TS11: Marsk S. . . 3C **66**
Blenheim Cl. TS11: Marsk S . . . 3C **66**
Blenheim Ct. TS17: Ing B 2F **149**
Blenheim M. TS10: Redc. 4B **48**
Blenheim Rd. TS4: Midd 4A **78**
Blenheim Rd. Sth.
TS4: Midd 5A **78**
Blenheim Ter. TS10: Redc. 4B **48**
Bletchley Cl. TS19: Stock T. . . . 4C **72**
Blind La. TS14: Pin 2E **137**
Blorenge Ct. TS17: Ing B. 2F **149**
Bluebell Cres. TS18: Stock T. . . 1A **98**
Blue Bell Gro. TS5: Midd. 2E **131**
TS19: Stock T 5C **72**
BLUE BELL INTERCHANGE . . . **3E 131**
Bluebell Way TS12: Skel 4E **89**
TS26: H'pool 4D **7**
Blue Ho. Point Rd.
TS18: Stock T. 4E **75**
(not continuous)
Blue Post Yd. TS18: Stock T . . . 1A **98**
Blythport Cl. TS18: Stock T. . . . 4C **74**
Boagey Wlk. TS24: H'pool. 4A **8**
Boar La. TS17: Ing B. 5C **128**
Boathouse Ct. TS18: Stock T. . . 2B **98**
Boathouse La.
TS18: Stock T 2B **98**
Boathouse Yd. *TS13: Stait*. . . . *1C 120*
(off High St.)
Bodiam Cl. TS17: Ing B. 4A **128**
Bodiam Dr. TS10: Redc 2F **65**
Bodmin Gro. TS26: H'pool. 1D **13**
Boeing Way TS18: Stock T. 5F **97**
BOHO ZONE 2E **77**
Bolam Gro. TS23: Bill 3E **39**
Bolckow Ind. Est. TS6: Gran . . . 2D **81**
Bolckow Rd. TS6: Gran 2D **81**
Bolckow St. TS1: Midd. 2E **77**
TS6: Est 2F **105**
TS12: Skel 5E **89**
TS14: Guis 1E **139**
Boldron Cl. TS18: Stock T. 3A **96**
Bollington Rd. TS4: Midd 5B **102**
Bolsover Rd. TS20: Nort 2B **74**
Boltby Cl. TS5: Midd 5E **101**
Boltby Way TS16: Eag 4B **126**
Bolton Cl. TS10: Redc 1E **65**
Bolton Ct. TS4: Midd 2F **101**
TS12: Skel 3E **89**
Bolton Gro. TS25: Seat C. 4E **21**
Bolton Way TS14: Guis 2F **139**
Bondene Gro. TS19: Stock T . . . 3A **72**
Bondfield Rd. TS6: Est 5D **81**
Bond St. TS24: H'pool 1F **15**
Bone St. TS18: Stock T 4B **74**
Bonington Cres. TS23: Bill 2D **39**
Bon Lea Trad. Est.
TS17: Thorn T 2D **99**
(not continuous)
Bonny Gro. TS8: Mart. 5F **133**
Bonnygrove Way
TS8: Coul N 5C **132**
Bonnyrigg Cl. TS17: Ing B. . . . 2B **150**
Bonnyrigg Wlk. TS25: H'pool. . . 4F **19**
BOOSBECK 3B **112**
Boosbeck Rd. TS12: Boo. 3C **112**
TS12: Skel 5B **88**
Bordesley Grn. TS3: Midd 5D **79**
Borough Rd. TS1: Midd 3E **77**
TS3: N Orm 4A **78**
TS4: Midd 4A **78**
TS10: Redc 5D **49**
Borrowby Ct. TS14: Guis 1D **139**
Borrowby La. TS13: Borr. 3B **120**
Borrowdale Gro. TS5: Midd. . . 4C **100**
TS16: Egg 2C **148**
Borrowdale Rd. TS6: Gran. 4F **81**
Borrowdale St. TS25: H'pool. . . 1B **20**
Borrowdale Wlk. TS6: Gran. . . . 4F **81**
Borton Wlk. TS19: Stock T. 4F **73**
Boscombe Gdns. TS8: Hem . . . 5F **131**
Boston Cl. TS25: H'pool. 5F **19**
Boston Dr. TS7: Mart. 4D **133**
Boston Wlk. TS20: Nort. 1C **74**
Boswell Gro. TS25: H'pool. 2E **19**
Boswell St. TS1: Midd 3F **77**
Bosworth Way TS23: Bill 4F **39**
Botany Way TS7: Nun 3A **134**
Bothal Dr. TS19: Stock T 3A **72**
Bothal Wlk. TS19: Stock T. 2A **72**
Bottle of Notes Sculpture. *3F 77*
(off Elm St.)
Bottomley Mall TS1: Midd. 2E **77**
BOULBY 1D **119**

Boulby Bank TS13: Boul 1C **118**
Boulby Barns Cotts.
TS13: Boul 1D **119**
(not continuous)
Boulby Dr. TS13: Loft 5C **92**
Boulby Rd. TS6: Midd 1D **61**
TS10: Redc 1F **63**
TS13: Carl H. 2A **92**
Boulby Wlk. TS6: Est 5F **81**
Boulevard, The TS1: Midd 3F **77**
Boundary Rd. TS1: Midd 2E **77**
TS6: Norm 3C **104**
Bournemouth Av.
TS3: Midd 3F **103**
Bournemouth Dr.
TS24: H'pool 2D **7**
Bourneville Dr.
TS19: Stock T 1C **72**
Bourton Ct. TS3: Midd 4D **103**
Bousdale Cotts. TS14: Guis 4A **138**
Bowes Ct. TS12: Skel 3A **88**
BOWESFIELD 4A 98
Bowesfield Bus. Pk.
TS18: Stock T 5A **98**
Bowesfield Cvn. Pk.
TS18: Stock T 3A **98**
Bowesfield Cres.
TS18: Stock T 3A **98**
Bowesfield Ind. Est.
TS18: Stock T 5A **98**
Bowesfield La.
TS18: Stock T 5A **98**
(Kingfisher Way)
TS18: Stock T 1A **98**
(Lightfoot Gro.)
Bowesfield Nth. Ind. Est.
TS18: Stock T 3B **98**
Bowesfield Ponds Nature Reserve
1A 128
Bowesfield Riverside Ind. Est.
TS18: Stock T 4A **98**
Bowes Grn. TS24: H'pool 2D **7**
Bowes Rd. TS2: Midd 1D **77**
TS23: Bill 4D **39**
Bowes Rd. Bus. Pk.
TS2: Midd 5D **57**
Bowfell Cl. TS16: Eag 4B **126**
Bowfell Rd. TS3: Midd 1C **102**
Bowhill Way TS23: Bill 3A **40**
Bowland Cl. TS7: Nun 4F **133**
Bowland Rd. TS12: Skel 2B **88**
Bowley Cl. TS6: Norm 2B **104**
Bowley Wlk. TS1: Midd 3D **77**
Bowline Ho. TS24: H'pool 2C **14**
Bowness Cl. TS25: H'pool 2B **20**
Bowness Gro. TS10: Redc 5C **48**
Bowood Cl. TS17: Ing B 4F **127**
Bowron St. TS20: Nort 3B **74**
Bowser St. TS24: H'pool 4C **14**
Bow St. TS1: Midd 4D **77**
TS14: Guis 2F **139**
Bow St. Bus. Cen.
TS14: Guis 2F **139**
Box Dr. TS7: Nun 4B **134**
Boxer Ct. TS6: S Ban 3A **80**
Boyne Ct. TS21: Sed 3C **22**
Boynston Gro. TS21: Sed 4D **23**
Boynton Rd. TS4: Midd 1A **102**
Brabazon Dr. TS11: Marsk S 3B **66**
Brabourn Gdns. TS8: Hem 5F **131**
Brackenberry Cres.
TS10: Redc 2E **65**
Brackenbury Wlk. TS6: Est 5F **81**
Bracken Cres. TS14: Guis 3B **138**
Brackenfield Ct. TS6: Est 3E **105**
Brackenhill Cl. TS7: Nun 5A **134**
Bracken Rd. TS19: Stock T 1E **73**
Brackenthwaite TS5: Midd 2B **130**
Bracknell Rd. TS17: Thorn T 4E **99**
Bradbury Rd. TS20: Nort 4B **54**
Bradfield Way TS10: Redc 3C **64**
Bradhope Rd. TS3: Midd 1B **102**
Brading Ct. TS17: Ing B 3F **127**
Bradley Ct. TS23: Bill 5F **39**
Bradley's Ter. TS9: Gt A 1D **167**
Bradshaw Ct. TS24: H'pool 3F **7**
Braehead TS16: Eag 5C **126**
Braemar Gro. TS6: Norm 5B **80**
Braemar Rd. TS5: Midd 3B **100**
TS23: Bill 4C **38**
(not continuous)
TS25: H'pool 4A **20**
Braeside TS15: K'ton 4D **161**
Braeworth Cl. TS15: Yarm 4F **149**
Brafferton Dr. TS23: Bill 2F **39**
Brafferton St. TS26: H'pool 3F **13**
Brafferton Wlk. TS5: Midd 1C **130**
Braid Cres. TS23: Bill 2D **55**
Braidwood Rd. TS6: Norm 2C **104**
Braithwaite Cl. TS12: Skel 2B **88**
Bramble Cl. TS8: Stain 5B **130**
Bramble Dykes TS10: Redc 4E **65**
Bramble Rd. TS19: Stock T 1E **73**
BRAMBLES FARM 4F 79
Brambling Cl. TS20: Nort 4F **53**
Bramcote Way
TS17: Thorn T 3C **128**
Bramfield Way TS17: Ing B 3A **128**
Bramham Down TS14: Guis 3E **139**
Bramley Ct. TS25: H'pool 4A **20**
Bramley Gro. TS7: Mart 2E **133**
Bramley Pde. TS18: Stock T 2A **98**
Brampton Cl. TS8: Hem 3E **131**
Bramwith Av. TS3: Midd 3D **103**
Brancepath Wlk. TS24: H'pool 3F **7**
Brancepeth Av. TS3: Midd 3C **102**
Brancepeth Cl. TS11: N Mar 2A **86**
Brancepeth Ct. TS23: Bill 4C **38**
Brandlings Ct. TS15: Yarm 3B **148**
Brandon Cl. TS23: Bill 3D **39**
TS25: H'pool 2D **31**
Brandon Rd. TS3: Midd 1F **103**
Brankin Ct. TS12: Skel 3F **89**
Branklyn Gdns.
TS17: Ing B 1B **150**
Branksome Av. TS5: Midd 4E **101**
Branksome Gro.
TS18: Stock T 3B **96**
Bransdale TS14: Guis 3A **138**
Bransdale Cl. TS19: Stock T 4E **73**
Bransdale Gro. TS10: Redc 1F **63**
TS25: Seat C 4E **21**
Bransdale Rd. TS3: Midd 1C **102**
Brantingham Dr.
TS17: Ing B 4E **127**
Brantwood Cl. TS17: Ing B 1C **150**
Brass Castle La.
TS8: Mart, Nun 3D **155**
Brass Wynd TS7: Nun 5F **133**
Brathay Wlk. TS10: Redc 1B **64**
Braygate Mill La. TS12: Brot 5E **91**
TS13: Carl H 5E **91**
Breakwater Ho.
TS24: H'pool 3D **15**
Brechin Dr. TS17: Thorn T 3D **129**
Brechin Gro. TS25: H'pool 4A **20**
Breckland Wlk. TS3: Midd 2D **103**
Breckon Hill Rd. TS4: Midd 4A **78**
Brecon Cres. TS17: Ing B 1F **149**
Brecon Dr. TS10: Redc 2A **64**
Brecon Gdns. TS6: Est 4D **81**
Brecongill Cl. TS24: H'pool 1B **14**
Brenda Rd. TS25: H'pool 1B **20**
Brendon Cres. TS23: Bill 1E **55**
Brendon Gro. TS17: Ing B 3B **150**
Brenkley Cl. TS20: Nort 4E **53**
Brent Ct. TS23: Bill 2C **54**
Brentford Ct. TS12: Brot 3C **90**
Brentford Rd. TS20: Nort 2A **74**
Brentnall St. TS1: Midd 3E **77**
Brereton Rd. TS4: Midd 4A **102**
Bretby Cl. TS4: Midd 3A **102**
Brettenham Av. TS4: Midd 5B **102**
(not continuous)
Breward Wlk. TS24: H'pool 2B **14**
Brewery St. TS24: H'pool 4B **14**
Brewery Ter. TS9: Stokes 1B **168**
Brewery Yd. TS15: Yarm 3B **148**
Brewsdale Rd. TS3: N Orm 3C **78**
Brian Honour Av.
TS24: H'pool 1A **14**
Briardene Av. TS5: Midd 4E **101**
Briardene Ct. TS19: Stock T 1A **72**
Briardene M. TS25: H'pool 2B **20**
Briardene Wlk.
TS19: Stock T 1A **72**
Briarfields Cl. TS26: H'pool 4E **13**
Briargate TS6: Est 1F **105**
Briar Gro. TS10: Redc 5C **48**
Briarhill Gdns. TS26: H'pool 2E **13**
Briar Rd. TS17: Thorn T 5C **98**
Briarvale Av. TS5: Midd 3D **101**
Briar Wlk. TS18: Stock T 2D **97**
TS26: H'pool 2A **14**
Brickton Rd. TS5: Midd 1B **100**
Bridge Ct. TS6: Norm 2C **104**
TS15: Yarm 2B **148**
Bridge Ho's. TS12: Skel 4A **88**
Bridgend Cl. TS6: Gran 3E **81**
Bridgepool Cl. TS24: H'pool 4B **8**
Bridge Rd. TS9: Stokes 1B **168**
TS10: Redc 3A **48**
TS18: Stock T 2B **98**
Bridge Rd. Retail Pk.
TS18: Stock T 2B **98**
Bridge St. TS9: Gt A 2C **166**
TS15: Yarm 2B **148**
TS17: Thorn T 2C **98**
TS24: H'pool 4D **15**
Bridge St. E. TS2: Midd 2F **77**
Bridge St. M. *TS9: Gt A* *2C 166*
(off Bridge St.)
Bridge St. W. TS2: Midd 2E **77**
Bridgewater TS15: Yarm 4A **150**
Bridgewater Ct. TS4: Midd 5A **78**
Bridnor Rd. TS3: Midd 3C **102**
Bridport Cl. TS18: Stock T 4D **75**
Bridport Gro. TS8: Hem 5F **131**
Brierley Dr. TS21: Thorpe T 4D **25**
TS22: Wyn 3E **25**
(Black Squares Dr.)
TS22: Wyn 4C **26**
(Salter Ho. Dr.)
Brierley Grn. TS7: Mart 4E **133**
(not continuous)
BRIERTON 3B 18
Brierton La. TS22: Bri 3B **18**
TS25: H'pool 3B **18**
Brierton Shops TS25: H'pool 3D **19**
Brierton Sports Cen. 3E 19
Brierville Rd. TS19: Stock T 3F **73**
Brigandine Cl. TS25: Seat C 4D **21**
Briggs Av. TS6: S Ban 3A **80**
Brigham Rd. TS3: Midd 2B **102**
Brighouse Bus. Village
TS2: Midd 5C **56**
Brighouse Rd. TS2: Midd 5C **56**
Brighton Cl. TS17: Thorn T 2B **128**
Bright St. TS1: Midd 3A **78**
TS18: Stock T 5A **74**
TS26: H'pool 3F **13**
Brignall Rd. TS18: Stock T 3F **97**
Brignell Rd. TS2: Midd 1D **77**
Brig Open TS24: H'pool 1F **15**
Brimham Cl. TS17: Ing B 5C **128**
Brimham Ct. TS10: Redc 1B **64**
Brimston Cl. TS26: H'pool 3D **13**
Brindle Cl. TS7: Mart 4E **133**
Brine St. TS4: Midd 4A **78**
Brinewells Grn. TS4: Midd 5B **78**
Brinkburn Ct. TS25: H'pool 5F **13**
Brinkburn Rd. TS20: Nort 2A **74**
TS25: H'pool 5A **14**
Brisbane Cres.
TS17: Thorn T 1B **128**
Brisbane Gro. TS18: Stock T 2D **97**
Briscoe Way TS8: Hem 4C **130**
Bristol Av. TS12: Salt 4C **68**
Bristol Wlk. TS26: H'pool 1E **13**

Bristow Rd. TS4: Midd. 2B **102**
Bristow St. TS3: N Orm 4C **78**
Britain Av. TS5: Midd. 4C **100**
Britannia Bus. Pk.
TS2: Midd 1C **76**
Britannia Cl. TS24: H'pool. 3C **14**
Britannia Ct. TS2: Midd. 1D **77**
Britannia Ho. TS24: H'pool 2D **15**
Britannia Pl. TS10: Redc 1E **63**
Britannia Rd. TS19: Stock T . . . 5F **73**
Britannia Ter. TS12: Brot. 2B **90**
Broadbent St. TS12: Brot. 3B **90**
Broad Cl. TS8: Stain 5B **130**
Broadfield Rd. TS24: H'pool 5F **9**
Broadgate Gdns.
TS5: Midd 3C **100**
Broadgate Rd. TS5: Midd 3C **100**
Broadhaven Cl. TS6: Est 5E **81**
Broadlands TS17: Ing B. 4A **128**
Broad Oaks Way
TS17: Ing B 5A **128**
Broadstone TS8: Mart 5E **133**
Broadway TS6: Gran 3E **81**
Broadway E. TS10: Redc 1E **63**
Broadway W. TS10: Redc 1D **63**
Broadwell Rd. TS4: Midd 1B **132**
Brock Cl. TS21: Stock T. 3D **53**
Brocklesby Rd. TS14: Guis . . . 4E **139**
Brockrigg Ct. TS14: Guis. 5D **109**
Broctune Gdns. TS12: Brot 2C **90**
Brodick Gro. TS25: H'pool. 4A **20**
Brodie Cl. TS17: Ing B. 4F **127**
Brogden Grn. TS3: Midd 2C **102**
Bromley Hill Cl. TS7: Nun. . . . 5A **134**
Bromley La. TS8: Newb. 4B **154**
Bromley Rd. TS18: Stock T. . . . 2D **97**
Brompton Av. TS14: Guis. 5F **109**
Brompton Gro.
TS18: Stock T 3C **96**
Brompton Rd. TS5: Midd. 1D **101**
Brompton St. TS5: Midd 5D **77**
Brompton Wlk.
TS25: Seat C 5D **21**
Bronaber Cl. TS17: Ing B. 5E **127**
Bronte Way TS23: Bill 3D **39**
Brookby Ct. TS18: Stock T. 5D **75**
Brookdale Rd. TS7: Mart. 3D **133**
Brookes, The TS15: Yarm 5C **148**
BROOKFIELD 2D **131**
Brookfield Av. TS5: Midd. 3C **130**
Brookfield Rd.
TS19: Stock T 5A **72**
Brooklime Av.
TS18: Stock T 1A **128**
Brooklime Cl. TS26: H'pool. 4D **7**
Brooksbank Av. TS10: Redc. . . . 5C **48**
Brooksbank Cl. TS7: Orm 1B **134**
Brooksbank Rd. TS7: Orm. . . . 1B **134**
Brookside TS12: Boo 2B **112**
Brookside Av. TS4: Midd 3F **101**
Brook St. TS2: Midd. 2F **77**
TS26: H'pool 3A **14**
Brookwood Way TS16: Eag . . . 1C **148**
Broomfield Av. TS16: Eag 5B **126**
Broomhead Ho.
TS17: Thorn T 1D 129
(off Fullerton Way)
BROOM HILL 3A **128**
Broom Hill *TS13: Stait. 1C 120*
(off High St.)
Broom Hill Av. TS17: Ing B . . . 5A **128**
Broomhill Gdns.
TS26: H'pool 2E **13**
Broomlee Cl. TS17: Ing B 2A **150**
Brotherswater Ct.
TS10: Redc 5B **48**
BROTTON 2B **90**
Brotton Rd.
TS12: Brot, Carl H 2D **91**
TS13: Carl H. 2E **91**
Brougham Cl. TS17: Ing B 3F **127**
Brougham Ent. Cen.
TS24: H'pool 1B **14**
Brougham Ter. TS24: H'pool . . . 2A **14**
Brough Cl. TS17: Thorn T 1E **129**
Brough Ct. TS4: Midd 2A **102**
TS27: H'pool 3D **7**
Brough Fld. Cl.
TS17: Ing B 3A **128**
Brough Rd. TS23: Bill. 5E **39**
Broughton Av. TS4: Midd. 5B **102**
Broughton Grn. TS10: Redc. . . . 2B **64**
Broughton Rd. TS9: Stokes . . . 2D **169**
TS22: Bill 5B **38**
Browning Av. TS25: H'pool 1E **19**
Brownsea Ct. TS17: Ing B 1B **150**
Browns Ter. TS13: Hind 5E **121**
TS13: Stait 1C **120**
Broxa Cl. TS10: Redc. 3B **64**
Bruce Av. TS5: Midd 2B **100**
Bruce Cres. TS24: H'pool 4A **8**
Brundall Cl. TS19: Stock T 3B **72**
Brunel Cl. TS24: H'pool. 5C **8**
Brunel Ho. *TS15: Yarm 3B 148*
(off The Old Market)
Brunel Rd. TS6: S Ban. 3F **79**
Brunel Wlk. TS19: Stock T 1B **72**
Brunner Ho. TS3: Midd 2D **103**
Brunner Rd. TS23: Bill. 5E **55**
Brunswick Av. TS6: S Ban 4B **80**
Brunswick Ct. *TS18: Stock T. . . 1A 98*
(off Brunswick St.)
Brunswick St. TS1: Midd 2F **77**
TS18: Stock T 1A **98**
TS24: H'pool 4C **14**
Bruntoft Av. TS24: H'pool. 3F **7**
Bruntons Mnr. Ct.
TS3: Midd. 1E **103**
Brus Cnr. TS24: H'pool 3A **8**
Brusselton Cl. TS5: Midd. 1C **130**
Brusselton Ct. TS18: Stock T. . . 2A **98**
Brylston Rd. TS3: Midd 5F **79**
Bryony Ct. TS14: Guis 3B **138**
Bryony Gro. TS7: Mart. 2C **132**
Buccleuch Cl. TS14: Guis 4E **139**
Buckfast Rd. TS12: Skel 4D **89**
Buckie Gro. TS25: H'pool 4A **20**
Buckingham Av. TS27: Hart 4F **5**
Buckingham Dr. TS6: Norm. . . 4C **104**
Buckingham Rd. TS10: Redc. . . 4C **48**
TS18: Stock T. 1F **97**
Buckland Cl. TS17: Ing B. 1C **150**
Buckleberry Cl.
TS24: H'pool 5A **8**
Buck St. TS2: Midd 1E **77**
Buckthorn Cres.
TS21: Stock T 4D **53**
Budworth Cl. TS23: Bill 2E **39**
Bulmer Cl. TS15: Yarm 5D **149**
Bulmer Ct. TS6: Norm. 2D **105**
Bulmer Pl. TS24: H'pool 4F **7**
Bulmer's Bldgs.
TS14: Guis. 1D 139
(off Park La.)
Bulmer Way TS1: Midd 3D **77**
Bungalows, The TS6: Gran 3E **81**
TS7: Orm 4A 104
(off Henry Taylor Ct.)
TS13: Port M 4F **121**
TS21: Long N. 1A **124**
Bunting Cl. TS17: Ing B. 5B **128**
TS26: H'pool 5E **7**
Burbank Ct. *TS24: H'pool 4C 14*
(off Burbank St.)
Burbank St. TS24: H'pool 4C **14**
Burdale Cl. TS16: Eag 4A **126**
Burdon Cl. TS19: Stock T 4C **72**
Burdon Gth. TS17: Ing B 4A **128**
Burdon Vw. TS16: Eag. 2A **148**
Burdon Way TS9: Stokes. 3D **169**
Burford Av. TS18: Stock T 3E **97**
Burgess St. TS18: Stock T. 5A **74**
Burgess Wlk. TS1: Midd 4A **78**
Burghley Ct. TS8: Hem. 4F **131**
Burghley Dr. TS17: Ing B. 4A **128**
Burke Pl. TS24: H'pool. 5E **9**
Burlam Rd. TS5: Midd. 1C **100**
Burley Cl. TS12: Skel. 4D **89**
Burnaby Cl. TS25: H'pool 2B **20**
Burneston Gro.
TS18: Stock T 2A **96**
Burnet Cl. TS17: Ing B. 4B **128**
Burnholme Av. TS3: Midd 5E **79**
Burnhope Rd. TS26: H'pool. . . . 3C **12**
Burniston Dr.
TS17: Thorn T 3B **128**
TS22: Bill 5A **38**
Burnmoor Dr. TS16: Eag 5B **126**
Burn Rd. TS25: H'pool. 5B **14**
Burnsall Rd. TS3: Midd 1B **102**
Burns Av. TS25: H'pool 1E **19**
Burn's Cl. TS27: Hart 3F **5**
Burnside Ct. TS18: Stock T. . . . 1E **97**
Burnside Gro. TS18: Stock T. . . 1E **97**
Burnside Ho. TS23: Bill 4F **55**
Burns Rd. TS6: Est. 5C **80**
Burnston Cl. TS26: H'pool. 2D **13**
Burnsville Rd. TS6: Gran. 3D **81**
Burns Wlk. TS6: Est. 5C **80**
Burntoft TS22: Wyn 2E **37**
Burn Valley App.
TS26: H'pool 5A **14**
Burn Valley Gro.
TS25: H'pool 5A **14**
Burn Valley Rd.
TS26: H'pool 5A **14**
Burn Wood Ct.
TS21: Long N. 1A **124**
Burringham Rd. TS20: Nort. . . . 5F **53**
Burton M. TS21: Sed 4D **23**
Burtonport Wlk.
TS18: Stock T 4C 74
(off Alnport Rd.)
Burtree Pk. TS25: Seat C 3E **21**
Burwell Dr. TS19: Stock T 4A **72**
Burwell Rd. TS3: Midd. 2F **103**
Burwell Wlk. TS25: H'pool 1E **31**
Burythorpe Cl. TS4: Midd 1A **102**
Busby Way TS15: Yarm 4F **149**
Bushmead Ter. TS3: Midd 3E **103**
Bush St. TS5: Midd 5D **77**
Bushton Cl. TS26: H'pool 2D **13**
Bute Av. TS25: H'pool 1A **20**
Bute Cl. TS17: Thorn T 2C **128**
Bute St. TS18: Stock T. 5A **74**
Butler St. TS20: Nort 2B **74**
Buttercup Av. TS22: Wyn. 3C **26**
Buttercup Cl. TS19: Stock T . . . 2C **72**
TS26: H'pool 4E **7**
Buttercup Gro. TS8: Stain 4B **130**
Butterfield Cl. TS16: Eag. 1B **148**
Butterfield Dr. TS16: Eag. 1B **148**
Butterfield Gro. TS16: Eag. . . . 1B **148**
Butterfly World
Stockton-on-Tees 2D **127**
Buttermere Av. TS5: Midd 4C **100**
Buttermere Rd. TS6: Gran 4F **81**
TS10: Redc 5B **48**
TS18: Stock T 5D **73**
Butterwick Gro. TS22: Wyn. . . . 4A **26**
Butterwick Rd. TS21: Sed 3D **23**
TS24: H'pool 3E **7**
Butterworth Ho.
TS17: Thorn T 1D 129
(off Master Rd.)
Butt La. TS14: Guis 2F **139**
Buttsfield Way TS23: Bill 2E **39**
Butts La. TS16: Egg. 2B **148**
TS27: Hart 3C **4**
Buxton Av. TS7: Mart. 4D **133**
Buxton Gdns. TS22: Bill. 5B **38**
Bydales Dr. TS11: Marsk S 4E **67**
Byelands St. TS4: Midd. 5A **78**
Byemoor Av. TS9: Gt A 3D **167**
Byemoor Cl. TS9: Gt A 3D **167**
Byfleet Av. TS3: Midd 4D **79**
Byland Cl. TS10: Redc. 2B **64**
TS14: Guis 2F **139**
Byland Gro. TS25: Seat C 4E **21**

Byland Rd. TS7: Nun 3B **134**
TS12: Skel 4D **89**
Bylands Gro. TS19: Stock T. . . . 1B **96**
Bylands Rd. TS6: Est. 1D **105**
Byland Way TS23: Bill 2A **56**
By-Pass Rd. TS23: Bill. 3D **55**
Byron Cl. TS23: Bill 2E **39**
Byron Ct. TS12: Brot 1B **90**
Byron St. TS26: H'pool. 3F **13**
Bywell Gro. TS7: Orm 4A **104**

C

Cabot Ct. TS17: Thorn T 2D **129**
Cadogan St. TS1: Midd 4D **77**
TS3: N Orm 4C **78**
Cadwell Cl. TS3: Midd. 2A **104**
Caernarvon Cl. TS6: Gran 4E **81**
Caernarvon Gro.
TS26: H'pool 1D **13**
Cairn Ct. TS2: Midd. 5D **57**
Cairn Rd. TS25: H'pool 5F **19**
Cairnston Rd. TS26: H'pool. . . . 3C **12**
Caister Ct. TS10: Redc. 3E **65**
Caistor Dr. TS25: H'pool 1F **31**
Caithness Rd. TS6: Norm 5B **80**
TS25: H'pool. 5F **19**
Calcott Cl. TS19: Stock T. 4C **72**
Calder Cl. TS22: Bill 4A **38**
Calderdale TS12: Skel 3C **88**
Calder Gro. TS4: Midd. 4B **102**
TS10: Redc 1B **64**
TS25: H'pool. 4F **19**
Caldey Gdns. TS17: Ing B 2E **149**
Caldicot Cl. TS6: Est 4E **81**
Caldwell Cl. TS8: Hem. 5E **131**
Caledonian Rd. TS25: H'pool. . . 1A **20**
Calf Fallow La. TS20: Nort 3F **53**
CALIFORNIA 5F 81
. . . . 1D 167
California Bungs. *TS6: Est . . . 1A **106***
(off Old Mines Rd.)
California Cl. TS18: Stock T . . . 5A **74**
California Ct. TS9: Gt A. 2D **167**
California Gro. TS9: Gt A 1D **167**
California Rd. TS6: Est 1F **105**
Callander Rd. TS25: H'pool 4F **19**
Calluna Gro. TS7: Mart 2C **132**
Calthorpe Ct. TS1: Midd 3D **77**
Calverley Rd. TS3: Midd 1F **103**
Calvert Cl. TS3: N Orm 4B **78**
Calvert's La. TS18: Stock T. . . . 5B **74**
Calvert's Sq. *TS18: Stock T. . . . 5B **74***
(off Calvert's La.)
Cambourne Cl. TS8: Hem 4E **131**
Cambrian Av. TS10: Redc 2A **64**
Cambrian Ct. TS17: Ing B 1F **149**
Cambrian Rd. TS23: Bill 1C **54**
Cambridge Av. TS5: Midd 3C **100**
TS7: Mart. 3D **133**
Cambridge Rd. TS3: Midd. 3C **78**
TS5: Midd 3B **100**
TS17: Thorn T 3C **98**
Cambridge Sq. TS5: Midd. . . . 3D **101**
Cambridge St. TS12: Salt 4C **68**
Cambridge Ter. TS2: Port C. . . . 4E **57**
Camden St. TS1: Midd 4A **78**
TS18: Stock T. 2F **97**
Camellia Cres. TS20: Nort. 1F **73**
Camelon St. TS17: Thorn T. . . . 3D **99**
Cameron Rd. TS24: H'pool 2B **14**
Cameron St. TS20: Nort 5A **54**
Campbell Ct. TS18: Stock T . . . 4C **74**
Campbell Gro. TS10: Redc 3C **64**
Campbell Rd. TS25: H'pool 4F **19**
Campion Cl. TS17: Ing B. 4B **128**
Campion Dr. TS14: Guis 3B **138**
Campion Gro. TS7: Mart 2C **132**
Campion St. TS26: H'pool. 4A **14**
Camsell Ct. TS5: Midd 1D **101**
Canberra Gro.
TS18: Stock T 2D **97**
Canberra Rd. TS7: Mart 3D **133**
Canewood TS3: Midd 1F **103**
Cannock Rd. TS3: Midd 2C **102**
Cannon Pk. Cl. TS1: Midd 3D **77**
Cannon Pk. Ind. Est.
TS1: Midd 3D **77**
Cannon Pk. Rd. TS1: Midd 3D **77**
Cannon Pk. Way TS1: Midd. . . . 3D **77**
Cannon St. TS1: Midd 3C **76**
TS5: Midd 4C **76**
Canon Gro. TS15: Yarm 5C **148**
Canterbury Gro. TS5: Midd . . . 1E **101**
Canterbury Rd. TS10: Redc 1F **65**
TS12: Brot 2C **90**
Canton Gdns. TS5: Midd 2D **131**
Canvey Wlk. TS14: Guis 3D **139**
Captain Cook and Staithes
Heritage Cen. 1C 120
Captain Cook Birthplace Mus.
. . . . 1D 133
Captain Cook Schoolroom Mus.
. . . . 2D 167
Captain Cook's Cl.
TS13: Stait 2B **120**
Captain Cook's Cres.
TS7: Mart 3E **133**
Captain Cook Sq. TS1: Midd . . . 3E **77**
Captain Cook's Way
TS9: Gt A 1D **167**
Captains Wlk. TS24: H'pool . . . 3D **15**
Carburt Rd. TS19: Stock T. 1A **72**
Carcut Rd. TS3: N Orm 3C **78**
Cardigan Cl. TS6: Est. 4E **81**
Cardigan Gro. TS26: H'pool. 5E **7**
Cardinal Gro. TS19: Stock T . . . 4F **71**
Cardwell Wlk.
*TS17: Thorn T 3C **98***
(off Walker St.)
Carew Cl. TS15: Yarm 1A **160**
Carey Cl. TS1: Midd 4D **77**
CARGO FLEET 3D 79
Cargo Fleet La.
TS3: Midd, N Orm 3D **79**
Cargo Fleet Rd. TS1: Midd 3A **78**
TS3: Midd 3A **78**
Carina Cres. TS18: Stock T 4F **97**
Carisbrooke Av. TS3: Midd . . . 1F **103**
Carisbrooke Rd.
TS26: H'pool 4D **13**
Carisbrooke Way
TS10: Redc. 1E **65**
Carlbury Av. TS5: Midd 1B **130**
Carlile Hill TS8: Hem 5D **131**
Carlile Wlk. TS20: Nort 3B **74**
CARLIN HOW 3F 91
Carlin Pk. TS13: Carl H 3E **91**
Carlisle St. TS25: Seat C 4E **21**
Carlow Cl. TS14: Guis 4E **139**
Carlow St. TS1: Midd. 5C **76**
CARLTON 5C 50
Carlton Av. TS22: Bill. 4B **38**
Carlton Bingo
Hartlepool 3B 14
Carlton Cl. TS14: Guis 5E **109**
TS18: Stock T 5A **74**
Carlton Dr. TS17: Thorn T 2B **128**
Carlton St. TS26: H'pool 4A **14**
Carlton Ter. TS15: Yarm 3B **148**
Carlton Village TS21: Carlt 5C **50**
Carlyle Rd. TS6: Est 5D **81**
Carmarthen Rd. TS3: Midd . . . 3E **103**
Carmel Gdns. TS5: Midd. 3D **131**
TS7: Nun 3B **134**
TS14: Guis 1E **139**
TS20: Nort 1C **74**
Carnaby Wlk. TS5: Midd 4E **101**
Carney St. TS12: Boo 3B **112**
Carnoustie Dr. TS16: Eag 5C **126**
Carnoustie Gro.
TS27: H'pool 2C **6**
Carnoustie Rd. TS11: N Mar . . . 2A **86**
Carnoustie Way TS8: Mart. . . . 4E **133**
Caroline M. TS10: Redc 4D **49**
Caroline St. TS26: H'pool 4B **14**
Carpenter Cl. TS15: Yarm 5E **149**
Carradale Cl. TS16: Eag 1C **148**
Carr Bri. Cl. TS16: Eag 2A **148**
Carriage Wlk. TS16: Eag. 4B **126**
Carrick Ct. TS2: Midd 5D **57**
Carricks Cnr. TS9: Stokes 2B **168**
Carrick St. TS24: H'pool. 4F **7**
Carrick's Yd. TS12: Skel 4B **88**
Carroll Wlk. TS25: H'pool 2D **19**
Carrol St. TS18: Stock T 5B **74**
Carron Gro. TS6: Norm 2C **104**
Carr St. TS18: Stock T. 1F **97**
TS26: H'pool 2A **14**
Carter's La. TS16: Eag. 5B **124**
Carthorpe Dr. TS23: Bill. 4E **39**
Cartmel Rd. TS10: Redc 1C **64**
Carvers Ct. TS12: Brot. 2C **90**
Carville Ct. TS19: Stock T 2B **72**
Casebourne Rd.
TS25: H'pool 1C **20**
Casper Ct. TS16: Eag. 5C **126**
Caspian Cl. TS17: Thorn T 4D **99**
Cassel Ct. TS23: Bill 2A **76**
Cass Ho. Rd. TS8: Hem. 1D **153**
Casson Ct. TS23: Bill. 4D **39**
Casson Way TS23: Bill. 4D **39**
Cassop Gro. TS5: Midd 1B **130**
Cassop Wlk. TS19: Stock T 2B **72**
Castle Cl. TS19: Stock T 4C **72**
Castle Ct. TS12: Boo 3B **112**
Castle Dyke Wynd
TS15: Yarm 3C **148**
Castlegate Cen.
TS18: Stock T 1B **98**
Castlegate Marine Club. 5B 74
Castlegate Quay
TS18: Stock T 1B **98**
Castlegate Quay Watersports Cen.
. . . . 1B 98
Castle Grange TS12: Skel 5B **88**
Castle Howard Cl.
TS27: H'pool 3D **7**
Castlemartin TS17: Ing B. 3F **149**
Castlereagh TS22: Wyn. 1C **36**
Castlereagh Cl.
TS21: Long N. 1A **124**
Castlereagh Rd.
TS19: Stock T. 4F **73**
Castlerigg Cl. TS12: Skel. 2C **88**
Castle Rd. TS10: Redc. 1E **65**
Castleton Av. TS5: Midd 3B **100**
Castleton Dr. TS22: Bill 5B **38**
Castleton Rd. TS6: Est. 5F **81**
TS18: Stock T. 3F **97**
TS25: Seat C 4E **21**
Castleton Wlk.
TS17: Thorn T 2B **128**
Castle Way TS4: Midd 2F **101**
TS18: Stock T 1B **98**
Castlewood TS3: Midd 2F **103**
Castle Wynd TS7: Nun. 5A **134**
Catcote Rd. TS25: H'pool. 3E **19**
Caterton Cl. TS15: Yarm 5E **149**
Cat Flatt La.
TS10: Marsk S, Redc 3F **65**
TS11: Marsk S 4A **66**
Cathedral Dr. TS19: Stock T . . . 4A **72**
Catherine Gro. *TS24: H'pool . . . 4C **14***
(off Sheerness Gro.)
Catherine Rd. TS24: H'pool. . . . 4C **14**
Catherine St. TS12: Ling 4E **113**
TS24: H'pool. 1F **15**
Cattersty Way TS12: Brot 1B **90**
Cattistock Cl. TS14: Guis 3F **139**
Caudwell Cl. TS19: Stock T. . . . 1A **72**
Causeway, The TS23: Bill 1D **55**
Cavendish Ho.
TS17: Thorn T 5B **74**
Cavendish Rd. TS4: Midd 3A **102**
Cavendish Wlk.
TS19: Stock T 1B **72**
Caversham Rd. TS4: Midd. . . . 4B **102**

Cawdor Cl. TS11: N Mar 2F **85**
TS17: Ing B 5F **127**
Cawood Dr. TS5: Midd 4E **101**
Cawthorn Cl. TS8: Hem 4C **130**
Cawthorne Pl. TS22: Wyn 3A **26**
Caxton Gro. TS25: H'pool 1E **19**
Caxton St. TS5: Midd 5E **77**
Cayton Cl. TS10: Redc 3B **64**
Cayton Dr. TS5: Midd 4E **101**
TS17: Thorn T 3B **128**
TS22: Bill 4B **38**
Cecil Ct. TS25: H'pool 2B **20**
Cecil St. TS1: Midd 3D **77**
TS18: Stock T 2A **98**
Cedar Cl. TS6: Est 1D **105**
Cedar Ct. TS17: Thorn T 4C **98**
Cedar Cres. TS16: Prest T 2D **127**
Cedar Dr. TS8: Thornt 1B **152**
Cedar Gro. DL2: Mid G 3A **144**
TS10: Redc 4E **49**
TS12: Brot 2A **90**
TS13: Loft 5B **92**
TS17: Thorn T 4C **98**
Cedar Ho. TS19: Stock T 3C **72**
Cedarhurst Dr. TS12: Ling 4E **113**
Cedar Rd. TS7: Mart 2F **133**
TS7: Orm 5B **104**
Cedar St. TS18: Stock T 5B **74**
Cedar Ter. TS2: Port C 5F **57**
Cedar Wlk. TS24: H'pool 1A **14**
Cedarwood Av.
TS9: Stokes 4C **164**
Cedarwood Glade
TS8: Stain 5C **130**
Cedarwood Rd. TS6: Norm 5B **80**
Celandine Cl. TS7: Mart 1C **132**
Celandine Gdns.
TS26: H'pool 4E **7**
Celandine Way
TS19: Stock T 3C **72**
CEMETERY RDBT. **4F 109**
Cennon Gro. TS17: Ing B 1F **149**
Centenary Cres. TS20: Nort . . . 1A **74**
Central Arc. TS15: Yarm 3B **148**
Central Av. TS5: Midd 1B **100**
TS23: Bill 3D **55**
Central M. TS1: Midd 3F **77**
Central Rd. TS24: H'pool 5D **9**
Central Sq. TS1: Midd 3F **77**
Central St. TS15: Yarm 3B **148**
Central Ter. TS10: Redc 3C **48**
Central Way TS9: Gt A 1D **167**
Central Way Bungs.
TS9: Gt A 1D **167**
Centre Ct. TS5: Midd 3C **130**
Centre Mall TS1: Midd 3E **77**
Centre Rd. TS8: Hem 4E **131**
Chadburn Grn. TS4: Midd 4F **101**
Chadburn Rd. TS20: Nort 2A **74**
Chadderton Cl. TS12: Boo 2B **112**
Chadderton Dr.
TS17: Thorn T 5E **99**
Chadwell Av. TS3: Midd 3D **103**
Chadwick Wlk.
TS19: Stock T 1B **72**
Chaffinch Cl. TS26: H'pool 5E **7**
Chalcot Wlk. TS3: Midd 5E **79**
Chaldron Way TS16: Eag 3A **126**
Chalfield Cl. TS17: Ing B 1C **150**
Chalford Oaks TS5: Midd 4A **100**
Chalk Cl. TS18: Stock T 2A **98**
Chalk Wlk. *TS18: Stock T 2A 98*
(off Chalk Cl.)
Challacombe Cres.
TS17: Ing B 3A **150**
Challoner Rd. TS15: Yarm 5B **148**
TS24: H'pool 1F **13**
Challoner Sq. TS24: H'pool 1F **13**
Chaloner M. TS14: Guis 2E **139**
Chaloner St. TS14: Guis 2E **139**
Chamomile Dr.
TS19: Stock T 2C **72**
Chancel Way TS6: Est 1E **105**
Chancery Ri.
TS17: Thorn T 2B **128**
Chandlers Cl. TS24: H'pool 3D **15**
Chandlers Ridge TS7: Nun . . . 4A **134**
Chandlers Wharf
TS18: Stock T 2B **98**
Chantry Cl. TS3: Midd 3C **102**
TS20: Nort 5A **54**
Chantry Sq. TS3: Midd 3D **103**
Chapelbeck Bungs.
TS14: Guis 2D **139**
Chapel Cl. TS3: Midd 3F **103**
TS11: Marsk S 4C **66**
Chapel Ct. TS23: Bill 4D **55**
Chapel Gdns. TS21: Carlt 5D **51**
Chapelgarth TS8: Stain 5C **130**
Chapell La. Nth. TS22: Wyn . . . 5A **28**
Chapell La. Sth. TS22: Wyn . . . 1A **38**
Chapel Pl. TS12: Moor 3B **142**
Chapel Rd. TS23: Bill 4D **55**
Chapel Row TS13: Loft 5C **92**
Chapel St. TS6: Laze 4C **82**
TS11: Marsk S 4C **66**
TS12: Brot 2C **90**
TS13: Skin 2A **92**
TS14: Guis 2E **139**
TS17: Thorn T 2C **98**
Chapel Yd. *TS13: Stait. 1C 120*
(off Staithes La.)
TS15: Yarm 3B **148**
Chapman Ct. TS3: Midd 1E **103**
Chapman St. TS20: Nort 1B **74**
Chards Cotts. TS12: Salt 1C **88**
Chard Wlk. TS3: Midd 3C **102**
Charlbury Rd. TS3: Midd 5D **79**
Charles St. TS10: Redc 3D **49**
TS11: N Mar 2A **86**
TS17: Thorn T 3C **98**
TS25: Seat C 4E **21**
Charlock TS8: Coul N 2C **154**
Charlotte Grange
TS26: H'pool 4A **14**
Charlotte St. TS2: Midd 2E **77**
TS10: Redc 3D **49**
TS12: Skel 4D **89**
TS26: H'pool 5A **14**
Charlton Cl. TS23: Bill 2A **56**
Charlton Rd. TS10: Redc 5F **47**
CHARLTONS 2F **141**
Charltonsfield TS12: Moor . . . 4B **142**
Charltons Gth. TS14: Guis 1E **139**
Charltons Pond (Nature Reserve)
. . . . 2F **55**
Charnley Grn. TS4: Midd 5A **102**
Charnwood Cl.
TS11: Marsk S 5C **66**
Charnwood Dr. TS7: Orm 1B **134**
Charrington Av.
TS17: Thorn T 3B **128**
Charterhouse St.
TS25: H'pool 1A **20**
Chart Ho. TS24: H'pool 3D **15**
Chartwell Cl. TS11: Marsk S . . . 3B **66**
TS17: Ing B 1C **150**
Charwood TS3: Midd 1F **103**
Chase, The TS10: Redc 5D **49**
TS19: Stock T 5B **72**
Chatham Gdns.
TS24: H'pool 1A **14**
Chatham Rd. TS16: Eag 4F **125**
TS24: H'pool 1F **13**
Chatham Sq. TS24: H'pool 1A **14**
Chathill Wlk. TS7: Orm 4A **104**
Chatsworth Ct.
TS19: Stock T 3D **73**
Chatsworth Gdns. TS22: Bill . . . 5C **38**
Chatton Cl. TS3: Midd 3D **103**
Chaucer Av. TS25: H'pool 1E **19**
Chaucer Cl. TS23: Bill 3D **39**
Chaytor Lee TS15: Yarm 4C **148**
Cheadle Wlk. TS3: Midd 2D **103**
Cheam Av. TS3: Midd 5D **79**
Cheddar Cl. TS6: Gran 4E **81**
Chedworth Ct. TS17: Ing B 3F **127**
Cheetham St. TS6: Gran 2D **81**
Chelford Cl. TS25: H'pool 5B **20**
Chelker Cl. TS26: H'pool 3C **12**
Chelmsford Av.
TS18: Stock T 1C **96**
Chelmsford Rd. TS5: Midd . . . 1E **101**
Chelmsford St.
TS17: Thorn T 2C **98**
Chelmsford Wlk. TS5: Midd . . . 2E **101**
Chelsea Gdns. TS20: Nort 4E **53**
Chelston Cl. TS26: H'pool 2C **12**
Cheltenham Av. TS7: Mart . . . 4D **133**
TS17: Thorn T 3C **98**
Cheltenham Cl. TS5: Midd 1F **101**
Cheltenham Rd.
TS18: Stock T 2E **75**
Chepstow Cl. TS23: Bill 5D **39**
Chepstow Wlk. TS26: H'pool 5E **7**
Cherelle Gdns. TS24: H'pool . . . 1A **14**
Cheriton Grn. TS3: Midd 5D **79**
Cherry Ct. TS19: Stock T 3A **74**
Cherry Fld. Dr. TS5: Midd 2D **101**
Cherry Gth. TS17: Ing B 4A **128**
Cherry Tree Apartments
TS26: H'pool 4E 7
(off Evergreen Cl.)
Cherry Tree Cl. TS7: Orm 4B **104**
Cherry Tree Dr. TS21: Sed 3D **23**
Cherry Tree Gdns.
TS20: Nort 1C **74**
Cherry Trees TS10: Redc 3B **48**
Cherry Wlk. TS24: H'pool 1A **14**
Cherrywood Av.
TS9: Stokes 5C **164**
Cherrywood Ct. TS5: Midd 2E **131**
Cherrywood Gro. TS6: Norm . . . 5B **80**
Chertsey Av. TS3: Midd 5D **79**
Chervil TS8: Coul N 1C **154**
Cherwell Ter. TS3: Midd 4E **79**
Chesham Cl. TS20: Nort 5B **54**
Chesham Gro. TS20: Nort 5C **54**
Chesham Rd. TS20: Nort 5B **54**
Chesham St. TS5: Midd 1E **101**
Cheshire Rd. TS20: Nort 1C **74**
Chesneywood TS3: Midd 1F **103**
Chesterfield Dr. TS8: Mart 5E **133**
Chester Rd. TS10: Redc 1F **65**
TS24: H'pool 2F **13**
TS26: H'pool 2F **13**
Chester St. TS1: Midd 5D **77**
Chesterton Av.
TS17: Thorn T 2B **128**
Chesterton Ct. TS20: Nort 1B **74**
Chesterton Rd. TS25: H'pool . . . 1E **19**
Chesterwood TS3: Midd 1F **103**
Chestnut Av. TS10: Redc 5E **49**
Chestnut Cl. TS6: Laze 4C **82**
TS12: Salt 5A **68**
Chestnut Dr. TS7: Mart 3E **133**
Chestnut Gro. TS12: Brot 2A **90**
TS17: Thorn T 4C **98**
Chestnut Rd. TS16: Prest T . . . 2C **126**
TS21: Sed 3D **23**
Chestnut Row TS25: Grea 3E **31**
Chestnut Sq. TS19: Stock T 3F **73**
Chetwode Ter. *TS3: Midd. 3E 103*
(off Ormesby Rd.)
Chevin Wlk. TS3: Midd 2C **102**
Cheviot Cres. TS23: Bill 2D **55**
Cheviot Dr. TS12: Skel 3C **88**
Chez Nous Av. TS25: H'pool . . . 1B **20**
Chichester Cl. TS25: H'pool 1F **31**
Chilcroft Cl. TS22: Bill 5A **38**
Childeray St. TS18: Stock T 1F **97**
Child St. TS12: Brot 2B **90**
TS14: Guis 2E **139**
Chillingham Ct. TS23: Bill 3E **39**
Chillingham Rd. TS12: Skel . . . 3B **88**
Chiltern Av. TS10: Redc 2A **64**
Chilton Cl. TS5: Midd 5C **100**
TS19: Stock T 1A **72**
Chiltons Av. TS23: Bill 4E **55**

Chine, The TS12: Salt 4B **68**
Chingford Av. TS3: Midd 2F **103**
Chingford Gro.
TS19: Stock T 4C **72**
Chipchase Rd. TS5: Midd 1D **101**
Chippenham Rd.
TS4: Midd 5A **102**
Chivers Ct. TS18: Stock T 4D **73**
Chopwell Cl. TS19: Stock T. . . . 1B **72**
Christchurch Dr.
TS18: Stock T 2B **96**
Christine Ho. TS17: Thorn T . . . 2B **98**
Christopher St. TS20: Nort 3B **74**
TS26: H'pool 3A **14**
Church Cl. TS7: Orm 4A **104**
TS8: Stain 5C **130**
TS11: Marsk S 4D **67**
TS13: Loft 5C **92**
TS16: Egg 2C **148**
TS17: Thorn T 3B **98**
TS24: H'pool. 1F **15**
Church Dr. TS9: Gt A 2C **166**
TS12: Boo 3C **112**
Churchend Cl. TS23: Bill 4D **55**
Church Farm Flats
TS21: Redm. 1B **70**
Church Fld. Way
TS17: Ing B 4A **128**
Church Howle Cres.
TS11: Marsk S 4E **67**
Churchill Cl. TS6: Est. 5E **81**
TS9: Gt A 1D **167**
TS22: Wyn 1E **37**
Churchill Dr. TS11: Marsk S . . . 4B **66**
Churchill Ho. TS17: Thorn T . . . 1C **98**
Churchill Rd. TS6: Est 5E **81**
Church La. DL2: Mid G 4A **144**
TS5: Midd 5C **100**
TS6: Est 3D **81**
TS6: Est, Gran 2D **81**
TS7: Nun 1B **156**
TS7: Orm 4F **103**
(not continuous)
TS9: Newt R. 2B **158**
TS11: Marsk S 3D **67**
TS12: Skel 4A **88**
TS14: Guis 1E **139**
TS21: Redm 1B **70**
Church M. TS23: Bill 4D **55**
Church Mt. TS6: Est. 1E **105**
Church Rd. TS16: Egg 2C **148**
TS18: Stock T 5B **74**
TS23: Bill. 4D **55**
Church Row TS13: Loft 5C **92**
TS22: Wolv. 2C **38**
TS24: H'pool 5B **14**
Church Sq. TS24: H'pool 3B **14**
Church St. TS10: Redc. 3A **48**
TS11: Marsk S 3C **66**
TS13: Stait 1C **120**
TS14: Guis 1F **139**
TS24: H'pool 3C **14**
TS25: Seat C 4E **21**
Church St. M. *TS14: Guis 1F 139*
(off Church St.)
Church St. Sth.
TS11: Marsk S. 4D **67**
Church Vw. TS18: Stock T. 4A **74**
TS21: Long N. 1A **124**
TS21: Sed 4C **22**
Church Wlk. TS3: Midd 5F **79**
TS3: N Orm 4C **78**
TS14: Guis 1F **139**
TS24: H'pool. 1F **15**
Churchyard Link Rd.
TS18: Stock T 1A **98**
Cinderwood TS3: Midd. 1F **103**
Cineworld Cinema
Middlesbrough 3A 78
(off Marton Rd.)
Cinnabar Rd. TS19: Stock T . . . 3B **72**
CLAIRVILLE. 5B **78**
Clairville Ct. TS4: Midd. 5A **78**
Clairville Rd. TS4: Midd 5A **78**
Clapham Grn. TS3: Midd. 1B **102**
Clapham Rd. TS15: Yarm 5B **148**
Claremont Ct. TS17: Thorn T. . . 1C **98**
Claremont Dr. TS7: Mart 4E **133**
TS26: H'pool. 4F **13**
Claremont Gdns.
TS19: Stock T 5B **72**
Claremont Gro. TS21: Sed. 5C **22**
Claremont Pk. TS26: H'pool. . . . 5F **13**
Clarence Rd. TS7: Nun 4B **134**
TS16: Eag. 4C **126**
TS24: H'pool 2B **14**
Clarence Row TS18: Stock T. . . 4B **74**
Clarences Community Farm . . . 4F **57**
Clarence St. TS18: Stock T. . . . 4B **74**
TS23: Bill. 3D **57**
TS24: H'pool. 5F **9**
Clarendon Rd. TS1: Midd 4E **77**
(not continuous)
TS17: Thorn T 5D **99**
TS20: Nort 2A **74**
Clarendon St. TS10: Redc. 3D **49**
Clarkson Ct. TS25: H'pool 3F **19**
Clarkson's Wood Nature Reserve
. . . . 2F **115**
Clark St. TS24: H'pool. 4C **14**
Claude Av. TS5: Midd 3D **101**
CLAVERING 2C **6**
Clavering Rd. TS27: H'pool. 2C **6**
Claxton Cl. TS19: Stock T 1A **72**
Claydon Gro. TS17: Ing B 1B **150**
Claygate TS23: Bill 3D **39**
Clay La. Commercial Pk.
TS6: S Ban. 1A **80**
Claymond Ct. TS20: Nort. 5A **54**
Claymore Rd. TS25: H'pool 5F **19**
Clayton Ct. TS18: Stock T 4A **98**
Claywood TS3: Midd 1F **103**
Cleadon Av. TS23: Bill 3E **39**
Cleadon Wlk. TS19: Stock T . . . 2B **72**
Clearpool Cl. TS24: H'pool 5C **8**
Clearwater Bus. Pk.
TS17: Thorn T 5C **74**
Clearwater Ho.
TS17: Thorn T 5B **74**
Cleasby Way TS16: Eag. 3A **126**
Cleatlam Cl. TS19: Stock T. . . . 2B **72**
Cleator Dr. TS14: Guis. 4D **139**
Clee Ter. TS23: Bill 1E **55**
Clements Ri. TS20: Nort 5F **53**
Clepstone Av. TS5: Midd 3C **100**
Clevecoat Wlk. TS27: Hart. 4F **5**
Clevegate TS7: Nun 4F **133**
Cleveland Av. TS5: Midd 3D **101**
TS9: Stokes 5C **164**
TS20: Nort 1B **74**
Cleveland Bus. Cen.
TS1: Midd. 3F **77**
Cleveland Cen., The
TS1: Midd. 3E **77**
Cleveland Cl. TS7: Orm. 5A **104**
Cleveland Ct. TS6: S Ban 2B **80**
Cleveland Dr. TS7: Mart 2D **133**
Cleveland Gdns. TS16: Eag . . . 5B **126**
Cleveland Gate Bus. Pk.
TS14: Guis 3E **139**
Cleveland Golf Course 3A **48**
Cleveland Ind. Est.
TS18: Stock T 4D **75**
Cleveland Ironstone Mus. 3A **92**
Cleveland Pl. TS14: Guis. 2F **139**
Cleveland Retail Pk.
TS6: S Ban. 4A **80**
Cleveland Rd. TS24: H'pool 5C **8**
Cleveland Sq. *TS1: Midd. 3E 77*
(off Cleveland Cen.)
Cleveland St. TS2: Midd 2F **77**
TS6: Est 1F **105**
TS6: Norm 2D **105**
TS9: Gt A. 1D **167**
TS10: Redc 3C **48**
TS12: Salt 4D **69**
Cleveland St. TS13: Live. 1A **116**
TS13: Loft 5C **92**
TS14: Guis. 1D **139**
TS24: H'pool. 5F **9**
Cleveland Vw. TS3: Midd 1E **103**
TS11: Marsk S 4A **66**
TS12: Skel 1A **112**
Cliff, The TS25: Seat C. 3E **21**
Cliff Cotts. TS5: Midd 2C **100**
TS11: Marsk S. 3D **67**
TS13: Port M 3F **121**
Cliff Cres. TS13: Loft. 5A **92**
Cliffden Ct. TS12: Salt. 4D **69**
Cliffe Av. TS13: Carl H 3E **91**
Cliffe Ct. TS25: Seat C 3E **21**
Cliffe St. TS12: Brot 2C **90**
Cliffe Ter. TS9: Gt A. 1D **167**
Cliff Ho. TS11: Marsk S. 3D **67**
Clifford Cl. TS24: H'pool 4F **7**
Clifford St. TS10: Redc 3C **48**
Cliffport Ct. TS18: Stock T. 4C **74**
Cliff Rd. TS13: Stait. 2C **120**
Cliff St. TS11: N Mar 2A **86**
Cliff Ter. TS11: Marsk S 3D **67**
TS13: Live 5A **92**
TS13: Skin 2A **92**
TS24: H'pool. 1F **15**
Cliffwood Cl. TS6: Est 2F **105**
Clifton Av. TS16: Prest T 3C **126**
TS18: Stock T. 3F **97**
TS22: Bill 5B **38**
TS26: H'pool. 4F **13**
Clifton Gdns. TS16: Prest T. . . 3D **127**
Clifton Ho. TS17: Thorn T 2B **98**
Clifton Pl. TS6: Est 2D **105**
Clifton St. TS1: Midd 4E **77**
Clip n climb. 3E **75**
Clive Cres. TS20: Nort. 1A **74**
Clive Rd. TS5: Midd 1D **101**
TS6: Est. 2D **105**
Clockwood Gdns.
TS15: Yarm 4D **149**
Cloisters, The
TS19: Stock T 4A **72**
Close, The TS4: Midd 2A **102**
TS13: Eas. 2A **118**
TS13: Live 5A **116**
TS21: Long N 1F **123**
Clough Cl. TS5: Midd 5C **76**
Clove Hitch Ho.
TS24: H'pool 2C **14**
Clover Ct. TS19: Stock T 3B **72**
Clover Dr. TS26: H'pool 2E **13**
Clover Hill Dr. TS13: Loft 5B **92**
Cloverwood Cl. TS7: Mart 3F **133**
Clydach Gro. TS17: Ing B. 2F **149**
Clyde Gdns. TS22: Bill. 4A **38**
Clyde Gro. TS18: Stock T. 3F **97**
Clyde Pl. TS24: H'pool 5D **9**
Clynes Rd. TS6: Gran. 4E **81**
Coach Ho. M. TS6: Norm 3C **104**
Coach Rd. TS12: Brot 1A **90**
Coal La. TS22: Wolv, Wyn 5E **27**
TS27: Elw. 4A **10**
(not continuous)
COAL LANE RDBT. **1B 38**
Coast Rd.
TS10: Marsk S, Redc 4E **49**
TS11: Marsk S 4E **49**
TS27: H'pool 1B **6**
Coate Cl. TS8: Hem 4C **130**
COATHAM
TS10 . . . . 3B **48**
TS21 . . . . 1E **125**
Coatham Av. DL2: Mid G 3A **144**
Coatham Cl. TS8: Hem 4E **131**
Coatham Ct. TS10: Redc 3F **47**
Coatham Dr. TS26: H'pool. 4D **13**
Coatham Gro. TS23: Bill 3E **39**
Coatham La. TS21: Elt. 4C **94**
Coatham Lodge TS10: Redc . . . 3A **48**
Coatham Marsh Nature Reserve
. . . . 4F **47**

Coatham Rd. TS10: Redc 3A **48**
TS19: Stock T 1B **72**
Coatham Va. TS16: Eag. 1A **148**
Coatsay Cl. TS19: Stock T. 2B **72**
Cobble Carr TS14: Guis. 2D **139**
Cobbles, The TS9: Stokes 1B **168**
Cobblestone Cl. TS8: Stain . . . 5C **130**
Cobblewood TS3: Midd 1F **103**
Cobb Wlk. TS24: H'pool. 5E **9**
Cobden St. TS17: Thorn T 3C **98**
TS18: Stock T 5A **74**
(not continuous)
TS26: H'pool. 3F **13**
Cobham St. TS1: Midd. 5E **77**
Cobwood TS3: Midd 1F **103**
Cockburn St. TS12: Ling 4E **113**
Cocken Rd. TS19: Stock T. 2B **72**
Cockerton Wlk.
TS19: Stock T 2B **72**
Cockfield Av. TS23: Bill 3F **39**
Cohen Ct. TS20: Nort 5F **53**
Colburn Wlk. TS6: Est 5F **81**
Colchester Rd. TS13: Eas 2A **118**
TS20: Nort 5B **54**
Coleby Av. TS4: Midd 5A **102**
Coledale Rd. TS3: Midd 2C **102**
Colenso St. TS26: H'pool. 5A **14**
Coleridge Av. TS25: H'pool 1B **20**
Coleridge Rd. TS23: Bill 2E **39**
Coleshill Cl. TS23: Bill. 5E **39**
Coleton Gdns. TS17: Ing B . . . 1B **150**
College Cl. TS27: Dalt P 1E **17**
College Ct. TS9: Stokes. 1C **168**
College Grn. TS2: Midd 2A **78**
College M. TS9: Stokes. 1B **168**
College Rd. TS3: Midd. 5E **79**
College Sq. TS9: Stokes 1C **168**
Colleton Wlk. TS3: Midd 2D **103**
Colliers Grn. TS4: Midd. 4B **78**
Collin Av. TS4: Midd 3F **101**
Collingham Dr. TS7: Nun. 1B **156**
Collingwood Chase
TS12: Brot 1B **90**
Collingwood Ct. TS2: Midd 5C **56**
Collingwood Rd. TS23: Bill 5D **55**
TS26: H'pool 3A **14**
Collingwood Wlk.
TS26: H'pool 3A **14**
Collins Av. TS20: Nort 1C **74**
Collinson Av. TS5: Midd 3A **100**
Colmans Nook TS23: Bill 2B **56**
Colmore Av. TS3: Midd 5A **80**
Colpitt Cl. TS20: Nort 5A **54**
Colsterdale Cl. TS23: Bill. 3E **39**
Coltman St. TS3: N Orm 4C **78**
Coltsfoot Cl. TS26: H'pool 4E **7**
Coltsfoot Dr. TS18: Stock T . . . 1A **128**
Columbia Dr. TS17: Thorn T . . . 1B **98**
Columbine Cl. TS7: Mart. 2C **132**
Colville St. TS1: Midd 4D **77**
Colwyn Cl. TS10: Redc 3D **65**
Colwyn Rd. TS20: Nort 5C **54**
TS26: H'pool 5A **14**
(not continuous)
Comfrey TS8: Coul N 1C **154**
Commerce Way TS6: S Ban. . . . 4A **80**
Commercial St. TS2: Midd 1E **77**
TS18: Stock T 5B **74**
TS24: H'pool 2D **15**
(Queen St.)
TS24: H'pool. 5F **9**
(Russell St.)
Commodore Way
TS24: H'pool 3D ***15***
(off Fleet Acv.)
Commondale Av.
TS19: Stock T. 3E **73**
Commondale Dr.
TS25: Seat C 5D **21**
Commondale Gro.
TS10: Redc 1A **64**
Compass Ho. TS24: H'pool 3D **15**
Compton Cl. TS20: Nort. 3B **74**
Compton Rd. TS25: H'pool 2D **19**
Comrie Rd. TS25: H'pool. 5F **19**
Concorde Ho. TS18: Stock T . . . 5F **97**
Concorde Way
TS18: Stock T. 5E **97**
Condercum Grn.
TS17: Ing B 3F **127**
Coney Cl. TS17: Ing B 5C **128**
Conifer Av. TS21: Sed 3D **23**
Conifer Cl. TS7: Orm 4B **104**
Conifer Cres. TS23: Bill 2C **54**
Conifer Dr. TS19: Stock T 2E **73**
Conifer Gro. TS23: Bill. 2C **54**
Conisborough Dr.
TS10: Redc. 2E **65**
Coniscliffe Ct. TS26: H'pool . . . 3D **13**
Coniscliffe Rd.
TS19: Stock T 2B **72**
TS26: H'pool 4C **12**
Coniston Av. TS10: Redc 5C **48**
Coniston Cres. TS21: Redm . . . 1B **70**
Coniston Gro. TS5: Midd 4C **100**
Coniston Rd. TS6: Gran 4F **81**
TS12: Skel 3B **88**
TS18: Stock T 4D **73**
TS25: H'pool 1C **20**
Connaught Ct. TS7: Nun 3B **134**
Connaught Rd. TS5: Midd 5B **76**
TS7: Nun 3A **134**
Conningsby Cl. TS25: H'pool . . . 1E **31**
Conrad Wlk. TS25: H'pool. 2D **19**
Consett Cl. TS19: Stock T 2B **72**
Consett Dryden Cl.
TS6: Norm 1D **105**
Consort Cl. TS19: Stock T 5C **72**
Constable Gro. TS23: Bill 3D **39**
Constance St. TS3: N Orm. 4B **78**
Constantine Ct. *TS1: Midd. 5E* ***77***
(off Linthorpe Rd.)
Convalescent St. TS12: Salt . . . 3C **68**
Conway Av. TS23: Bill 5E **39**
Conway Rd. TS10: Redc 1D **65**
Conway Wlk. TS26: H'pool 1E **13**
Conwy Gro. TS17: Ing B. 1F **149**
Conyers Cl. TS15: Yarm. 5B **148**
Conyers Ct. TS12: Brot 2C **90**
Conyers Way TS3: N Orm 4B **78**
Cook Cres. TS20: Nort. 1A **74**
Cookgate TS7: Nun 3F **133**
Cook's Ct. TS7: Orm 4B **104**
Coombe Hill TS11: N Mar 2A **86**
Coombe Way TS18: Stock T . . . 2A **96**
Co-operative Cl. *TS13: Loft. . . . 5B* ***92***
(off Deepdale Rd.)
Co-operative Ter. TS13: Loft . . . 5C **92**
Cooper Cl. TS6: Est 2E **105**
Copeland Cl. TS12: Skel 3C **88**
Copeland Ct. TS2: Midd 5D **57**
Copgrove Cl. TS3: Midd. 1C **102**
Copley Cl. TS19: Stock T. 2B **72**
Copley Wlk. TS3: Midd 3D **103**
Copnor Wlk. TS3: Midd 3D **103**
Copperwood TS3: Midd 2F **103**
Copperwood Cl.
TS27: H'pool 2C **6**
Coppice, The TS8: Coul N 3F **131**
(not continuous)
TS22: Wyn 5D **27**
Coppice Rd. TS4: Midd 2A **102**
Copse, The TS14: Guis 2B **138**
TS24: H'pool 1A **14**
Copse Cl. TS17: Ing B 4B **128**
Copse La. TS17: Ing B. 4B **128**
Copsewood Wlk.
TS9: Stokes 5C **164**
Coquet Cl. TS10: Redc. 2F **65**
TS17: Ing B 2B **150**
Coral Gro. TS17: Thorn T 4D **99**
Coral Ho. TS24: H'pool 3D **15**
Coral St. TS1: Midd 4E **77**
TS12: Salt 3C **68**
Coral Way TS10: Redc. 2E **65**
Corbridge Cl. TS8: Hem. 4E **131**
Corbridge Ct. TS19: Stock T . . . 2B **72**
Corby Av. TS5: Midd 4A **100**
Corby Ho. TS4: Midd 2A **102**
Corby Lodge TS20: Nort. 4F **53**
Corder Rd. TS5: Midd 5B **76**
Corfe Cres. TS23: Bill 5D **39**
Corfu Way TS10: K'ham 3F **63**
Coris Cl. TS7: Mart 2C **132**
Cormland Cl. TS20: Nort. 1C **74**
Cormorant Dr. TS10: Redc. 2E **65**
Corncroft M. TS6: Gran 2E **81**
Cornfield Rd. TS5: Midd 2E **101**
TS17: Thorn T 3B **98**
TS19: Stock T 5A **72**
Cornfields Ho. TS6: Est 3E **105**
Cornflower Cl. TS26: H'pool 4D **7**
Cornforth Av. TS3: Midd 3D **103**
Cornforth Cl. TS19: Stock T. . . . 2B **72**
Cornforth Gro. TS23: Bill 3F **39**
Corngrave Cl.
TS11: Marsk S 4E **67**
Cornhill Wlk. TS7: Orm 4A **104**
Cornriggs Wlk.
TS19: Stock T 1B **72**
Cornsay Cl. TS5: Midd. 5B **100**
TS19: Stock T 2B **72**
Cornwall Cl. TS7: Nun. 3A **134**
Cornwall Cres. TS23: Bill. 2F **55**
Cornwall Gro. TS20: Nort 1C **74**
Cornwallis Cl. TS12: Brot 1C **90**
Cornwall Rd. TS14: Guis. 3D **139**
Cornwall St. TS25: H'pool 1A **20**
Corona Ct. TS18: Stock T. 4E **97**
Coronation Av. TS13: Hind. . . . 5E **121**
Coronation Ct. TS6: Norm 2D **105**
Coronation Cres.
TS15: Yarm 5A **148**
Coronation Dr. TS25: Seat C . . . 5D **15**
Coronation Grn. TS3: Midd . . . 4F **103**
Coronation Rd. TS13: Loft. 5B **92**
Coronation St. TS3: N Orm 4C **78**
TS13: Carl H. 3F **91**
Coronation Ter. TS14: Guis . . . 1E **139**
Corporation Rd. TS1: Midd 3E **77**
TS10: Redc 4A **48**
TS24: H'pool 5E **9**
Corporation St.
TS18: Stock T 5A **74**
Corsham Wlk. TS3: Midd 3D **103**
Cortland Rd. TS7: Nun. 3C **134**
Coryton Wlk. TS3: Midd 3D **103**
Costain Gro. TS20: Nort 4B **54**
Costa St. TS1: Midd. 5D **77**
Cotcliffe Way TS7: Mart. 1A **156**
Cotgarth Way
TS19: Stock T 2A **72**
Cotherstone Cl. TS16: Eag. . . . 5F **125**
Cotherstone Dr. TS5: Midd . . . 2C **130**
Cotherstone Rd.
TS18: Stock T. 3F **97**
Cotswold Av. TS3: Midd 5D **79**
Cotswold Cres. TS23: Bill 2D **55**
Cotswold Dr. TS10: Redc. 1A **64**
TS12: Skel 3C **88**
Cottage Farm TS19: Stock T . . . 1D **97**
Cottersloe Rd. TS20: Nort. 4B **54**
Cottingham Dr. TS3: Midd. 5D **79**
Cottonwood TS3: Midd. 1F **103**
Coulby Farm Way
TS8: Coul N 5B **132**
Coulby Mnr. Farm
TS8: Coul N 3A **132**
(not continuous)
Coulby Mnr. Way
TS8: Coul N 3F **131**
COULBY NEWHAM 4B **132**
Coulson Cl. TS15: Yarm. 1B **160**
Coulthard Ct. TS6: S Ban. 2A **80**
Coulton Gro. TS22: Bill 5A **38**
Council of Europe Blvd.
TS17: Stock T, Thorn T . . . 5B **74**
Coundon Grn. TS19: Stock T . . . 2B **72**
Countisbury Rd. TS20: Nort. . . . 3E **53**

County Court
Hartlepool 3B **14**
Middlesbrough 3F 77
(part of Combined Courts)
Courageous Cl.
TS25: Seat C 3D **21**
Court, The TS12: Salt. 4C **68**
Courtney Wlk. TS3: Midd. 5E **79**
Court Rd. TS4: Midd 2A **102**
Covent Cl. TS6: Norm 4C **104**
Coverdale TS8: Hem 5D **131**
Coverdale Bldgs. TS12: Brot. . . 2C **90**
Coverdale Rd.
TS19: Stock T 1C **96**
Covert, The TS8: Coul N 1C **154**
COWBAR 1C **120**
Cowbar Bank TS13: Stait 1C **120**
Cowbar Cotts. TS13: Stait 1B **120**
Cowbar La.
TS13: Boul, Stait. 1F **119**
Cowbridge La.
TS23: Cowp B 3B **40**
Cow Cl. La. TS12: Moor 4C **142**
(not continuous)
Cow Close Wood Nature Reserve
. . . . 5D **143**
Cowdray Cl. TS14: Guis 4F **139**
Cowley Cl. TS16: Prest T. 1D **127**
TS25: Seat C 2E **21**
Cowley Rd. TS5: Midd. 5D **101**
COWPEN BEWLEY 4C **40**
Cowpen Bewley Rd.
TS23: Cowp B, Bill 4C **40**
Cowpen Bewley Woodland Pk.
. . . . 2C **40**
Cowpen Bewley Woodland Pk.
Vis. Cen. 3C **40**
Cowpen Cres. TS19: Stock T. . . 2B **72**
Cowpen La.
TS23: Bill, Cowp B 3E **55**
Cowpen La. Est. TS23: Bill. 2F **55**
Cowpen La. Ind. Est.
TS23: Bill 5A **40**
Cowpen Marsh Nature Reserve
. . . . 4F **41**
Cowper Gro. TS25: H'pool. 2D **19**
Cowper Rd. TS20: Nort 3C **74**
Cowscote Cres. TS13: Loft 4A **92**
Cowshill Grn. TS19: Stock T . . . 2B **72**
Cowton Way TS16: Eag 3B **126**
Coxgreen Cl. TS19: Stock T. . . . 2B **72**
Coxhoe Rd. TS23: Bill 5F **39**
Coxmoor Way TS11: N Mar 2F **85**
Coxwold Cl. TS5: Midd 5E **101**
Coxwold Rd. TS18: Stock T. . . . 1D **97**
Coxwold Way TS23: Bill. 2B **56**
Crabtree Wlk. TS7: Nun 1D **135**
Cradley Dr. TS5: Midd 3C **130**
Cradoc Gro. TS17: Ing B 1F **149**
Cragdale Rd. TS3: Midd 1C **102**
CRAGGHALL RDBT. **2D 91**
Craggs St. TS4: Midd. 3A **78**
TS19: Stock T. 4F **73**
Cragside TS12: Brot 2C **90**
TS21: Sed 5C **22**
Cragside Ct. TS17: Ing B. 1B **150**
Cragston Cl. TS26: H'pool. 2D **13**
Cragston Ct. TS10: Redc 4E **65**
Craigearn Rd. TS6: Norm 1C **104**
Craigweil Cres.
TS19: Stock T. 3F **73**
Crail Wlk. TS25: H'pool 4F **19**
Craister Rd. TS20: Nort. 4B **74**
Cramlington Cl. TS8: Hem. . . . 4E **131**
Cranage Cl. TS5: Midd 3B **100**
Cranberry TS8: Coul N. 5D **133**
Cranbourne Dr. TS10: Redc 4E **65**
Cranbourne Ter.
TS18: Stock T. 2F **97**
Cranbrook TS8: Mart 5E **133**
Cranesbill Av. TS26: H'pool. 4E **7**
Cranfield Av. TS3: Midd. 4F **79**
(not continuous)
Cranford Av. TS6: S Ban 4B **80**
Cranford Cl. TS6: S Ban. 4B **80**
Cranford Gdns. TS5: Midd 4B **100**
Cranleigh Rd. TS18: Stock T . . . 1E **97**
Cranmore Rd. TS3: Midd. 5C **78**
Cranstock Cl. TS22: Bill. 5A **38**
Cranswick Cl. TS23: Bill. 2F **39**
Cranswick Dr. TS5: Midd 5E **101**
Cranwell Gro.
TS17: Thorn T 3D **129**
Cranwell Rd. TS25: H'pool 5D **19**
Cranworth Grn.
TS17: Thorn T 2D **99**
Cranworth St. TS17: Thorn T. . . 2C **98**
Crathorne Cres. TS5: Midd . . . 1B **100**
Crathorne Pk. TS6: Norm 2C **104**
Crathorne Rd. TS20: Nort 5B **54**
Craven St. TS1: Midd 4D **77**
Craven Va. TS14: Guis. 3E **139**
Crawcrook Wlk.
TS19: Stock T 2B **72**
Crawford St. TS25: Seat C 4E **21**
Crawley Rd. TS17: Thorn T 4E **99**
Crayke Rd. TS18: Stock T 2D **97**
Crazy Corner 4D **129**
Creekwood TS3: Midd 1F **103**
Cremorne Cl. TS7: Mart. 2C **132**
Crescent, The DL2: Mid G 2C **144**
TS5: Midd 2D **101**
TS7: Nun 3B **134**
TS7: Orm 4F **103**
TS10: Redc. 4E **49**
TS11: Marsk S 4D **67**
TS12: Salt 5C **68**
TS16: Eag. 1B **148**
TS17: Thorn T 4C **98**
TS21: Carlt 5C **50**
TS26: H'pool 3E **13**
Crescent Av. TS23: Bill. 4E **55**
Crescent Rd. TS1: Midd. 5C **76**
Cresswell Cl. TS8: Hem. 4E **131**
Cresswell Ct. TS26: H'pool 3D **13**
Cresswell Dr. TS26: H'pool 3D **13**
Cresswell Rd. TS6: Gran 2E **81**
TS26: H'pool 3D **13**
Crest, The TS26: H'pool 2D **13**
Crestwood TS3: Midd. 2F **103**
TS10: Redc 4D **65**
Cribyn Cl. TS17: Ing B 1F **149**
Crickethollow Cl. TS24: H'pool . . . 5F **7**
Cricket La. TS6: Norm. 3C **104**
Crieff Wlk. TS25: H'pool 4F **19**
Crimdon Beck Cl.
TS18: Stock T 4D **75**
Crimdon Cl. TS8: Hem. 5E **131**
Crimdon Wlk. TS19: Stock T . . . 1A **72**
Crinklewood TS3: Midd 2F **103**
Crispin Ct. TS12: Brot 2C **90**
TS21: Sed 4D **23**
Crisp St. TS20: Nort. 2B **74**
Crocus Gdns. TS26: H'pool 5E **7**
Croft, The TS7: Mart 3D **133**
Croft Av. TS5: Midd 4B **100**
Croft Dr. TS7: Nun 4B **134**
Crofton Ct. TS18: Stock T 4D **75**
CROFT ON HEUGH 1F **15**
Crofton Rd. TS18: Stock T. 4D **75**
Croft Rd. TS16: Eag. 1B **148**
Crofts, The TS21: Stil. 2B **50**
Croft St. TS18: Stock T 4B **74**
Croft Ter. TS24: H'pool. 1F **15**
Cromer Ct. TS16: Eag 1C **148**
Cromer St. TS4: Midd 4A **78**
Cromer Wlk. TS10: Redc. 2B **64**
TS25: H'pool 5E **19**
Cromore Cl. TS17: Thorn T . . . 2C **128**
Cromwell Av. TS13: Loft 5D **93**
TS18: Stock T 4B **74**
Cromwell Grn.
TS18: Stock T 5B **74**
Cromwell Rd. TS6: S Ban 3A **80**
Cromwell St. TS3: N Orm 4B **78**
TS24: H'pool 5C **14**
Cromwell Ter.
TS17: Thorn T 3C **98**
Crookershill Cl. TS7: Nun 5A **134**
Crookhall Wlk.
TS19: Stock T 2B **72**
CROOKSBARN 3B **54**
Crooks Barn La. TS20: Nort. . . . 3A **54**
Crook St. TS20: Nort 4A **54**
Cropton Cl. TS10: Redc 3B **64**
Cropton Way TS8: Coul N 4B **132**
Crosby Ct. TS16: Eag. 5D **127**
Crosby Ter. TS2: Port C 5A **58**
Crosby Wlk. TS17: Thorn T 3C **98**
Crosby Way TS10: Redc 1B **64**
Crossbeck Ter. TS6: Norm. . . . 2D **105**
Crossbeck Way TS7: Orm 4B **104**
Crosscliff TS8: Hem 4E **131**
Cross Fell TS10: Redc 1B **64**
Crossfell Rd. TS3: Midd 2C **102**
Crossfields TS8: Coul N. 1B **154**
Cross La. TS9: L Ayt 4E **167**
TS13: Loft 3B **92**
Cross Row TS12: Boo 3B **112**
TS16: Egg 2C 148
(off Back La.)
Cross St. TS6: Est 1F **105**
TS14: Guis 2E **139**
TS20: Nort 5B **54**
TS21: Sed 4D **23**
TS23: Bill. 3D **57**
Crossthwaite Gdns.
TS12: Skel 2C **88**
Crosswell Pk. TS17: Ing B 2F **149**
Crosswood Av. TS6: Norm. . . . 3D **105**
Crowhurst Cl. TS14: Guis. 4E **139**
Crowland Av. TS3: Midd 2A **104**
Crowland Rd. TS25: H'pool 1D **31**
Crow La. TS6: Old L. 5A **82**
Crown Hall Apartments
TS24: H'pool 4C **14**
Crowood Av. TS9: Stokes. 5C **164**
Croxdale Gro. TS19: Stock T . . . 1B **96**
Croxdale Rd. TS23: Bill 4E **39**
Croxden Gro. TS3: Midd 3E **103**
Croxton Av. TS25: H'pool 1F **31**
Croxton Cl. TS19: Stock T 5F **71**
Croydon Rd. TS1: Midd 5A **78**
Crummackdale TS17: Ing B. . . 3B **150**
Crummock Rd. TS10: Redc 5C **48**
Culgaith Av. TS3: Midd 1C **102**
Cullen Rd. TS25: H'pool. 4F **19**
Culloden Way TS23: Bill 4A **40**
Culross Gro. TS19: Stock T 5F **71**
Cumberland Cres. TS23: Bill. . . 3D **55**
Cumberland Gro. TS20: Nort . . . 4F **53**
Cumberland Ho. TS5: Midd . . . 2E **101**
Cumberland Rd. TS5: Midd . . . 1E **101**
Cumbernauld Rd.
TS17: Thorn T 4E **99**
Cumbria Wlk. TS25: H'pool 5B **14**
Cumnor Wlk. TS3: Midd 5D **79**
Cundall Rd. TS26: H'pool. 3F **13**
Cunningham Cl. TS12: Brot. . . . 1B **90**
Cunningham Ct. TS21: Sed 2C **22**
Cunningham Dr.
TS17: Thorn T 3D **129**
Curlew La. TS20: Nort. 3A **54**
Curson St. TS6: Est 2F **105**
Curthwaite TS5: Midd 2A **130**
Custom Ho. TS2: Midd. 1F **77**
Cuthbert Cl. TS17: Thorn T 3C **98**
Cutler Cl. TS7: Mart. 2E **133**
Cygnet Dr. TS18: Stock T. 5A **98**
Cypress Ct. TS19: Stock T. 3A **74**
Cypress Rd. TS7: Mart. 2E **133**
TS10: Redc. 5F **49**

D

Dabholm Rd. TS6: Midd 5E **45**
Dacre Cl. TS17: Thorn T 5C **98**
Dahlia Pl. TS23: Bill 1D **55**

Daimler Dr. TS23: Bill . . . 5B **40**
Daisy Cl. TS26: H'pool . . . 4E **7**
Daisy Ct. TS19: Stock T. . . . 3C **72**
Daisy La. TS7: Orm . . . 4B **104**
Dalaro Ct. TS10: K'ham . . . 4A **64**
Dalby Cl. TS10: Redc. . . . 3C **64**
TS22: Bill . . . 5A **38**
Dalby Ct. TS8: Coul N . . . 5B **132**
Dalby Vw. TS8: Coul N . . . 5B **132**
Dalby Way TS8: Coul N . . . 5B **132**
Dalcross Ct. TS8: Hem. . . . 5E **131**
(not continuous)
Dale Cl. TS19: Stock T . . . 2A **72**
Dale Gth. TS11: Marsk S . . . 5E **67**
Dale Gro. TS19: Stock T . . . 1B **96**
DALEHOUSE . . . 2B **120**
Dalehouse Bank
TS13: Stait . . . 3B **120**
Dales, The TS19: Stock T . . . 3E **73**
Dales Pk. Rd. TS8: Hem . . . 5C **130**
Daleston Av. TS5: Midd. . . . 3D **101**
Daleston Cl. TS26: H'pool . . . 2C **12**
Dale St. TS1: Midd. . . . 3E **77**
TS11: N Mar. . . . 1A **86**
Dale Ter. TS12: Ling . . . 4E **113**
Daleville Cl. TS4: Midd . . . 3F **101**
Dalewood Wlk.
TS9: Stokes . . . 5C **164**
Daley Cl. TS24: H'pool . . . 2B **14**
Dalkeith Cres. TS8: Hem . . . 3E **131**
Dalkeith Rd. TS25: H'pool. . . . 3E **19**
Dallas Ct. TS8: Hem . . . 5E **131**
(not continuous)
Dallas Rd. TS25: H'pool . . . 3E **19**
Dalmuir Cl. TS16: Eag. . . . 5C **126**
Dalry Gro. TS25: H'pool. . . . 4E **19**
Dalston Ct. TS7: Orm. . . . 4B **104**
Dalton Bk. La. TS22: Clax . . . 2D **17**
TS27: Dalt P. . . . 2D **17**
Dalton Ct. TS10: Redc . . . 4F **65**
Dalton Gro. TS20: Nort . . . 2A **74**
TS23: Bill . . . 3E **39**
Dalton Hgts. TS27: Dalt P . . . 1E **17**
Dalton La. TS27: Dalt P. . . . 2C **16**
TS27: Elw, Hart. . . . 4F **5**
DALTON PIERCY . . . 1E **17**
Dalton St. TS26: H'pool. . . . 4A **14**
Daltry Cl. TS15: Yarm . . . 5E **149**
Dalwood Ct. TS8: Hem. . . . 5E **131**
Dam St. TS13: Loft . . . 5C **92**
Danby Dale Av.
TS10: Redc . . . 1A **64**
Danby Gro. TS17: Thorn T. . . . 4D **99**
TS25: Seat C . . . 4E **21**
Danby Rd. TS6: Est . . . 5F **81**
TS20: Nort . . . 3B **74**
Danby Wlk. TS23: Bill . . . 5C **38**
Danby Wynd TS15: Yarm . . . 3B **148**
Danes Brook Ct.
TS17: Ing B . . . 3B **150**
Danesfort Av. TS14: Guis . . . 2D **139**
Daniel Ct. TS4: Midd . . . 5A **78**
Dante Rd. TS7: Mart . . . 2B **132**
Daphne Rd. TS19: Stock T . . . 3A **74**
Darbyshire Cl.
TS17: Thorn T . . . 1C **128**
Darcy Cl. TS15: Yarm . . . 1A **160**
Darenth Cres. TS3: Midd. . . . 2D **103**
Darlington Bk. La.
TS19: Stock T . . . 4D **71**
TS21: Stock T, Whinn H . . . 1A **94**
Darlington La.
TS19: Stock T . . . 3B **72**
(not continuous)
TS20: Nort . . . 1F **73**
Darlington Rd.
TS18: Stock T . . . 3A **96**
TS21: Elt. . . . 4E **95**
TS21: Long N . . . 1F **123**
TS21: Stock T . . . 3A **96**
Darlington St.
TS17: Thorn T . . . 2C **98**
TS24: H'pool. . . . 1F **15**
Darlington Ter. *TS13: Stait . . . 1C 120*
(off High St.)
Darnall Grn. TS4: Midd . . . 5B **102**
Darnbrook Way TS7: Nun. . . . 4F **133**
Darnton Dr. TS4: Midd. . . . 5B **102**
Darras Wlk. TS3: Midd . . . 5D **79**
Dartmouth Gro. TS10: Redc . . . 2D **65**
Darvel Rd. TS25: H'pool . . . 3E **19**
Darwen Ct. TS8: Hem . . . 5E **131**
Darwin Cl. TS19: Stock T . . . 1B **72**
Darwin Gro. TS25: H'pool . . . 1D **19**
Dauntless Cl. TS25: Seat C . . . 3E **21**
Davenport Rd. TS15: Yarm . . . 1A **160**
Daventry Av. TS19: Stock T. . . . 2E **73**
David Lloyd Leisure
Stockton-on-Tees . . . 5D **75**
David Rd. TS20: Nort. . . . 2C **74**
Davison Cl. TS22: Wyn . . . 2E **37**
Davison Dr. TS24: H'pool. . . . 3F **7**
Davison St. TS1: Midd. . . . 3E **77**
TS12: Ling . . . 4E **113**
Davy Cl. TS18: Stock T . . . 3A **98**
Davy Rd. TS6: S Ban . . . 3F **79**
Dawdon Cl. TS19: Stock T. . . . 1B **72**
Dawley Cl. TS17: Thorn T . . . 4E **99**
Dawlish Cl. TS10: Redc. . . . 3A **64**
Dawlish Dr. TS25: H'pool . . . 5A **20**
Dawlish Grn. TS4: Midd . . . 5B **102**
Dawn Cl. TS20: Nort . . . 3A **54**
Dawson Ho. TS23: Bill. . . . 1D **55**
Dawson Sq. TS5: Midd . . . 1B **100**
Dawson's Wharf TS2: Midd . . . 1E **77**
Daylight Rd. TS19: Stock T. . . . 3D **73**
Days Ter. TS12: Brot . . . 2B **90**
Day St. TS12: Brot. . . . 3B **90**
Deacon Gdns. TS25: Seat C. . . . 5E **21**
Deacon St. TS3: N Orm . . . 4C **78**
Deal Cl. TS19: Stock T. . . . 2E **73**
Deal Ct. TS4: Midd . . . 2A **102**
Deal Rd. TS10: Redc . . . 2E **65**
TS23: Bill . . . 4D **39**
Dean Fall Cl. TS26: H'pool . . . 4E **7**
Deansgate TS6: Est . . . 1A **106**
Dean St. TS18: Stock T . . . 1F **97**
De Brus Ct. TS3: N Orm. . . . 3B **78**
TS12: Salt . . . 3C **68**
Debruse Av. TS15: Yarm . . . 1A **160**
De Brus Pk. TS8: Mart . . . 2E **155**
De Brus Way TS14: Guis . . . 1E **139**
Deepdale TS14: Guis. . . . 3A **138**
Deepdale Av. TS4: Midd . . . 2F **101**
(not continuous)
TS6: Gran . . . 4F **81**
TS18: Stock T. . . . 4E **75**
Deepdale La.
TS13: Skin, Loft . . . 3A **92**
Deepdale Rd. TS13: Loft. . . . 4A **92**
Deepdene Gro. TS10: Redc . . . 3F **65**
Deepgrove Wlk. TS6: Est. . . . 5F **81**
Dee Rd. TS6: Est. . . . 5D **81**
Deerpool Cl. TS24: H'pool. . . . 5C **8**
De Haviland Way
TS25: Seat C . . . 1E **33**
De Havilland Av.
TS18: Stock T. . . . 5E **97**
De Havilland Dr.
TS11: Marsk S . . . 3A **66**
Deighton Gro. TS23: Bill . . . 4D **39**
Deighton Rd. TS4: Midd . . . 1B **132**
De La Mare Dr. TS23: Bill . . . 2D **39**
Delamere TS22: Wyn . . . 4B **26**
Delamere Dr.
TS11: Marsk S . . . 5B **66**
Delamere Rd. TS3: Midd. . . . 3D **103**
Delarden Rd. TS3: Midd . . . 5D **79**
Delaval Rd. TS23: Bill . . . 5F **39**
Dell Cl. TS7: Mart . . . 3C **132**
Dellfield Cl. TS3: Midd . . . 3C **102**
Del Strother Av.
TS19: Stock T. . . . 4E **73**
Denbigh Rd. TS23: Bill. . . . 4E **39**
Dene Cl. TS17: Thorn T. . . . 4E **99**
Dene Gth. TS27: Dalt P . . . 1E **17**
Dene Gro. TS10: Redc. . . . 4D **49**
Dene Rd. TS4: Midd . . . 2A **102**
Deneside Cl. TS15: Yarm . . . 4D **149**
Denevale TS15: Yarm . . . 4D **149**
Dene Wlk. TS11: Marsk S . . . 4B **66**
Denham Grn. TS3: Midd . . . 5D **79**
Denholme Av.
TS18: Stock T. . . . 3E **97**
Denmark St. TS2: Midd. . . . 2D **77**
Dennison St. TS18: Stock T. . . . 3F **97**
Densham Dr. TS18: Stock T. . . . 2F **97**
Denshaw Cl. TS19: Stock T. . . . 5A **72**
Dentdale Cl. TS15: Yarm. . . . 1B **160**
Denton Cl. TS5: Midd . . . 2B **130**
TS19: Stock T . . . 1B **72**
Dent St. TS26: H'pool . . . 3B **14**
Denver Dr. DL2: Mid G . . . 1B **144**
Depot Rd. TS2: Midd . . . 1E **77**
Derby, The TS7: Mart. . . . 1B **132**
Derby Av. TS5: Midd . . . 2A **100**
Derby Cl. TS17: Thorn T . . . 3D **99**
Derby Rd. TS14: Guis . . . 3D **139**
Derby St. TS18: Stock T . . . 5A **74**
TS25: H'pool . . . 1B **20**
Derby Ter. TS17: Thorn T . . . 2D **99**
Derwent Av. TS14: Guis. . . . 3C **138**
Derwent Cl. TS21: Redm. . . . 1B **70**
Derwent Pk. TS13: Loft. . . . 5D **93**
Derwent Rd. TS10: Redc. . . . 5A **48**
TS12: Skel . . . 4B **88**
TS17: Thorn T . . . 5D **99**
Derwent St. TS1: Midd . . . 4D **77**
TS3: N Orm . . . 4C **78**
TS20: Nort . . . 2A **74**
TS26: H'pool . . . 3B **14**
Derwentwater Av.
TS5: Midd . . . 4C **100**
Derwentwater Rd. TS6: Gran. . . 4F **81**
Desford Grn. TS3: Midd. . . . 1D **103**
Desmond Rd. DL2: Mid G . . . 3A **144**
Deva Cl. TS4: Midd . . . 2B **102**
Devon Cl. TS10: Redc . . . 1B **64**
Devon Cres. TS12: Skel. . . . 4A **88**
TS23: Bill . . . 2F **55**
Devonport Gdns.
DL2: Mid R. . . . 4A **144**
Devonport Rd. TS5: Midd. . . . 2F **101**
TS18: Stock T . . . 4C **74**
Devon Rd. TS6: Gran . . . 4E **81**
TS14: Guis. . . . 3D **139**
Devonshire Rd. TS5: Midd . . . 1D **101**
Devonshire St.
TS18: Stock T. . . . 3F **97**
Devon St. TS25: H'pool . . . 1B **20**
Dewberry TS8: Coul N. . . . 1D **155**
Dewberry Cl. TS26: H'pool . . . 4D **7**
Dew La. TS7: Orm. . . . 5A **104**
Diamond Ct. TS18: Stock T . . . 5F **97**
DIAMOND HALL RDBT. . . . **5E 23**
Diamond Rd. TS1: Midd . . . 4E **77**
TS17: Thorn T . . . 4D **99**
Diamond St. TS12: Salt. . . . 3C **68**
Dickens Ct. TS23: Bill . . . 3D **39**
Dickens Gro. TS25: H'pool. . . . 1F **19**
Dickens St. TS24: H'pool . . . 3F **7**
Didcot Cl. TS10: Redc . . . 4E **65**
Dikes La. TS9: Gt A . . . 2F **167**
Diligence Way TS16: Eag . . . 4B **126**
Dillside TS19: Stock T. . . . 3C **72**
Dimmingdale Rd.
TS12: Moor . . . 5C **142**
Dinas Ct. TS17: Ing B. . . . 1F **149**
Dingleside TS19: Stock T . . . 4C **72**
Dinsdale Av. TS5: Midd. . . . 5C **100**
Dinsdale Ct. TS23: Bill. . . . 4F **39**
Dinsdale Dr. TS16: Eag . . . 5C **126**
Dinsdale Rd. TS19: Stock T . . . 1B **72**
Diomed Ct. TS7: Mart . . . 1C **132**
Dionysia Rd. TS3: Midd. . . . 5C **78**
Dipton Grn. TS4: Midd. . . . 5B **102**
Dipton Rd. TS19: Stock T . . . 1A **72**
Dishforth Cl. TS17: Thorn T . . 3D **129**
Dixon Gro. TS3: Midd . . . 5C **78**

Dixons Bank
TS7: Mart, Nun 3E **133**
Dixon St. TS12: Brot 2B **90**
TS12: Skel 3C **88**
TS13: Carl H 3F **91**
TS18: Stock T 5A **74**
Dobson Pl. TS24: H'pool 3E **7**
Dobson Ter. TS10: Redc 4D **49**
Dockside Rd. TS3: Midd 2C **78**
TS6: Midd 1F **79**
Dockside Rd. Ind. Est.
TS3: Midd 2C **78**
Dock St. TS2: Midd 2F **77**
Dodford Rd. TS8: Hem 5E **131**
Dodsworth Wlk. TS27: H'pool 3D **7**
Doncaster Cres.
TS19: Stock T 2F **73**
Donegal Ter. TS1: Midd 5C **76**
Donington Grn. TS3: Midd 2A **104**
Dorado Cl. TS18: Stock T 4E **97**
Dorchester Cl. TS8: Midd 2B **132**
TS19: Stock T 2E **73**
Dorchester Dr. TS24: H'pool 2D **7**
Doric Ho. TS21: Sed 4C **22**
Dorkings, The TS9: Gt Bro 5F **169**
Dorlcote Pl. TS20: Nort 2B **74**
Dorman Gdns. TS5: Midd 2D **101**
Dorman Mus. 5E **77**
Dorman Rd. TS6: Est 1E **105**
Dorman's Cres. TS10: Redc 5F **47**
DORMANSTOWN 1E **63**
Dorman Way TS12: Skel 5E **89**
Dorma Pk. Bungs.
TS25: Grea 3E **31**
Dormor Way TS6: S Ban 3E **79**
(not continuous)
Dornoch Sands TS5: Midd 3B **130**
Dorothy St. TS3: N Orm 4C **78**
Dorothy Ter. *TS17: Thorn T 3C* ***98***
(off Langley Av.)
Dorrien Cres. TS3: Midd 5C **78**
Dorset Cl. TS5: Midd 1D **101**
TS10: Redc 1B **64**
Dorset Cres. TS23: Bill 1F **55**
Dorset Rd. TS12: Skel 4A **88**
TS14: Guis 4C **138**
TS20: Nort 1C **74**
Dorset St. TS25: H'pool 1B **20**
Douglas Cl. TS18: Stock T 5F **97**
Douglas St. TS4: Midd 4A **78**
(not continuous)
Douglas Ter. TS6: Norm 2D **105**
Douglas Wlk. *TS20: Nort 3B* ***74***
(off Headlam Ct.)
Dovecote Cl. TS11: Marsk S 4C **66**
Dovecot St. TS18: Stock T 1F **97**
Dovedale Av. TS6: Gran 4F **81**
Dovedale Cl. TS20: Nort 1C **74**
Dovedale Rd. TS20: Nort 1C **74**
Dove La. TS20: Nort 4A **54**
Dover Cl. TS10: Redc 2E **65**
TS23: Bill 5C **38**
Dover Rd. TS19: Stock T 2F **73**
(not continuous)
Dover St. TS24: H'pool 3C **14**
Dovey Ct. TS17: Ing B 1F **149**
Downe St. TS13: Live 5A **92**
Downfield Way TS11: N Mar 2F **85**
Downham Av. TS3: Midd 3C **102**
Downham Gro. TS25: H'pool 5E **19**
Downholme Gro.
TS18: Stock T 3C **96**
Downside Rd. TS5: Midd 3A **100**
Dowson Rd. TS24: H'pool 2F **7**
Doxford Wlk. TS8: Hem 5E **131**
Doyle Wlk. TS25: H'pool 2D **19**
Doyle Way TS19: Stock T 4A **72**
Dragon Ct. TS20: Nort 5B **54**
Drake Cl. TS11: Marsk S 4E **67**
Drake Ct. TS2: Midd 2C **76**
Drake Ho. TS24: H'pool 3D **15**
Drake Rd. TS20: Nort 1A **74**
Draycott Av. TS5: Midd 3D **131**
Draycott Cl. TS10: Redc 3B **64**
TS20: Nort 5E **53**
Drayton Rd. TS25: H'pool 2D **19**
Dresser La. TS5: Midd 2D **101**
Driffield Way TS23: Bill 2F **39**
Driftwell Dr. TS19: Stock T 4A **72**
Drive, The TS8: Stain 5C **130**
TS11: Marsk S 4B **66**
TS17: Thorn T 2B **128**
TS25: Grea 3E **31**
Droitwich Av. TS19: Stock T 2E **73**
Drovers La. TS21: Redm 1B **70**
Drovers Way Caravan Pk.
TS21: Elt 1E **125**
Druridge Gro. TS10: Redc 2F **65**
Dryburn Rd. TS19: Stock T 1A **72**
Dryden Cl. TS23: Bill 2E **39**
Dryden Rd. TS25: H'pool 2E **19**
Duchy Rd. TS26: H'pool 3C **12**
Duddon Sands TS5: Midd 3B **130**
Duddon Wlk. TS19: Stock T 5F **73**
Dudley Rd. TS23: Bill 4D **39**
Dudley Wlk. *TS10: Redc 2E* ***65***
(off Carisbrooke Way)
Dufton Rd. TS5: Midd 1C **100**
Dugdale St. TS18: Stock T 4C **74**
Duhallow Cl. TS14: Guis 4E **139**
Dukeport Ct. *TS18: Stock T 4C* ***74***
(off Alnport Rd.)
Dukes Ct. TS17: Thorn T 5D **129**
Duke St. TS26: H'pool 2F **13**
Dukesway TS17: Thorn T 5D **129**
Dulas Cl. TS10: Redc 3E **65**
Dulverton Cl. TS17: Ing B 3B **150**
Dulverton Way TS14: Guis 3F **139**
Dumbarton Av.
TS19: Stock T 2F **73**
Dumfries Rd. TS25: H'pool 4F **19**
Dunbar Av. TS4: Midd 5B **102**
Dunbar Ct. TS13: Eas 2A **118**
Dunbar Dr. TS16: Eag 1C **148**
Dunbar Rd. TS23: Bill 5D **39**
TS25: H'pool 3E **19**
Duncan Av. TS10: Redc 5A **48**
Duncan Pl. TS13: Loft 5B **92**
Duncan Rd. TS25: H'pool 3E **19**
Duncombe Rd. TS4: Midd 3A **78**
Dundas Arc. TS1: Midd 2F **77**
Dundas St. TS1: Midd 3E **77**
(not continuous)
TS10: Redc 3C **48**
TS11: N Mar 1A **86**
TS13: Loft 5B **92**
TS19: Stock T 4F **73**
TS24: H'pool 4C **14**
Dundas St. E. TS12: Salt 4C **68**
Dundas St. W. TS12: Salt 4C **68**
Dundas Ter. TS11: Marsk S 5C **66**
TS11: N Mar 1A **86**
Dundee Rd. TS25: H'pool 4F **19**
Dunedin Av. TS18: Stock T 2B **96**
Dunedin Ho. TS17: Thorn T 1B **98**
Dunelm Ct. TS21: Sed 4C **22**
Dunelm Rd. TS19: Stock T 3C **72**
Duneside TS19: Stock T 3C **72**
Dunford Cl. TS19: Stock T 1B **72**
Dunholm Av. TS3: Midd 3A **104**
Dunkeld Cl. TS19: Stock T 1B **72**
Dunkerque Mall TS1: Midd 2E **77**
Dunkery Cl. TS17: Ing B 3A **150**
Dunlane Cl. TS5: Midd 5B **76**
Dunlin Cl. TS20: Nort 3B **54**
Dunlin Ho. TS24: H'pool 3D **15**
Dunlin Rd. TS26: H'pool 5E **7**
Dunmail Rd. TS10: Redc 5B **48**
TS19: Stock T 5F **73**
Dunmoor Gro. TS17: Ing B 2A **150**
Dunmow Av. TS3: Midd 3E **103**
Dunnet Cl. TS10: Redc 4C **64**
Dunning Rd. TS1: Midd 3F **77**
Dunning St. TS1: Midd 3F **77**
Dunoon Cl. TS19: Stock T 2F **73**
Dunoon Rd. TS25: H'pool 3E **19**
Dunottar Av. TS16: Prest T 3C **126**
DUNSDALE 1D **109**
Dunsdale Cl. TS6: Est 2E **105**
TS11: Marsk S 4E **67**
Dunsley Cl. TS3: Midd 1B **102**
Dunsley Ct. TS14: Guis 1E **139**
Dunsley Dr. TS23: Bill 4E **39**
Dunsmore Cl. TS8: Malt 2F **151**
Dunsop Av. TS4: Midd 5B **102**
Dunstable Cl. TS19: Stock T 2E **73**
Dunstable Rd. TS5: Midd 5B **76**
Dunster Ho. TS3: Midd 2D **103**
Dunster Rd. TS23: Bill 4E **39**
Dunston Cl. TS14: Guis 4E **139**
Dunston Rd. TS19: Stock T 1B **72**
TS26: H'pool 3D **13**
Durham Ho. TS4: Midd 2A **102**
Durham La.
TS16: Eag, Prest T 4A **96**
TS21: Elt, Prest T, Stock T
4A **96**
Durham La. Ind. Pk.
TS16: Eag 3A **126**
Durham Rd. TS6: Est 5E **81**
TS10: Redc 1F **65**
TS12: Brot 2C **90**
TS19: Stock T 5C **52**
TS21: Sed 2C **22**
(Neville Dr.)
TS21: Sed 4B **22**
(Sands Hall Rdbt.)
TS21: Stock T, Thorpe L, Thorpe T
3C **34**
TS22: Wolv 2C **38**
Durham Rd. By-Pass
TS18: Stock T 3E **73**
TS19: Stock T 3E **73**
Durham St. TS2: Midd 1F **77**
TS18: Stock T 5A **74**
TS24: H'pool 5E **9**
DURHAM TEES VALLEY AIRPORT
2D **145**
Durham Tees Valley Bus. Cen.
TS19: Stock T 4A **74**
Durham University
Queen's Campus Sports Cen.
1D **99**
Durham University
Queen's Campus, Stockton
5D **75**
Durness Gro. TS25: H'pool 3E **19**
Durnford Rd. TS3: Midd 2F **103**
Duxford Rd. TS5: Midd 2B **100**
DW Fitness
Middlesbrough 3A 78
(off Marton Rd.)
DYKE HOUSE 1A **14**

E

Eaglebridge Ct. TS22: Wyn 2E **37**
Eagle Ct. TS18: Stock T 5F **97**
Eagle Pk. TS8: Mart 5F **133**
(not continuous)
EAGLESCLIFFE 5C **126**
Eaglescliffe Cl. TS11: N Mar 2F **85**
Eaglescliffe Golf Course 4C **126**
Eaglescliffe Ind. Est.
TS16: Eag 3C **126**
Eaglescliffe Station (Rail) 3C **126**
Eaglesfield Rd.
TS25: H'pool 3D **19**
Eamont Gdns. TS26: H'pool 4A **14**
Eamont Rd. TS20: Nort 5A **54**
Eamont Ter. TS26: H'pool 5A **14**
Earle Cl. TS15: Yarm 4E **149**
Earl's Ct. TS20: Nort 1B **74**
Earls Ct. Rd. TS8: Hem 5E **131**
Earlsdon Av. TS5: Midd 1B **130**
Earlsferry Rd. TS25: H'pool 3D **19**
Earls Nook TS23: Bill 1A **56**
Earlston Wlk. TS25: H'pool 3D **19**

Earl St. TS24: H'pool 4D **9**
Earlsway TS17: Thorn T. 5E **129**
Earn Wlk. TS25: H'pool 3D **19**
Earsdon Cl. TS20: Nort 5E **53**
EASBY 5F **167**
Easby Av. TS5: Midd 3E **101**
Easby Cl. TS6: Est 5A **82**
TS10: Redc 2B **64**
TS14: Guis 2F **139**
Easby Ct. TS12: Skel 3E **89**
Easby Gro. TS6: Est. 1D **105**
TS17: Thorn T 4D **99**
Easby La. TS9: Gt A, L Ayt. . . . 2C **166**
Easby Rd. TS23: Bill. 1E **55**
Easdale Ct. TS17: Thorn T. 5E **99**
Easdale Wlk. TS5: Midd 3E **101**
EASINGTON 2A **118**
Easington Rd. TS19: Stock T. . . 5B **52**
TS24: H'pool 1C **6**
Easson Rd. TS10: Redc 5C **48**
Easson St. TS4: Midd 1A **102**
East Av. TS23: Bill 4D **55**
Eastbank Rd. TS7: Orm 5B **104**
Eastbourne Av. TS16: Egg 2C **148**
Eastbourne Gdns.
TS3: Midd. 3F **103**
Eastbourne Rd. TS5: Midd. . . . 2E **101**
TS19: Stock T 3A **74**
(not continuous)
Eastbury Cl. TS17: Ing B 1C **150**
East Cres. TS5: Midd. 2B **100**
TS13: Loft 5D **93**
Eastcroft TS3: Midd 1C **102**
Eastcroft Rd. TS6: Gran 2E **81**
East Dr. TS17: Thorn T 1D **99**
East End TS9: Stokes. 1C **168**
TS21: Sed 4D **23**
Easter Pk. TS2: Midd. 1C **76**
TS17: Thorn T 5E **129**
EASTERSIDE 5B **102**
Easterside Rd. TS4: Midd 5B **102**
E. Farm Cl. TS6: Norm 3D **105**
Eastfield Rd. TS11: Marsk S . . . 4B **66**
Eastfields TS9: Stokes. 1C **168**
Eastgate Rd. TS5: Midd. 3C **100**
Eastham Sands TS5: Midd. . . . 3B **130**
Eastland Av. TS26: H'pool 5F **13**
Eastland Vw. TS3: Midd. 5E **79**
Eastleigh TS17: Thorn T 1E **129**
East Lodge TS5: Midd 5F **77**
E. Lodge Gdns. TS11: Redc. . . . 4B **64**
EAST LOFTUS 5D **93**
Eastlowthian St. TS2: Port C . . . 5F **57**
East Mdws. TS11: Marsk S 4D **67**
E. Middlesbrough Ind. Est.
TS3: N Orm 3E **79**
(Telford Rd.)
TS3: N Orm 4D **79**
(Westerby Rd.)
Easton St. TS17: Thorn T 3D **99**
East Pde. TS12: Skel 4B **88**
TS21: Sed 3D **23**
TS24: H'pool 5D **9**
E. Pastures Cotts.
TS12: Skel 5A **90**
Eastport Rd. TS18: Stock T 4C **74**
East Pct. TS23: Bill 1D **55**
East Row TS5: Midd. 2B **100**
TS6: Est 1F **105**
East Scar TS10: Redc. 2E **65**
East Side TS7: Nun 2C **156**
East St. TS11: Marsk S 4D **67**
TS13: Loft 5C **92**
East Ter. *TS12: Skel. 4B 88*
(off Wood's Yd.)
TS12: Skel 4B **88**
(Grasmere Cres.)
East Vw. DL2: Mid R 4A **144**
East Vw. Ter. TS4: Midd 1A **102**
TS25: Seat C 3E **21**
Eastwell Cl. TS21: Sed 4D **23**
Eastwood Rd. TS3: Midd 2A **104**
Ebchester Cl. TS19: Stock T . . . 5B **52**
Eccleston Wlk. TS4: Midd 5A **102**
Eckert Av. TS5: Midd 2A **100**
Eckford Wlk. TS25: H'pool 3E **19**
Eddison Way TS8: Hem 5E **131**
(not continuous)
Eddleston Wlk. TS25: H'pool. . . 3D **19**
Eden Dr. TS21: Sed 4D **23**
Edenhall Gro. TS10: Redc 2C **64**
Eden Ho. TS23: Bill 4D **55**
Eden Rd. TS4: Midd 2F **101**
TS12: Skel 3C **88**
Eden St. TS12: Salt 4C **68**
TS24: H'pool 4B **14**
Eden Way TS22: Bill. 4A **38**
Eder Rd. TS20: Nort. 2B **74**
Edgar St. TS20: Nort 2B **74**
TS25: H'pool 1C **20**
Edgehill Gdns. TS12: Brot. 2B **90**
Edgehill Way TS23: Bill 4A **40**
Edgeworth Ct. TS8: Hem 5F **131**
Edgley Rd. TS18: Stock T 2B **96**
Edinburgh Av. TS5: Midd. 3D **101**
Edinburgh Cl. TS7: Nun. 3A **134**
Edinburgh Gro.
TS25: H'pool 4C **20**
Edison Dr. TS19: Stock T. 1B **72**
Edith St. TS5: Midd 4B **76**
Edmondbyers Rd.
TS19: Stock T 5B **52**
Edmondsley Wlk.
TS19: Stock T 5C **52**
Edmundsbury Rd.
TS5: Midd. 1F **101**
Ednam Gro. TS25: H'pool 3E **19**
Edridge Grn. TS3: Midd 5E **79**
Edston Dr. TS14: Guis 5F **109**
Edward Kitching Ter.
TS9: Gt A 1D 167
(off Cliffe Ter.)
Edwards Ct. TS5: Midd 2E **101**
Edwards St. TS6: Est 2F **105**
TS18: Stock T 2A **98**
Edward St. TS3: N Orm 4C **78**
TS6: S Ban 3B **80**
Edzell Wlk. TS25: H'pool. 3D **19**
Egerton Cl. TS20: Nort. 4E **53**
Egerton Rd. TS26: H'pool 4C **12**
Egerton St. TS1: Midd 5F **77**
Egerton Ter. TS25: Grea 3E **31**
EGGLESCLIFFE 2C **148**
Egglescliffe Bank
TS16: Egg 2B **148**
Egglescliffe Cl.
TS19: Stock T 5C **52**
Egglescliffe Ct. TS16: Egg. . . . 2C **148**
Eggleston Ct. TS2: Midd 1C **76**
TS12: Skel 4D **89**
Egglestone Ct. TS23: Bill 4E **39**
Egglestone Dr. TS16: Eag 5A **126**
Egglestone Ter.
TS18: Stock T. 1F **97**
Eggleston Rd. TS10: Redc. 3C **64**
Eglington Rd. TS6: Gran 2E **81**
Eglinton Av. TS14: Guis 3E **139**
Egmont Rd. TS4: Midd. 5A **78**
Egton Av. TS7: Nun 4F **133**
Egton Cl. TS10: Redc. 3C **64**
Egton Dr. TS25: Seat C 5D **21**
Egton Rd. TS20: Nort. 2B **74**
Eider Cl. TS17: Ing B. 5B **128**
TS26: H'pool 1D **13**
Elcho St. TS26: H'pool. 3A **14**
Elcoat Rd. TS20: Nort 4B **54**
Elder Ct. TS1: Midd 3F **77**
Elder Gro. TS10: Redc 3F **65**
TS19: Stock T. 2E **73**
Elderslie Wlk. TS25: H'pool . . . 3D **19**
Elderwood Ct. TS4: Midd 3F **101**
Elderwood Gdns. TS6: Norm. . . 5B **80**
Eldon Gro. TS26: H'pool. 4F **13**
Eldon St. TS17: Thorn T 2C **98**
Eldon Wlk. TS17: Thorn T. 3D **99**
Eleanor Pl. TS18: Stock T 2A **98**
Elemere Ct. TS23: Bill 4E **39**
Elgin Av. TS3: Midd. 3D **103**
TS6: Gran. 2C **80**
Elgin Rd. TS17: Thorn T 3D **129**
TS25: H'pool 3E **19**
Eliot Ct. TS23: Bill 3D **39**
Elishaw Grn. TS17: Ing B 2A **150**
Elizabeth St. TS17: Thorn T. . . . 3C **98**
Elizabeth Ter. TS3: N Orm. 4B **78**
Elizabeth Way TS25: Seat C . . . 4D **21**
Elkington Cl.
TS17: Thorn T 1D **129**
Elkington Wlk. TS3: Midd 2A **104**
Elland Av. TS4: Midd 5B **102**
Ellary Wlk. TS25: H'pool 3D **19**
Ellen Av. TS18: Stock T 2F **97**
Ellenport Ct. TS18: Stock T. . . . 4C **74**
Ellerbeck Av. TS7: Mart 5F **133**
Ellerbeck Ct. TS9: Stokes 3D **169**
Ellerbeck Way TS7: Orm 4B **104**
TS9: Stokes 3D **169**
Ellerburne St.
TS17: Thorn T 3D **99**
Ellerby Cl. TS10: Redc. 2C **64**
Ellerby Grn. TS3: Midd 1C **102**
Ellerby Rd. TS6: Est. 5F **81**
Ellers Bank TS11: Upleat 2C **110**
Ellerton Cl. TS5: Midd 5E **101**
Ellerton Rd. TS18: Stock T 3A **96**
Ellesmere Wlk. TS3: Midd. 5E **79**
Ellett Ct. TS24: H'pool 4F **7**
Ellicott Wlk. TS18: Stock T 2A **98**
Elliot St. TS1: Midd 3F **77**
TS10: Redc 3B **48**
TS12: Skel 5B **88**
Elliott St. TS26: H'pool 3A **14**
Elliotts Yd. *TS13: Stait. 1C 120*
(off High St.)
Ellis Gdns. TS8: Hem. 5E **131**
Ellison St. TS26: H'pool. 5A **14**
Elm Av. TS21: Sed 3D **23**
Elm Cl. TS6: Norm. 5C **80**
TS12: Salt 4A **68**
Elm Dr. TS7: Mart 2D **133**
Elmfield Gdns. TS25: H'pool . . . 3F **19**
Elm Gro. TS17: Thorn T. 4C **98**
TS26: H'pool 3E **13**
Elm Ho. TS18: Stock T. 5B **74**
Elmhurst Gdns. TS8: Hem 5E **131**
(not continuous)
Elm Rd. TS10: Redc. 4E **49**
TS14: Guis 1E **139**
Elmstone Gdns. TS8: Hem. . . . 5E **131**
(not continuous)
Elm St. TS1: Midd 3F **77**
TS6: S Ban. 2A **80**
ELM TREE 3C **72**
Elm Tree Av. TS19: Stock T. . . . 3B **72**
Elm Tree Cen. TS19: Stock T. . . 4C **72**
Elm Tree Pk. TS25: Seat C. 3E **21**
Elm Wlk. TS13: Loft. 5B **92**
Elmwood TS8: Coul N 3B **132**
Elmwood Av. *TS5: Midd. 1B 100*
(off Greenbank Av.)
Elmwood Cl. TS9: Stokes 5C **164**
Elmwood Ct. TS19: Stock T. . . . 3B **72**
Elmwood Gro.
TS19: Stock T 4D **73**
Elmwood Pl. TS26: H'pool. 1E **13**
Elmwood Rd. TS16: Prest T. . . 2C **126**
TS26: H'pool 2E **13**
Elphin Wlk. TS25: H'pool 3D **19**
Elsdon Gdns. TS17: Ing B 2A **150**
Elsdon St. TS18: Stock T 1F **97**
Elstob Cl. TS19: Stock T 5B **52**
Elstone Rd. TS4: Midd. 3A **78**
Elterwater Cl. TS10: Redc 5B **48**
Eltham Cres.
TS17: Thorn T 3E **129**
Eltisley Grn. TS3: Midd 5E **79**
ELTON 4E **95**
Elton Cl. TS19: Stock T 5C **52**
Elton Gro. TS19: Stock T 1A **96**

ELTON INTERCHANGE 3F **95**
Elton La. TS16: Eag 1B **148**
ELTON PARK 5F **71**
Elton Rd. TS22: Bill 4B **38**
Elton St. TS10: Redc 4C **48**
Eltringham Rd. TS26: H'pool 4A **14**
Elvan Gro. TS25: H'pool 3E **19**
Elvington Cl. TS23: Bill 1F **39**
Elvington Grn. TS3: Midd 1E **103**
ELWICK 4C **10**
Elwick Av. TS5: Midd 5C **100**
Elwick Cl. TS10: Redc 4F **65**
TS19: Stock T 5B **52**
Elwick Ct. TS26: H'pool 5A **14**
Elwick Gdns. TS19: Stock T 5B **52**
Elwick Rd. TS24: H'pool 4E **13**
TS26: H'pool 2A **12**
TS27: Elw 3E **11**
Ely Cres. TS10: Redc 5F **49**
TS12: Brot 2C **90**
Ely St. TS4: Midd 4A **78**
Embleton Av. TS5: Midd 4C **100**
Embleton Cl. TS19: Stock T 5B **52**
Embleton Ct. TS10: Redc 2D **65**
Embleton Gro. TS22: Wyn 2E **37**
Embleton Rd. TS22: Bill 4B **38**
Embleton Wlk.
*TS19: Stock T 5B **52***
(off Embleton Cl.)
Embsay Cl. TS4: Midd 3A **102**
TS17: Ing B 2B **150**
Emerald St. TS1: Midd 4E **77**
TS12: Salt 3C **68**
Emerson Av. TS5: Midd 3E **101**
Emerson Ct. TS24: H'pool 3F **7**
Emily St. TS1: Midd 3F **77**
Emma Simpson Ct.
TS18: Stock T 3C **96**
Emmerson St. TS5: Midd 1E **101**
Emmetts Gdns.
TS17: Ing B 1B **150**
Empire Sq. TS24: H'pool 4C **14**
Emsworth Dr. TS16: Eag 5A **126**
Endeavour, The TS7: Nun 3A **134**
Endeavour Cl. TS25: Seat C 3E **21**
Endeavour Dr. TS7: Orm 5B **104**
Endeavour Ho.
TS17: Thorn T 1B **98**
Enderby Gdns. TS8: Hem 5E **131**
Endeston Rd. TS3: Midd 3E **103**
Endrick Rd. TS25: H'pool 3D **19**
Endsleigh Dr. TS5: Midd 3A **100**
Enfield Chase TS14: Guis 3D **139**
Enfield Gro. TS6: Norm 4C **104**
Enfield Shop. Cen.
TS14: Guis 3E **139**
Enfield St. TS1: Midd 4D **77**
Ennerdale Av. TS5: Midd 4C **100**
Ennerdale Cres. TS12: Skel 3B **88**
Ennerdale Rd.
TS18: Stock T 5D **73**
Ennis Rd. TS10: Redc 5E **47**
Ennis Sq. TS10: Redc 5E **47**
Enron Ho. TS17: Thorn T 1C **98**
Ensign Ct. TS24: H'pool 3D **15**
Enterpen Cl. TS15: Yarm 4F **149**
Enterprise Cen. Annexe
TS2: Midd 1E **77**
Enterprise Ct. TS6: S Ban 1A **80**
Enterprise Ho. *TS25: H'pool 1C **20***
(off Thomlinson Rd.)
Epping Av. TS3: Midd 3D **103**
Epping Cl. TS11: Marsk S 4C **66**
TS17: Thorn T 2C **128**
Epsom Av. TS4: Midd 5B **102**
Epsom Rd. TS10: Redc 2D **65**
Epworth Grn. TS3: Midd 1E **103**
Erica Gro. TS7: Mart 1C **132**
Eric Av. TS17: Thorn T 3D **99**
Eridge Rd. TS14: Guis 3F **139**
Eriskay Wlk. TS25: H'pool 3D **19**
Eris Rd. TS18: Stock T 5E **97**
Erith Gro. TS4: Midd 1B **132**
Ernest St. TS26: H'pool 2A **14**
Ernest Wlk. TS26: H'pool 2A **14**
Errington Gth.
*TS11: Marsk S 5E **67***
(off Hambleton Cres.)
Errington St. TS12: Brot 3B **90**
Errol St. TS1: Midd 5F **77**
TS24: H'pool 3B **14**
Erskine Rd. TS25: H'pool 3D **19**
Escomb Cl. TS19: Stock T 5B **52**
Escombe Av. TS4: Midd 5B **102**
Escombe Rd. TS23: Bill 2E **39**
Escomb Ho. TS4: Midd 2A **102**
Esha Ness Ct. TS25: H'pool 3D **19**
Esher Av. TS6: Norm 4C **104**
Esher St. TS1: Midd 4A **78**
Eshton TS22: Wyn 3B **26**
Eshwood Sq. TS1: Midd 3E **77**
Esk Cl. TS14: Guis 3D **139**
Eskdale TS8: Hem 5D **131**
Eskdale Cl. TS15: Yarm 1B **160**
Eskdale Ct. TS25: H'pool 3D **19**
Eskdale Rd. TS10: Redc 1F **63**
TS25: H'pool 4D **19**
Eskdale Ter. TS12: Ling 4E **113**
*TS14: Guis 1E **139***
(off Hedley St.)
Esk Grn. TS16: Eag 1B **148**
Esk Gro. TS25: H'pool 3E **19**
Esk Rd. TS20: Nort 1A **74**
Esk St. TS3: N Orm 4C **78**
Esk Ter. *TS13: Loft 5D **93***
(off Tees St.)
Esplanade TS10: Redc 3C **48**
Essex Av. TS6: Gran 3D **81**
Essex Cres. TS23: Bill 2F **55**
Essex Gro. TS20: Nort 1C **74**
Essexport Rd.
TS18: Stock T 4C **74**
Essex St. TS1: Midd 5D **77**
ESTON 1E **105**
Eston Leisure Cen. 4C **80**
Eston Leisure Complex 4C **80**
Eston Rd.
TS6: Est, Laze, Old L 1A **106**
(not continuous)
TS6: Gran 1C **80**
Eston Sports Academy 4C **80**
Eston Vw. TS3: Midd 2D **103**
Etal Wlk. TS12: Skel 3A **88**
Etherley Cl. TS19: Stock T 5B **52**
Etherley Wlk. TS19: Stock T 5B **52**
(not continuous)
Eton Rd. TS5: Midd 2C **100**
TS18: Stock T 2F **97**
Eton St. TS25: H'pool 1A **20**
Ettersgill Cl. TS16: Eag 5A **126**
Ettington Av. TS3: Midd 4D **103**
Etton Rd. TS23: Bill 1E **39**
Ettrick Wlk. TS25: H'pool 3D **19**
Evans St. TS6: Gran 3D **81**
Evendale TS14: Guis 3A **138**
Evenwood Cl. TS19: Stock T 5B **52**
Evenwood Gdns.
TS5: Midd 2D **131**
Everett St. TS26: H'pool 2F **13**
Evergreen Cl. TS26: H'pool 4D **7**
Evergreen Wlk. *TS4: Midd 3F **101***
(off Pinewood Av.)
Evergreen Way TS8: Mart 5D **133**
Everingham Rd.
TS15: Yarm 1A **160**
Eversham Rd. TS6: Gran 2E **81**
Eversley Wlk. TS3: Midd 3D **103**
Evesham Rd. TS3: Midd 3D **103**
Evesham Way TS23: Bill 3A **40**
Evolution 5A **28**
Ewbank Dr. TS18: Stock T 1F **97**
Ewbank Gdns. TS18: Stock T 1F **97**
Exchange Pl. TS1: Midd 2F **77**
Exchange Sq. TS1: Midd 2F **77**
Exchange Yd. TS18: Stock T 1A **98**
Excercise4less 4B **52**
Exeter Rd. TS5: Midd 1F **101**
TS6: Est 1E **105**
Exeter St. TS12: Salt 4C **68**
TS24: H'pool 4C **14**
Exford Cl. TS17: Ing B 3B **150**
Exmoor Gro. TS26: H'pool 1D **13**
Exmouth Cl. TS10: Redc 3A **64**
Eyebright Cl. TS26: H'pool 4D **7**
Ezard St. TS19: Stock T 4A **74**

F

Fabian Ct. Shop. Cen.
TS6: Est 5E **81**
Fabian Rd. TS6: Est 5C **80**
Faceby Pl. TS20: Nort 3B **74**
Faceby Wlk. TS3: Midd 2C **102**
Fagg St. TS18: Stock T 5A **74**
Fairbridge St. TS1: Midd 3E **77**
Fairburn Cl. TS19: Stock T 5A **72**
Fairburn Rd. TS6: Norm 2C **104**
Fairdene Av. TS19: Stock T 5A **72**
Fairfax Ct. TS8: Hem 1E **153**
TS15: Yarm 3B **148**
Fairfax Rd. DL2: Mid G 1B **144**
FAIRFIELD 4B **72**
Fairfield Av. TS5: Midd 3B **100**
TS7: Orm 5A **104**
Fairfield Cl. TS10: Redc 1C **64**
TS19: Stock T 5B **72**
Fairfield Rd. TS9: Stokes 1B **168**
TS13: Stait 2C **120**
TS19: Stock T 5B **72**
Fairmead TS10: Redc 3A **64**
TS15: Yarm 5A **148**
Fairstone Av. TS19: Stock T 4A **72**
Fairthorn Av. TS19: Stock T 5A **72**
Fairview TS21: Long N 1A **124**
Fairview Gdns. TS20: Nort 4D **53**
Fairville Rd. TS19: Stock T 4A **72**
Fairway TS18: Stock T 2F **97**
Fairway, The TS8: Mart 4E **133**
TS12: Salt 5B **68**
TS16: Eag 5C **126**
Fairwell Rd. TS19: Stock T 3A **72**
Fairwood Pk. TS8: Mart 5E **133**
Fairy Cove Ter. *TS24: H'pool 5F **9***
(off Cove Wlk.)
Fairy Cove Wlk. TS24: H'pool 5F **9**
Fairy Dell TS7: Mart 4C **132**
Fakenham Av. TS5: Midd 3B **100**
Falcon Ct. TS18: Stock T 4A **98**
Falcon Ct. Office Pk.
TS18: Stock T 5F **97**
Falcon La. TS20: Nort 3A **54**
Falcon Rd. TS3: N Orm 4E **79**
TS26: H'pool 1D **13**
Falcon Wlk. TS15: Hilt 1E **163**
(not continuous)
Falcon Way TS14: Guis 2A **138**
Falkirk Rd. TS25: H'pool 4E **19**
Falkirk St. TS17: Thorn T 3D **99**
Falklands Cl.
TS11: Marsk S 4B **66**
Falkland St. TS1: Midd 4D **77**
Fallow Cl. TS17: Ing B 5B **128**
Fallows Ct. TS1: Midd 3D **77**
Fall Way TS6: Norm 4C **104**
Falmouth Cl. TS10: Redc 2B **64**
Falmouth Gro. TS26: H'pool 1E **13**
Falmouth St. TS1: Midd 5F **77**
Falston Cl. TS23: Bill 4C **38**
Fanacurt Rd. TS14: Guis 3B **138**
Fancy Bank TS14: Slape 2C **140**
Fane Cl. TS19: Stock T 5B **72**
Fane Gro. TS5: Midd 5C **100**
Faraday Dr. TS19: Stock T 1B **72**
Faraday St. TS1: Midd 4D **77**
Farah Rd. TS24: H'pool 2A **14**
Faray Grn. TS17: Thorn T 4E **99**
Fareham Cl. TS25: H'pool 1F **31**
Farfield Mnr. TS21: Sed 1C **22**

Farfields Cl. TS21: Long N . . . 1F **123**
Farington Dr. TS7: Mart 3F **133**
Farleigh Cl. TS23: Bill 4E **39**
Farley Dr. TS5: Midd 5A **100**
Farmbank Rd. TS7: Orm 1B **134**
Farmcote Ct. TS8: Hem 1D **153**
(not continuous)
Farm Gth. TS9: Gt A 1D **167**
Farm La. TS17: Ing B 5B **128**
TS18: Stock T 1D **97**
Farmside M. TS8: Mart 1E **155**
Farnborough Av. TS5: Midd . . . 3C **100**
Farndale Ct. TS4: Midd 2A **102**
Farndale Cres. TS4: Midd 2A **102**
Farndale Dr. TS14: Guis 3A **138**
Farndale Gdns. TS12: Ling . . . 4E **113**
Farndale Grn. TS19: Stock T . . . 3E **73**
Farndale Rd. TS4: Midd 2A **102**
TS7: Nun 3B **134**
TS25: Seat C 4E **21**
Farndale Sq. TS10: Redc 1F **63**
Farndale Wlk. TS6: Est 5F **81**
Farne Ct. TS17: Ing B 1B **150**
Farnell Gro. TS25: H'pool 3E **19**
Farne Wlk. *TS14: Guis 3D 139*
(off Dorset Rd.)
Farnham Cl. TS16: Eag 5A **126**
Farnham Wlk. TS3: Midd. 3C **102**
Faronia Wlk. TS18: Stock T . . . 5D **75**
Farrer St. TS18: Stock T 4A **74**
Farrier Cl. TS17: Ing B 5B **128**
Farrier M. TS6: Laze 4C **82**
Farr Wlk. TS25: H'pool 4E **19**
Farthingale Way TS8: Hem . . . 1D **153**
Fastnet Gro. TS24: H'pool 4C **14**
Fauconberg Cl. TS23: Bill 2B **56**
Fauconberg Way
TS15: Yarm 5A **148**
Faulder Wlk. TS25: H'pool 2B **20**
Faverdale Av. TS5: Midd 2B **130**
Faverdale Cl. TS1: Midd 3E **77**
TS19: Stock T 3C **72**
Faversham Cl. TS8: Hem. 1E **153**
Fawcett Av. TS8: Stain. 5C **130**
Fawcett Rd. TS17: Thorn T . . . 1D **129**
Fawcett Way
TS17: Thorn T 1D **129**
Fawcus Ct. TS10: Redc 1F **63**
(not continuous)
Faygate Ct. TS8: Hem 5D **131**
Fearby Rd. TS18: Stock T 3A **96**
Fearnhead TS8: Mart 5E **133**
Felbrigg La. TS17: Ing B 1B **150**
Felby Av. TS3: Midd 4D **103**
Felixstowe Cl. TS25: H'pool . . . 1E **31**
Fell Briggs Dr.
TS11: Marsk S 4C **66**
Fellston Cl. TS26: H'pool 2D **13**
Felton La. TS19: Stock T. 3A **72**
Fencote Gdns.
TS19: Stock T 5B **72**
Fenham Ct. TS7: Orm 4A **104**
Fen Moor Cl. TS8: Hem 4C **130**
Fenner Cl. TS11: Marsk S 5F **67**
FENS 1D **31**
Fens, The TS27: Hart. 3B **6**
Fens Ct. TS25: H'pool 5F **19**
Fens Cres. TS25: H'pool 5F **19**
Fenton Cl. TS6: S Ban 2A **80**
TS17: Ing B 1B **150**
Fenton Ct. TS12: Boo 3C **112**
Fenton Rd. TS25: H'pool 1D **31**
Fenton St. TS12: Boo 3B **112**
Ferguson Way TS21: Redm. . . . 1B **70**
Fermenter Rd. TS23: Bill. 3C **56**
Ferndale TS19: Stock T. 3C **72**
Ferndale Av. TS3: Midd 4E **79**
Ferndale Cl. TS11: N Mar 2A **86**
Ferndale Ct. TS3: Midd 5F **79**
Fernhill Rd. TS6: Est 2F **105**
Fernie Rd. TS14: Guis 4E **139**
TS20: Nort 4B **54**
Fern St. TS1: Midd. 4F **77**
Fernville Cl. TS25: H'pool 1E **19**
Fernwood TS8: Coul N. 2B **154**
TS10: Redc 3D **65**
Fernwood Av. TS25: H'pool 1A **20**
Ferranti Wlk. TS19: Stock T . . . 1B **72**
Ferry Rd. TS2: Midd. 1F **77**
TS24: H'pool 1E **15**
Fescue Cl. TS18: Stock T 1A **128**
Fewston Cl. TS3: Midd 1C **102**
TS26: H'pool 3C **12**
Field Cl. TS17: Thorn T 4E **99**
Fieldfare La. TS20: Nort 3B **54**
(not continuous)
Fieldfare Rd. TS26: H'pool 5E **7**
Field Good Campsite
TS14: Guis 1D **109**
Field Head TS10: Redc 1B **64**
Fielding Ct. TS23: Bill 3D **39**
Fieldview Cl. TS2: Port C 4E **57**
Fife Gro. TS25: H'pool. 4D **19**
Fife Rd. TS20: Nort 4A **54**
Fife St. TS1: Midd 3A **78**
Filey Cl. TS10: Redc 2F **65**
Finchale Av. TS3: Midd 3E **103**
TS23: Bill 5D **39**
Fincham Cl. TS20: Nort. 5E **53**
Finchdale Cl. TS10: Redc 4E **65**
Finchfield Cl. TS16: Eag 5B **126**
Finchlay Ct. TS5: Midd 3D **131**
Finchley Rd. TS20: Nort 4B **54**
Findlay Gro. TS25: H'pool 4E **19**
Finkle St. TS18: Stock T 1B **98**
Finsbury St. TS1: Midd 4D **77**
Firbeck Wlk. TS17: Thorn T. . . 3C **128**
Firby Cl. TS20: Nort. 4E **53**
TS24: H'pool 5C **8**
Fircroft Ct. TS13: Loft 1B **116**
Fir Gro. TS10: Redc. 3A **64**
TS17: Thorn T 4C **98**
Firlands, The TS11: Marsk S. . . 3D **67**
Fir Rigg Dr. TS11: Marsk S 4C **66**
Firs, The TS12: Boo. 4B **112**
Firsby Ct. TS8: Hem. 5E **131**
(not continuous)
Firsby Wlk. TS3: Midd. 1D **103**
First Foulsyke TS13: Loft. 5E **93**
Firtree Av. TS6: Norm 3D **105**
Fir Tree Cl. TS15: Hilt 1F **163**
Firtree Dr. TS6: Norm 3C **104**
Firtree Rd. TS19: Stock T 3E **73**
Fishbourne Gro.
TS17: Ing B 4E **127**
Fisherman's Sq. TS10: Redc. . . 4D **49**
Fishpond Rd.
TS11: Redc, Year 5B **64**
Fiske Ct. TS5: Midd 3C **130**
Fitzwilliam Cl.
TS11: Marsk S 4D **67**
Fitzwilliam St. TS10: Redc 4D **49**
Five Acres TS8: Stain. 5B **130**
Flamborough Ho.
TS4: Midd 2A **102**
Flatts La. TS6: Norm, Nun . . . 3D **105**
TS7: Nun 3D **105**
(Bankfields Rd.)
TS7: Nun 1D **135**
(Crabtree Wlk.)
Flatts La. Dr. TS6: Norm. 4D **105**
Flatts Lane Woodland Country Pk.
. . . . 5E **105**
Flatts Lane Woodland Country
Pk. Nature Reserve 1C **134**
Flatts Lane Woodland Country
Pk. Vis. Cen. 5E **105**
Flaxton Ct. TS26: H'pool 5A **14**
Flaxton St. TS26: H'pool 5A **14**
Fleck Way TS17: Thorn T 4D **129**
Fleet, The TS10: Redc. 1E **63**
TS17: Thorn T 4E **99**
Fleet Av. TS24: H'pool. 3C **14**
Fleet Bri. Rd. TS18: Stock T . . . 1C **74**
TS20: Nort 1C **74**
TS23: Bill 5C **54**
Fleetham Gro.
TS18: Stock T 2A **96**
Fleetham Pl. TS1: Midd 3D **77**
Fleetham St. TS1: Midd 3D **77**
(Fleetham Pl.)
TS1: Midd. 4E **77**
(Kingston St.)
Fleet Ho. TS3: Midd 1F **103**
Fleet St. TS3: N Orm 3C **78**
Fleetwood Wlk. TS10: Redc . . . 2B **64**
Fleming Cl. TS19: Stock T. 2C **72**
Fleming Rd. TS6: S Ban 4A **80**
Fleming St. TS10: Redc. 3B **48**
Fletcher St. TS1: Midd. 3F **77**
Fletcher Wlk. TS25: H'pool 2D **19**
Flexley Av. TS3: Midd 3F **103**
Flint Wlk. TS26: H'pool. 1D **13**
Flixton Gro. TS22: Bill 5A **38**
Flodden Way TS23: Bill 3A **40**
Flora St. TS6: Est. 1E **105**
Florence Ct. TS17: Ing B 1B **150**
Florence Ho.
TS17: Thorn T 1C **98**
Florence St. TS2: Midd 2E **77**
Florida Gdns. TS5: Midd 4D **101**
Flotilla Ho. *TS24: H'pool. 3D 15*
(off Admiral Way)
Flounders Rd. TS15: Yarm . . . 5A **148**
FOGGY FURZE 2B **20**
Folkestone Cl. TS8: Hem. 5E **131**
Folland Dr. TS11: Marsk S 3B **66**
Fonteyn Ct. TS8: Hem 5E **131**
Fontwell Cl. TS19: Stock T 3A **72**
Forber Rd. TS4: Midd. 4F **101**
Forcett Cl. TS5: Midd. 2C **130**
Fordon Pl. TS4: Midd. 4A **102**
Ford Pl. TS18: Stock T. 4A **74**
Ford St. TS18: Stock T. 4A **74**
Fordwell Rd. TS19: Stock T. . . . 3A **72**
Fordyce Rd. TS8: Hem 5D **131**
(not continuous)
TS25: H'pool 4D **19**
Fordy Gro. TS17: Thorn T 5C **98**
Foreland Point TS17: Ing B . . . 3A **150**
Forest Dr. TS7: Orm. 1B **134**
Forester Cl. TS25: Seat C 3D **21**
Foresters Cl. TS22: Wyn 2D **37**
FORESTER'S LODGE RDBT. 3B **26**
Forest La. TS15: K'ton. 5A **160**
Forest M. TS17: Thorn T 2D **129**
Forest Pk. TS21: Stil 1B **50**
Forfar Av. TS4: Midd 1B **132**
Forfar Rd. TS25: H'pool. 4D **19**
Forge, The TS12: Brot. 2C **90**
Forget-Me-Not Gro.
TS19: Stock T 3D **73**
Formby Cl. TS27: H'pool 2C **6**
Formby Grn. TS4: Midd 4A **102**
Formby Wlk. TS16: Eag. 4C **126**
Forres Wlk. TS25: H'pool 4D **19**
Forster Ho. TS1: Midd 3F **77**
Forth Gro. TS25: H'pool. 4E **19**
Forth Rd. TS10: Redc 5A **48**
Fortrose Cl. TS16: Eag. 1C **148**
Forty Foot Rd. TS2: Midd 2D **77**
Forum Ct. TS3: N Orm. 4B **78**
Forum Leisure Cen. 1E **55**
Fosdyke Grn. TS3: Midd 2A **104**
Fossfeld TS19: Stock T 3A **72**
Foster St. TS12: Brot. 3A **90**
Foston Cl. TS20: Nort. 4F **53**
Foston Way TS18: Thorn T 5D **75**
Foundation Cl. TS10: Redc 2D **65**
Founders Ct. TS25: Grea 3E **31**
Foundry Way TS14: Guis 3D **139**
Fountain Ct. TS1: Midd 3F **77**
Fountains Av. TS17: Ing B. . . . 5C **128**
Fountains Cl. TS14: Guis. 2E **139**
(not continuous)
Fountains Ct. TS12: Skel 4D **89**
Fountains Cres. TS6: Est. 1D **105**
Fountains Dr. TS5: Midd 4D **101**
Fountain St. TS14: Guis. 2E **139**

Four Winds Ct. TS26: H'pool . . . 3D **13**
Fowler Cl. TS15: Yarm. 5E **149**
Fox Almshouses TS20: Nort . . . 5B **54**
Foxberry Av. TS5: Midd 2B **130**
Fox Cl. TS17: Ing B 4C **128**
Foxglove Cl. TS19: Stock T 3C **72**
TS26: H'pool 5D **7**
Foxgloves TS8: Coul N. 5C **132**
Foxheads Ct. TS1: Midd 3D **77**
Fox Hills TS12: Brot. 2C **90**
Fox Howe TS8: Coul N. 3B **132**
(not continuous)
Foxrush Cl. TS10: Redc. 3C **64**
Foxrush Farm Community Woodland 2F 63
Fox St. TS20: Nort. 1B **74**
Foxton Cl. TS15: Yarm. 4E **149**
Foxton Dr. TS23: Bill 2E **39**
Foxwood Dr. TS19: Stock T. . . . 3C **72**
Frampton Grn. TS3: Midd 4D **103**
France St. TS10: Redc. 3D **49**
Francis Wlk. *TS17: Thorn T. . . . 3C 98*
(off Cuthbert Cl.)
Frankfield M. TS9: Gt A. 2D **167**
Frankfield Pl. TS9: Gt A 1D **167**
Franklin Cl. TS18: Stock T. 2B **96**
Franklin Ct. TS17: Thorn T . . . 2D **129**
Fransham Rd. TS3: Midd 1D **103**
Fraser Ct. TS25: H'pool. 4D **19**
Fraser Gro. TS25: H'pool. 4D **19**
Fraser Rd. TS18: Stock T 3D **97**
Frederick St. TS3: N Orm 4C **78**
TS17: Thorn T 2C **98**
TS18: Stock T 4A **74**
Frederic St. TS24: H'pool 5E **9**
Fredric Ter. TS23: Bill 3D **57**
Freebrough Rd.
TS12: Moor 3B **142**
Freemantle Gro.
TS25: H'pool 4B **20**
Freight Rd. TS6: Midd 1E **61**
Fremantle Cres. TS4: Midd . . . 3F **101**
Fremington Wlk.
TS4: Midd 1B **132**
Frensham Dr. TS25: H'pool 2B **20**
Freshingham Cl. TS8: Hem . . . 5E **131**
Freville St. TS24: H'pool. 4C **14**
Friarage Gdns. TS24: H'pool . . . 1F **15**
Friar St. TS24: H'pool 1F **15**
Friarswood Cl. TS15: Yarm . . . 4E **149**
Friar Ter. TS24: H'pool. 1F **15**
Friendship La. TS24: H'pool . . . 1F **15**
Frimley Av. TS3: Midd. 1D **103**
Fritillary Pl. TS21: Nort. 3D **53**
Frobisher Cl. TS11: Marsk S . . . 5F **67**
Frobisher Rd.
TS17: Thorn T 2D **129**
Frocester Ct. TS17: Ing B 3E **127**
Frome Rd. TS20: Nort. 2B **74**
Front, The DL2: Mid R. 4A **144**
TS25: Seat C. 4F **21**
Front St. TS13: Carl H 3F **91**
TS21: Sed 4D **23**
TS25: Grea 3E **31**
TS27: Hart 4F **5**
Frosterley Gro. TS23: Bill. 3F **39**
Fry St. TS1: Midd 3F **77**
Fryup Cres. TS14: Guis 4D **139**
Fuchsia Gro. TS19: Stock T. . . . 5C **72**
Fudan Way TS17: Thorn T. 1C **98**
Fulbeck Cl. TS25: H'pool 3F **19**
Fulbeck Ct. TS23: Bill. 1F **55**
Fulbeck Rd. TS3: Midd 2A **104**
Fulford Gro. TS11: N Mar. 2F **85**
Fulford Way TS8: Mart. 5F **133**
Fuller Cres. TS20: Nort 5F **53**
Fullerton Way
TS17: Thorn T 1D **129**
Fulmar Head TS14: Guis 2B **138**
Fulmar Ho. TS24: H'pool. 3D **15**
Fulmar Rd. TS20: Nort 3A **54**
Fulmerton Cres. TS10: Redc . . . 4C **64**
FULTHORPE. 4A 36
Fulthorpe Av. TS24: H'pool 3E **7**
Fulthorpe Gro. TS22: Wyn. 2D **37**
Fulthorpe Rd. TS20: Nort. 5F **53**
Fulwood Av. TS4: Midd 3A **102**
Fun City
Stockton-on-Tees 1A 98
(off Skinner St.)
Fun Shack 3E 75
Furlongs, The TS10: Redc. 5D **49**
Furness St. TS24: H'pool. 2B **14**

G

Gable Ct. TS17: Thorn T 4D **99**
Gables, The TS4: Midd 1A **102**
TS7: Mart. 3C **132**
TS10: Redc 3B **48**
TS21: Sed 2C **22**
Gadebridge Cl. TS17: Ing B . . . 5F **127**
Gainford Av. TS5: Midd 3E **101**
Gainford Rd. TS19: Stock T. . . . 1C **96**
TS23: Bill 5F **39**
Gainford St. TS26: H'pool 4B **14**
Gainsborough Cl.
TS6: Norm. 4D **105**
Gainsborough Cres.
TS23: Bill. 3D **39**
Gainsborough Rd.
TS7: Mart. 2C **132**
Gaisgill Cl. TS7: Orm 4B **104**
Gala Bingo
Middlesbrough 5C 78
Gala Cl. TS25: Seat C 2E **21**
Galava Wlk. TS17: Ing B 5E **127**
Galgate Cl. TS7: Mart 3E **133**
GALLEY HILL 3B 138
Galleys Fld. Ct. TS24: H'pool . . . 5F **9**
Galloway Sands TS5: Midd . . . 3B **130**
Galsworthy Rd.
TS25: H'pool 2D **19**
Ganstead Way TS23: Bill 2F **39**
Ganton Cl. TS11: N Mar. 1A **86**
TS22: Bill 5A **38**
Garbutt St. TS18: Stock T 4B **74**
Garden Cl. TS9: Stokes 1B **168**
TS17: Thorn T 3B **98**
Gardenia Way TS23: Bill 5D **39**
Garden Pl. TS6: Norm. 2D **105**
Gardens, The TS4: Midd 3A **102**
Gardner Ho. TS25: H'pool 3D **19**
Garforth Cl. TS20: Nort 4F **53**
Garland Ho. TS24: H'pool 2C **14**
Garmon Cl. TS17: Ing B. 1F **149**
Garnet St. TS1: Midd 4E **77**
TS12: Salt 3C **68**
Garrett Wlk. TS1: Midd 4D **77**
Garrick Gro. TS25: H'pool 2E **19**
Garrowby Rd. TS3: Midd 2C **102**
Garsbeck Way TS7: Orm 4B **104**
Garsdale Cl. TS15: Yarm. 1B **160**
Garsdale Grn. TS3: Midd. 1D **103**
Garside Dr. TS24: H'pool. 4A **8**
Garstang Cl. TS7: Mart 3F **133**
Garston Gro. TS25: H'pool. 4B **20**
Garth, The TS8: Coul N 1B **154**
TS9: Stokes 1B **168**
TS11: Marsk S. 3C **66**
TS12: Brot 2C **90**
TS20: Nort 5A **54**
TS21: Sed 3D **23**
Garth Cl. TS21: Carlt 5C **50**
Garth Ends TS13: Stait. 1C **120**
Garth Wlk. TS3: Midd 2C **102**
Garvin Cl. TS3: Midd. 2C **102**
Gascoyne Cl. TS7: Mart. 2E **133**
Gaskell La. TS13: Loft. 5B **92**
Gatenby Dr. TS5: Midd 2C **130**
Gatesgarth Cl. TS24: H'pool 5B **8**
Gatley Wlk. TS16: Prest T. . . . 2D **127**
Gatwick Grn. TS3: Midd 1D **103**
Gayle Moor Cl. TS17: Ing B. . . 3B **150**
Gayton Sands TS5: Midd 3B **130**
Gedney Av. TS3: Midd. 4D **103**
Geltsdale TS5: Midd 2C **130**
Gemini Cen. TS24: H'pool. 4B **14**
Geneva Dr. TS10: Redc 5C **48**
Gentian Way TS19: Stock T. . . . 3C **72**
George Stephenson Blvd.
TS19: Stock T 1B **72**
George Stephenson Ct.
TS18: Stock T 4A **98**
George Stephenson Ho.
TS17: Thorn T 1B **98**
George St. TS10: Redc 4D **49**
TS14: Guis. 1D **139**
TS17: Thorn T 2C **98**
TS24: H'pool 3C **14**
George Ter. TS12: Brot 3B **90**
Georgiana Cl. TS17: Thorn T. . . 2C **98**
Georgian Theatre, The 5B 74
Geranium Cl. TS23: Bill. 5D **39**
GERRICK 5E 143
Gerrie St. TS12: Boo 3C **112**
Ghyll, The TS27: Elw. 4D **11**
Gibb Sq. TS24: H'pool 5F **9**
Gibraltar Rd. TS16: Eag. 4F **125**
Gibson Gro. TS24: H'pool 2D **7**
Gibson St. TS3: N Orm 4C **78**
Gifford St. TS5: Midd. 1E **101**
Gilberti Pl. TS24: H'pool 3F **7**
Gilkes St. TS1: Midd 3E **77**
Gilkes Wlk. TS4: Midd. 4B **102**
Gillercomb TS10: Redc 4C **64**
Gilling Rd. TS19: Stock T 5B **72**
Gilling Wlk. TS3: Midd 1C **102**
Gilling Way TS10: Redc. 2E **65**
Gillpark Gro. TS25: Seat C 4D **21**
Gill St. TS12: Salt 5C **68**
TS14: Guis 1E **139**
TS24: H'pool 4B **14**
Gilmonby Rd. TS3: Midd. 4D **103**
Gilmour St. TS17: Thorn T 3C **98**
Gilpin Ho. TS20: Nort 5A **54**
Gilpin Rd. TS17: Thorn T. 4C **98**
Gilpin Sq. TS19: Stock T 3F **73**
Gilside Rd. TS23: Bill. 5F **39**
Gilsland Cl. TS5: Midd 2B **130**
Gilsland Gro. TS6: Norm. 2D **105**
Gilwern Ct. TS17: Ing B 2F **149**
Girrick Cl. TS8: Hem 5C **130**
Girton Av. TS3: Midd 4D **103**
Gisborne Gro. TS18: Stock T. . . 2C **96**
Gisburn Av. TS3: Midd. 3D **103**
Gisburn Rd. TS23: Bill 5F **39**
Gladesfield Rd. TS20: Nort. . . . 2B **74**
Gladstone Ind. Est.
TS17: Thorn T 2C **98**
Gladstone St. TS6: Est. 1F **105**
TS12: Brot 3A **90**
TS13: Carl H. 3F **91**
TS13: Loft 5C **92**
TS17: Thorn T 2C **98**
TS18: Stock T 2A **98**
TS24: H'pool. 1F **15**
Gladys Worthy Cl.
TS25: H'pool 1E **19**
Glaisdale Av. TS5: Midd 4E **101**
TS10: Redc. 1F **63**
TS19: Stock T. 3E **73**
Glaisdale Cl. TS6: Est 5A **82**
Glaisdale Gro. TS25: Seat C . . . 4E **21**
Glaisdale Rd. TS6: Est 5A **82**
TS15: Yarm 4E **149**
Glamis Gro. TS4: Midd 3A **102**
Glamis Rd. TS23: Bill 4C **38**
Glamis Wlk. TS25: H'pool 4E **19**
Glamorgan Gro.
TS26: H'pool 1D **13**
Glasgow St. TS17: Thorn T 2C **98**
Glastonbury Av. TS6: Est. 1E **105**
Glastonbury Ho. TS3: Midd . . . 3E **103**
Glastonbury Rd. TS12: Skel . . . 4D **89**
Glastonbury Wlk.
TS26: H'pool 1E **13**
Gleaston Cres. TS4: Midd 4A **102**

Gleaston Wlk. TS4: Midd. 4A **102**
GLEBE. 4E 53
Glebe, The TS20: Nort. 4E **53**
Glebe Gdns. TS8: Stain 5C **130**
TS13: Eas. 3A **118**
Glebe Gth. TS13: Eas. 2A **118**
Glebe Rd. TS1: Midd 4D **77**
TS9: Stokes 2C **168**
Gledstone TS22: Wyn 3A **26**
Glen, The TS16: Egg 2C **148**
Glenarm Rd. TS22: Wyn 4F **27**
Glenbury Gro. TS10: Redc 4F **65**
Glencairn Gro. TS25: H'pool . . . 4D **19**
Glendale TS14: Guis 4A **138**
Glendale Av. TS26: H'pool 4F **13**
Glendale Rd. TS5: Midd 4E **101**
Glendue Cl. TS7: Nun 4A **134**
Gleneagles Cl. TS22: Bill. 5A **38**
Gleneagles Ct. TS4: Midd 4A **102**
Gleneagles Rd. TS4: Midd. . . . 4F **101**
TS11: N Mar. 1A **86**
TS27: H'pool 2C **6**
Glenfall Cl. TS22: Bill 5A **38**
Glenfield Cl. TS19: Stock T. . . . 5A **72**
Glenfield Dr. TS5: Midd 4E **101**
Glenfield Rd. TS19: Stock T . . . 5A **72**
Glenfield Ter. TS13: Loft 5D **93**
Glenhow Gdns. TS12: Salt. 4C **68**
Glenluce Cl. TS16: Eag 5C **126**
Glenmor Gro. TS6: Norm. 1C **104**
Glenn Cres. TS7: Mart. 3D **133**
Glenside TS12: Salt. 4D **69**
Glenston Cl. TS26: H'pool 2C **12**
Glentower Gro.
TS25: Seat C 4D **21**
Glentworth Av. TS3: Midd 2A **104**
Glevum Av. TS17: Ing B. 5E **127**
Globe Theatre 5A 74
Gloucester Cl. TS7: Nun 3A **134**
Gloucester Rd. TS14: Guis . . . 4D **139**
Gloucester St. TS25: H'pool . . . 1A **20**
Gloucester Ter. TS23: Bill 1F **55**
Glyder Ct. TS17: Ing B 1F **149**
Goals Soccer Cen.
Middlesbrough 5B 76
Goathland Dr. TS25: Seat C. . . . 5D **21**
Goathland Gro. TS14: Guis . . . 4D **139**
Goathland Rd. TS6: Est 5F **81**
Gofton Pl. TS6: Est 4D **81**
Gold Crest TS14: Guis 2B **138**
Goldcrest Cl. TS17: Ing B 5B **128**
TS26: H'pool 5D **7**
Golden Boy Green Community Cen.
. . . . 2B 80
GOLDEN FLATS 5B 20
Golden Flatts Apartments
TS25: H'pool 4C **20**
Golden Lion M.
TS9: Stokes 1C **168**
Golden Mdws. TS25: H'pool . . . 4B **20**
Golden Way TS13: Loft 5C **92**
Goldfinch Rd. TS26: H'pool. 5D **7**
Goldrill Gdns. TS10: Redc. 1B **64**
Goldsmith Av. TS24: H'pool. 3E **7**
Goldsmith Cl. TS23: Bill 3D **39**
Gooch Cl. TS19: Stock T 1B **72**
Goodrich Way TS17: Ing B . . . 5A **128**
Goodwin Cl. TS10: Redc 4B **64**
Goodwin Wlk. TS24: H'pool. . . . 4C **14**
Goodwood Rd. TS10: Redc 2D **65**
Goodwood Sq.
TS17: Thorn T 2F **99**
Gooseberry Cl. TS26: H'pool. . . . 4E **7**
Goose Gth. TS16: Eag 1B **148**
Goose Pastures
TS15: Yarm 4C **148**
Gooseport Rd.
TS18: Stock T 4C **74**
Gordon Cres. TS6: Gran. 3E **81**
Gordon Rd. TS10: Redc. 4A **48**
Gore Sands TS5: Midd. 2A **130**
Gorman Rd. TS5: Midd 1D **101**
Gorsefields Ct. TS6: Est. 3E **105**
Gorton Cl. TS23: Bill 4C **38**
Gosford M. TS2: Midd 2E **77**
Gosford St. TS2: Midd 2F **77**
Gosforth Av. TS10: Redc 4D **49**
Goshawk Rd. TS26: H'pool 5D **7**
Gough Cl. TS1: Midd 4D **77**
Goulton Cl. TS15: Yarm 4E **149**
Gower Wlk. TS26: H'pool. 5E **7**
Gowsers Dr. TS15: Yarm 1A **160**
Grace Cl. TS25: Seat C 5E **21**
Graffenberg St. TS10: Redc . . . 3D **49**
Grafton Cl. TS14: Guis. 3E **139**
Graham St. TS13: Live. 5A **92**
TS24: H'pool 5E **9**
Graham Wlk. TS25: H'pool 4E **19**
Grainger Cl. TS16: Eag 4B **126**
Grainger St. TS24: H'pool 2B **14**
Grainton Ct. TS18: Stock T 5D **75**
Grammar School La.
TS15: Yarm 4B **148**
Grampian Rd. TS12: Skel 3C **88**
TS23: Bill 1D **55**
Granary, The TS22: Wyn 5C **26**
Grange Av. TS18: Stock T 4D **73**
TS23: Bill 4E **55**
TS26: H'pool. 3F **13**
Grange Bus. Cen., The
TS23: Bill 3F **55**
Grange Cl. TS6: Gran. 3E **81**
TS26: H'pool 3E **13**
Grange Cres. TS7: Mart. 3D **133**
Grange Dr. TS9: Stokes 1B **168**
Grange Est. TS6: Laze 3C **82**
Grange Farm TS8: Coul N 3B **132**
Grange Farm Rd. TS6: Gran . . . 3E **81**
GRANGEFIELD 5D 73
Grangefield Rd.
TS18: Stock T 5D **73**
Grangefields TS12: Brot 2A **90**
Grange La. TS13: Loft 3E **93**
Grange Rd. TS1: Midd 3E **77**
(not continuous)
TS17: Thorn T 3C **98**
TS20: Nort 1B **74**
TS26: H'pool. 3F **13**
GRANGETOWN 3E 81
Grangetown By-Pass
TS6: Midd, Gran. 2B **80**
Grange Vw. TS22: Wolv. 3C **38**
Grangeville Av.
TS19: Stock T 5A **72**
Grange Wood TS8: Coul N 3F **131**
Grantham Av. TS26: H'pool 4F **13**
Grantham Grn. TS4: Midd 5B **102**
Grantham Rd. TS20: Nort 4F **53**
Grantley Av. TS3: Midd 5A **80**
Grant St. TS10: Redc. 3C **48**
Granville Av. TS26: H'pool. 3F **13**
Granville Gro. TS20: Nort 1B **74**
Granville Pl. TS26: H'pool 3F **13**
Granville Rd. TS1: Midd 5E **77**
Granville Ter. TS10: Redc 3D **49**
Granwood Rd. TS6: Est 2F **105**
Grasby Cl. TS3: Midd. 2A **104**
Grasmere Av. TS5: Midd 5C **100**
Grasmere Cres. TS12: Skel 4B **88**
Grasmere Dr. TS6: Norm. 1C **104**
Grasmere Rd. TS10: Redc. 5C **48**
TS18: Stock T. 5E **73**
Grasmere St. TS26: H'pool 5A **14**
Grass Cft. TS21: Long N 1A **124**
Grassholme Av. *TS5: Midd . . . 1B 100*
(off Greenbank Av.)
Grassholme Rd.
TS26: H'pool 3C **12**
Grassholme Way TS16: Eag. . . 4F **125**
Grassholm Rd. TS20: Nort 1B **74**
Grassington Grn.
TS17: Ing B 3B **150**
Grassington Rd. TS4: Midd . . . 3A **102**
Gravel Hole Nature Reserve
. . . . 2A 54
Graygarth Rd. TS3: Midd. 2C **102**
Gray's Rd. TS18: Stock T. 5E **73**
Gray St. TS2: Midd. 2F **77**
GRAYTHORP 4C 32
Graythorp Ind. Est.
TS25: H'pool 4D **33**
Graythorp Rd. TS25: H'pool. . . . 4C **32**
Great Auk TS14: Guis. 2B **138**
GREAT AYTON 2D 167
Gt. Ayton Rd.
TS9: Nun, Gt A. 4C **156**
Great Ayton Station (Rail) . . . 2F 167
GREAT BROUGHTON 5F 169
Gt. Charles Gdns.
TS13: Loft 5C **92**
GREATHAM 3E 31
Greatham Av.
TS18: Stock T 4D **75**
Greatham Cl. TS5: Midd 2D **131**
Greatham St. TS25: H'pool 1C **20**
Greear Garth TS14: Guis 2D **139**
Green, The TS4: Midd 3A **102**
TS9: Gt A 2D **167**
TS10: Redc. 1E **63**
TS11: Marsk S 4B **66**
TS12: Salt 1B **88**
TS15: K'ton 4D **161**
TS16: Egg 2C **148**
TS17: Thorn T 1C **128**
TS20: Nort 4A **54**
TS21: Long N. 1A **124**
TS22: Wolv. 2C **38**
TS23: Bill 4D **55**
TS23: Cowp B 4C **40**
TS25: Grea 3E **31**
TS25: Seat C 3E **21**
TS27: Elw. 4D **11**
Greenabella Marsh (Nature Reserve)
. . . . 1D 43
Greenacre Cl. TS9: Gt A 3C **166**
TS11: Marsk S. 4C **66**
Greenacres TS8: Stain. 5B **130**
Greenbank Av. TS5: Midd 1B **100**
Greenbank Ct. TS26: H'pool . . . 3E **13**
Greenbank Ter. TS12: Boo. . . . 2B **112**
Green Cl. TS7: Nun 4A **134**
Greencroft TS10: Redc. 3A **64**
Greencroft Wlk. TS3: Midd . . . 3E **103**
Green Dragon La.
TS18: Stock T 5B 74
(off Green Dragon Yd.)
Green Dragon Mus. 5B 74
Green Dragon Yd.
TS18: Stock T 5B **74**
Green Farm Cl. TS22: Wolv. . . . 2C **38**
Greenfield Dr. TS16: Eag. 5B **126**
Greenfields Way
TS18: Stock T 1A **96**
Greenfinch Cl. TS26: H'pool 5E **7**
Greenford Wlk. TS3: Midd. . . . 2A **104**
Greenham Cl. TS3: Midd. 2A **104**
Greenhead Cl. TS8: Hem. 3E **131**
Greenhow Gro. TS25: Seat C. . . 4E **21**
Greenhow Rd. TS3: Midd 1C **102**
Greenhow Wlk. TS10: Redc. . . . 2B **64**
Greenland Av. TS5: Midd. 2A **100**
Greenland Rd. TS24: H'pool 5C **8**
(not continuous)
Greenlands Rd. TS10: Redc . . . 5E **49**
Green La. TS5: Midd 4B **100**
TS7: Nun 5E **155**
TS8: Newb, Nun 5E **155**
TS9: L Ayt 5C **166**
TS10: Marsk S, Redc 3A **66**
TS12: Skel 5B **88**
TS15: Yarm 2A **160**
TS17: Thorn T 5B **98**
TS19: Stock T 2D **73**
Greenlea TS27: Elw. 4C **10**
Green Leas TS21: Carlt 5C **50**
Greenlee Cl. TS17: Ing B. 2A **150**
Greenock Cl. TS11: N Mar 2F **85**
Greenock Rd. TS25: H'pool 4E **19**
Green Rd. TS12: Skel 4B **88**

Green's Beck Rd.
TS18: Stock T 2C 96
Green Scar TS10: Redc 3E 65
Greensforge Dr.
TS17: Ing B 4F 127
Greens Gro. TS18: Stock T 2C 96
Greenshank Cl. TS26: H'pool . . . 5D 7
Greenside TS6: Norm 4C 104
TS17: Ing B 5B 128
TS25: Grea 3E 31
Greenside Vw. TS12: Boo 2B 112
Green's La. TS18: Stock T. 1C 96
Greenstones Rd. TS10: Redc. . . 2E 65
Green St. TS24: H'pool 5C 14
Greens Valley Dr.
TS18: Stock T 2C 96
Green Ter. TS25: Seat C. 4E 21
Green Vale Gro.
TS19: Stock T 1A 96
Green Way TS7: Nun 4A 134
Greenway TS6: Est. 1E 105
TS17: Ing B 5B 128
Greenway, The TS3: Midd 5F 79
Greenway Ct. TS3: Midd 5F 79
Greenwood Av. TS5: Midd. . . . 3D 101
Greenwood Rd.
TS18: Stock T 2C 96
TS23: Bill 1F 55
TS24: H'pool 2B 14
Greenwood Wlk. TS10: Redc. . . 2C 64
Grenadier Cl. TS18: Stock T . . . 5D 73
Grendale Ct. TS13: Loft. 5C 92
Grendon Wlk. TS3: Midd 4D 103
Grenville Cl. TS11: Marsk S . . . 5E 67
Grenville Rd.
TS17: Thorn T 2D 129
Gresham Rd. TS1: Midd 4D 77
Gresley Ct. TS12: Salt 4C 68
Greta Av. TS25: H'pool 2A 20
Greta Rd. TS10: Redc 5A 48
TS12: Skel 3C 88
TS20: Nort 5A 54
Greta St. TS1: Midd. 4D 77
TS12: Salt 5C 68
Gretton Av. TS4: Midd 5B 102
Grewgrass La.
TS11: Marsk S, N Mar 4D 65
Greyfriars Ct. TS24: H'pool 3E 7
Greylands Av. TS20: Nort 1B 74
Greymouth Cl.
TS18: Stock T 2C 96
Greys Ct. TS17: Ing B 1B 150
Greystoke Ct. TS5: Midd 4C 100
Greystoke Gro. TS10: Redc. . . . 3C 64
Greystoke Wlk. TS10: Redc. . . . 3C 64
Greystone Rd. TS6: Gran 2F 81
GREYSTONES RDBT. 5B 82
Grey St. TS20: Nort 2B 74
Grey Towers Dr. TS7: Nun 5A 134
Grey Towers Farm Cotts.
TS7: Nun 5B 134
Grey Towers Gdns.
TS7: Nun 2B 156
Grey Towers Hall TS7: Nun . . . 2B 156
GREY TOWERS RDBT. 1C 156
Greywood Cl. TS27: H'pool 2C 6
Gribdale Rd. TS3: Midd. 1D 103
Griffin Rd. TS4: Midd. 1A 102
Griffiths Cl. TS15: Yarm. 1B 160
Griffiths Rd. TS6: Gran 4E 81
Grimston Wlk. TS3: Midd 1B 102
Grimwood Av. TS3: Midd. 4E 79
GRINDON 3D 35
Grindon La.
TS21: Thorpe T 3C 34
Grinkle Av. TS3: Midd 3D 103
Grinkle Ct. TS14: Guis 1E 139
Grinkle La. TS13: Eas 5F 117
Grinkle Rd. TS10: Redc 5F 47
Grinton Rd. TS18: Stock T. 3B 96
Grisedale Cl. TS5: Midd 2C 130
Grisedale Cres. TS6: Gran. 4F 81
TS16: Egg 2C 148
Gritten Sq. TS24: H'pool 4C 8
Groom Ter. TS25: H'pool 5A 20
Grosmont Cl. TS10: Redc 3C 64
Grosmont Dr. TS23: Bill 5C 38
Grosmont Pl. TS6: Est 5F 81
Grosmont Rd. TS6: Est. 5F 81
TS25: Seat C 5E 21
Grosvenor Ct. TS17: Ing B. . . . 2B 150
Grosvenor Gdns.
TS6: Norm 2D 105
TS26: H'pool 3A 14
(off Grosvenor St.)
Grosvenor Pl. TS14: Guis 2D 139
Grosvenor Rd. TS5: Midd 2C 100
TS19: Stock T 1C 96
TS22: Bill 5B 38
Grosvenor Sq. TS14: Guis. . . . 2D 139
Grosvenor St. TS26: H'pool. . . . 3A 14
(not continuous)
Grosvenor Ter.
TS13: Carl H 3F 91
Grove, The TS5: Midd 3D 131
TS7: Mart. 5D 103
TS9: Gt A 2C 166
TS14: Guis 4B 138
TS15: Yarm 5C 148
TS25: Grea 3E 31
TS26: H'pool. 3F 13
Grove Bank TS15: K'ton. 4C 160
Grove Cl. TS26: H'pool. 4F 13
Grove Hill TS13: Skin 2A 92
Grove Rd. TS3: N Orm. 4B 78
TS10: Redc 4D 49
TS13: Skin 2A 92
Groves, The TS18: Stock T 2F 97
Groves St. TS24: H'pool. 1F 15
Grove St. TS18: Stock T. 2F 97
Grove Ter. TS20: Nort 2B 74
Grundales Dr.
TS11: Marsk S 4C 66
Guernsey Wlk. TS14: Guis . . . 3D 139
Guildford Ct. TS6: Norm 4D 105
Guildford Rd. TS6: Norm. 4C 104
TS23: Bill 4C 38
Guillemot Cl. TS26: H'pool 5D 7
GUISBOROUGH 2E 139
Guisborough By-Pass
TS14: Guis 1C 138
Guisborough Ct. TS6: Est. 1F 105
Guisborough Forest
& Walkway Vis. Cen. . . . 3F 137
Guisborough Ho.
TS4: Midd 2B 102
Guisborough La.
TS12: Skel 1F 111
Guisborough Leisure Cen. . . . 5F 109
Guisborough Mus., The 1E 139
Guisborough Priory (remains)
. . . . 1F 139
Guisborough Rd. TS7: Nun . . . 5A 134
TS9: Gt A 2C 166
TS12: Moor 3A 142
TS12: Salt 5B 68
Guisborough St. TS6: Est. 2F 105
Guisborough Swim & Fitness Cen.
. . . . 1D 139
Guiseley Way TS16: Eag 3B 126
Gullane Gro. TS25: H'pool. 4E 19
Gulliver Rd. TS25: H'pool 2D 19
Gun Gutter TS13: Stait. 1C 120
Gunnergate Cl. TS12: Salt. 4A 68
Gunnergate La. TS7: Mart. . . . 4C 132
TS8: Coul N 4C 132
Gunnerside Rd.
TS19: Stock T 5A 72
Gunners Va. TS22: Wyn 4A 26
Gurney Ho. TS1: Midd 3F 77
Gurney St. TS1: Midd. 3F 77
TS11: N Mar. 1A 86
Guthrie Av. TS5: Midd 3A 100
Guthrie Wlk. TS25: H'pool. 4D 19
Gwynn Cl. TS19: Stock T. 4A 72
Gym World 2A 78
Gypsy La. TS7: Mart, Nun 3E 133
Gypsy Lane Station (Rail) . . . 2A 134

H

Hackforth Rd. TS18: Stock T . . . 3B 96
Hackness Wlk. TS5: Midd 4E 101
Hackworth Ct. TS18: Stock T. . . 4A 74
Hadasia Gdns.
TS19: Stock T 5C 72
Haddon Rd. TS23: Bill 5C 38
Haddon St. TS1: Midd 5F 77
Hadleigh Cl. TS21: Sed 5C 22
Hadleigh Cres. TS4: Midd 2A 102
Hadleigh Wlk. TS17: Ing B . . . 5A 128
Hadlow Wlk. *TS3: Midd. 1D 103*
(off Homerton Rd.)
Hadnall Cl. TS5: Midd 5A 100
Hadrian Way TS17: Ing B 4E 127
Hadston Cl. TS10: Redc 3D 65
Haffron Av. TS18: Stock T 4B 74
HAGG FARM RDBT. 2E 89
Hailsham Av.
TS17: Thorn T 5D 129
Haldane Gro. TS25: H'pool 4E 19
Halegrove Ct. TS18: Stock T . . . 5A 98
Hale Rd. TS23: Bill. 4E 39
Halidon Way TS23: Bill 4F 39
Halifax Cl. TS11: Marsk S 4B 66
Halifax Rd. TS17: Thorn T. . . . 2D 129
Hall Cl. TS11: Marsk S 4C 66
TS21: Carlt 5C 50
Hall Close, The TS7: Orm 4A 104
Hallcroft Cl. TS23: Bill. 4D 55
Hall Dr. TS5: Midd 5C 100
Hall Farm Cl. TS22: Wolv 3B 38
Hallgarth TS9: Gt Bro. 5F 169
Hallgarth Cl. TS5: Midd. 2C 130
Hallgate Cl. TS18: Stock T 3A 96
Hall Grounds TS13: Loft 5C 92
Hallifield St. TS20: Nort 2B 74
Hall Lea TS21: Sed 3C 22
Hall Moor Cl. TS15: K'ton 4D 161
Halton Cl. TS23: Bill. 2E 39
Halton Ct. TS3: Midd 5A 80
TS23: Bill 2E 39
Halyard Way TS3: Midd. 2B 78
Hambledon Cres. TS12: Skel. . . 3C 88
Hambledon Rd. TS5: Midd . . . 2B 100
Hambleton Av. TS10: Redc 2A 64
Hambleton Cres.
TS11: Marsk S 5E 67
Hambleton Ga. TS9: Stokes . . 2C 168
Hambletonian Yd.
TS18: Stock T 1A 98
(off West Row)
Hambleton Rd. TS7: Nun. 3B 134
Hambleton Sq. TS23: Bill 1C 54
Hamilton Ct. TS21: Thorpe T . . . 2E 51
Hamilton Gro. TS6: Norm 5B 80
TS10: Redc 4A 48
Hamilton Rd. TS19: Stock T . . . 3F 73
TS25: H'pool 4E 19
Hammond Cl. TS7: Mart 3C 132
Hampden St. TS6: S Ban. 3A 80
Hampden Way
TS17: Thorn T 2D 129
Hampshire Grn. TS20: Nort. . . . 2C 74
Hampstead, The TS10: Redc. . . 2E 65
Hampstead Gdns.
TS26: H'pool 3E 13
Hampstead Gro. TS6: Norm . . 4C 104
Hampstead Rd. TS6: Norm . . . 4C 104
Hampstead Way TS5: Midd . . . 3B 130
Hampton Cl. TS7: Nun. 3A 134
Hampton Gro. TS10: Redc. 5E 49
Hampton Rd. TS18: Stock T . . . 2E 97
Hamsterley Rd.
TS19: Stock T 2C 72
Hamsterley Way TS12: Skel . . . 3C 88
Hanbury Cl. TS17: Ing B 5B 128
Handale Cl. TS14: Guis. 2A 140

Handale Ho. Rd. TS13: Eas . . . 5F **117**
Handley Cl. TS18: Stock T 1F **127**
TS25: Seat C 1E **33**
Hankin Rd. TS3: N Orm 4B **78**
Hanover Ct. TS20: Nort 5F **53**
Hanover Gdns. TS5: Midd 2C **100**
Hanover Ho. TS12: Salt 3C **68**
Hanover Pde. TS20: Nort 5F **53**
Hanover Point TS20: Nort 5F **53**
Hanson Ct. TS10: Redc 4C **48**
Hanson Gro. TS3: Midd 5F **79**
Hanson Sq. TS24: H'pool 3C **14**
Hanson St. TS10: Redc 4C **48**
Hanzard Dr. TS22: Wyn 5E **27**
Harbottle Cl. TS17: Ing B 2A **150**
Harbourne Gdns.
TS5: Midd 2D **131**
Harbour Wlk. TS24: H'pool 2C **14**
Harcourt Rd. TS6: S Ban 3F **79**
Harcourt St. TS26: H'pool 3F **13**
Hardale Gro. TS10: Redc. 1A **64**
Harding Row TS20: Nort 1B **74**
Hardknott Gro. TS10: Redc 5B **48**
HARDWICK 1B 72
Hardwick Av. TS5: Midd 4C **100**
Hardwick Ct. TS26: H'pool. 5C **12**
Hardwick Hall Country Pk.
Sedgefield 3B 22
Hardwick Pk. Vis. Cen. 4B 22
Hardwick Rd. TS6: S Ban 2A **80**
TS19: Stock T 1C **72**
TS21: Sed 3C **22**
TS23: Bill 5F **39**
Hardy Gro. TS23: Bill. 3D **39**
Harebell Cl. TS12: Skel 5E **89**
TS17: Ing B 4B **128**
Harehills Rd. TS5: Midd 2B **100**
Haresfield Way
TS17: Ing B 5B **128**
Hareshaw Cl. TS17: Ing B 2A **150**
Harestones TS22: Wyn 4B **26**
Harewood Cres.
TS19: Stock T 3B **72**
Harewood Ho. TS4: Midd 2B **102**
Harewood Rd.
TS17: Thorn T 2D **99**
Harewood St. TS1: Midd 5E **77**
Harewood Way TS10: Redc 2E **65**
Harford St. TS1: Midd 5D **77**
Harker Cl. TS15: Yarm. 5B **148**
Harland Pl. TS20: Nort 5B **54**
Harlech Cl. TS6: Est. 5E **81**
Harlech Ct. TS17: Ing B. 1F **149**
Harlech Gro. TS11: N Mar. 2A **86**
Harlech Wlk. TS26: H'pool 1E **13**
Harley Ct. TS18: Stock T 4F **97**
Harlow Cres. TS17: Thorn T . . . 5E **99**
Harlsey Cres.
TS18: Stock T 3C **96**
Harlsey Gro. TS18: Stock T. . . . 3C **96**
Harlsey Rd. TS18: Stock T 3C **96**
Harold Hornsey Sq.
TS24: H'pool 1A ***14***
(off Tommy McGuigan Gro.)
Harpenden Wlk. TS3: Midd . . . 1D **103**
Harper Pde. TS18: Stock T 3D **97**
Harpers Grn. TS20: Nort 4D **53**
Harper Ter. TS18: Stock T 3D **97**
Harrier Cl. TS17: Thorn T 1C **128**
TS26: H'pool 1D **13**
Harriet Ho. *TS17: Thorn T. 1B* ***98***
(off Sorbonne Cl.)
Harrington Rd. TS10: Redc 3C **64**
Harris Ct. TS17: Thorn T. 4D **99**
Harris Gro. TS25: H'pool 4E **19**
Harrison Pl. TS24: H'pool 4F **7**
Harrison St. TS3: N Orm 4C **78**
Harris St. TS1: Midd 3E **77**
Harris Wlk. *TS14: Guis 3D* ***139***
(off Dorset Rd.)
Harrogate Cres. TS5: Midd . . . 2E **101**
Harrowgate La.
TS19: Stock T 3A **72**
Harrow Rd. TS5: Midd 3C **100**
TS18: Stock T. 1E **97**
Harrow St. TS25: H'pool 1A **20**
Harsley Wlk. TS3: Midd 1D **103**
HART 4F 5
Hart Av. TS26: H'pool. 2E **13**
HARTBURN 2D 97
Hartburn Av. TS18: Stock T 1D **97**
Hartburn Ct. TS5: Midd 1C **130**
Hartburn La. TS18: Stock T 2E **97**
Hartburn M. TS18: Stock T 2C **96**
Hartburn Village
TS18: Stock T 3D **97**
Hart Church. 3A 6
Hart Cl. TS19: Stock T. 2D **73**
Harter Cl. TS7: Nun 4A **134**
Hartfields Mnr. TS26: H'pool 5E **7**
Hartforth Av. TS5: Midd 2C **130**
Hartington Cl.
TS17: Thorn T 3C **98**
Hartington Rd. TS1: Midd 3E **77**
TS18: Stock T 1A **98**
Hartington St. TS13: Loft. 4A **92**
Hartland Gro. TS3: Midd 3E **103**
Hart La. TS26: H'pool 4A **6**
TS27: Hart 4A **6**
Hart La. Cotts. TS26: H'pool . . . 2F **13**
HARTLEPOOL. 4B 14
Hartlepool Art Gallery. 3C 14
Hartlepool Cl. TS19: Stock T. . . 2C **72**
Hartlepool Crematorium
TS25: H'pool 3A **20**
Hartlepool Golf Course 1E 7
Hartlepool Ind. Est.
TS24: H'pool 5A **8**
Hartlepool Power Station Vis. Cen.
. . . . 4F 33
Hartlepool Rd. TS21: Sed 1C **24**
TS22: Wyn 1C **24**
Hartlepool St Hilda's Parish Church
. . . . 1F 15
(off Church Cl.)
Hartlepool's Maritime Experience
. . . . 2C 14
Hartlepool Station (Rail) 3C 14
Hartlepool Town Hall Theatre
. . . . 3B 14
Hartlepool United FC 3B 14
Hartley Cl. TS26: H'pool 3A **14**
Hartley St. TS26: H'pool 3A **14**
Hartoft Sq. TS26: H'pool 2A **14**
Harton Av. TS22: Bill 5A **38**
Harton Cl. TS10: Redc 1E **63**
Hart Pastures TS27: Hart. 4A **6**
Hart Reservoirs (Nature Reserve)
. . . . 4D 7
Hart Rd. TS27: H'pool 3D **7**
Hartsbourne Cres.
TS11: N Mar. 2F **85**
Hartside Gdns. TS26: H'pool. . . 2D **13**
Hartside Gro. TS19: Stock T . . . 2E **73**
HART STATION 2D 7
Hartville Rd. TS24: H'pool. 1C **6**
Hartwith Dr. TS19: Stock T 5B **52**
Harvard Av. TS17: Thorn T 1C **98**
Harvester Cl. TS25: Seat C 2D **21**
Harvester Ct. TS7: Mart. 1B **132**
Harvey Ct. TS10: Redc. 1F **63**
Harvey Wlk. TS25: H'pool 2D **19**
Harvington Chase
TS8: Coul N 4B **132**
Harwal Rd. TS10: Redc 4A **48**
Harwell Cl. TS4: Midd 3A **102**
Harwell Dr. TS19: Stock T. 3A **72**
Harwich Cl. TS10: Redc. 2F **65**
Harwich Gro. TS25: H'pool 4B **20**
Harwood Ct. TS2: Midd. 1D **77**
TS18: Stock T. 5E **75**
Hasguard Way TS17: Ing B . . . 2E **149**
Hasledon Gro. TS21: Sed 5C **22**
Hastings, The TS6: Norm 2D **105**
Hastings Cl. TS7: Nun. 3A **134**
TS17: Thorn T 3C **128**
Hastings Ho. TS3: Midd. 3E **103**
Hastings Pl. TS24: H'pool 4F **7**
Hastings Way TS23: Bill 4A **40**
Haswell Av. TS25: H'pool 2B **20**
Haswell Ct. TS20: Nort 3B **74**
Hatchlands Pk. TS17: Ing B. . . 4A **128**
Hatfield Av. TS5: Midd. 4C **100**
Hatfield Cl. TS16: Eag 5A **126**
TS25: H'pool 5B **20**
Hatfield Rd. TS23: Bill 5F **39**
Hatherley Ct. TS3: Midd 5E **79**
Hatterall Ct. TS17: Ing B 2F **149**
Hauxley Cl. TS10: Redc. 2F **65**
Hauxwell's Yd. TS15: Yarm. . . 3B **148**
Havelock St. TS17: Thorn T. . . . 3C **98**
TS24: H'pool 4D **15**
Haven Grn. TS24: H'pool. 4D **9**
Haven Wlk. TS24: H'pool 4D **9**
Haverthwaite TS5: Midd 2B **130**
HAVERTON HILL. 3D 57
Haverton Hill Ind. Est.
TS23: Bill 4D **57**
Haverton Hill Rd.
TS18: Stock T 2A **76**
TS23: Bill 2A **76**
Havilland Rd.
TS17: Thorn T 2D **129**
Haweswater Rd. TS10: Redc. . . 5B **48**
Hawford Cl. TS17: Ing B 5C **128**
Hawker Cl. TS25: Seat C 5E **21**
Hawkesbury Cl.
TS18: Stock T 2C **96**
Hawkins Cl. TS11: Marsk S 5E **67**
Hawkridge Cl. TS17: Ing B . . . 3B **150**
TS26: H'pool 2A **14**
Hawkridge St. TS26: H'pool . . . 3A **14**
Hawk Rd. TS3: N Orm 4D **79**
Hawkshead Rd. TS10: Redc . . . 5C **48**
Hawkstone TS8: Mart. 1E **155**
Hawkstone Cl. TS14: Guis 3E **139**
TS22: Bill 5A **38**
Hawnby Cl. TS19: Stock T. 5A **72**
Hawnby Rd. TS5: Midd 3E **101**
Hawthorn Av. TS17: Thorn T . . . 5C **98**
TS23: Bill 3D **55**
Hawthorn Cres. TS7: Mart. . . . 2E **133**
Hawthorn Dr. TS12: Brot 2A **90**
TS14: Guis 3B **138**
Hawthorne Rd.
TS19: Stock T. 3F **73**
Hawthorn Gro. TS15: Yarm . . . 4D **149**
Hawthorn Pl. TS16: Egg 2C **148**
Hawthorn Rd. TS10: Redc 5E **49**
TS21: Sed 3D **23**
Hawthorns, The TS9: Gt A. . . . 1D **167**
Hawthorn Wlk. TS24: H'pool . . . 1A **14**
Haxby Cl. TS5: Midd 5E **101**
Haxby Ct. TS14: Guis 5F **109**
Haxby Wlk. TS24: H'pool. 5C **8**
Hayburn Cl. TS10: Redc. 2E **65**
TS17: Ing B 1C **150**
Haydock Pk. Rd.
TS17: Thorn T 2F **99**
Haydon Grn. TS23: Bill 2D **39**
Hayfield Cl. TS26: H'pool 3E **13**
Hayling Gro. TS10: Redc 3E **65**
Hayling Way TS18: Stock T 1F **95**
Haymore St. TS5: Midd 1E **101**
Hayston Rd. TS26: H'pool 2C **12**
Hazelbank TS8: Coul N 3B **132**
Hazel Ct. TS1: Midd. 3F **77**
TS20: Nort 1B **74**
Hazeldene Av. TS18: Stock T. . . 3E **97**
Hazel Gdns. TS12: Brot. 2A **90**
Hazel Gro. TS7: Mart 3F **133**
TS10: Redc. 4E **49**
TS17: Thorn T 4C **98**
TS24: H'pool 1A **14**
Hazelgrove Residential Pk.
TS12: Salt 3B **68**
Hazelhen Cl. TS26: H'pool 5D **7**
Hazelmere Cl. TS22: Bill 4A **38**
Hazel Rd. TS19: Stock T 3F **73**

Hazel Slade TS16: Eag 5C **126**
Hazelwood Ct. TS5: Midd 2E **131**
Hazelwood Ri. TS24: H'pool 5F **9**
Headingley Ct. TS25: Seat C . . . 5E **21**
Headlam Ct. TS20: Nort 3B **74**
Headlam Rd. TS20: Nort 3B **74**
TS23: Bill 4F **39**
Headlam Ter. TS16: Eag 2B **148**
HEADLAND, THE. 1F **15**
Headland Prom. TS24: H'pool. . . 4D **9**
Headlands, The
TS11: Marsk S 3D **67**
Headland Sports Hall 1F **15**
Head St. TS1: Midd 3E **77**
Healaugh Pk. TS15: Yarm 5D **149**
Heath, The TS20: Nort. 2A **74**
Heather Cl. TS19: Stock T 1E **73**
TS22: Wyn 2C **26**
Heather Dr. TS5: Midd 5C **100**
Heatherfields Rd. TS6: Est . . . 3E **105**
Heather Gro. TS12: Skel 5E **89**
TS24: H'pool. 1F **13**
Heathfield Cl. TS16: Eag 5B **126**
Heathfield Dr. TS25: H'pool. . . . 1A **20**
Heath Rd. TS3: Midd 3B **78**
Heathrow TS17: Thorn T 5E **99**
Heathrow Cl. DL2: Mid G. 1A **144**
Heaton Rd. TS23: Bill 2D **39**
Hebburn Rd. TS19: Stock T. . . . 2C **72**
Hebron Ct. TS9: Stokes 1A **168**
Hebron Dr. TS9: Stokes 1A **168**
Hebron Rd. TS5: Midd 2F **101**
TS9: Stokes 1A **168**
Heddon Gro. TS17: Ing B. 3A **150**
Hedingham Cl. TS4: Midd 2A **102**
Hedley Cl. TS15: Yarm 1B **160**
Hedley Ct. TS15: Yarm 2B **148**
Hedleyhope Wlk.
TS19: Stock T 2C **72**
Hedley St. TS14: Guis 1E **139**
Heighington Cl.
TS19: Stock T 2C **72**
Helen Ho. TS17: Thorn T. 1B **98**
Hellhole La. TS21: Thorpe T. . . 1D **51**
Helmsley Cl. TS5: Midd. 4E **101**
Helmsley Dr. TS14: Guis. 1D **139**
Helmsley Gro.
TS19: Stock T 4C **72**
Helmsley Lawn *TS10: Redc. . . . 1E* ***65***
(off Carisbrooke Way)
Helmsley Rd. TS9: Stokes. . . . 1C **168**
Helmsley St. TS24: H'pool 1A **14**
Helston Ct. TS17: Thorn T. 5E **99**
Hembury Ct. TS17: Ing B. 4F **127**
Hemel Cl. TS17: Thorn T. 4E **99**
Hemingford Gdns.
TS15: Yarm 5D **149**
HEMLINGTON. 5E **131**
HEMLINGTON GRANGE 2E **153**
Hemlington Grn.
TS19: Stock T 2C **72**
Hemlington Hall Rd.
TS8: Hem. 4C **130**
Hemlington Lake & Recreation Cen.
. . . . 5D **131**
Hemlington La. TS8: Hem 3E **131**
(not continuous)
Hemlington Rd. TS8: Stain . . . 5C **130**
TS9: Stokes 3C **164**
HEMLINGTON VILLAGE 5A **132**
Hemlington Village Rd.
TS8: Hem. 5A **132**
Hempstead Cl.
TS17: Thorn T 4E **99**
Henderson Gro.
TS24: H'pool 2B **14**
Henley Gro. TS17: Thorn T 3C **98**
Henley Rd. TS5: Midd 2C **100**
Henrhyd Cl. TS17: Ing B 2F **149**
Henrietta Cl. TS17: Thorn T . . . 2C **98**
Henrietta St. TS24: H'pool. 5E **9**
Henry Bolckow Vis. Cen. 1D **133**
Henry Pease Ct. TS12: Salt. . . . 4A **68**
Henry Smith's Ter.
TS24: H'pool. 5F **9**
Henry St. TS3: N Orm 5C **78**
TS6: S Ban 2B **80**
TS10: Redc 3B **48**
Henry Taylor Ct. TS7: Orm . . . 4A **104**
Henshaw Dr. TS17: Ing B 2A **150**
Hensley Ct. TS20: Nort 4E **53**
Heortnesse Rd. TS24: H'pool . . . 4C **8**
Hepple Cl. TS23: Bill 2D **39**
Herbert St. TS3: N Orm 4C **78**
Herbert Wlk. TS24: H'pool. 2B **14**
Hereford Cl. TS5: Midd 1E **101**
Hereford Rd. TS14: Guis 3D **139**
Hereford St. TS25: H'pool 1B **20**
Hereford Ter. TS23: Bill 2F **55**
Heriot Grange TS25: H'pool. . . . 4E **19**
Heriot Gro. TS25: H'pool 4E **19**
Hermitage Pl. TS20: Nort 4A **54**
Herne Cl. TS10: Redc 3E **65**
Heron Ct. TS18: Stock T. 1F **97**
Heron Ga. TS14: Guis 2B **138**
Heronspool Cl. TS24: H'pool. . . . 5C **8**
Herrington Rd. TS23: Bill. 2E **39**
Herschell St. TS10: Redc 4C **48**
Hershall Dr. TS3: Midd 1E **103**
Hertford Rd. TS20: Nort. 1A **74**
Hesketh Av. TS4: Midd 5B **102**
Hesleden Av. TS5: Midd 2B **130**
Hesledon Cl. TS19: Stock T . . . 2D **73**
Heslington Gdns.
TS14: Guis 5E **109**
Heslop St. TS17: Thorn T 3D **99**
Heswall Rd. TS23: Bill. 5F **39**
Hetton Cl. TS23: Bill 4D **39**
Heugh Battery Mus. 1F **15**
Heugh Chare TS24: H'pool. 1F **15**
Hewitt's Bldgs. TS14: Guis . . . 1E **139**
Hewley St. TS6: Est. 2D **105**
Heworth Dr. TS20: Nort 4E **53**
Hexham Dr. TS6: Est 1E **105**
Hexham Grn. TS3: Midd. 3F **103**
Hexham Wlk. TS23: Bill. 5D **39**
Heysham Gro. TS10: Redc. 3F **65**
Heythrop Dr. TS5: Midd 4A **100**
TS14: Guis 3E **139**
Heywood St. TS5: Midd. 4C **76**
Hibernian Gro. TS25: H'pool . . . 4E **19**
Hickling Gro. TS19: Stock T . . . 3B **72**
Hidcote Gdns. TS17: Ing B . . . 1B **150**
Highbank Rd. TS7: Orm. 1B **134**
High Barrass *TS13: Stait 1C* ***120***
(off High St.)
Highbury Av. TS5: Midd. 4E **101**
High Chu. M. TS15: Yarm 3B **148**
High Chu. Wynd
TS15: Yarm 3B **148**
HIGH CLARENCE. 4E **57**
Highcliffe Gro. TS11: N Mar . . . 2A **86**
High Farm Cl. TS21: Carlt 5C **50**
High Farm Vw. TS6: S Ban 4B **80**
High Fell TS10: Redc. 1B **64**
Highfield Cl. TS16: Eag 5B **126**
Highfield Cres.
TS18: Stock T 2C **96**
Highfield Dr. TS16: Eag 5B **126**
Highfield Gdns. TS16: Eag . . . 5B **126**
Highfield Rd. TS4: Midd 1A **102**
(not continuous)
TS6: Est 1E **105**
TS11: Marsk S 4B **66**
TS18: Stock T 2C **96**
High Force Rd. TS2: Midd. 1C **76**
Highgate TS6: Est 1A **106**
High Gill Rd. TS7: Nun 2A **134**
High Godfalter Hill
TS7: Nun 2C **134**
HIGH GRANGE 3D **39**
High Grange Av. TS23: Bill 4D **39**
High Grange Ho. TS23: Bill. . . . 4D **39**
High Green TS9: Gt A 2D **167**
Highland Rd. TS25: H'pool 4E **19**
High La. TS8: Malt. 2E **151**
HIGH LEVEN. 4B **150**
Highlight, The TS24: H'pool . . . 2C **14**
Highmead Wlk. TS3: Midd . . . 4D **103**
High Newham Ct.
TS19: Stock T 1B **72**
High Newham Rd.
TS19: Stock T 1B **72**
High Peak TS14: Guis 4F **139**
Highpoint Pk. TS24: H'pool. . . . 2B **14**
High Rifts TS8: Stain 5B **130**
High Row TS13: Loft 4A **92**
High Stone Cl. TS10: Redc 2E **65**
High St. TS2: Port C. 5F **57**
TS6: Est 5A **82**
TS6: Est, Norm. 2C **104**
TS6: Laze 4C **82**
TS7: Orm 4F **103**
TS9: Gt A 2C **166**
TS9: Gt Bro. 5F **169**
TS9: Stokes 1B **168**
TS10: Redc 3C **48**
TS11: Marsk S 3C **66**
TS12: Boo 2B **112**
TS12: Brot 2B **90**
TS12: Ling 3D **113**
TS12: Moor 2B **142**
TS12: Skel 4B **88**
TS13: Hind 5E **121**
TS13: Loft 5C **92**
TS13: Skin 2A **92**
TS13: Stait 1C **120**
TS15: Yarm 2B **148**
TS18: Stock T 5B **74**
TS20: Nort 5B **54**
TS21: Sed 4D **23**
TS22: Wolv. 2C **38**
TS24: H'pool. 1F **15**
TS25: Grea 2E **31**
High St. West TS10: Redc. 3A **48**
HIGH THROSTON 1C **12**
High Throston Golf Course. . . . 1C **12**
Hilcott Cl. TS17: Ing B. 4A **128**
Hilda Pl. TS12: Salt. 4C **68**
Hilda Wlk. TS24: H'pool 4D **15**
Hilden Pk. TS17: Ing B 4A **128**
Hilderthorpe TS7: Nun 3F **133**
Hilderthorpe Cl.
TS17: Ing B 4A **128**
Hildewell TS13: Hind. 5E **121**
Hildyard Cl. TS9: Stokes 5B **164**
Hillbrook Cres. TS17: Ing B. . . 4A **128**
Hill Cl. TS12: Skel 4B **88**
Hill Cres. TS10: Redc 5E **47**
Hillcrest Av. TS18: Stock T 1C **96**
Hillcrest Dr. TS7: Nun 2B **134**
TS13: Loft 1B **116**
Hillcrest Gro. TS27: Elw 3C **10**
Hillel Wlk. TS5: Midd 2D **131**
Hill Ho. Farm TS20: Nort. 2B **74**
Hillingdon Rd. TS3: Midd 4D **103**
Hillington Gro. TS17: Ing B. . . 4A **128**
Hillmorton Rd. TS17: Ing B. . . 4A **128**
Hillocks La. TS12: Moor 3B **142**
Hill Ri. DL2: Mid R 4A **144**
Hill Rd. TS23: Bill 4D **55**
Hills, The TS12: Skel. 4B **88**
Hillsford Cl. TS17: Ing B 4A **128**
Hillside Cl. TS11: N Mar 3F **85**
Hillside Rd. TS20: Nort. 4B **54**
Hillston Cl. TS26: H'pool. 2C **12**
Hill St. TS1: Midd 3E **77**
TS10: Redc 3B **48**
Hill St. E. TS18: Stock T 4C **74**
Hill St. Shop. Cen.
TS1: Midd. 2E **77**
Hills Vw. Rd. TS6: Est 1F **105**
Hill Vw. TS17: Ing B 5A **128**
TS25: Grea 4F **31**
Hillview *TS3: Midd 3D* ***103***
(off Delamere Rd.)
Hill Vw. Rd. TS14: Guis. 2E **139**
Hill Vw. Ter. TS11: N Mar 2A **86**
Hillway TS17: Ing B. 4A **128**

Hillwood Ct. TS17: Thorn T . . . 1D **129**
Hilston Cl. TS17: Ing B 5A **128**
HILTON 1F **163**
Hilton La. TS15: High L 4B **150**
HINDERWELL 4E **121**
Hinderwell Av. TS10: Redc 5A **48**
Hinderwell La.
TS13: Hind, Stait 3C **120**
Hindhead TS16: Eag 5C **126**
Hindpool Cl. TS24: H'pool 5B **8**
Hinton Av. TS5: Midd 1B **100**
Hinton Ct. TS14: Guis 1F **139**
Hirdman Gro. TS24: H'pool 2E **7**
Hird Rd. TS15: Yarm 5A **148**
Hirds Dr. TS13: Loft 5B **92**
Hive Cl. TS19: Stock T 2F **73**
HM Bark Endeavour 1B **98**
HMP Holme House
TS18: Stock T 2D **75**
HMP Kirklevington Grange
TS15: K'ton 1D **161**
HMS Trincomalee 2C **14**
Hobdale Ter. TS12: Skel 2B **112**
Hob Hill Cl. TS12: Salt 5B **68**
Hob Hill Cres. TS12: Salt 5B **68**
Hob Hill La.
TS11: Salt, Upleat 3E **87**
TS12: Salt 3E **87**
Hobson Av. TS10: Redc 2E **63**
Hodges Ho. TS1: Midd 2F **77**
Hodgeson's Yd.
TS18: Stock T 1B ***98***
(off Finkle St.)
Hodgson Ct. TS6: Est 2F **105**
Hogarth Cl. TS23: Bill 3D **39**
Holbeck Av. TS5: Midd 2D **131**
Holbeck Wlk.
TS17: Thorn T 3E **129**
Holburn Pk. TS19: Stock T 2D **73**
Holdenby Dr. TS3: Midd 4D **103**
Holden Cl. TS6: Gran 2D **81**
Holdernesse TS22: Wyn 4A **26**
Holder St. TS10: Redc 4C **48**
Holdforth Cl. TS24: H'pool 5F **7**
Holdforth Ct. TS24: H'pool 5F **7**
Holdforth Rd. TS24: H'pool 5F **7**
Holey Cl. TS8: Hem 4D **131**
Holgate, The TS5: Midd 5D **77**
Holland Rd. TS25: H'pool 1E **31**
Hollies, The TS10: Redc 5E **49**
TS12: Skel 5E **89**
TS23: Bill 4D **55**
Hollinside Cl. TS19: Stock T . . . 2D **73**
Hollinside Rd. TS23: Bill 4F **39**
Hollins La. TS5: Midd 2C **100**
Hollis Ct. TS8: Coul N 4B **132**
Hollowfield TS8: Coul N 3A **132**
(not continuous)
Hollowfield Sq.
TS8: Coul N 4A **132**
Hollybush Av. TS17: Ing B 4C **128**
Hollybush Est. TS12: Skel 3D **89**
Hollygarth TS9: Gt A 2C **166**
Hollygarth Cl. TS9: Gt A 2C **166**
Holly Hill Cl. TS7: Orm 5B **104**
Hollyhurst Av. TS4: Midd 3F **101**
Holly La. TS8: Stain 5C **130**
Hollymead Dr. TS14: Guis 1E **139**
Hollymount TS23: Bill 4D **55**
TS26: H'pool 3E **13**
Holly Pond Cl. TS15: Yarm . . . 2A **160**
Hollystone Ct. TS23: Bill 3E **39**
Holly St. TS1: Midd 4F **77**
TS20: Nort 1B **74**
Holly Ter. TS2: Port C 4E **57**
Hollytree M. TS14: Guis 2E **139**
Hollywalk Av. TS6: Norm 3C **104**
Hollywalk Cl. TS6: Norm 3C **104**
Hollywalk Dr. TS6: Norm 2D **105**
Hollywood Bowl
Stockton-on-Tees 1A **100**
Holmbeck Rd. TS12: Skel 4E **89**
Holme Ct. TS3: Midd 4F **103**
Holmefields Rd. TS6: Est 3E **105**
Holme Ho. Rd.
TS18: Stock T 3D **75**
Holme Land TS17: Ing B 3A **128**
Holmes Cl. TS17: Thorn T 5B **98**
Holmeside Gro. TS23: Bill 3F **39**
Holmside Wlk.
TS19: Stock T 2C **72**
Holms La. TS21: Carlt 3C **50**
Holmwood Av. TS4: Midd 3F **101**
Holnest Av. TS3: Midd 2D **103**
Holnicote Cl. TS17: Ing B 3B **150**
Holt, The TS8: Coul N 3F **131**
Holtby Wlk. TS3: Midd 1D **103**
(Fransham Rd.)
TS3: Midd 4D **103**
(Hillingdon Rd.)
Holt Cl. TS5: Midd 3B **130**
Holt St. TS24: H'pool 5B **14**
Holwick Rd. TS2: Midd 2C **76**
Holyhead Ct. TS6: Est 4D **81**
Holyhead Dr. TS10: Redc 3E **65**
Holyrood Cl. TS17: Thorn T 3D **99**
Holy Rood Ct. TS4: Midd 1A **102**
Holyrood Cres. TS27: Hart 4F **5**
Holyrood La. TS4: Midd 1A **102**
Holyrood Wlk. TS25: H'pool . . . 4E **19**
Holystone Dr. TS17: Ing B 2A **150**
Holywell Grn. TS16: Eag 5C **126**
Homebryth Ho. TS21: Sed 3D **23**
Homerell Cl. TS10: Redc 2E **65**
Homer Gro. TS25: H'pool 2E **19**
Homerton Rd. TS3: Midd 1D **103**
Homestall TS21: Sed 1C **22**
Homestead Gth.
TS17: Ing B 3A **128**
Honddu Ct. TS17: Ing B 2F **149**
Honey Bee Cl. TS19: Stock T . . . 2F **73**
Honeycomb Av.
TS19: Stock T 2F **73**
Honey Pot Cl. TS21: Whit 3A **50**
Honeypot Cl. TS22: Wyn 3C **26**
Honeypot Gro. TS19: Stock T . . . 2F **73**
Honeysuckle Cl. TS26: H'pool . . . 4D **7**
Honeysuckle Ct. TS20: Nort . . . 1A **74**
Honey Way TS19: Stock T 2F **73**
Hong Kong Rd. TS16: Eag 4F **125**
Honister Cl. TS19: Stock T 4F **73**
Honister Gro. TS5: Midd 5B **100**
Honister Rd. TS10: Redc 5B **48**
Honister Wlk. TS16: Eag 1C **148**
Honiton Way TS25: H'pool 5F **19**
Hood Cl. TS24: H'pool 2E **7**
Hood Dr. TS6: S Ban 3B **80**
Hoope Cl. TS15: Yarm 1B **160**
Hope Gdns. TS18: Stock T 3A **98**
Hope St. TS18: Stock T 2F **97**
TS23: Bill 3D **57**
TS24: H'pool 3C **14**
Hopgill Wlk. TS10: Redc 1B **64**
Hopkins Av. TS3: Midd 5E **79**
Hopps St. TS26: H'pool 2A **14**
Hordenburn Cl.
TS18: Stock T 5E **75**
Horden Rd. TS23: Bill 5F **39**
Hornbeam Cl. TS7: Orm 4B **104**
Hornbeam Wlk.
TS19: Stock T 1E **73**
Hornby Av. TS21: Sed 5C **22**
Hornby Cl. TS1: Midd 3E **77**
TS25: Seat C 2E **21**
Horncliffe Row TS5: Midd 2B **100**
Horndale Cl. TS10: Redc 4E **65**
Hornleigh Gro. TS10: Redc 4A **48**
Hornsea Cl. TS23: Bill 2F **39**
Hornsea Gro. TS10: Redc 4A **48**
HORSE & JOCKEY RDBT. 5C **52**
Horseclose La. TS21: Carlt 5E **51**
Horsefield St. TS4: Midd 3A **78**
Horse Shoe Pond
TS22: Wyn 4B **26**
Horsley Pl. TS24: H'pool 4F **7**
Horsley Way TS23: Bill 2E **39**
Hoskins La. TS4: Midd 4B **102**
Hoskins Way TS3: Midd 1E **103**
Hospital Cl. TS25: Grea 3E **31**
Hospital Cotts. TS25: Grea 3E **31**
Hough Cres. TS17: Thorn T 5C **98**
Houghton Banks
TS17: Ing B 3A **128**
Houghton Grn.
TS19: Stock T 2C **72**
Houghton St. TS24: H'pool 5B **14**
Hoveton Cl. TS19: Stock T 3C **72**
Hovingham Dr. TS14: Guis . . . 5E **109**
Hovingham St. TS3: N Orm 4C **78**
Howard Ct. TS4: Midd 2A **102**
Howard Dr. TS11: Marsk S 5E **67**
Howard Pl. TS20: Nort 3B **74**
Howard St. TS1: Midd 4D **77**
TS24: H'pool 4D **9**
Howard Wlk. TS23: Bill 5D **55**
Howbeck La. TS24: H'pool 5A **8**
Howcroft Av. TS10: Redc 2E **63**
Howden Dike TS15: Yarm 5D **149**
Howden Rd. TS24: H'pool 2E **7**
Howden Wlk. TS18: Stock T . . . 5A **74**
Howe Hill Bank TS9: Seam . . . 5C **154**
Howe St. TS1: Midd 5E **77**
Howgill Wlk. TS3: Midd 1C **102**
Howlbeck Bungs.
TS14: Guis 1D ***139***
(off Howlbeck Rd.)
Howlbeck Rd. TS14: Guis 1D **139**
Hoylake Cl. TS11: N Mar 2A **86**
Hoylake Rd. TS4: Midd 4F **101**
Hoylake Way TS16: Eag 1C **148**
Hub, The 3C **48**
Hubbard Wlk. TS4: Midd 3A **78**
Huby Ct. TS14: Guis 5E **109**
Huby Vs. TS19: Stock T 3B **72**
Huckelhoven Ct.
TS24: H'pool 4C **14**
Huckelhoven Way
TS24: H'pool 4C **14**
Hudeshope Cl.
TS18: Stock T 5E **75**
Hudson Ho. TS17: Thorn T . . . 1D **129**
Hudson Quay TS3: Midd 2A **78**
Hudson St. TS2: Midd 1F **77**
Hudswell Gro.
TS18: Stock T 3C **96**
Hugill Cl. TS15: Yarm 5D **149**
Hugo Ct. TS18: Stock T 3A **76**
Hulam Cl. TS19: Stock T 2D **73**
Hulton Cl. TS7: Mart 3F **133**
Humber Cl. TS13: Loft 5D **93**
Humber Gro. TS22: Bill 4A **38**
Humber Rd. TS17: Thorn T 5D **99**
Humbledon Rd.
TS19: Stock T 2D **73**
Hume Ho. TS18: Stock T 4A **74**
Hume St. TS18: Stock T 4A **74**
(not continuous)
Humewood Gro. TS20: Nort . . . 4B **54**
Hummersea Cl. TS12: Brot 2B **90**
Hummersea La. TS13: Loft 5C **92**
Hummershill La.
TS11: Marsk S 4D **67**
Hundale Cres. TS10: Redc 3D **65**
Hunley Av. TS12: Brot 1B **90**
Hunley Cl. TS12: Brot 1B **90**
Hunley Hall Golf Course 1C **90**
Hunstanton Gro.
TS11: N Mar 2F **85**
Huntcliffe Av. TS10: Redc 5A **48**
Huntcliffe Dr. TS12: Brot 1A **90**
Hunter Ho. Ind. Est.
TS25: H'pool 1D **33**
Huntersgate TS6: Est 1A **106**
Hunters Grn. TS16: Eag 5A **126**
HUNTER'S HILL 4E **139**
Hunter St. TS26: H'pool 3A **14**
Huntingdon Grn. TS20: Nort . . . 1C **74**
Huntley Cl. TS3: Midd 4E **103**
Huntley Rd. TS25: H'pool 4E **19**

Huntsman Dr. TS2: Port C 3B **58**
Hunwick Cl. TS5: Midd 1B **130**
Hunwick Wlk. TS19: Stock T . . . 2C **72**
Hurn Wlk. TS17: Thorn T 1E **129**
Huron Cl. TS4: Midd 1A **102**
Hurricane Ct. TS18: Stock T . . . 5F **97**
Hurst Pk. TS10: Redc 2D **65**
Hurworth Cl. TS19: Stock T. . . . 5A **72**
Hurworth Rd. TS4: Midd 3A **102**
TS23: Bill 2A **40**
Hury Rd. TS20: Nort 5A **54**
Hustler Rd. TS5: Midd. 3C **130**
Hutchinson St. TS12: Brot. 2B **90**
TS18: Stock T 5A **74**
Hutone Pl. TS24: H'pool 2E **7**
Hutton Av. TS26: H'pool. 3F **13**
Hutton Cl. TS17: Thorn T. 4C **98**
Hutton Ct. TS26: H'pool. 3A **14**
HUTTON GATE 4B **138**
Hutton Gro. TS10: Redc. 2E **63**
TS18: Stock T 2D **97**
Hutton La. TS14: Guis 4B **138**
Hutton Rd. TS4: Midd 5B **78**
TS6: Est 5A **82**
Hutton St. TS13: Skin 2A **92**
TS24: H'pool 4C **8**
HUTTON VILLAGE 5C **138**
Hutton Village Rd.
TS14: Guis 4B **138**
Huxley Wlk. TS25: H'pool 1E **19**
Hylton Av. TS12: Skel 3A **88**
Hylton Gro. TS20: Nort 2A **74**
Hylton Rd. TS23: Bill 5F **39**
TS26: H'pool 5C **12**
Hythe Cl. TS10: Redc. 3F **65**

I

Ian Gro. TS25: H'pool 5E **19**
Ian St. TS17: Thorn T 3D **99**
Ibbetson St. TS24: H'pool 5F **9**
Iber Gro. TS25: H'pool. 5E **19**
Ibrox Gro. TS25: H'pool 5F **19**
Ibstone Wlk. TS19: Stock T. . . . 5C **52**
Ickworth Ct. TS17: Ing B 1B **150**
Ida Rd. TS3: Midd 5B **78**
Ida St. TS20: Nort 2A **74**
Ilam Ct. TS17: Ing B 1B **150**
Ilderton Rd. TS18: Thorn T 5D **75**
Ilford Rd. TS19: Stock T 5C **52**
Ilford Way TS3: Midd. 3D **103**
Ilfracombe Dr. TS10: Redc 2A **64**
Ilkeston Wlk. TS19: Stock T . . . 5C **52**
Ilkley Gro. TS14: Guis 4D **139**
TS25: H'pool 4B **20**
Ilston Grn. TS3: Midd 3D **103**
Imeson St. TS6: Est 2F **105**
Imperial Av. TS6: S Ban. 1F **79**
TS17: Thorn T 3D **99**
TS20: Nort 2B **74**
Imperial Cres. TS20: Nort 2B **74**
Imperial Rd. TS23: Bill 5D **55**
Inchcape Rd. TS25: H'pool 5E **19**
Inch Gro. TS25: H'pool. 5E **19**
Ingham Gro. TS25: H'pool. 1D **31**
Ingleborough La.
TS17: Ing B 2B **150**
INGLEBY BARWICK 5B **128**
Ingleby Barwick Golf Academy
. . . . 3F **127**
Ingleby Cl. TS6: Est. 5A **82**
Ingleby Ct. *TS10: Redc 3C 48*
(off Station Rd.)
Ingleby Gro. TS18: Stock T. . . . 2D **97**
Ingleby Ho. TS4: Midd. 2B **102**
Ingleby Rd. TS4: Midd. 5B **78**
TS9: Gt Bro. 5F **169**
TS25: Seat C 5E **21**
Ingleby Way TS17: Ing B. 5A **128**
Inglefield TS25: H'pool 5A **20**
Ingleside M. TS12: Salt. 4C **68**
Ingleton Rd. TS19: Stock T 5C **52**
Inglewood Av.
TS11: Marsk S 5C **66**
Inglewood Cl. TS3: Midd 1A **104**
Ingoldsby Rd. TS3: Midd 2A **104**
Ingram Gro. TS17: Ing B 2A **150**
Ingram Rd. TS3: Midd 1C **102**
Ingrove Cl. TS19: Stock T 5C **52**
INGS, THE 3F **65**
Ings Av. TS3: Midd. 5E **79**
Ings La. TS9: Stokes 4F **169**
TS12: Brot 2C **90**
(not continuous)
TS15: Yarm 5A **148**
Ings M. TS10: Redc. 4D **49**
Ings Rd. TS10: Redc 4D **49**
Inkerman St. TS18: Stock T. . . . 5A **74**
Innes Rd. TS25: H'pool 5E **19**
Innes St. TS2: Midd 1E **77**
Innovation Av. TS18: Stock T. . . 4E **97**
Innovation Centre, The
TS10: K'ham 4A **64**
TS25: H'pool. 1F **31**
Innovation Ct. TS18: Stock T. . . 4E **97**
Inskip Wlk. TS19: Stock T. 1C **72**
Institute Ter. TS6: Gran 2E **81**
Instow Cl. TS19: Stock T. 1C **72**
Intelect Ct. TS2: Midd 2C **76**
Intrepid Cl. TS25: Seat C. 2D **21**
Inverness Rd. TS25: H'pool. . . . 5E **19**
Ipswich Av. TS3: Midd. 3D **103**
Irene St. TS13: Carl H 3F **91**
Iron Masters Way TS1: Midd. . . 4C **76**
Ironmasters Way TS21: Stil. . . . 1A **50**
Ironstone Way TS13: Live 1A **116**
Irstead Wlk. TS19: Stock T 5C **52**
Irthing Cl. TS17: Ing B. 2A **150**
Irvin Av. TS12: Salt 4A **68**
Irvine Rd. TS3: Midd 5C **78**
TS25: H'pool 5E **19**
Islay Ct. TS17: Thorn T. 4D **99**
Islay Gro. TS25: H'pool 5E **19**
Islington Wlk. TS4: Midd. 5B **102**
Italy St. TS2: Midd. 2E **77**
Ivanhoe Cres. TS25: H'pool. . . . 5E **19**
Iveston Gro. TS22: Bill. 5A **38**
Iveston Wlk. TS19: Stock T. . . . 5C **52**
Ivy Cl. TS20: Nort 2A **74**
Ivy Cotts. TS15: Hilt. 1E **163**
TS16: Egg 2C **148**
Ivy Dr. TS18: Thorn T 5D **75**
Ivy Gro. TS24: H'pool. 5F **7**

J

Jacklin Wlk. TS16: Eag 5C **126**
Jack Simon Way TS5: Midd. . . 3B **130**
Jackson Dr. TS9: Stokes 5B **164**
Jacksons Landing
TS24: H'pool 2C **14**
Jackson St. TS12: Brot 3B **90**
TS13: Loft 1D **117**
TS25: H'pool 1A **20**
Jacques Ct. TS24: H'pool. 1F **15**
James Cook Ho. TS1: Midd 3F **77**
James Cook Sculpture *2D 167*
(off High Grn.)
James Ct. TS9: Gt A 1D **167**
Jameson Rd. TS20: Nort. 4A **54**
TS25: H'pool 4D **19**
James St. TS3: N Orm. 4B **78**
TS24: H'pool 4D **15**
Jamison Av. TS10: Redc 3C **64**
Jane Wlk. TS20: Nort 3C **74**
Japonica Way TS20: Nort 2A **74**
Jarsling Ho. TS24: H'pool 2C **14**
Jarvis Wlk. TS25: H'pool. 4D **19**
Jasmine Cl. TS26: H'pool 4E **7**
Jasmine Flds. TS15: K'ton. . . . 3E **161**
Jasmine Gro. TS7: Mart 2C **132**
Jasmine Rd. TS19: Stock T 3F **73**
Jasper Gro. TS21: Stil 1B **50**
Jay Av. TS17: Thorn T 1E **151**
Jaywood Cl. TS27: H'pool 2B **6**
JD Sports Domes 1E **33**
Jedburgh Rd. TS25: H'pool 4D **19**
Jedburgh St. TS1: Midd 3F **77**
Jefferson St. TS3: N Orm 4C **78**
Jenner Dr. TS19: Stock T. 2C **72**
Jennings, The TS6: Norm 2D **105**
Jenny Frisk Rd. TS12: Boo . . . 4C **112**
Jersey St. TS24: H'pool. 3C **14**
Jersey Wlk. TS14: Guis. 3D **139**
Jervaulx Rd. TS12: Skel 4D **89**
Jesmond Av. TS5: Midd. 3C **100**
Jesmond Est. TS24: H'pool 1A **14**
Jesmond Gdns. TS24: H'pool. . . . 5F **7**
Jesmond Gro. TS18: Stock T. . . 3C **96**
Jesmond M. TS26: H'pool. 2A **14**
Jesmond Rd. TS26: H'pool 2F **13**
Jesmond Sq. TS24: H'pool. 1F **13**
Jobson St. TS26: H'pool 2A **14**
Jocelyn Way TS5: Midd 3B **130**
Joe Allon Cl. TS24: H'pool 1A **14**
John Boyle Rd. TS6: S Ban 1B **80**
John Howe Gdns.
TS24: H'pool 4E **7**
Johnson Gro. TS20: Nort 5F **53**
Johnsons Sq. TS12: Moor. . . . 2B **142**
Johnson St. TS1: Midd. 3E **77**
TS26: H'pool 4B **14**
Johnson's Yd. TS14: Guis 2E **139**
Johnston Av. TS12: Salt. 4B **68**
John St. TS9: Gt A. 1D **167**
TS12: Skel 4D **89**
TS13: Loft 5C **92**
TS18: Stock T 5A **74**
TS24: H'pool 3C **14**
John Walker Rd. TS21: Sed . . . 1D **23**
John Walker Sq.
TS18: Stock T 1B **98**
Joicey Ct. TS26: H'pool. 3A **14**
Jones Rd. TS6: S Ban 2B **80**
TS24: H'pool. 4F **7**
Joppa Gro. TS25: H'pool 4E **19**
Jowitt Rd. TS24: H'pool 4F **7**
Joyce Rd. TS24: H'pool 3E **7**
Jubilee Bank TS7: Orm 4A **104**
Jubilee Ct. TS6: Est 2F **105**
Jubilee Gro. TS22: Bill. 5C **38**
Jubilee Homes TS25: H'pool. . . 5A **14**
Jubilee Rd. TS6: Est 2F **105**
Jubilee St. TS3: N Orm 4C **78**
Jubilee St. Sth. TS3: N Orm . . . 4C **78**
Junction Rd. TS19: Stock T. . . . 5C **52**
TS20: Nort 5C **52**
Juniper Cl. TS10: Redc 3E **65**
Juniper Gro. TS7: Mart 2F **133**
TS21: Elt. 4E **95**
Juniper Wlk. TS25: H'pool 4D **19**
Jura Gro. TS25: H'pool 4E **19**
Jute Gro. TS25: H'pool 4D **19**
Jutland Rd. TS25: H'pool. 4B **20**

K

Kader Av. TS5: Midd 1B **130**
Kader Cotts. TS5: Midd 1C **130**
Kader Farm Rd. TS5: Midd . . . 1C **130**
Kader Pde. TS5: Midd 1B **130**
Kailey Vw. TS4: Midd 1A **102**
Kathleen St. TS25: H'pool 1B **20**
Kearsley Cl. TS16: Prest T . . . 1D **127**
Keasdon Cl. TS3: Midd 1B **102**
Keats Rd. TS6: Est. 2D **105**
Kebock Wlk. TS25: H'pool. 4D **19**
Kedleston Cl. TS19: Stock T . . . 3D **73**
Kedlestone Pk. TS8: Mart 5E **133**
Kedward Av. TS3: Midd 4E **79**
Keepersgate TS6: Est 1A **106**
Keepers La. TS17: Ing B 5B **128**
Keighley Av. TS7: Mart 1B **132**
Keilder Cl. TS10: Redc 3B **64**
Keilder Ri. TS8: Hem. 4F **131**
Keir Hardie Cl. TS6: S Ban 2B **80**

Keir Hardie Cres.
TS6: S Ban . . . 2B **80**
Keithlands Av. TS20: Nort . . . 1B **74**
Keith Rd. TS4: Midd . . . 3F **101**
Keithwood Cl. TS4: Midd . . . 3F **101**
Kelbrook Wlk. TS3: Midd . . . 1E **103**
Keld Cl. TS17: Ing B . . . 3B **150**
Kel Dennis Cl. TS6: Est . . . 5D **81**
Keld Gro. TS19: Stock T . . . 1A **96**
Kelfield Av. TS3: Midd . . . 1E **103**
Kelgate Ter. TS8: Stain . . . 5B **130**
Kelling Cl. TS23: Bill . . . 3E **39**
Kelloe Cl. TS19: Stock T . . . 1C **72**
Kells Gro. TS25: H'pool . . . 4D **19**
Kelsall Cl. TS3: Midd . . . 3E **103**
Kelso Ct. TS3: Midd . . . 2C **102**
Kelso Gro. TS25: H'pool . . . 4D **19**
Kelsterne Cl. TS15: Yarm . . . 5E **149**
Kelvin Gro. TS3: Midd . . . 3D **103**
TS25: H'pool . . . 4D **19**
Kemplah Ho. TS14: Guis . . . 2E **139**
Kempston Way TS20: Nort . . . 5E **53**
Kendal Ct. TS4: Midd . . . 2A **102**
Kendal Gro. TS10: Redc . . . 1C **64**
Kendal Rd. TS18: Stock T . . . 4D **73**
TS25: H'pool . . . 1B **20**
Kenilworth Av. TS3: Midd . . . 3E **103**
Kenilworth Flats TS23: Bill . . . 5E **39**
Kenilworth Rd. TS23: Bill . . . 5E **39**
Kenilworth Way TS10: Redc . . . 2F **65**
Kenley Gdns. TS20: Nort . . . 4E **53**
Kenmore Rd. TS3: Midd . . . 2A **104**
Kennedy Cres. TS13: Carl H . . . 2A **92**
Kennedy Gdns. TS23: Bill . . . 1E **55**
Kennedy Gro. TS20: Nort . . . 1F **73**
Kennthorpe TS7: Nun . . . 3F **133**
Kensington Av. TS6: Norm . . . 3D **105**
Kensington Ct. TS24: H'pool . . . 5F **7**
Kensington Rd. TS5: Midd . . . 5D **77**
TS18: Stock T . . . 2F **97**
Kent Av. TS25: H'pool . . . 1B **20**
Kent Cl. TS7: Nun . . . 3B **134**
Kent Gro. TS20: Nort . . . 1C **74**
Kentmere Av. TS12: Skel . . . 2C **88**
Kentmere Rd. TS3: Midd . . . 2C **102**
Kenton Cl. TS18: Stock T . . . 3C **96**
Kentport Ct. TS18: Stock T . . . 4C **74**
Kentra Cl. TS10: Redc . . . 3E **65**
Kent Rd. TS14: Guis . . . 3D **139**
Kenville Gro.
TS19: Stock T . . . 4A **72**
Kenwood Cres. TS17: Ing B . . . 5A **128**
Kepier Cl. TS19: Stock T . . . 1C **72**
Kepple Av. TS3: Midd . . . 2C **102**
Kepwick Cl. TS5: Midd . . . 5E **101**
Kerr Cres. TS21: Sed . . . 2C **22**
Kerr Gro. TS25: H'pool . . . 4D **19**
Kerridge Cl. TS11: Marsk S . . . 4C **66**
Kerry Cl. TS6: Est . . . 4D **81**
Kesteven Rd. TS4: Midd . . . 1B **132**
TS25: H'pool . . . 5D **19**
Kestrel Av. TS3: N Orm . . . 4D **79**
Kestrel Cl. TS20: Nort . . . 3A **54**
TS26: H'pool . . . 5C **6**
Kestrel Hide TS14: Guis . . . 2B **138**
Keswick Gro. TS5: Midd . . . 5C **100**
Keswick Rd. TS6: Norm . . . 1C **104**
TS10: Redc . . . 1C **64**
TS23: Bill . . . 4D **55**
Keswick St. TS26: H'pool . . . 5A **14**
Kettleness Av. TS10: Redc . . . 5A **48**
Kettlewell Cl. TS23: Bill . . . 4D **39**
Ketton Rd. TS19: Stock T . . . 1C **72**
Ketton Row TS1: Midd . . . 3D **77**
Keverstone Cl.
TS19: Stock T . . . 1D **73**
Keverstone Gro. TS23: Bill . . . 2F **39**
Kew Gdns. TS20: Nort . . . 4E **53**
Kew Ri. TS6: Norm . . . 4C **104**
Keynsham Av. TS3: Midd . . . 3E **103**
Kielder Cl. TS22: Bill . . . 5A **38**
Kielder Rd. TS26: H'pool . . . 3C **12**
Kilbride Cl. TS17: Thorn T . . . 4E **99**
Kilbridge Cl. TS11: N Mar . . . 2A **86**
Kilburn Rd. TS4: Midd . . . 3A **102**
TS18: Stock T . . . 2D **97**
Kildale Ct. TS3: N Orm . . . 3B **78**
Kildale Gro. TS10: Redc . . . 1A **64**
TS19: Stock T . . . 1A **96**
TS25: Seat C . . . 5D **21**
Kildale Rd. TS4: Midd . . . 1A **102**
TS23: Bill . . . 2D **55**
Kildare Ho. TS4: Midd . . . 2B **102**
Kildare St. TS1: Midd . . . 5C **76**
Kildwick Gro. TS3: Midd . . . 3E **103**
Kilkenny Rd. TS14: Guis . . . 3E **139**
Killerby Cl. TS19: Stock T . . . 1D **73**
Killinghall Gro.
TS18: Stock T . . . 1A **96**
Killinghall Row DL2: Mid G . . . 1A **144**
Kilmarnock Rd.
TS25: H'pool . . . 5D **19**
Kilmory Wlk. TS25: H'pool . . . 4D **19**
Kilnwick Cl. TS23: Bill . . . 2F **39**
Kilsyth Gro. TS25: H'pool . . . 4D **19**
KILTON . . . 5E **91**
Kilton Cl. TS10: Redc . . . 1E **65**
TS19: Stock T . . . 1D **73**
Kilton Ct. TS4: Midd . . . 2F **101**
Kilton Dr. TS12: Brot . . . 2C **90**
Kilton La. TS12: Brot, Carl H . . . 2C **90**
TS12: Ling, Live . . . 4F **113**
TS13: Carl H . . . 3F **91**
KILTON LA. RDBT. . . . **3C 90**
KILTON THORPE . . . 1C **114**
Kilton Thorpe La.
TS12: Brot . . . 1C **114**
Kilvington Gro. TS7: Mart . . . 5A **134**
Kilwick St. TS24: H'pool . . . 5B **14**
Kimberley Dr. TS3: Midd . . . 1D **103**
Kimberley St. TS26: H'pool . . . 5A **14**
Kimble Dr. TS17: Thorn T . . . 2C **128**
Kimblesworth Wlk.
TS19: Stock T . . . 1D **73**
Kimmerton Av. TS5: Midd . . . 1C **130**
Kinbrace Rd. TS25: H'pool . . . 4D **19**
Kindersley St. TS3: N Orm . . . 4C **78**
Kinderton Gro. TS20: Nort . . . 5E **53**
Kindlewood Gdns.
TS14: Guis . . . 2E **139**
Kingcraft Rd. TS7: Mart . . . 1B **132**
King Edward's Rd.
TS1: Midd . . . 4E **77**
King Edward's Sq.
TS1: Midd . . . 4E **77**
King Edward Ter.
TS11: Marsk S . . . 4D **67**
Kingfisher Cl. TS26: H'pool . . . 5D **7**
Kingfisher Dr. TS14: Guis . . . 2A **138**
Kingfisher Ho. TS24: H'pool . . . 3D **15**
Kingfisher Way
TS18: Stock T . . . 5A **98**
King Georges Ter.
TS6: S Ban . . . 1F **79**
King Oswy Dr. TS24: H'pool . . . 2D **7**
Kingsbridge Cres.
TS5: Midd . . . 2B **100**
Kings Cl. TS6: Laze . . . 4C **82**
Kings Ct. TS20: Nort . . . 5B **54**
Kingsdale Cl. TS15: Yarm . . . 1B **160**
Kingsdown Way
TS11: N Mar . . . 2A **86**
Kings Ho. TS1: Midd . . . 3F **77**
Kingsley Av. TS25: H'pool . . . 2F **19**
Kingsley Cl. TS6: Gran . . . 4E **81**
Kingsley Rd. TS6: Gran . . . 4E **81**
TS18: Stock T . . . 1C **96**
King's M. East TS3: N Orm . . . 4B **78**
King's M. West TS3: N Orm . . . 4B **78**
Kingsport Cl. TS18: Stock T . . . 4D **75**
Kings Rd. TS3: N Orm . . . 4B **78**
TS5: Midd . . . 1C **100**
TS22: Bill . . . 5C **38**
Kingston Av. TS5: Midd . . . 3D **101**
Kingston Rd. TS20: Nort . . . 3B **74**
Kingston St. TS1: Midd . . . 4E **77**
King St. TS6: S Ban . . . 2A **80**
TS10: Redc . . . 3D **49**
TS17: Thorn T . . . 3C **98**
TS18: Stock T . . . 5B **74**
TS25: H'pool . . . 1C **20**
Kingsway TS23: Bill . . . 1D **55**
Kingsway Av. TS6: S Ban . . . 4B **80**
Kininvie Cl. TS10: Redc . . . 4C **64**
Kininvie Wlk. TS19: Stock T . . . 1D **73**
Kinkerdale Rd. TS6: Midd . . . 2F **61**
Kinloch Rd. TS6: Norm . . . 1C **104**
Kinloss Cl. TS17: Thorn T . . . 1E **129**
Kinloss Wlk. TS17: Thorn T . . . 1E **129**
Kinmel Cl. TS10: Redc . . . 3E **65**
Kinross Av. TS3: Midd . . . 3E **103**
Kinross Gro. TS25: H'pool . . . 4D **19**
Kinterbury Cl. TS25: Seat C . . . 2D **21**
Kintra Rd. TS25: H'pool . . . 4D **19**
Kintyre Dr. TS17: Thorn T . . . 2C **128**
Kintyre Wlk. *TS14: Guis . . . 4C 138*
(off Dorset Rd.)
Kinver Cl. TS3: Midd . . . 2C **102**
Kipling Gro. TS19: Stock T . . . 1B **96**
Kipling Rd. TS25: H'pool . . . 1E **19**
Kirby Av. TS5: Midd . . . 2B **100**
Kirby Bri. TS9: Kirkb . . . 4E **169**
Kirby Cl. TS6: Est . . . 5A **82**
TS23: Bill . . . 5F **39**
Kirby Wlk. TS10: Redc . . . 2C **64**
Kirkbridge Way TS17: Ing B . . . 4F **127**
Kirkbright Cl. TS12: Ling . . . 4E **113**
Kirkby La. TS9: Gt Bro . . . 5F **169**
TS9: Kirkb . . . 5D **169**
Kirkdale TS14: Guis . . . 3A **138**
TS17: Thorn T . . . 1C **98**
Kirkdale Cl. TS19: Stock T . . . 4E **73**
Kirkdale Way TS5: Midd . . . 5E **101**
Kirkfell Cl. TS16: Eag . . . 4B **126**
Kirkgate Rd. TS5: Midd . . . 3C **100**
Kirkham Rd. TS7: Nun . . . 3B **134**
Kirkham Row TS4: Midd . . . 4B **102**
Kirk Hill TS21: Carlt, Redm . . . 1B **70**
Kirklands, The
TS11: Marsk S . . . 3D **67**
Kirkland Wlk. TS3: Midd . . . 3D **103**
KIRKLEATHAM . . . 5A **64**
Kirkleatham Av.
TS11: Marsk S . . . 3D **67**
Kirkleatham Bus. Pk.
TS10: K'ham . . . 4A **64**
Kirkleatham By-Pass
TS10: K'ham, Redc . . . 1A **84**
Kirkleatham La.
TS10: K'ham, Redc . . . 4A **48**
Kirkleatham Memorial Park & Crematorium
TS11: Year . . . 5B **64**
Kirkleatham Mus. & Owl Cen. . . . 5A **64**
Kirkleatham St. TS10: Redc . . . 4A **48**
KIRKLEVINGTON . . . 4D **161**
Kirklevington Grange
TS15: K'ton . . . 1D **161**
Kirklevington Hall Dr.
TS15: K'ton . . . 2D **161**
Kirklevington Wlk.
TS19: Stock T . . . 1C **72**
Kirknewton Cl.
TS19: Stock T . . . 1D **73**
Kirknewton Gro.
TS17: Ing B . . . 2A **150**
Kirknewton Rd. TS6: Norm . . . 2C **104**
Kirk Rd. TS15: Yarm . . . 5E **149**
Kirkstall Av. TS3: Midd . . . 3E **103**
Kirkstall Ct. TS12: Skel . . . 4D **89**
Kirkstone Ct. TS24: H'pool . . . 5A **8**
Kirkstone Gro. TS10: Redc . . . 1C **64**
TS24: H'pool . . . 5F **7**
Kirkstone Rd. TS3: Midd . . . 2C **102**
Kirk St. TS21: Stil . . . 2A **50**
Kirkwall Cl. TS19: Stock T . . . 4F **71**
Kirkwood Dr. TS10: Redc . . . 4E **65**
Kirriemuir Rd. TS25: H'pool . . . 4D **19**

Kitchen Gdn., The
TS26: H'pool 3E **13**
Kittiwake Cl. TS26: H'pool 1D **13**
Knaith Cl. TS15: Yarm 1A **160**
Knapton Av. TS22: Bill 5A **38**
Knaresborough Av.
TS7: Mart. 4D **133**
Knaresborough Cl.
TS27: H'pool 3D **7**
Knayton Gro. TS19: Stock T . . . 1A **96**
Knebworth Ct. TS17: Ing B . . . 5A **128**
Knighton Ct. TS17: Thorn T. . . . 5E **99**
Knightsbridge Gdns.
TS26: H'pool 3E **13**
Knightsport Rd.
TS18: Stock T 4C **74**
Knitsley Wlk. TS19: Stock T . . . 1C **72**
Knole Rd. TS23: Bill. 5E **39**
Knotty Hill Golf Course 1B **22**
Knowles Cl. TS15: K'ton 4C **160**
Knowles St. TS18: Stock T 5B **74**
Kreuger All. TS3: N Orm 4B **78**
Kyle Av. TS25: H'pool 1A **20**
Kyle Gdns. TS20: Nort 4F **53**

L

Laburnum Av. TS17: Thorn T. . . 5C **98**
Laburnum Ct. TS18: Stock T . . . 1F **97**
Laburnum Gro. TS2: Port C 5F **57**
Laburnum Rd. TS6: Norm 5C **80**
TS7: Orm 5B **104**
TS10: Redc. 4E **49**
TS12: Brot 2A **90**
TS16: Prest T. 2C **126**
Laburnum St. TS26: H'pool 3A **14**
Lacey Gro. TS26: H'pool 2F **13**
Lackenby La.
TS6: Est, Gran, Old L 5A **82**
Lackenby Rd. TS6: Laze 4C **82**
Ladgate Grange TS3: Midd . . . 2D **103**
Ladgate La. TS3: Midd 5C **102**
TS4: Midd 5C **102**
TS5: Midd. 2E **131**
TS8: Midd. 2E **131**
Ladle, The TS4: Midd 5D **103**
Ladyfern Way TS20: Nort. 1F **73**
Lady Hullocks Ct.
TS9: Stokes 2B **168**
Lady Mantle Cl. TS26: H'pool . . . 4C **6**
Ladyport Grn. TS18: Stock T. . . 4C **74**
Ladysmith St. TS25: H'pool. . . . 1C **20**
Lagonda Ct. TS23: Bill. 5C **40**
Lagonda Rd. TS23: Bill 5B **40**
Laindon Av. TS4: Midd 1B **132**
Laing Cvn. Site TS10: Redc. . . . 4F **47**
Laing Cl. TS6: Gran. 2D **81**
Laing St. TS18: Stock T. 5A **74**
Laird Rd. TS25: H'pool 4D **19**
Lakeland Wlk. TS25: H'pool . . . 1B **20**
Lakes Av. TS10: Redc 5C **48**
Lakeston Cl. TS26: H'pool. 2D **13**
Lamberd Rd. TS24: H'pool. 3F **7**
Lambert Ter. TS13: Eas 2A **118**
Lambeth Rd. TS5: Midd 2D **101**
Lambfield Way TS17: Ing B. . . 3A **128**
Lamb La. TS17: Ing B 1A **150**
Lambourne Dr. TS7: Mart 2E **133**
Lambton Cres. TS21: Sed 4C **22**
(not continuous)
Lambton Lodge TS21: Sed 4C **22**
Lambton Rd. TS4: Midd. 1A **102**
(not continuous)
TS19: Stock T. 4F **73**
TS23: Bill 5F **39**
Lambton St. TS6: Norm. 2D **105**
TS24: H'pool 4C **14**
Lambton Ter. TS4: Midd 1A **102**
Lammermuir Rd. TS23: Bill. . . . 1C **54**
Lamonby Cl. TS7: Nun. 4F **133**
Lamont Gro. TS25: H'pool. 4C **18**
Lamport Cl. TS18: Stock T 4D **75**
Lamport St. TS1: Midd 4C **76**
Lanark Cl. TS19: Stock T. 4B **72**
Lanark Rd. TS25: H'pool 4C **18**
Lanberry Grn. TS4: Midd. 1B **102**
Lancaster Ct. TS24: H'pool 1B **14**
Lancaster Dr. TS11: Marsk S. . . 3B **66**
Lancaster Ho. TS6: Est 4E **81**
Lancaster Lodge
TS17: Thorn T 1C 128
(off Martinet Rd.)
Lancaster Rd. TS5: Midd. 2E **101**
TS16: Eag. 4E **125**
TS24: H'pool 1B **14**
Lancaster Rd. Nth.
TS24: H'pool 5B **8**
Lancaster Way
TS17: Thorn T 3D **129**
Lancefield Rd. TS20: Nort. 4B **54**
Lanchester Av. TS23: Bill. 4C **38**
Lanchester Rd. TS6: Gran. 2D **81**
Landseer Dr. TS23: Bill 3D **39**
Lane, The TS21: Sed. 3D **23**
Lane End Cotts.
TS15: K'ton 1D **161**
Lanehouse Rd.
TS17: Thorn T 4C **98**
Lane Pl. TS6: Gran 3D **81**
Laneside Rd. TS18: Stock T . . . 2C **96**
LANGBAURGH 5F **157**
Langbaurgh Cl. TS9: Gt A 1D **167**
Langbaurgh Ct. TS12: Salt. 3C **68**
Langdale TS14: Guis 3A **138**
Langdale Cl. TS16: Egg. 1B **148**
Langdale Cres. TS6: Gran 5F **81**
Langdale Gro. TS5: Midd 4D **101**
Langdale Rd. TS23: Bill. 4E **55**
Langdon Sq. TS8: Coul N 3B **132**
Langdon Way TS16: Eag 5A **126**
Langham Wlk.
TS19: Stock T 5A **72**
Langleeford Way
TS17: Ing B 2A **150**
Langley Av. TS17: Thorn T 3D **99**
Langley Cl. TS10: Redc. 3C **64**
Langley Ct. TS3: Midd. 3D **103**
Langridge Cres. TS3: Midd . . . 2C **102**
Langsett Av. TS3: Midd 2C **102**
Langthorne Gro.
TS18: Stock T 2A **96**
Langthorpe TS7: Nun 3F **133**
Langthwaite Wlk.
TS10: Redc 3C **64**
Langton Av. TS22: Bill 5A **38**
Langton Cl. TS4: Midd 1F **101**
Lanrood Grn. TS4: Midd 1B **102**
Lansbury Cl. TS6: S Ban 3A **80**
Lansbury Gro. TS24: H'pool . . . 2B **14**
Lansdowne Ct. TS4: Midd 5A **78**
TS26: H'pool 4A **14**
Lansdowne Rd. TS4: Midd 5A **78**
TS12: Brot 3C **90**
TS15: Yarm 4D **149**
TS17: Thorn T 4E **99**
TS26: H'pool 4A **14**
Lansdown Way TS23: Bill. 4F **39**
Lanshaw Grn. TS4: Midd. 1B **102**
Lantsbery Dr. TS13: Live 1A **116**
Lanyard, The TS24: H'pool 3C **14**
Lapwing La. TS20: Nort. 3A **54**
Lapwing Rd. TS26: H'pool. 1D **13**
Larch Cl. TS7: Mart 2F **133**
Larch Ct. TS15: Yarm. 1A **160**
Larch Cres. TS16: Prest T 2D **127**
Larches, The TS6: Norm 5B **80**
TS7: Orm 5B **104**
TS10: Redc. 5E **49**
TS19: Stock T 3C **72**
Larch Gro. TS24: H'pool 5A **8**
Larch Rd. TS14: Guis 1D **139**
TS19: Stock T 3A **74**
Larch Ter. TS2: Port C 5F **57**
Lark Dr. TS14: Guis 2A **138**
Larkhall Sq. TS20: Nort. 2B **74**
Larkspur Cl. TS26: H'pool 4D **7**
Larkspur Rd. TS7: Mart 2B **132**
Larkswood Rd. TS10: Redc 4C **64**
Larpool Cl. TS26: H'pool 3F **13**
Lartington Way TS16: Eag. . . . 5A **126**
Larun Beat, The
TS15: Yarm 5C **148**
Larvik Ct. TS13: Skin. 2A **92**
Lastingham Av. TS6: Est 1E **105**
Latham Rd. TS5: Midd 1D **101**
Latimer Cl. TS15: Yarm. 1A **160**
Latimer La. TS14: Guis 3C **138**
Lauder Cl. TS19: Stock T. 4B **72**
Lauderdale Dr. TS14: Guis. . . . 3F **139**
Lauder Ho. TS19: Stock T 4B **72**
Lauder St. TS24: H'pool 3B **14**
Laura St. TS1: Midd. 5F **77**
Laureate Cl. TS25: H'pool 1F **19**
Laurel Av. TS4: Midd 3A **102**
TS17: Thorn T 5C **98**
Laurel Cl. TS12: Salt 5C **68**
Laurel Cres. TS12: Brot. 2A **90**
Laurel Gdns. TS25: H'pool. 2E **19**
Laurel Pk. TS13: Loft. 5B **92**
Laurel Rd. TS7: Mart. 3D **133**
TS10: Redc. 5F **49**
TS12: Salt 5C **68**
TS16: Prest T. 2C **126**
TS19: Stock T. 3F **73**
Laurels, The TS25: H'pool 5F **13**
Laurel St. TS1: Midd 4F **77**
Laurelwood Rd.
TS18: Thorn T 5D **75**
Lavan Ct. TS10: Redc 3E **65**
Lavan Sands TS5: Midd. 3B **130**
Lavender Cl. TS18: Stock T. . . . 1A **98**
Lavender Ct. TS11: Marsk S . . . 5D **67**
Lavender La. TS22: Wyn. 3C **26**
Lavender Rd. TS3: Midd 5C **78**
Lavender Way TS20: Nort 1A **74**
Lavernock Cl. TS10: Redc 2E **65**
Law Courts
Teesside 3F **77**
Lawns, The TS24: H'pool. 1F **15**
Lawns Gill TS12: Skel 4A **88**
Lawnswood Rd. TS3: Midd . . . 1A **104**
Lawrence Rd. TS17: Thorn T. . . 5B **98**
(not continuous)
Lawrence St. TS10: Redc 4D **49**
TS18: Stock T 2A **98**
Lawrenny Gro. TS17: Ing B . . . 2F **149**
Lawson Cl. TS6: S Ban 3B **80**
Lawson Ind. Est.
TS3: N Orm 3C **78**
(Fleet St.)
TS3: N Orm 4C **78**
(Leven Rd.)
Lawson Rd. TS25: Seat C 3E **21**
Lawson St. TS18: Stock T 1A **98**
Lawson Way TS3: N Orm. 3C **78**
Lax Ter. TS22: Wolv. 2C **38**
Laxton Cl. TS23: Bill 4D **39**
Laycock St. TS1: Midd. 4C **76**
Layland Rd. TS12: Skel 4E **89**
LAZENBY. 4C **82**
Lazenby Bank Local Nature Reserve
. . . . 1D **107**
Lazenby Bank Rd.
TS6: Laze, Guis 5C **82**
TS14: Guis 5D **83**
Lazenby Rd. TS24: H'pool 2E **7**
Leahope Ct. TS17: Thorn T . . . 2E **129**
Lealholm Cres. TS3: Midd. . . . 4E **103**
Lealholme Gro.
TS19: Stock T 1B **96**
Lealholm Rd. TS25: H'pool 4A **20**
Lealholm Wlk. TS6: Est 5F **81**
Lealholm Way TS14: Guis. . . . 4D **139**
Leamington Dr.
TS25: H'pool 1B **20**
Leamington Gro. TS3: Midd. . . 3F **103**
Leamington Pde.
TS25: H'pool 1B **20**

Leam La. TS19: Stock T 3A **72**
Learning La. TS6: Norm 5C **80**
Leas, The TS10: Redc 2E **65**
TS21: Sed 5C **22**
Leas Gro. TS24: H'pool 4D **9**
Leas Wlk. TS24: H'pool 4D **9**
Leazon Hill TS17: Ing B 4A **128**
Leckfell Cl. TS7: Mart 4F **133**
Ledbury Dr. TS5: Midd 3D **131**
TS17: Thorn T 2C **128**
Ledbury Way TS14: Guis 4D **139**
Leeds St. TS18: Stock T 5A **74**
Leeholme Gdns. TS23: Bill 1F **55**
Leeholme Rd. TS23: Bill 1E **55**
Leeming Rd. TS5: Midd 2C **100**
Lee Rd. TS6: Gran 1D **81**
Lees Rd. TS1: Midd 4D **77**
Leeway, The TS3: Midd 3B **78**
Leicester Ho. TS6: Est 4E **81**
Leicester Rd. TS20: Nort 1C **74**
Leicester Way TS16: Eag 2A **148**
Leighton Rd. TS6: Gran 3E **81**
TS18: Stock T 3A **96**
Leighton Ter. TS27: H'pool 3D **7**
Leinster Rd. TS1: Midd 5C **76**
Leith Wlk. TS17: Thorn T 3D **129**
Lenham Cl. TS22: Bill 4A **38**
Lennox Cres. TS23: Bill 2D **55**
Lennox Wlk. TS25: H'pool 4C **18**
(not continuous)
Leo Gro. TS18: Stock T 4F **97**
Leonard Ropner Dr.
TS19: Stock T 5F **71**
Lerwick Cl. TS19: Stock T 5F **71**
Letch Cl. TS21: Stock T 4F **51**
Letch La.
TS21: Carlt, Stock T 5D **51**
Letch Rd. TS20: Nort 4B **54**
Letchworth Dr.
TS19: Stock T 1C **72**
Letitia Ind. Est. TS5: Midd 4C **76**
Letitia St. TS5: Midd 4B **76**
Leven Bank Rd.
TS15: Yarm, Ing B 5F **149**
TS17: Yarm 5F **149**
LEVEN BRIDGE 4B **150**
Leven Cl. TS9: Stokes 1C **168**
TS16: Eag 2B **148**
Leven Ct. TS9: Gt A 3E **167**
Levendale Cl. TS15: Yarm 4E **149**
Leven Gro. TS17: Thorn T 5D **99**
TS25: H'pool 4D **19**
Leven M. TS9: Stokes 2B **168**
Leven Rd. TS3: N Orm 4C **78**
TS9: Stokes 2A **168**
TS14: Guis 3D **139**
TS15: Yarm 4C **148**
TS20: Nort 5A **54**
Levenside TS9: Gt A 2C **166**
TS9: Stokes 2B **168**
(not continuous)
Levenside Pl. TS9: Stokes 2B **168**
Leven St. TS1: Midd 4C **76**
TS6: S Ban 2A **80**
TS12: Salt 4C **68**
TS23: Bill 3D **57**
Levens Wlk. TS10: Redc 1C **64**
Leven View Residential Pk.
TS17: Ing B 3A **150**
Leven Wynd TS9: Stokes 2B **168**
Leveret Cl. TS17: Ing B 4C **128**
Levick Ct. TS5: Midd 3C **100**
Levick Cres. TS5: Midd 4A **100**
Levington Ct. TS15: K'ton 4E **161**
Levington M. TS15: K'ton 4E **161**
Levington Wynd TS7: Nun 4A **134**
Levisham Cl. TS5: Midd 5E **101**
TS18: Stock T 2D **97**
Lewes Way TS23: Bill 3A **40**
Lewis Gro. TS25: H'pool 2D **19**
Lewis Rd. TS5: Midd 1D **101**
Lewis Wlk. TS14: Guis 3D **139**
Lexden Av. TS5: Midd 4A **100**
Lexington Ct. TS20: Nort 2B **74**
Leybourne Ter.
TS18: Stock T 1F **97**
Leyburn Gro. TS18: Stock T 3B **96**
Leyburn St. TS26: H'pool 5A **14**
Libanus Ct. TS17: Ing B 1F **149**
Lichfield Av. TS6: Est 5E **81**
TS16: Eag 5A **126**
Lichfield Rd. TS5: Midd 2F **101**
Liddel Ct. TS24: H'pool 4A **8**
Lifestyle Fitness 2C **14**
Lightfoot Cres. TS24: H'pool 4E **7**
Lightfoot Gro. TS18: Stock T 1A **98**
Light Pipe Hall Rd.
TS18: Stock T 1F **97**
(not continuous)
Lilac Av. TS17: Thorn T 5C **98**
TS21: Sed 3D **23**
Lilac Cl. TS6: Laze 4C **82**
TS12: Salt 5A **68**
TS21: Carlt 4D **51**
Lilac Cres. TS12: Brot 2A **90**
Lilac Gro. TS3: Midd 5E **79**
TS10: Redc 5E **49**
Lilac Rd. TS6: Norm 5C **80**
TS7: Orm 5B **104**
TS16: Prest T 2C **126**
TS19: Stock T 3E **73**
Lile Gdns. TS21: Sed 4E **23**
Lily Pot Cl. TS22: Wyn 3C **26**
Limber Grn. TS3: Midd 3A **104**
Limbrick Av. TS19: Stock T 5A **72**
Limbrick Ct. TS19: Stock T 5B **72**
Lime Cl. TS7: Mart 2D **133**
Lime Cres. TS6: Norm 1C **104**
TS24: H'pool 1A **14**
Lime Gro. TS19: Stock T 5B **72**
Limeoak Way TS18: Stock T 4C **74**
Limerick Rd. TS10: Redc 1D **63**
Lime Rd. TS6: Norm 5B **80**
TS10: Redc 4E **49**
TS14: Guis 1D **139**
TS16: Prest T 2D **127**
Limes Cres. TS11: Marsk S 5D **67**
Limes Rd. TS5: Midd 2E **101**
Limetree Ct. TS4: Midd 3F **101**
Limetrees Cl. TS2: Port C 4E **57**
Limpton Ga. TS15: Yarm 5C **148**
Linby Av. TS3: Midd 3C **102**
Lincoln Cres. TS23: Bill 2F **55**
Lincoln Gro. TS20: Nort 1C **74**
Lincoln Pl. TS17: Thorn T 4C **98**
Lincoln Rd. TS10: Redc 1F **65**
TS14: Guis 3D **139**
TS25: H'pool 5D **19**
Lincombe Dr. TS5: Midd 3D **131**
Linden Av. TS9: Gt A 2C **166**
TS18: Stock T 3E **97**
Linden Cl. TS9: Gt A 1C **166**
Linden Ct. TS17: Thorn T 4C **98**
Linden Cres. TS7: Mart 3C **132**
TS9: Gt A 2C **166**
Linden Gro. TS5: Midd 2D **101**
TS9: Gt A 2C **166**
TS17: Thorn T 4C **98**
TS26: H'pool 4F **13**
Linden Gro. Ct. TS9: Gt A 1C **166**
Linden Ho. TS12: Brot 2A **90**
Linden Rd. TS9: Gt A 2C **166**
TS12: Brot 2A **90**
Lindisfarne Av.
TS17: Thorn T 4D **99**
Lindisfarne Cl. TS27: H'pool 3D **7**
Lindisfarne Rd. TS3: Midd 3E **103**
Lindrick TS8: Mart 5E **133**
Lindrick Ct. TS6: Est 2E **105**
Lindrick Dr. TS27: H'pool 2C **6**
Lindrick Rd. TS11: N Mar 2F **85**
Lindsay Rd. TS25: H'pool 4C **18**
Lindsay St. TS18: Stock T 2A **98**
Lindsey Ct. TS12: Brot 3C **90**
Lingberry Gth. TS13: Loft 5C **92**
Ling Cl. TS7: Mart 1C **132**
LINGDALE 4E **113**
Lingdale Cl. TS19: Stock T 4E **73**
Lingdale Dr. TS25: Seat C 5D **21**
Lingdale Gro. TS10: Redc 1F **63**
Lingdale Ind. Est.
TS12: Ling 4E **113**
Lingdale Rd. TS12: Ling 3C **112**
TS17: Thorn T 5D **99**
Lingfield Ash TS8: Coul N 5B **132**
Lingfield Dr. TS16: Eag 5A **126**
Lingfield Rd. TS15: Yarm 4E **149**
TS19: Stock T 5A **72**
Lingfield Way TS8: Coul N 5C **132**
Lingholme TS10: Redc 1B **64**
Lingmell Rd. TS10: Redc 2C **64**
Lingwood Ct.
TS17: Thorn T 1D **129**
Link, The TS3: Midd 3F **103**
Link Cen. *TS18: Stock T* *4A* ***74***
(off Farrer St.)
Links, The TS12: Salt 1B **88**
TS25: Seat C 5E **21**
Linkway, The TS23: Bill 1E **55**
Linley Ct. TS20: Nort 3A **54**
Linlithgow Cl. TS14: Guis 4D **139**
Linmoor Av. TS3: Midd 1E **103**
Linnet Ct. TS20: Nort 3B **54**
Linnet Rd. TS26: H'pool 5E **7**
Linshiels Gro. TS17: Ing B 2A **150**
LINTHORPE 1D **101**
Linthorpe M. TS1: Midd 3E **77**
Linthorpe Rd. TS1: Midd 5E **77**
(not continuous)
TS5: Midd 1E **101**
Linton Av. TS7: Mart 3C **132**
Linton Cl. TS19: Stock T 3A **72**
Linton Rd. TS6: Norm 2B **104**
Linwood Av. TS9: Stokes 5C **164**
Linwood Ct. TS14: Guis 1E **139**
Lion Bri. Cl. TS22: Wyn 2E **37**
Lion Ct. TS22: Wyn 5E **27**
Lismore Gdns.
TS17: Thorn T 4D **99**
Lister St. TS24: H'pool 4A **14**
TS26: H'pool 4A **14**
Lithgo Cl. TS25: Seat C 2E **21**
LITTLE AYTON 3E **167**
Lit. Ayton La.
TS9: Gt A, L Ayt 3E **167**
Littleboy Dr. TS17: Thorn T 4E **99**
Lit. Brown St. *TS18: Stock T* *1A* ***98***
(off West Row)
Littlecote TS17: Ing B 3F **127**
Little Crake TS14: Guis 2B **138**
Little Grebe TS14: Guis 2A **138**
LITTLE MALTBY 3C **150**
Lit. Moorsholm La.
TS12: Moor 4F **113**
Little Pasture TS17: Ing B 4A **128**
Little Ross TS17: Thorn T 4D **99**
Lit. York St. TS18: Stock T 1A **98**
Littondale TS8: Hem 5D **131**
Littondale Ct. TS17: Ing B 3A **150**
LIVERTON 5A **116**
Liverton Av. TS5: Midd 5C **76**
Liverton Cres.
TS17: Thorn T 3B **128**
TS22: Bill 4B **38**
Liverton La.
TS13: Live 5A **116** & 1F **143**
Liverton Mill Bank
TS12: Moor 1D **143**
LIVERTON MINES 1A **116**
Liverton Rd. TS13: Live 2A **116**
(Lantsbery Dr.)
TS13: Live 5A **92**
(Liverton Ter.)
TS13: Loft 5B **92**
Liverton Ter. TS13: Live 1A **116**
Liverton Ter. Sth.
TS13: Live 1A **116**
Liverton Whin TS12: Salt 4A **68**
Livingstone Rd. TS3: N Orm 4C **78**

Lizard Gro. TS24: H'pool 4C **14**
Lizard Wlk. TS24: H'pool. 4C **14**
Lloyd St. TS2: Midd. 2D **77**
Lobelia Cl. TS7: Orm. 4B **104**
Lobster Rd. TS10: Redc. 3B **48**
Loch Gro. TS25: H'pool 4D **19**
Lockerbie Wlk.
TS17: Thorn T 2C **128**
Locke Rd. TS10: Redc 4B **48**
Lockheed Cl. TS18: Stock T. . . 1F **127**
Lockheed Ct. TS18: Stock T. . . . 5F **97**
Lockton Cl. TS8: Hem 5C **130**
Lockton Cres.
TS17: Thorn T 3B **128**
Lockwood Ct. TS6: Est. 2E **105**
Locomotion Ct. TS16: Eag. . . . 4B **126**
Lodge Farm Rd. TS6: Est. 1F **105**
Lodge Rd. TS6: Est 1E **105**
Lodge St. TS18: Stock T 1A **98**
Lodore Gro. TS5: Midd 5B **100**
LOFTUS 5B **92**
Loftus Bank
TS13: Carl H, Loft, Skin . . . 3F **91**
Loftus Ho. TS4: Midd. 2A **102**
Loftus Leisure Cen. 4A **92**
Logan Dr. TS19: Stock T 5C **72**
Logan Gro. TS25: H'pool 4D **19**
Lomond Av. TS23: Bill 2E **55**
Londonderry Rd.
TS19: Stock T. 4F **73**
Londonderry St.
TS24: H'pool. 1F **15**
Longacre Cl. TS12: Skel 2C **88**
Longbank Rd. TS7: Orm 5B **104**
Longbeck La.
TS11: N Mar, Year 2C **84**
Longbeck Rd.
TS11: Marsk S 5B **66**
LONGBECK RDBT. **5B 66**
Longbeck Station (Rail) 4B **66**
Longbeck Trad. Est.
TS11: Marsk S 4B **66**
Longbeck Way
TS17: Thorn T 3E **129**
Longcroft Wlk. TS3: Midd 5D **79**
Longfellow Rd. TS23: Bill 3D **39**
Longfellow Wlk.
TS25: H'pool 3D **19**
Longfield Vw. TS6: Norm 4C **104**
Longford Cl. TS23: Bill. 4E **39**
Longford St. TS1: Midd 5C **76**
LONGHILL 2C **20**
Longhill Ind. Est.
TS25: H'pool 1C **20**
(not continuous)
Longhirst TS8: Coul N 5C **132**
LONGLANDS 4A **78**
Longlands Rd. TS3: Midd 5A **78**
TS4: Midd 5A **78**
Long La. TS12: Moor. 2C **142**
TS15: K'ton. 5F **161**
Longleat Wlk. TS17: Ing B . . . 5A **128**
LONG NEWTON 1A **124**
Long Newton La.
TS16: Eag. 1A **124**
TS21: Eag, Long N. 1A **124**
Long Row TS13: Port M. 4F **121**
Longscar Wlk.
TS24: H'pool 4C **14**
Longshaw Cl. TS17: Ing B. 5C **128**
Longthwaite Cl. TS12: Skel 3C **88**
Long Wlk. TS15: Yarm. 4D **149**
Longworth Way TS14: Guis . . . 5F **109**
Lonsdale Ct. TS25: H'pool. 5B **14**
Lonsdale St. TS1: Midd. 5D **77**
Loraine Cl. TS11: Marsk S. 5E **67**
Lord Av. TS17: Thorn T 4D **129**
Lord Cl. TS5: Midd. 3B **130**
Lord Nelson Cl.
TS25: Seat C 3D **21**
Lord Nelson's Yd.
TS15: Yarm 3B **148**
Lord St. TS10: Redc. 3C **48**
Lorimer Cl. TS17: Ing B. 5B **128**
Lorne Ct. TS18: Stock T. 3E **97**
Lorne St. TS1: Midd 4D **77**
Lorne Ter. TS12: Brot 2C **90**
Lorrain Gro. TS20: Nort. 4C **54**
Lorton Rd. TS10: Redc 2C **64**
Lothian Gro. TS10: Redc 4A **48**
Lothian Rd. TS4: Midd. 5A **78**
Lovaine St. TS1: Midd. 4D **77**
Lovat Av. TS10: Redc. 5A **48**
Lovat Gro. TS25: H'pool 4D **19**
Love La. TS22: Wyn 2C **26**
Low Church Wynd
TS15: Yarm 2B **148**
Low Cleveland St.
TS13: Live 5A **92**
Lowcross Av. TS14: Guis 4C **138**
Lowcross Dr. TS9: Gt Bro. 5F **169**
Lowdale La. TS24: H'pool 2C **6**
Lowell Cl. TS23: Bill 2E **39**
Lwr. East St. TS2: Midd 2F **77**
Lwr. Feversham St.
TS2: Midd. 2F **77**
Lwr. Gosford St. TS2: Midd 2F **77**
Lower Promenade
TS12: Salt 3D **69**
Lowestoft Way TS10: Redc 3A **64**
Loweswater Cres.
TS18: Stock T 4D **73**
Loweswater Gro.
TS10: Redc 5C **48**
Low Farm Cl. TS8: Thornt 1B **152**
Low Farm Dr. TS10: Redc 2B **64**
Lowfield Av. TS3: Midd 5E **79**
LOWFIELDS
TS6 . . . . 5C **80**
TS17 . . . . 4B **128**
Lowfields Av. TS17: Ing B 4A **128**
(not continuous)
Lowfields Grn. TS17: Ing B. . . 5B **128**
Lowfields Wlk. TS17: Ing B. . . 4B **128**
Low Fold TS10: Redc. 1B **64**
LOW GRANGE
TS6 . . . . 3C **80**
TS23 . . . . 4E **39**
Low Grange Av. TS23: Bill 2E **39**
Low Green TS9: Gt A 2B **166**
Lowick Cl. TS19: Stock T. 4B **72**
Low La. TS5: Midd. 3C **130**
TS8: Thornt 1E **151**
TS15: Thorn T 1E **151**
TS17: High L, Thorn T . . . 4B **150**
TS17: Stain. 1E **151**
Lowmead Wlk. TS3: Midd. . . . 4D **103**
Lowood Av. TS7: Mart 3C **132**
Lowson St. TS21: Stil 1B **50**
Low Stanghow Rd.
TS12: Ling 5E **113**
Lowther Cl. TS22: Bill 4A **38**
Lowthian Rd. TS24: H'pool 3A **14**
TS26: H'pool 3A **14**
LOW THROSTON 1E **13**
Loxley Rd. TS3: Midd 1A **104**
Loyalty Cl. TS25: H'pool 2B **20**
Loyalty Ct. TS25: H'pool 2B **20**
Loyalty M. TS25: H'pool 2B **20**
Loyalty Rd. TS25: H'pool. 3B **20**
Loy La. TS13: Loft 5E **93**
Lucan St. TS24: H'pool 3B **14**
Luccombe Cl. TS17: Ing B. . . . 3B **150**
Lucerne Ct. TS7: Mart 2C **132**
Lucerne Dr. TS14: Guis 3B **138**
Lucerne Rd. TS10: Redc 5C **48**
Luce Sands TS5: Midd. 3B **130**
Lucia La. TS14: Guis. 3C **138**
Ludford Av. TS3: Midd. 3D **103**
Ludham Gro. TS19: Stock T . . . 3C **72**
Ludlow Cres. TS10: Redc 1E **65**
Ludlow Rd. TS23: Bill 5D **39**
Luff Way TS10: Redc 2E **65**
Lufton Cl. TS17: Ing B 4E **127**
Lullingstone Cres.
TS17: Ing B 3F **127**
Lulsgate TS17: Thorn T 1E **129**
Lulworth Cl. TS10: Redc 3E **65**
Lulworth Gro. TS24: H'pool. 2D **7**
Lumley Rd. TS10: Redc. 4D **49**
TS23: Bill 5E **39**
Lumley Sq. TS24: H'pool 1F **15**
Lumley St. TS13: Loft 4A **92**
Lumley Ter. TS14: Guis 1F **139**
Lumpsey Cl. TS12: Brot. 2B **90**
Lundy Ct. TS17: Ing B 1B **150**
Lundy Wlk. *TS14: Guis 3D* ***139***
(off Dorset Rd.)
Lunebeck Wlk.
TS17: Thorn T 3E **129**
Lunedale Av. TS5: Midd 4D **101**
Lunedale Rd. TS23: Bill. 2D **55**
Lune Rd. TS16: Eag. 2B **148**
TS20: Nort 1A **74**
Lune St. TS12: Salt 4C **68**
Lustram Vale TS19: Stock T . . . 3E **73**
Lustrum Av. TS18: Stock T. 3F **75**
Lustrum Retail Pk.
TS18: Stock T. 3F **75**
Lutton Cres. TS22: Bill. 5A **38**
Luttrell Ho. TS3: Midd 2C **102**
Lutyens Sq. TS19: Stock T 1B **72**
Lycium Cl. TS7: Mart. 1C **132**
Lydbrook Rd. TS5: Midd 1B **100**
Lydd Gdns. TS17: Thorn T. . . . 1E **129**
Lyme Pk. TS17: Ing B 5A **128**
Lynas Pl. TS10: Redc 3C **48**
Lyn Cl. TS17: Ing B 3B **150**
Lyndale TS14: Guis 4A **138**
Lyndon Way TS18: Stock T 5A **72**
Lynmouth Cl. TS8: Hem. 4C **130**
Lynmouth Rd. TS20: Nort 4E **53**
Lynmouth Wlk. TS26: H'pool . . . 1E **13**
Lynnfield Rd. TS26: H'pool 3B **14**
Lynn St. TS24: H'pool 3C **14**
Lynn St. Nth. *TS24: H'pool 3C* ***14***
(off Lynn St.)
Lynn St. Sth. TS24: H'pool 4C **14**
Lynton Ct. TS26: H'pool. 1E **13**
Lynwood Av. TS5: Midd 4E **101**
Lynx Way TS18: Stock T 4E **97**
Lysander Cl.
TS11: Marsk S 4B **66**
Lytham Wlk. TS16: Eag 5C **126**
Lythe Pl. TS4: Midd 4A **102**
Lythe Wlk. TS6: Est 5F **81**
Lyttleton Dr. TS18: Stock T 2C **96**
Lytton Ct. TS4: Midd 4B **78**
Lytton St. TS4: Midd 4A **78**

M

Mablethorpe Cl. TS10: Redc . . . 2B **64**
Macaulay Rd. TS25: H'pool. . . . 2D **19**
McAuley Ct. TS3: Midd 1C **102**
Mac Bean St. TS3: N Orm 4C **78**
McClean Av. TS10: Redc 5F **47**
McCreton St. TS3: N Orm 5C **78**
McDonald Pl. *TS24: H'pool 1F* ***15***
(off Cliff Ter.)
Mackie Dr. TS14: Guis 5F **109**
Macklin Av.
TS23: Bill, Cowp B 1A **56**
McLean Rd. TS12: Brot 2C **90**
Macnay St. TS12: Salt 4C **68**
Macrae Rd. TS25: H'pool 5C **18**
Maddocks Cl.
TS17: Thorn T 1D **129**
Maddren Way TS5: Midd. 1D **101**
Madison Sq. TS19: Stock T 4B **72**
Magdalene Dr. TS27: Hart 3F **5**
Magdalen St. TS3: N Orm 4B **78**
Magister Rd.
TS17: Thorn T 1C **128**
Magistrates' Court
Hartlepool 3B **14**
Teesside 3F **77**
Magnis Cl. TS17: Ing B 5F **127**

Magnolia Ct. TS10: Redc. 4E **65**
TS18: Stock T. 1F **97**
Maidstone Dr. TS7: Mart 2E **133**
Mainsforth Dr. TS5: Midd 1D **131**
TS23: Bill 2F **39**
Mainsforth Flats
TS24: H'pool 4D **15**
Mainsforth Ter. TS24: H'pool. . . 3C **14**
TS25: H'pool 1D **21**
Mainside TS21: Redm 1B **70**
Maize Beck Wlk.
TS18: Stock T 4D **75**
Major Cooper Ct.
TS25: Seat C 4E **21**
Major St. TS18: Stock T 4B **74**
Majuba Rd. TS10: Redc. 3A **48**
Making Tracks BMX **5E 47**
Malcolm Dr. TS19: Stock T 3A **72**
Malcolm Gro. TS10: Redc 5E **49**
TS17: Thorn T 5D **99**
Malcolm Rd. TS25: H'pool 5D **19**
Malden Rd. TS20: Nort 5B **54**
Maldon Rd. TS5: Midd. 1B **100**
Malham Gill TS10: Redc 1B **64**
Malham Gro. TS17: Ing B 5C **128**
Malin Gro. TS10: Redc 4C **64**
Mallaig Vw. TS19: Stock T 4B **72**
Mallard Cl. TS14: Guis 3A **138**
Mallard Ct. TS10: Redc 1F **63**
Mallard La. TS20: Nort 4A **54**
Mallards, The TS8: Hem 1A **154**
Malleable Way
TS18: Stock T 5D **75**
Malling Rd. TS20: Nort 2B **74**
Malling Wlk. TS3: Midd 1D **103**
Mallory Cl. TS1: Midd 3D **77**
Mallory Rd. TS20: Nort 5A **54**
Mallowdale TS7: Mart, Nun . . . 4F **133**
Malltraeth Sands
TS5: Midd 2A **130**
Malmo Ct. TS10: K'ham 4F **63**
Malta Rd. TS16: Eag 4F **125**
MALTBY **1F 151**
Maltby Ct. TS14: Guis 1D **139**
Maltby Ho. TS4: Midd 2A **102**
Maltby Pl. TS17: Thorn T 4C **98**
Maltby Rd. TS8: Thornt 1A **152**
Maltby St. TS3: N Orm 4C **78**
Maltings, The TS25: H'pool. . . . 5B **14**
Malton Dr. TS19: Stock T 3A **72**
Malton Ter. TS21: Sed. 4D **23**
Malvern Av. TS10: Redc 2A **64**
TS12: Skel 3C **88**
Malvern Cl. TS9: Stokes 2B **168**
Malvern Dr. TS5: Midd 2C **130**
TS9: Stokes 2B **168**
Malvern Rd. TS18: Stock T 1E **97**
TS23: Bill 1C **54**
Mandale Ct. TS18: Stock T 3E **75**
Mandale Ho. TS17: Thorn T . . . 3D **99**
TS24: H'pool 2C **14**
Mandale Ind. Est.
TS17: Thorn T 2C **98**
Mandale Retail Pk.
TS18: Stock T 4D **75**
Mandale Rd. TS5: Midd. 4A **100**
TS17: Thorn T 2B **98**
MANDALE RDBT. **4A 100**
Manfield Av. TS5: Midd 2A **100**
Manfield St. TS18: Stock T 1F **97**
Manitoba Gdns. TS4: Midd 5A **78**
Manless Ter. TS12: Skel 5B **88**
Manners St. TS24: H'pool 1F **15**
Manning Cl. TS17: Thorn T . . . 1D **129**
Manning Way
TS17: Thorn T 1D **129**
Manor Cl. TS9: Stokes. 1C **168**
TS22: Wolv. 3C **38**
TS27: Elw. 4D **11**
Manor Ct. TS12: Moor. 3B **142**
TS22: Wolv. 3C **38**
Manor Dr. TS15: Hilt 1E **163**
TS21: Stil 2B **50**
Mnr. Farm Way
TS8: Coul N 3A **132**
Manor Flds. TS22: Wyn. 3A **26**
TS27: Dalt P 1E **17**
Manor Gth. TS15: K'ton. 4D **161**
Manor Gth. Dr. TS26: H'pool . . . 3E **13**
Manor Ga. TS21: Long N. 1A **124**
Manor Grn. TS6: Norm 1D **105**
Manor Gro. TS9: Gt Bro 5F **169**
Manor Ho. M. TS15: Yarm. . . . 3B **148**
Manor Pl. TS19: Stock T 4B **72**
Manor Rd. TS26: H'pool 3D **13**
Manorside TS9: Stokes 1C **168**
Manor St. TS1: Midd 4D **77**
Manor Wlk. TS21: Stil 2B **50**
Manor Way TS23: Bill 2B **56**
Manor Wood TS8: Coul N. 3F **131**
Mansepool Cl. TS24: H'pool 4B **8**
Mansfield Av. TS17: Thorn T. . . 2D **99**
Mansfield Rd. TS6: Est 2E **105**
Manston Ct. DL2: Mid G 1A **144**
Man's Yd. TS13: Stait 1C **120**
Manton Av. TS5: Midd 3B **100**
Mapel Ct. TS19: Stock T 3C **72**
Maple Av. TS4: Midd 3F **101**
TS17: Thorn T 5C **98**
Maple Gdns. TS14: Guis 1D **139**
Maple Gro. TS12: Brot. 2A **90**
TS21: Sed 3D **23**
Maple Rd. TS19: Stock T. 3F **73**
Maple Sq. TS10: Redc. 4D **49**
Maple St. TS1: Midd 4F **77**
Mapleton Cl. TS10: Redc. 4C **64**
Mapleton Cres. TS10: Redc. . . . 4B **64**
Mapleton Dr. TS8: Hem. 4D **131**
(not continuous)
TS20: Nort 4F **53**
Mapleton Rd. TS24: H'pool 1B **14**
(not continuous)
Maplewood Dr. TS6: S Ban 4A **80**
Maplin Vw. TS19: Stock T. 4B **72**
Marchlyn Cres. TS17: Ing B. . . 1F **149**
Mardale TS8: Hem 5D **131**
Mardale Av. TS25: H'pool 5A **20**
Mardale Wlk. TS10: Redc 3C **64**
Margaret St. TS3: N Orm. 4B **78**
Margill Cl. TS7: Mart. 2E **133**
Margrove Heritage Cen. **5A 112**
MARGROVE PARK. **5A 112**
Margrove Pk. Cvn. Site
TS12: Boo 5A **112**
Margrove Ponds Nature Reserve
. . . . **4A 112**
Margrove Rd. TS12: Boo 2F **141**
Margrove Wlk. TS3: Midd 3D **103**
Margrove Way TS12: Brot 1A **90**
Marham Cl. TS3: Midd. 3F **103**
Maria Dr. TS19: Stock T 4A **72**
Maria St. TS3: N Orm 4C **78**
Marigold Gro. TS19: Stock T. . . 3C **72**
Marina Av. TS10: Redc 3A **48**
Marina Gateway TS24: H'pool . . . 3C **14**
Marina Vw. TS24: H'pool. 3C **14**
Marina Way TS18: Stock T 5C **74**
TS24: H'pool 1B **14**
Marine Ct. TS12: Salt 3C **68**
Marine Cres. TS24: H'pool. 1F **15**
Marine Dr. TS24: H'pool 4D **9**
Marine Pde. TS12: Salt 4C **68**
Mariners Ct. TS11: Marsk S . . . 3C **66**
Mariners Point TS24: H'pool . . . 2D **15**
Marine Ter. TS13: Skin 1A **92**
Marion Av. TS5: Midd 3C **100**
TS16: Eag. 1B **148**
Maritime Av. TS24: H'pool 3C **14**
Maritime Cl. TS24: H'pool. 3D **15**
Maritime Rd. TS18: Stock T . . . 4B **74**
Mark Av. TS20: Nort 3A **54**
Markby Grn. TS3: Midd 3A **104**
Market Pl. TS3: N Orm 4B **78**
TS9: Stokes 1B **168**
TS14: Guis 1E **139**
TS24: H'pool 4B **14**
Market St. TS6: S Ban 2A **80**
Market Wlk. *TS3: N Orm 4B 78*
(off Conyers Way)
Markham Sq. TS19: Stock T . . . 4B **72**
Marlborough Av.
TS11: Marsk S 3C **66**
Marlborough Cl. TS23: Bill 4D **55**
Marlborough Ct. TS12: Skel . . . 3C **88**
Marlborough Rd.
TS7: Mart. 3C **132**
TS12: Skel 3C **88**
TS18: Stock T. 2F **97**
Marlborough St.
TS25: H'pool 1A **20**
Marley Cl. TS19: Stock T. 4C **72**
Marley Wlk. TS27: H'pool 3D **7**
Marlowe Rd. TS25: H'pool 2D **19**
Marlsford Gro. TS5: Midd 4B **100**
Marmaduke Pl. TS20: Nort 4A **54**
Marmion Cl. TS25: H'pool. 2B **20**
Marquand Rd. TS6: S Ban. 3B **80**
Marquis Gro. TS20: Nort 4F **53**
Marquis St. TS24: H'pool. 1F **15**
Marrick Rd. TS3: Midd 3D **103**
TS18: Stock T 3B **96**
Marsden Cl. TS4: Midd 3A **102**
TS17: Ing B 1C **150**
Marshall Av. TS3: Midd 5E **79**
Marshall Cl. TS12: Salt 4B **68**
TS24: H'pool 3E **7**
Marshall Ct. TS3: Midd 4F **79**
Marshall Dr. TS12: Brot. 1A **90**
Marshall Gro.
TS18: Stock T. 4E **73**
Marsh Ho. Av. TS23: Bill 1E **39**
Marsh Ho. La. TS25: Grea 4F **31**
Marsh La. TS23: Cowp B. 4C **40**
Marsh Rd. TS1: Midd 3D **77**
(not continuous)
TS3: N Orm 3C **78**
Marsh St. TS1: Midd 3D **77**
Marske By-Pass
TS11: Marsk S 4E **65**
MARSKE-BY-THE-SEA **4C 66**
Marske Cen. **4C 66**
Marske La. TS11: Marsk S 1D **87**
TS12: Skel 4F **87**
TS19: Stock T 2A **72**
Marske Mill La. TS12: Salt 4B **68**
Marske Mill Ter. TS12: Salt. . . . 5C **68**
Marske Pde. TS19: Stock T. . . . 3A **72**
Marske Rd.
TS11: Marsk S, Salt 1E **87**
TS12: Salt. 1E **87**
Marske Station (Rail) **5C 66**
Marske St. TS25: H'pool 5B **14**
Marston Ct. TS18: Stock T. 4F **75**
Marston Rd. TS12: Brot. 2C **90**
TS18: Stock T. 4E **75**
Martham Cl. TS19: Stock T 3C **72**
Martindale TS5: Midd 2B **130**
Martindale Cl. TS27: Elw. 3C **10**
Martindale Gro. TS16: Egg . . . 1C **148**
Martindale Pl. TS6: Gran. 4E **81**
Martindale Rd. TS6: Gran 5E **81**
Martindale Way TS10: Redc . . . 4C **64**
Martinet Ct. TS17: Thorn T . . . 1C **128**
Martinet Rd. TS17: Thorn T. . . 1C **128**
Martin Gro. TS25: H'pool. 1F **19**
Martinhoe Cl. TS17: Ing B. . . . 4B **150**
Marton Av. TS4: Midd 4D **103**
Marton Burn Rd. TS4: Midd. . . 2F **101**
Marton Cres. TS6: Est 2F **105**
Marton Dale Ct. TS7: Mart. . . . 3E **133**
Marton Dr. TS22: Bill 5B **38**
Marton Gill TS12: Salt 4A **68**
MARTON GROVE. **1F 101**
Marton Gro. TS12: Brot 1A **90**
Marton Gro. Rd. TS4: Midd . . . 1F **101**
MARTON IN CLEVELAND **3E 133**
MARTON INTERCHANGE **2D 133**
Marton Moor Cnr.
TS7: Nun 5A **134**

Marton Moor Rd. TS7: Nun . . . 4B **134**
Marton Pk. TS4: Midd 2B **102**
Marton Rd. TS1: Midd 3A **78**
TS4: Midd 1A **102**
Martonside Way TS4: Midd . . . 3A **102**
Marton St. TS24: H'pool 2A **14**
MARTON VILLAGE 2C 132
Marton Way TS4: Midd 3B **102**
Marway Rd. TS12: Brot 1A **90**
Marwood Dr. TS9: Gt A 3C **166**
TS12: Brot 1A **90**
Marwood Sq. TS19: Stock T . . . 4B **72**
Mary Jaques Ct. TS4: Midd . . . 1A **102**
Marykirk Rd.
TS17: Thorn T 3D **129**
Maryport Cl. TS18: Stock T 4C **74**
Mary Rose Cl. TS25: Seat C . . . 3D **21**
Mary St. TS18: Stock T 1F **97**
TS26: H'pool 3A **14**
Masefield Rd. TS25: H'pool . . . 2D **19**
Masham Gro. TS19: Stock T . . . 1A **96**
Mason St. TS6: Norm 2D **105**
Mason Wlk. TS24: H'pool 2B **14**
Massey Rd. TS17: Thorn T 1C **98**
Massidon Gro. TS6: Norm. . . . 3D **105**
Master Rd. TS17: Thorn T. . . . 1C **128**
Masterton Dr. TS18: Stock T . . . 2B **96**
Mastiles Cl. TS17: Ing B 3A **150**
Matfen Av. TS7: Nun 3A **134**
Matfen Ct. TS21: Sed. 3C **22**
Matford Av. TS3: Midd. 5E **79**
Matlock Av. TS7: Mart. 4D **133**
Matlock Gdns. TS22: Bill 4C **38**
Mattison Av. TS5: Midd 1B **100**
Maxton Rd. TS6: S Ban 3A **80**
Maxwell Ct. *TS18: Stock T. 3F **97***
(off Devonshire St.)
TS25: H'pool 5D **19**
Maxwell Pl. TS10: Redc 1E **63**
Maxwell Rd. TS3: N Orm. 4E **79**
TS25: H'pool 5D **19**
Mayberry Gro. TS5: Midd 3E **101**
Maybray King Wlk.
TS20: Nort 5B **54**
Mayes Wlk. TS15: Yarm 1B **160**
Mayfair Av. TS4: Midd. 1A **102**
TS6: Norm 4C **104**
Mayfield Cl. TS16: Eag 5A **126**
Mayfield Cres. TS16: Eag 5A **126**
Mayfield Rd. TS7: Nun 2A **134**
Mayflower Cl. TS24: H'pool. . . . 3C **14**
Mayflower Ct. TS8: Hem 3D **131**
Mayflower Ho. TS24: H'pool . . . 3D **15**
Maygate TS6: Est. 1A **106**
Maynard Gro. TS22: Wyn. 4F **25**
Maynard St. TS13: Carl H 3F **91**
May St. TS24: H'pool. 1B **14**
Maze La. TS17: Thorn T 1E **99**
Mead Cres. TS17: Thorn T. 4E **99**
Meadfoot Dr. TS5: Midd 2C **130**
Meadow, The TS25: H'pool 2A **20**
Meadowbank Rd.
TS7: Orm 5B **104**
Meadow Cl. TS7: Orm 5A **104**
TS14: Guis 2E **139**
Meadowcroft Rd.
TS6: Norm 2B **104**
Meadowdale Cl. TS2: Port C . . . 4E **57**
Meadow Dale Ct.
TS12: Ling 4E **113**
Meadow Dr. TS7: Orm 5B **104**
TS26: H'pool 4D **13**
Meadow End TS16: Eag. 4B **126**
Meadowfield TS9: Stokes 5C **164**
Meadowfield Ct.
TS9: Stokes 5C **164**
TS25: Seat C 5E **21**
Meadowfield Dr. TS16: Eag. . . 4B **126**
Meadowfields Cl.
TS11: Marsk S 4D **67**
Meadowgate TS6: Est 1A **106**
Meadowgate Dr.
TS26: H'pool 3E **13**
Meadow Hill TS21: Sed. 1C **22**
Meadowings, The
TS15: Yarm 4B **148**
Meadowlands Cl.
TS13: Eas. 3A **118**
Meadow Rd. TS11: Marsk S . . . 5D **67**
TS19: Stock T 5C **72**
Meadows, The TS8: Coul N. . . 5C **132**
TS10: Redc 1B **64**
TS21: Sed 5C **22**
TS22: Wyn. 3B **26**
Meadows Wlk. TS26: H'pool 5E **7**
Meadowsweet La.
TS19: Stock T 3B **72**
Meadowsweet Rd.
TS26: H'pool 4D **7**
Meadow Va. Cl.
TS15: Yarm 5B **148**
Meadow Vw. Rd.
TS5: Midd 1B **100**
Meadow Wlk. TS21: Carlt 5C **50**
Meadway TS10: Redc 3B **64**
Measham Cl. TS20: Nort 5F **53**
Meath St. TS1: Midd 5C **76**
Meath Way TS14: Guis 3D **139**
Mecca Bingo
Hartlepool 3C 14
Stockton-on-Tees 1B 98
Medbourne Cl. TS6: Est. 2F **105**
Medbourne Gdns.
TS5: Midd 2D **131**
Medina Cl. TS19: Stock T 4B **72**
Medina Gdns. TS5: Midd. 2E **131**
Medway Cl. TS12: Skel 2C **88**
Medway Ho. TS23: Bill 4D **55**
Medwin Cl. TS12: Brot 1A **90**
Megarth Rd. TS5: Midd. 1D **101**
Meggitts La. TS10: K'ham 2E **63**
Melbourne Cl. TS7: Mart 3E **133**
Melbourne St. TS1: Midd 4C **76**
TS18: Stock T 5A **74**
Melbreak Gro. TS5: Midd 5B **100**
Meldreth Ho. TS12: Salt 5C **68**
Meldrum Sq. TS19: Stock T . . . 4B **72**
Meldyke La. TS8: Stain 5C **130**
Meldyke Pl. TS8: Stain 5C **130**
Melford Gro. TS17: Ing B 1B **150**
Melgrove Way TS21: Sed 5C **22**
Melksham Sq.
TS19: Stock T 4B **72**
Mellanby La. TS25: Grea. 3E **31**
Mellor St. TS19: Stock T 4F **73**
Melrose Av. TS5: Midd 3C **100**
TS23: Bill 5E **39**
Melrose Cres. TS14: Guis 2A **140**
Melrose Dr. TS18: Stock T. 3E **97**
Melrose Ho. TS1: Midd 3F **77**
Melrose St. TS1: Midd. 3F **77**
TS25: H'pool 1A **20**
Melsonby Av. TS3: Midd 3E **103**
Melsonby Ct. TS23: Bill. 3A **40**
Melsonby Gro.
TS18: Stock T 2A **96**
Melton Rd. TS19: Stock T 4B **72**
Melton Wlk. TS8: Hem 4D **131**
Melville Wlk. TS20: Nort. 3C **74**
Memorial Dr. TS7: Mart 2D **133**
Mendip Av. TS12: Skel. 3C **88**
Mendip Dr. TS10: Redc 2A **64**
Mendip Rd. TS23: Bill 1D **55**
Merchant Ho. *TS24: H'pool. . . . 3D **15***
(off Quayside)
Meredith Av. TS6: Norm 3C **104**
Mereston Cl. TS26: H'pool 2C **12**
Merganser Rd. TS26: H'pool. . . . 5D **7**
Meridian Way TS18: Stock T. . . 5D **73**
Merion Dr. TS11: N Mar. 2F **85**
Merioneth Cl. TS17: Ing B 1F **149**
Merlay Cl. TS15: Yarm 1A **160**
Merlin Cl. TS14: Guis 2A **138**
Merlin Rd. TS3: N Orm 4D **79**
TS19: Stock T 4B **72**
Merlin Way TS26: H'pool. 4C **6**
Merriman Grn. TS24: H'pool. . . . 3D **7**
Merring Cl. TS18: Stock T. 1A **96**
Merrington Av. TS5: Midd 2B **130**
Merryweather Ct.
TS15: Yarm 3C **148**
Merry Weather's Yd.
TS14: Guis 2E **139**
Mersehead Sands
TS5: Midd 2B **130**
Mersey Rd. TS10: Redc. 4B **48**
Merton Rd. TS5: Midd 2B **100**
Merville Av. TS19: Stock T 1C **96**
Meryl Gdns. TS25: H'pool 5A **20**
Messines La. TS21: Stil. 2A **50**
Metcalfe Cl. TS15: Yarm 1B **160**
Metcalfe Rd. TS6: S Ban 3F **79**
Metz Bri. Cvn. Site
TS2: Midd 2C **76**
Metz Bri. Rd. TS2: Midd 2D **77**
Mews, The TS7: Orm. 5A **104**
TS11: Marsk S 4D **67**
TS16: Eag. 3C **126**
Mexborough Cl.
TS19: Stock T 3D **73**
Meynell Av. TS14: Guis 3B **138**
Meynell's Cotts.
TS15: Yarm 3B **148**
Meynell Wlk. TS15: Yarm 5B **148**
Mickey Barron Cl.
TS24: H'pool 2A **14**
Mickleby Cl. TS7: Nun. 4F **133**
MICKLE DALES. 4E 65
Mickledales Dr.
TS11: Marsk S 4C **66**
MICKLEDALES RDBT. 4D **65**
Micklemire La. TS25: Grea 4F **31**
Mickleton Dr. TS16: Eag 5A **126**
Mickleton Rd. TS2: Midd. 5C **56**
Micklow Cl. TS10: Redc 3C **64**
Micklow La. TS13: Loft 5C **92**
Micklow Ter. TS13: Loft 5D **93**
Midbourne Rd.
TS19: Stock T 3A **74**
Middle Av. TS23: Bill. 4D **55**
Middlebank TS21: Thorpe T . . . 2D **51**
Middlebank Rd. TS7: Orm. . . . 5B **104**
Middle Beck TS3: Midd 2E **103**
Middlefield Rd.
TS11: Marsk S 4B **66**
TS19: Stock T 2C **72**
Middlegate TS24: H'pool 1F **15**
Middle Gill TS6: Norm 3D **105**
Middleham Ct. TS25: H'pool . . . 4B **20**
Middleham Rd.
TS19: Stock T 1C **96**
Middleham Way TS10: Redc . . . 1F **65**
Middle Rd. TS17: Ing B. 5B **128**
MIDDLESBROUGH 2E 77
Middlesbrough Bus Station . . . 3E 77
Middlesbrough By-Pass
TS1: Midd. 2E **77**
TS3: Midd 3A **78**
TS4: Midd 3A **78**
Middlesbrough FC 2B 78
Middlesbrough Leisure Pk. 3A 78
Middlesbrough Municipal Golf Cen.
. . . . 1F 131
Middlesbrough RC Cathedral
. . . . 5C 132
Middlesbrough Rd.
TS6: S Ban 3F **79**
TS7: Nun, Guis. 2D **135**
TS14: Guis 2E **137**
TS17: Thorn T 2D **99**
Middlesbrough Rd. E.
TS6: S Ban. 2A **80**
(not continuous)
Middlesbrough Sports Village
. . . . 5C 102
Middlesbrough Station (Rail)
. . . . 2F 77
Middlesbrough Tennis
& Badminton Club 1A 102

Middlesbrough Theatre 2E 101
Middlesbrough Transporter Bridge Vis. Cen. 1F 77
Middle St. TS18: Stock T. 5A 74
MIDDLETON 1C 14
Middleton Av. TS5: Midd 3B 100
TS17: Thorn T 3C 128
TS22: Bill 5B 38
Middleton Cl. TS16: Eag 5F 125
Middleton Ct. TS15: Yarm 5C 148
Middleton Dr. TS14: Guis. 3F 139
Middleton Grange La.
TS24: H'pool 3B 14
(not continuous)
Middleton Grange Shop. Cen.
TS24: H'pool 4B 14
Middleton La. DL2: Mid G. . . . 3A 144
MIDDLETON ONE ROW 4A 144
MIDDLETON-ON-LEVEN 4F 163
Middleton Rd. TS24: H'pool . . . 2B 14
MIDDLETON ST GEORGE 1A 144
Middleton Wlk.
TS18: Stock T. 1F 97
Middleton Woods
DL2: Mid G. 2B 144
Middleway TS17: Thorn T 2C 98
Middlewood Cl. TS27: H'pool . . . 2C 6
Middridge Gro. TS23: Bill 3F 39
Midfield, The TS5: Midd 5D 77
Midfield Vw. TS19: Stock T. . . . 4B 72
Midhurst Rd. TS3: Midd 1A 104
Midlothian Rd. TS25: H'pool. . . 4C 18
Midville Wlk. TS3: Midd 2A 104
Miers Av. TS24: H'pool 4F 7
Milbank Cl. TS27: Hart 3A 6
Milbank Ct. TS18: Stock T. 5A 74
Milbank Rd. TS24: H'pool 1B 14
Milbank St. TS6: S Ban 2A 80
TS18: Stock T 5A 74
Milbank Ter. TS10: Redc 3C 48
Milbourne Ct. TS21: Sed 2C 22
Milburn Cres. TS20: Nort 2A 74
Milburns Yd. *TS9: Stokes 1B 168*
(off High St.)
Mildenhall Cl. TS25: H'pool . . . 2E 31
MILE HOUSE 2E 73
Miles St. TS6: S Ban 2B 80
Milfoil Cl. TS7: Mart 2B 132
Milford Ho. TS3: Midd. 4D 79
Milford Wlk. TS10: Redc 2B 64
Mill, The TS9: Gt A 2D 167
Millais Gro. TS23: Bill. 2D 39
Millbank TS13: Skin. 4F 91
Millbank La.
TS17: Thorn T 1C 128
Millbank Ter. TS21: Whit. 3A 50
Millbeck Ho. TS20: Nort 5B 54
Millbeck Way TS7: Orm. 4B 104
Millbrook Av. TS3: Midd 4F 79
(not continuous)
Millclose Wlk. TS21: Sed 1D 23
Mill Cotts. TS21: Thorpe T 2D 51
Mill Ct. TS23: Bill. 5E 55
TS25: Grea 3E 31
Millennium Ct. TS9: Stokes. . . 2E 169
Millennium Green Vw.
TS3: Midd. 2E 103
Miller Cl. TS15: Yarm 5D 149
Miller Cres. TS24: H'pool 3D 7
Millers La. TS12: Ling. 2A 142
Millers Row TS10: Redc 3C 64
Millfield Cl. TS16: Eag 1B 148
TS17: Thorn T 3E 99
Millfield Rd. TS3: N Orm. 5C 78
Millford Rd. TS20: Nort 1F 73
Millgin Ct. TS17: Ing B 4B 128
Millholme Av. TS12: Skel 3D 89
Millholme Cl. TS12: Brot 3A 90
Millholme Dr. TS12: Brot 3A 90
MILLHOLME RDBT. 4F 89
Millholme Ter. TS12: Brot. 3A 90
Mill House Leisure Cen. 3B 14
Millington Cl. TS23: Bill. 1F 39
Mill La.
DL2: Long N, Mid G. 1A 144
(not continuous)
DL2: Mid G. 1C 144
TS13: Skin 3A 92
TS20: Nort 4B 54
TS21: Bis, Stil, Whit. 4A 50
TS21: Long N. 1A 144
TS22: Wolv. 3B 38
TS23: Bill 4E 55
Mill Mdw. Ct. TS20: Nort 5B 54
Millpool Cl. TS24: H'pool 5C 8
Mill Riggs TS9: Stokes 1C 168
Mills St. TS1: Midd 4C 76
Millston Cl. TS26: H'pool 2C 12
Millstone Cl. TS10: Redc. 3E 65
Mill St. TS14: Guis. 2E 139
TS20: Nort 5A 54
Mill St. E. TS18: Stock T. 5B 74
Mill St. W. TS18: Stock T 5A 74
Mill Ter. TS9: Gt A. 2C 166
TS21: Thorpe T 2D 51
TS25: Grea 3E 31
Mill Vw. TS13: Loft 5B 92
Mill Wynd TS15: Yarm. 3B 148
Milner Gro. TS24: H'pool. 2B 14
Milner Rd. TS20: Nort. 4A 54
Milne Wlk. TS25: H'pool 4C 18
Milton Cl. TS12: Brot. 1A 90
Milton Rd. *TS26: H'pool 3B 14*
(off York Rd.)
TS26: H'pool 3A 14
(Thornville Rd.)
Milton St. TS12: Salt 4C 68
MIMA 3F 77
Minch Rd. TS25: H'pool 5D 19
Miners Garth TS13: Live 1A 116
Minerva M. TS15: Yarm 3C 148
Miniott Wlk. TS8: Hem 4D 131
Minskip Cl. TS14: Guis 5E 109
Minsterley Dr. TS5: Midd 5A 100
Missenden Gro. TS3: Midd . . . 3F 103
Mitchell Av. TS17: Thorn T . . . 1D 129
Mitchell St. TS26: H'pool 4A 14
Mitford Cl. TS7: Orm. 4B 104
Mitford Ct. TS21: Sed 2C 22
Mitford Cres. TS19: Stock T . . . 2A 72
Moat, The TS23: Bill 1A 56
Moat St. TS18: Stock T. 1B 98
Moffat Rd. TS25: H'pool 5C 18
Monach Rd. TS25: H'pool. 5D 19
Monarch Gro. TS7: Mart 2E 133
Mond Cres. TS23: Bill 5D 55
Mond Ho. TS3: Midd 2D 103
Monkland Cl. TS1: Midd 3E 77
Monkseaton Dr. TS22: Bill. 5C 38
Monksfield TS23: Bill. 4E 55
Monkton Ri. TS14: Guis. 5F 109
Monkton Rd. TS25: H'pool. 5C 18
Monmouth Dr. TS16: Eag. 5C 126
Monmouth Gro. TS26: H'pool . . . 5E 7
Monmouth Rd. TS6: Est 4D 81
Monreith Av. TS16: Eag. 5C 126
Montague St. TS1: Midd 3A 78
TS24: H'pool. 5F 9
Montagu's Harrier
TS14: Guis 2B 138
Montgomery Gro.
TS26: H'pool 1E 13
Montreal Pl. TS4: Midd 1A 102
Montrose Cl. TS7: Mart. 3C 132
Montrose St. TS1: Midd. 3F 77
TS12: Salt 5C 68
Moorbeck Way TS7: Orm. 4B 104
Moorberries TS15: Hilt. 1F 163
Moor Cl. TS12: Moor. 3B 142
TS15: K'ton 4D 161
Moorcock Cl. TS6: Est 2F 105
Moorcock Row TS12: Ling. . . . 3D 113
Moore St. TS10: Redc. 3D 49
Moorgate TS6: Est. 1A 106
Moor Grn. TS7: Nun. 5A 134
Moorhen Rd. TS26: H'pool 1D 13
Moorhouse Est.
TS18: Prest T. 5D 97
Moor Pde. TS24: H'pool. 5F 9
Moor Pk. TS7: Nun 4A 134
TS16: Eag. 1C 148
Moor Rd. TS3: Midd 3B 78
MOORSHOLM 3B 142
Moorsholm La. TS13: Live. . . . 5E 115
Moorsholm Way TS10: Redc. . . 2C 64
Moorside Cl. TS10: Redc. 4F 65
Moorston Cl. TS26: H'pool 2C 12
Moor Ter. TS24: H'pool 1F 15
Moortown Rd. TS4: Midd. 4A 102
TS11: N Mar. 2F 85
Moor Vw. TS6: Norm. 3D 105
TS13: Hind 5E 121
Moor Vw. Ct. TS13: Hind 5E 121
Moray Cl. TS4: Midd 2A 102
Moray Rd. TS20: Nort 1F 73
Mordales Dr. TS11: Marsk S . . . 5E 67
Morehead Ter. TS13: Eas 2B 118
Moreland Av. TS23: Bill. 1D 55
Moreland Cl. TS22: Wolv 2C 38
Moreland St. TS24: H'pool 5C 14
Moresby Cl. TS4: Midd 3B 102
Moresby Wlk. TS17: Ing B. . . . 4E 127
Morgan Dr. TS14: Guis 3E 139
Morison Gdns. TS24: H'pool 5F 9
Morlais Ct. TS17: Ing B 2F 149
Morland Fell TS10: Redc. 1B 64
Morley Carr Dr.
TS15: Yarm 1A 160
Morpeth Av. TS4: Midd 1B 132
Morris Cres. TS19: Stock T 1C 72
Morrison Rd. TS14: Guis 1F 139
Morrison St. TS21: Stil 1B 50
Morris Rd. TS6: Est 2E 105
Mortain Cl. TS15: Yarm. 5E 149
Mortimer Dr. TS20: Nort 5F 53
Morton Carr La. TS7: Nun. . . . 3C 134
(not continuous)
Morton Cl. TS14: Guis. 3C 138
Morton St. TS26: H'pool 3A 14
Morven Vw. *TS19: Stock T 4B 72*
(off Mosston Rd.)
Morville Ct. TS17: Ing B 1B 150
Mosbrough Cl.
TS19: Stock T 3D 73
Mosedale Rd. TS6: Gran 5E 81
Moses St. TS3: N Orm. 4B 78
Mosman Ter. TS3: N Orm 4C 78
Mossdale Gro. TS14: Guis. . . . 3A 138
Moss Gdns. TS8: Hem. 4D 131
Mosston Rd. TS19: Stock T. . . . 4B 72
Moss Way TS18: Stock T. 5E 97
Mosswood Cres. TS5: Midd. . . 1B 130
Motherwell Rd.
TS25: H'pool 5D 19
Moulton Gro. TS19: Stock T . . . 5A 72
Mount, The TS6: Norm 3C 104
Mountbatten Cl. TS24: H'pool . . . 5C 8
Mount Gro. TS20: Nort 4B 54
MOUNT LEVEN 4E 149
Mt. Leven Rd. TS15: Yarm . . . 4E 149
MOUNT PLEASANT 2B 74
Mt. Pleasant TS13: Carl H 3F 91
TS13: Stait. 1C 120
(off High St.)
TS14: Guis. 4D 109
TS21: Stil 2A 50
Mt. Pleasant Av.
TS11: Marsk S. 4D 67
Mt. Pleasant Bungs.
TS19: Stock T 5C 52
Mt. Pleasant Cl. TS21: Stil 2A 50
Mt. Pleasant Grange
TS18: Stock T 3A 98
Mt. Pleasant Gro. TS21: Stil . . . 2B 50
Mt. Pleasant Rd. TS20: Nort. . . 2B 74
Mt. Pleasant Wlk. TS21: Stil. . . 2A 50
Mt. Pleasant Way
TS8: Coul N 1C 154
TS9: Stokes 3E 169

Mountstewart TS22: Wyn 1E **37**
Mountston Cl. TS26: H'pool . . . 2D **13**
Mourie Wood Way
TS15: Yarm 1A **160**
Mowbray Dr. TS8: Hem 4D **131**
Mowbray Gro. TS19: Stock T. . . 2A **72**
Mowbray Rd. TS20: Nort 2A **74**
TS25: H'pool 1D **31**
Mowden Cl. TS19: Stock T 3D **73**
Moyne Gdns. TS25: H'pool 5B **14**
Mr Twister's 4B **20**
Mucky La. TS14: Guis 5B **110**
Muirfield TS7: Nun 4A **134**
Muirfield Cl. TS11: N Mar 2A **86**
TS27: H'pool 2C **6**
Muirfield Rd. TS16: Eag 5C **126**
Muirfield Wlk. TS27: H'pool 2C **6**
Muirfield Way TS4: Midd. 4A **102**
Muir Gro. TS25: H'pool 5D **19**
Muker Gro. TS19: Stock T 1A **96**
Mulberry Ct. TS4: Midd 3F **101**
Mulberry Ri. TS26: H'pool. 4C **6**
Mulberry Wynd
TS18: Stock T. 3F **97**
Mulgrave Ct. TS14: Guis 5E **109**
Mulgrave Rd. TS5: Midd 2E **101**
TS26: H'pool. 3F **13**
Mulgrave Wlk. *TS6: Est. 5F 81*
(off Sleights Cres.)
TS10: Redc 2B **64**
Mullroy Rd. TS25: H'pool 4C **18**
Munro Gro. TS25: H'pool. 5D **19**
Murdock Rd. TS3: N Orm. 4F **79**
Muriel St. TS1: Midd 5F **77**
TS10: Redc 4D **49**
TS13: Carl H 3F **91**
Murray St. TS26: H'pool 3A **14**
Murton Cl. TS17: Thorn T 2B **128**
Murton Gro. TS22: Bill. 5B **38**
Murton Pk. Ct.
TS11: Marsk S 3D **67**
Murton Scalp Rd.
TS12: Boo 3C **112**
Mus. of Hartlepool 2C **14**
Museum Rd. TS24: H'pool. 3B **14**
Musgrave St. TS24: H'pool 4D **15**
Musgrave Ter. TS22: Wolv. 2C **38**
Musgrave Wlk. TS24: H'pool. . . . 4C **14**
Muston Cl. TS5: Midd 5E **101**
Myrddin-Baker Rd. TS6: Est . . . 5E **81**
Myrtle Ct. TS17: Thorn T. 4C **98**
Myrtle Gro. TS17: Thorn T. 4C **98**
Myrtle Rd. TS16: Prest T. 2C **126**
TS19: Stock T. 3F **73**
Myrtle St. TS1: Midd 4F **77**
Myton Rd. TS17: Ing B 1A **150**
Myton Wlk. TS8: Hem 4D **131**
Myton Way TS17: Ing B. 4F **127**

N

Nab Cl. TS6: Est. 2E **105**
Nairnhead Cl. TS8: Hem 4D **131**
NAISBERRY 2C **12**
Naisberry Est. TS26: H'pool . . . 2C **12**
Nantwich Cl. TS8: Hem. 4D **131**
Napier St. TS5: Midd 5E **77**
TS6: S Ban 2A **80**
TS20: Nort 2B **74**
Naseby Ct. TS12: Brot. 3C **90**
TS23: Bill 3A **40**
Nash Gro. TS25: H'pool 2E **19**
Nature's World 2E **131**
Navenby Gro. TS25: H'pool. . . . 1D **31**
Navigation Point Shop. & Hotel Cen.
TS24: H'pool 2D **15**
Navigation Way
TS17: Thorn T 1E **99**
Navigator Ct. TS18: Stock T . . . 4A **98**
Naylor Rd. TS21: Sed 4D **23**
Neasham Av. TS7: Mart. 4D **133**
TS23: Bill 3F **39**
Neasham Cl. TS18: Stock T. . . . 5B **74**
Neasham Ct. TS9: Stokes 5B **164**
Neasham La. TS9: Stokes 5B **164**
Neath Ct. TS17: Ing B 2F **149**
Nederdale Cl. TS15: Yarm. . . . 1B **160**
Needles Cl. TS10: Redc. 4B **64**
Nelson Av. TS23: Bill 2C **56**
Nelson Cl. TS12: Brot 1C **90**
Nelson Ct. TS6: S Ban 2A **80**
Nelson Farm La.
TS27: H'pool 2B **6**
Nelson Sq. TS20: Nort. 5A **54**
Nelson St. TS6: S Ban 2F **79**
Nelson St. Ind. Est.
TS6: S Ban 2A **80**
Nelson Ter. TS10: Redc 3B **48**
TS18: Stock T 5A **74**
Neptune Cen. (Swimming Baths)
. . . . 1D **103**
Neptune Cl. TS25: Seat C 2D **21**
Neptune Ho. TS24: H'pool. 2D **15**
Nesbyt Rd. TS24: H'pool 3F **7**
Nesham Av. TS5: Midd 2B **100**
Nesham Rd. TS1: Midd 4C **76**
TS24: H'pool. 5F **9**
Nessfield Pl. TS7: Nun 3C **134**
Netherby Cl. TS15: Yarm 4E **149**
Netherby Ga. TS26: H'pool 2E **13**
Netherby Grn. TS3: Midd 3E **103**
NETHERFIELDS 2A **104**
Netherfields Cres.
TS3: Midd 2A **104**
Netley Gro. TS3: Midd 3F **103**
Nevern Cres. TS17: Ing B 2E **149**
Neville Dr. TS21: Sed 2C **22**
Neville Gro. TS14: Guis. 3C **138**
Neville Rd. TS18: Stock T 3A **76**
Neville's Ct. TS5: Midd 3D **101**
Nevis Wlk. TS17: Thorn T 4D **99**
Newark Rd. TS25: H'pool 1D **31**
Newark Wlk. TS20: Nort 1C **74**
Newbank Cl. TS7: Orm 5B **104**
Newbiggin Cl. TS16: Eag 5F **125**
Newbiggin Rd. TS23: Bill. 2E **39**
Newbridge Ct. TS5: Midd. 4E **101**
Newbrook TS12: Skel. 5B **88**
NEW BROTTON 1A **90**
Newburgh Ct. TS23: Bill. 1A **56**
Newburn Bri. Ind. Est.
TS25: H'pool 5D **15**
Newbury Av. TS5: Midd 2B **100**
Newbury Rd. TS12: Brot 3B **90**
Newbury Way TS23: Bill. 4F **39**
NEWBY 4B **154**
Newby Cl. TS5: Midd 4E **101**
TS20: Nort 5A **54**
Newby Gro. TS17: Thorn T 4D **99**
Newby Ho. TS4: Midd 2A **102**
Newby La. TS8: Newb 4E **153**
Newcomen Ct. TS10: Redc 3B **48**
Newcomen Grn. TS4: Midd . . . 1A **102**
Newcomen Gro. TS10: Redc . . . 3C **48**
Newcomen Rd. TS6: S Ban 3F **79**
Newcomen Ter. TS10: Redc . . . 3B **48**
TS13: Loft 5B **92**
New Company Row
TS13: Skin 2A **92**
New Dales Cl. TS15: Yarm . . . 1A **160**
New Earswick St.
TS19: Stock T 1C **72**
Newfield Cres. TS5: Midd 1B **130**
Newgale Cl. TS17: Ing B 2E **149**
Newgate TS6: Est. 1F **105**
New Grove Ter. TS13: Skin 2A **92**
Newham Av. TS5: Midd 4D **101**
Newham Cres. TS7: Mart 3D **133**
NEWHAM GRANGE 4E **73**
Newham Grange Av.
TS19: Stock T. 4E **73**
Newham Grange Country Farm
. . . . 3A **132**
Newham Way TS8: Coul N 4F **131**
Newhaven Cl. TS8: Hem 4D **131**
Newhaven Ct. TS24: H'pool. . . . 4C **14**
Newholm Ct. TS25: H'pool 4A **20**
Newholme Ct. TS14: Guis 1D **139**
Newholm Way TS10: Redc 2B **64**
Newick Av. TS3: Midd 1D **103**
Newington Rd. TS4: Midd 3A **102**
Newlands Av. TS20: Nort. 1B **74**
TS26: H'pool. 4F **13**
Newlands Gro. TS10: Redc 5B **48**
(not continuous)
Newlands Rd. TS1: Midd. 4A **78**
TS12: Skel 1A **112**
TS16: Eag. 1B **148**
Newley Ct. TS3: Midd 2A **104**
Newlyn Grn. TS3: Midd 3E **103**
Newlyn Way TS10: Redc 3F **65**
Newmarket Av.
TS17: Thorn T 2F **99**
Newmarket Rd. TS10: Redc . . . 1D **65**
NEW MARSKE 1A **86**
NEWPORT 4C **76**
Newport Cl. TS17: Ing B 2E **149**
Newport Cres. TS1: Midd. 3E **77**
Newport Ho. TS17: Thorn T. . . . 2B **98**
Newport Ind. Est. TS1: Midd . . . 4D **77**
Newport Rd. TS1: Midd 4C **76**
TS5: Midd 4B **76**
Newport Sth. Bus. Pk.
TS1: Midd 4C **76**
Newport Way TS1: Midd 3C **76**
Newquay Cl. TS8: Hem 4D **131**
TS26: H'pool 2E **13**
Newquay Dr. TS10: Redc. 3B **64**
New Rd. TS14: Guis. 2E **139**
TS23: Bill 5D **55**
New Row TS14: Dun 1D **109**
Newsam Cres. TS16: Eag 1B **148**
Newsam Rd. TS16: Eag. 1B **148**
NEW SKELTON 4D **89**
NEWSTEAD 3D **139**
Newstead Av. TS19: Stock T . . . 3D **73**
Newstead Farm La.
TS14: Guis 2C **138**
Newstead Rd. TS4: Midd. 5A **78**
New St. TS17: Thorn T 2C **98**
NEWTON 4F **73**
NEWTON BEWLEY 5F **29**
Newton Cl. TS6: Est. 2F **105**
Newtondale TS14: Guis 3A **138**
Newton Dr. TS17: Thorn T. . . . 2B **128**
Newton Gro. TS22: Bill 5B **38**
Newton Hanzard Long Dr.
TS22: Wyn 2B **26**
Newton Hanzard Short Dr.
TS22: Wyn 3C **26**
Newton Mall *TS1: Midd. 3E 77*
(off Cleveland Cen.)
Newton Rd. TS9: Gt A 1D **167**
TS10: Redc 2B **64**
NEWTON UNDER ROSEBERRY
. . . . 2C **158**
Newton Wlk. TS20: Nort 3B **74**
Newtown Av. TS19: Stock T. . . . 4F **73**
Nicholson Way TS24: H'pool. . . . 3E **7**
Nicklaus Dr. TS16: Eag 5C **126**
Nidderdale TS12: Skel. 2B **88**
Nightingale Cl. TS26: H'pool. . . . 5C **6**
Nightingale Dr.
TS19: Stock T 2C **72**
Nightingale Rd. TS6: Est 5E **81**
Nightingale Wlk. TS20: Nort . . . 4A **54**
Nimbus Cl. TS7: Mart 2C **132**
Nine Acres TS27: Hart 4E **5**
Nolan Ho. TS18: Stock T 4A **74**
Nolan Pl. TS18: Stock T 4A **74**
Nolton Ct. TS17: Ing B 2F **149**
Nookston Cl. TS26: H'pool 1D **13**
Norcliffe St. TS3: N Orm 4C **78**
Norfolk Cl. TS10: Redc 1B **64**
TS12: Skel 4A **88**
TS25: H'pool 1B **20**
Norfolk Cres. TS3: Midd. 3F **103**
Norfolk Pl. TS3: Midd 1C **102**

Norfolk St. TS18: Stock T. 1F **97**
Norfolk Ter. TS23: Bill 2F **55**
Norham Wlk. TS7: Orm 4A **104**
NORMANBY. 2D **105**
Normanby Ct. TS7: Mart 3C **132**
Normanby Hall Pk.
TS6: Norm 3C **104**
Normanby Rd.
TS6: Est, S Ban 1A **80**
TS7: Orm 3A **104**
NORMANBY TOP. 4E **105**
Norman Ter. TS6: S Ban. 2F **79**
Nth. Albert Rd. TS20: Nort. 3F **53**
Northallerton Rd.
TS17: Thorn T 4D **99**
Northall St. TS18: Stock T. 3E **97**
Northampton Ho. TS6: Est. 4E **81**
Northampton Wlk.
TS25: H'pool 5B **14**
North Av. TS12: Salt. 4B **68**
Northbank Cres. TS7: Orm . . . 5B **104**
Northbourne Rd.
TS19: Stock T. 3F **73**
Northbrook Ct. TS26: H'pool . . . 4E **13**
North Burn Cl.
TS18: Stock T 4D **75**
North Cl. TS21: Thorpe T. 1E **51**
TS27: Elw. 3C **10**
Northcote St.
TS18: Stock T. 2F **97**
Northdale Ct. TS3: Midd 1E **103**
North Dr. TS7: Orm 4A **104**
TS26: H'pool 3E **13**
North End TS21: Sed 4C **22**
Northern Rd. TS5: Midd. 1B **100**
Northern Route TS5: Midd. . . . 1B **100**
North Fen TS10: Redc 1B **64**
Northfield Cl. TS9: Stokes. . . . 1B **168**
Northfield Dr. TS9: Stokes. . . . 1B **168**
Northfield Rd.
TS11: Marsk S 4B **66**
TS22: Bill 5C **38**
Northfleet Av. TS3: Midd 5E **79**
Northgate TS14: Guis. 1E **139**
TS24: H'pool 5E **9**
Northgate Rd. TS5: Midd. 3D **101**
North Grn. TS18: Stock T. 2A **98**
Northiam Cl. TS8: Hem 4D **131**
Northland Av. TS26: H'pool 4F **13**
North La. TS27: Elw. 4D **11**
(Elwick Rd.)
TS27: Elw. 3C **10**
(North Cl.)
Northleach Dr. TS8: Hem 4D **131**
Nth. Liverton Ind. Est.
TS13: Live 1A **116**
NTH. LODGE RDBT. 5F **109**
North Mt. Pleasant St.
TS20: Nort 2B **74**
NORTH ORMESBY 4C **78**
Nth. Ormesby By-Pass
TS3: N Orm 3B **78**
Nth. Ormesby Rd.
TS4: Midd 3A **78**
Northpark TS23: Bill. 2E **39**
North Pk. Rd. TS21: Sed 3C **22**
Nth. Point M. *TS9: Stokes. . . . 1B* ***168***
(off Stone Hall Cl.)
Northport Rd. TS18: Stock T . . . 4C **74**
North Ridge TS12: Skel 3B **88**
North Rd. TS1: Midd 2D **77**
TS2: Midd 2D **77**
TS9: Stokes 1B **168**
TS13: Loft 5C **92**
TS25: Seat C 3E **21**
North Row TS6: Laze 4C **82**
Nth. Shore Innovation Cen.
TS18: Stock T 5C **74**
Nth. Shore Link
TS18: Stock T 5C **74**
Nth. Shore Rd.
TS18: Stock T 5B **74**
North Side TS13: Stait. 1C **120**
Northside Bus. Pk.
DL2: Mid G 2D **145**
NORTH SKELTON 4F **89**
Nth. Skelton Rd. TS12: Skel . . . 4D **89**
Nth. Slip Rd. TS6: Est. 3D **81**
North St. TS2: Midd 1F **77**
TS6: S Ban 1A **80**
TS18: Stock T 5A **74**
Nth. Tees Industrial Est.
TS18: Stock T 4A **76**
Nth. Tees Nature Pk.. . . . . 3E **41**
North Ter. TS10: Redc 3C **48**
TS12: Skel 4A **88**
TS13: Loft 3C **92**
Northumberland Gro.
TS20: Nort 3F **53**
TS25: H'pool 5B **14**
Northumberland Rd.
TS17: Thorn T 4C **98**
Northumberland Wlk.
TS25: H'pool 5B **14**
North Vw. TS10: Redc 1A **66**
TS27: Dalt P. 1E **17**
Northwold Cl. TS25: H'pool 1E **31**
North Wood TS5: Midd 5D **101**
NORTON 5B **54**
Norton Av. TS20: Nort 1F **73**
Norton Ct. TS20: Nort 2B **74**
Norton Dr. TS19: Stock T. 3A **72**
Norton Golf Course. 2D **53**
NORTON GRANGE 2A **74**
Norton Hall TS20: Nort 4B **54**
NORTON JUNC. 3B **54**
Norton Junc. Cotts.
TS20: Nort 4D **53**
Norton Rd. TS18: Stock T 5B **74**
TS20: Nort 4B **74**
Norton Sports Complex 3F **53**
Norwich Av. TS19: Stock T 3B **72**
Norwich Rd. TS5: Midd 1E **101**
TS10: Redc. 1F **65**
Norwood Cl. TS19: Stock T 3B **72**
Norwood Rd. TS3: Midd 1A **104**
Nottingham Dr. TS10: Redc 1E **65**
Nottingham Wlk.
TS25: H'pool 5B **14**
Nuffield Rd. TS23: Bill. 1A **56**
Nugent Av. TS1: Midd 4C **76**
Nuneaton Dr. TS8: Hem. 4D **131**
Nunnington Cl. TS17: Ing B. . . 5B **128**
Nuns St. TS24: H'pool 1F **15**
NUNTHORPE 4A **134**
Nunthorpe By-Pass
TS7: Nun 5B **134**
Nunthorpe Gdns. TS7: Nun . . . 4B **134**
Nunthorpe Station (Rail) 3B **134**
NUNTHORPE VILLAGE. 2C **156**
Nursery Dr. TS22: Wyn 4E **25**
Nursery Gdns. TS15: Yarm . . . 5D **149**
Nursery La. TS5: Midd 1C **100**
TS18: Stock T. 1E **97**
Nutfield Cl. TS8: Hem 4D **131**
Nuthatch Cl. TS26: H'pool. 1D **13**
Nut La. TS4: Midd 5A **78**
Nutley Rd. TS23: Bill 5F **39**
Nyson St. TS1: Midd 5E **77**

O

Oak Av. TS7: Mart 3E **133**
Oakdale TS7: Orm 4B **104**
Oakdale Rd. TS11: N Mar 2F **85**
Oakdene Av. TS18: Stock T 3E **97**
Oakdene Cl. TS6: Norm. 2D **105**
Oakenshaw Dr. TS5: Midd. . . . 1C **130**
Oakesway TS24: H'pool. 5A **8**
Oakesway Bus. Pk.
TS24: H'pool 5A **8**
Oakesway Ind. Est.
TS24: H'pool 4A **8**
Oakfield Av. TS16: Eag 4B **126**
Oakfield Cl. TS16: Eag. 4B **126**
Oakfield Gdns. TS7: Orm. 2B **104**
Oakfield Rd. TS3: N Orm. 4B **78**
Oak Gro. TS24: H'pool 1F **13**
Oakham Grn. TS20: Nort 1C **74**
Oak Hill TS8: Coul N 4C **132**
Oakhurst Cl. TS17: Ing B. 5C **128**
Oakland Av. TS25: H'pool 2A **20**
Oaklands TS9: Gt A 1D **167**
Oaklands, The DL2: Mid R . . . 4A **144**
Oaklands Av. TS20: Nort 1B **74**
Oaklands Rd. TS6: Norm. 4D **105**
Oaklea Cl. TS20: Nort 5A **54**
Oakley Cl. TS8: Hem 4D **131**
TS14: Guis 4F **139**
Oakley Gdns. TS24: H'pool 1A **14**
Oakley Rd. TS12: Boo 3C **112**
Oakley Wlk. TS6: Est 2E **105**
Oakridge TS7: Orm 4B **104**
Oakrise TS7: Orm 3B **104**
Oak Rd. TS10: Redc. 5E **49**
TS12: Brot 1A **90**
TS14: Guis. 1D **139**
TS16: Prest T. 2D **127**
Oaks, The DL2: Mid G 2C **144**
TS8: Hem. 4D **131**
Oaksham Dr. TS23: Bill 2E **39**
Oakstead TS25: H'pool 3C **20**
Oak St. TS1: Midd 3F **77**
OAK TREE 2C **144**
Oaktree Cl. DL2: Mid G 2C **144**
Oak Tree Cres. TS21: Sed 3D **23**
Oaktree Gro. TS18: Stock T. . . . 3B **96**
Oak Wlk. TS13: Loft. 4B **92**
Oakwell Gdns. TS20: Nort. 5A **54**
Oakwell Rd. TS20: Nort. 5A **54**
Oakwood Cl. TS27: H'pool. 3C **6**
Oakwood Ct. TS7: Mart 3F **133**
Oakwood Gdns. TS6: Norm . . . 1B **104**
Oakworth Grn. TS4: Midd 3A **102**
Oatfields Ct. TS6: Est. 3E **105**
Oatlands Gro. TS13: Eas 3A **118**
Oban Av. TS25: H'pool. 1A **20**
Oban Rd. TS3: Midd 1D **103**
Oberhausen Mall
TS1: Midd. 3E **77**
Occupation Rd. TS6: Est 3F **105**
Ocean Rd. TS24: H'pool 1C **6**
Ochil Ter. TS23: Bill. 2E **55**
Offerton Dr. TS8: Hem 4E **131**
Okehampton Dr. TS7: Mart . . . 3C **132**
Oldbury Gro. TS8: Hem 4E **131**
Old Cemetery Rd.
TS24: H'pool 3B **8**
Old College Apartments, The
TS5: Midd 2D **101**
Old Convent Gdns.
TS4: Midd 1A **102**
Old Durham Rd. TS21: Sed 1C **22**
Old Flatts La. TS6: Norm 5D **105**
Oldford Cres. TS5: Midd 5C **100**
Oldgate TS6: Est 1A **106**
Oldham Cl. TS12: Boo. 2C **112**
Oldham St. TS12: Boo. 3B **112**
OLD LACKENBY 5A **82**
Old Market, The
TS15: Yarm 3B **148**
Old Middlesbrough Rd.
TS6: S Ban 3F **79**
Old Mill Wynd TS9: Gt A. 3D **167**
Old Mines Rd. TS6: Est 1F **105**
Old Picture Ho. Ct.
TS20: Nort 1B **74**
Old Pier Lighthouse 2F **15**
Old Pier (Pilot's Pier) 2F **15**
Old Rectory Gdns.
TS15: Yarm 4B **148**
Old Rd. TS23: Bill 5D **55**
Old Row *TS6: Est. 1F* ***105***
(off The Square)
OLD SALTBURN 4D **69**
Old Station M. TS16: Eag 2B **148**
Old Station Rd. TS6: S Ban 1F **79**
Oldstead Ct. TS8: Hem 4D **131**

Old Stockton Rd.
TS23: Cowp B 3C **30**
Old Stokesley Rd.
TS7: Nun 1B **156**
Old Stubble, The
TS13: Stait 1C **120**
OLD TOWN 4C 14
Oliver St. TS5: Midd 1D **101**
TS6: S Ban 3A **80**
Olive St. TS24: H'pool 1F **15**
Olliver St. TS10: Redc. 4D **49**
Olney Wlk. TS3: Midd 3D **103**
On Target Paintball 3E 135
Ontario Cres. TS10: Redc 5C **48**
Onyx Cl. TS25: Seat C 2D **21**
Opus Pk. TS18: Stock T 5F **97**
Orange Gro. TS20: Nort. 2A **74**
Orchard, The TS12: Skel 3C **88**
TS17: Ing B 4F **127**
TS21: Sed 4D **23**
Orchard Cl. TS9: Gt A 5A **158**
TS21: Carlt. 5D **51**
TS21: Sed 4D **23**
Orchard Dr. TS14: Guis 2F **139**
ORCHARD ESTATE 5A 126
Orchard Gro. TS6: Est 1D **105**
Orchard M. TS16: Eag 1A **148**
Orchard Rd. TS5: Midd 2D **101**
TS10: Redc 5C **48**
TS17: Thorn T 1B **128**
TS19: Stock T 5B **72**
Orchard Way TS7: Orm 4A **104**
Orchid Cl. TS22: Wyn 2C **26**
Orchid Gro. TS19: Stock T. 3B **72**
Orchid Rd. TS26: H'pool 4E **7**
Orde Wingate Way
TS19: Stock T 4A **74**
Ordsall Grn. TS3: Midd 3E **103**
Oriel Cl. TS5: Midd 3D **101**
Orkney Wlk. TS14: Guis. 4C **138**
Orkney Way TS17: Thorn T 4D **99**
Orleans Gro. TS7: Mart 2E **133**
Orme Ct. TS3: N Orm. 3C **78**
ORMESBY 4A 104
Ormesby Bank TS7: Orm 5A **104**
Ormesby Hall 5F 103
Ormesby Rd. TS3: Midd 5C **78**
TS6: Norm 3C **104**
TS25: H'pool 4A **20**
Ormesby Sports Complex . . . 2B 104
Ormston Av. TS3: Midd 3E **103**
Orpington Rd. TS3: Midd. 3E **103**
Orton Gro. TS22: Bill 5A **38**
Orwell Cl. TS12: Skel 3D **89**
Orwell Gdns. TS19: Stock T . . . 1B **96**
Orwell St. TS1: Midd 4C **76**
Orwell Wlk. TS25: H'pool 2E **19**
Osborne Rd. TS5: Midd 1D **101**
TS18: Stock T. 2F **97**
TS26: H'pool 4A **14**
Osbourne Cl. TS8: Hem. 4D **131**
Osprey Cl. TS14: Guis 2A **138**
TS20: Nort 3B **54**
Osprey Ho. TS24: H'pool. 3D **15**
Osprey Way TS26: H'pool 5E **7**
Ostler Cl. TS17: Ing B 5B **128**
Oswestry Grn. TS4: Midd 1B **132**
Otley Av. TS3: Midd 3E **103**
Ottawa Rd. TS4: Midd 5A **78**
Otterburn Gdns. TS5: Midd . . . 2D **131**
Otterburn Way TS23: Bill 3F **39**
Otterhill Ct. TS8: Hem. 3D **131**
Otterington Cl. TS27: Hart. 3A **6**
Otterpool Cl. TS24: H'pool. 5B **8**
Otter Way TS17: Ing B. 4C **128**
Oughton Cl. TS15: Yarm 5E **149**
Oulston Rd. TS18: Stock T 1D **97**
Ouseport Rd.
TS18: Stock T 4C **74**
Ouston St. TS24: H'pool 4B **14**
Outram St. TS1: Midd 4D **77**
TS18: Stock T. 2F **97**
Ouzel Cl. TS26: H'pool 5D **7**
Oval, The TS5: Midd 3C **130**
TS22: Wyn 5B **26**
TS26: H'pool. 4F **13**
Oval Grange TS26: H'pool 3E **13**
Oval Vw. TS4: Midd. 4B **102**
Overbrook TS9: Gt A 2C **166**
Overcombe Way TS10: Redc . . . 2B **64**
Overdale TS14: Guis 4A **138**
Overdale Cl. TS10: Redc 4C **64**
Overdale Rd. TS3: Midd 2C **102**
Overmans Cotts. TS13: Skin . . . 3A **92**
Overton Way TS18: Stock T. . . . 2A **98**
Owens Rd. TS6: S Ban 3F **79**
Owington Gro. TS23: Bill 2A **40**
Owletts Ct. TS17: Ing B 2B **150**
Owls Gro. TS17: Ing B 2F **149**
Owton Cl. TS25: H'pool 4F **19**
OWTON MANOR 5E 19
Owton Mnr. La.
TS25: H'pool 4D **19**
OXBRIDGE 1F 97
Oxbridge Av. TS18: Stock T. . . . 1D **97**
(not continuous)
Oxbridge Ct. TS18: Stock T. . . . 1D **97**
Oxbridge Ind. Est.
TS18: Stock T. 1F **97**
(Oxbridge La.)
TS18: Stock T. 5F **73**
(Wrynose Gdns.)
Oxbridge La. TS18: Stock T. . . . 1F **97**
(Mary St.)
TS18: Stock T 1C **96**
(Preston Rd.)
Ox Cl. Cotts. TS12: Salt. 4A **68**
Oxendale Rd. TS10: Redc 1B **64**
Oxfield TS8: Coul N 3B **132**
Oxford Rd. TS5: Midd 2B **100**
TS17: Thorn T 3C **98**
TS25: H'pool 1E **19**
Oxford St. TS1: Midd. 5D **77**
TS6: S Ban 2A **80**
TS12: Boo 3B **112**
TS12: Salt 4C **68**
TS25: H'pool 1B **20**
(not continuous)
Oxford St. Lwr. TS25: H'pool. . . 5C **14**
Oxgang Cl. TS10: Redc 3C **64**
Oxhill Cl. TS8: Malt 2F **151**
Oxhill Farm TS8: Malt 2F **151**
Oxley St. TS10: Redc. 3D **49**
OXYGEN CORNER. 5A 56
Oxygym Fitness Club 1F 55
Oysterman Ho. TS24: H'pool. . . 2C **14**

P

Pacific Dr. TS17: Thorn T 4C **98**
Paddock, The DL2: Mid G 3A **144**
TS7: Nun 5B **134**
TS9: Stokes 5C **164**
TS16: Eag. 4C **126**
TS27: Elw. 3C **10**
Paddock Grn. TS22: Wyn. 4B **26**
Paddock Wood TS8: Coul N. . . 3A **132**
Padstow Cl. TS26: H'pool 2D **13**
Pages M. TS12: Salt 3C **68**
Paignton Cl. TS8: Midd 2B **132**
Paignton Dr. TS25: H'pool 5F **19**
Palace Cl. TS20: Nort 2A **54**
Palace Row TS27: Hart 4F **5**
Palin Cl. TS4: Midd 3A **78**
Palladium Bldgs.
TS4: Midd. 2F **101**
PALLISTER 5D 79
Pallister Av. TS3: Midd 5E **79**
Pallister Ct. TS3: Midd. 4F **79**
Palmers Cl. TS13: Stait. 2B **120**
Palmers Sq. TS13: Hind 5E **121**
Palmerston Ct.
TS17: Thorn T 3C **98**
Palmerston St.
TS18: Stock T 5A **74**
Palmer St. TS1: Midd 4E **77**
Palmer Wlk. TS16: Eag 5C **126**
Palm Gro. TS19: Stock T. 5B **72**
Palm St. TS1: Midd 4F **77**
Palm Ter. TS2: Port C 4E **57**
Panmore Wlk. TS16: Eag. 4C **126**
Pannal Cl. TS11: N Mar 2F **85**
Pannal Wlk. TS16: Eag 5C **126**
Pannell Av. TS5: Midd. 3B **100**
Pannell Cl. TS27: H'pool 2C **6**
Pannell Pl. TS27: H'pool 2C **6**
Pannierman La. TS7: Nun. . . . 4D **165**
TS9: Gt A, Stokes. 4D **165**
Parade, The TS26: H'pool 3E **13**
Parish Row TS25: Grea 3E **31**
Paris Pl. TS7: Mart 2C **132**
Park, The TS22: Wolv 2C **38**
Park Av. TS6: S Ban. 5B **80**
TS10: Redc 4D **49**
TS17: Thorn T 3D **99**
TS22: Wyn 5B **26**
TS26: H'pool 3E **13**
Park Av. Nth. TS3: Midd. 3F **103**
Park Av. Sth. TS3: Midd 3A **104**
Park Ct. TS10: Redc. 1F **63**
Park Cres. TS21: Stil 2B **50**
Parkdale Way TS5: Midd 4E **101**
Park Dr. TS19: Stock T 2D **73**
TS26: H'pool 3D **13**
PARK END 3D 103
Parkers Yd. TS14: Guis 2E **139**
PARKFIELD 3F 97
Parkfield Av. TS5: Midd. 4D **101**
Parkfield Rd. TS18: Stock T . . . 2A **98**
Parkfield Way
TS18: Stock T 2A **98**
Parkgate TS6: Est 1A **106**
Parkinson Ho. *TS1: Midd. 2F 77*
(off Central M.)
Parkin St. TS18: Stock T 5A **74**
Parklands TS3: Midd 1D **103**
Parklands, The TS10: Redc. . . . 3D **65**
Parklands Av. TS23: Bill 4D **55**
Parklands Cl. TS3: Midd 1D **103**
Parklands Ct. TS16: Eag 2B **148**
Parklands Way
TS26: H'pool 4C **12**
Park La. TS1: Midd 5E **77**
TS13: Eas. 3B **118**
TS14: Guis 2C **138**
Park M. TS26: H'pool. 3E **13**
Parkmore Leisure Club 4C 126
Park Ri. TS9: Gt A. 2D **167**
Park Rd. TS12: Brot. 3A **90**
TS17: Thorn T 5C **98**
TS18: Stock T. 2F **97**
TS24: H'pool. 4F **13**
TS26: H'pool. 4F **13**
Park Rd. Nth. TS1: Midd 5E **77**
(not continuous)
Park Rd. Sth. TS4: Midd 1F **101**
TS5: Midd. 1E **101**
Parkside TS1: Midd 5F **77**
TS3: Midd. 4E **103**
TS14: Guis 1E **139**
TS21: Long N. 1F **123**
TS23: Bill 5E **39**
Parkside Ct. TS17: Thorn T. . . . 5E **99**
Parkside W. TS1: Midd 5F **77**
Park Sq. TS9: Gt A. 2D **167**
TS26: H'pool. 2F **13**
Parkstone Cl. TS11: N Mar 2A **86**
Parkstone Gro. TS24: H'pool. . . . 2D **7**
Parkstone Pl. TS16: Eag 1C **148**
Parkston Ho. TS23: Bill 3D **55**
Park St. TS1: Midd. 3E **77**
Park Ter. TS12: Brot 3B **90**
TS13: Loft 5C **92**
TS17: Thorn T 3C **98**
TS18: Stock T 1B **98**
Park Twr. Apartments
TS24: H'pool 4B **14**
Park Va. Rd. TS4: Midd 1F **101**

Park Vw. TS15: Yarm 5B **148**
TS18: Stock T 2F **97**
TS21: Sed 4C **22**
TS23: Bill 1D **55**
Parkview Rd. E.
TS25: H'pool 4C **20**
Parkview Rd. W.
TS25: H'pool 4B **20**
Park Vw. Ter. TS14: Guis. 2D **139**
Park Vw. W. Ind. Est.
TS25: H'pool 4B **20**
Parkway, The
TS6: Est, Norm. 4E **105**
TS7: Mart, Orm 2D **133**
TS8: Coul N 3A **130**
TS12: Salt 4A **68**
TS17: Thorn T 3A **130**
Parkway Ct. TS8: Coul N 5B **132**
Parkway Dr. TS6: Norm. 3D **105**
Parkway Gro. TS3: Midd 1D **103**
PARKWAY JUNC. INTERCHANGE
. . . . **4F 129**
Parkway Shop. Cen.
TS8: Coul N 4B **132**
Parkway Village
TS8: Coul N 4B **132**
Parkwood Dr. TS18: Stock T . . . 3D **97**
Park Wynd TS4: Midd 5C **102**
Parliament Cl.
TS18: Stock T 2A **98**
Parliament Rd. TS1: Midd. 4C **76**
Parliament St.
TS18: Stock T 2A **98**
Parliament Wlk.
TS18: Stock T 2A **98**
Parracombe Cl.
TS17: Ing B 3B **150**
Parrington Pl. TS6: Laze 4C **82**
Parsely Nook TS26: H'pool 5E **7**
Parsons Ct. TS6: S Ban 4A **80**
Parsons Wlk. TS20: Nort. 4A **54**
Parton St. TS24: H'pool. 1A **14**
Partridge Av. TS5: Midd 2C **130**
Partridge Cl. TS17: Ing B 5B **128**
Passfield Cres. TS6: S Ban 2B **80**
Pasture, The TS17: Ing B 4A **128**
Pasture Cl. TS11: Marsk S 4A **66**
Pasture Fld. TS21: Sed 1D **23**
Pasture La. TS6: Laze 3C **82**
Pastures, The TS8: Coul N . . . 5C **132**
(not continuous)
Patey Ct. TS5: Midd. 2D **101**
Patten La. TS14: Guis 1E **139**
Patten St. TS6: Norm 2D **105**
Patterdale Av. TS5: Midd. 4C **100**
TS19: Stock T. 4E **73**
Patterdale St. TS25: H'pool. . . . 1B **20**
Pattison Ct. TS4: Midd. 1A **102**
Pauntley Dr. TS5: Midd 3C **130**
Pavilion Cl. TS25: Seat C 5D **21**
Pavilion Shop. Cen.
TS17: Thorn T 1D **129**
Paxton Cl. TS18: Stock T. 4B **74**
Peacocks Cl. TS9: Stokes 5B **164**
Peakston Cl. TS26: H'pool. 2D **13**
Pearl St. TS1: Midd 4E **77**
TS12: Salt 3C **68**
Pearson Cl. TS18: Stock T. 2A **98**
Pearson St. TS1: Midd. 3C **76**
Pearson Ville TS9: Gt A. 2D **167**
Pearson Wlk. *TS18: Stock T . . . 2A 98*
(off Pearson Cl.)
Pearson Way TS17: Thorn T . . . 1C **98**
Pear Tree Ct. TS11: N Mar 1A **86**
Pease Ct. TS12: Ling 4E **113**
TS14: Guis 4B **138**
TS16: Eag. 4B **126**
Pease Gdns. TS4: Midd. 4B **102**
Pease St. TS12: Ling 4E **113**
Pease Wlk. TS18: Stock T. 2A **98**
Peaton St. TS3: N Orm 4C **78**
Pecten Ct. TS13: Live 1A **116**
Peebles Av. TS25: H'pool 1A **20**
Peelers Ct. TS14: Guis. 5E **109**
Peel St. TS1: Midd. 4E **77**
TS17: Thorn T 3C **98**
Pegasus Av. TS18: Stock T 4F **97**
Pegasus Ho. TS22: Wyn 5A **28**
Pegman Cl. TS14: Guis 5F **109**
Peirse Cl. TS4: Midd 4A **78**
Peirson Ct. TS10: Redc 3B **48**
Peirson St. TS10: Redc 3B **48**
Pelham St. TS1: Midd 4E **77**
Pelton Cl. TS23: Bill 2D **39**
Pemberton Cres.
TS4: Midd 3A **102**
Pembroke Dr. TS17: Ing B 3F **149**
Pembroke Gro. TS26: H'pool. . . . 5E **7**
Pembroke Rd. TS20: Nort 1A **74**
Pembroke Way TS10: Redc 5E **49**
Penarth Wlk. TS26: H'pool 1D **13**
Penberry Gdns.
TS17: Ing B 2F **149**
Penders La. TS15: K'ton 3E **161**
Penderyn Cres.
TS17: Ing B 2F **149**
Pendle Cl. TS12: Skel 3B **88**
Pendle Cres. TS23: Bill 1E **55**
Pendock Cl. TS5: Midd 2C **130**
Penhill Cl. TS3: Midd 1C **102**
Penhill Rd. TS18: Stock T 2B **96**
Penistone Rd. TS3: Midd. 3E **103**
Penllyn Way TS8: Hem 3E **131**
Pennal Gro. TS17: Ing B 5E **127**
Pennard Grn. TS3: Midd 1E **103**
Pennine Av. TS18: Stock T. 3F **75**
Pennine Cres. TS10: Redc. 1B **64**
Pennine Ho. TS18: Stock T 5F **97**
Pennine Way TS12: Skel 3C **88**
TS17: Ing B 3A **150**
Pennington Cl. TS23: Bill. 4E **39**
Pennydarren Way
TS17: Ing B 5F **127**
Penny La. TS18: Stock T. 2A **98**
Pennyman Cl. TS6: Norm 2C **104**
Pennyman Ct. TS3: Midd 4F **103**
Pennyman Grn. TS8: Malt 2F **151**
Pennyman Wlk.
TS11: Marsk S 4D **67**
Pennyman Way TS8: Stain . . . 5C **130**
Pennypot La. TS16: Prest T. . . 1D **127**
Pennyroyal Rd.
TS18: Stock T 1A **128**
Penrhyn St. TS26: H'pool 5B **14**
Penrith Cl. TS10: Redc 1C **64**
Penrith Rd. TS3: Midd. 1D **103**
Penrith St. TS24: H'pool 4D **9**
Penryn Cl. TS12: Skel 3D **89**
Pensby Av. TS4: Midd 1B **132**
Penshaw Cl. TS17: Ing B. 5C **128**
Penshaw Ct. TS23: Bill. 2E **39**
Penshurst Pl. TS23: Bill 5F **39**
Pentilly St. TS24: H'pool 5F **9**
Pentland Av. TS10: Redc. 2A **64**
TS12: Skel 3C **88**
TS23: Bill. 1D **55**
Penton Ct. TS23: Bill 3E **39**
Penwick Cl. TS15: Yarm 5B **148**
Penwick Wlk. TS15: Yarm. . . . 5B **148**
Penyghent Way
TS17: Ing B 3B **150**
Percy St. TS1: Midd. 4E **77**
TS26: H'pool. 2F **13**
Peregrine Ct. TS14: Guis. 2B **138**
Perry Av. TS17: Thorn T 4D **129**
Perth Cres. TS7: Mart 3D **133**
Perth Gro. TS18: Stock T. 2D **97**
Pert Rd. TS24: H'pool 2E **7**
Petch Cl. TS1: Midd. 4D **77**
Petch's Cotts. TS13: Live. 5A **116**
Petch St. TS18: Stock T. 5F **73**
Petrel Cres. TS20: Nort. 3A **54**
Petworth Cres. TS17: Ing B. . . 1B **150**
Pevensey Cl. TS4: Midd 4A **102**
Peveril Rd. TS23: Bill 5D **39**
Pexton Cl. TS8: Hem 4C **130**
Pheasant Cl. TS17: Ing B 5B **128**
Pheasant Flds La.
TS12: Skel 2E **89**
Phillida Ter. TS5: Midd 1F **101**
Phillips Av. TS5: Midd 2E **101**
Phillips Rd. TS24: H'pool 2A **14**
Phillips Tank Farm Local Wildlife Site
. . . . **1B 42**
Phoenix Cl. TS25: H'pool. 5E **19**
Phoenix Gdns.
TS18: Stock T 1D **97**
Phoenix Pk. TS8: Hem 3E **131**
Phoenix Sidings
TS19: Stock T 5A **74**
Phoenix Wlk. TS18: Stock T . . . 1D **97**
Phyllis Mohan Ct.
TS3: Midd 3D **103**
Pickering Gro. TS25: H'pool . . . 4B **20**
Pickering St. TS23: Bill 3D **57**
Picktree Gdns. TS25: H'pool . . . 3F **19**
Picton Av. TS5: Midd 3B **100**
TS22: Bill 4B **38**
Picton Cl. TS15: Yarm 2A **160**
Picton Cres. TS17: Thorn T . . . 3B **128**
Picton Pl. TS20: Nort. 5B **54**
Picture Ho. TS23: Bill 4D **55**
Piddington Cl. TS17: Ing B . . . 4F **127**
Piercebridge Cl.
TS19: Stock T 3C **72**
Pikeston Cl. TS26: H'pool 2D **13**
Pilgrim St. TS24: H'pool 4C **14**
Pilkington St. TS3: N Orm 4C **78**
Pillowell Cl. TS26: H'pool 1E **13**
PINCHINTHORPE **3E 137**
Pinder Cl. TS20: Nort 5A **54**
Pine Cl. TS10: Redc. 4E **49**
Pine Ct. TS19: Stock T. 3C **72**
Pineda Cl. TS5: Midd 3D **131**
Pine Gro. TS24: H'pool 5F **7**
Pine Hill TS8: Coul N. 4C **132**
PINE HILLS **3A 138**
Pinehurst Way TS11: N Mar. . . . 2F **85**
Pine Ridge Av. TS21: Sed 2D **23**
Pine Rd. TS7: Orm. 4B **104**
TS14: Guis 1D **139**
Pinero Gro. TS25: H'pool 2D **19**
Pines, The TS15: Yarm 4C **148**
Pine St. TS1: Midd. 3F **77**
TS3: N Orm 3D **79**
TS20: Nort 5B **54**
Pine Tree Gro. DL2: Mid G . . . 2A **144**
Pine Wlk. TS13: Loft 4B **92**
Pinewood Av. TS4: Midd 3F **101**
Pinewood Cl. TS13: Eas 3A **118**
TS27: H'pool 2C **6**
Pinewood Rd. TS7: Mart 2F **133**
TS16: Prest T. 3C **126**
Pinewood Wlk.
TS9: Stokes 5C **164**
Pinfold St. TS18: Stock T 4B **74**
Pintail Cl. TS26: H'pool. 1D **13**
Piper Ct. TS19: Stock T. 1C **72**
Piper Knowle Rd.
TS19: Stock T 1A **72**
Piper Knowle Vw.
TS19: Stock T 5B **52**
Pipit Cl. TS17: Ing B 5A **128**
Pippins, The TS22: Wolv. 2C **38**
Pipstrelle Ct. TS21: Stock T . . . 3D **53**
Pirbright Gro. TS8: Hem 4E **131**
Place in the Park, The. **4E 13**
Planetree Ct. TS7: Mart. 2E **133**
Plantation Rd.
TS10: K'ham, Redc 5B **64**
(not continuous)
Plantations, The TS22: Wyn . . . 4A **26**
Player Ct. TS16: Eag 5C **126**
Playlin Cl. TS15: Yarm. 4E **149**
Plumer Dr. TS20: Nort. 5A **54**
Plymouth Gro. TS26: H'pool . . . 1E **13**
Plymouth Wlk. TS26: H'pool . . . 1E **13**
Pochin Rd. TS6: Gran 1D **81**
Poldon Ter. TS23: Bill 2E **55**

Pond Farm Cl. TS13: Hind 5F **121**
Pontac Rd. TS11: N Mar 1A **86**
Poole Gdns. TS7: Nun 1B **156**
TS26: H'pool 3A **14**
POOLE RDBT. **5B 134**
Poole Ter. TS7: Nun. 1B **156**
Pope Gro. TS25: H'pool. 1D **19**
Poplar Ct. TS15: Yarm 2B **148**
Poplar Gro. TS6: S Ban 4B **80**
TS10: Redc. 4E **49**
TS12: Brot 2A **90**
TS18: Stock T. 2F **97**
Poplar Pl. TS14: Guis 1C **138**
Poplar Rd. TS16: Eag 1B **148**
TS17: Thorn T 4C **98**
Poplars, The TS8: Thornt 1B **152**
TS22: Wolv. 2C **38**
Poplars La. TS21: Carlt 5C **50**
Poplars Rd. TS5: Midd. 2E **101**
Poplar Ter. TS2: Port C 4E **57**
Poppy Cl. TS7: Orm. 3B **104**
TS26: H'pool 4D **7**
Poppy La. TS19: Stock T. 3C **72**
Porlock Rd. TS23: Bill 5C **38**
Porret La. TS13: Hind 5D **121**
Porrett Cl. TS24: H'pool. 2E **7**
Portchester Cl. TS17: Ing B. . . 4E **127**
PORT CLARENCE 5F **57**
Port Clarence Rd.
TS2: Midd, Port C 3D **57**
Porthleven Way TS10: Redc . . . 3F **65**
Portland Cl. TS7: Mart. 3C **132**
TS10: Redc 4C **64**
TS16: Eag. 1C **148**
Portland Gro. TS24: H'pool 2D **7**
Portland Ho. TS3: Midd 4E **79**
Portland Wlk. TS10: Redc 4C **64**
Portmadoc Wlk. TS26: H'pool. . . 1D **13**
Portman Ri. TS14: Guis 4E **139**
Portman Rd. TS20: Nort 1A **74**
Portman St. TS1: Midd 4E **77**
PORT MULGRAVE 4F 121
PORTRACK 4D 75
Portrack Bk. La.
TS18: Stock T. 2E **75**
Portrack Ct. TS18: Stock T 4B **74**
Portrack Grange Cl.
TS18: Stock T. 4F **75**
Portrack Grange Rd.
TS18: Stock T. 4E **75**
Portrack Ind. Est.
TS18: Stock T. 3F **75**
(not continuous)
PORTRACK INTERCHANGE **2F 75**
Portrack Interchange Bus. Pk.
TS18: Stock T. 3E **75**
Portrack Interchange Retail Pk.
TS18: Stock T. 3F **75**
Portrack La. TS18: Stock T 4B **74**
Portrack Marsh Nature Reserve
. . . . 4F 75
Portrack Retail Pk.
TS18: Stock T 4D **75**
Portrack Trade Pk.
TS18: Stock T. 3E **75**
Portrush Cl. TS4: Midd. 4F **101**
TS11: N Mar 2F **85**
Portsmouth Rd. TS16: Eag. . . . 4F **125**
Port Sunlight Gro.
TS19: Stock T 1C **72**
Potteries, The TS5: Midd 2D **101**
Potter Wlk. TS24: H'pool 2B **14**
Pottery M. *TS5: Midd 1D* ***101***
(off Benson St.)
Pottery St. TS17: Thorn T 3B **98**
Pottery Wharf TS17: Thorn T. . . 3B **98**
Potto Cl. TS15: Yarm 4E **149**
Pounder Pl. TS24: H'pool. 4F **7**
Powburn Cl. TS19: Stock T 3A **72**
Powell St. TS26: H'pool. 5A **14**
Powerleague
Stockton-on-Tees. 4F 97
Powlett Rd. TS24: H'pool 5A **8**
Pragnell Ct. TS10: Redc. 3F **65**
Preen Dr. TS5: Midd 4B **100**
Premier Pde. TS19: Stock T . . . 1A **96**
Premier Rd. TS3: Midd 2D **103**
TS7: Orm 5A **104**
TS19: Stock T 5C **72**
Prescot Rd. TS3: Midd. 3F **103**
Preseli Gro. TS17: Ing B 2F **149**
Preston Ct. TS12: Brot. 2B **90**
Preston Farm Bus. Pk.
TS18: Stock T. 4F **97**
Preston Farm Ind. Est.
TS18: Stock T. 5E **97**
(not continuous)
Preston Farm Local Nature Reserve
. . . . 2F 127
Preston La. TS18: Prest T. . . . 1D **127**
(not continuous)
PRESTON-ON-TEES. 2D 127
Preston Park Mus. 2D 127
Preston Pk. Skatepark. 2D 127
Preston Rd. TS18: Stock T 1C **96**
Preston Way TS9: Stokes 5B **164**
Prestwick Cl. TS4: Midd 4A **102**
Prestwick Ct. DL2: Mid G 1A **144**
TS16: Eag. 1C **148**
Preswick Cl. TS11: N Mar 2F **85**
Price Av. TS5: Midd 3B **100**
Price Rd. TS10: Redc. 1E **63**
Priestcrofts TS11: Marsk S 4E **67**
Priestfield Av. TS3: Midd. 4E **103**
Primary Vw. TS3: Midd 1C **102**
Primrose Cl. TS14: Guis 3B **138**
Primrose Grn.
TS18: Stock T 1A **98**
PRIMROSE HILL. 3A 74
Primrose Hill TS13: Skin. 2A **92**
Primrose Hill Bus. Pk.
TS19: Stock T 4A **74**
Primrose Rd. TS26: H'pool 4D **7**
Primrose St. TS19: Stock T 4F **73**
Primrose Ter. TS12: Salt 4C **68**
Princeport Rd.
TS18: Stock T 4C **74**
Prince Regent St.
TS18: Stock T 1A **98**
Princes Rd. TS1: Midd 4D **77**
TS12: Salt 5C **68**
Princess Av. TS18: Stock T 4B **74**
Princes Sq. TS17: Thorn T . . . 3D **129**
Princess St. TS17: Thorn T 2C **98**
TS24: H'pool. 1F **15**
Prince's Wharf
TS17: Thorn T 1C **98**
Princeton Dr. TS17: Thorn T . . . 1C **98**
Principal Rd. TS10: Redc 2D **65**
Prior Ct. TS23: Bill. 3A **40**
Priors Wood TS14: Guis 1C **138**
Priorwood Gdns.
TS17: Ing B 2B **150**
Priory Cl. TS14: Guis. 1E **139**
Priory Ct. TS14: Guis 1F **139**
TS20: Nort 5A **54**
TS24: H'pool 5C **8**
(Telford Cl.)
TS24: H'pool. 1F **15**
(Union St.)
Priory Dr. TS8: Stain 5C **130**
Priory Gdns. TS20: Nort 5A **54**
Priory Gro. TS10: Redc 4A **48**
Priory Pl. TS1: Midd 3E **77**
Priory Rd. TS5: Midd. 3A **100**
Priory St. TS1: Midd 3E **77**
PRISSICK 4B 102
Prissick St. TS24: H'pool 1F **15**
Pritchett Rd. TS3: Midd 3F **103**
Proctor's Ct. TS25: Seat C 4F **21**
Progress Ho. TS17: Thorn T . . . 5C **74**
Promenade TS24: H'pool 4D **15**
(Bridge St.)
TS24: H'pool. 5F **9**
(Moor Pde.)
TS25: H'pool 4D **15**
Prospect, The TS5: Midd 3E **101**
Prospect Pl. TS3: Midd 2D **79**
TS12: Ling 4E **113**
TS12: Skel 5A **88**
TS14: Guis 2E **139**
TS20: Nort 2B **74**
Prospect Ter. TS6: Est 1F **105**
TS11: Marsk S 4D **67**
TS12: Ling 4E **113**
Prospect Way TS25: H'pool 4B **20**
Protear Gro. TS20: Nort. 4C **54**
Providence Dr.
TS14: Guis 3D **139**
PS Wingfield Castle 2C 14
Puddlers Rd. TS6: S Ban 1A **80**
Pulford Rd. TS20: Nort. 5F **53**
Pump La. TS15: K'ton 4E **161**
Punch St. TS1: Midd 3C **76**
Pursglove Ter. TS14: Guis 1F **139**
Purves Pl. TS24: H'pool 4A **8**
Pybus Pl. TS10: Redc 3C **48**
Pym St. TS6: S Ban 3A **80**
Pytchley Rd. TS14: Guis 3E **139**

Q

Quads 4 All 4B 18
QUAKERS GROVE 4D 165
Quarry Bank Rd.
TS11: Upleat 4C **86**
Quarry Dr. TS8: Stain. 5C **130**
Quarry La.
TS11: Marsk S, Upleat 2D **87**
QUARRY LANE RDBT. **1D 87**
Quarry Rd. TS16: Prest T 3D **127**
Quarry Wood Local Nature Reserve
TS18: Prest T. 3D **127**
Quayside TS18: Stock T. 1B **98**
TS24: H'pool 3D **15**
Quay St. TS2: Midd 2A **78**
Quebec Gro. TS4: Midd 1A **102**
TS23: Bill 3E **39**
Quebec Rd. TS18: Stock T 3D **97**
Queen Anne Ter.
TS18: Stock T 2D **97**
Queen Elizabeth Way
TS17: Ing B 3F **127**
TS18: Stock T. 3F **127**
Queens Av. TS17: Thorn T. 3C **98**
Queensberry Av.
TS26: H'pool. 4F **13**
Queensbury Cl. TS10: Redc . . . 3A **64**
Queens Ct. *TS24: H'pool 4F* ***7***
(off Warren Rd.)
Queens Dr. TS9: Stokes. 5C **164**
TS21: Sed 5B **22**
TS22: Bill 5C **38**
Queensland Av. TS10: Redc . . . 5D **49**
Queensland Gro.
TS18: Stock T 2D **97**
Queensland Rd.
TS25: H'pool 4A **20**
Queen's Mdw. TS25: H'pool. . . . 2F **31**
Queens Meadow Bus. Pk.
TS25: H'pool. 2F **31**
Queen's Pde. TS24: H'pool 4B **14**
QUEENS PARK 4B 74
Queensport Cl.
TS18: Stock T 4D **75**
Queens Rd. TS5: Midd 2D **101**
TS13: Loft 4B **92**
Queens Sq. TS2: Midd 2F **77**
Queens Ter. TS2: Midd. 2F **77**
TS2: Port C. 5F **57**
Queen St. TS6: Laze 4C **82**
TS6: S Ban. 2A **80**
TS10: Redc 3B **48**
TS12: Boo 3B **112**
TS13: Carl H. 3F **91**
TS18: Stock T 5B **74**
TS24: H'pool. 1F **15**
(Rowell St.)

Queen St. TS24: H'pool 2D **15**
(Slake Ter.)
TS25: Seat C 3E **21**
Queen's Wlk. TS18: Stock T . . . 5B **74**
Queensway TS3: N Orm 3E **79**
TS12: Salt 4A **68**
TS23: Bill 1D **55**
(not continuous)
TS25: Grea 3E **31**
Queensway Ct. TS3: N Orm 3E **79**
Queensway Ho. TS3: N Orm . . . 4E **79**
Queen Ter. TS25: Seat C 4E **21**
Quenby Rd. TS23: Bill 5E **39**
Quorn Cl. TS14: Guis 4E **139**

R

Raby Cl. TS27: Hart 4A **6**
Raby Ct. TS4: Midd 1A **102**
Raby Gdns. TS24: H'pool 1F **13**
(not continuous)
Raby Rd. TS10: Redc 5E **49**
TS18: Stock T 1D **97**
TS24: H'pool 1A **14**
TS26: H'pool 2B **14**
Raby Sq. TS24: H'pool 1A **14**
Raby St. TS24: H'pool 1F **15**
Racecourse, The TS22: Wyn . . . 4E **25**
Race Ter. TS9: Gt A 2C **166**
Radcliffe Av. TS19: Stock T 1E **73**
Radcliffe Cres.
TS17: Thorn T 1C **98**
Radcliffe Ter. TS24: H'pool 1F **15**
Radford Cl. TS19: Stock T 4D **53**
Radlett Av. TS19: Stock T 1D **73**
Radnor Cl. TS19: Stock T 1E **73**
Radnor Grn. TS3: Midd 4E **103**
Radnor Gro. TS26: H'pool 1D **13**
Radstock Av. TS19: Stock T 5E **53**
Radyr Cl. TS19: Stock T 4C **52**
Raeburn St. TS26: H'pool 3F **13**
Rafton Dr. TS27: H'pool 2D **7**
Raglan Cl. TS19: Stock T 4C **52**
Raglan Ter. TS23: Bill 5E **39**
Ragpath La. TS19: Stock T 4D **53**
RAGWORTH 1F **73**
Ragworth Pl. TS20: Nort 4A **54**
Ragworth Rd. TS20: Nort 5A **54**
Railway Cotts. TS7: Nun 4B **134**
TS11: Marsk S 5B **66**
TS13: Carl H 3E **91**
TS13: Loft 5D **93**
TS13: Skin 3A **92**
TS16: Eag 2B **148**
Railway Ho's. TS2: Port C 1A **78**
Railway Ter. TS12: Brot 3B **90**
TS12: Skel 4F **89**
TS13: Loft 1D **117**
(Jackson St.)
TS13: Loft 5B **92**
(Stable Ct.)
TS16: Eag 3C **126**
TS17: Thorn T 2C **98**
Rainbow Casino 1A **100**
Rainbow La. TS10: Redc 3B **48**
Rainbow Leisure Cen. 4B **132**
Raincliffe Ct. TS8: Coul N 4B **132**
Raines Ct. TS4: Midd 1B **102**
Rainford Av. TS19: Stock T 1E **73**
Rainham Cl. TS3: Midd 5A **80**
TS17: Ing B 2B **150**
Rainsford Cres. TS3: Midd 5F **79**
Rainton Av. TS5: Midd 1C **130**
Rainton Dr. TS17: Thorn T 2B **128**
Rainton Gro. TS18: Stock T 2A **96**
Raisbeck Cl. TS11: Marsk S . . . 4C **66**
Raisbeck Gro.
TS19: Stock T 1B **72**
Raisby Cl. TS5: Midd 2B **130**
Raisdale Cl. TS17: Thorn T . . . 1D **129**
Raisegill Cl. TS3: Midd 1B **102**
Raithwaite Cl. TS14: Guis 1D **139**
Raithwaite Ho. TS14: Guis . . . 1E **139**
Rake Av. TS19: Stock T 5D **53**
Raleigh Cl. TS11: Marsk S. 5F **67**
Raleigh Ct. TS2: Midd 2C **76**
Raleigh Rd. TS20: Nort 1A **74**
Raleigh Wlk. TS20: Nort 1A **74**
Ralfland Way TS7: Nun 4A **134**
Ralph Sq. TS19: Stock T 3D **73**
Rampside Av. TS19: Stock T . . . 4D **53**
Ramsbury Av. TS19: Stock T . . . 5D **53**
Ramsey Cres. TS15: Yarm 5B **148**
Ramsey Gdns. TS17: Ing B . . . 2E **149**
Ramsey Rd. TS10: Redc 1F **63**
Ramsey Vw. TS20: Nort 1C **74**
Ramsey Wlk. *TS14: Guis. 3D **139***
(off Dorset Rd.)
Ramsgate TS18: Stock T 1A **98**
Randolph St. TS12: Salt 5C **68**
Raskelf Av. TS19: Stock T 1D **73**
Rathnew Av.
TS19: Stock T 5C **52**
Raunds Av. TS19: Stock T 1D **73**
Raven Cl. TS14: Guis 3A **138**
Ravendale Rd. TS3: Midd 2F **103**
Raven La. TS20: Nort 4A **54**
Ravenscar Cres.
TS19: Stock T 1F **73**
Ravenscroft Av. TS5: Midd . . . 3E **101**
Ravensdale TS5: Midd 2B **130**
Ravensworth Av.
TS6: Norm 1C **104**
Ravensworth Cres.
TS24: H'pool 1D **7**
Ravensworth Gro.
TS18: Stock T 2A **96**
Ravensworth Rd. TS23: Bill 5E **39**
Ravenwood Cl. TS27: H'pool 2B **6**
Rawcliffe Av. TS5: Midd 3C **130**
Rawley Dr. TS10: Redc 3A **64**
Rawlings Ct. TS24: H'pool 4A **8**
Rawlinson Av. TS23: Bill 4E **55**
Rawlinson St. TS13: Carl H 2F **91**
Ray Ct. TS19: Stock T 1C **72**
Raydale TS8: Hem 5C **130**
Raydale Beck TS17: Ing B 3B **150**
Raylton Av. TS7: Mart 4D **133**
Reading Rd. TS20: Nort 2A **74**
Rear High St. TS12: Skel 4B **88**
Rear Norton Rd.
*TS18: Stock T 5A **74***
(off Norton Rd.)
Recreation Vw.
TS12: Moor 3B **142**
Rectory Av. TS14: Guis 2D **139**
Rectory Cl. TS14: Guis 2D **139**
Rectory La. TS14: Guis 3D **139**
TS21: Long N 1A **124**
Rectory La. Ind. Est.
TS14: Guis 3E **139**
Rectory Row TS21: Sed 4D **23**
Rectory Way TS25: Seat C 5E **21**
Red Admiral Cl.
TS19: Stock T 3B **72**
Redbrook Av. TS19: Stock T . . . 5D **53**
Redbrook Vs. TS19: Stock T . . . 5D **53**
REDCAR 3C **48**
Redcar & Cleveland Leisure
& Community Heart 3C **48**
Redcar Av. TS11: Marsk S 4B **66**
TS19: Stock T 1E **73**
Redcar Beach Pk.
TS10: Redc 3A **48**
Redcar Beacon 3C **48**
Redcar Bears Speedway 3E **79**
Redcar Borough Park Bowling Club
. . . . 5D **49**
Redcar Bus Station 3D **49**
Redcar Central Station (Rail)
. . . . 4C **48**
Redcar Cl. TS25: H'pool 5A **14**
Redcar East Station (Rail) 5E **49**
Redcar La. TS10: Redc 4D **49**
Redcar Racecourse 5C **48**
Redcar Rd. TS6: S Ban 2A **80**
TS10: Redc, Marsk S 3E **65**
TS11: Marsk S 3E **65**
TS14: Dun, Guis 5D **85**
TS14: Guis 1E **139**
TS17: Thorn T 5C **98**
(not continuous)
Redcar Rd. E. TS6: S Ban 2B **80**
Redcar Rd. W. TS6: S Ban 2A **80**
Redcar St. TS2: Midd 2F **77**
Redditch Av. TS19: Stock T 5E **53**
Rede Ho. TS1: Midd 3F **77**
Redesdale Ct. TS2: Midd 5D **57**
Redesdale Gro.
TS17: Ing B 2A **150**
Red Hall La. TS15: Cast 3A **162**
Redheugh Ho.
TS17: Thorn T 2B **98**
Redhill Rd. TS19: Stock T 1D **73**
Red Ho. TS19: Stock T 5D **53**
Redland Cl. TS18: Stock T 1A **96**
Red Lion St. TS10: Redc 3C **48**
REDMARSHALL 1B **70**
Redmarshall Rd. TS21: Bis 1A **70**
TS21: Stock T 3E **71**
TS21: Whit 3A **50**
Redmarshall St. TS21: Stil 2A **50**
Redmayne Cl. TS23: Bill 4E **39**
Redmire Rd. TS18: Stock T 1D **97**
Redruth Av. TS19: Stock T 1E **73**
Redshank Cl. TS26: H'pool 5D **7**
Redstart Cl. TS26: H'pool 5E **7**
Redwing La. TS20: Nort 3B **54**
Redwing Rising TS14: Guis . . . 2B **138**
Redwood Cl. TS27: H'pool 1C **6**
Redwood Ct. TS7: Mart 2E **133**
Redwood Dr. TS12: Salt 5A **68**
Redworth Rd. TS23: Bill 5F **39**
Redworth St. TS24: H'pool 4C **14**
Reed Cl. TS20: Nort 1C **74**
Reedsdale Cl. TS10: Redc 4F **65**
Reedston Rd. TS26: H'pool 2C **12**
Reed St. TS17: Thorn T 2C **98**
TS24: H'pool 4C **14**
Reef Ho. TS24: H'pool 2C **14**
Reepham Cl. TS19: Stock T . . . 5C **52**
Reeth Rd. TS5: Midd 3C **100**
TS18: Stock T 3C **96**
Regal Cl. TS25: Seat C 5F **21**
Regency Av. TS6: Norm 3D **105**
Regency Dr. TS25: H'pool 3B **20**
Regency M. TS10: Redc 3C **48**
Regency Pk. TS17: Ing B 2C **150**
Regency W. Mall
*TS18: Stock T 1A **98***
(off Prince Regent St.)
Regent Cinema
Redcar 3C **48**
Regent Ct. TS6: Gran 4E **81**
Regent M. *TS18: Stock T. 1A **98***
(off Prince Regent St.)
Regent Rd. TS4: Midd 2A **102**
Regent Sq. TS24: H'pool 1F **15**
Regent St. TS18: Stock T 5A **74**
TS24: H'pool 1F **15**
Regent Wlk. TS10: Redc 3C **48**
Reid Ter. TS14: Guis 1E **139**
Reigate Av. TS5: Midd 3E **101**
Reigate Cl. TS19: Stock T 5D **53**
Relton Way TS26: H'pool 3E **13**
Renfrew Rd. TS20: Nort 5B **54**
Rennie Rd. TS6: S Ban 4F **79**
Renown Wlk. TS6: S Ban 3B **80**
Renvyle Av. TS19: Stock T 5C **52**
Repton Av. TS19: Stock T 1D **73**
Repton Rd. TS3: Midd 5A **80**
Resolution, The TS7: Nun 3A **134**
Resource Cl. TS6: S Ban 3B **80**
Retford Cl. TS19: Stock T 5D **53**
Retford Gro. TS25: H'pool 5E **19**
Rettendon Cl. TS19: Stock T . . . 5E **53**
Revesby Rd. TS3: Midd 3F **103**
Reynolds Ct. TS23: Bill 3D **39**

Reynoldston Av.
TS19: Stock T 4D **53**
Reystone Yd. TS17: Thorn T . . . 2C **98**
Rhinog Gro. TS17: Ing B 5F **127**
Rhobell Vw. TS17: Ing B 5E **127**
Rhodes Ct. TS17: Thorn T 2D **129**
Rhondda Av. TS19: Stock T 1E **73**
Rhoose Ga. TS17: Thorn T 5E **99**
Rhyl Cl. TS19: Stock T. 5E **53**
Rialto Ct. TS18: Stock T 2B **98**
Ribble Cl. TS22: Bill 4A **38**
Ribbleton Cl. TS7: Mart 3F **133**
Ribchester Cl.
TS19: Stock T 5D **53**
Riccarton Cl. TS19: Stock T . . . 5C **52**
Richard Ct. TS26: H'pool. 4A **14**
Richard Hind Wlk.
TS18: Stock T. 3F **97**
Richard Ho. TS17: Thorn T 1B **98**
Richardson Hall *TS9: Gt A . . . 2D* ***167***
(off The Green)
Richardson Rd.
TS17: Thorn T 5B **98**
TS18: Stock T. 2F **97**
Richardson St. TS26: H'pool . . . 2A **14**
Richard St. TS12: Skel. 4F **89**
TS26: H'pool 4A **14**
Richmond Cl. TS6: Est 1D **105**
Richmond Ct. TS4: Midd 2A **102**
TS6: Gran. 4E **81**
Richmond Cres. TS23: Bill. 5E **39**
Richmond Pl. TS17: Thorn T . . . 5E **99**
Richmond Rd. TS10: Redc. 5E **49**
TS18: Stock T. 2E **97**
Richmond St. TS2: Midd 1E **77**
TS18: Stock T 4A **74**
TS25: H'pool 1B **20**
Ricknall Cl. TS5: Midd. 2B **130**
Ridge, The TS8: Coul N. 2B **154**
TS12: Salt 1C **88**
Ridge La. TS13: Stait. 5C **118**
Ridgeway TS8: Coul N. 5A **132**
Ridings, The TS4: Midd. 1B **102**
Ridley Av. TS5: Midd 4C **100**
Ridley Ct. TS20: Nort. 4A **54**
TS26: H'pool 2A **14**
Ridley Dr. TS20: Nort. 5F **53**
Ridley M. TS20: Nort. 5B **54**
Ridley St. TS10: Redc 3C **48**
Ridley Ter. TS13: Skin 2A **92**
Ridlington Way TS24: H'pool. . . . 2E **7**
Ridsdale Av. TS19: Stock T. . . . 1D **73**
Rievaulx Av. TS23: Bill 5C **38**
Rievaulx Cl. TS19: Stock T 5D **53**
Rievaulx Dr. TS5: Midd 4E **101**
Rievaulx Rd. TS12: Skel 3D **89**
Rievaulx Wlk. TS6: Est 1D **105**
Rievaulx Way TS14: Guis. 2F **139**
RIFT HOUSE 2E **19**
Rifts Av. TS12: Salt 4B **68**
Riftswood Dr.
TS11: Marsk S 4B **66**
Rigby Ho. TS15: Yarm 4B **148**
Rigg, The TS15: Yarm 5C **148**
Riggston Pl. TS26: H'pool. 2D **13**
Riley St. TS18: Stock T 1F **97**
Rillington Cl. TS19: Stock T . . . 5C **52**
Rillston Cl. TS26: H'pool. 2D **13**
Rillstone Way TS10: Redc. 4E **65**
Rimdale Dr. TS19: Stock T 4A **72**
Rimswell Pde.
TS19: Stock T 4A **72**
Rimswell Rd. TS19: Stock T . . . 3A **72**
Ring Rd., The TS19: Stock T. . . 2E **73**
TS20: Nort 2E **73**
Rings, The TS17: Ing B 4F **127**
Ring Stones Cl.
TS26: H'pool 4E **7**
Ringway TS17: Thorn T 1E **129**
Ringway Gro. DL2: Mid G 1A **144**
Ringwood Cres.
TS19: Stock T. 1E **73**
Ringwood Rd. TS3: Midd. 1A **104**
Ripley Cl. TS12: Skel. 3B **88**
Ripley Ct. TS3: Midd 5A **80**
Ripley Rd. TS20: Nort 4F **53**
Ripon Cl. TS19: Stock T 1D **73**
TS25: H'pool 4C **20**
Ripon Rd. TS7: Nun. 3B **134**
TS10: Redc. 1F **65**
TS12: Brot 2C **90**
Ripon Way TS6: Est 5F **81**
Rise, The TS7: Nun 3A **134**
Rishton Cl. TS19: Stock T 1D **73**
Rissington Wlk.
TS17: Thorn T 1E **129**
Ritchie Humphreys Dr.
TS24: H'pool 2A **14**
Rium Ter. TS24: H'pool 3B **14**
Rivendell Cl. TS23: Bill 5D **39**
River Ct. TS2: Midd 5C **56**
Rivergreen Bus. Cen.
TS25: H'pool. 1F **31**
Riverhead Av. TS19: Stock T. . . 1D **73**
Riversdene TS9: Stokes. 2A **168**
Riverside TS18: Stock T 1B **98**
Riverside Bus. Pk.
TS2: Midd 1D **77**
(not continuous)
Riverside M. TS15: Yarm 2B **148**
TS17: Thorn T 3B **98**
Riverside Pk. Ind. Est.
TS2: Midd 5D **57**
Riverside Pk. Rd. TS2: Midd. . . 2C **76**
Riverside Pk. Trad. Est.
TS2: Midd 1D **77**
Riverside Quay
TS17: Thorn T 1B **98**
Riverside Rd. TS2: Seal S 3E **59**
Riverside Stadium 2B 78
Riverslea TS9: Stokes 2A **168**
Riverston Cl. TS26: H'pool 2C **12**
Riversway TS7: Mart 2E **133**
River Tees Watersports Cen.
. . . . 5C 74
Riverton Croft
TS18: Thorn T 5D **75**
R-Kade Scatepark 3B 48
Robert Av. TS6: Gran. 3D **81**
Roberts Ho. TS17: Thorn T 1C **98**
TS18: Stock T. 5E **97**
Robertson Ho. TS20: Nort 5A **54**
Robert St. TS17: Thorn T. 2C **98**
Robin Cl. TS17: Ing B 5B **128**
Robinson Cl. TS25: H'pool 2B **20**
Robinson Ct. TS13: Loft 5D **93**
Robinson St. TS12: Skel 3C **88**
TS13: Loft 5D **93**
Robinson's Yd. *TS12: Skel 4B* ***88***
(off High St.)
Robinson Ter. TS13: Loft. 5C **92**
Robson Av. TS17: Thorn T. . . . 5D **129**
Robson Ct. TS24: H'pool 5A **8**
Robson St. TS23: Bill. 3D **57**
Rochdale Av. TS19: Stock T . . . 5E **53**
Rochdale Cl. TS3: Midd 2D **103**
Rochester Ct. TS17: Ing B. . . . 2A **150**
TS17: Thorn T 1C **98**
Rochester Dr. TS10: Redc 1E **65**
Rochester Rd. TS5: Midd. 2E **101**
TS19: Stock T. 5E **53**
TS23: Bill 5E **39**
Rockall Av. TS19: Stock T 5C **52**
Rockbourne Way
TS17: Ing B 4F **127**
Rockcliffe Ct. TS13: Eas 3A **118**
Rockcliffe Ter. TS13: Carl H . . . 2A **92**
Rockcliffe Vw. TS13: Carl H . . . 2A **92**
Rocket Ter. TS10: Redc 3A **48**
Rockferry Cl. TS19: Stock T . . . 5C **52**
Rockingham Ct. TS5: Midd . . . 4B **100**
Rockliffe Rd. TS5: Midd 2C **100**
Rockpool Cl. TS24: H'pool. 4B **8**
Rockport Ct. TS18: Stock T 4C **74**
Rockwood Cl. TS14: Guis. 3F **139**
Rodmell Cl. TS3: Midd 2A **104**
Rodney Cl. TS12: Brot 2C **90**
TS23: Bill 5D **55**
Rodney St. TS26: H'pool 3A **14**
Roebuck Cl. TS17: Ing B 4C **128**
Roecliffe Gro.
TS19: Stock T 5B **52**
Roedean Dr. TS16: Eag 1C **148**
Rogeri Pl. TS24: H'pool 3F **7**
Roger La. TS8: Malt 2F **151**
TS15: Hilt 4F **151**
Rokeby Av. TS4: Midd 3A **102**
Rokeby St. TS18: Stock T 2F **97**
TS24: H'pool 4C **8**
Roker St. TS24: H'pool 4B **14**
Roker Ter. TS18: Stock T. 2F **97**
Rollesby Way TS18: Stock T . . . 5D **75**
Rolleston Av. TS19: Stock T . . . 5C **52**
Romaine Pk. TS24: H'pool 4C **8**
Romaldkirk Rd. TS2: Midd 2C **76**
Romanby Av. TS19: Stock T . . . 1E **73**
Romanby Cl. TS24: H'pool 4C **8**
Romanby Gdns. TS5: Midd . . . 3E **131**
Roman Rd. TS5: Midd. 1D **101**
Roman Ter. TS5: Midd. 2D **101**
Romany Rd. TS9: Gt A 1D **167**
Romax Ind. Units
TS18: Stock T 4D **75**
Romford Rd. TS19: Stock T. . . . 5D **53**
Romney Cl. TS10: Redc. 2E **65**
Romney Grn. TS23: Bill. 3D **39**
Romney St. TS1: Midd. 4E **77**
Romsey Rd. TS19: Stock T 1E **73**
Rona Gdns. TS17: Thorn T 4D **99**
Ronaldshay Ter.
TS11: Marsk S. 4D **67**
Rookery, The TS16: Eag 2B **148**
Rookery Dale TS12: Boo 2B **112**
Rook La. TS20: Nort 3A **54**
Rookwood Rd. TS7: Nun 3B **134**
Ropery Rd. TS24: H'pool. 4C **8**
Ropery St. TS18: Stock T 5A **74**
Ropner Av. TS18: Stock T 2E **97**
Ropner Gdns. DL2: Mid G 4A **144**
Roscoe Rd. TS23: Bill 5E **55**
Roscoe St. TS1: Midd 4A **78**
Rose Av. TS11: Marsk S 4A **66**
Rosebank TS26: H'pool 5F **13**
Rosebay Cl. TS26: H'pool 4E **7**
Rosebay Ct. TS14: Guis. 3B **138**
Roseberry Av. TS9: Gt A 1E **167**
TS9: Stokes 5D **165**
Roseberry Ct. TS9: Stokes . . . 3D **169**
Roseberry Cres. TS6: Est 5A **82**
TS9: Gt A 5A **158**
TS20: Nort 4B **54**
Roseberry Dr. TS8: Stain. 5C **130**
TS9: Gt A 1D **167**
Roseberry Flats TS23: Bill. 1D **55**
Roseberry La. TS9: Newt R. . . 3C **158**
Roseberry M. TS26: H'pool 3F **13**
Roseberry Mt. TS14: Guis 2C **138**
Roseberry Rd. TS4: Midd 5A **78**
(not continuous)
TS9: Gt A 1D **167**
TS10: Redc 2A **64**
TS20: Nort 4B **54**
TS23: Bill 1C **54**
TS26: H'pool. 3F **13**
Roseberry Topping 3D 159
Roseberry Vw.
TS9: Newt R. 2C **158**
TS17: Thorn T 3C **98**
Rosebud Cl. TS26: H'pool 4D **7**
Rosebury M. TS7: Nun 3B **134**
Rose Cott. Gdns.
TS8: Stain 5B **130**
Rosecroft Av. TS13: Loft 1B **116**
Rosecroft La. TS13: Loft 1B **116**
Rosedale Av. TS4: Midd. 1F **101**
TS26: H'pool. 4F **13**
Rosedale Cl. TS12: Skel 3C **88**
TS21: Sed 2D **23**
Rosedale Ct. TS9: Stokes 3D **169**

Rosedale Cres. TS13: Loft 4B **92**
TS14: Guis 3B **138**
Rosedale Gdns. TS12: Ling . . . 4E **113**
TS19: Stock T 5D **53**
TS23: Bill 4D **39**
Rosedale Gro. TS10: Redc. 1F **63**
Rosedale La. TS13: Port M . . . 4E **121**
Rosedale Rd. TS7: Nun. 3B **134**
Rosegarth Ct. TS9: Gt Bro 5F **169**
ROSE HILL. 4C **148**
ROSEHILL 2B **96**
Rose Hill TS8: Newb 4B **154**
Rosehill TS9: Gt A. 2D **167**
TS13: Hind 5E **121**
Rose Hill Dr. TS9: Stokes 2B **168**
Rose Hill Way TS9: Stokes . . . 2B **168**
Roseland Cres. TS7: Mart 1E **133**
Roseland Dr. TS7: Mart 1E **133**
Rosemary Cotts.
TS11: Marsk S 5D **67**
Rosemary Nook TS26: H'pool . . . 5E **7**
Rosemoor Cl. TS7: Mart 3C **132**
Rosemount Rd. TS11: N Mar . . . 2F **85**
Roseneath Av.
TS19: Stock T 4D **53**
Rose St. TS1: Midd 3E **77**
TS18: Stock T 1A **98**
Rose Ter. TS16: Egg 2C **148**
Roseville Ct. TS17: Ing B 5A **128**
Rose Wlk. TS12: Salt. 5D **69**
Roseway, The TS12: Salt. 5C **68**
Rosewood Cl. TS7: Orm 4B **104**
Rosewood Ct. TS7: Mart 2E **133**
ROSEWORTH. 5D **53**
Roseworth TS9: Gt Bro. 5F **169**
Rosgill TS10: Redc 1B **64**
Rosiere Gro. TS10: Redc. 5C **48**
Roslyn Av. TS3: Midd 2D **103**
Rossall St. TS25: H'pool 1A **20**
Rossendale Cl.
TS11: Marsk S 5C **66**
Rossetti Way TS23: Bill 3D **39**
Rossett Wlk. TS3: Midd. 2C **102**
(not continuous)
Rossett Way TS10: Redc 1B **64**
Ross Gro. TS25: H'pool 4B **20**
Rosslare Rd. TS19: Stock T . . . 5C **52**
Rosslyn Ct. TS18: Stock T. 3E **97**
ROSSMERE 4F **19**
Rossmere Learner Swimming Pool
. . . . 4F **19**
Rossmere Way TS25: H'pool . . . 4F **19**
Ross Rd. TS18: Stock T. 3D **75**
Ross Saltburn Rd.
TS17: Thorn T 4D **99**
Ross St. TS1: Midd 4D **77**
Rosthwaite TS5: Midd 2B **130**
Rosthwaite Av.
TS19: Stock T. 5E **53**
Rosthwaite Cl. TS24: H'pool 5B **8**
Rosthwaite Dr. TS12: Skel. 2C **88**
Rostrevor Av. TS19: Stock T . . . 4D **53**
Rothbury Av. TS19: Stock T. . . . 5D **53**
Rothbury Cl. TS17: Ing B. 2B **150**
Rothbury Rd. TS3: Midd 2C **102**
Rothbury St. TS23: Bill 1D **55**
Rotherham Av.
TS19: Stock T 1D **73**
Rothesay Dr. TS10: Redc. 2E **65**
Rothesay Gro. TS7: Nun 2B **134**
Rothwell Cres.
TS19: Stock T 1D **73**
Rothwell M. TS6: Est. 1F **105**
Rottingdean Cl.
TS19: Stock T 5D **53**
Roundhay Dr. TS16: Eag 5C **126**
ROUND HILL 2F **149**
Roundhill Av. TS17: Ing B 1F **149**
Roundhill Cl. TS26: H'pool 3C **12**
Roundsway TS7: Mart 2E **133**
Rounton Grn. TS3: Midd 2C **102**
Rounton Gro. TS19: Stock T . . . 1B **96**
Rousham Gdns. TS5: Midd . . . 2B **100**
Routledge Ct. TS24: H'pool. 5A **8**
Routledge Rd. TS20: Nort. 3C **74**
Rowallane Gdns.
TS17: Ing B 2B **150**
Rowan Av. TS14: Guis. 3B **138**
Rowan Dr. TS9: Gt A 1D **167**
Rowan Gro. TS8: Stain 5B **130**
Rowan Oval TS21: Sed 3D **23**
Rowan Rd. TS16: Eag 1B **148**
TS19: Stock T 3A **74**
Rowanton Pl. TS26: H'pool 2D **13**
Rowanwood Ct. TS5: Midd . . . 2E **131**
Rowan Yd. TS20: Nort. 5B **54**
Rowell St. TS24: H'pool. 1F **15**
Rowen Cl. TS17: Ing B. 1F **149**
Rowland Keld TS14: Guis 4B **138**
Rowlands Gro. TS23: Bill. 2A **40**
Roworth Rd. TS3: Midd 1A **104**
Roxburgh Cl. TS6: Norm 5B **80**
ROXBY 5E **119**
Roxby Av. TS3: Midd 4E **103**
TS14: Guis 4D **139**
Roxby Cl. TS10: Redc 2C **64**
TS19: Stock T. 1F **73**
TS25: Seat C 5D **21**
Roxby La. TS13: Rox, Stait . . . 5E **119**
Royal George Dr.
TS16: Eag. 4A **126**
Royce Av. TS23: Bill. 5B **40**
Royce Ct. TS23: Bill. 5B **40**
Royd, The TS15: Yarm. 5B **148**
Royston Av. TS3: Midd. 4E **103**
Royston Cl. TS19: Stock T. 1F **73**
Royston Gro. TS25: H'pool 1D **31**
Ruberry Av. TS19: Stock T. 5C **52**
Ruby St. TS1: Midd 4E **77**
TS12: Salt 3C **68**
Rudby Cl. TS15: Yarm 4E **149**
Rudd Cl. TS22: Wyn. 1F **37**
Rudds Pl. TS5: Midd 1E **101**
Rudland Wlk. TS6: Est. 5F **81**
Rudston Av. TS22: Bill 4A **38**
Rudston Cl. TS17: Thorn T . . . 2B **128**
Rudyard Av. TS19: Stock T 5C **52**
Rufford Cl. TS7: Mart. 3F **133**
TS14: Guis 4E **139**
TS17: Ing B 5C **128**
Ruff Tail TS14: Guis. 2B **138**
Rugby Rd. TS18: Stock T. 1F **97**
Rugby St. TS25: H'pool 1A **20**
Rugby Ter. TS2: Port C 4E **57**
Rugeley Cl. TS19: Stock T 1D **73**
Ruislip Cl. TS19: Stock T 1D **73**
Runciman Rd. TS24: H'pool. 4F **7**
Runcorn Av. TS19: Stock T 1D **73**
Runfold Cl. TS19: Stock T. 4C **52**
Runnymead Grn.
TS3: Midd. 4E **103**
Runnymede TS7: Nun 4A **134**
Runnymede Cl.
TS19: Stock T 5D **53**
Runswick Av. TS5: Midd 2C **130**
TS10: Redc 5A **48**
TS19: Stock T 1D **73**
Runswick La. TS13: Hind. 5F **121**
Runswick Rd. TS6: Est. 5F **81**
Rupert St. TS18: Stock T. 4C **74**
Rushleigh Av. TS5: Midd. 5B **100**
Rushmere TS8: Mart 5E **133**
Rushmere Heath TS16: Eag. . . 1C **148**
Rushpool Cl. TS10: Redc. 2B **64**
Rushyford Av. TS19: Stock T. . . 1D **73**
Ruskin Av. TS5: Midd 4B **100**
TS12: Salt 4B **68**
Ruskin Ct. TS19: Stock T. 1B **72**
Ruskin Gro. TS25: H'pool. 1F **19**
Russell St. TS1: Midd 3F **77**
TS18: Stock T 5A **74**
(not continuous)
TS24: H'pool 5E **9**
Russell Wlk. TS17: Thorn T . . . 3C **98**
TS25: H'pool 5B **14**
(not continuous)
Rustington Cl.
TS19: Stock T 5D **53**
Ruswarp Av. TS19: Stock T. . . . 1D **73**
Ruswarp Cl. TS6: Est. 1F **105**
Ruswarp Gro. TS25: Seat C 5E **21**
Ruswarp Rd. TS6: Est 1F **105**
Ruth Av. TS3: Midd 1E **103**
Rutherglen Wlk. TS16: Eag . . . 1C **148**
Ruthin Cl. TS19: Stock T 5E **53**
Rutland Av. TS7: Mart 3C **132**
Rutland Cl. TS19: Stock T 5E **53**
Rutland Ct. TS1: Midd 3F **77**
Ryan Av. TS18: Stock T 4B **74**
Ryan Ct. TS26: H'pool 3A **14**
Ryans Row TS11: Marsk S 4B **66**
Ryan Wlk. TS18: Stock T. 4B **74**
Rydal Av. TS5: Midd 4C **100**
TS6: Gran 4F **81**
TS10: Redc 5B **48**
TS23: Bill 5E **55**
Rydal Rd. TS12: Skel. 3B **88**
TS18: Stock T. 5E **73**
Rydal St. TS26: H'pool 5A **14**
Rydal Way TS21: Redm. 1B **70**
Ryder Cl. TS11: N Mar. 2F **85**
Ryde Rd. TS19: Stock T 5D **53**
Rye Cl. TS16: Eag 2B **148**
Ryedale TS14: Guis. 4B **138**
Ryedale Cl. TS15: Yarm 1B **160**
Ryedale St. TS3: N Orm 4C **78**
Ryefields Ho. TS6: Est. 3E **105**
Ryehill Cl. TS7: Nun 5A **134**
Ryehill Gdns. TS26: H'pool 2E **13**
Ryehills Dr. TS11: Marsk S 3E **67**
Rye Hill Way TS8: Coul N 2C **154**
Ryelands Pk. TS13: Eas. 3A **118**
Ryhill Wlk. TS7: Orm. 4A **104**
Ryhope Av. TS19: Stock T. 5D **53**
Rylstone Ct. TS4: Midd 3A **102**
Ryton Cl. TS17: Thorn T 2B **128**

S

Sabatier Cl. TS17: Thorn T 1C **98**
Sacriston Cl. TS23: Bill 4C **38**
Sadberge Gro.
TS19: Stock T 5A **72**
Sadberge Rd. TS18: Stock T . . . 3F **97**
Sadberge St. TS3: N Orm 4C **78**
Saddler Cl. TS17: Ing B. 5B **128**
Saddleston Cl. TS26: H'pool . . . 2D **13**
Sadler Dr. TS7: Mart 3C **132**
Sadler Forster Way
TS17: Thorn T 4D **129**
Sadler St. TS25: H'pool. 5D **15**
Saffron Wlk. TS25: Seat C 3E **21**
St Abb's Wlk. TS24: H'pool 4C **14**
St Aidan's Cres. TS22: Bill. 2C **54**
St Aidan's Dr. TS1: Midd 3E **77**
St Aidan's St. TS1: Midd 4E **77**
TS25: H'pool 1B **20**
St Aidan's Vw. TS12: Boo 3C **112**
St Albans Cl. TS10: Redc 3B **64**
St Albans Ct. TS1: Midd 3D **77**
St Andrew's Cl. TS16: Eag. . . . 1C **148**
St Andrew's Gro.
TS27: H'pool 2D **7**
St Andrews Rd. TS7: Mart. . . . 3D **133**
TS11: N Mar. 1A **86**
St Andrew's Rd. E.
TS6: Gran 3E **81**
St Andrew's Rd. W.
TS6: Gran 3E **81**
St Annes Gdns. DL2: Mid G. . . 3A **144**
St Annes Rd. TS11: N Mar. . . . 2A **86**
St Ann's Ct. TS24: H'pool 4D **15**
ST ANN'S HILL. 4C **74**
St Anns Ind. Est.
TS18: Stock T 4C **74**
St Ann's Ter. TS18: Stock T. . . . 4C **74**
St Anthonys TS3: Midd. 2E **103**
St Austell Cl. TS8: Hem. 4C **130**

St Barnabas Rd. TS5: Midd . . . 1D **101**
St Bees Wlk. *TS24: H'pool 4C 14*
(off Longscar Wlk.)
St Bega's Glade
TS26: H'pool 3E **13**
St Bernard Rd.
TS18: Stock T 1A **98**
St Brides Ct. TS17: Ing B 2F **149**
St Catherines Ct.
TS3: Midd 1C **102**
TS24: H'pool 4C **14**
St Columba's Av. TS22: Bill 2C **54**
St Columba's Ct.
TS25: H'pool 2E **19**
St Crispins Ct.
TS19: Stock T. 3E **73**
St Cuthbert Av. TS7: Mart 4F **133**
St Cuthbert Ct.
TS17: Thorn T 3C **98**
St Cuthbert's Av. TS23: Bill 2C **54**
St Cuthberts Church and Turner Mausoleum 5A **64**
St Cuthbert's Rd.
TS18: Stock T 2A **98**
(not continuous)
St Cuthbert St. TS24: H'pool 5E **9**
St Cuthbert's Wlk.
TS13: Live 1A **116**
St David's Cl. TS23: Bill. 2C **54**
St Davids Gro. TS17: Ing B . . . 2F **149**
St David's Rd. TS6: Gran 2E **81**
St David's Wlk.
TS26: H'pool 1D **13**
St David's Way TS5: Midd. . . . 5D **101**
St Edmund's Grn. TS21: Sed . . . 3D **23**
(not continuous)
St Edmund's Ter. TS21: Sed . . . 4D **23**
St Francis Cl. TS5: Midd 2B **100**
St Francis Ga. TS25: H'pool . . . 2B **20**
St George's Bungs.
TS6: Gran. 3E **81**
St George's Cres.
TS11: N Mar. 2A **86**
St George's Rd. TS6: Gran. 3E **81**
St George's Rd. W.
TS6: Gran. 3E **81**
St George's Sq. TS6: S Ban. . . . 2A **80**
St Georges Ter. TS13: Live . . . 1A **116**
St George Way DL2: Mid G . . . 2C **144**
St Germain's Grange
TS11: Marsk S. 4D **67**
St Germain's Gro.
TS11: Marsk S. 4D **67**
St Germain's La.
TS11: Marsk S. 4D **67**
St Helen's Cl. TS6: Est 1D **105**
St Helen's St. TS24: H'pool 5E **9**
St Helens Wlk. TS13: Live. . . . 1A **116**
St Hilda Chare TS24: H'pool . . . 1F **15**
St Hilda Cres. TS24: H'pool. . . . 1F **15**
ST HILDA'S 1F **77**
St Hilda's Pl. TS13: Loft 5C **92**
St Hilda's Ter. TS13: Loft 4A **92**
St Hilda St. TS24: H'pool. 1F **15**
St Ives Cl. TS8: Midd. 2B **132**
TS10: Redc. 3F **65**
St James Cl.
TS21: Thorpe T 1D **51**
St James Ct. TS6: Gran. 2D **81**
TS19: Stock T 2D **73**
St James Gro. TS27: Hart 4F **5**
St James Ho. TS18: Stock T . . . 4C **74**
St James' M. TS1: Midd 5D **77**
St Joan's Gro. TS25: H'pool . . . 2B **20**
St Johns Cl. TS4: Midd 3A **78**
TS18: Stock T 4A **74**
St John's Ga. *TS1: Midd 3A 78*
(off Woodside St.)
St John's Gro. TS10: Redc 5D **49**
St Johns Pk. TS21: Stil 2B **50**
St Johns Row TS6: Gran 3E **81**
St John's Way
TS19: Stock T. 2F **73**
St Josephs Ct. TS10: Redc 5B **48**
TS26: H'pool 3A **14**
St Leonards Cl. TS13: Live . . . 1A **116**
St Leonards Rd.
TS14: Guis 3C **138**
St Luke's Av. TS17: Thorn T . . . 3D **99**
St Luke's Cotts. TS4: Midd . . . 2A **102**
St Lukes Ct. TS26: H'pool 2F **13**
St Lukes Cres. TS21: Sed 1C **22**
St Margarets Cl.
DL2: Mid G. 3A **144**
St Margaret's Gro.
TS5: Midd 4D **101**
TS6: S Ban. 4B **80**
TS10: Redc 1D **65**
TS17: Thorn T 1D **129**
TS25: H'pool 2B **20**
St Margaret's Way
TS12: Brot 2B **90**
St Mark's Cl. TS11: Marsk S . . . 4C **66**
TS19: Stock T 4B **72**
St Mark's Ct. TS17: Thorn T . . . 1B **98**
St Mark's Ho. TS17: Thorn T. . . 1B **98**
St Martins Cl. TS13: Live. 1A **116**
St Martin's Way
TS15: K'ton 4D **161**
St Mary's Cl. TS18: Stock T . . . 4B **74**
St Mary's Ct. TS5: Midd 3D **101**
TS6: Gran. 3E **81**
TS24: H'pool. 1F 15
(off Northgate)
St Marys Ga. Bus. Pk.
TS20: Nort 4B **74**
St Mary St. TS24: H'pool 1F **15**
St Mary's Wlk. TS5: Midd 4D **101**
St Matthews Ct. TS6: Gran 2D **81**
St Mawes Cl. TS26: H'pool 2D **13**
St Michael's Cl. TS13: Live . . . 1A **116**
St Michael's Ct. TS20: Nort. . . . 2B **74**
St Michael's Gro.
TS20: Nort 2B **74**
St Nicholas Ct. TS6: Gran 2D **81**
St Nicholas Gdns.
TS15: Yarm 5E **149**
St Oswald's Cres. TS23: Bill . . . 2C **54**
St Oswalds St. TS24: H'pool . . . 2A **14**
St Patrick's Cl. TS6: Gran 3E **81**
St Patrick's Rd. TS6: Gran. 3E **81**
St Pauls Ct. TS6: Gran. 3E **81**
TS19: Stock T. 4F **73**
St Pauls Rd. TS1: Midd. 3D **77**
TS17: Thorn T 3C **98**
TS19: Stock T. 4F **73**
TS26: H'pool 4A **14**
St Paul's St. TS19: Stock T 5F **73**
St Paul's Ter. TS19: Stock T . . . 4F **73**
St Peter's Gro. TS10: Redc 5D **49**
St Peter's Ho.
TS17: Thorn T 1D **129**
St Peter's Rd. TS18: Stock T . . . 2F **97**
St Stephens Cl. TS20: Nort 3A **54**
St Thomas Gro. TS10: Redc . . . 5D **49**
St Vincent Ter. TS10: Redc 4B **48**
Salcombe Cl. TS8: Midd 2B **132**
Salcombe Dr. TS25: H'pool 5A **20**
Salcombe Way TS10: Redc 3E **65**
Salisbury Ct. TS1: Midd 3D **77**
Salisbury Gro. TS10: Redc 5F **49**
Salisbury Pl. TS26: H'pool 1E **13**
Salisbury St. TS17: Thorn T . . . 3D **99**
Salisbury Ter. TS6: S Ban 2F **79**
TS20: Nort 2B **74**
Salis Cl. TS5: Midd 3B **130**
Saltaire Ter. TS25: Grea. 4F **31**
Saltburn Bank TS12: Salt. 3D **69**
SALTBURN-BY-THE-SEA 4C **68**
Saltburn Cliff Lift 3D **69**
Saltburn Gill Nature Reserve 1E **89**
Saltburn Golf Course 5B **68**
Saltburn La. TS12: Salt. 4D **69**
TS12: Salt, Skel 3C **88**
SALTBURN LANE RDBT. 2C **88**
Saltburn Leisure Cen. 5B **68**
Saltburn Miniature Railway . . . 4D **69**
Saltburn Rd.
TS12: Brot, Salt 4D **69**
Saltburn Station (Rail) 4C **68**
Saltburn Valley Woodland Cen. 5D **69**
Saltcote TS7: Mart. 2E **133**
Saltergill La. TS15: K'ton 3A **160**
Salter Ho. Dr. TS22: Wyn 4C **26**
(not continuous)
Salter Ho's. TS22: Wyn 4C **26**
Saltern Wetlands 2B **42**
SALTERSGILL 3F **101**
Saltersgill Av. TS4: Midd 3F **101**
Saltersgill Cl. TS4: Midd 3F **101**
Salter's La. TS21: Fish, Sed . . . 2D **23**
Salter Wlk. TS24: H'pool. 5E **9**
Saltholme Cl. TS2: Port C 4E **57**
Saltholme Nature Reserve 3F **57**
Saltholme Wild Bird Discovery Cen. 2A **58**
Saltney Rd. TS20: Nort 5F **53**
Salton Cl. TS5: Midd 2B **100**
Saltram Cl. TS17: Ing B. 1B **150**
Saltram Gro. TS7: Mart 2C **132**
Saltscar TS10: Redc. 2E **65**
Saltview Ter. TS2: Port C 5A **58**
Saltwater Ct. TS4: Midd 5B **78**
Saltwells Cres. TS4: Midd. 5B **78**
Saltwells Rd. TS4: Midd 4A **78**
Samaria Gdns. TS5: Midd 2D **131**
Sambrook Gdns.
TS5: Midd 2D **131**
Samphire St. TS2: Port C. 5F **57**
Samuelson Ho. TS3: Midd . . . 2D **103**
Samuel St. TS19: Stock T 4F **73**
Sanctuary Cl. TS5: Midd 5C **100**
Sandalwood Ct. TS5: Midd . . . 2E **131**
Sandbanks Dr. TS24: H'pool 2D **7**
Sanderson Gro. TS13: Loft 5D **93**
Sanderson's Yd. TS13: Loft. . . . 5C **92**
Sandford Cl. TS4: Midd 4A **102**
Sandgate Ind. Est.
TS25: H'pool 5D **15**
(not continuous)
Sandhall Cl. TS23: Bill. 2E **39**
Sandholme TS12: Ling 4E **113**
Sandling Ct. TS7: Mart 2E **133**
Sandmartin La. TS20: Nort 3B **54**
Sandmoor Cl. TS6: Est. 2E **105**
Sandmoor Rd. TS11: N Mar. . . . 2F **85**
Sandown Pk. TS10: Redc 1D **65**
Sandown Rd. TS23: Bill. 4D **39**
Sandown Way TS17: Thorn T. . . 2F **99**
Sandpiper Cl. TS10: Redc 3E **65**
Sandpiper Ho. TS24: H'pool . . . 3D **15**
Sandpiper Wlk. TS2: Port C. . . . 4E **57**
Sandport Wlk.
TS18: Stock T 4C 74
(off Alnport Rd.)
Sandringham Ho.
TS3: Midd 3D **103**
Sandringham Rd.
TS3: Midd 3D **103**
TS6: Gran. 4E **81**
TS10: Redc 4C **48**
TS12: Ling 5F **113**
TS17: Thorn T 3D **99**
TS18: Stock T. 1F **97**
TS26: H'pool 3A **14**
Sandsend Rd.
TS6: Est 5F **81**
TS10: Redc 1A **64**
SANDS HALL RDBT. 4B **22**
Sandwell Av. TS3: Midd. 3F **103**
Sandwell Chare
TS24: H'pool. 1F **15**
Sandwich Gro. TS27: H'pool 2D **7**
Sandwood Pk. TS14: Guis 4A **138**
Sandy Bank TS21: Sed. 4A **22**
Sandy Flatts Ct. TS5: Midd . . . 2E **131**
Sandy Flatts La. TS5: Midd . . . 2E **131**

Sandy La.
TS11: Guis, N Mar 5D **85**
(not continuous)
TS22: Bill 5B **38**
(not continuous)
Sandy La. W. TS22: Bill 3F **37**
Sandy Leas La. TS21: Elt 5A **70**
Saphwood Wlk. TS5: Midd . . . 3B **130**
Sapley Cl. TS17: Thorn T 2C **128**
Sarah St. TS25: H'pool 1C **20**
Sargasso Wlk.
TS17: Thorn T 4D **99**
Sark Wlk. *TS14: Guis 3D 139*
(off Hutton La.)
Saro Pl. TS25: Seat C 1E **33**
Satley Rd. TS23: Bill 2F **39**
Saunton Av. TS10: Redc 3E **65**
Saunton Rd. TS23: Bill 1F **55**
Saville Cl. TS22: Wyn 3A **26**
Sawley Gro. TS18: Stock T 2A **96**
Sawtry Rd. TS3: Midd 3F **103**
Saxby Rd. TS20: Nort 2B **74**
Saxonfield TS8: Coul N 4B **132**
Saxon Way TS3: N Orm 3C **78**
Scafell Grn. TS17: Thorn T 4D **99**
Scalby Gro. TS10: Redc 2E **65**
TS19: Stock T 5A **72**
Scalby Rd. TS3: Midd 1B **102**
Scaling Ct. TS14: Guis 1D **139**
Scampton Cl.
TS17: Thorn T 2B **128**
Scanbeck Dr. TS11: Marsk S . . . 3D **67**
Scarborough St. TS6: S Ban . . . 3A **80**
TS13: Loft 5A **92**
TS17: Thorn T 3C **98**
TS24: H'pool 3C **14**
Scarteen Cl. TS14: Guis 3D **139**
Scarth Cl. TS12: Ling 4E **113**
Scarth Wlk. TS18: Stock T 5F **73**
Scarthwood Cl.
TS17: Ing B 5C **128**
Scawfell Gro. TS25: H'pool 1B **20**
Scholars Ct. TS15: Yarm 3B **148**
Scholars Ga. TS14: Guis 4D **139**
Scholars Ri. TS4: Midd 4B **102**
School Av. TS5: Midd 2B **100**
School Cl. TS11: Marsk S 4D **67**
TS18: Stock T 2A **98**
TS21: Thorpe T 2D **51**
School Cft. TS1: Midd 2F **77**
School La. TS9: Gt A 2D **167**
TS13: Live 1A **116**
School Wlk. TS18: Stock T 2A **98**
Schooner Ct. TS24: H'pool 3D **15**
Scotforth Cl. TS7: Mart 3F **133**
Scotney Ct. TS5: Midd 2B **100**
Scotney Rd. TS23: Bill 5D **39**
Scotswood Ho.
TS17: Thorn T 2B **98**
Scott Dr. TS20: Nort 5F **53**
Scott Gro. TS25: H'pool 2D **19**
Scotton Cl. TS18: Stock T 3A **96**
Scotton Ct. TS3: Midd 2A **104**
Scott Rd. TS6: Norm 2B **104**
Scott's Rd. TS2: Midd 2A **78**
TS3: Midd 2A **78**
Scott St. TS10: Redc 4D **49**
Scrafton Pl. TS11: Marsk S 4D **67**
Scruton Cl. TS18: Stock T 2B **96**
Scugdale Cl. TS15: Yarm 1B **160**
Sculptor Cres. TS18: Stock T . . . 4E **97**
Scurfield Rd. TS19: Stock T . . . 1A **72**
Seaford Cl. TS10: Redc 3E **65**
Seaham Cl. TS10: Redc 3F **65**
TS20: Nort 4E **53**
Seaham St. TS20: Nort 4B **74**
Seaham Vw. TS20: Nort 4E **53**
Sealand Cl. TS17: Thorn T . . . 3D **129**
Seal Sands Link Rd.
TS23: Bill, Cowp B 2D **39**
Seal Sands Rd. TS2: Seal S . . . 1B **58**
Seamer Cl. TS5: Midd 4E **101**
Seamer Gro. TS18: Stock T 2D **97**
Seamer Rd.
TS8: Thornt, Newb 1B **152**
TS15: Hilt, Seam 1F **163**
Seathwaite TS5: Midd 3B **130**
SEATON CAREW **4E 21**
Seaton Carew Golf Course **5F 21**
Seaton Carew Rd.
TS2: Port C, Seal S 5A **58**
Seaton Cl. TS10: Redc 2F **65**
TS13: Stait 2C **120**
TS19: Stock T 5A **72**
Seaton Cres. TS13: Stait 2C **120**
Seaton Crew Station (Rail) . . . **4D 21**
Seaton Gth. TS13: Stait 1C **120**
Seaton La. TS25: H'pool 4B **20**
Seatonport Ct.
TS18: Stock T 4C **74**
Seaton St. TS1: Midd 4F **77**
Seaton Ter. TS12: Ling 5E **113**
Seaview Pk. Homes
TS24: H'pool 1C **6**
Sea Vw. Ter. TS6: Gran 1D **81**
TS24: H'pool 5E **9**
Second Foulsyke TS13: Loft . . . 5F **93**
Sedgebrook Gdns.
TS3: Midd 3A **104**
SEDGEFIELD **4D 23**
Sedgefield Ind. Est.
TS21: Sed 2D **23**
Sedgefield Racecourse **5A 22**
Sedgefield Rd. TS5: Midd 2C **130**
Sedgefield Way
TS18: Stock T 3E **75**
Sedgemoor Rd. TS6: Est 3E **105**
Sedgemoor Way TS23: Bill 3A **40**
Sedgewick Cl. TS24: H'pool 3A **8**
Sefton Rd. TS3: Midd 1A **104**
Sefton Way TS15: Yarm 5A **148**
Selbourne St. TS1: Midd 4D **77**
Selby Gro. TS25: H'pool 3A **20**
Selby Rd. TS7: Nun 3B **134**
Selkirk Cl. TS4: Midd 4F **101**
(not continuous)
Selset Av. TS3: Midd 4E **103**
Selset Cl. TS26: H'pool 3C **12**
Selwood Cl. TS17: Thorn T . . . 2D **129**
Selworthy Grn. TS17: Ing B . . . 3B **150**
Selwyn Dr. TS19: Stock T 2A **72**
Semmerwater Gro.
TS10: Redc 5C **48**
Sennybridge Gro.
TS17: Ing B 2F **149**
Serenity Hollow TS12: Boo . . . 2B **112**
Serenity Touring Cvn. & Camping Pk.
TS13: Hind 5E **121**
Serpentine Gdns.
TS26: H'pool 2E **13**
Serpentine Rd. TS26: H'pool . . . 3E **13**
(not continuous)
Severn Dr. TS14: Guis 3C **138**
Severn Gro. TS12: Skel 3D **89**
TS22: Bill 4A **38**
Severn Rd. TS10: Redc 4A **48**
Severn Way TS10: Redc 4A **48**
Severs Dr. TS8: Stain 5C **130**
Severs St. TS6: S Ban 2F **79**
Seymour Av. TS16: Eag 2A **148**
Seymour Cl. TS11: Marsk S 5F **67**
Seymour Cres. TS16: Eag 1A **148**
Seymour Dr. TS16: Eag 1A **148**
Seymour Gro. TS16: Eag 2A **148**
Seymour Hill Ter. *TS13: Loft . . . 5C 92*
(off North Rd.)
Shackleton Cl.
TS17: Thorn T 2D **129**
Shadforth Dr. TS23: Bill 3F **39**
Shadwell Cl. TS6: Norm 4C **104**
Shaftesbury Rd. TS6: Est 5D **81**
Shaftesbury St.
TS18: Stock T 2A **98**
Shakespeare Av. TS6: Gran 3F **81**
TS25: H'pool 1A **20**
Shaldon Cl. TS10: Redc 3E **65**
Shambles, The
TS18: Stock T 1B **98**
Shandon Pk. TS8: Mart 5D **133**
Shannon Ct. TS25: Grea 3E **31**
Shannon Cres.
TS19: Stock T 4A **72**
Shannon Lea DL2: Mid G 1A **144**
Shapwick Pl. TS17: Ing B 4F **127**
Sharp Cres. TS24: H'pool 4A **8**
Sharrock Cl. TS3: N Orm 4B **78**
Shaw Cres. TS6: Gran 4F **81**
Shawcross Av. TS6: Gran 3D **81**
Shaw Gro. TS25: H'pool 2D **19**
Shearwater La. TS20: Nort 3A **54**
Sheepdene TS22: Wyn 4A **26**
Sheepfoote Hill
TS15: Yarm 4B **148**
Sheerness Gro.
TS24: H'pool 4C **14**
Sheerness Way TS10: Redc 3E **65**
Shelley Cl. TS23: Bill 2D **39**
Shelley Cres. TS6: Est 5C **80**
Shelley Gro. TS25: H'pool 1F **19**
Shelley Rd. TS4: Midd 3F **101**
Shelton Ct. TS3: Midd 2F **103**
Shepherd Cl. TS17: Thorn T . . . 5B **98**
Shepherd Ct. TS12: Boo 3C **112**
Shepherdson Ct. TS6: S Ban . . . 2A **80**
Shepherdson Way
TS3: Midd 2B **78**
Shepton Cl. TS17: Thorn T 5E **99**
SHERATON **4A 4**
Sheraton Bank TS27: Sher 3A **4**
Sheraton Hall Est. TS27: Sher . . . 3A **4**
Sheraton Pk. TS19: Stock T 2E **73**
Sheraton St. TS18: Stock T 1F **97**
Sherborne Wlk. TS5: Midd . . . 2B **100**
Sherburn Av. TS23: Bill 3E **39**
Sherburn Cl. TS5: Midd 1C **130**
Sheridan Gro. TS25: H'pool 1F **19**
Sheriff St. TS26: H'pool 3A **14**
Sheringham Ct. TS10: Redc 3F **65**
Sherwood Cl. TS7: Orm 1B **134**
Sherwood Dr.
TS11: Marsk S 4B **66**
Sherwood Rd.
TS17: Thorn T 2C **128**
Shetland Av. TS17: Thorn T . . . 4D **99**
Shetland Cl. TS5: Midd 3D **131**
Shevington Gro. TS7: Mart . . . 3E **133**
Shibden Rd. TS3: Midd 5C **78**
Shields Ter. TS24: H'pool 4C **8**
Shildon Cl. TS23: Bill 4D **39**
Shincliffe Rd. TS23: Bill 3F **39**
Shinwell Cres. TS6: S Ban 3A **80**
Shipham Cl. TS10: Redc 3E **65**
Ship Inn Yd. TS18: Stock T 1A **98**
Shoreham Cl. TS10: Redc 3E **65**
Shoreswood Wlk.
TS5: Midd 2D **131**
Short Cl. TS18: Stock T 4F **97**
Shotley Cl. TS23: Bill 4D **39**
Shotton Ct. TS23: Bill 5F **39**
Showcase Cinema
Stockton-on-Tees **1A 100**
Shrewsbury Rd. TS3: Midd . . . 2F **103**
Shrewsbury St.
TS25: H'pool 1A **20**
Shropshire Wlk.
TS25: H'pool 5B **14**
Sidcup Av. TS3: Midd 4E **103**
Siddington Wlk. TS3: Midd . . . 1E **103**
Sideling Tails TS15: Yarm 5B **148**
Sidings Cl. TS24: H'pool 3D **15**
Sidlaw Av. TS12: Skel 3C **88**
Sidlaw Rd. TS23: Bill 5C **38**
Sidmouth Cl. TS8: Midd 1B **132**
Silton Cl. TS10: Redc 1F **63**
Silton Gro. TS18: Stock T 2D **97**
Silverbirch Rd. TS26: H'pool 4D **7**
Silver Chambers
TS18: Stock T 5B 74
(off Silver St.)

Silver Ct. *TS18: Stock T* *5B* ***74***
(off Silver St.)
Silverdale TS7: Nun. 4F **133**
Silver St. TS9: Stokes 1B **168**
TS15: Yarm 3B **148**
TS18: Stock T 5B **74**
TS24: H'pool 4B **14**
Silverton Rd. TS14: Guis 4F **139**
Silverwood Cl. TS27: H'pool 2C **6**
Silverwood Ct.
TS17: Thorn T 3C **98**
Simcox Ct. TS2: Midd 2C **76**
Simonside Gro.
TS17: Ing B 2B **150**
Simonside Wlk. TS7: Orm. . . . 4A **104**
Simpson Cl. TS6: S Ban 3B **80**
Simpson Grn. TS6: S Ban 3A **80**
Simpson St. TS5: Midd 1E **101**
Sinclair Rd. TS25: H'pool 3D **19**
Sinderby Cl. TS23: Bill. 4E **39**
Sinderby La. TS7: Mart 1F **155**
Sinnington Cl. TS14: Guis 3E **139**
Sinnington Rd.
TS17: Thorn T 2C **128**
Sir Douglas Pk.
TS17: Thorn T 1C **128**
Sir Hugh Bell Ct.
TS10: Redc. 3E **47**
Sir William Turner's Ct.
TS10: K'ham 5A **64**
Siskin Cl. TS20: Nort. 3A **54**
TS26: H'pool 1D **13**
Sitwell Wlk. TS25: H'pool 2D **19**
Skeeby Cl. TS18: Stock T 3B **96**
SKELTON. **4B 88**
Skelton / Brotton By-Pass
TS12: Brot, Skel. 3A **88**
SKELTON CASTLE RDBT. **3A 88**
Skelton Ct. TS14: Guis. 5E **109**
Skelton Dr. TS10: Redc 1E **65**
TS11: Marsk S 4E **67**
Skelton Ellers TS12: Skel 2C **110**
TS14: Guis, Skel. 4A **110**
SKELTON GREEN **5B 88**
SKELTON HIGH GREEN **5A 88**
Skelton Ind. Est.
TS12: Skel 3E **89**
Skelton Rd. TS12: Brot 4F **89**
Skelton St. TS24: H'pool 3F **7**
Skelwith Rd. TS3: Midd. 2C **102**
Skerne Rd. TS20: Nort. 1A **74**
TS24: H'pool 4A **8**
(not continuous)
Skerries Cres. TS10: Redc 3B **64**
Skiddaw Cl. TS16: Eag 4B **126**
Skiddaw Ct. TS7: Nun 3F **133**
Skinner St. TS18: Stock T 1A **98**
SKINNINGROVE **2A 92**
Skinningrove Bank Rd.
TS13: Loft 1A **92**
Skiplam Cl. TS8: Hem 4C **130**
Skipper Gro. TS21: Nort 3D **53**
Skipper's La.
TS6: Norm, S Ban. 3F **79**
Skipper's La. Ind. Est.
TS6: S Ban 3F **79**
(not continuous)
Skipton Rd. TS23: Bill 5D **39**
Skirbeck Av. TS3: Midd 3A **104**
Skirlaw Rd. TS15: Yarm 5B **148**
Skomer Ct. TS10: Redc 3E **65**
Skottowe Cres. TS9: Gt A 1C **166**
Skottowe Dr. TS9: Gt A 1C **166**
Skripka Dr. TS22: Bill. 5A **38**
Skye Wlk. TS14: Guis 4C **138**
Skylark Cl. TS26: H'pool 5E **7**
Slake Ter. TS24: H'pool. 2D **15**
Slaley Cl. TS11: N Mar 2F **85**
SLAPEWATH **2D 141**
Slater Rd. TS6: Gran 4F **81**
Slater Wlk. TS6: Gran 4F **81**
Slayde, The TS15: Yarm 5C **148**
Sledmere Cl. TS23: Bill 2F **39**
Sledmere Dr. TS5: Midd 4E **101**
Sledwick Rd. TS23: Bill 5F **39**
Sleightholme Cl.
TS18: Stock T. 5E **75**
Sleights Ct. TS14: Guis 1E **139**
Sleights Cres. TS6: Est 5F **81**
Slingsby Cl. TS5: Midd 5E **101**
Slip Inn Bank TS8: Midd 2A **132**
Slippery Hill *TS13: Stait* *1C* ***120***
(off High St.)
Slip Rd. TS6: Est 3D **81**
Slipway, The TS18: Stock T. . . . 5C **74**
Smirks Yd. TS20: Nort. 5B **54**
Smith's Dock Pk. Rd.
TS6: Norm 2C **104**
Smith's Dock Rd. TS6: Midd . . . 4F **59**
Smith St. TS1: Midd. 3E **77**
TS18: Stock T 5A **74**
Smurthwaites Yd.
TS20: Nort 5B **54**
Sneck Ga. La. TS8: Newb 4B **154**
Snipe La. TS13: Eas. 5F **117**
Snipe St. TS10: Redc. 3E **47**
Snowberry Cl. TS20: Nort 1F **73**
Snowden St. TS6: Est 5D **81**
Snowdon Cres. TS10: Redc. . . . 1B **64**
Snowdon Gro. TS17: Ing B. . . . 1F **149**
TS24: H'pool 2D **7**
Snowdon Rd. TS2: Midd 2E **77**
Snowdrop Av. TS22: Wyn 3C **26**
Snowdrop Cl. TS19: Stock T . . . 3B **72**
Snowdrop Pl. TS18: Stock T . . . 1A **98**
Snowdrop Rd. TS26: H'pool 4D **7**
SOBER HALL **3B 150**
Sober Hall Av. TS17: Ing B . . . 2A **150**
Somerby Ter. TS3: Midd 1D **103**
Somersby Cl. TS24: H'pool 4C **8**
Somerset Cres. TS12: Skel 4A **88**
Somerset Rd. TS6: Gran 4E **81**
TS14: Guis. 3D **139**
TS20: Nort 1A **74**
Somerset St. TS1: Midd 4A **78**
Somerset Ter. TS23: Bill 2F **55**
Somerville Av. TS3: Midd 3F **103**
Soppett St. TS10: Redc 4C **48**
Sopwith Cl. TS18: Stock T 4F **97**
Sorbonne Cl.
TS17: Thorn T 1B **98**
Sorrel Cl. TS19: Stock T 3B **72**
Sorrel Ct. TS7: Mart. 1C **132**
Sorrell Gro. TS14: Guis 3B **138**
Sotherby Rd. TS3: N Orm 4D **79**
TS6: S Ban. 4D **79**
Southampton St.
TS10: Redc 4D **49**
South Av. TS10: Redc 1E **63**
TS21: Stil 2A **50**
TS23: Bill 4D **55**
SOUTH BANK. **2A 80**
Sth. Bank Bus. Cen.
TS6: S Ban. 2A **80**
Sth. Bank By-Pass
TS3: N Orm 3D **79**
TS6: S Ban. 3D **79**
Sth. Bank Rd. TS3: N Orm. 3C **78**
South Bank Station (Rail) **1A 80**
Southbrooke Av.
TS25: H'pool. 2F **19**
Southburn Ter. TS25: H'pool . . . 5B **14**
South Ct. TS6: S Ban 2A **80**
South Cres. TS24: H'pool. 1F **15**
Southdean Cl. TS8: Hem 4E **131**
Southdean Dr. TS8: Hem 3E **131**
South Dr. TS7: Mart. 2D **133**
TS7: Orm 4A **104**
TS26: H'pool 3E **13**
South End TS25: Seat C 5F **21**
Southend TS4: Midd 2A **102**
Southerndale Rd.
TS10: Redc 1B **64**
Southfield Cres. TS20: Nort . . . 2B **74**
Southfield La. TS1: Midd. 4E **77**
(not continuous)
Southfield Rd. TS1: Midd 4E **77**
TS11: Marsk S 4D **67**
TS20: Nort 2B **74**
Southfield Ter. TS9: Gt A. 1D **167**
Sth. Gare Rd. TS10: Redc 1A **46**
Southgate TS6: Est 1A **106**
TS24: H'pool 1E **15**
South Grn. TS18: Stock T 2A **98**
South Lackenby TS6: Old L 5A **82**
Southland Av. TS26: H'pool 4F **13**
Southlands Dr. TS7: Nun. 2B **134**
Southlands Leisure
& Community Cen. **3E 103**
SOUTH LOFTUS **5C 92**
Southmead Av. TS3: Midd 4E **103**
South Mt. Pleasant St.
TS20: Nort 2B **74**
South Pde. TS25: H'pool 5B **14**
South Pk. Av. TS6: Norm. 3D **105**
Southport Cl. TS18: Stock T . . . 4D **75**
South Rd. TS20: Nort. 1B **74**
TS26: H'pool 4A **14**
(not continuous)
Southside Retail Pk.
TS18: Stock T. 4E **75**
South St. TS6: Est 2F **105**
TS14: Guis. 2D **139**
TS21: Stil 2A **50**
Sth. Tees Bus. Cen.
TS6: S Ban. 1A **80**
Sth. Tees Imperial Food Pk.
TS6: S Ban 1F **79**
South Tees Motorsports Pk. **2E 79**
South Tees MX Pk. **2E 79**
South Ter. TS6: S Ban 2A **80**
TS10: Redc. 4E **49**
TS12: Skel 4A **88**
(not continuous)
Sth. Town La. TS13: Loft. 1C **116**
South Vw. TS13: Loft. 5C **92**
TS16: Eag. 2B **148**
TS21: Sed 4D **23**
TS23: Bill 4D **55**
TS27: Hart 4F **5**
Southview Farm Camp
& Caravan Site
TS9: Gt Bus 4A **168**
South Vw. Ter. TS3: N Orm 4C **78**
Southwark Cl. TS6: Norm 4C **104**
South Way TS20: Nort. 1C **74**
Southway TS6: Midd 2E **83**
Southwell Ct. TS1: Midd 3D **77**
Southwell Rd. TS5: Midd. 2F **101**
Southwell Sq. TS5: Midd 2F **101**
Southwick Av. TS4: Midd. 1B **132**
Southwold Cl. TS10: Redc. 2A **64**
Southwood TS8: Coul N. 2B **154**
Sovereign Intl. Bus. Pk.
TS25: H'pool 4C **20**
Sowerby Cres. TS9: Stokes . . . 1A **168**
Sowerby Way TS16: Eag 4B **126**
Spain Hill TS11: Marsk S 4D **67**
Spalding Rd. TS25: H'pool 1D **31**
Spalding Wlk. TS20: Nort 1C **74**
Spark (Childrens Arts Cen.) . . . **4D 73**
Spark Sq. TS19: Stock T 3D **73**
Spaunton Cl. TS8: Hem 4C **130**
Spearman Wlk.
TS27: H'pool 3D **7**
Speeding Dr. TS24: H'pool 2D **7**
Speedwell Cl. TS26: H'pool. 4E **7**
Speeton Av. TS5: Midd 5E **101**
Speeton Cl. TS23: Bill 2E **39**
Spell Cl. TS15: Yarm 4F **149**
Spenborough Rd.
TS19: Stock T 3D **73**
Spence Ct. TS9: Gt A. 1D **167**
Spencerbeck Ho. TS7: Orm . . . 4B **104**
Spencer Cl. TS11: Marsk S 3C **66**
Spencerfield Cres.
TS3: Midd. 5F **79**
Spencer Hall TS18: Stock T. . . . 1B **98**
Spencer Rd. TS6: Est 5D **81**

Spennithorne Rd.
TS18: Stock T 1D **97**
Spenser Gro. TS25: H'pool 1F **19**
Spilsby Cl. TS25: H'pool 1E **31**
Spinnaker Ho. *TS24: H'pool . . . 3D 15*
(off Quayside)
Spinney, The DL2: Mid G. 1B **144**
TS18: Stock T 3D **97**
TS26: H'pool 4C **12**
Spital, The TS15: Yarm 4B **148**
Spitalfields TS15: Yarm. 5B **148**
SPITAL FLATT 5D **149**
Spital Ga. TS15: Yarm. 5C **148**
Spitfire Cl. TS11: Marsk S. 4B **66**
SPITFIRE RDBT. 2C **128**
Splash 5B **74**
Springbank Rd. TS7: Orm 5B **104**
Spring Bank Wood
TS22: Wyn 4B **26**
Spring Cl. TS17: Thorn T. 3C **98**
Springfield TS9: Stokes. 1C **168**
Springfield Av. TS12: Brot. 3A **90**
TS18: Stock T. 3E **97**
Springfield Cl. TS16: Eag 5B **126**
Springfield Gdn.
TS9: Stokes 1C **168**
Springfield Gro.
TS15: K'ton 3E **161**
Springfield Ho.
TS9: Stokes 1C **168**
Springfield Rd. TS5: Midd. . . . 1B **100**
Spring Gdn. Cl. TS7: Orm 1B **134**
Spring Gdn. La. TS7: Orm. . . . 1A **134**
Spring Gdn. Rd.
TS25: H'pool 1B **20**
Springhead Ter. TS13: Loft 5C **92**
Springhill TS7: Orm. 4B **104**
Springhill Gro. TS17: Ing B . . . 2B **150**
Springholme TS7: Orm 4B **104**
TS18: Stock T. 2F **97**
Springholme Yd.
TS18: Stock T. 2F **97**
Spring La. TS21: Sed. 5C **22**
Springlea TS7: Orm. 4B **104**
Spring Lodge Gdns.
TS14: Guis 2B **138**
Springmead TS7: Orm. 4B **104**
Spring Ri. TS6: Norm 4C **104**
Springston Rd. TS26: H'pool. . . 2D **13**
Spring St. TS2: Midd 2F **77**
TS18: Stock T. 2F **97**
Springvale Ter. TS5: Midd. . . . 2B **100**
Springwalk TS7: Orm 4B **104**
Spring Way TS18: Stock T. 3E **97**
Springwell Cl. TS23: Bill 1F **39**
Springwell Flats
TS26: H'pool 1E **13**
Springwood Rd. TS14: Guis. . . 2E **139**
Spruce Rd. TS19: Stock T 1E **73**
Spurn Wlk. TS24: H'pool 4C **14**
Spurrey Cl. TS17: Ing B. 4B **128**
Squadron Ct.
TS17: Thorn T 1C **128**
Square, The TS6: Est. 1F **105**
TS13: Skin 2A **92**
TS18: Stock T 5B **74**
(not continuous)
TS21: Sed 4D **23**
Stable, The TS16: Eag. 3C **126**
Stable Ct. TS13: Loft. 5B **92**
Stable M. TS10: Redc 4D **49**
Stables, The TS17: Ing B. 1E **149**
TS22: Wyn 5B **26**
Stadium Ct. TS6: S Ban. 4A **80**
Stafford Cl. TS17: Thorn T. 3B **98**
Stafford Rd. TS6: Gran. 4E **81**
TS14: Guis 3D **139**
Stafford St. TS18: Stock T. 2A **98**
Staincliffe Rd. TS25: Seat C . . . 3E **21**
Staindale TS14: Guis. 3A **138**
Staindale Cl. TS15: Yarm 4E **149**
Staindale Gdns.
TS19: Stock T. 4E **73**
Staindale Pl. TS25: H'pool. 2F **19**
Staindale Rd. TS17: Thorn T. . . 5D **99**
Staindrop Ct. TS23: Bill 3C **38**
Staindrop Dr. TS5: Midd 1C **130**
Staindrop St. TS24: H'pool 4C **14**
Stainforth Ct. TS3: Midd 4D **103**
Stainforth Gdns.
TS17: Ing B 5C **128**
Stainmore Cl. TS19: Stock T . . . 5F **73**
STAINSBY 2E **129**
Stainsby Ga. TS17: Thorn T. . . . 4E **99**
Stainsby Grange Ho.
TS17: Thorn T 1E 129
(off Allensway)
Stainsby Rd. TS5: Midd. 3A **100**
Stainsby St. TS17: Thorn T 3C **98**
STAINTON 5C **130**
Staintondale Av. TS10: Redc . . . 1F **63**
Stainton Gro. TS20: Nort. 2A **74**
STAINTON INTERCHANGE . . . 4C **130**
Stainton Rd. TS22: Bill 5B **38**
Stainton St. TS3: N Orm 4C **78**
Stainton Way TS7: Mart. 4E **133**
TS8: Coul N, Hem, Mart, Stain
. . . . 4C **130**
STAITHES 1C **120**
Staithes and Runswick Lifeboat
Station. 1C **120**
Staithes Ct. TS24: H'pool 4D **15**
Staithes Gateway Cen.
TS13: Stait 1C **120**
Staithes La. TS13: Stait. 2C **120**
Staithes Rd. TS10: Redc 5F **47**
Stakesby Cl. TS14: Guis 5D **109**
Stamford Ct. TS23: Bill. 3F **39**
Stamford St. TS1: Midd. 4A **78**
Stamford Wlk. TS25: H'pool . . . 5E **19**
Stamp St. TS18: Stock T 5A **74**
Stanford Cl. TS17: Thorn T 2C **98**
Stanghow La. Flats
TS12: Ling, Skel. 4C **88**
Stanghow Rd.
TS12: Ling, Skel. 4C **88**
Stanhope Av. TS26: H'pool 4A **14**
Stanhope Gdns. TS4: Midd . . . 2B **102**
Stanhope Gro. TS5: Midd 3D **101**
Stanhope Rd. TS18: Stock T . . . 4E **73**
TS23: Bill 5F **39**
Stanhope St. TS12: Salt. 4C **68**
Stanley Cl. TS17: Thorn T. 3C **98**
Stanley Gro. TS9: Gt A 3D **165**
TS10: Redc 4D **49**
Stanley Rd. TS25: H'pool 2B **20**
Stanley St. TS20: Nort. 5A **54**
Stanley Wlk. TS18: Stock T. . . . 5A **74**
Stanmore Av. TS4: Midd 4A **102**
Stanmore Gro. TS25: Seat C . . . 4D **21**
Stannage Gro.
TS17: Thorn T 5C **98**
Stanstead M.
TS17: Thorn T 1E **129**
Stanstead Way
TS17: Thorn T 1E **129**
Stansted Gro. DL2: Mid G 1A **144**
Stanway Cl. TS17: Ing B 4F **127**
Stapleford Rd. TS3: Midd 3A **104**
Stapleton St. TS20: Nort 3A **54**
Stapylton Ct. TS6: Gran. 2D **81**
Stapylton St. TS6: Gran. 2D **81**
Starbeck Cl. TS11: N Mar 2F **85**
Starbeck Wlk.
TS17: Thorn T 3E **129**
Starbeck Way TS7: Orm 3B **104**
Startforth Rd. TS2: Midd 1C **76**
Station App. TS24: H'pool 3C **14**
Station Cl. TS11: Marsk S 5C **66**
Station Cres. TS23: Bill 2D **55**
Station La. TS12: Skel. 3C **88**
TS25: Seat C 4D **21**
Station Pde. TS23: Bill. 2C **54**
Station Rd. TS6: Est. 2E **105**
TS6: Midd. 5E **61**
TS9: Gt A 2D **167**
Station Rd. TS9: Stokes. 1C **168**
TS10: Redc 3C **48**
TS13: Hind 5E **121**
TS13: Loft 5B **92**
TS16: Eag. 3C **126**
TS20: Nort 3A **54**
TS21: Sed 5A **22**
(not continuous)
TS23: Bill 2C **54**
TS25: Grea 4E **31**
Station Rd. Ind. Est.
TS9: Stokes 4D **169**
Station Sq. TS12: Salt 4C **68**
Station St. TS1: Midd. 2E **77**
TS12: Salt 4C **68**
TS17: Thorn T 2C **98**
TS20: Nort 4B **74**
Station Vs. TS11: Marsk S. 5C **66**
Staveley Ct. TS3: Midd 1C **102**
Staveley Gro. TS19: Stock T . . . 2E **73**
Staveley Wlk. TS7: Orm 4A **104**
Stavordale Rd.
TS19: Stock T. 4F **73**
Steavenson St. *TS13: Carl H . . . 3F 91*
(off Dixon St.)
Steele Cres. TS6: S Ban 2B **80**
Steer Ct. TS23: Bill 3D **39**
Stephenson Ct. TS6: S Ban 4A **80**
Stephenson Ho.
TS15: Yarm 3B 148
(off The Old Market)
Stephenson Ind. Est.
TS25: H'pool 2D **33**
Stephenson St. TS1: Midd 4F **77**
TS17: Thorn T 2C **98**
TS24: H'pool 5C **8**
Stephenson Way
TS18: Stock T 1B **98**
Stephens Rd. TS6: S Ban 2B **80**
Stephen St. TS26: H'pool. 2F **13**
Sterne Cotts. TS12: Skel 4B **88**
Stevenage Cl. TS17: Thorn T. . . 4E **99**
Stevenson Cl. TS15: Yarm 4E **149**
Stewart Ct. TS20: Nort. 3B **74**
Stewart Pk. Av. TS4: Midd. . . . 5C **102**
Stewart Rd. TS20: Nort 3B **74**
Stileston Cl. TS26: H'pool 2D **13**
STILLINGTON 2A **50**
Stillington Ind. Est.
TS21: Stil 1A **50**
Stirling Rd. TS10: Redc. 5E **49**
Stirling St. TS25: H'pool 1B **20**
Stirling Way TS17: Thorn T. . . 3D **129**
Stockdale Av. TS10: Redc 1F **63**
Stockton Almhouse, The
TS18: Stock T 1A **98**
Stockton Bus. Cen.
TS18: Stock T 1A **98**
STOCKTON GRANGE. 4D **73**
STOCKTON-ON-TEES. 1B **98**
Stockton Riverside College
Sports Cen. 4F **39**
Stockton Riverside College
Sports Cen. 1C 98
(off Harvard Av.)
Stockton Rd. DL2: Sadb. 1C **122**
TS5: Midd. 1F **99**
TS21: Long N 1F **123**
TS21: Sed, Thorpe L 4D **23**
(not continuous)
TS21: Sed, Thorpe L 4A **24**
TS22: Newt B. 1D **39**
TS25: H'pool 5B **14**
Stockton Station (Rail) 4A **74**
Stockton St. TS2: Midd 2E **77**
TS23: Bill. 3D **55**
TS24: H'pool 3B **14**
Stockton-Thornaby By-Pass
TS17: Thorn T 3A **96**
TS18: Stock T, Thorn T . . . 3A **96**
Stockwell Av.
TS17: Thorn T 4D **129**
Stockwith Cl. TS3: Midd 3A **104**

STOKESLEY 1B **168**
Stokesley By-Pass
TS9: Stokes 5D **165**
Stokesley Cres. TS23: Bill. 3D **55**
Stokesley Golf Course 2E **169**
Stokesley Ind. Pk.
TS9: Stokes 3D **169**
Stokesley Leisure Cen.
& Swimming Pool 2D **169**
Stokesley Rd. TS7: Mart 1C **132**
TS7: Nun 5B **134**
TS8: Hem, Newb 5A **132**
TS8: Newb 3D **155**
TS9: Gt A 3C **166**
TS14: Guis 3F **137**
TS25: Seat C 4E **21**
Stoneacre Av. TS17: Ing B. . . . 1B **150**
Stonebridge Cres.
TS17: Ing B 3A **128**
Stonechat Cl. TS17: Ing B 5A **128**
TS26: H'pool. 5F **7**
Stone Ct. TS21: Stil 1A **50**
Stonecrop Cl. TS18: Stock T . . . 2D **97**
Stonedale TS12: Skel 2B **88**
Stonedale Wlk. TS5: Midd. . . . 2B **130**
Stonegate TS6: Est 1A **106**
Stone Hall Cl. TS9: Stokes . . . 1B **168**
Stonehouse Cl.
TS15: Yarm 5D **149**
Stonehouse Ind. Est.
TS12: Ling 4F **113**
Stonehouse St. TS5: Midd. . . . 1E **101**
Stoneleigh Av. TS5: Midd 4B **100**
Stone Row TS13: Skin 2A **92**
Stone St. TS4: Midd 3A **78**
Stonethwaite Cl.
TS24: H'pool 5B **8**
Stoneyhurst Av. TS5: Midd . . . 3A **100**
Stonor Wlk. TS3: Midd. 4E **103**
Stornoway Cl. TS19: Stock T . . . 5F **71**
Stotfold St. TS26: H'pool. 4A **14**
Stotfold Wlk. TS5: Midd 2A **130**
Stoupe Gro. TS10: Redc. 2F **65**
Stourport Cl. TS18: Stock T. . . . 4C **74**
Stowe St. TS1: Midd 4E **77**
Stowmarket Cl.
TS25: H'pool. 1F **31**
Strait La. TS8: Stain 4B **130**
Straker St. TS26: H'pool 3A **14**
Strand, The TS10: Redc. 2F **65**
STRANGHOW 5E **113**
STRANTON 5C **14**
Stranton TS24: H'pool 5B **14**
(not continuous)
Stranton St. TS17: Thorn T 3C **98**
Stratford Cres. TS5: Midd 1B **100**
Stratford Rd. TS25: H'pool 1A **20**
Strathaven Dr. TS16: Eag 5C **126**
Strathmore Dr. TS15: K'ton . . . 4D **161**
Stratton Cl. TS12: Brot 2B **90**
Strauss Rd. TS6: S Ban 2B **80**
Strawberry Apartments
TS26: H'pool 4C **6**
Stray, The TS21: Long N 1A **124**
Streatlam Rd. TS23: Bill 4F **39**
Strensall Cl. TS11: N Mar 2A **86**
Stripe, The TS9: Stokes. 1B **168**
Strome Cl. TS17: Ing B 1C **150**
Strona Wlk. TS14: Guis. 3D **139**
Stuart St. TS24: H'pool 2B **14**
Stubbs Cl. TS23: Bill 3D **39**
Studland Dr. TS24: H'pool. 2D **7**
Studland Rd. TS10: Redc. 3F **65**
Studley Rd. TS5: Midd. 2C **100**
TS17: Thorn T 5D **99**
TS19: Stock T. 4F **73**
TS25: H'pool 5B **14**
Stump Cross TS14: Guis 2D **139**
Sturt Dr. TS20: Nort 5F **53**
Sudbury TS8: Mart. 4E **133**
Sudbury Rd. TS20: Nort 5C **54**
Suffolk Cl. TS12: Skel 5B **88**
TS25: H'pool 1B **20**
Suffolk Rd. TS5: Midd 2F **101**
Suffolk St. TS18: Stock T. 1F **97**
Sugar Loaf Cl. TS17: Ing B . . . 1F **149**
Suggitt St. TS26: H'pool. 3F **13**
Sulby Av. TS3: Midd 2D **103**
Summerfield Gro.
TS17: Thorn T 1D **129**
Summerhill Country Pk. 1D **19**
Summerhill Country Pk. Vis. Cen.
. . . . 5D **13**
Summerhill La.
TS25: H'pool 5E **13**
Summerhouse Sq.
TS20: Nort 5A **54**
Summer La. TS22: Wyn 2C **26**
Sundell Ct. TS18: Stock T 1F **97**
Sunderland Rd. TS22: Wolv . . . 2C **38**
Sundew Ct. TS18: Stock T. . . . 1A **128**
Sundial M. TS22: Wolv 2C **38**
Sun Gdns. TS17: Thorn T 3B **98**
Sunley Av. TS4: Midd 2A **102**
Sunningdale Ct. TS6: Est. 1E **105**
Sunningdale Dr. TS16: Eag . . . 5C **126**
Sunningdale Gro.
TS27: H'pool 3D **7**
Sunningdale Ho. TS4: Midd. . . 4F **101**
TS6: Est 2E **105**
Sunningdale Rd. TS4: Midd. . . 4F **101**
TS11: N Mar. 2A **86**
Sunningdale Wlk.
TS16: Eag. 5C **126**
(not continuous)
Sunniside TS24: H'pool 1F **15**
Sunnybank Rd. TS7: Orm 5B **104**
Sunnybrow Av. TS23: Bill 3D **55**
Sunnyfield TS7: Orm 4A **104**
TS9: Gt A 2C **166**
Sunnyfield Gdns.
TS13: Eas. 2A **118**
Sunnyfield Nurseries
*TS9: Gt A 3C **166***
(off Easby La.)
Sunnygate TS6: Est 1A **106**
Sunny Row TS13: Port M. 4E **121**
Sunnyside TS8: Coul N. 4F **131**
(not continuous)
Sunnyside Gro.
TS18: Stock T 3C **96**
Sunstar Gro. TS7: Mart 2C **132**
Sun St. TS17: Thorn T. 3B **98**
TS18: Stock T. 2F **97**
Surbiton Rd. TS18: Stock T 4F **71**
TS19: Stock T. 4F **71**
Surgery La. TS24: H'pool 4A **8**
Surrey Rd. TS20: Nort. 1C **74**
Surrey St. TS1: Midd. 5D **77**
Surrey Ter. TS23: Bill. 2E **55**
Surtees Bus. Cen.
TS18: Stock T 3A **98**
Surtees St. TS18: Stock T 1A **98**
TS24: H'pool 4C **14**
Surtees Way TS18: Stock T. . . . 3A **98**
Sussex St. TS2: Midd. 2E **77**
TS25: H'pool 1B **20**
Sussex Wlk. TS20: Nort. 2C **74**
Sutherland Gro. TS20: Nort. . . . 3A **54**
Sutton Pl. TS23: Bill. 5F **39**
Sutton Way TS4: Midd 4F **101**
Swainby Cl. TS5: Midd 5E **101**
Swainby Rd. TS20: Nort 3B **74**
TS25: Seat C 5E **21**
Swain Ct. DL2: Mid G 1A **144**
Swainson Pl. TS24: H'pool 3B **14**
Swainson St. TS24: H'pool 3B **14**
Swainston Cl. TS5: Midd. 1B **130**
TS22: Wyn 3A **26**
Swale Av. TS17: Thorn T. 5D **99**
Swalebrooke Av.
TS25: H'pool 1E **19**
Swale Cl. TS16: Eag 2B **148**
Swaledale Cl. TS17: Ing B . . . 2B **150**
Swaledale Cres. TS23: Bill 2D **55**
Swale Rd. TS20: Nort 5A **54**
Swallow Cl. TS14: Guis. 2A **138**
TS26: H'pool 5D **7**
Swallowfields TS8: Coul N . . . 1A **154**
Swallow La. TS20: Nort. 4A **54**
Swanage Cl. TS8: Midd. 2B **132**
Swanage Dr. TS10: Redc 3F **65**
Swanage Gro. TS24: H'pool 2D **7**
Swan Av. TS19: Stock T. 1B **72**
Swancer Ct. TS22: Wyn. 4B **26**
Swan Ho. TS17: Thorn T 1C **98**
SWAN'S CORNER RDBT. **2C 134**
SWART HOLE RDBT. **5E 27**
Sweet Pea Cl. TS22: Wyn 2B **26**
Swift Gro. TS25: H'pool 2E **19**
Swilly La. TS12: Skel. 4B **88**
Swinburne Rd. TS16: Eag 3C **126**
TS25: H'pool 2E **19**
Swinburn Rd. TS20: Nort. 3A **74**
Swinburn's Yd. TS15: Yarm. . . 3B **148**
Swindale La.
TS12: Ling, Moor. 3A **142**
Swinton Rd. TS18: Stock T 3B **96**
Swyfte Cl. TS21: Sed. 4D **23**
Sycamore Av. TS12: Salt 5A **68**
TS17: Thorn T 5C **98**
Sycamore Cres. TS6: Norm. . . . 5C **80**
Sycamore Dr. TS12: Brot. 2A **90**
Sycamore Rd. TS5: Midd. 2E **101**
TS7: Orm 5B **104**
TS10: Redc. 4E **49**
TS16: Prest T. 2D **127**
TS19: Stock T. 2E **73**
Sycamores, The
TS25: H'pool. 2F **19**
Sycamore Ter. TS2: Port C 4E **57**
Sycamore Way
TS19: Stock T 1C **72**
Sydenham Rd.
TS18: Stock T. 2E **97**
TS25: H'pool 1B **20**
(not continuous)
Sydney Cl. TS5: Midd 2B **100**
Sydney Rd. TS7: Mart 3D **133**
Sydney St. TS18: Stock T 5A **74**
Sylvan M. TS22: Wyn 4B **26**
Sylvan Wlk. TS3: Midd 4E **103**
Symons Cl. TS18: Stock T. 1A **96**
Synthonia Sports Ground 3F **55**
Syon Ct. TS5: Midd 2B **100**
Syon Gdns. TS20: Nort 4E **53**

T

Tai Hua Ct. TS4: Midd 3A **78**
Tailrigg Cl. TS19: Stock T 4F **73**
Talbenny Gro. TS17: Ing B. . . . 2F **149**
Talbot Ho. *TS24: H'pool. 1F **15***
(off Northgate)
Talbot M. TS6: Est. 4D **81**
Talbot St. TS1: Midd 4A **78**
TS20: Nort 3B **74**
Talgarth Rd. TS20: Nort. 4B **54**
Talisker Gdns. TS10: Redc 3D **65**
Talisman Cl. TS16: Eag 4A **126**
Talland Cl. TS27: H'pool 3C **6**
Talybont Gro. TS17: Ing B 1F **149**
Tamarisk Cl. TS17: Ing B. 4B **128**
Tame Rd. TS3: N Orm 3C **78**
Tameside TS9: Stokes 5B **164**
Tame St. TS23: Bill 3D **57**
Tamworth Rd. TS23: Bill 4E **39**
Tanfield Rd. TS25: H'pool 2A **20**
Tanhill Wlk. TS3: Midd 2D **103**
Tankersley Rd. TS11: N Mar . . . 2A **86**
Tankerville St. TS26: H'pool . . . 3A **14**
Tanner Cl. TS17: Ing B 5B **128**
Tansley Av. TS3: Midd 1E **103**
TANTON 2B **164**
Tanton Gro. TS22: Bill 5A **38**
Tanton Rd.
TS9: Seam, Stokes. 3A **164**
TS9: Stokes 4C **164**

Tanwell Cl. TS19: Stock T 4B **72**
Tanya Gdns. TS5: Midd 2E **131**
TS19: Stock T 5C **72**
Taransay Vw. TS17: Thorn T . . . 4D **99**
Tarell Ct. TS17: Ing B. 2F **149**
Tarnston Rd. TS26: H'pool 2D **13**
Tarring St. TS18: Stock T. 1F **97**
Tarr Steps TS17: Ing B. 3B **150**
Task Ind. Est. TS18: Stock T . . . 4B **74**
Task Rd. TS18: Stock T 4C **74**
Tasman Dr. TS18: Stock T. 2B **96**
Tasmania Sq. TS7: Mart 3E **133**
Tatham Cl. TS7: Nun 4A **134**
Taunton Cl. TS8: Midd 2B **132**
Taunton Gro. TS26: H'pool 1D **13**
Taunton Va. TS14: Guis 4E **139**
Taurus Cl. TS18: Stock T 4F **97**
Tavistock Cl. TS27: H'pool. 3C **6**
Tavistock Rd. TS5: Midd 1D **101**
Tavistock St. TS5: Midd. 1D **101**
Tawney Cl. TS6: Est. 4D **81**
Tawney Rd. TS6: Est 4D **81**
Taybrooke Av. TS25: H'pool 1F **19**
Teak St. TS1: Midd. 4F **77**
Tealby Wlk. TS3: Midd 2A **104**
Teal Ct. TS10: Redc 3E **47**
Teare Cl. TS1: Midd. 4D **77**
Teasel Ct. TS19: Stock T 3C **72**
Tebay Cl. TS7: Orm 4A **104**
Tedder Av. TS17: Thorn T 2D **129**
Tedworth Cl. TS14: Guis 4E **139**
Tees & Hartlepool Yacht Club 3D **15**
Tees Bank Av.
TS16: Prest T. 3D **127**
Tees Barrage International White Water Cen. 5E **75**
Tees Barrage Way
TS17: Thorn T 5E **75**
Tees Bay Bus. Pk.
TS25: H'pool 3D **33**
Tees Bay Retail Pk.
TS25: H'pool 3C **20**
Teesbrooke Av. TS25: H'pool . . . 2F **19**
Tees Ct. TS6: S Ban 4F **79**
TEESDALE 1C **98**
Teesdale Av. TS23: Bill 2D **55**
TS26: H'pool. 4F **13**
Teesdale Ho. TS17: Thorn T . . . 1C **98**
Teesdale Lodge
TS17: Thorn T 1C **98**
Teesdale Ter. TS17: Thorn T . . . 3D **99**
Tees Dock Rd. TS6: Midd 2C **60**
Teesgate TS17: Thorn T. 5E **99**
Teesmouth Field Study Cen. 4E **33**
Teesmouth (Seal Sands) National Nature Reserve 2F **43**
Tees (Newport) Bri. App. Rd.
TS18: Stock T 2A **76**
TEESPORT 2C **60**
Teesport Commerce Pk.
TS6: Midd 5F **59**
Teesport Rd. TS6: Midd 3F **61**
Tees Reach TS17: Thorn T 1C **98**
Tees Rd. TS10: Redc 5B **48**
TS14: Guis 3C **138**
TS25: H'pool, Seat C 2C **42**
Teesside Airport Station (Rail) 1E **145**
Teesside Crematorium
TS5: Midd. 1E **131**
Teesside Golf Course 3E **99**
Teesside Ho. TS1: Midd. 3F **77**
Teesside Ind. Est.
TS17: Thorn T 4E **129**
Teesside Leisure Pk.
TS17: Thorn T 1A **100**
Teesside Pk. Dr.
TS17: Thorn T 2F **99**
TEESSIDE PK. INTERCHANGE 2E **99**
Teesside Shopping Pk.
TS17: Thorn T 2F **99**
Teesside Small Gauge Railway 1E **127**
Tees St. TS6: S Ban. 1A **80**
TS13: Loft 5D **93**
TS23: Bill 3D **57**
TS24: H'pool 3B **14**
Tees Viaduct TS18: Stock T. . . . 3A **76**
Tees View Point 1E **79**
TEESVILLE 5B **80**
Teesway TS18: Stock T 3F **75**
Teignmouth Cl. TS27: H'pool. . . . 3C **6**
Telford Cl. TS24: H'pool 5C **8**
Telford Rd. TS3: N Orm 3E **79**
Temperance Ter.
TS24: H'pool. 5F **9**
Tempest Ct. TS22: Wyn 1E **37**
Tempest Rd. TS24: H'pool. 3E **7**
Temple Ct. TS20: Nort. 4B **74**
Templeton Cl. TS27: H'pool. 3C **6**
Tenby Cl. TS6: Est 5E **81**
Tenby Rd. TS10: Redc 2A **64**
Tenby Wlk. TS26: H'pool 1E **13**
Tenby Way TS16: Eag 1C **148**
Tennant St. TS18: Stock T. 5A **74**
Tennis World Middlesbrough 5C **102**
Tennyson Av. TS6: Gran. 3E **81**
TS25: H'pool. 1F **19**
Tennyson Cl. TS6: Gran 4E **81**
Tennyson Rd. TS23: Bill 2D **39**
Tennyson St. TS1: Midd. 5E **77**
Ternbeck Way
TS17: Thorn T 3E **129**
Tern Gro. TS10: Redc. 2E **65**
Terrace, The TS27: Dalt P 1F **17**
TS27: Elw. 4C **10**
Terry Dicken Ind. Est.
TS9: Stokes 3D **169**
Test Valley Ct. TS22: Wyn 4F **27**
Tetcott Cl. TS14: Guis 4E **139**
Tewkesbury Av. TS7: Mart. . . . 4D **133**
Thackeray Gro. TS5: Midd. . . . 3E **101**
Thackeray Rd. TS25: H'pool . . . 1D **19**
Thames Av. TS14: Guis 3C **138**
TS17: Thorn T 5D **99**
TS24: H'pool 5A **8**
Thames Rd. TS10: Redc 5A **48**
TS12: Skel 3C **88**
TS22: Bill 4A **38**
Thatch La. TS17: Ing B 4C **128**
The . . . .
Names prefixed with 'The' for example 'The Acres' are indexed under the main name such as 'Acres, The'
Theakston Gro.
TS18: Stock T 2A **96**
Theatre Yd. *TS18: Stock T. 5B 74*
(off Calvert's La.)
Thetford Av. TS3: Midd 3F **103**
Thetford Rd. TS25: H'pool 1E **31**
Thimbleby Cl. TS7: Mart 5A **134**
Thinford Gdns. TS5: Midd 2D **131**
Thirlby Cl. TS3: Midd. 2C **102**
Thirlby Way TS14: Guis 5E **109**
Thirlmere Av. TS5: Midd 4C **100**
Thirlmere Ct. TS23: Bill 5E **55**
Thirlmere Cres.
TS6: Norm 2D **105**
Thirlmere Dr. TS12: Skel. 4B **88**
Thirlmere Rd. TS10: Redc. 5B **48**
Thirlmere St. TS26: H'pool 5A **14**
Thirlwall Dr. TS17: Ing B. 2A **150**
Thirsk Gro. TS25: H'pool. 3B **20**
Thirsk Rd. TS9: Stokes 3A **168**
TS15: K'ton, Yarm 5C **148**
Thistle Cl. TS26: H'pool 4D **7**
Thistle Grn. TS18: Stock T 5B **74**
Thistle Ri. TS8: Coul N 3F **131**
Thistle Rd. TS19: Stock T 1E **73**
Thistle St. TS1: Midd. 4F **77**
Thomas St. TS3: N Orm. 4C **78**
TS12: Skel 4D **89**
TS18: Stock T 4A **74**
Thomas Wright Way
TS21: Sed 1C **22**
Thomlinson Rd.
TS25: H'pool 1C **20**
Thompson Gro. TS24: H'pool . . . 5A **8**
Thompsons Cl. TS22: Wolv 2C **38**
Thompson's Rd. TS12: Skel. . . . 5B **88**
Thompson St. TS18: Stock T . . . 4A **74**
TS24: H'pool 5B **14**
Thomson Av. TS5: Midd. 1B **100**
Thomson St. TS14: Guis 2D **139**
Thorgill Cl. TS4: Midd 3F **101**
Thorington Gdns.
TS17: Ing B 1C **150**
THORNABY-ON-TEES. 1D **129**
Thornaby Pavilion Leisure Cen. 1D **129**
Thornaby Pl. TS17: Thorn T . . . 2B **98**
Thornaby Pool 4B **98**
Thornaby Rd. TS17: Thorn T. . . 2C **98**
Thornaby Station (Rail). 2C **98**
THORNABY VILLAGE 1C **128**
Thornberry Ct. TS5: Midd 2C **100**
Thornbrough Cl.
TS18: Stock T 3B **96**
Thornbury Cl. TS10: Redc 4F **65**
TS27: H'pool 2C **6**
Thorn Cl. TS17: Ing B 4B **128**
Thorndike Rd. TS6: Est 5E **81**
Thorndyke Av. TS4: Midd. 3A **102**
Thornfield Cl. TS16: Eag 5A **126**
Thornfield Gro. TS5: Midd. . . . 3C **100**
Thornfield Rd. TS5: Midd 3C **100**
Thornhill Gdns.
TS26: H'pool 2E **13**
Thornhill Pl. TS26: H'pool. 2E **13**
Thornley Av. TS23: Bill. 2E **39**
Thorn Rd. TS19: Stock T 1E **73**
Thorn Side TS17: Ing B 4B **128**
Thornthwaite TS5: Midd 3B **130**
Thornthwaite Cl. TS12: Skel . . . 3B **88**
THORNTON 1B **152**
Thornton Cl. TS8: Thornt. 1B **152**
Thornton Cotts.
TS8: Thornt 1B **152**
Thornton Cres. TS22: Bill. 5B **38**
Thornton Gth. TS15: Yarm. . . . 5C **148**
Thornton Gro. TS20: Nort 2A **74**
Thornton Rd.
TS8: Thornt, Stain 1B **152**
Thornton St. TS3: N Orm. 4C **78**
TS26: H'pool 4A **14**
Thornton Va. TS8: Thornt 1B **152**
THORNTREE. 1F **103**
Thorntree Av. TS3: Midd 4E **79**
(not continuous)
Thorntree Ct. TS17: Thorn T . . . 5D **99**
Thorntree Ho. TS3: Midd. 1E **103**
Thorn Tree La. TS25: Grea. 4F **31**
Thorntree Rd. TS17: Thorn T. . . 4C **98**
Thornville Rd. TS26: H'pool . . . 3A **14**
Thornwood Av. TS17: Ing B. . . 4B **128**
THORPE LARCHES 1B **34**
Thorpe M. TS20: Nort 5B **54**
Thorpe Rd. TS21: Carlt 4D **51**
Thorpe St. TS24: H'pool 5D **9**
THORPE THEWLES 2E **51**
Thorpe Wood (Nature Reserve) 4F **35**
Thorphill Way TS23: Bill 3E **39**
Three Acres TS17: Thorn T 1C **98**
Three Tuns Wynd
TS9: Stokes 1B **168**
Throckley Av. TS5: Midd 1C **130**
Thropton Cl. TS23: Bill. 3C **38**
THROSTON 5E **9**
Throston Cl. TS26: H'pool 5F **7**
THROSTON GRANGE. 5E **7**
Throston Grange La.
TS26: H'pool 1D **13**

Throston St. TS24: H'pool 1F **15**
Thrush Rd. TS10: Redc 4C **48**
Thrushwood Cres.
TS11: Marsk S 5E **67**
Thruxton Way TS20: Nort. 5F **53**
Thurlestone TS8: Mart 4F **133**
Thurlow Grange TS21: Sed 4D **23**
Thurlow Rd. TS21: Sed 4D **23**
Thurnham Gro. TS7: Mart 3E **133**
Thursby Dr. TS7: Orm 4A **104**
Thursby Gro. TS25: H'pool 1D **31**
Thurso Cl. TS19: Stock T. 5F **71**
Thwaites La. TS10: Redc 5D **49**
Thweng Way TS14: Guis 3C **138**
Tibbersley Av. TS23: Bill 4E **55**
Tibthorpe TS7: Nun 3F **133**
Tick Hills La. TS13: Live 5A **116**
Tidkin La. TS14: Guis 3C **138**
Tilbury Rd. TS6: S Ban. 2F **79**
TILERY 3C **74**
Tilery Ct. TS20: Nort 3B **74**
Tilery Rd. TS20: Nort. 3B **74**
Tilery Way TS20: Nort 3B **74**
Tilery Wood TS22: Wyn. 4B **26**
Timberscombe Cl.
TS17: Ing B 3A **150**
Timothy Ct. TS18: Stock T. 2A **98**
Timothy Hackworth Ct.
TS16: Prest T. 3C **126**
Tindale TS14: Guis 3A **138**
Tindale Cl. TS15: Yarm 1B **160**
Tindale Wlk. TS5: Midd. 2C **130**
Tintagel Cl. TS27: H'pool 3C **6**
Tintern Av. TS23: Bill. 5D **39**
Tintern Rd. TS12: Skel 4D **89**
Tipton Cl. TS17: Thorn T 5E **99**
Tirril Way TS7: Mart. 4F **133**
Titan Ho. *TS26: H'pool 4B **14***
(off York Rd.)
Tithe Barn Rd.
TS19: Stock T 1A **72**
Tiverton Gro. TS26: H'pool 1E **13**
TOCKETTS 3F **109**
Tocketts Mill Cvn. Pk.
TS14: Guis. 2B **110**
Tocketts Mill Country Pk. 2B **110**
Tocketts Water Mill. 2B **110**
Toddington Dr. TS20: Nort 5E **53**
TOD POINT 3C **46**
Tod Point Rd. TS10: Redc 3E **47**
Tofts Cl. TS11: Marsk S 4E **67**
Tofts Farm E. Ind. Est.
TS25: H'pool 1D **33**
Tofts Farm W. Ind. Est.
TS25: H'pool 2C **32**
Tofts Rd. E. TS25: H'pool 1D **33**
Tofts Rd. W. TS25: H'pool 3C **32**
Tollerton Cl. TS19: Stock T 4D **73**
TOLLESBY 2C **132**
Tollesby Bri. TS8: Coul N 3B **132**
Tollesby La. TS7: Mart 1B **132**
(Harvester Ct.)
TS7: Mart. 3C **132**
(Okehampton Dr.)
Tollesby Rd. TS5: Midd 3E **101**
Tom Browns Yd.
TS15: Yarm 2B **148**
Tomlinson Way TS3: Midd 5F **79**
Tommy McGuigan Gro.
TS24: H'pool 2A **14**
Topcliffe Dr. TS5: Midd 2C **130**
Topcliffe Rd. TS17: Thorn T. . . 1E **129**
Topcliffe St. TS26: H'pool 3F **13**
Top Corner Sports. 4E **79**
Topcroft Cl. TS3: Midd. 4E **103**
Topham Grn. TS3: Midd. 1C **102**
Topping Cl. TS24: H'pool. 4D **9**
Torbay Cl. TS8: Midd 1B **132**
Torbay Wlk. TS26: H'pool 1E **13**
Torcross Cl. TS27: H'pool 3C **6**
Torcross Way TS10: Redc 3E **65**
Toronto Cres. TS4: Midd 1A **102**
Torquay Av. TS25: H'pool. 5F **19**
Torver Mt. TS7: Mart 4F **133**
Torver Way TS12: Skel. 2C **88**
Torwell Dr. TS19: Stock T 4B **72**
Total Fitness
Stockton-on-Tees 2D **99**
Tothill Av. TS3: Midd 2A **104**
Totnes Cl. TS27: H'pool. 3C **6**
Tourist Info. Cen.
Great Ayton 2D **167**
Hartlepool 3C **14**
Middlesbrough 3F **77**
Saltburn-by-the-Sea 4D **69**
Staithes 1C **120**
Stockton-on-Tees 1B **98**
Tovil Cl. TS19: Stock T 2A **72**
Tower Chamber Apartments
*TS24: H'pool 3C **14***
(off Tower St.)
Tower Flats *TS24: H'pool. 3C **14***
(off Tower St.)
Tower Grn. TS2: Midd 1F **77**
Tower Ho. TS17: Thorn T. 2B **98**
Tower St. TS18: Stock T 1B **98**
TS24: H'pool 3C **14**
Town Cl. TS9: Stokes. 1B **168**
Townend TS21: Sed 1C **22**
Town End Cl. TS15: K'ton 4E **161**
TOWN FARM 1E **103**
Town Farm Ct. TS21: Sed 4C **22**
Town Grn. TS12: Skel 4A **88**
Town Hall Ct. TS15: Yarm 3B **148**
Town House, The
*TS18: Stock T 1A **98***
(off Skinner St.)
Town Sq. TS8: Coul N 4B **132**
TS23: Bill 1D **55**
Town Wall TS24: H'pool. 1E **15**
Towthorpe TS7: Nun. 3F **133**
Trafalgar Ct. TS6: S Ban 2A **80**
Trafalgar Ho. TS24: H'pool 3D **15**
Trafalgar Ter. TS10: Redc 4B **48**
Tralee Cl. TS10: K'ham 4F **63**
Tranmere Av. TS3: Midd 1E **103**
Transporter Way TS4: Midd. . . . 5A **78**
Tranter Rd. TS4: Midd 3F **101**
Travellers Ga. TS25: H'pool . . . 3B **20**
Trecastell TS17: Ing B 2F **149**
Tredegar Wlk. TS26: H'pool . . . 1D **13**
TREEBRIDGE RDBT. **4C 156**
Trees Pk. Village
DL2: Mid G. 1E **145**
Trefoil Cl. TS14: Guis 3B **138**
Trefoil Ct. TS20: Nort. 2A **74**
Trefoil Wood TS7: Mart 1C **132**
Tregarth Cl. TS4: Midd. 3F **101**
Tremaine Cl. TS27: H'pool 3C **6**
Trenchard Av.
TS17: Thorn T 2C **128**
Trenholme Cl. TS17: Ing B . . . 3B **128**
Trenholme Rd. TS4: Midd 5B **78**
Trent Av. TS17: Thorn T. 5D **99**
Trentbrooke Av.
TS25: H'pool. 2F **19**
Trentham Av. TS3: Midd. 2F **103**
Trent Rd. TS10: Redc. 5A **48**
Trent St. TS20: Nort. 2A **74**
Tresco Wlk. TS14: Guis 3C **138**
Trevarrian Dr. TS10: Redc 3E **65**
Trevine Gdns. TS17: Ing B 2F **149**
Trevino Ct. TS16: Eag 5C **126**
Trevithick Cl. TS16: Eag 4A **126**
Trevose Cl. TS10: Redc. 3D **65**
Triangle, The TS14: Guis. 2B **138**
Trident Bus. Cen.
TS2: Midd 1D **77**
Trident Cl. TS24: H'pool 3D **15**
Trigo Cl. TS7: Mart 2C **132**
Trimdon Av. TS5: Midd 1B **130**
Trinity Ct. TS14: Guis. 1E **139**
Trinity M. TS3: N Orm 4B **78**
TS17: Thorn T 1C **98**
Trinity St. TS18: Stock T 1A **98**
TS24: H'pool. 5F **9**
Trinity Wlk. TS10: Redc. 3C **64**
Tristram Av. TS25: H'pool 1F **19**
Tristram Cl. TS6: Norm 2C **104**
Troisdorf Way TS10: K'ham 4A **64**
Troon Cl. TS4: Midd 4F **101**
TS22: Bill 5A **38**
Troutbeck Rd. TS10: Redc 1B **64**
Trout Hall La. TS12: Skel. 5B **88**
Troutpool Cl. TS24: H'pool 5C **8**
Troutsdale Cl. TS15: Yarm. . . . 1B **160**
True Lovers Wlk.
TS15: Yarm 2B **148**
Trueman Ct. TS5: Midd 3C **100**
truGym
Stockton-on-Tees. 5E **97**
Trunk Rd. TS6: Est, S Ban 4F **79**
TS6: Midd, Redc. 2F **81**
TS10: Redc. 2F **81**
Trunk Rd. Dormanstown Ind. Est.
TS10: Redc. 5E **47**
Truro Dr. TS25: H'pool 5F **19**
Tudor Ct. TS3: Midd. 1A **104**
Tulip Cl. TS18: Stock T 1A **98**
TS26: H'pool 4D **7**
Tuned In 3B **48**
Tunstall Av. TS23: Bill 3E **39**
TS26: H'pool. 2F **13**
Tunstall Gdns. TS10: Redc. 4F **65**
Tunstall Gro. TS26: H'pool. 2E **13**
Tunstall Hall La.
TS26: H'pool 4D **13**
Tunstall La. TS7: Nun 4F **155**
Tunstall Rd. TS18: Stock T 3B **96**
Tunstall St. TS3: N Orm. 4C **78**
Turford Av. TS3: Midd 5E **79**
Turnberry Av. TS16: Eag 1C **148**
Turnberry Dr. TS11: N Mar. 3F **85**
Turnberry Gro. TS27: H'pool 2C **6**
Turnberry Way TS8: Mart. 5E **133**
Turnbull St. TS24: H'pool 2B **14**
Turnbull Way TS4: Midd 4C **102**
Turner Cl. TS23: Bill 3D **39**
Turner St. TS10: Redc 3C **48**
Turner Ter. TS6: Laze. 4C **82**
Turner Wlk. TS25: H'pool 2D **19**
Turnpike Wlk. TS21: Sed 1C **22**
Turnstall Av. TS26: H'pool 2F **13**
Turnstile, The TS5: Midd. 5D **77**
Turton Rd. TS15: Yarm 5B **148**
Tuson Wlk. TS24: H'pool 2B **14**
Tweed Av. TS17: Thorn T 5D **99**
Tweed Ho. *TS18: Stock T 4C **74***
(off Tweedport Rd.)
Tweedport Rd.
TS18: Stock T 4C **74**
Tweed Rd. TS10: Redc 5A **48**
Tweed St. TS12: Salt 4C **68**
TS13: Loft 5D **93**
Tweed Wlk. TS24: H'pool 2A **14**
Twinleaf Apartments
TS26: H'pool 4D **7**
Twizziegill Vw. TS13: Eas 3A **118**
Tynebrooke Av. TS25: H'pool. . . 2E **19**
Tyne Ct. TS6: S Ban 4F **79**
Tynedale Cl. TS12: Skel. 3C **88**
Tynedale St. TS18: Stock T 1F **97**
Tyneport Grn. *TS18: Stock T . . . 4C **74***
(off Eastport Rd.)
Tyne Rd. TS10: Redc 5B **48**
Tyne St. TS6: S Ban 2A **80**
TS13: Loft 5D **93**
Tyreman Ct. TS13: Skin. 3A **92**
Tyrone Rd. TS19: Stock T 4A **72**

U

Uldale Dr. TS16: Egg. 1C **148**
Ullapool Cl. TS19: Stock T. 5F **71**
Ulla St. TS1: Midd 5E **77**
Ullswater Av. TS5: Midd 4C **100**
Ullswater Cl. TS6: Gran 4F **81**
Ullswater Dr. TS12: Skel 3B **88**

Ullswater Gro. TS10: Redc 5C **48**
Ullswater Rd. TS18: Stock T . . . 5E **73**
TS23: Bill 4E **55**
TS25: H'pool 1C **20**
Underwood Ct. TS5: Midd 3C **100**
Union Rd. TS24: H'pool 4C **8**
Union St. TS1: Midd 4D **77**
TS14: Guis 1E **139**
TS18: Stock T 4C **74**
TS24: H'pool. 1F **15**
University Blvd.
TS17: Thorn T 1B **98**
University of Teesside
Clarendon Rd. 4F **77**
Victoria Rd. 4F **77**
UPLEATHAM 5C **86**
Upleatham Church 5D **87**
Upleatham Gro.
TS19: Stock T 1B **96**
Upleatham St. TS12: Salt 4C **68**
Up. Albion St. TS6: S Ban 2A **80**
Up. Branch St. TS6: S Ban 2A **80**
(not continuous)
Up. Church St. TS24: H'pool . . . 3B **14**
Up. Garth Gdns.
TS14: Guis 2E **139**
Up. Graham St. TS6: S Ban. . . . 2A **80**
(not continuous)
Up. Green La.
TS17: Thorn T 1C **128**
Up. Jackson St. TS6: S Ban. . . . 2A **80**
Up. Napier St. TS6: S Ban. 2A **80**
Up. Norton Rd.
TS18: Stock T 4B **74**
Up. Oxford St. TS6: S Ban. 2A **80**
Up. Princess St. TS6: S Ban . . . 2A **80**
Uppingham St. TS25: H'pool. . . 1A **20**
Upsall Cotts. TS14: Guis 2F **135**
Upsall Gro. TS19: Stock T. 1B **96**
Upsall Pde. TS19: Stock T. 5B **72**
Upsall Rd. TS3: Midd 2D **103**
TS7: Nun 3B **134**
Upton Ct. TS17: Ing B 1B **150**
Upton Hill TS13: Boul, Loft . . . 1B **118**
Upton St. TS1: Midd. 4F **77**
Upton Wlk. TS25: H'pool 1E **31**
Urford Cl. TS15: Yarm 5E **149**
Urlay Gro. TS5: Midd. 1D **131**
URLAY NOOK 4F **125**
Urlay Nook Rd. TS16: Eag 4F **125**
Urswick Cl. TS4: Midd 2F **101**
Usk Ct. TS17: Ing B 1F **149**
Usway Ct. TS17: Ing B. 2A **150**
Usworth Ind. Est.
TS25: H'pool 3B **20**
Usworth Rd. TS25: H'pool. 3B **20**
Uvedale Rd. TS6: S Ban 3B **80**
Uxto La. TS12: Moor 1B **142**

V

Vale, The TS4: Midd 3F **101**
TS19: Stock T 3C **72**
TS26: H'pool 4D **13**
Vale Dr. TS17: Thorn T 4E **99**
Valiant Way TS17: Thorn T . . . 3C **128**
Valley Av. TS13: Loft. 4A **92**
Valley Cl. TS11: Marsk S 3D **67**
TS15: Yarm 4D **149**
TS26: H'pool 4C **12**
Valley Dr. TS15: Yarm. 4D **149**
TS26: H'pool 5C **12**
Valley Gdns. TS11: Marsk S . . . 3D **67**
TS16: Eag. 1A **148**
TS19: Stock T 3D **73**
Valley Gdns. (Italian Garden)
. . . . 4D **69**
Valley Rd. TS4: Midd. 2F **101**
Vancouver Gdns.
TS4: Midd 5A **78**
Vancouver Ho. TS1: Midd 3F **77**
Vane Cl. TS22: Wyn. 1E **37**
Vane Ct. TS21: Long N. 1F **123**
Vane St. TS18: Stock T 5A **74**
TS24: H'pool 5E **9**
Vanguard Ct. TS18: Stock T. . . . 5F **97**
Van Mildert Way
TS18: Stock T. 3F **97**
Varo Ter. TS18: Stock T 1F **97**
Vaughan Ct. TS6: Gran 2D **81**
Vaughan Shop. Cen.
TS3: Midd 2A **104**
Vaughan St. TS1: Midd 3E **77**
TS12: Skel 4E **89**
Vaynor Dr. TS17: Ing B 1F **149**
Venables Rd. TS14: Guis 1D **139**
Ventnor Av. TS25: H'pool. 2A **20**
Ventnor Ct. TS10: Redc 2B **64**
Ventnor Rd. TS5: Midd 2D **101**
Venture Ct. TS25: H'pool 2F **31**
Verbena Dr. TS23: Bill 5D **39**
Verner Cl. TS24: H'pool. 1C **6**
Verner Rd. TS24: H'pool 1C **6**
Vernon Ct. TS8: Stain 5C **130**
Veronica St. TS3: N Orm 4B **78**
Verwood Cl. TS19: Stock T 2A **72**
Veryan Rd. TS23: Bill. 5F **39**
Viaduct, The TS17: Thorn T. . . . 1E **99**
Viburnum Cl. TS10: Redc 4E **65**
Vicarage Av. TS19: Stock T 5F **73**
Vicarage Ct. TS25: H'pool 5B **14**
Vicarage Dr. TS11: Marsk S . . . 4D **67**
Vicarage Gdns.
TS25: H'pool 5B **14**
Vicarage Row TS25: Grea 3E **31**
Vicarage St. TS19: Stock T 4F **73**
Vicars Cl. TS21: Thorpe T 2D **51**
Vickers Cl. TS11: Marsk S. 3B **66**
TS18: Stock T. 5F **97**
Vickers La. TS25: Seat C. 5D **21**
Victoria Apartments
TS1: Midd. 5F **77**
Victoria Av. TS10: Redc. 5D **49**
TS20: Nort 2A **74**
Victoria Cl. TS3: Midd. 5C **78**
TS11: N Mar. 1A **86**
Victoria Gdns. TS3: Midd. 3F **103**
Victoria Gro. TS19: Stock T. . . . 4C **72**
Victoria Homes
TS25: H'pool 5A **14**
Victoria Ho. TS17: Thorn T 1C **98**
TS18: Stock T 5B ***74***
(off Bath La.)
Victoria Pk.
Harlepool. 3B **14**
Victoria Pl. TS24: H'pool 1F **15**
Victoria Rd. TS1: Midd 4E **77**
TS12: Salt 1C **88**
TS16: Eag. 4C **126**
TS17: Thorn T 3C **98**
TS19: Stock T 4C **72**
TS24: H'pool 3A **14**
TS26: H'pool 3A **14**
Victoria St. TS1: Midd 4C **76**
TS6: S Ban. 2A **80**
TS18: Stock T 5A **74**
TS24: H'pool. 1F **15**
TS25: Seat C 4E **21**
Victoria Ter. TS2: Port C 5F **57**
TS12: Salt 5C **68**
TS13: Loft 5D **93**
TS24: H'pool 3C **14**
Victor Way TS17: Thorn T. . . . 2D **129**
Victory Sq. TS24: H'pool 4B **14**
Victory Ter. TS10: Redc. 4B **48**
Vienna Ct. TS10: K'ham. 4F **63**
Viewley Cen. TS8: Hem. 4E **131**
Viewley Cen. Rd.
TS8: Hem 4E **131**
Viewley Hill Av. TS8: Hem. . . . 4F **131**
Village, The TS7: Mart 2D **133**
Village Grn., The
TS7: Mart. 5A **134**
TS21: Whit. 3A **50**
Village Grn. Vw. TS7: Mart . . . 5A **134**
Village Paddock
TS18: Stock T 3D **97**
Villa Rd. TS3: Midd 5F **79**
Villa Ter. TS18: Stock T. 1A **98**
Villiers St. TS24: H'pool 4B **14**
Vincent Rd. TS5: Midd. 2F **101**
TS23: Bill 3D **39**
Vincent St. TS24: H'pool. 4C **8**
Vine Cl. TS14: Guis 3E **139**
Vinovia Pl. TS17: Ing B 4E **127**
Viola Cl. TS26: H'pool. 4D **7**
Violet Cl. TS20: Nort 2A **74**
Virginia Cl. TS19: Stock T. 2D **73**
Virginia Estate DL2: Mid G . . . 1B **144**
Virginia Gdns. TS5: Midd 2D **131**
Viscount Cl. TS24: H'pool 5B **8**
Vision Retail Pk.
TS24: H'pool 2C **14**
Vollum Ri. TS24: H'pool 5E **9**
Voltigeur Dr. TS27: Hart 3A **6**
Vue Bus. Pk. TS25: H'pool 1C **20**
Vue Cinema
Hartlepool 3C **14**
Vulcan St. TS2: Midd. 1E **77**
Vulcan Way TS17: Thorn T . . . 3D **129**

W

Wade Av. TS18: Stock T 4B **74**
Wainfleet Rd. TS25: H'pool. . . . 1D **31**
Wainstones Cl. TS9: Gt A 3C **166**
Wainstones Ct.
TS9: Stokes 3D **169**
TS15: Yarm 5D **149**
Wainstones Dr. TS9: Gt A 3C **166**
Wainstones Wlk. TS13: Loft . . . 4C **92**
Wainwright Cl. TS25: Seat C . . . 2E **21**
Wainwright Wlk.
TS25: Seat C 2E **21**
Wakefield Rd. TS5: Midd. 1E **101**
Wake St. TS3: N Orm 4C **78**
Waldon St. TS24: H'pool 5B **14**
Waldridge Gro. TS23: Bill 2A **40**
Walk, The TS27: Elw 4C **10**
Walkers Row TS14: Guis 1E **139**
Walker St. TS10: Redc 3C **48**
TS17: Thorn T 3C **98**
Walkley Av. TS17: Thorn T 5C **98**
Waller Ct. TS24: H'pool. 4A **8**
Wallington Ct. TS23: Bill 3E **39**
Wallington Dr. TS21: Sed 3C **22**
Wallington Rd. TS23: Bill 2D **39**
Wallington Wlk. TS23: Bill. 2E **39**
Wallington Way TS23: Bill 3E **39**
Wallis Rd. TS6: S Ban 3F **79**
Walmer Cres. TS11: N Mar 2F **85**
Walnut Cl. TS17: Thorn T 5C **98**
Walnut Gro. TS10: Redc 5E **49**
Walpole Rd. TS25: H'pool 1E **19**
Walpole St. TS1: Midd. 4E **77**
Walsham Cl. TS19: Stock T. . . . 3C **72**
Walsingham Ct. TS23: Bill 4D **55**
Walter St. TS18: Stock T 2F **97**
Waltham Av. TS18: Stock T. . . . 1C **96**
Walton Av. TS5: Midd 3D **101**
Walton Ct. TS18: Stock T 4D **75**
Waltons, The TS9: Gt A 3E **167**
Walton St. TS18: Stock T 4D **75**
Walton Ter. TS14: Guis 2E **139**
Walworth Cl. TS10: Redc. 1E **65**
Walworth Gro. TS5: Midd 5C **100**
Wand Hill TS12: Boo 2C **112**
Wand Hill Gdns. TS12: Boo. . . 2C **112**
Wandhills Av. TS12: Skel. 3E **89**
Wansbeck Gdns.
TS26: H'pool 5A **14**
Wansford Cl. TS23: Bill 2F **39**
Wanstead Cl. TS11: Marsk S. . . 3C **66**
Warbler Cl. TS17: Ing B 5A **128**
Warcop Cl. TS7: Nun 4F **133**
Wardale Av. TS5: Midd 2C **130**
Wardell Cl. TS15: Yarm. 5D **149**

Wardman Cres. TS10: Redc . . . 5E **49**
Ward St. TS12: Moor. 3B **142**
Warelands Way TS4: Midd 5B **78**
Warelands Way Ind. Est.
TS4: Midd 5B **78**
Ware St. TS20: Nort 3B **74**
Warkworth Dr. TS26: H'pool . . . 3D **13**
Warkworth Rd. TS23: Bill 4C **38**
Warren, The TS13: Hind 5E **121**
WARRENBY 3E **47**
Warrenby Ct. TS10: Redc 3E **47**
Warrenby Ind. Est.
TS10: Redc. 3E **47**
Warren Cl. TS24: H'pool 5A **8**
Warren Ct. TS24: H'pool 5A **8**
Warrenport Rd.
TS18: Stock T 4C **74**
Warren Rd. TS24: H'pool. 4F **7**
Warren St. TS1: Midd 4D **77**
TS24: H'pool 5E **9**
Warrior Dr. TS25: Seat C. 2D **21**
WARRIOR PARK. 3D **21**
Warrior Ter. *TS12: Salt 4C 68*
(off Cleveland St.)
Warsett Cres. TS12: Skel. 4E **89**
Warsett Rd. TS11: Marsk S 4E **67**
Warton St. TS3: N Orm 4C **78**
Warwick Cl. TS16: Eag 2B **148**
Warwick Cres. TS23: Bill 2F **55**
Warwick Gro. TS20: Nort. 1C **74**
TS26: H'pool. 4F **13**
Warwick Rd. TS10: Redc. 1D **65**
TS14: Guis 3D **139**
Warwick St. TS1: Midd 5D **77**
(not continuous)
TS6: S Ban 3A **80**
Wasdale Cl. TS24: H'pool 5B **8**
Wasdale Dr. TS16: Egg 1C **148**
Wasdale Gro. TS19: Stock T . . . 2E **73**
Washford Cl. TS17: Ing B 3A **150**
Washington Av.
DL2: Mid G. 2B **144**
Washington Gro. TS20: Nort . . . 1F **73**
Washington St. TS2: Midd. 2E **77**
Wasp Nest Yd.
TS18: Stock T 5B 74
(off Silver St.)
Wass Way TS16: Eag. 4B **126**
Watchgate TS7: Nun 4A **134**
Water Avens Way
TS18: Stock T 1A **128**
Watercress Cl. TS26: H'pool 4D **7**
Waterford Rd. TS20: Nort 2A **74**
Waterford Ter. TS1: Midd 5C **76**
Water La. TS13: Loft. 5C **92**
(not continuous)
Waterlily Ct. TS26: H'pool 4E **7**
Waterloo Ho. TS17: Thorn T . . . 2B **98**
Waterloo Rd. TS1: Midd 4E **77**
(not continuous)
Waterside, The DL2: Mid G. . . 2B **144**
TS17: Thorn T 2B **98**
Waterside Way TS26: H'pool. . . 1C **12**
Watersmeet Cl.
TS17: Ing B 4B **150**
Watling Cl. TS20: Nort. 5F **53**
Watness Av. TS12: Skel. 3E **89**
Watson Gro. TS17: Thorn T. . . . 3B **98**
Watson St. TS1: Midd 3F **77**
Wattie Moore Gro.
TS24: H'pool 1A **14**
Watton Cl. TS25: H'pool 2E **31**
Watton Rd. TS17: Thorn T. 5E **99**
Waveney Gro. TS12: Skel 3D **89**
Waveney Rd. TS10: Redc 1A **64**
Waverley St. TS1: Midd 4D **77**
TS18: Stock T. 2F **97**
Waverley Ter. TS25: H'pool 1F **19**
Waverton Gdns. TS10: Redc . . . 3C **64**
Waymar Cl. TS5: Midd 2C **100**
Wayside Rd. TS3: Midd. 5A **80**
Wear Ct. TS6: S Ban 4F **79**
Wear Cres. TS16: Eag 2B **148**
Weardale TS14: Guis. 4A **138**
Weardale Cres. TS23: Bill. 3D **55**
Weardale Gro. TS5: Midd 3E **101**
Weardale Pl. TS18: Stock T . . . 4E **73**
Weare Gro. TS21: Stil 2B **50**
Wearport Grn.
TS18: Stock T 4C 74
(off Eastport Rd.)
Wear St. TS6: S Ban 2A **80**
Weary Bank TS15: Mid L. 5D **163**
Weastell St. TS5: Midd 1E **101**
Weatherhead Av.
TS5: Midd 3A **100**
Weaver Cl. TS17: Ing B. 4C **128**
Weaverham Rd. TS20: Nort. . . . 1F **73**
Weavers Ct. TS9: Stokes 1B **168**
Weaverthorpe TS7: Nun. 3F **133**
Webb Rd. TS6: S Ban. 3F **79**
Webster Av. TS5: Midd 2F **101**
Webster Rd. TS6: Est. 2E **105**
TS22: Bill 5C **38**
Webster St. TS18: Stock T 1A **98**
Weddell Ct. TS17: Thorn T 4C **98**
Welbeck Ct. TS12: Skel. 3D **89**
Welburn Av. TS4: Midd 2A **102**
Welburn Gro. TS7: Orm. 4A **104**
Welbury Cl. TS18: Stock T 2B **96**
Welland Cl. TS5: Midd 2C **130**
Welland Cres.
TS19: Stock T 3B **72**
Welland Rd. TS10: Redc 1A **64**
TS25: H'pool 1E **31**
Wellbrook Cl. TS17: Ing B. . . . 1C **150**
Wellburn Ct. TS19: Stock T. . . . 5B **72**
Wellburn Rd. TS19: Stock T . . . 5A **72**
Welldale Cres.
TS19: Stock T 4B **72**
Welldeck Gdns.
TS26: H'pool. 3F **13**
Welldeck Rd. TS26: H'pool 3F **13**
Wellesley Rd. TS4: Midd. 4A **78**
Wellfield Grn. TS19: Stock T. . . 1B **72**
Wellgarth M. TS21: Sed 1C **22**
Well House, The
TS11: Upleat 5C **86**
Wellington Cl.
TS11: Marsk S 3B **66**
Wellington Ct.
TS18: Stock T. 5E **97**
Wellington Dr. TS22: Wyn. 1D **37**
Wellington Ho. TS22: Wyn 5A **28**
Wellington Sq.
TS18: Stock T 5A **74**
Wellington St. TS2: Midd 2E **77**
TS18: Stock T 5A **74**
(not continuous)
Wellington Wlk.
TS18: Stock T 5A **74**
Well La. TS8: Newb, Seam . . . 5E **153**
TS9: Seam 5E **153**
Wellmead Rd. TS3: Midd. 5F **79**
Wells Av. TS24: H'pool 4A **8**
Wells Cl. TS6: Est 1E **105**
Well's Cotts. TS16: Egg. 2C **148**
Wells Gro. TS10: Redc. 1F **65**
Wellspring Cl. TS5: Midd 1B **130**
Wells St. TS24: H'pool. 5F **9**
Welton Ho. TS3: Midd 2A **104**
Welwyn Cl. TS19: Stock T. 1C **72**
Wembley Ct. TS18: Stock T. . . . 1F **97**
Wembley St. TS1: Midd. 4C **76**
Wembley Way TS6: Norm 4C **104**
TS18: Stock T. 1F **97**
Wembury Cl. TS10: Redc. 3E **65**
Wensleydale TS12: Skel 3B **88**
Wensleydale Gdns.
TS17: Thorn T 5E **99**
Wensleydale Gro.
TS17: Ing B 3B **150**
Wensleydale St.
TS25: H'pool 1B **20**
Wensley Rd. TS18: Stock T. . . . 1D **97**
Wentworth Ct. TS6: Est 2E **105**
Wentworth Cres.
TS11: N Mar. 2F **85**
Wentworth Gro. TS27: H'pool . . . 3D **7**
Wentworth St. TS1: Midd 4D **77**
Wentworth Way TS16: Eag . . . 1C **148**
Wesley Mall TS1: Midd 3E **77**
Wesley Pl. TS20: Nort. 1B **74**
Wesley Row TS1: Midd 3D **77**
Wesley Sq. *TS13: Stait 1C 120*
(off Beckside)
TS24: H'pool 3B **14**
Wesley Ter. TS13: Carl H. 3F **91**
West Av. TS12: Salt 4B **68**
TS23: Bill 4D **55**
Westbank Rd. TS7: Orm 5B **104**
Westbeck Gdns. TS5: Midd . . . 3E **101**
W. Beck Way TS8: Coul N 3B **132**
Westborough Gro.
TS18: Stock T 2A **96**
Westbourne Gro.
TS3: N Orm 4B **78**
TS6: S Ban. 4B **80**
TS10: Redc 3C **48**
Westbourne Rd. TS5: Midd . . . 2B **100**
TS25: H'pool 1A **20**
Westbourne St.
TS18: Stock T. 2F **97**
Westbrooke Av.
TS25: H'pool. 2F **19**
Westbrooke Gro.
TS25: H'pool 2A **20**
Westbury St. TS17: Thorn T . . . 2C **98**
W. Coatham La. TS10: Redc. . . 1D **63**
Westcott St. TS18: Stock T 2A **98**
West Cres. TS5: Midd 2B **100**
Westcroft TS3: Midd 1C **102**
Westcroft Rd. TS6: Gran 2D **81**
Westdale Rd.
TS17: Thorn T 1D **129**
WEST DYKE. 4C **48**
W. Dyke Rd. TS10: Redc 3C **48**
West End TS9: Stokes 2B **168**
TS14: Guis. 2D **139**
TS21: Sed 4C **22**
West End Av. TS14: Guis. 2D **139**
West End Cl. TS13: Hind 5E **121**
West End Gdns.
TS15: Yarm 2B **148**
West End Way
TS18: Stock T. 4E **97**
Westerby Rd. TS3: N Orm. 3D **79**
Westerdale Av. TS10: Redc. . . . 1A **64**
TS19: Stock T. 4E **73**
Westerdale Ct. TS14: Guis . . . 2C **138**
Westerdale Rd. TS3: Midd . . . 1C **102**
TS25: Seat C 5D **21**
Westerham Gro. TS4: Midd. . . 4A **102**
Westerleigh Av.
TS19: Stock T 5B **72**
Westerton Grn.
TS19: Stock T 1B **72**
Westerton Rd. TS23: Bill 2E **39**
W. Farm Cl. TS6: Norm. 3D **105**
WESTFIELD 5A **48**
Westfield Av. TS10: Redc 4C **48**
Westfield Cl. TS6: Norm 2B **104**
Westfield Ct. TS10: Redc. 1E **63**
(not continuous)
TS19: Stock T. 3E **73**
Westfield Cres.
TS19: Stock T. 2E **73**
Westfield Rd. TS6: Norm 2C **104**
TS9: Stokes 1B **168**
TS11: Marsk S 4A **66**
TS13: Loft 5B **92**
Westfields TS25: H'pool 3D **19**
Westfield Ter. TS13: Loft. 5B **92**
Westfield Wlk. TS13: Loft. 4B **92**
Westfield Way TS10: Redc 1E **63**
TS13: Loft 4B **92**
West Gth. TS21: Carlt 5C **50**
Westgarth Cl.
TS11: Marsk S 4C **66**

Westgate TS14: Guis 2D **139**
TS15: Yarm 2B **148**
Westgate Mall TS14: Guis 2E **139**
Westgate Rd. TS5: Midd 3C **100**
TS14: Guis 1E **139**
WESTGATE RDBT. **1F 81**
West Grn. TS9: Stokes 2B **168**
W. Hartlepool Rd.
TS22: Wolv 2C **38**
Westholme Ct. TS23: Bill 4F **39**
Westland Av. TS26: H'pool 5F **13**
Westlands TS9: Stokes 2A **168**
TS15: K'ton 4D **161**
Westlands Av. TS20: Nort 1B **74**
Westlands Rd. TS16: Eag 1B **148**
Westland Way TS18: Stock T . . . 4F **97**
West La. TS5: Midd 5B **76**
(not continuous)
TS6: Gran 2D **81**
(not continuous)
Westlowthian St.
TS2: Port C 5F **57**
West M. TS15: Yarm 3B **148**
Westminster Cl. TS6: Est 5E **81**
Westminster Oval
TS20: Nort 3A **54**
Westminster Rd.
TS5: Midd 1E **101**
W. Moor Cl. TS15: Yarm 4E **149**
Westmoreland Gro.
TS20: Nort 3F **53**
Westmoreland St.
TS25: H'pool 5B **14**
Westmoreland Wlk.
TS25: H'pool 5B **14**
Westmorland Rd.
TS5: Midd 1D **101**
TS10: Redc 1C **64**
Weston Av. TS3: Midd 4E **79**
Weston Ct. TS9: Stokes 3E **169**
Weston Cres. TS20: Nort 2B **74**
WEST PARK **3C 12**
West Pk. TS26: H'pool 4D **13**
West Pk. Av. TS13: Loft 5B **92**
West Pk. La. TS21: Sed 4C **22**
Westpoint Rd.
TS17: Thorn T 1C **98**
Westport Cl. TS18: Stock T 4C **74**
West Pct. TS23: Bill 1D **55**
Westray TS8: Mart 5E **133**
Westray St. TS13: Carl H 3F **91**
West Rd. TS13: Loft 5A **92**
TS23: Bill 4D **55**
West Row TS5: Midd 2B **100**
TS6: Est 1F **105**
TS18: Stock T 1A **98**
TS25: Grea 4E **31**
West Scar TS10: Redc 2D **65**
West Side TS7: Mart 2D **133**
TS7: Nun 2C **156**
West St. TS2: Midd 1E **77**
TS2: Port C 5F **57**
TS6: Est 1F **105**
TS6: Norm 2D **105**
TS11: Marsk S 3D **67**
TS15: Yarm 2B **148**
TS21: Stil 1A **50**
West Ter. TS3: N Orm 4B **78**
TS9: Gt A 2C **166**
TS10: Redc 3C **48**
TS11: N Mar 2A **86**
TS12: Skel 4A **88**
WEST VIEW **4F 7**
West Vw. TS10: Redc 4D **49**
West Vw. Cl. TS16: Eag 5B **126**
West Vw. Rd. TS24: H'pool 3E **7**
TS27: H'pool 3B **6**
West Vw. Ter. TS16: Eag 1B **148**
TS25: Seat C 4E **21**
Westward Cl. TS1: Midd 3E **77**
Westwick Ter. TS4: Midd 1B **132**
Westwood Av. TS5: Midd 3D **101**
TS7: Nun 3B **134**
West Wood Dr. TS6: Norm . . . 3D **105**
Westwood La. TS17: Ing B . . . 1C **150**
Westwood Way TS27: H'pool . . . 2C **6**
Westworth Cl. TS15: Yarm 5E **149**
Wetherall Av. TS15: Yarm 1B **160**
Wetherby Cl. TS18: Stock T 3E **75**
Wetherby Grn. TS7: Orm 3A **104**
Wetherell Cl. TS11: Marsk S . . . 5E **67**
Wetherfell Cl. TS17: Ing B . . . 3A **150**
Wethers Nook TS26: H'pool 4E **7**
Weymouth Av. TS8: Midd 1B **132**
Weymouth Dr. TS24: H'pool 2D **7**
Weymouth Rd.
TS18: Stock T 1C **96**
Whaddon Chase TS14: Guis . . . 3F **139**
Wharfdale TS12: Skel 2C **88**
Wharfdale Av. TS23: Bill 3D **55**
Wharfedale Cl. TS17: Ing B . . . 3B **150**
Wharf St. TS18: Stock T 1B **98**
Wharton Cl. TS15: Yarm 5E **149**
Wharton Cott. TS12: Skel 2C **88**
Wharton Cotts. TS12: Boo 5B **112**
Wharton Pl. TS12: Boo 2C **112**
Wharton St. TS12: Skel 5F **89**
TS24: H'pool 3B **14**
Wharton Ter. TS24: H'pool 1A **14**
(not continuous)
Wheatacre Cl.
TS11: Marsk S 5E **67**
Wheatear Dr. TS10: Redc 3D **65**
Wheatear La. TS17: Ing B 5A **128**
Wheatfields Ho. TS6: Est 3E **105**
Wheatlands TS9: Gt A 1D **167**
Wheatlands Cl. TS14: Guis . . . 3F **139**
Wheatlands Dr.
TS11: Marsk S 4C **66**
TS13: Eas 3A **118**
Wheatlands Pk. TS10: Redc . . . 3D **65**
WHEATLANDS RDBT. **4D 65**
Wheatley Cl. TS5: Midd 2D **131**
Wheatley Rd. TS19: Stock T . . . 1B **72**
Wheatley Wlk.
TS19: Stock T 1B **72**
Wheeldale Av. TS10: Redc 1A **64**
Wheeldale Cres.
TS17: Thorn T 5D **99**
Wheldrake Cl. TS14: Guis 5E **109**
Whernside TS7: Mart 4F **133**
TS12: Skel 3B **88**
Whernside Cres.
TS17: Ing B 3B **150**
Whessoe Rd. TS19: Stock T . . . 1C **72**
Whessoe Wlk.
TS19: Stock T 1C **72**
Whickam Rd. TS19: Stock T . . . 1B **72**
Whinchat Cl. TS17: Ing B 5B **128**
TS26: H'pool 5F **7**
Whinchat Tail TS14: Guis 2B **138**
Whinfell Av. TS16: Eag 4B **126**
Whinfell Cl. TS7: Mart 4F **133**
Whinfield Cl. TS19: Stock T . . . 3A **72**
Whinflower Dr. TS20: Nort 4F **53**
Whingroves TS17: Thorn T 4F **99**
Whinlatter Cl.
TS19: Stock T 5F **73**
Whin Mdws. TS24: H'pool 3E **7**
WHINNEY BANKS **3B 100**
Whinney Banks Rd.
TS5: Midd 2A **100**
WHINNEY HILL **5A 70**
Whinnies Local Nature Reserve, The
. . . . **1A 144**
Whinny Bank TS9: Gt A 1E **159**
Whinston Cl. TS26: H'pool 2C **12**
Whinstone Dr. TS8: Stain 5C **130**
Whinstone Vw. TS9: Gt A 1D **167**
Whinstone Vw.
Camping & Caravan Site
TS9: Gt A 4F **157**
Whin St. TS1: Midd 3E **77**
Whisperdale Ct. TS3: Midd . . . 1E **103**
Whistlewood Cl.
TS25: H'pool 2A **20**
Whistlewood Way
TS3: Midd 1C **102**
Whitburn St. TS24: H'pool 5B **14**
Whitby Av. TS6: Est 5E **81**
TS14: Guis 2F **139**
Whitby Cl. TS12: Skel 4D **89**
Whitby Cres. TS10: Redc 1F **65**
Whitby Gro. TS24: H'pool 4C **14**
Whitby Rd. TS7: Nun 3B **134**
TS13: Eas, Loft 5D **93**
TS14: Guis 2F **139**
Whitby St. TS24: H'pool 3C **14**
Whitby St. Sth. TS24: H'pool . . . 4C **14**
Whitby Wlk. TS24: H'pool 4C **14**
Whitchurch Cl. TS17: Ing B . . . 3A **150**
Whitebeam Ct. TS4: Midd 3F **101**
Whitecliffe Ter. TS13: Loft 5B **92**
Whitecliff Wood Nature Reserve
. . . . **5A 92**
Whitegate Cl. TS13: Stait 2C **120**
Whitehall Rd. TS16: Eag 3A **126**
White Hart Ct. *TS27: Hart 4F 5*
(off Clevecoat Wlk.)
Whitehaven Ct. TS10: Redc 2B **64**
White Ho. Cft. TS21: Long N . . . 5A **94**
White Ho. Dr. TS21: Sed 4D **23**
Whitehouse Dr.
TS19: Stock T 4D **73**
White Ho. Rd.
TS17: Thorn T 1B **128**
Whitehouse Rd. TS22: Bill 4A **38**
Whiteoaks Cl. TS10: Redc 4F **65**
Whitestone Bus. Pk.
TS4: Midd 4A **78**
White Stone Cl. TS10: Redc . . . 2E **65**
White St. TS3: Midd 5C **78**
Whitewater Way
TS17: Thorn T 5E **75**
Whitfield Av. *TS4: Midd 4A 78*
(off Marton Rd.)
Whitfield Bldgs. *TS4: Midd 4A 78*
(off Park Va. Rd.)
Whitfield Cl. TS16: Eag 5B **126**
Whitfield Dr. TS25: H'pool 2B **20**
Whitfield Rd. TS20: Nort 4F **53**
Whithorn Gro. TS8: Hem 3E **131**
Whitley Rd. TS17: Thorn T . . . 2D **129**
Whitrout Rd. TS24: H'pool 3E **7**
Whitstable Gdns.
TS10: Redc 3A **64**
WHITTON **3A 50**
Whitton Cl. TS5: Midd 5B **100**
Whitton Gro. TS21: Stil 2A **50**
Whitton La. TS21: Stil, Whit . . . 3A **50**
Whitton Rd. TS19: Stock T 5C **72**
TS21: Redm 4A **50**
Whitwell Cl. TS18: Stock T 2A **98**
Whitwell Pl. TS12: Ling 4F **113**
Whitwell Ter. TS14: Guis 1E **139**
Whitworth Gdns.
TS25: H'pool 3F **19**
Whitworth Rd. TS6: Gran 2D **81**
(not continuous)
Whorlton Cl. TS14: Guis 4D **139**
Whorlton Rd. TS2: Midd 5D **57**
TS22: Bill 5B **38**
Wibsey Av. TS3: Midd 4E **103**
Wickets, The TS7: Mart 2C **132**
TS25: Seat C 5E **21**
Wicklow St. TS1: Midd 5C **76**
Widdrington Ct.
TS19: Stock T 2A **72**
Wigton Sands TS5: Midd 3B **130**
Wilder Gro. TS25: H'pool 1D **19**
Wildon Grange TS7: Mart 1A **156**
Wilken Cres. TS14: Guis 5F **109**
Wilkinson St. TS12: Ling 4D **113**
WILLEY FLATT **1B 160**
Willey Flatt La.
TS15: Yarm 5B **148**
William Crosthwaite Av.
TS17: Thorn T 1D **151**
Williams Av. TS5: Midd 2B **100**

Williams St. TS12: Skel 4F **89**
William St. TS2: Midd 2E **77**
TS6: Est 1F **105**
TS10: Redc 4D **49**
TS12: Skel 4D **89**
TS18: Stock T 1A **98**
(not continuous)
TS24: H'pool 4C **14**
William Ter. TS20: Nort. 2B **74**
William Turner Rd.
TS10: Redc 2D **65**
Willington Dr. TS24: H'pool 3F **7**
Willowbank TS8: Coul N 5B **132**
Willow Bri. Cl. TS21: Carlt 5D **51**
Willow Chase, The
TS21: Long N 1F **123**
Willow Cl. TS12: Salt. 5A **68**
TS17: Thorn T 5C **98**
Willowdene Av.
TS18: Stock T. 3E **97**
Willow Dr. TS6: Norm 3C **104**
TS12: Brot 2A **90**
Willow Flats TS26: H'pool. 4D **7**
Willow Gro. TS24: H'pool 1A **14**
Willow Rd. TS14: Guis. 1E **139**
TS19: Stock T. 3F **73**
Willows, The TS7: Mart. 3D **133**
TS10: Redc. 5E **49**
TS19: Stock T 3D **73**
TS21: Sed 5C **22**
Willow Sage Ct.
TS18: Stock T 1A **128**
Willows Av. TS8: Malt 1F **151**
Willows Ct. TS17: Thorn T. . . . 5E **129**
Willows Rd. TS5: Midd 2E **101**
Willow Ter. TS2: Port C 4E **57**
Willow Wlk. TS13: Loft 4B **92**
TS24: H'pool 1A **14**
Wilmire Rd. TS22: Bill. 5C **38**
Wilmore Rd. TS10: Redc. 4C **48**
Wilrock Av. TS7: Mart 4E **133**
Wilson Pl. TS4: Midd. 4B **102**
Wilson St. TS1: Midd. 3E **77**
TS12: Brot 2B **90**
TS12: Ling 4E **113**
TS14: Guis. 2D **139**
TS17: Thorn T 2D **99**
TS26: H'pool. 3F **13**
Wilson Ter. TS13: Skin 2A **92**
Wilstrop Grn. TS3: Midd 4D **103**
WILTON. 4F **83**
Wilton Av. TS10: Redc. 1D **63**
TS26: H'pool. 4F **13**
Wilton Bank TS12: Salt 4A **68**
Wilton Castle TS10: Wilt 4E **83**
Wilton Golf Course. 4D **83**
Wilton Grn. TS6: Laze 4B **82**
Wilton La. TS14: Guis, Wilt 3E **83**
Wilton Rd. TS26: H'pool 4A **14**
Wilton St. TS1: Midd 5E **77**
TS10: Redc 3C **48**
Wilton Village TS10: Wilt 4E **83**
Wilton Way TS6: Est 5F **81**
Wilton Works TS6: Midd 4D **63**
Wiltshire Rd. TS12: Skel 4A **88**
Wiltshire Wlk. TS20: Nort 2C **74**
Wiltshire Way TS26: H'pool . . . 1D **13**
Wimbledon Ct. TS5: Midd 3C **100**
Wimbledon Rd. TS5: Midd . . . 3C **100**
Wimpole Rd. TS19: Stock T. . . . 4F **71**
Wincanton Rd. TS10: Redc 1D **65**
Winchester Rd. TS5: Midd. . . . 1F **101**
TS10: Redc. 1F **65**
TS12: Brot 2C **90**
Winchester Wlk.
TS26: H'pool 1E **13**
Windermere Av. TS10: Redc . . . 5C **48**
TS21: Redm 1B **70**
TS23: Bill 4E **55**
Windermere Dr. TS12: Skel. . . . 3B **88**
Windermere Rd.
TS5: Midd 2D **101**
TS18: Stock T 5D **73**
Windermere Rd.
TS25: H'pool 2B **20**
(not continuous)
Windleston Dr. TS3: Midd 4D **103**
Windlestone Ho. *TS23: Bill 5F **39***
(off Windlestone Rd.)
Windlestone Rd. TS23: Bill 5F **39**
Windmill Ter. TS20: Nort. 2B **74**
Windmill Way
TS17: High L 3C **150**
Windsor Ct. TS5: Midd. 2E **101**
TS6: Gran 4E **81**
TS12: Salt 4D **69**
Windsor Cres. TS7: Nun 3A **134**
Windsor Dr. TS12: Ling 4F **113**
Windsor Oval TS17: Thorn T . . . 5C **98**
Windsor Rd. TS5: Midd 1D **101**
TS6: Est 2D **105**
TS10: Redc. 1E **65**
TS12: Salt 4C **68**
TS17: Thorn T 5C **98**
TS18: Stock T. 2E **97**
Windsor St. TS1: Midd. 4E **77**
TS23: Bill 3D **57**
TS26: H'pool 4B **14**
Windsor Ter. *TS13: Loft 5D **93***
(off Tweed St.)
Windward Way TS2: Midd 2F **77**
Windy Hill La.
TS11: Marsk S 4D **67**
Wingate Av. TS23: Bill 3F **39**
Wingate Wlk. TS3: Midd 5E **103**
Wingfield Cl. TS24: H'pool 3A **8**
Wingrove TS15: Yarm 3B **148**
Winkies Castle Mus. 4C **66**
Winpenny Cl. TS15: Yarm 5E **149**
Winsford Ct. TS17: Ing B. 3B **150**
Winslade Av. TS3: Midd. 4F **79**
Winston Av. TS23: Bill 3E **39**
Winston Churchill Cl.
TS17: Thorn T 2D **129**
Winston Ct. TS24: H'pool 4D **9**
Winston Dr. TS6: Est 1E **105**
Winston St. TS18: Stock T. 2F **97**
Winterbottom Av.
TS24: H'pool 4A **8**
Winter Cl. TS15: Yarm. 1A **160**
TS25: H'pool 2B **20**
Wintersweet Gdns.
TS20: Nort 1F **73**
Winterton Av. TS21: Sed 1D **23**
Winterton Cotts. TS21: Sed. . . . 1D **23**
Winthorpe Gro.
TS25: H'pool 1D **31**
Wisbech Cl. TS25: H'pool 2D **31**
Wiske Cl. TS19: Stock T 3B **72**
Witcombe Cl. TS17: Ing B 4E **127**
Witham Av. TS16: Prest T 3C **126**
Witham Gro. TS25: H'pool. 1E **31**
Witham Lodge
TS16: Prest T. 3C **126**
Witton Ct. TS23: Bill. 5F **39**
Witton Pk. TS18: Stock T. 3A **98**
Woburn Gro. TS3: Midd 3F **103**
TS25: H'pool 5A **20**
Woking Cl. TS6: Norm. 4D **105**
Wolfe Rd. TS20: Nort 1A **74**
Wollaton Rd. TS23: Bill 5F **39**
Wolsey Dr. TS20: Nort. 4E **53**
Wolsey Ho. TS24: H'pool. 1F **15**
Wolsingham Dr. TS5: Midd . . . 2D **131**
TS17: Thorn T 5E **99**
WOLVISTON 2C **38**
Wolviston Bk. La. TS23: Bill . . . 2D 39
TS23: Bill, Cowp B 2A **40**
Wolviston Ct. TS22: Bill. 5B **38**
WOLVISTON INTERCHANGE . . . 1A 38
Wolviston Mill La.
TS22: Bill, Wolv 4A **38**
Wolviston Rd.
TS22: Bill, Wolv 4C **38**
TS23: Bill 5C **38**
TS25: H'pool 1A **20**
WOLVISTON RDBT. 2D 39
WOLVISTON SERVICES 1B 38
Wolviston Wlk.
TS19: Stock T 1B **72**
Woodale Cl. TS14: Guis. 5E **109**
Woodbank Rd. TS7: Orm. 5B **104**
Woodbine Cl. TS9: Gt A 1D **167**
Woodbine Ter. TS25: Grea 3E **31**
Woodborough La.
TS19: Stock T 3D **73**
Woodbrook Cl.
TS11: N Mar. 2F **85**
Woodburn Cl. TS8: Hem 3E **131**
Woodchester Gro.
TS17: Ing B 4E **127**
Woodcock Cl. TS6: Est. 3E **105**
Wood Ct. TS13: Loft 5C **92**
Woodend Ct. TS22: Wyn 4C **26**
Woodford Cl.
TS11: Marsk S 4B **66**
Woodford Grn. TS16: Eag 1C **148**
Woodford Wlk.
TS17: Thorn T 3C **128**
Woodgarth TS6: Est. 1D **105**
Woodgate Cl. TS25: Grea 2E **31**
Woodhall Gro.
TS18: Stock T 3B **96**
Woodham Grn.
TS19: Stock T 1B **72**
Woodham Rd. TS23: Bill 3E **39**
Woodhay Av. TS5: Midd 3A **100**
Woodhouse Rd.
TS14: Guis 1C **138**
WOODHOUSE RDBT. 2B 138
Woodland Grn. TS5: Midd. . . . 2A **100**
Woodland M. TS21: Sed 2D **23**
Woodlands, The TS7: Nun. . . . 5B **134**
TS17: Thorn T 5C **98**
Woodlands Dr. TS6: Norm. . . . 3E **105**
TS15: Yarm 4D **149**
Woodlands Grn.
DL2: Mid G. 1A **144**
Woodlands Gro.
TS26: H'pool 3D **13**
Woodlands Rd. TS1: Midd. 5F **77**
TS6: Norm 4D **105**
Woodland St. TS18: Stock T . . . 2F **97**
Woodlands Wlk.
TS9: Stokes 5C **164**
Woodland Vw. TS7: Mart. 1A **156**
Woodland Way
TS21: Long N 1F **123**
Woodlea TS8: Coul N. 5B **132**
Woodley Gro. TS7: Orm 1B **134**
Woodmere Rd.
TS19: Stock T 4D **73**
Woodrow Av. TS7: Mart. 3D **133**
TS12: Salt 4B **68**
Woodrush TS8: Coul N. 2C **154**
Woodside TS7: Orm. 4F **103**
TS10: Redc 3C **64**
TS12: Brot 2A **90**
TS17: Ing B 4B **128**
TS22: Wyn 4B **26**
Woodside Gro.
TS18: Stock T 3C **96**
Woodside St. TS1: Midd 3A **78**
Woodstock Ct.
TS18: Stock T 4B **98**
Woodstock Way
TS27: H'pool 2C **6**
Wood St. TS1: Midd. 2F **77**
TS6: Gran. 2D **81**
TS24: H'pool. 1F **15**
TS25: H'pool 5D **15**
Wood's Yd. TS12: Skel 4B **88**
Woodvale TS8: Coul N. 4D **133**
(not continuous)
Wood Vw. TS13: Loft. 5C **92**
Woodville Av. TS4: Midd 3F **101**
Woolcotts Cl. TS17: Ing B 3B **150**
Wooler Cres. TS23: Bill 4E **55**
Wooler Rd. TS26: H'pool 3E **13**

Woolsington Dr.
DL2: Mid G. 1A **144**
Worcester Gdns.
TS25: H'pool 1B **20**
Worcester St. TS1: Midd 5D **77**
Wordsworth Av.
TS25: H'pool. 1F **19**
Wordsworth Cl. TS23: Bill 2D **39**
Wordsworth Rd. TS6: Est 5D **81**
Wordsworth Va. TS5: Midd . . . 5B **100**
Works Rd. TS3: Midd 3D **79**
Worsall Cl. TS15: Yarm 4B **148**
Worsall Gro. TS18: Stock T. . . . 3C **96**
Worsall Rd. TS15: Yarm 5A **148**
Worset Gro. TS10: Redc 4E **65**
Worset La. TS26: H'pool 1C **12**
TS27: Elw. 5D **5**
Worsley Cl. TS16: Prest T. . . . 2D **127**
Worsley Cres. TS7: Mart. . . . 4D **133**
Worthing Ct. TS18: Stock T. . . . 1A **98**
Worthing St. Sth. Bank
TS18: Stock T. 1F **97**
Wray St. TS4: Midd 3A **78**
Wrekenton Cl.
TS19: Stock T 1B **72**
Wren Cl. TS18: Stock T 1F **97**
Wrensfield Rd.
TS19: Stock T. 5F **73**
Wren St. TS18: Stock T 1F **97**
Wren Ter. TS13: Loft 5D **93**
Wrentree Cl. TS10: Redc. 3D **65**
Wrightson Ho. TS3: Midd 2D **103**
TS17: Thorn T 1D **129**
Wrightson St. TS20: Nort 1B **74**
Wroxham Cl. TS19: Stock T . . . 3C **72**
Wroxton Av. TS5: Midd 3C **100**
Wroxton Cl. TS5: Midd 3B **100**
Wrynose Gdns.
TS19: Stock T. 5F **73**
Wycherley Av. TS5: Midd 3C **100**
Wycherley Cl. TS7: Orm 1B **134**
Wychgate TS6: Est. 1A **106**
Wychwood Cl.
TS17: Thorn T 2D **129**
Wycliffe Ct. TS15: Yarm 5D **149**
Wye Carr Dr. TS15: Yarm 1A **160**
Wye Cl. TS19: Stock T. 3B **72**
Wykeham Av. TS14: Guis 4D **139**
Wykeham Cl. TS10: Redc 3B **64**
TS22: Bill 5A **38**
Wykeham Ct. TS12: Skel. 4D **89**
Wykeham Way
TS8: Coul N 3B **132**
Wyke La. TS7: Nun 1B **156**
Wykes Cl. TS21: Sed. 4D **23**
Wylam Ct. TS18: Stock T. 4A **98**
Wylam Rd. TS20: Nort. 1A **74**
Wylam St. TS1: Midd 4D **77**
Wynd, The TS8: Stain 5B **130**
TS11: Marsk S 4D **67**
TS22: Wyn 4B **26**
Wynde, The TS19: Stock T 3A **72**
Wynn's Gth. TS14: Guis 1F **139**
Wynnstay Gdns.
TS24: H'pool 1A **14**
Wynyard Av. TS22: Wyn 1A **38**
Wynyard Bus. Pk.
TS22: Wyn 5F **27**
Wynyard Ct. TS21: Thorpe T . . . 2E **51**
Wynyard Ho. *TS22: Wolv. 2C* ***38***
(off Durham Rd.)
Wynyard M. TS25: H'pool 4E **19**
Wynyard Pk. TS22: Wyn 5A **28**
Wynyard Rd.
TS21: Thorpe T, Bill 2E **51**
TS22: Wolv, Wyn 3D **37**
TS25: H'pool 4D **19**
Wynyard St. TS20: Nort. 4B **74**
WYNYARD VILLAGE **5B 26**
Wynyard Woodland Pk. **4E 35**
Wynyard Woodland Pk. Observatory
. . . . **5E 35**
Wynyard Woodland Pk. Vis. Cen.
. . . . **5E 35**
Wynyard Woods TS22: Wyn . . . 3A **26**
Wyverne Ct. TS25: H'pool 3A **20**

Y

Yale Cres. TS17: Thorn T 1C **98**
Yard, The TS13: Loft 5B **92**
YARM **3B 148**
Yarm Bk. La. TS21: Stock T. . . . 4F **71**
Yarm Cl. TS25: H'pool 2A **20**
Yarm Golf Academy **1E 161**
Yarm La. TS9: Gt A 2E **165**
TS18: Stock T 1A **98**
TS21: Sed. 5F **23**
Yarmouth Cl. TS25: H'pool 2E **31**
Yarmouth Dr. TS10: Redc 2B **64**
Yarm Rd. DL2: Mid G. 1A **144**
(not continuous)
TS15: Hilt 5E **151**
TS16: Eag, Prest T 2B **148**
TS18: Prest T, Stock T 4E **97**
Yarm Station (Rail). **1C 160**
Yarm St. TS18: Stock T 1A **98**
Yarrow Dr. TS18: Stock T 1A **128**
Yeadon Gro. TS17: Thorn T . . . 1E **129**
Yeadon Wlk. DL2: Mid G. 1A **144**
YEARBY **2B 84**
Yearby Bank
TS14: Year, Dun 2C **84**
Yearby Cl. TS5: Midd. 5B **100**
TS6: Est 2E **105**
Yearby Cres.
TS11: Marsk S 4E **67**
Yearby M. TS11: Year 1B **84**
Yearby Rd. TS11: Year. 2B **84**
Yenton Cl. TS23: Bill 4D **55**
Yeoman St. TS10: Redc. 4D **49**
TS12: Skel 3C **88**
Yeoman Ter.
TS11: Marsk S 4C **66**
Yeovil Wlk. *TS26: H'pool. 1E* ***13***
(off Torbay Gro.)
Yew St. TS1: Midd 3E **77**
Yew Tree Av. TS10: Redc. 3A **64**
Yew Tree Gro. TS7: Mart 3F **133**
Yew Wlk., The
TS21: Long N 1F **123**
Yoredale Cl. TS17: Ing B. 2B **150**
York Apartments
TS17: Thorn T 1C **128**
York Cres. TS23: Bill 3E **55**
York Flatlets TS24: H'pool. . . . 4B **14**
York Pl. TS24: H'pool. 2F **15**
York Rd. TS5: Midd 2F **101**
TS7: Nun 3B **134**
TS10: Redc. 3F **47**
TS12: Brot 2C **90**
TS26: H'pool 3B **14**
York St. TS18: Stock T. 1A **98**
York Ter. TS10: Redc 3A **48**
(not continuous)
Yorkway TS17: Thorn T 2C **98**
Young St. TS26: H'pool 3A **14**
Yukon Gdns. TS4: Midd 5A **78**

Z

Zetland Cotts.
TS11: Marsk S. 3D **67**
Zetland Ct. *TS12: Salt. 4D* ***69***
(off Dundas St. E.)
Zetland Lifeboat Mus. **3D 49**
Zetland M. TS12: Salt 4C **68**
Zetland Pl. TS1: Midd 2F **77**
Zetland Rd. TS1: Midd. 2F **77**
TS10: Redc. 1F **65**
TS11: Marsk S 4D **67**
TS13: Loft 5B **92**
TS19: Stock T. 3F **73**
TS26: H'pool. 3F **13**
Zetland Row TS13: Skin 2A **92**
Zetland Ter. TS11: N Mar 1A **86**
TS12: Salt 4C **68**
TS13: Loft 5B **92**
Zinc Works Rd. TS25: Seat C. . . 3F **33**

MIX
Paper from responsible sources
FSC® C016201
FSC
www.fsc.org

The representation on the maps of a road, track or footpath is no evidence of the existence of a right of way.

SAFETY CAMERA INFORMATION

PocketGPSWorld.com's CamerAlert is a self-contained speed and red light camera warning system for SatNavs and Android or Apple iOS smartphones/tablets. Visit www.cameralert.com to download.

Safety camera locations are publicised by the Safer Roads Partnership which operates them in order to encourage drivers to comply with speed limits at these sites. It is the driver's absolute responsibility to be aware of and to adhere to speed limits at all times.

By showing this safety camera information it is the intention of Geographers' A-Z Map Company Ltd. to encourage safe driving and greater awareness of speed limits and vehicle speed. Data accurate at time of printing.

HOSPITALS, HOSPICES and selected HEALTHCARE FACILITIES covered by this atlas.

N.B. Where it is not possible to name these facilities on the map, the reference given is for the road in which they are situated.

BUTTERWICK HOSPICE &
BUTTERWICK HOUSE CHILDREN'S HOSPICE . . .2C **72**
Middlefield Road
STOCKTON-ON-TEES
TS19 8XN
Tel: 01642 607742

CARTER BEQUEST (PRIMARY CARE) HOSPITAL 3D **101**
Cambridge Road
MIDDLESBROUGH
TS5 5NH
Tel: 01642 850911

EAST CLEVELAND PRIMARY CARE HOSPITAL 3B **90**
Alford Road
Brotton
SALTBURN-BY-THE-SEA
TS12 2FF
Tel: 01287 676205

GUISBOROUGH PRIMARY CARE HOSPITAL 1E **139**
Northgate
GUISBOROUGH
TS14 6HZ
Tel: 01287 284000

HARTLEPOOL AND DISTRICT HOSPICE 5A **8**
Alice House
Wells Avenue
HARTLEPOOL
TS24 9DA
Tel: 01429 855555

JAMES COOK UNIVERSITY HOSPITAL 3B **102**
Marton Road
MIDDLESBROUGH
TS4 3BW
Tel: 01642 850850

MINOR INJURIES UNIT (HARTLEPOOL) 4B **14**
Park Road
HARTLEPOOL
TS24 7PW
Tel: 01429 890947

NHS WALK-IN CENTRE (HARTLEPOOL) 4B **14**
One Life Hartlepool
Park Road
HARTLEPOOL
TS24 7PW
Tel: 01429 890947

NHS WALK-IN CENTRE (STOCKTON) 2B **72**
High Newham Road
Tithebarn House
STOCKTON-ON-TEES
TS19 8RH
Tel: 01642 525480

ROSEBERRY PARK 2B **102**
Marton Road
MIDDLESBROUGH
TS4 3AF
Tel: 01642 837300

SANDWELL PARK HOSPITAL .2B **14**
Lancaster Road
HARTLEPOOL
TS24 8LN
Tel: 01429 285601

SEDGEFIELD COMMUNITY HOSPITAL 2C **22**
Salters Lane
Sedgefield
STOCKTON-ON-TEES
TS21 3EE
Tel: 01740 626600

TEES HOSPITAL 4E **53**
Junction Road
STOCKTON-ON-TEES
TS20 1PX
Tel: 01642 918404

TEESSIDE HOSPICE 3D **101**
1 Northgate Road
MIDDLESBROUGH
TS5 5NW
Tel: 01642 816777

TEES VALLEY TREATMENT CENTRE 5E **77**
Linthorpe Road
One Life
MIDDLESBROUGH
TS1 3QY
Tel: 01642 737855

THE PRIORY HOSPITAL 1D **145**
Middleton St. George
DARLINGTON
DL2 1TS
Tel: 01325 333192

UNIVERSITY HOSPITAL OF HARTLEPOOL 5F **7**
Holdforth Road
HARTLEPOOL
TS24 9AH
Tel: 01429 266654

UNIVERSITY HOSPITAL OF NORTH TEES 2C **72**
Hardwick Road
STOCKTON-ON-TEES
TS19 8PE
Tel: 01642 617617

WEST LANE HOSPITAL 1C **100**
Acklam Road
MIDDLESBROUGH
TS5 4EE
Tel: 01642 352000